The Poetry Handbook

A Guide to Reading Poetry for Pleasure and Practical Criticism

Second Edition

JOHN LENNARD

OXFORD
UNIVERSITY PRESS

OXFORD
UNIVERSITY PRESS

Great Clarendon Street, Oxford OX2 6DP

Oxford University Press is a department of the University of Oxford.
It furthers the University's objective of excellence in research, scholarship,
and education by publishing worldwide in

Oxford New York

Auckland Cape Town Dar es Salaam Hong Kong Karachi
Kuala Lumpur Madrid Melbourne Mexico City Nairobi
New Delhi Shanghai Taipei Toronto

With offices in

Argentina Austria Brazil Chile Czech Republic France Greece
Guatemala Hungary Italy Japan South Korea Poland Portugal
Singapore Switzerland Thailand Turkey Ukraine Vietnam

Oxford is a registered trade mark of Oxford University Press
in the UK and in certain other countries

Published in the United States
by Oxford University Press Inc., New York

First published 1996
Paperback edition reprinted with corrections 1996
Second edition with companion website 2005

British Library Cataloguing in Publication Data
Data available

Library of Congress Cataloging in Publication Data
Lennard, John.
The poetry handbook : a guide to reading poetry for pleasure and
practical criticism / John Lennard.—2nd ed.
p. cm.
Includes bibliographical references and index.
ISBN 0-19-926538-0 (acid-free paper)
1. English poetry—History and criticism—Theory, etc.—Handbooks, manuals, etc.
2. History language—Versification—Handbooks, manuals, etc. 3. Criticism—
Authorship—Handbooks, manuals, etc. 4. Poetry—Explication—Handbooks,
manuals, etc. 5. Books and reading—Handbooks, manuals, etc.
6. Poetics—Handbooks, manuals, etc. I. Title.
PR502.L38 2005
808.1—dc22 2005021580

Typeset by RefineCatch Limited, Bungay, Suffolk
Printed in Great Britain on acid-free paper by
Clays Ltd, St Ives plc

ISBN 978-0-19-926538-1

5

For

ANNE BOWLER PUGH and ANNE BARTON

who taught me far more than these basics ;

and for the late, much missed

JEREMY MAULE

who told me to write them down.

Cricket is an art. Like all arts
it has a technical foundation. To enjoy it
does not require technical knowledge, but
analysis that is not technically based is mere impressionism.

C. L. R. JAMES, *Beyond a Boundary*

Acknowledgements to the Second Edition

As well as renewing my thanks to those without whom this book would not exist at all, and giving proper thanks to those readers of the first edition whose feedback showed me how to do better, I must give special and happy thanks to Francis, David, and Jacqui Ingledew, whose friendship and exceptionally generous hospitality allowed me at last to visit Walcott's Caribbean. Francis was also instrumental in my invitation to teach online for Fairleigh Dickinson University—far and away the most interesting thing to have happened to me professionally in years, and the single most important impulse to revision. Jay Parini freely lent me his encyclopaedic anthologist's knowledge of American poetry, and I have gratefully seized suggestions and ideas from Anne Henry, Alison Hennegan, and Dave Palfrey, who knows a great deal more about computers than I do. David Colclough very kindly supplied his article on Donne for the new *DNB* ahead of its publication, and Richard Todd, an editor of the variorum Donne, read the sections on 'The Flea' and reassured me about their accuracy and sense. Alex Lindsay fielded questions about Dryden ; Fiona Green allowed me to pick her poetic brains and let me borrow for months on end her facsimile of Dickinson's fascicles ; and Anne Barton lent me her rare copy of *The Girlhood of Shakespeare's Heroines*. Without Fiona Kinnear there would be no website.

Formal thanks are also due to Professor Jon Stallworthy, one of the editors of the *Norton Anthology* (as well as a lovely poet and once upon a time one of my doctoral examiners), for liaison about the timing and content of its fifth edition.

'Nearing Forty' is reproduced from Derek Walcott's *Collected Poems 1948–84* (New York: Farrar, Straus and Giroux, 1986). Copyright © 1986 by Derek Walcott. Reprinted by permission of Farrar, Straus and Giroux, Inc. and Faber and Faber Ltd. 'Sestina' is reproduced from Elizabeth Bishop's *The Complete Poems: 1927–1979* (New York: Farrar, Straus and

Giroux; London: Chatto & Windus, 1983). Copyright © 1979, 1983 by Alice Helen Methfessel. Reprinted by permission of Farrar, Straus and Giroux, Inc. 'September Song' is reproduced from Geoffrey Hill's *King Log* (London: André Deutsch, 1968). Copyright © 1994 by Geoffrey Hill. Reprinted by kind permission of André Deutsch, Houghton Mifflin Co., and Penguin Books Ltd.

John Lennard
Kingston, W. I.
June 2005

Acknowledgements to the First Edition

Beyond the debts acknowledged in the dedication I would like to thank those students who have harassed me into clarity, especially Dan Fugallo, Tess Grant, Rob Morris, Penny Taylor, and Nicky White ; and those brave students, Adam Barnes, Andy Miller, and Simon Oastler, who have allowed their timed work to appear in the last chapter. My warmest thanks also to Jonathan Lloyd for reading many first drafts, and to Ljubica Dimitrijevic for putting up with me while he did so ; to the anonymous first reader at OUP for the most helpful report I have ever had ; to Jonathan Steinberg for boundless encouragement ; to John Creaser for valuable commentary on the entire manuscript ; to William Clocksin for help with the mathematical formula ; to John Lyons for help with the Greek ; to Gabriel Gbadamosi for a persuasive argument about phrasing ; to Francis Ingledew for help with Walcott's West Indian experience ; to Hugh Stevens for suggestions about Walcott and gender ; to Frances Whistler for spotting (and being very kind about) a number of careless mistakes ; and to Mary Luckhurst for everything.

J.C.L.
Cambridge
August 1995

Contents

Preface to the Second Edition

Since publication in 1996 *The Poetry Handbook* has by most accounts done its work reasonably well. As reviewers ignore textbooks, feedback was slow, but interesting when it did come, very positively, from teachers and students using the *Handbook* as a coursetext ; reader-reviews at Amazon.com were also good. The competition has sharpened a little, but sales remain strong and poetry is hardly a cutting-edge technology with necessarily short-lived manuals—so why (besides marketing imperatives) should there now be a second edition?

To begin with, if teachers and students alike were strongly positive, teachers had at least one recurrent doubt. Few actively disliked Walcott's 'Nearing Forty', with specific analysis of which every chapter ends—many came to appreciate it and acknowledged my reasons for choosing it—yet most felt that for some students it was an unhappy choice, and would have preferred an older canonical poem. Feedback also provided local rebukes about poets slighted and forms omitted, with some corrections of fact, regrets that more American poems were not cited, and requests for chapter-by-chapter exercises in versification and/or practical criticism. I also had my own dissatisfactions with this or that bit, and a growing awareness of having short-changed some things rather more than I had intended.

All this invited but didn't compel a new edition. The alleged problem with 'Nearing Forty' is putatively more serious, but to those who argue that a finely wrought and honest poem about the compromises of middle age is inappropriate for youthful students, as to students who tell me they aren't yet nearing forty themselves, I give the reply a teacher once gave me : *Yes of course, but I think you'll find that's not true.* Walcott's extended syntax, formalism, erudition, and cultural complexity, as well as the imagination required by his subject from younger readers, certainly make his poem a formidable proposition, but, frankly, so much the better. Difficulties are also opportunities : all welcome the cultural and ethnic dimensions Walcott inherently activates, and younger students occasioned difficulty must be offset against mature students for once afforded a lesser rather than a greater barrier ; besides, every poem has weaknesses as well as strengths, and no choice among the many with potent claims and capacities would satisfy all. Errors should be corrected and serious omissions rectified, but why otherwise admit change when there can be no logical end to it?

The crux in 1996 was limitation to a single exemplary poem. A further modern poem or poems would have incurred copyright fees OUP was not then willing to bear, while any additional poems treated as 'Nearing Forty' is treated would have raised the word-count by many thousands, threatening price and market-profile. Some feeders-back were alert to this as a danger, and ended by cautioning me against their own special pleadings because the value of *The Poetry Handbook* lay substantially in its brevity and brisk tones ; do not, they said, sacrifice its racing lines by making it carry everyone's burdens—but (changing metaphors mid-stream) they seemed to countenance some growth all the same, especially if mild pruning were also possible.

This makes good and marketing sense, and a slight expansion-with-revisions would probably have been agreed—were it not that we are all willy-nilly amid a techno-revolution that is swiftly transforming our media of data-storage and -retrieval, and so our modes and practices of writing and reading. In personal practice that means that while in 1996 I was under no pressure, from myself or OUP, to gear *The Poetry Handbook* either to online resources or to web-pedagogy, both considerations now press on all decision-making about textbooks. Additionally, I have since 2002 been formally teaching online, and in all teaching obliged explicitly to confront changes in what 'research' actually is for readers who turn to the World Wide Web (WWW, 'the Web') before having recourse to a print-library.

All pages, whether on paper or screen, have normative limits (deriving from technology, practical convenience, and commercial viability) that constrain how text is embodied and affect how it can be conceived. The limits of the *metal page*[1]—the archetype at any given time of pages printed using Gutenberg's movable metal type—were dictated by the basic requirement for a separate metal type-piece for each character and necessarily centralised production, and so (despite technological improvements and the switch from hand- to machine-presses) were fundamentally unchanged for 500 years (1470–1970). They were also therefore among the principal determinants of the printed *codex*, or bound book, including most poetry (and pretty much all canonical

[1] Italicised terms appear in the Glossary.

poetry) throughout modern history—but they have changed now, and the limits of the *e-page* remain to be established. I doubt if the codex or hard copy will cease to be used any time soon—handwriting, after all, has hardly been destroyed by print—but their roles have already changed and in part diminished, and their influences on the forms we give to data and texts have been (and will continue to be) variously challenged and complemented. How rapidly and severely poetry in itself will be affected by word-processor composition, laser-printing, and the e-page is moot, under exponential exploration, and well worth pondering even if one's own tastes are conservative ; a few particular developments are now mentioned in the text, but it is the broader impact of the Web on practical criticism that has for me truly justified a new edition.

The critical decision was that the *Handbook* should be accompanied by a dedicated website, http://www.oup.com/uk/literature/poetry, where the poems I quote or cite are wherever possible (given copyright issues) gathered or hyperlinked. Readers with convenient access to the Web (which now includes most students facing formal exams) can thus read as much of my evidence as they wish, contextualise it all, and assess for themselves the strength of my generalisations and observations. (The website is in its nature capable of currency, and such matters as new volumes from or deaths of poets will be recorded there long before print can catch up.)

Systematic use of *The Norton Anthology of Poetry* (still the most widely used print-resource) is far too valuable to abandon, and it has itself again been updated, but voiding the general restriction to the *Norton* that I observed in 1996 has allowed a far wider range of poetic reference while retaining confidence that relevant information, exemplary poems, and publication-details are for almost all readers at most a google away. There have been considerable knock-on effects in all directions ; in particular, a systematic expansion of the 'exemplary poems' became compelling, and OUP agreed that two might incur additional *permissions* costs. The sections on 'Nearing Forty' have been substantially retained, but each chapter now considers, in addition, one or more of a small group of canonical poems : Donne's 'The Flea', Keats's 'Ode on Melancholy', Dickinson's 'I heard a Fly buzz—when I died—', Owen's 'Anthem for Doomed Youth', Bishop's 'Sestina', and Hill's 'September Song'. These are quoted in full when first discussed, and reconsidered to enrich particular chapters. The print edition has therefore increased in bulk and remains fully autonomous, but just as those who used the first edition in conjunction with the *Norton* profited, so those who use this second edition in conjunction with the *Norton* or with the website will profit.

The greater range of reference, quoting more poems (especially Renaissance material) at length or in full, and the ready availability online of digital facsimiles, have also forced me to confront issues of textual modernisation, marginalised in 1996 by a general reliance on the *Norton*. Now, while *Norton* references may still be provided, the text I quote will typically come from the first (or last authorised) edition, so readers will regularly be confronted by old orthography. In Marlowe's *Hero and Leander* (printed 1598), for example, 'deceives' appears as "deceaues", showing both different spelling and the positional use of 'u' and 'v' as graphs of the same letter ; *long-s* (ſ) is also retained.[2] It looks odd when you're unused to it, but it rarely takes more than a second to work out what a word is, and anything genuinely difficult is glossed. For poems first printed after 1800 there isn't usually much in it, though Browning, for example, reworked his own texts quite heavily, and features such as italicisation and capitalisation are often edited away. My reasons for preferring fairly stringently unmodernised texts are variously suggested throughout my text, and formally set out in *The Drama Handbook* (OUP, 2002) ; here I will say only that modernisation destroys as much as it clarifies, and that the availability of digital imaging is already exerting a perceptible pressure on university teachers to expect familiarity with at least the general appearance and features of early editions. There is also an advantage in that scholarly editions of poetry, however published, always provide basic bibliographical information about their source texts, for which in many cases there are standard abbreviations. To keep pages and argument as clear as possible, I have therefore often felt free to give only summary details of the source (as, for Shakespeare, 'text from F1, 1623') ; fuller details are intrinsically provided by the links on the website.

Readers will also be confronted by unmodernised punctuation, which is treated systematically in Chapter 4 and elsewhere as necessary. Older conventions of punctuation are generally far more coherent than critics tend to allow, and while at first appearance (often in rela-

[2] Before *c.* 1630 the Roman alphabet was reckoned to have 24 letters, i/j and u/v each counting as one (which explains why 'W', double-u, is formed as a double-v) : 'i' was used initially and medially, 'j' terminally (thus 'Iulius' and 'maior', but 'viij'), while 'v' was used initially, 'u' medially and terminally (thus 'vnto' and 'vpon', but 'loue', 'haue', 'glou[e]'). Meaning is not affected, but care is sometimes needed, as with 'Iove' (Jove) and 'love'. Before *c.*1800 's' and 'ſ' were variant lower-case or *minuscule* (p. 100) forms of the same letter : the upper-case form was always 'S', but in lower-case 'ſ' was used initially and medially, *short-s* terminally (thus 'ſuffers', 'loſs').

tively brief quotations) unexpected marks in unpredicted places may seem anomalous, familiarity breeds both understanding and respect. In some critical books with 'unmodernised' quotations, the uses of inverted commas are nevertheless modernised into conformity with the style of the main text ; not here. Inverted commas in quotations are retained as is, whether single, double, or admixed. My own practice in the main text is exemplified by 'deceives' and "deceaues" in the last paragraph : 'deceives' (with single inverted commas) because that is the normal modern spelling of the word in question, which needs to be clearly indicated to assist easy reading, but is not a quotation ; "deceaues" (with double inverted commas) because that is a quotation from Marlowe, the fidelity of which I guarantee. Single inverted commas may do slightly variant duty, as around some titles or as '*scare quotes*' (p. 130), but in the main text double inverted commas always indicate exact quotations.[3]

I have, however, made one systematic exception to a policy of exact quotation, by making consistent in quotations, and extending to my own practice, a welcome feature of many pre-1939 texts, the use of spaces before as well as after semi-colons, colons, and question- and exclamation-marks. I personally find it extremely helpful as a reader for articulation of sense to be thus displayed, in verse and prose, and as a teacher know how vital it can be in enabling a competent sense of grammatical construction to develop ; as computers now permit me to provide OUP with the text directly, as attachments, and for such conventions to be preserved in production, it becomes possible to adapt personal practice without financial penalty, and seems foolish not to do so.

Besides the exemplary poems, the major addition is of exercises : versification, requiring only a pen and paper (and not even that if you can concentrate hard enough), offers no challenge to the print edition, but, with the website available, to restrict analytical exercises to those possible without a computer is unacceptable. Some such exercises (or where history, biography, and gender are concerned, a commentary in lieu) are provided, but other and interactive exercises are and will be available online. In some instances, of course, the computer is merely a handy tool for doing what could be done anyway—highlighting or colour-coding, for example—but through labour- and time-saving,

[3] Strictly speaking, only *photoquotations* are wholly unmodernised—in any re-setting there is almost always a *de facto* modernisation of type-fount, some aspects of layout, and the general *bibliographical codes* (p. 96)—but I have been as stringent as possible in preserving alphanumerics, punctuation, and details of layout.

clarity, and interactivity, online exercises can also encourage and advance analytical competence in ways we are still discovering.

The only major cut from the first print edition is of the student-essays, transferred to the website, where they are joined by a much wider range of examples provided by students at various levels using the *Handbook*. Other (interactive) materials have been and will be added to the site. It is not yet clear what may simply be a form of bonus-track, nor how the Web may most profitably be exploited, but there is fearsome invigoration in the scale of this change, and it will be extremely interesting to see in a few years what the interactive aspects of the website have generated.[4] Particularly in dealing with layout, punctuation, and rhyme there are compelling pedagogic opportunities here, but there is also a severe danger of over-expansion : text online cannot profitably be read any faster than print, the time available to students to read course-texts and research their essays has not grown, and how they choose to deploy it remains to be seen.

I have extensively reworked most of Chapters 1–8 (Metre–Syntax) to address the assorted complaints and my own second thoughts, but later chapters have changed far less, though all text has been curry-combed and emended as necessary. The material on exams has been changed to reflect the transfer of student essays to the website and include material on written work devised for *The Drama Handbook*. To summarise the methodological changes :

- *Norton Anthology* references are retained and updated to the 5th edition (2004) ; *Oxford Anthology* references have been cut.
- Where there is a *Norton* reference no other is provided for citations, nor for modern quotations unless the text I quote differs (in which case there is a footnote). For unmodernised older texts only a brief parenthetical reference is usually provided, but for modern texts <u>not</u> in the *Norton* full bibliographical data is given in footnotes on first occurrence, and short-title references thereafter.
- Sources cited in footnotes throughout without bibliographical detail (including anthologies cited by editor and/or short-title as the source of poetic quotations) are fully detailed in the 'Select Bibliography and Further Reading'. To minimise footnote clutter

[4] Consider a movement in eight years from three student essays, predicated on one university system and included against conventions of academic monography, to the proto-normative provision of a website with a varied collection of such essays, offering future examinees access to their peers, not within one school or university but around the world.

standard abbreviations have been used, notably 'U[niversity]' and 'P[ress]'. See also the list of Abbreviations, p. xx.

- Again to minimise clutter, cross-references appear simply as parentheses of the form '(p. xxi)'
- Specific directions to a page of the website are occasionally indicated by the Wingdings computer-mouse (🖰).

The chapter-glossaries, main glossary, initial use of italics for technical terms, and use of underlining for emphasis, are retained ; all are explained in the Introduction (p. xxi).

The one change I bitterly regret is the record of Jeremy Maule's death in my renewed dedication. Few have done more for their students, or been kinder to their friends.

John Lennard
Kingston, W. I.
June 2005

Abbreviations

BCE	Before Common Era (= BC)
CE	Common Era (= AD)
ch.	chapter
FSG	Farrar, Straus and Giroux
IT	information technology
LRB	London Review of Books
ME	Middle English
MS/S	Manuscript/s
OE	Old English
OED	Oxford English Dictionary
OED2	Oxford English Dictionary, 2nd edition, 1989
OUP	Oxford University Press
P.	Press
RKP	Routledge and Kegan Paul
Sh. OED	Shorter Oxford English Dictionary
TESL	teaching English as a Second Language
TS/S	typescript/s
U.	University

Introduction

This book is for anyone who wants to read poetry with a better understanding of its craft and technique ; it is also a textbook and crib for school and undergraduate students facing exams in practical criticism. Teaching the practical criticism of poetry at several universities, and talking to students about their previous teaching, has made me sharply aware of how little consensus there is about the subject. Some teachers do not distinguish practical criticism from critical theory, or regard it as a critical theory, to be taught alongside psychoanalytical, feminist, Marxist, and structuralist theories ; others seem to do very little except invite discussion of 'how it feels' to read poem *x*. And as practical criticism (though not always called that) remains compulsory in most English Literature coursework and exams, at school and university, this is an unwelcome state of affairs.

For students there are many consequences. Teachers at school and university may contradict one another, and too rarely put the problem of differing viewpoints and frameworks for analysis in perspective ; important aspects of the subject are omitted in the confusion, leaving otherwise more than competent students with little or no idea of what they are being asked to do. How can this be remedied without losing the richness and diversity of thought which, at its best, practical criticism can foster ? What are the basics ? How may they best be taught ?

My own answer is that the basics are an understanding of and ability to judge the elements of a poet's craft. Profoundly different as they are, Chaucer, Shakespeare, Pope, Dickinson, Eliot, Walcott, and Plath could readily converse about the techniques of which they are common masters ; few undergraduates I have encountered know much about metre beyond the terms 'blank verse' and 'iambic pentameter', much about form beyond 'couplet' and 'sonnet', or anything about rhyme more complicated than an assertion that two words do or don't. The commonest fault of their own writing is an inability to use any punctuation beyond full-stops and commas (parentheses, colons, semi-colons, dashes, and hyphens might as well not exist) and a consequent tendency to connect clauses in endless series at the cost of all subtlety. Yet it is exactly techniques of ordering to which (as to the other elements of craft—layout and lineation, diction and syntax, deployments of biography and history) close reading must attend.

To name and define the elements of poetic craft is, of course, in part a set of ideological decisions, but the influence of ideology on metre or rhyme is very much slower than its influence on what is put into metre or made to rhyme. I do not believe a craft-based practical criticism to be incompatible with or opposed to theoretical approaches ; rather, it is a helpful precursor of them all, a foundation-course in reading. To interpret a given use of form, or a rhyme, or some metrical device may involve, for any particular reader, reference to Freud, Marx, de Saussure, or de Beauvoir ; it must first be noticed by the reader, and it is much easier to notice things of which you have some knowledge. And while theoretical criticisms may seek to account for a text without detailed reference to its technique, to how it has achieved its texture, practical criticism—if the term means anything at all—cannot avoid that engagement with technique we call close reading. Close reading is itself only a beginning, to be followed by more distant readings, but it is a sensible place to start.

If what is to be taught is the value and uses of the poet's tools, the method must be their itemisation, description, and demonstration. The basic list of tools represented by my chapter-titles is not in dispute—metre, form, lineation, rhyme, and so on are fundamental constituents of most Western poetry—but to some issues, notably layout and punctuation, I give more attention than is usual because I find it helpful to do so ; to others, notably class- and gender-conscious analysis, I attend less than is now usual because I have little to add to what others have said. These personal choices are balanced out in the suggestions for further reading, and I have generally tried to describe and explain with an even hand.

I use (wherever possible) material in the 5th edition of *The Norton Anthology of Poetry* (2004) which remains the fullest, most widely used single volume. Full texts of all poems quoted or cited are, wherever possible, provided (or linked) on the companion-website at http://www.oup.com/uk/literature/poetry. To avoid crippling copyright fees and keep the book reasonably short quotations are as brief as possible, use of either the *Norton* or the website is assumed, and readers are intended to have one or other available as they read.

PAGE-REFERENCES OF THE FORM (N999) ARE TO THE *NORTON ANTHOLOGY*. 🖰 INDICATES A DIRECTION OR REFERENCE TO THE WEBSITE.

Occasionally, when they represent the readiest source, the 3rd and 4th editions of the *Norton* (1983, 1996) are cited in the form '3N000' or '4N000'. All readers are strongly advised to consult in full any poem cited or excerpted, for unless you look up these poems (looking carefully at how a particular tool is used in an individual poem, seeing how my generalisations relate to the specifics of its use) your understanding will be sketchy. Needing regularly to consult poems, it is best to treat this book as a short guided tour, to be taken at no more than a chapter a day—and only that fast if you are in a hurry. My advice would be to take a month or more, working through each chapter in short but regular sessions, going on to the next only when happy that you have absorbed the last. In face-to-face teaching I normally spread out the chapters over a whole term as one among several subjects (a practice candidates for exams are particularly advised to follow) ; between this first course and exams there would be other courses to deepen students' knowledge and develop their confidence. In short, any student who reads this book cover-to-cover in a sitting (except as revision) will be wasting their time. I also require students facing closed exams regularly to write a timed (1-hour) answer, so they become wholly familiar with the contours of that hour, and their timing of answers quite automatic. This has proven benefits, but if you are facing an exam you and your teachers must decide how much practice you need.

At the end of each chapter I look at the topic of the chapter at work in Derek Walcott's 'Nearing Forty' and two or three other poems drawn from a small canonical group, so that technical readings are built up chapter by chapter. These recurrent poems, from Donne's 'The Flea' to Hill's 'September Song', are invoked only in the chapters they best illuminate, but the sequential development of complementary technical readings makes it easier to understand the interrelation of elements within poems of varying ages. Even for 'Nearing Forty', covered in every chapter, there remain aspects of the poem I ignore : but any reading which did claim to be complete would have to include most (if not all) of what I do say. It may seem odd to privilege a poem about a mid-life crisis for students, but I find it works well in both class and individual teaching, and the growing enthusiasm of students working on the poem seems to me a valuable proof of practical criticism. It is not only that familiar and accessible poems can be read more deeply with a knowledge of their craft ; such knowledge also makes accessible to any reader poems which may at first seem obscure or unrewarding. 'Nearing Forty' is printed in full on pages 22–3, as it appears in Walcott's *Collected Poems 1948–84* ; the other recurrent poems are printed in full where they are first invoked, and all are on the website.

One of my purposes is to introduce students to the technical vocabulary of poetry and its criticism. This vocabulary, though perhaps offputting, is essential if technical knowledge is to be usable in exams, and to make accurate argument about poetic techniques possible, between students as well as with teachers. Without it practical criticism becomes inevitably long-winded and inexact—imagine trying to discuss music without names for notes, keys, and instruments—so the matter must be tackled ; at the same time it is true there are disputes about nomenclature, terms that are ambiguous or duplicated, and some that are missing. Where there are alternatives to my own choice, or where (in a few instances) I offer *coinages* (terms of my own invention), my decisions are explained in a footnote. As with any professional *lexicon* (the vocabulary of a specific trade or activity) these technical terms are mutually supporting : the more of them you know, the easier it is to learn a new one ; conversely, the first few are often awkward, or defined by unknown others. All technical terms are *italicised* (set in slanting *italic* letters) on their first appearance[1] : to avoid confusion I have therefore not used italics for non-technical words I simply want to stress, but have underlined them. (Titles and foreign words, however, are italicised in the conventional way.) I have tried to introduce technical vocabulary in a helpful order, and where I have had to introduce a term before the chapter which deals with it properly I usually italicise, and in tougher or important cases provide a short definition in the text or a footnote with a reference to the pages where it is dealt with in full. The commonest and most useful technical terms introduced in each chapter are grouped and defined in a sub-glossary at the end of each chapter ; all are defined and indexed in the Glossary at the back. To assist historical awareness all poets' dates are also provided with their index entry.

One word I might be expected to have used in a technical sense I have deliberately avoided. An 'image', according to the *Shorter Oxford English Dictionary* (definition 4), is 'A counterpart, copy M[iddle]

[1] The names of punctuation-marks, at pp. 111–40, are (for reasons of layout) given in bold.

E[nglish] ; a symbol, emblem, representation 1566 ; a type, typical example, embodiment 1548' : the word has been used by critics in all these and many other ways. So inconsistent has that use been, covering everything from the meaning of a single word to a meaning arising from a whole poem, that 'image' does not seem to me truly a technical term, and I have not found it difficult to avoid. It remains true, though, that almost all the techniques I discuss (metrical, formal, syntactical, whatever) will probably first be apprehended by a reader as components or substructures of an 'image' (of one or another kind) that the poem (or poet) has communicated to them.

There is also one word I probably use too much that doesn't readily fit into a particular chapter : irony. It is notoriously hard to define exactly : common to most definitions is a contrast between what is (or is said or done) and what might be expected to be (or to be said or done) ; difficulty of definition arises because the word always invokes this double state of being and perceiving. The Japanese characters for 'irony' literally mean 'skin-and-muscle', the surface you see and the power hidden beneath it ; my rule-of-thumb definition is that irony is 'the preservation of distance'—the corollary is that whenever you use the word you should be able to specify how and between what and what a distance is being preserved. I find this definition helpful in teaching and recommend it—but a word of warning, for many critics assume this preserved distance is necessarily undermining, antagonistic to one or other pole of the irony, as if the ironic was no more than a sarcastic response to thwarted expectation. In modern writing this is too often the case, but far less so in older work. A Renaissance writer like Donne may be acutely aware of the distance between himself and God, and use irony to figure it : to characterise this agonised relationship as 'undermining' is reductive, and it has nothing whatever to do with sarcasm. Donne knew very well that God was behind him in both senses, albeit sometimes at a distance—so in talking of irony you should remember that its modern sense is often lax and misleading.

Finally, please try to enjoy the poems as you learn to see and hear at work within them the techniques with which they are written. Twain once said that humour is like a frog—you can dissect it but it tends to die in the process ; some have felt the same of poetry, that analysis spoils pleasure. I find the opposite, that understanding redoubles admiration ; in any case, if you don't enjoy what you study, learning will be slow.

1
Metre

> to a poet there may be no more important element of a poem.
>
> JON STALLWORTHY (N2029)

> (Rod upon mild silver rod, like meter
> Broken in fleet cahoots with subject-matter)
>
> JAMES MERRILL, 'The Book of Ephraim', 'F'[1]

Rhythm is basic : hearing our hearts beat, feeling our lungs breathe, walking, dancing, sex, and sport—all create and require a sense of rhythm. In all speech rhythmic patterns help us pick out phrase and meaning from strings of syllables, and to create and shape these rhythms, manipulating readers with words underpinned by them, is part of a poet's job. All poets use rhythm and all readers of poetry hear rhythm, whether or not they are conscious of doing so, but *prosody*, the description and analysis of poetic rhythms, can be as complicated as musical notation, and different languages require different sorts of prosody.

In the classical languages prosody was *quantitative*, based on vowel length or quantity. In Anglo-Saxon (or *Old English*) prosody was *qualitative*, based on patterns of stress or accent (with other complex rules concerning alliteration, p. 202). In Slavic languages, like Russian, words can be very long, because such *synthetic* languages build a lot of meaning into one word by adding prefixes and inflecting endings, but there is also a rule which allows only one stress per word, however long—so Russian poetry is usually analysed with a basis in accent but many variants. In Romance languages, like French, rules of stress are more flexible than Russian but more rigid than English ones, and French

[1] *The Changing Light at Sandover* (1982; New York: Atheneum, 1984), 20.

poetry is usually analysed in *syllabic* prosody, according to the number of syllables in each line.

Modern English is a very *analytical* language, one which distributes meaning among many words and has a grammar dependent on prepositions and word-order rather than inflected endings (pp. 263–4). Its prosody has varied as the language and culture have evolved : medieval Middle English is usually analysed accentually, mixed with other rules concerning alliteration and/or rhyme (p. 165), and accentual systems apply as late as John Skelton (?1460–1529), whose tumbling prosody is sometimes called *Skeltonics*—but the main post-medieval system of prosody in English is the *accentual-syllabic*. This is a qualitative prosody, which disregards syllable length and is instead concerned with formal patterns of *un/stressed beats*, the syllables on which emphatic accent is (not) placed. Syllables matter, because each beat will be pronounced as one syllable, but it is possible to conflate or multiply syllables : 'thickening', for example, could have two syllables (thickening) or three (thick-en-ing) ; some words can be shortened by substituting an apostrophe (') for one or more letters, as *cannot* → *can't*, *of* → *o'*, or *never* → *ne'er*. This is called *elision* (the verb is to *elide*, and missing letters are *elided*), but you can't usually elide stresses in the same way.

Accentual-syllabic prosody isn't remotely perfect, but has proven the most popular and useful system. It is *neoclassical*, derived from Greek and/or Roman writings, which accounts for its many strengths, flexibility, and widespread acceptance, but some scholars argue forcefully that some aspects are ill-adapted to English, and alternatives should be considered (p. 12). Scholars often disagree in analysing prosody, partly because it's genuinely complicated, like the drum- and bass-lines in a song but with rhythm created by words, not played behind them. As with music there is a technical vocabulary that puts people off, but without knowing the words you can't talk about the rhythms usefully or write about them compactly in timed work. But your real guide must always be your own ears : don't hesitate to read a poem aloud as you work (or mouth it silently in an exam), and if I ask you to read something aloud please do so : rhythm is much easier to speak and hear than describe, and reading lines of poetry aloud—making your mouth say what your eyes see—will help you think about them.

In accentual-syllabic prosody the basic unit of poetry is the *line*, clearly visible on the page, which may be defined as 'a single sequence of characters read from left to right'. Lines are analysed by breaking the *metre*,[2] the rhythmic pattern, down into the repetition of a basic unit, a *foot*, and saying how many *feet* make up a line. For example, this line from Shakespeare's 'Sonnet 12' (N258 ; text from Q1, 1609, omitting a *drop-cap*.[3]) :

When I doe count the clock that tels the time,

would usually be spoken like this (stressed beats are in CAPITAL LETTERS, or 'caps') :

When I doe COUNT the CLOCK that TELS the TIME

This is analysed as five feet, each comprising an unstressed followed by a stressed beat, the *ictus* (Latin, 'a blow or stroke') ; I have separated the feet with vertical slashes :

When I | doe COUNT | the CLOCK | that TELS | the TIME

This kind of foot is an *iamb* (pronounced e-AMB) and there are five of them, so the line is an *iambic pentameter* (Greek πεντε [pente], 'five'). If there are only four iambs, as in this line from *The Winter's Tale* (text from F1,1623, where it is italicised as a song) :

When DAF- | faDILS | beGIN | to PEERE,

then the line is an *iambic tetrameter* (Greek τετταρα [tettara], 'four'), and so on.

The basic feet and line-lengths you need to know are these[4] ; 'u' indicates an unstressed beat and 'x' an ictus[5] :

ux : *iamb*, from which the adjective is *iambic*
xu : *trochee, trochaic*
xx : *spondee, spondaic*
uu : *pyrrhic, pyrrhic*

---

[2] This word is confusing : in the US it is always 'meter' ; in the UK 'meter' and 'metre' are distinct. On its own, meaning 'rhythmic pattern in general', it is 'metre', but as a suffix, meaning 'a measurement', is 'meter' (as in 'pentameter').

[3] A large initial letter (here the W of 'When') occupying more than one line.

[4] The named triple and quadruple feet, most uncommon and some very rare, are in full:
triple feet : *tribrach* (uuu) ; *dactyl* (xuu) ; *amphibrach* (uxu) ; *anapæst* (uux) ; *antibacchius* (xxu) ; *amphimacer* (xux) ; *bacchius* (uxx) ; *molossus* (xxx) ;
quadruple feet : *proceleusmatic* (uuuu) ; *first* (xuuu), *second* (uxuu), *third* (uuxu), and *fourth paeon* (uuux) ; *ionic (a) majore* (xxuu) ; *ditrochee* (xuxu) ; *choriamb* (xuux) ; *antispast* (uxxu) ; *diamb* (uxux) ; *ionic (a) minore* (uuxx) ; *first* (uxxx), *second* (xuxx), *third* (xxux), and *fourth epitrite* (xxxu) ; *dispondee* (xxxx).

[5] Different notations may be used, as 'x' for an unstressed beat and '/' for an ictus. Always check what system a particular author is using.

uux : *anapæst, anapæstic*
xuu : *dactyl, dactylic*

one foot per line	:	*monometer*, adjective	*monometric*
two feet per line	:	*dimeter*	*dimetric*
three feet per line	:	*trimeter*	*trimetric*
four feet per line	:	*tetrameter*	*tetrametric*
five feet per line	:	*pentameter*	*pentametric*
six feet per line	:	*hexameter*	*hexametric*
seven feet per line	:	*heptameter*	*heptametric*
eight feet per line	:	*octameter*	*octametric*

There is an easy way of remembering which foot is which, by pronouncing the name of each to embody its rhythm. The word i-AMB is an iamb, an unstressed beat followed by an ictus ; the word TRO-chee (TRO-key) is a trochee, an ictus followed by an unstressed beat ; SPONDEE is a spondee, two equally stressed beats ; pyrrhic (pih-rick) is really a spondee (no word has no stress) but pronounced quickly is as near a pyrrhic as any word can be ; and an-a-PÆST (an-a-PEEST) is an anapæst. For dactyls use the adjective DAC-tyl-ic, or remember that it comes from Greek δακτιλοζ [daktilos], 'a finger', and is long-short-short (stress-unstress-unstress), like finger-joints.[6]

A full description of a line identifies the kind and number of feet, and immediately tells you what the basic pattern is : a trochaic trimeter will be three trochees, 'xu | xu | xu' ; an anapæstic dimeter (like ll. 3–4 of a limerick) will be two anapæsts, 'uux | uux', and so on. That is the basic pattern, but not every line described as an iambic pentameter (or whatever) will exactly follow it : a sequence of completely regular lines

[6] Another useful mnemonic is Coleridge's 'Metrical Feet', written for his sons ; each line is in the foot it names. As a classicist Coleridge refers to 'longs' and 'shorts' rather than un/stressed beats (Greek and Latin prosody depend on vowel length), and includes the *amphibrach(ys)* (uxu) and *amphimacer* (xux) :

> Trochee trips from long to short;
> From long to long in solemn sort
> Slow Spondee stalks; strong foot! yet ill able
> Ever to come up with Dactyl trisyllable.
> Iambics march from short to long;—
> With a leap and a bound the swift Anapæsts throng;
> One syllable long, with one short at each side,
> Amphibrachys hastes with a stately stride;—
> First and last being long, middle short, Amphimacer
> Strikes his thundering hoofs like a proud high-bred Racer.

There are also remarkable verses exemplifying complex metres by Tennyson, usually called 'In Quantity'.

would sound monotonous and artificial. So to describe a poem as 'in iambic pentameter' means that the pattern of five iambs is the template a poet has used as the basis of each line, which readers can use to identify variations, effects at work in a particular line. There is an analogy with time-signature and syncopation in music, or you might think of the template as default-settings a poet will then modify.

Many combinations of feet and line-lengths are possible, but iambic pentameter (five iambs), and tetrameter (four iambs) are much the commonest. Spondees and pyrrhics are never used as basic metres, because lines made from them would be all *ictūs* (ik-toos),[7] which would sound like a dalek, or all unstressed beats, which is impossible. Instead spondees and pyrrhics are used within iambic and trochaic lines to vary the rhythm, acting as a *distinguishing* foot to the ear, just as SMALL CAPITALS or *italic* are distinguishing *faces* of type to the eye.[8] An iamb in an otherwise trochaic line, or a trochee in an iambic line, is called an *inverted* foot, and will also act as a distinguishing foot.[9] Both distinguishing and inverted feet are varieties of *substitute* feet, those which replace a regular foot.

Lines made up of iambic and anapæstic feet produce a *rising rhythm*, because stressed beats, for which the voice tends to be pitched slightly higher, come after unstressed beats, when the voice is pitched lower. If you read aloud these lines in iambic pentameter from Marlowe's *Hero and Leander* (N239 ; text from Q2, 1598), you'll hear your voice rise with each stress and drop down to rise again with the next :

> Her vaile was artificiall flowers and leaues,
> Whoſe workmanſhip both man and beaſt deceaues.
>
> Her VAILE | was ART- | iFI- | ciall FLOWERS | and LEAUES,
> Whose WORK- | manSHIP | both MAN | and BEAST | deCEAUES.

It sounds silly when exaggerated, but rising rhythm is the basic pattern of sound in most English speech. We all talk in iambs and anapæsts,

---

[7] Latin 5th declension plurals are formed with long 'u', shown by a macron ; cf. status, statūs.

[8] A fount of type (font in the US) is a design for a complete set of letters and numbers. This book is printed in Stone Serif ; this is Comic sans MS ; and this is Westminster. Each fount has designs for all lower-case and UPPER-CASE letters (or 'large caps') and numerals, in roman, *italic* and SMALL CAPS, each a (*type-*)*face* of that fount. Each face comes in different sizes, called points ; the main text of the book is in 12-point : it could be 14-, 16-, or even 18-point, but that would waste paper.

[9] An anapæst in a dactylic line, or a dactyl in an anapæstic, would also be inverted feet.

and as you listen to others | you WILL | be A- | ble EA- | siLY | to HEAR | the RIS- | ing RHY- | thm IN | their WORDS. This is how most native speakers of English would normally speak those words ; it is also a natural sequence of nine iambs. This explains why iambic metres are most popular with poets, because they sound most like ORdinARy SPEECH in PEOple's MOUTHS.

Lines of trochees and dactyls produce a *falling rhythm*, with voice pitched higher on each opening ictus and lower on each following unstressed beat. It is rare to hear anyone talk conversationally in English in trochees, and sounds strange ; in poetry strangeness can be harnessed to good use. Longfellow's *The Song of Hiawatha* (1855, N954) is famous partly for its trochaic tetrameter ; this is from book III, 'Hiawatha's Childhood' (I haven't indicated the ictūs because every line is regular ; if you read the lines aloud you will hear your voice create the falling rhythm) :

By the shore of Gitche Gumee,
By the shining Big-Sea-Water,
Stood the wigwam of Nokomis,
Daughter of the Moon, Nokomis.
Dark behind it rose the forest,
Rose the black and gloomy pine-trees,
Rose the firs with cones upon them;
Bright before it beat the water,
Beat the clear and sunny water,
Beat the shining Big-Sea-Water.

You can hear the falling rhythm become a chant, helped along by the repetitions. It doesn't sound natural—but there's no reason it should, and as Longfellow was writing about Hiawatha and his wife Minnehaha, both strongly trochaic names, it made sense for him to choose a trochaic metre.[10]

Browning sought a very different effect in 'Soliloquy of the Spanish Cloister' (N1010), one of the great hate-poems in English ; the metre is again trochaic tetrameter :

---

[10] Longfellow was influenced by the Finnish epic *Kalevala* ; an OUP reader tells me that "In trochaic tetrameter, both alliterative and repetitive in phrasing, it was the last oral epic tradition to be collected in Europe, by Lönnrot in the early nineteenth century, and therefore of great interest to philologists of the time and Longfellow's model." In Finnish, first syllables of words are always stressed, and falling rhythms closest to common speech ; things are otherwise in English, as Longfellow found out. See the 'Editor's Preface' in the illustrated 1909 edition (🖱).

There's a great text in Galatians,
  Once you trip on it, entails
Twenty-nine distinct damnations,
  One sure if another fails :

THERE'S a | GREAT text | IN Ga- | LAtians,
  ONCE you | TRIP on I IT, en- | TAILS
TWENty- | NINE dis- | TINCT dam- | NAtions,
  ONE sure | IF a- | NOTHer | FAILS :

It sounds more natural than *Hiawatha* (Browning was a better poet) but still odd, and the whole poem shows the monk speaking the lines to be pretty odd himself ; metrical oddity suggests mental oddity, unusual stresses as much as actual words betraying his obsessions—to begin with, there is no such text in Galatians. Trochaic effects vary, but it's always worth asking what use of falling rhythm a poet is making.

Notice that the second and fourth lines in Browning's stanza are missing their last unstressed beat (or have an incomplete fourth trochee). You could argue therefore that the poem isn't all in trochaic tetrameter, because every other line is trochaic *sesquitrimeter* (with 3½ trochees),[11] but as it's common to omit a final unstressed beat people mostly don't bother ; in the same way, iambic and anapæstic lines can miss their first unstressed beat. Such lines are *catalectic* (from Greek καταληκτικοζ [catalektikos], 'to leave off'), and are common ; it's almost always unstressed beats at the beginning or end of the line that are missing.

Lines can also be *hypermetric* (from Greek υπερ [hyper], 'over-', + 'meter'), with an extra beat, like Shakespeare's famous line from *Hamlet* (text from F1) :

To be, or not to be, that is the Queſtion :
To BE, | or NOT | to BE, | THAT is | the QUES- | tion :

'THAT is', the fourth foot, is inverted, a trochee, but the others are regular iambs, and the line works as an iambic pentameter despite the fact that '-tion' is an eleventh beat. Such additional beats used to be called *feminine endings* if unstressed, and *masculine endings* if stressed ; these sexist terms are easily replaced by *stressed* and *unstressed hyperbeats*.

Feet with two beats (iambs and trochees) create *duple* metres, whose basic pattern is an alternation of stressed and unstressed beats ;

[11] You can add *sesqui-* (from Latin, *semis que*, meaning 'and-a-half') to any line-length—sesquimonometers, lines of 1½ feet; sesquidimeters, 2½, etc.

similarly, feet with three beats (mainly anapæsts and dactyls) create *triple* metres, and in English rising triple metres tend to be comic because of the tripping rhythm produced by consecutive unstressed beats. Limericks, for example, are in anapæstic trimeter (ll. 1–2 + 5) and dimeter (ll. 3–4) : read aloud this, by Edward Lear, and you'll hear the triple rhythm (all lines are catalectic, with the first unstressed beat missing, which is common in limericks) :

> There WAS | an Old MAN | with a BEARD,
> Who SAID, | "It is JUST | as I FEARED!—
>   Two OWLS | and a HEN,
>   Four LARKS | and a WREN,
> Have ALL | built their NESTS | in my BEARD!" (N1041)

The connection between triple rhythm and comedy is strong but not unbreakable ; it's possible, for example, to write serious limericks, or ones about such a bitter subject that they aren't at all funny however they trip off the tongue (pp. 29, 76).

These technical terms make it possible to write about rhythms you hear, but only in very boring poems will all lines conform exactly to the prescribed metrical pattern. For one thing, writing an exactly iambic line means any longer word/s in the line must alternate un/stressed syllables, as "AL-ter-NAT-ing" does. This leaves a wide but nevertheless restricted choice of vocabulary ("vo-CAB-u-la-ry" would be out). It would not mean, though, that every word must be iambic, because a trochaic word could be split across two iambs, as "unctuous" and "vapor" are in this line from *Paradise Lost* (IX. 635 ; N439) :

> ComPACT | of UNC- | tuous VA- | por, WHICH | the NIGHT

Both "unctuous" and "vapor" must be pronounced trochaically, as 'UNCtuous' and 'VApor'—you cannot naturally say them iambically, as 'uncTUOUS' or 'vaPOR'—but by putting the stressed syllable of each word in one foot and the unstressed in the next, Milton fits both into a regular iambic line. This is one way of enlivening regular lines, and in reading you hear simultaneously the *cadence* (Latin, *cadere*, to fall) of trochaic words, the falling rhythm they try to generate (which slows you down), and the rising rhythm of iambic metre (which keeps you going). In this way it is possible to fit iambic words into trochaic lines, and vice versa ; anapæstic and dactylic words are a different problem, and it is common for poets in one or another way to distort the prescribed rhythm.

This variability and irregularity can sometimes make it difficult to decide what the basic metre is. For example, "Hoping for love, longing for change" (HOping for LOVE, LONGing for CHANGE) could be described as an iambic tetrameter with substitute trochees in first and third place ('xu ux xu ux'), or as a trochaic tetrameter with substitute iambs in second and fourth place ('xu ux xu ux'). Both descriptions are accurate, and nothing in the line itself indicates one is better than another ; what usually makes one description clearly more helpful is context, for if the line appears in a sequence of predominantly iambic (or trochaic) lines, there is little point in supposing that for one line the poet changed the basic foot. You should therefore never try to identify a metre from one line—especially not the first, often irregular precisely because it is first ; instead read a dozen or so lines and decide which template best fits what you are hearing. The vast majority of poems written before 1900, and many written later, do have a consistent template which isn't difficult to identify, and you can then begin to spot variations.

Once you know the basic foot and line-length, you confront three aspects of metre. The first is the prescribed pattern of stress, as 'ux | ux | ux | ux | ux' for iambic pentameter : the template (or default-setting). The second is the way you would speak the words of the line in everyday conversation, the normal pronunciation of the words (settings you superimpose on some or all of the default-settings). The third is created by the interaction of the first two, the rhythm of that particular line described prosodically ; working it out is called *scanning* the line, and the final pattern on which you decide is your *scansion*.

Sometimes prescribed pattern of stress and normal pronunciation are identical, in which case there is no problem. Sometimes they differ, and normal pronunciation will then usually overturn prescribed pattern to create a substitute foot of some kind. This must be so, for you cannot easily mispronounce words to make them fit : "VOC-a-BU-la-RY" is at first incomprehensible as a sound, then irritating or stupid. It is possible, especially in song-lyrics, hymns, and strongly oral poems such as *ballads* (where pitch and stress may be very stylized in performance) to force slight changes of pronunciation, usually for the sake of rhyme. In verse 19 of 'The Twa Sisters', an old Scottish ballad—"The miller quickly drew the dam, [/] And there he found a drowned woman"[12]—the last word would normally be a trochee (WOman), but the rhyme

---

[12] A line-break is usually represented by a *solidus* or *forward slash* (/) : p. 127. Within inverted commas, square brackets (*crotchets*) indicate an editorial insertion/emendation.

with "dam" prods a reader towards an iamb (woMAN) ; in the last verse "then" rhymes with "Ellen", forcing the name from 'ELLen' to 'ellEN'. An accent thus forced to move along by one or more beats is *wrenched* : they rarely sound good but can be useful, even necessary, in a particular poem. Scanning a line therefore involves identifying first the pattern of the metre, then which feet (if any) are altered from their prescribed value by the actual words (identify the default-settings and which have been overridden).

Even with twentieth- and twenty-first-century poetry in *free verse*, with variable or less strictly observed metres where the usefulness of accentual-syllabic prosody (or any neoclassical system) may be limited, it should not be forgotten. As a rule of thumb, if the template seems to be changing every few lines complete metrical analysis is likely to be lengthy and complex, and (especially in exams) you are probably best off confining yourself to a straightforward observation of the metre as free verse while pointing out any particularly striking or pleasing local effects—but even then don't turn your ears off completely. Sometimes there will be groups of lines in a regular metre : in Eliot's 'The Love Song of J. Alfred Prufrock' (N1340), for example, lines vary from three (l. 45) to twenty syllables (l. 102) in length ; but ll. 112–18, where Prufrock talks about Hamlet, and ll. 125–31, the last seven, are blocks of regular iambic pentameter. As the metre in which much of *Hamlet* is written it is appropriate (or ironic, as Prufrock is explaining how he isn't like Prince Hamlet) for lines invoking it to be in iambic pentameter ; regularity and commonness of metre also help Prufrock to find a place where he can stop, as the irregularity of many earlier lines reflects the way in which, uncertain and worried, he rambles on.

A related example is the last line of John N. Morris's '*Hamlet* at Sea', describing a performance of Shakespeare's play on the *Dragon*, sailing in convoy with the *Hector* to the East Indies in 1607.[13] For the performance most sailors from both ships went aboard the *Dragon* ; some had to stay on the *Hector* to man it but could see lights and hear noise, and as these sailors strain to hear *Hamlet* across the water :

It sounds like happiness at a distance.

The poem is in free verse, so metre is variable, but many lines, including this one, are in iambic pentameter—as one might expect in a

[13] In Morris, *A Schedule of Benefits* (New York: Atheneum, 1987). This performance of *Hamlet* is the earliest known outside Britain ; see Gary Taylor, 'Hamlet in Africa 1607', in Ivo Kamps and Jyotsna Singh, eds, *Travel Knowledge: European 'Discoveries' in the Early Modern Period* (New York: Palgrave, 2001) and online (🖱).

poem about *Hamlet*. The prescribed pattern of stresses is therefore five iambs :

It SOUNDS | like HAP- | piNESS | at A | disTANCE.

but in ordinary speech the line would usually be spoken like this :

It SOUNDS | like HAP- | piness | at a | DIStance.

As you can see, prescription and ordinary speech are identical in the first two feet, "It SOUNDS | like HAP-", so there is no problem and the result is two iambs. But in the third foot, the prescribed iamb is not matched by the ordinary speech : "happiness" is usually pronounced 'HAP-pi-ness', with only one stress, on the first syllable (i.e. it is dactylic) ; '-pi-ness', here the foot, is thus a pyrrhic, two unstressed beats. The prescription wants to make that pyrrhic into an iamb by stressing "-ness", so giving 'HAP-pi-NESS' two stresses, on the first and last syllables. This is unusual, but not obviously wrong, a pronunciation which can be understood and doesn't offend the ear unless grossly exaggerated. You could insist it be scanned as a pyrrhic ; I would allow it as a weak iamb, with a relatively light ictus (-piNESS rather than -piNESS).

The clash between prescription and speech is stronger in the fourth foot. An iamb is prescribed, to make it "at A", but in speech it would be another pyrrhic, without a stress on either word, and pronounced quite quickly, as short, unstressed words tend to be. Making the foot into an iamb by stressing "A" would slow the line (which might or might not be acceptable) ; it would also affect meaning, insisting that this distance was 'a distance', not 'the distance' or 'two distances'—which clarifies nothing, and disturbs the usual rhythm of the phrase (at a DIStance, ti-ti-TUM-ti). Because it is common, the way that phrase is normally spoken carries a lot of weight : this foot must be scanned as a pyrrhic, and the prescribed iambic ictus goes missing. (If you decided to scan the third foot as a pyrrhic, consider whether you really want two pyrrhics, four unstressed beats, in a row.)

In the fifth foot the clash between prescription and speech is absolute. The prescription wants an iamb, "disTANCE", but the word is usually pronounced as a trochee. "DIStance", and cannot acceptably become iambic. So the foot has to be a trochee, an inversion in this iambic line which therefore ends with an unstressed beat, not the ictus one would expect with iambs : for the last line of the poem to trail off in the unstressed sibilance of "-tance" sounds rather wistful, inviting readers to remember that the sailors to whom *The Tragicall Historie of*

Hamlet sounds like happiness would rather be watching the performance on the *Dragon* than keeping watch on the *Hector*. The line as a whole deviates increasingly from the prescribed pattern—iamb, iamb, weak iamb, pyrrhic, trochee :

```
u    x    |u    x |u  x | u u | x   u
It SOUNDS like HAPpiNESS at a DIStance.
```

The loss of rising rhythm in the weak third, stressless fourth, and inverted fifth feet also makes the line sound wistful rather than assertively regular. Scanned thus, the line sounds well in making good sense ; its relations of sound and sense are coherently expressed.

Many readers of modern verse, and many critics (who should know better), seem to think neoclassical prosody has no relevance after *Modernism*, but when metrical poetry was joined by free-verse poetry it didn't die away—nor even slacken much. It is true that reaction against the iambic pentameter was a part of Modernism, and that neoclassical prosody was and is widely attacked and variously subverted ; it is also true that the pentameter survives pretty much unscathed, often (as in Eliot and Morris) keeping cheerful company with free verse. So do many other metres, and knowledge of them is as indispensable in reading and assessing contemporary work as in confronting the *canon* of older work—but if that knowledge is to be useful, its limitations as well as its strengths must be appreciated.

The various attempts to propose a wholly different basis on which to approach rhythm, including those founded on musical time-values and various linguistic or statistical approaches, have yet to find widespread acceptance and are patently less adequate than the system/s they abandon. The outstanding modern prosodic theorist, Derek Attridge, summarises the alternatives usefully in *The Rhythms of English Poetry*, and is dismissive, moving on to clearly superior ideas of his own about ways of approaching the rhythms of poems which consciously abandon foot-based prosodies : for such poems his thinking is invaluable, but they are relatively few in number, and Attridge's complex approach does not obviously deal better with poems whose authors were thinking neoclassically than the neoclassical system he also slights. There is certainly a genuine problem, common in neoclassical systems, in that the basic conceptual apparatus had to be translated from quantity to quality, and subsequently evolved into a very different system in which some of the basic concepts are permanently wrenched—but if the evolved terminology is taken as a means to an end, a way of seeking to communicate what you can hear in a line, it is a powerful tool.

The object lesson in recognising the limits of neoclassical prosody is Gerard Manley Hopkins, who famously articulated a theory of *sprung rhythm* to describe the metrics he had developed in the 1870s–1880s. Hopkins's terminology and notation are primarily neoclassical, explaining various circumstances in which additional, usually unstressed beats can be added to feet or lines, and many students down the years have spent days puzzling out what they think he means, and how it supposedly all works. My advice is not to bother, because it doesn't : Hopkins appears here under 'Lineation' (p. 166), because what he had in fact done was to abandon post-Renaissance neoclassical prosody altogether, and revert to an adapted Old or Middle English accentual model that doesn't bother much with unstressed beats at all, instead requiring a combination of numbers of accents and alliteration within a particular kind of line that isn't foot-based. Hopkins's attempt to provide a neoclassical model of un-neoclassical practice is politically and intellectually interesting, but prosodically a mare's nest of irrelevance and laxity that is far more hindrance than help in understanding with ear, mouth, and pen what he might have been up to. It's his poems that matter, not his retrospective rationalisations, but it does not follow from Hopkins's horrible theoretical self-traducement that the terminology he abused is useless or incorrigibly complex.

Clearly, some free-verse poets need special prosodic attention. Eliot developed and influentially disseminated (partly in verse-drama) an accentual system, for which Old and Middle English prosodic models are needed as often as neoclassical ones, and a distinct American accentual line descends from Whitman via W. C. Williams, as a distinct Irish one was imported into British poetry principally by Yeats (pp. 167–70). With globalisation, all these models and analytical systems (and more, from other local and regional traditions) have become more readily available to all, so that with almost any modern poet, as much as with a musician, the sampled or experimental use of many different metrical frameworks should be expected. But just as figurative art has not been displaced by abstraction, nor tonal music by atonal, so neoclassical metrics continue to appear among and often to dominate other modes of composition and shaping ; in the professionally competent close reading of poetry knowledge of them is a simple necessity.

Prosody is now for many students an unfamiliar subject, and some of the things you can describe with it (such as dactylic octameter) are very rare ; equally, some (particularly iambic tetrameter and pentameter, spondees, pyrrhics, and inverted feet) are things every reader of English poetry will frequently encounter. Whatever better prosodic systems may eventually be devised for English, the neoclassical system I have been describing will remain necessary, and not only because it is what poets from Chaucer to Auden and beyond understood themselves to be doing ; it endured for so long, and continues to endure, because it is, taken rightly, a superbly flexible tool allowing readers of poetry to describe what their voices and ears can make of a line. Used with habitual care about the distinction of a prescribed metre and a worked-out scansion, it can also accommodate without a qualm the individual accents and speaking voices of every reader, however varied (a matter also considered under 'Rhyme')—and in that alone is far more politically correct, in the best way, than some of its (supposed) rivals. It has often been written about tediously and badly, and its classroom teaching, when attempted at all, is too often timid and abstract : but it need not be so. Read aloud oneself, then again ; listen to others read, including when possible the author or a professional reader ; all that is at stake is to be able to analyse and describe what you are in any case doing as you search the words for their pulse by lodging them in your own rhythms of breath and hearing.

Exemplary Poems

1. John Donne, 'The Flea', from *Songs and Sonets in Poems, by J. D. with Elegies on the Authors Death* (London: John Marriot, 1633), 230–1 (N309). Drop-cap. omitted, line-numbers added. Various *manuscripts* (handwritten texts) of the poem have multiple minor variants, but as none are *autograph* (in Donne's hand) I opt for 1633, without assuming spelling, punctuation, etc. to be necessarily Donne's.

Marke but this flea, and marke in this,
How little that which thou deny'ſt me is ;
It ſuck'd me first, and now ſucks thee,
And in this flea, our two bloods mingled bee ;
Thou know'ſt that this cannot be ſaid
A ſinne, nor ſhame nor loſſe of maidenhead,
   Yet this enjoyes before it wooe,
   And pamper'd ſwells with one blood made of two
   And this, alas, is more then wee would doe.

Oh ſtay, three lives in one flea ſpare,
Where wee almoſt, yea more then maryed are.
This flea is you and I, and this
Our mariage bed, and mariage temple is ;
Though parents grudge, and you, w'are met,
And cloiſterd in theſe living walls of Jet.
  Though uſe make you apt to kill mee,
  Let not to that, ſelfe murder added bee,
  And ſacrilege, three ſinnes in killing three.

Cruell and ſodaine, hast thou ſince
Purpled thy naile, in blood of innocence ?
Wherein could this flea guilty bee,
Except in that drop which it ſuckt from thee ?
Yet thou triumph'ſt, and ſaiſt that thou
Find'ſt not thy ſelfe, nor mee the weaker now ;
  'Tis true, then learne how falſe, feares bee ;
  Juſt ſo much honor, when thou yeeld'ſt to mee,
  Will waſt, as this flea's death tooke life from thee.

Donne's poem of persuasion and remonstrance became famous in the twentieth century as a rude canonical text, delightfully favouring sex and disparaging virginity, but to his contemporaries the metre was as interesting as the content. Such *Carpe Diem* poems (Latin, 'seize the day'), enjoining a reluctant woman to co-operate, were as common as unrequited poets—Herrick's 'To the Virgins, to Make Much of Time' and Marvell's 'To his Coy Mistress' (N357, 478) are other famous examples—and even using the intimate travels of a flea as a pretext was (in an age of fleas) pretty obvious. Donne's argument, however, becomes sufficiently vehement to put his metre under considerable pressure.

In his *Conversations with Drummond of Hawthornden* (1619), a record of table-talk during a visit to Scotland, Ben Jonson—who knew Donne well—called him "the first poet in the world in some things" but insisted that "Donne, for not keeping of accent, deserved hanging".[14] People are rightly amused by Jonson's doubtless well-lubricated severity, but as a playwright he had reasons to worry about clarity of rhythm, and his exasperation with Donne is understandable by anyone trying to scan 'The Flea'. Almost any stress-pattern could be argued for the first four words (from 'MARK but this flea' to 'Mark but this FLEA'),

[14] Ian Donaldson, ed., *Ben Jonson* (Oxford and New York: OUP, 1985), 597, 596.

and many other (bits of) lines also seem disconcertingly malleable in the mouth—but even so an iambic pattern can quickly be discerned. Trochees might just seem possible for 'MARK but | THIS flea', but carry on and they go plainly wrong :

. . . AND marke | IN this
HOW lit- | TLE that | WHICH thou | DE-ny'ſt | ME is;

None of these template-trochees could survive into an agreed scansion ('lit-TLE' and 'DE-ny'ſt' are as absurd as 'dis-TANCE'), but after those first four unstable words (and openings are often unstable) iambs, if debatable, are nevertheless clearly speakable :

. . . and MARKE | in THIS
How LIT- | tle THAT | which THOU | deNY'ST | me IS;
It SUCK'D | me FIRST, | and NOW | ſucks THEE,
And IN | this FLEA, | our TWO | bloods MING- | led BEE;

This is not the scansion, remember, only a template with which your voice must engage—even in these few lines "which thou", "me is", "me first" and several more feet could plainly become spondees—but the fact that an iambic template is speakable without obvious impossibility suggests strongly it is right (as unspeakability showed trochees must be wrong). Applying iambs also reveals consistent alternation in line-lengths between tetrameters (ll. 1, 3, 5, 7 of each stanza) and pentameters (ll. 2, 4, 6, 8–9), and however many feet you might want to substitute in your scansion that rules out as basic feet anything triple or quadruple.[15]

Despite Donne's problems with "keeping accent", therefore, his iambs remain audible, but reading aloud also makes it clear that speed is essential ; despite the careful and rational arrangement of argument in *stanzas* (See this flea . . . Don't kill it! . . . Now that you have . . .) each stage is under pressure. The difficulty in scanning 'Marke but this flea' is precisely about how many stresses in what pattern—that is, how to manage with vocal force a balance between playfully rational argument and serious desire. "Oh stay [. . .]" is in its nature a sudden interjection as the woman reaches out to squash Donne's argument, and the whole pleading stanza that follows invites hasty (as it debars ponderous) speech. Only in the final stanza, where Donne takes unexpectedly severe offence at the wanton killing of the flea (witless slaughter posing

[15] Though it is theoretically possible to produce alternating lines of 8 and 10 beats with catalectic and hypermetric anapæstic or dactylic trimeters.

as a counter-argument), am I willing to let my voice really slow down, and the more it does so—especially in the final three lines, which can profitably be deliberately, even coldly spoken—the greater the problem of settling on a scansion.

It is precisely such shimmying accents that make Donne so rewarding a poet to hear read well, but faced with a Donne poem under exam conditions I would be chary (unless the question were specifically prosodic) of delving too deeply. Closeness to impassioned speech makes for uncertain complexity, and under time-pressure it may be as well to join Jonson in letting Donne's prosody go hang—yet at the same time many of his poems cleave more closely to regularity than this one. Even here the iambic beat is quite strong enough for "Cruell and ſodaine" to leap into auditory focus : "Cruell" (helped by its spelling) drags out over both beats as a near-spondee (or is the line catalectic ?), while the brutally trochaic "ſodaine" (equally helped) is broken over the foot-division and chopped-off by a comma ('CRU-ell | and SOD- | aine, . . .), reflecting the sudden pressure needed to kill a flea, and the jet of blood that results if it has just sucked. One might also without too much detail venture an argument that (except for l. 16) the final three lines of each stanza tend to be metrically more regular than the first six, reflecting a division of labour : each first six lines tell the story, and are sped (hence additionally stressed) by action ; each last three reach a conclusion, and are slowed (hence more readily regular) by judgement. If you train your ears even a little, such an argument will be readily available even on one quick *sotto voce* reading in an exam-room ; elsewhere, with time and sound available, there are many worse and few better ways of coming to Donne than through reading him aloud, and to do so well is willy-nilly to scan him, whether you ever write it down.

2. Wilfred Owen, 'Anthem for Doomed Youth' (1917) ; text of Owen's final draft, British Library MS 43720 (N1386). Line-numbers added.

What passing-bells for these who die as cattle?
—Only the monstrous anger of the guns.
Only the stuttering rifles' rapid rattle
Can patter out their hasty orisons.
No mockeries now for them ; no prayers nor bells ;
Nor any voice of mourning save the choirs,—
The shrill demented choirs of wailing shells ;
And bugles calling for them from sad shires.

What candles may be held to speed them all ?
Not in the hands of boys, but in their eyes
Shall shine the holy glimmers of goodbyes.
The pallor of girls' brows shall be their pall ;
Their flowers the tenderness of patient minds,
And each slow dusk a drawing-down of blinds.

Owen's famous sonnet is popular and memorable partly for its familiar form. Sonnets conventionally have 14 lines of iambic pentameter ; here there are some oddities of form, but prosodically a fierce iambic regularity. The first foot may be a spondee, but iambs immediately reassert themselves (WHAT PAS- | ing BELLS | for THOSE | who DIE | as CAT - | tle) ; "Only" may open ll. 2–3 with trochees, but all other trochaic words (passing-, monstrous, rifles' rapid rattle, patter, mourning, wailing, bugles) and the amphibrachic "demented" (deMENted, uxu) are split among regular iambs. Again, if Owen creates obvious prosodic effects with "stuttering" and "mockeries" (which demand substitute anapæsts, or must be syllabically compressed as 'stutt'ring' and 'mock-'ries'), those effects are local, and stand out precisely because of the otherwise rigid iambic regularity. The point is also clear in l. 7, "The SHRILL | deMEN- | ted CHOIRS | of WAIL- | ing SHELLS", where there is a real temptation in reading aloud to give undue emphasis to 'shrill', making it sound its meaning, but the voice is restrained from overdoing it by the encompassing regularity of the beat. Owen's metre is under discipline, and surviving drafts of the poem (🖱) show him progressively tightening it to leave only those well-braced local effects—plus the total effect of maintaining such prosodic regularity despite the passionate content.

This is the metrical aspect of the central (if surprisingly little-remarked) paradox of 'Anthem for Doomed Youth', bluntly caught in the very idea of writing a sonnet about the grotesque and terrible meat-machine of trench-warfare. Much as Owen's elegiac and enraged impulse is bound within what Wordsworth called "the Sonnet's scanty plot of ground" (N796), so individual lines are bound tightly to their templates, and readers invited to a scansion with (by my count) 65 of 70 feet as regular iambs and at most five substitute feet, all in ll. 1–5. After "shrill" in l. 7, moreover, there isn't even any temptation to metrical irregularity : ll. 8–12 are stringently iambic, and neither the slight slurring of "flowers" (l. 13) as it contracts into one stressed beat, nor the trochaic cadence of "a drawing-down of" (l. 14) can disturb the sonority of the final two lines. Reading aloud, I find anger and speed decreasing, and sentiment increasing (the formal shift in the last six lines is clear)—but both initial passion and later quiescence must be held within a clear and determined regularity, and in as much as they colour one's reading voice, must do so behind metrical bars.

The march of Owen's iambs might be interpreted as just that, a soldier's beat marching him "up the line to death" (as Sassoon has it in 'Base Details'), or more largely as embodying the ossified military logic that recklessly killed millions, including, eventually, Owen himself. I also suspect Owen had to write metrically to write at all, not simply because that was how almost all the poetry he knew was written, but because to write otherwise would be to risk ranting in desperation—metre as guiding foot-holes rather than metrical bars. But a different thought is suggested by another striking moment of untoward iambic regularity, worth fullish quotation, in Browning's 'Porphyria's Lover' (N1009 ; text from *Dramatic Lyrics*, 1842) :

Be sure I looked up at her eyes
Proud, very proud ; at last I knew
Porphyria worshipped me ; surprise
Made my heart swell, and still it grew
While I debated what to do.
That moment she was mine, mine, fair,
Perfectly pure and good : I found
A thing to do, and all her hair
In one long yellow string I wound
Three times her little throat around,
And strangled her. No pain felt she ;
I am quite sure she felt no pain.
As a shut bud that holds a bee
I warily oped her lids ; again
Laughed the blue eyes without a stain.

> And I untightened next the tress
>   About her neck ; her cheek once more
> Blushed bright beneath my burning kiss :
> I propped her head up as before [. . .]

There is one hammering moment, the triple stress of "mine, mine, fair," ending l. 36 with a spondee and "Perfectly" inverting the first foot of l. 37 ; infinitely more terrifying is the quite undisturbed metre everywhere else. Even the moment of murder registers in this gynocide's words only as a full-stop, and does not trouble (or even fill) its regular tetrameter ; if the immediately repeated assurance suggests anxiety ("No pain felt she ; [/] I am quite sure she felt no pain."), metre and punctuation express only calm certainty. What Browning catches is a capacity for monstrous indifference, an egotism unable to recognise the claims of another life—and that sounds close in kind, if not scale, to the central concern of Owen's 'Anthem'. One might therefore argue for Owen's metrical self-constraint as (besides bars and footholds) in its very unsuitability a primary means of registering abnormality and wrongness, in some measure taking hold and making reportable, but acknowledging also that it can only hold up against the slaughter a frame any imagination of it must exceed.

3. Derek Walcott, 'Nearing Forty', from *The Gulf and Other Poems* (1969) and *Collected Poems 1948–84* (New York: Farrar, Straus and Giroux, 1986), 136–7.

'Nearing Forty' alone is treated in <u>every</u> chapter, and so will be treated more closely here. Before I say anything at all about it please read the poem carefully for yourself. It is printed on the next two facing pages as it appears in Walcott's *Collected Poems 1948–84*.[16]

[16] I have preserved as far as possible the hierarchy of faces, though the fount is not the same and line-numbers are added. One misprint, the transposition of a semi-colon and a comma in ll. 14–15, has been corrected by collation with the first British edition of *The Gulf* (London: Jonathan Cape, 1969), 67–8.

Nearing Forty

[*for John Figueroa*]

The irregular combination of fanciful invention may delight awhile by that novelty of which the common satiety of life sends us all in quest. But the pleasures of sudden wonder are soon exhausted and the mind can only repose on the stability of truth . . .
—SAMUEL JOHNSON

Insomniac since four, hearing this narrow,
rigidly metred, early-rising rain
recounting, as its coolness numbs the marrow,
that I am nearing forty, nearer the weak
vision thickening to a frosted pane,
nearer the day when I may judge my work
by the bleak modesty of middle age
as a false dawn, fireless and average,
which would be just, because your life bled for
the household truth, the style past metaphor
that finds its parallel however wretched
in simple, shining lines, in pages stretched
plain as a bleaching bedsheet under a guttering rainspout; glad for the sputter
of occasional insight, you who foresaw
ambition as a searing meteor

will fumble a damp match and, smiling, settle
for the dry wheezing of a dented kettle,
for vision narrower than a louvre's gap,
then, watching your leaves thin, recall how deep
prodigious cynicism plants its seed,
gauges our seasons by this year's end rain
which, as greenhorns at school, we'd
call conventional for convectional;
or you will rise and set your lines to work
with sadder joy but steadier elation,
until the night when you can really sleep,
measuring how imagination
ebbs, conventional as any water clerk
who weighs the force of lightly falling rain,
which, as the new moon moves it, does its work
even when it seems to weep.

Metre

'Nearing Forty' could be said to be in free verse, but strongly tends to iambic pentameter. The poem is printed and scanned opposite in a way I find helpful when working intensively on metre. Instead of dividing words into feet with vertical slashes, ictūs and unstressed beats are grouped to reproduce the pattern of words, so that you can easily see my scansion of each. Thus "Insomniac", becomes 'uxuu' ('In-SOM-ni-ac'), representing an iamb ('In-SOM-') and a pyrrhic ('-ni-ac'). As the basic rhythm is duple, with no necessity for triple substitutions, to see what feet make up each line you simply divide beats into pairs : l. 3, "recounting, as its coolness numbs the marrow," is scanned as 'uxu, u u xu x u xu,' ; put in foot-divisions ('ux | u, u | u x | u x | u x | u') and it is shown (despite the trochaic "coolness" and "marrow") as four iambs, a pyrrhic, and an unstressed hyperbeat. Punctuation-marks are included with the scansion to help you see where you are in the line ; numbers on the far right give the beats per line (in l. 19 there is a choice about how to pronounce "narrower", so that number could be one higher).

The lines vary in length from 7 to 12 beats, but more than half (18/32) have 10. Another nine have 11 beats, of which seven can be scanned as hypermetric iambic pentameters with unstressed (ll. 1, 3, 11, 17, 18), or stressed (ll. 15, 26) hyperbeats. Therefore 25/32 lines are scannable as iambic pentameter, clearly the dominant metre. Working numbers out exactly takes time, but to know the big answer you need only read aloud as far as l. 7—with practice your ear will by then hear rising iambic rhythm, and all but one line as pentametric.

Once basic metre has been identified, the first thing to notice is that ll. 13–14 and 28–9 deviate from it in the same, striking way : l. 13, with 12 beats the longest, is immediately followed by a line with only 8 beats, so the two lines have 20 beats : as two pentameters would usually have. In other words, although the lines are irregular :

plain as a bleaching bedsheet under a gutter- 12
ing rainspout; glad for the sputter 8

they could easily be made regular :

plain as a bleaching bedsheet under a 10
guttering rainspout; glad for the sputter 10

Insomniac since four, hearing this narrow,	uxuu u x, xu u xu,	11
rigidly metred, early-rising rain	xxx xu, xu-xu x	10
recounting, as its coolness numbs the marrow,	uxu, u u xu x u xu	11
that I am nearing forty, nearer the weak	u x u xu xu, xu u x	11
vision thickening to a frosted pane,	xu xux u u xu x,	10
nearer the day when I may judge my work	xu u x u x u x u x	10
by the bleak modesty of middle age	u u x xuu u xu x	10
as a false dawn, fireless and average,	u u x x, xu u xuu	10
which would be just, because your life bled for	u x x x, ux u x x u	10
the household truth, the style past metaphor	u xu x, u x x xuu	10
that finds its parallel however wretched	u x u xuu uxu xu	11
in simple, shining lines, in pages stretched	u xu, xu x, u xu x	10
plain as a bleaching bedsheet under a gutter-	x u u xu xu xu u xu-	12
ing rainspout; glad for the sputter	u xu; x u u xu	8
of occasional insight, you who foresaw	u uxuu xu, x u xx	11
ambition as a searing meteor	uxu u u xu xuu	10
will fumble a damp match and, smiling, settle	u xu u x x u, xu, xu	11
for the dry wheezing of a dented kettle,	u u x xu u u xu xu,	11
for vision narrower than a louvre's gap,	u xu xu u u xu x,	10
then, watching your leaves thin, recall how deep	x, xu u x x, ux x x	10
prodigious cynicism plants its seed,	uxu xuxu x u x,	10
gauges our seasons by this year's end rain	xu u xu u u x x x	10
which, as greenhorns at school, we'd	x, u xu u x, x	7
call conventional for convectional;	x uxuu x uxuu;	10
or you will rise and set your lines to work	u x u x u x u x u x	10
with sadder joy but steadier elation,	u xu x u xxx xxx,	11
until the night when you can really sleep,	ux u x u x u xu x,	10
measuring how imagination	xuu x uxuxu	9
ebbs, conventional as any water clerk	x, uxuu u xu xu x	11
who weighs the force of lightly falling rain,	u x u x u xu xu x,	10
which, as the new moon moves it, does its work	x, x u x x x u, x u x	10
even when it seems to weep.	xu x x x u x.	7

But the rhyme is then misplaced, and with 'guttering' split between lines, as "gutter- [/] ing", there is mid-word a half-pause, an air-bubble in the piping. The effect is accentuated by the trochees and trochaic words in ll. 12–14 (compare ll. 25 and 27, both notably regular), but is made to imitate rainwater flowing from a gutter by being embodied in lines of odd length.

There is confirmation in ll. 28–29, which repeat the effect to a different but still watery end :

measuring how imagination 9
ebbs, conventional as any water clerk 11

Again neither line has the right number of beats, but they have between them the right number for two lines. You might be alerted to what is going on here by trying to scan l. 29 : if you start at the beginning it's awkward, and the result is a very irregular line of two trochees, a pyrrhic, two more trochees, and a stressed hyperbeat :

EBBS, con- | VENTion- | al as | ANy | WAter | CLERK

Begin after the comma, shifting all foot-divisions along by one beat, and the line becomes an iambic pentameter with one pyrrhic and an initial stressed hyperbeat :

EBBS, | conVENT- | ional | as AN- | y WA- | ter CLERK

This makes far better sense, and the previous line is readily scanned as a catalectic iambic pentameter, with the first foot inverted and the ictus of the last iamb missing :

MEASur- | ing HOW | iMAG- | iNA- | tion

The stressed hyperbeat beginning l. 29, "EBBS", would complete the truncated final iamb of 28 : both would then be pentameters, and the comma would coincide with the line-break :

MEASur- | ing HOW | iMAG- | iNA- | tion EBBS, 10
conVENT- | ional | as AN- | y WA- | ter CLERK 10

So when Walcott wrote the lines as they are, with one foot split between the two lines :

MEASur- | ing HOW | iMAG- | iNA- | tion 9
EBBS, | conVENT- | ional | as AN- | y WA- | ter CLERK 11

he allowed the last ictus of l. 28 to ebb down to the beginning of l. 29, and left the unstressed '-tion' trailing, as if the strongly iambic word 'imagination' itself ebbed away. In this way the foot split between lines rhythmically illustrates their meaning, yet as a rather imaginative thing to do contradicts the idea that the poet's imagination is ebbing (p. 334).

There is a different sort of metrical device in l. 2 : "rigidly" is usually pronounced as a dactyl, "RIG-id-ly", but I scan it as three consecutive stresses and begin with two spondees :

RIGID- | LY ME- | tred EAR- | ly-RIS- | ing RAIN

I could scan the first foot as a trochee and the second as an iamb, "RIGid- | ly ME-", which would preserve my usual pronunciation, but "rigid-" is not strongly trochaic—weaker, say, than "metred" or "-rising"—so making it a spondee, which sounds all right, seems a better compromise with the prescribed iamb. Once admitted as a spondee, it sounds odd to scan '-ly' as unstressed, and pronounce "rigidly" as 'RIG-ID-ly' ; odder than scanning it as three lightly stressed beats, 'rig-id-ly'. It's debatable, and pitch is as important as weight of stress : what persuades me to scan the line as two spondees and three iambs is that "rigidly metred" is itself then rigidly metred, as rising rhythm returns with "early-rising rain". Because the poem is partly about writing poetry, such metrical self-reference seems satisfying. (Both "early-" and "-rising" are trochaic words divided between feet, so rising rhythm is preserved.)

There is again confirmation when Walcott uses a similar technique in l. 26 :

with sadder joy but steadier elation,

I scan this as three iambs, two spondees and a stressed hyperbeat :

with SAD- | der JOY | but STEAD- | IER | ELA- | TION,

"steadier" is normally pronounced as a dactyl, 'STEAD-i-er' ; "elation" as an amphibrach, 'e-LA-tion' ; arguably, then, the line should have a pyrrhic and an unstressed hyperbeat :

with SAD- | der JOY | but STEAD- | ier | eLA- | tion,

This is possible, but I don't like it. The pyrrhic is very weak, and 'eLA-tion' falls dismally away, so this scansion does nothing to help and everything to defeat meaning. But if, as with "rigidly metred", you let your voice pick up the iambic stress on "stead-" and carry it as two light spondees and a stressed hyperbeat, scansion moves from the trochaic cadence of "sadder" lying across two iambs to a steadier beat in keeping with the note of general resolution which begins at l. 25.

Finally, there is a problem in l. 19, "for vision narrower than a louvre's gap" : "narrower" would also usually be pronounced as a dactyl, 'NAR-row-er', but if it occupies three beats the scansion becomes very awkward. If instead it is compressed into two, as the trochaic 'NARR-'wer', the line can readily be scanned with the third foot as a pyrrhic :

for VIS- | ion NARR- | ower than | a LOU- | vre's GAP,

The elision compressing "narrower" is awkward to say but metrically satisfying because "narrower" is compressed into a narrower space than it would like ; the opposite of "thickening" in l. 5 ("vision thickening to a frosted pane"), which could have two syllables, 'thicke-ning', but here has to be pronounced as three, 'thick-en-ing', to thicken the line up to its proper size. Alternatively, using speed rather than elision, "ower than" could be thought a substitute anapæst (ow-er THAN) or tribrach (uuu).

Exercises : Metrical composition and analysis

1. You will learn more about prosody by trying to write metrically than in any other way. As a first step try 10 lines in iambic pentameter : by all means allow yourself leeway, but not too much. The lines need not be continuous (twos or threes are easier than longer groups) and need not rhyme ; just concentrate on the duple iambic pulse (ti-TUM ti-TUM . . .) and pentametric length. Reading the lines aloud as you work is necessary, and there's nothing wrong with counting beats on your fingers ; you may also find it helpful to use the system of capitalising stressed syllables (or an equivalent) as you write.

2. Next try trochaic tetrameter or pentameter, which you'll find harder. The easiest way is to string together trochaic words (Charlie Chaplin's famous waddle . . .), but the exact coincidence of words and feet soon sounds dull, and as you warm up try to fit in iambic words (Chaplin's walk, unique and waddling . . .). Enjambment is also a defence against trochaic clang (Chaplin, masterclown who waddled / jauntily through many movies / crying softly, losing-out, and / starving . . .).

3. To investigate triple rhythm the best vehicle is the limerick, a famously obscene form that need never be dull. What matters is the skipping ti-ti- of the anapæsts : Lear's opening formula, 'There was an . . .', is always usable, but if l. 1 is catalectic, ll. 2 + 5 should match ; ll. 3–4 should also pair. Rhyme matters, but there's no point worrying ; maintaining triple rhythm throughout should take precedence. Names are readily worked in ; try your own as well as tempting targets (In *The Poetry Handbook* I read / that John Donne must be taken at speed : / which is all very well / were it not for the smell / of his feet catechising his creed.).

4. To extend prosody into critical practice, pick a short poem and scan it thoroughly, noting uncertainties and viable alternative scansions. Test your results by reading the whole poem aloud with one variant, then another. If there is someone you can work with, each select a poem the other doesn't know, scan, and read to one another, ears open and texts in hands : challenge decisions you don't understand, and try to work out why disagreements arise, noting particularly where accent has led someone to a decision you would not have taken.

5. Find a text of Clare's 'An Invite to Eternity' (🖱) and try to scan it, paying particular attention to ll. 1–4 : what exactly is the problem, and how might it most clearly (and economically) be stated ? Without giving away too much, there is an instability that makes any constant metre hard to identify but relates suggestively to other oddities in the poem. Remember that the purpose of the terminology is not simply to 'be correct', but to enable you comprehensibly to describe (perhaps under time-pressure) what it is you can hear and how it is you want to speak. Working in a pair or group, hearing an/other voice/s tackle the lines, is very helpful. (I know of no available recording of Clare's poem, but if you repeat the exercise with other problematical poems check for available readings on the Web and in libraries—Richard Burton did some wonderful readings

of Donne, for example, and James Mason once tackled Browning with very interesting results. One doesn't have to agree with their scansions, but if you disagree it is excellent practice to work out why, and how most persuasively to state your case.)

Chapter Glossary

accent : the emphasis or stress placed on a beat.

accentual-syllabic : the kind of prosody principally used in English.

anapæst, anapæstic : a foot of three beats, two unstressed and the last stressed (uux) ; the metre produced by such feet.

beat : a word or syllable/s bearing one stress (x) or unstress (u).

cadence : a fall, in tone, pitch etc.

catalectic : of a line, missing one or more beats.

dimeter : a line of two feet.

distinguishing : of a foot, type-face, or fount, different from that normally used.

duple : of a foot, having two beats ; the rhythm produced by such feet.

elision : omission, as of one or more letters from a word (usually indicated with an apostrophe) ; the verb is 'to elide'.

falling rhythm : that produced by feet with unstressed beats following stressed beats.

feminine : of an ending, with one or more unstressed hypermetrical beats.

foot : a prosodic unit of stressed and/or unstressed beats, the component of a line.

free verse : poetry in which the metre varies.

heptameter : a line of seven feet.

hexameter : a line of six feet.

hyperbeats : those beats in a line which are surplus to the metre ; stressed and unstressed hyperbeats are politically corrected masculine and feminine endings.

hypermetric : of a line in a given metre, with one or more hyperbeats.

iamb, iambic : a foot of two beats, an unstressed followed by a stressed (ux) ; the metre produced by such feet.

ictus : the stressed beat of a foot ; the plural is ictūs (ik-toos).

inverted : of a foot, the reverse of that normally used in a given line.

line : a single sequence of characters read from left to right.

line-break : the turn of one line into the next ; notated as '/'.

masculine : of an ending, with one or more stressed hypermetrical beats.

metre : the rhythmic pattern of beats.

neoclassical : derived from Greek and/or Latin writings.

pentameter : a line of five feet.

prosody : the study and notation of metre.

pyrrhic : a foot of two unstressed beats (uu).

rising rhythm : that produced by feet with stressed beats following unstressed beats.

scansion : the individual metrical pattern of a particular line or poem.

spondee : a foot of two stressed beats (xx).

stressed : of a beat, spoken emphatically, often with the voice pitched slightly higher than for an unstressed beat.

substitute foot : any foot used as a replacement for one of the regular feet in a given line ; includes inverted and distinguishing feet.

tetrameter : a line of four feet.

trimeter : a line of three feet.

triple : of a foot, having three beats ; the rhythm produced by such feet.

trochee, trochaic : a foot of two beats, a stressed followed by an unstressed (xu) ; the metre produced by such feet.

u : notation for an unstressed beat.

unstressed : of a beat, spoken unemphatically, often more rapidly and with the voice pitched slightly lower than for a stressed beat.

wrenched accent : occurs when the requirements of metrical stress (and/or rhyme) prevail over the natural stress of a word or words.

x : notation for a stressed beat.

2

Form

To choose a form is to acquire two sets of entangled baggage. 'Internal baggage' exists because a decision about form prescribes one or more of structure, metre, rhyme, punctuation, and tone : if, for example, you decide to write a *sonnet*, you probably aim to write 14 iambic pentameters, with a choice of *rhyme-schemes* reflecting different ways of structuring the lines[1] ; about 140 syllables after you begin you must stop. 'External baggage' exists because forms become historically associated with particular content. Sonnets have served as love-poems and in courtship from Petrarch's fourteenth-century Italian, through Elizabethan sequences by Spenser, Sidney, and Shakespeare, to Elizabeth Barrett Browning's *Sonnets from the Portuguese* (N190, 213, 257, 947) : so when Yeats used sonnet-form for Leda's brutal rape (N1200), he created tension between form and content, his choice of form in itself ironising his poem.

Poetry in free verse is often also in *open form*, which doesn't mean no form, but that it is not predetermined. Just as Eliot occasionally used iambic pentameter in 'The Love Song of J. Alfred Prufrock', so he used it in ll. 77–102 of *The Waste Land* (N1346) to parody a speech from Shakespeare's *Antony and Cleopatra*, and *heroic quatrains* (iambic pentameters rhyming *abab*) in ll. 235–46 (p. 43). In *The Waste Land* as a whole he created a new form, of five parts with the fourth short, later developed in *Four Quartets*. As with 'free' verse, 'open' form doesn't mean don't think about it : all lines have rhythm/s, and all poems form/s.

Poems may be *stichic*, a simple sequence of lines, or *stanzaic*, in lines grouped by spaces above and below ; in Italian *stanza* means 'room, or stopping-place', and if a poem is a house, stanzas are rooms. Spenser

[1] *Rhyme-schemes* indicate which lines rhyme with which : l. 1 and all lines rhyming with it are *a* ; the second rhyme-word and all its rhyming lines are *b*, and so on. Thus limericks are *aabba*, showing ll. 1–2 + 5 rhyme, as do ll. 3–4 ; Robert Browning's lines on p. 7 are *abab*.

only half-completed *The Faerie Queene* (N165), but at *c.* 35,000 lines it is one of the longest poems in English, written in the *Spenserian stanza*, eight iambic pentameters + a hexameter (or *alexandrine*) rhyming *ababbcbcc* :

Like as a ſhip, whom cruell tempeſt driues
  Vpon a rocke with horrible diſmay,
  Her ſhattered ribs in thouſand peeces riues,
  And ſpoyling all her geares and goodly ray°, *array*
  Does make her ſelfe miſſortunes piteous pray.
  So downe the cliffe the wretched Gyant tumbled;
  His battred ballances° in peeces lay, *scales*
  His timbered bones all broken rudely rumbled,
So was the high aſpyring with huge ruine humbled.
  (v.ii.50; text from *The Second Parte*, 1596, p. 210)

It may seem a severe constraint to use such a form, and it certainly affected what Spenser could say as well as how he could say it. The longer final line is a definite end to the stanza (read it aloud and you'll hear what I mean), and makes it difficult to *enjamb* (carry syntax over) from one stanza to the next—so much so that Spenser never did it : his every stanza is *end-stopped* (the opposite of enjambment, punctuation ending the sense with the line), all but five with full-stops. The 35,000 lines have 400,000+ beats ; when Spenser decided to use this stanza he effectively committed himself to a full-stop every 92 beats ; he could have others, but couldn't omit that regular one. Yet the form was a help and opportunity : instead of pages stretching blankly away, he was confronted, once he created his stanza-form, with a series of empty moulds ready to be filled with words and articulated with punctuation ; once filled, each would have structural integrity and strength. Far from being repetitious or dull, it is a pleasure of reading *The Faerie Queene* to see Spenser manage the internal structure of his stanza, favouring one variant or another at different times. The *ababbcbcc* rhyme-scheme comprises interlocking sets of four lines (or *quatrains*), *abab* and *bcbc*, plus the alexandrine : in the stanza above a full-stop ends l. 5, so its individual structure isn't the obvious *abab—bcbc—c*, but the curious *ababb—cbcc*. If you miss this structural variation the poem can seem dull, but if you notice it there is always something interesting going on.

It is easy to think of forms as objects, as if a poet wanting one looked through a catalogue : a misleading habit. Spenser created his stanza-form (hence its name) ; it is a possibility he exploited, subject to challenge and local variation as much as the metrical template of iambs, and the range of possible forms is huge, because any specified element may be varied, creating sub-groups which overlap. A quatrain must have four lines, but metre can be variously prescribed, and the lines made to rhyme in 15 combinations ; even sticking to the four major English feet in line-lengths between trimeters and pentameters, there are nearly 5,000 sub-types, from iambic trimeters rhyming *aaaa* to dactylic pentameters rhyming *abcd*. For a stanza of five lines the possible number of rhyme-schemes alone rises to 52, for one of six to 203 ; with combinations of metres also rising exponentially the number of variant types soon becomes astronomical[2]—so much so that only a tiny fraction have ever been used.

This is often forgotten. Sonnets, for example, are commonly discussed as if the three most popular kinds (*Petrarchan, Shakespearian*, and *Spenserian*, pp. 48–9) were all there were, but one may arrange 14 iambic pentameters in any one of 190,899,322 ways, all sonnets. The major variants are popular, and named, because they have proven particularly useful and influential, but are more like small charted areas on a large, mostly blank map than ready-made objects. Pick ten sonnets by different authors—say, Wyatt, Spenser, Sidney, Shakespeare, and Wordsworth—and chances are you'll find ten rhyme-schemes ; to reduce such variety to three is absurd. Poets know better :

If by dull rhymes our English must be chaind
And, like Andromeda, the Sonnet sweet,
Fetterd, in spite of pained Loveliness ;
Let us find out, if we must be constrain'd,
Sandals more interwoven & complete
To fit the naked foot of Poesy ;
Let us inspect the Lyre & weigh the stress
Of every chord & see what may be gained
By ear industrious & attention meet,
Misers of sound & syllable no less,
Than Midas of his coinage, let us be
Jealous° of dead leaves in the bay wreath Crown ; *intolerant*
So if we may not let the Muse be free,
She will be bound with Garlands of her own.

(John Keats, text from letter-journal,
14 Feb.–3 May 1819 ; N916)

[2] The number of rhyme-schemes $r(n)$ for a stanza of n lines is $r(n) = \sum_{i=2}^{n} i \left\{ {n-1 \atop i-1} \right\}$ where $\left\{ {n \atop k} \right\}$ denotes a Stirling Number of the Second Kind.

This unusual rhyme-scheme, *abcabdcabcdede*, is nameless, and obviously intended by Keats to differ from any existing sonnet rhyme-scheme ; his sonnet 'On the Sonnet' exemplifies the experimentation it recommends. All he did is shift a 3×4 arrangement to a 4×3 one—the rhymes divide with the heavier punctuation, *abc;abd;cab-cde;de*—but form (unlike multiplication) is not commutative, and readers are pointedly reminded that any particular form is a tiny, temporarily frozen portion of an endlessly fluid medium, only seeming a solid object through its repeated use by different poets. It may seem easier to think of forms as fixed objects, but to do so will handicap and diminish your reading.

Given this fluidity, there is no wholly satisfactory way of cataloguing forms ; the easiest is to take as an index the number of lines whose proportions and relations are specified. In *isometric* stanzas line-length is constant ; in *heterometric* stanzas it varies, so you may in notating stanza-forms need to record the number of beats with the rhyme :

The King sits in Dumferling town,	*a*	8 beats
Drinking the blude-reid wine:	*b*	6
"O, whar will I get guid sailor,	*c*	8
To sail this ship of mine?"	*b*	6

This, from 'Sir Patrick Spens' (N103), is an iambic quatrain rhyming *abcb* ; the first and third lines are tetrametric, the second and fourth trimetric ; it notates as *a8b6c8b6*.

One-line forms

No major stichic forms use trimeters or tetrameters, which are too short to say much in. Despite the classical dactylic hexameter, in English those using a line longer than a pentameter are rare, but Blake's 'Book of Thel' (N737) and Clough's *Amours de Voyage* (N1051) are examples. To understand those poets' choices, however (p. 163), one must start with the unrhymed iambic pentameter they implicitly reject, the *blank verse* of Marlowe, Shakespeare, Jonson, and other *Jacobethan* dramatists[3] ; the best-known and most influential form in English.

[3] English usage of *verse* (from Latin *vertere*, 'to turn' → *versus*, 'a furrow ; a line of writing') is odd. Technically and biblically ('chapter and verse') 'a verse' is a single unit, typically a line, but also 'a (given) poet's craftwork in general', and 'a stanza' (usually of a hymn or song). Sometimes 'verse' is all but synonymous with 'poetry' (from Greek ποιηίν [poiein], 'to make'), but the radical sense of a furrow, one of many similar units achieved by effort, informs a half-distinction typically between

A classic instance of 'a minute to learn and a lifetime to master', blank verse is iambically close to ordinary speech, strong yet flexible, and as good for a poem of only a few lines as an epic of ten thousand. It is weighty, the decasyllabic line (+ hyperbeats) giving space for complete clauses and expansive oratory, but as readily energetic and momentous as sonorous and grave. You need only recall a few famous Shakespearian lines—"When we haue ſhuffel'd off this mortall coile", "The qualitie of mercy is not ſtrain'd", "Cry, God for *Harry*, England, and S. *George*"—to realise they are memorable precisely as lines, individual *verses* possessed of unitary integrity and strength.

Blank verse is also called *heroic verse*,[4] and since developing as a dramatic form in the late-sixteenth century, and being influentially chosen by Milton (against the contemporary odds) for his Christian epic *Paradise Lost*, has been in continuous use. Wordsworth chose it for his meditative verse-autobiography *The Prelude*, Tennyson for his Arthurian *Idylls of the King*, Browning for many *dramatic monologues* (pp. 57–8), including the 21,000 lines of *The Ring and the Book*, and Masefield for many Trojan and Arthurian poems such as 'The Surprise'.[5] Its dramatic use has declined sharply since Ibsen's promotion of tragic prose, though Fry used it for religious drama and it turns up in translations of classical plays. In poetry it remains common, but is often interpreted by critics as consciously alluding to a better, statelier past in a kind of nostalgia : which is true of Eliot's use in *The Waste Land* but as a general claim nonsensically forgets how close blank verse can be to everyday speech. Frost repeatedly chose blank verse, for 'The Death of the Hired Man', 'The Wood-Pile', 'Birches' (N1232, 1233), and, famously, 'Mending Wall' :

> Something there is that doesn't love a wall,
> That sends the frozen-ground-swell under it,
> And spills the upper boulders in the sun;
> And makes gaps even two can pass abreast. (N1227)

'narrative' or 'dramatic verse' (longer, plainer, doing a job) and 'lyric poetry' (shorter, prettier, purer) that can be a basis for snobbishly disdaining 'verse' while professing to admire 'poetry', or infra-diggishly admitting to writing 'verse' while disclaiming any pretension as a 'poet'. *Versification*, 'the art and craft of casting into verse', i.e. into a metrical form (cf. 'dramatisation'), is sometimes used to imply a result at best metrically correct and passionless, at worse talentless or vulgar (cf. 'novelisation') ; to refer to someone as a 'versifier' or 'versifying' also implies amateurish lack of talent or purpose (but that is true of the rarer *poetise/r, poetising*).

[4] The adjective 'heroic' applied to any form means its line is iambic pentameter.

[5] *Selected Poems* (Manchester: Carcanet, 1984) ; *Arthurian Poets: John Masefield* (Woodbridge and New York: Boydell Press, 1994).

Frost's easy mix of colloquialism, precision, and ready gravitas ("He says again, 'Good fences make good neighbors.' ") has influenced experiments with blank verse by poets as diverse as Schwartz, Nemerov (N1626), Sexton, Wilbur (N1633), and (most recently) Jim Powell.[6] Another great modern master of the form, Walcott, is equally concerned with colloquial gravitas but also with accents and creole grammars, obliging blank verse to accommodate and empower West Indian speech :

> You ever look up from some lonely beach
> and see a far schooner? Well, when I write
> this poem, each phrase go be soaked in salt;
> I go draw and knot every line as tight
> As ropes in this rigging; in simple speech
> My common language go be the wind,
> My pages the sails of the schooner *Flight*.
>
> ('The Schooner *Flight*', i. 70–6 ; N1826)

A purist might argue that an explicit rhyme (beach/speech) debars this as truly blank verse, but the rhyme is occasional, and it is a metrical motor, rising iambs under pentametric discipline, that makes this (like much of Walcott's verse) so compelling. Still very much alive, his influence has yet fully to develop ; as it does, blank verse will develop internationally with it.

By definition, blank verse is not stanzaic, but long blank-verse poems often have *verse-paragraphs*, which as in prose function as units of argument or emotion (p. 112).

Two-line forms

The basic two-line form is the *couplet*, usually rhyming, which may be *open*, when the syntax runs on from couplet to couplet, as in Chaucer's 'Prologue' to *The Canterbury Tales* (N19), but increasingly became *closed*, units of syntax as well as form, as in the major poems of Dryden and Pope (N500, 596). Closed couplets (where there may be *internal enjambment*, between first and second lines, but not *external* or *couplet enjambment*, between successive couplets) tend to sound assertive and epigrammatic : Shakespeare used them on stage to end blank-verse speeches, and on paper to conclude sonnets. A dominant form in both poetry and drama throughout the later seventeenth and eighteenth centuries, couplets went out when Romanticism came in. More

[6] Powell, *It was Fever that Made the World* (Chicago: U Chicago P, 1989).

recently open couplets have returned to favour, but often with less than full-rhyme,[7] and with persistent enjambment, internal and external, producing a rippling effect rather than the clear point-by-point sequence of closed couplets.

Chaucer, Shakespeare, Dryden, and Pope all preferred *heroic couplets*, where pentameters give the space to say a lot and accommodate polysyllables without bursting. Once an almost automatic choice for serious public verse, they are now used more discriminatingly. Browning deployed them in 'My Last Duchess' (N1012), another of his chillingly well-ordered murderers' monologues, and Owen in 'Strange Meeting' (N1389), an extraordinary excursion from the trenches to hell ; more recently, Tony Harrison preferred them for his riddling tribute 'A Kumquat for John Keats', where they let him savour his question :

> Whole, straight off the tree, sweet pulp and sour skin—
> or was it sweet outside, and sour within?
> For however many kumquats that I eat
> I'm not sure if it's flesh or rind that's sweet, (N1875)[8]

Couplets in iambic tetrameter are also popular, and were used to perfection by Marvell, who wrote of lying in a garden in summer that it had the effect of :

> Annihilating all that's made
> To a green Thought in a green Shade.
>
> (N485; text from *Miscellaneous Poems*, 1681)

Full-rhyme and completed syntax give a strong sense of closure, but the scale of the thought the couplet manages so elegantly to capture seems too big for its tetrameters ; from the early eighteenth century tetrametric couplets tend to be used comically or satirically, heroic couplets tragically and epically (though they could therefore be debunked in *mock-epics*, such as Pope's 'The Rape of the Lock', N604). Swift was fond of the tetrametric couplet, and explained in his 'Verses on the Death of Dr Swift' that he <u>had</u> to be comic :

> In Pope, I cannot read a Line,
> But with a Sigh, I wish it mine:

---

[7] In *full-rhyme* the last stressed vowel and all following sounds are identical in two or more words—bat/cat, hiss/miss, imperium/delirium, frantic/Atlantic. In *half-rhyme* either the last stressed vowel (lust/lost) or the following sounds (bite/fire) differ (pp. 191–2).

[8] There is an illustrated edition (Newcastle: Bloodaxe, 1981).

> When he can in one Couplet fix
> More Senſe than I can do in Six
> It gives me ſuch a jealous Fit,
> I cry, Pox take him, and his Wit.
>
> (N578; text from Dublin edition, 1739)

More recently two poets have rescued tetrameters from levity : Eliot used them mainly in quatrains, but Harrison, in film/poems[9] and the chilling war-poem 'A Cold Coming', has (with the most brutal rhymes I know, pp. 206–08) fully restored tetrametric couplets to gravity.

Couplets using trimeters or shorter lines are rare in their own right, but occur as components of other forms. In 'An Horatian Ode' (N486; p. 159), Marvell alternated couplets in iambic tetrameter and trimeter, the extreme brevity of trimetric couplets making even tetrametric ones seem spacious. A similar effect is heard in ll. 3–4 of limericks, a couplet in anapæstic dimeter, where syntactical proximity of rhyme-words combines with triple rhythm to accelerate the form into its punch-line. In Donne's 'A Valediction of weeping' (N300) ll. 5–6 of each stanza form a couplet in iambic dimeter.

Couplets using a longer line have been widely used, particularly *fourteeners*, in iambic heptameter. The length of heptameters tends to make their rhythm sound rather galumphing, as in Golding's sixteenth-century translation of Ovid, but they can be very effective. The stanza of Kipling's 'Tommy' (N1181 ; p. 164) is made from four fourteener-couplets (with ll. 5–6 + 8 hypermetric), long lines giving space for the colloquial idiom of a private. Long trochaic couplets are rarer, but Tennyson used sesquiheptametric ones for 'Locksley Hall'.

There are also heterometric couplets. *Poulter's Measure*, popular in the sixteenth century, combined a hexameter and heptameter (*a12a14*) ; though used by Wyatt and Queen Elizabeth (N142) it proved unwieldy and was fatally mocked by Sidney in 'What Length of Verse?' (N210). All combinations are possible, but lines rarely differ by more than one foot and effects must be judged on merit ; Nash, in 'Columbus' (N1438), rhymes lines of 17 and 55 beats :

> And, just as he thought, her disposition was very malleable,
> And she said, Here are my jewels, and she wasn't penurious like Cornelia the mother of the Gracchi, she wasn't referring to her children, no, she was referring to her jewels, which were very valuable,

[9] *The Shadow of Hiroshima and other film/poems* (London: Faber, 1995) and *Prometheus* (London: Faber, 1998).

There is also an excellent form which prescribes inequality, the *clerihew*, invented by Edmund Clerihew Bentley ; a quatrain of two unequal but otherwise unspecified couplets, its first line is always someone's name, to comment on whom is the purpose. Among the best is Bentley's own about Nell Gwynne, the mistress of Charles II :

Nell
fell
when Charles the Second (or 'Charles II')
beckoned.

Readily shaped from the daily news, clerihews can be as severe as you wish ('Michael Jackson / was once a black son. / Now he's quite / white.') ; easy to do, hard to do well, they can with practice become a familiar joy.

Three-line forms

There are two basic three-line forms, the *triplet*, where all lines rhyme *(aaa)*, and the *tercet*, where one or more do not *(aab, aba, abb, abc)*. They are distinguished because the effect of triple rhyme is distinct.

Heroic triplets are commonest as a variation among heroic couplets, as in Pope's 'Epistle to Dr Arbuthnot', ll. 323–5 (N633), and are often indicated by a *brace* (}). The triple rhyme, usually emphatic, can easily go over the top and sound insistent-because-uncertain, but that can itself be exploited, as by Schnackenberg in 'Supernatural Love' (N2003). Heterometric triplets occur often in the stanza-forms invented by Donne : in 'The Canonisation' (N296) ll. 5–7 of each stanza form a triplet, with two lines in iambic tetrameter and the third heroic (*a8a8a10*) ; in 'A Valediction of weeping' (N300) each stanza ends with a triplet of the type *a10a10a14*. Such heterometrics, especially when a longer line delays the third rhyme, can lessen the triplet's thumping insistence ; even so, Donne's fondness for them chimes with other aggressive qualities of his work, and the triplets of Bishop's 'Roosters'[10] (*a4a6a8*) similarly remain forceful. Falling rhythm can also soften rhyme, and Browning used triplets in catalectic trochaic octameter for 'A Toccata of Galuppi's' (N1017). At the other extreme, Herrick's 'Upon his departure hence' (N2031), five triplets in iambic monometer, amplifies and exploits its clanging rhymes.

Linked tercets rhyming *aba bcb cdc* etc. form *terza rima*, used by Dante for *The Divine Comedy* ; in Italian the metre is syllabic, in English

[10] *Complete Poems* (1983; London: Chatto and Windus, 1991).

usually heroic, and *terza rima* readily carries narrative (though Shelley used it lyrically in 'Ode to the West Wind', N872). The rippling effect of its interlocking *chain-rhyme* persists even in radical variations : Eliot replaced rhyme with a pattern of stressed and unstressed hyperbeats in part II of *Little Gidding*, ll. 80–151 (N2041, pp. 204–05), Hardy's tercets in 'Friends Beyond' are catalectic trochaic octameters sandwiching a tetrameter (*a15b7a15*), and the legacy of such experiments in freeing form can be heard in the colloquially loose *terza rima* of Walcott's *Omeros* (N1827). W. C. Williams created an influential blank tercet, as in his love-poem *Asphodel, That Greeny Flower* (N1276; p. 88) ; broadly iambic, with lines ranging from mono- to tetrameters and the second and third lines progressively indented, it isn't often closely imitated but its blankness and layout recur widely, as in Zarin's 'The Ant Hill' (N2013). As the form departs from Dante, however, it loses its association with speaking to and hearing the dead—which is what attracted Eliot and Hardy in the first place. Less gloomily, heterometric tercets of the type *a8a8b6* (or equivalent) may be paired to make stanzas, as in Suckling's 'A Ballad upon a Wedding' (N454), and Auden created an alarmingly unstable pair, approximately *a12b12c7d14e14c7*, for 'At the Grave of Henry James' ; effects obtained with such irregular tercets are very variable, and must be judged on merit. Tercets also occur in Petrarchan sonnets, and as the stanza-form of *villanelles* (p. 52).

There is also the *haiku*, a syllabic form specifying lines of five, seven, and five syllables (no prescribed feet or beats), with an equivalent of the Western *volta* or *turn*, a moment of disjunction from which a new or redirected sense develops, ideally after the first or second lines. Of sixteenth-century Japanese origin, haiku are meditative, competitive, and may be linked with a 7 + 7-syllable couple in sequences (*renga*) ; Pound discovered them through the celebrated Bashō (Matsuo Munefusa, 1644–94) and Kobayashi Issa (Kobayashi Nobuyuki, 1763–1828), and influentially embodied an understanding of their principles in the "*hokku*-like sentence" of 'In a Station of the Metro' (N1297, 2036). They have since become widely popular in the West, as (like clerihews) short and easy yet capable of any content :

> Helpful little books
> illustrate this Japanese
> three-line form of verse.

Four-line forms

Four lines make a *quatrain*, the commonest form both in its own right (as in many hymns) and as a component of larger forms. Like squares and other structures based on the number 4, the quatrain is both strong and pleasing ; its enormous variety has been very widely explored, and the major variants of rhyme provide necessary subdivisions.

Monorhymed quatrains, with one rhyme throughout (*aaaa*), are rare : the rhyme-clang is worse than with triplets, but Donne used them in ll. 7–10 of 'The Anniversary' stanza (N303) ; freestanding examples include D. G. Rossetti's 'The Woodspurge' and Updike's 'I Missed His Book' (N1105, 1846). A heterometric triplet + verse quatrain, typically *a8a8a8b4* as in John Betjeman's 'Slough',[11] or *a8a8a8b6*, as in Snodgrass's 'Magda Goebbels (30 April 1945)' (p. 161), is more interestingly malleable, and (like heterometric tercets) readily pairs in *aaabcccb* forms.

Quatrains in which only two lines rhyme (*abac* or *abcb*[12]) have no agreed name, but may be called *single-rhymed*. In any regular metre they are easy to construct and use for narrative ; the type *a8b6c8b6* (alternating tetrameters and trimeters, as in 'Sir Patrick Spens', p. 36) is the *ballad stanza* or *common metre*, a staple of ballads and hymns. Making the first line trimetric *(a6b6c8b6)* produces *short metre*, making all trimetric *half-metre*, and making all tetrametric *long metre*, disturbingly used by Eliot in 'Whispers of Immortality' and 'Sweeney Among the Nightingales'. Dickinson (N1110) was a gifted user of single-rhymed quatrains.

Cross-rhymed quatrains (*abab*) are harder to write well : unless the metre is long or the poet skilled, tick-tock rhyme will soon become obvious and insistent. It will also tend to drag, because the third line, while advancing the poem, rhymes back to the first, and the fourth to the second : always looking back, the poem is likely to fall over. The modern master is again Eliot, who made the difficulty work for him in part III of *The Waste Land* (ll. 235–48) describing the joyless copulation of a young man and a typist :

> The time is now propitious, as he guesses,
> The meal is ended, she is bored and tired,
> Endeavours to engage her in caresses
> Which still are unreproved, if undesired.
> Flushed and decided, he assaults at once;
> Exploring hands encounter no defence;
> His vanity requires no response,
> And makes a welcome of indifference. (N1351)

---

[11] First collected in *Continual Dew* (London: John Murray, 1937).

[12] Quatrains rhyming *aabc, abca, abbc,* and *abcc* are also single-rhymed, but rare.

The metrically regular lines are chimed along in the first quatrain by stressed polysyllabic rhymes, their rhythm as remorseless as the man and as tired as the typist. Matching the man's rising excitement (but hardly passion), the second quatrain is metrically a little disturbed and somewhat faster, but remains remorseless enough to plough through the tolling rhymes, still just *abab* but very close to *aaaa*. The result memorably indicts an indifferent lust.

Couplet-rhymed quatrains (*aabb*) split dully in the middle, rarely a desirable effect (though Rich found it right for 'Aunt Jennifer's Tigers', N1791). If one couplet embraces the other, however, so ll. 1 + 4 rhyme while 2 + 3 pair in the middle, you have the interesting *abba*. When paired in the *octave* of Petrarchan sonnets sequential couplets (*-bbaabb-*) become prominent ; used singly, mirror-symmetry of rhyme would split the quatrain centrally, *ab-ba*, but finds the *-bb-* couplet fastened across the breaking-point, giving to the lines the tension of an arch and the sense of coming back to the ground (or even home, like a return to the tonic key in music) at the end of each stanza. It is properly *chiasmic* rhyme,[13] but I call such quatrains *arch-rhymed*. Tennyson used ones in iambic tetrameter for *In Memoriam A.H.H.* (N996), and that variant is the *Tennysonian stanza*. It also occurs in *Onegin stanzas* (pp. 51–2).

Last come two imports by nineteenth-century Orientalists, the Persian *rubai* and Malay *pantun* or *pantoum*. The *rubai* enjoyed a brief but intense English vogue following Fitzgerald's translation of *The Rubaiyat of Omar Khayyam of Naishápúr* (1859, N961), and is also called the *(Omar) Khayyam stanza*. It uses *aaba* quatrains, in English usually heroic ; Swinburne in 'Laus Veneris' paired the *b*-lines (*aaba ccbc dded ffef* . . .), and in 'Relics' created an enlarged *terza rima* by cycling the rhymes (*aaba bbcb ccdc* . . .). Pantoums require ll. 2 + 4 of each (supposedly cross-rhymed) quatrain to recur as ll. 1 + 3 of the next (*1234 2546 5768* . . . as well as *abab bcbc cdcd* . . .) ; the final stanza must incorporate the orphaned lines from the first in reverse order (*x3y1*), so the very first and last lines are identical. It was introduced to French poetry by Fouinay and Hugo, and to English by Dobson's 'In Town' : the *New Princeton Encyclopedia of Poetry and Poetics* cites a Malay proverb, "a p[antun] is like a hawk with a chicken, it takes its time about striking", adding that "the cross rhymes scissor the couplets". In Malay, with complex segmentation and metrics, the pantoum has a rich history, and French poetry has accommodated it ; three fine American

[13] From Greek *χιασμός* [chiasmus], 'a diagonal arrangement'; 'chi' is the Greek 'X' [*x*].

poets, Justice in 'Pantoum of the Great Depression' (N1687), Ashbery in 'Pantoum', and Kumin in 'Pantoum, with Swan' found its repetitions so difficult to manage interestingly that all used blank quatrains. Pantoums don't begin to compete as a repetitive form with twelve-bar blues, but do create a distinctive mood, and recent examples like Kumin's or Lilley's 'Mint in Box: A Pantoum Set' suggest it is rooting itself.[14]

Five- to twelve-line forms

The potential range of longer forms is vast, but few have been much used, and most are built from verses, couplets, tercets or triplets, and quatrains ; their properties reflect the properties and placing of those components, as a gearbox expresses the ratios of its cogs. Even the heterometric limerick (five anapæstic lines in the form *a9a9b6b6a9*) may be regarded as two couplets and a verse, or even a triplet interrupted by a couplet. Readers who find such stanza-analysis difficult might try highlighting or otherwise displaying the components to see how they interlock (especially easy on screen), or reading stanzas aloud with over-emphatic rhymes (and gestures) to hear their interweaving.

Besides limericks, five-line stanzas are uncommon and have no agreed name, but may be called *pentains*.[15] Larkin used loosely iambic pentains rhyming *abbab* for 'Annus Mirabilis' ; Coleridge varied the common metre of 'The Rime of the Ancient Mariner' (N812) with (among others) an iambic pentain of the form *a8b6c8c8b6* ; Parini used blank pentains in 'Groundings: A Sequence'.[16] As so few of the 50,000+ possible pentains have ever been used, good ones must be undiscovered. I found for myself an iambic pentain of the form *a8b8a8b8b10*, dubbed a *long five* : a cut-down version of the Spenserian stanza, shorter and in tetra- + pentameter (rather than heroic + alexandrine), it enables stanza-enjambment and is useful for narrative (and oddly, elegy, pp. 66–7) ; readers who versify might experiment with it, or pentains of their own discovery.

The six-line *sestet* completes Petrarchan sonnets, where it usually consists of two tercets, and is a freestanding narrative and lyric stanza, often in quatrain + couplet form, *abab-cc* ; the quatrain narrates and the couplet summarises or comments, as in Shakespeare's *Venus and Adonis*.

---

[14] Dobson, Justice, and Ashbery are all in Strand and Boland, *Making of a Poem* ; Kumin, *The Long Marriage* (New York and London: Norton, 2002) ; Lilley, *Versary* (Applecross and Cambridge: Salt, 2002).

[15] *Cinquain* would be logical, given 'quatrain . . . sestet', but was used by Adelaide Crapsey for a syllabic form (*a2b4c6d8e2*) she invented ; see Hollander, *Rhyme's Reason*, 25.

[16] *Anthracite Country* (New York: Random House, 1982).

Larkin's 'An Arundel Tomb' (N1650) uses a fine tetrametric sestet rhyming *abbcac* distinguished by the long delay in the *a*-rhyme, which (as in cross-rhymed quatrains) turns the stanza back into itself and slows it ; Larkin used this against the acceleration of the *-bb---* couplet to help control pace and generate a very mellow, elegiac tone. The creation of sestets from heterometric tercets by Suckling and Auden was mentioned (p. 42) ; when the third and sixth lines are shorter *bobs* or *bob-lines*, this 3 + 3 sestet is excellently comic. Sestets are also the component-stanza of *sestinas* (pp. 52–3).

The principal seven-line *heptet* is *rhyme royal*, heroic and rhyming *ababbcc*, used by Chaucer for *Troilus and Criseyde*, Wyatt for both surviving versions of 'They Flee from me', James I of Scotland for 'The Kingis Quair' (hence the name), Shakespeare for *The Rape of Lucrece*, Wordsworth for 'Resolution and Independence', and Auden for 'A Letter to Lord Byron' and some of 'The Shield of Achilles' (N67, 127, 790, 1479). At its best rhyme royal balances readings of it as tercet + couplets *(aba-bb-cc)* or as quatrain + tercet (*abab-bcc*), fusing narration (associated with quatrains) and moral commentary (associated with the summary epigrammatism of couplets) to produce morally charged action. All other heptets are conspicuous in their rarity, though 7–7 sonnets are an obvious variant of 8–6 ones.

Eight-line *octets* may simply be double-quatrains : heroic in the arch-rhymed *octave* of Petrarchan sonnets (*abbaabba*) and the cross-rhymed *Sicilian stanza* (*abababab*) ; tetrametric, like Macauley's cross-rhymed *abab-cdcd* in *Horatius*, the single-rhymed *abcb-defe* of 'Tom o'Bedlam's Song' (N124), and Snodgrass's bobbed *aaab6-cccd6* in 'Magda Goebbels' (p. 161) ; even trimetric, like Larkin's (rather irregular) *abcd-efgd* in 'MCMXIV' (N1653). The tetrametric couplet-rhymed octets of Marvell's 'The Garden' (N484), 'Upon the Hill and Grove at *Bill-borow*', and 'Upon Appleton House' (p. 60) are sturdy 4 × 4 squares, *aabbccdd* : 'Appleton House' explicitly rejects Petrarchan stanza-complexities in its opening lines—"Within this sober Frame expect [/] Work of no Forrain *Architect*".[17] The more complex Franco-Italian octets, such as the *triolet* (*abaaabab*, l. 1 repeated as ll. 4 + 7, l. 2 as l. 8 + variant metric specifications), have mostly been used comically, as in W. E. Henley's 'Easy is the triolet',[18] Hopkins's 'The Child is Father to the Man', and Cope's 'Valentine' (N1948).

The principal English octet, however, is an Italian import, *ottava*

[17] Text from *Miscellaneous Poems* (1681), omitting a drop-cap.
[18] Hollander, *Rhyme's Reason*, 83–4.

rima, heroic and rhyming *abababcc* (cross-rhymed sestet + couplet). As the stanza of Byron's *Beppo* and *Don Juan* (N837) it is now often supposed comic, and the argument advanced that triple rhymes, acceptable in richly rhyming Italian, are forced—and so comic—in English. This, frankly, is silly : Byron could be deadly serious when he wanted, and learned *ottava rima* not only from his friend Frere's satirical *Whistlecraft* (imitating Pulci's fifteenth-century mock-heroic *Morgante Maggiore*), but also from two great Elizabethan translations, Harington's of Ariosto's *Orlando Furioso* (1591), a fantastical romance, and Fayrfax's of Tasso's *Il Goffredo* (1600),[19] an altogether earnest epic of the First Crusade. In neither translation is English *ottava rima* intrinsically comic, but (as happened to tetrametric couplets between Marvell and Eliot) poets lost sight of how to use *ottava rima* seriously, and since *Don Juan* it has certainly tended to be used comically (as by James Agee in 'John Carter'[20]). An honourable exception goes to Yeats, who with the help of less-than-full rhymes[21] and at the cost of some dignified pomposity in the couplets, managed serious *ottava rima* in 'Sailing to Byzantium' and 'Among School Children' (N1199) ; his choice of form can be read as ironic, like that of sonnet-form for 'Leda and the Swan', and in using *ottava rima* for short poems he productively dislocated a form previously used only for long poems into new possibilities.

At nine lines there is the Spenserian stanza of *The Faerie Queene* (*ababbcbcc12*, p. 34), used by Keats in 'The Eve of St Agnes' (N907), Shelley in 'Adonais' (N879), and Tennyson in 'The Lotos-Eaters' (N988). Two linked heroic quatrains, *abab-bcbc*, allow narration, and the stanza is strongly bound by its central couplet + outliers, *-b-bb-b--* ; the alexandrine provides variety, and space to finish or comment on the action of the stanza, but prevents stanza-enjambment. Majestic and self-contained, it rolls sonorously along with much decoration and harmony, especially with Keats at the wheel.

Keats also invented a range of ten- and eleven-line stanzas. All are heroic, 'Ode on Melancholy' (N937, p. 68) rhyming *ababcdecde*, 'Ode on a Grecian Urn' (N938) *ababcdedce*, 'To Autumn' (N939) *ababcdedcce*, and (with line 8 reduced to a trimeter) 'Ode to a Nightingale' (N935) *ababcdec6de*. Narrative (such as it is) tends to be dealt with in the initial cross-rhymed quatrain, and emotional commentary supplied in the tercets (the relative absence of which toughens the longer 'Autumn'

19 Subtitled *Gerusalemma Liberata* ; Fayrfax's translation was *Jerusalem Delivered*.

20 *Collected Poems* (London: Calder and Boyars, 1972).

21 See pp. 39n. 7, 191–2.

stanza)—so most of these stanza forms resemble slightly cut-down sonnets. 'Ode to Psyche' (N933) runs through five forms of 11–18 lines, verse-paragraphs as much as stanzas ; it is loosely *Pindaric* (p. 54), but detailed explanation would take pages. What is again striking is that despite the numberless possibilities, few forms of this length are much used, and rarely deviate from the obvious 4–3–3 or 4–4–3 patterns exemplified by Keats ; perhaps, as in football, many formations are possible and few truly workable, but the reluctance to experiment is so great that I suspect external inhibitions of some kind (perhaps related to the general prevalence of decimal units).

Finally, anything twelve lines long is a *douzaine*, the stanza of the *canzone* (p. 53). If single stanzas, douzaines usually do little more than stack couplets, like Bradstreet's 'To My Dear and Loving Husband' (N465) ; Tennyson, however, used a triple-quatrain structure stunningly in 'Mariana' (N982), *ababcddcefef*, preventing the outlying cross-rhymes' usual brisk advancement of narrative by binding them to the central arch-rhyme and repeating the last quatrain wholesale in every stanza as a burden. Douzaine simply means 'dozen' in French, and in standard French alexandrines a dozen lines form a 12 × 12 square ; the most famous freestanding English example, however, Shakespeare's six-couplet sonnet 126, is heroic and interesting primarily in its pointed failure to have 14 lines.

Longer closed forms

There are five more finite forms : sonnets, *Onegin stanzas, villanelles, sestinas*, and *canzoni*. All are iambic, the sonnet, villanelle, sestina, and *canzone* usually heroic, while Onegin stanzas are tetrametric. Additionally, medieval literature has a group of finite forms requiring line-repetitions, such as the *rondel*, (*Chaucerian*) *roundel, roundelay*, and *rondeau*, little used in English since the Renaissance save for a late nineteenth-century flurry including Dobson's 'The Wanderer'[22] and Swinburne's astonishing *Century of Roundels* (1883).

Until the seventeenth century 'sonnet' (from Italian *sonetto*,'a little sound') meant any short lyric poem ; the particular form used by Petrarch—14 lines forming an octave of linked arch-rhymed quatrains, *abbaabba* + a sestet of linked tercets, *cdecde, cdedce*, or *cdeedc*—slowly became a restrictive norm, the *Petrarchan sonnet*. It was (and is) normal to have a turn between octave and sestet, giving a tangential relationship between parts or a degree of spin to the whole ; the asymmetric

[22] In F. Stillman, *Poet's Manual*.

8–6 form proved flexible and satisfying, as did the internal structures, the octave readable as two quatrains *(abba-abba)* or three couplets with binding rhymes fore-and-aft *(a-bb-aa-bb-a)*, and the sestet variable at need.

The great Elizabethan vogue for sonneteering produced two major variants named after their most famous practitioners ; the better known is the *Shakespearian* sonnet,[23] three cross-rhymed quatrains + couplet, *ababcdcdefefgg*. The *terminal* couplet (which Shakespeare almost always closed) has its usual tendency to summarise or comment on the quatrains, and hence to moralise ; the turn usually comes at ll. 12–13. It is easy to think the 4–4–4–2 form a greater break from the Petrarchan 8–6 than it really is : many Shakespearian sonnets reproduce the 8–6 division with a heavy stop and a secondary but more central turn at l. 8, allowing the third quatrain to develop away from the first two. In the second major variant, the *Spenserian* sonnet, quatrains are chain-rhymed, *ababbcbccdcdee*, which does tend to undermine any 8–6 division and makes the end of l. 12 the most probable place for the turn, but partly restores in ll. 4–5 + 8–9 the medial couplets of the Petrarchan octave. In sequence—Spenser's was the *Amoretti* (N190)—the Spenserian sonnet is more fluid (or nimble) and less itemising than the Shakespearian, but pays in lessened authority and clarity.

Hundreds more variants have been tried. Sidney began *Astrophel and Stella* (N213) with an 'alexandrine sonnet' in iambic hexameter ; Hopkins produced what he called *curtal sonnets*, such as 'Pied Beauty' (N1167), ten lines dividing 6–4½ to reproduce sonnet-structure in miniature ; Lowell wrote blank sonnets ; and Baugh (among others) with the 6–8 of 'There's a Brown Girl in the Ring' beautifully reversed the Petrarchan imbalance. Meredith in *Modern Love* (N1107) re-challenged the limitation to 14 lines with sonnets constructed as four arch-rhymed quatrains, the *Meredithian* sonnet adopted by Harrison in *The School of Eloquence* (N1872) ; also extending the form, often satirically, are *caudate* ('tailed') sonnets, typically adding one or more tercets (as Milton did in 'On the New Forcers of Conscience under the Long Parliament'). The major variants continue to be respectfully used, but in the hands of the experimental cummings (N1393), or of Morgan, Heaney (N1905), O'Siadhail, Muldoon (N1979), and Harrison, who demand attention to the relations between regional poet and classical

[23] It was invented by Henry Howard, Earl of Surrey (1517–47), and popularised by his sonnets in *Tottel's Miscellany* (1557, N137), a very influential anthology.

form, any variety can acquire irony (as in 'Leda and the Swan', but more delicate). Potent ironies also attend the sonnets of Hill (N1834) and Soyinka.[24]

Facing such challenges, it helps to consider notation. If variant forms are simply 8–6 and 4–4–4–2 (or 8,6 and 4,4,4,2) punctuation serves only to separate, and isn't indicating relationship between parts, nor any turn : as it could. In both cases the mark needed is the semi-colon : the notation 8 ; 6 accurately records the Petrarchan turn of octave into sestet, and 4 ; 4 ; 4 : 2 the Shakespearian itemization of quatrains + summary couplet. Particular variants can also be recorded : a Shakespearian sonnet with a heavy turn between its second and third quatrains, and the third + couplet acting as a sestet (mixed Petrarchan-Shakespearian form), would be 4, 4 ; 4, 2. Still stranger beasts, such as Hill's 3 . 4 . (3) 3 . 1 (p. 72) can be just as readily notated, so always ask yourself which mark is most accurate and helpful : fuller notation aids clear thinking (and can save valuable time in exams).

Thus equipped one can go sonneteering, but the territory is vast. Serious explorers should use a dedicated anthology and proper history, but beware traffic round Shakespeare, whose volume of sonnets has in the last 150 years received more critical attention than any other book—some revelatory, most a shocking waste of trees. Casual adventurers need only an outline history, in brief, that sonnets filtered, then poured into Elizabethan England from Humanist Italy via the mid-sixteenth-century *Pléiade* school of poets in France, their major English sponsors being Wyatt and Surrey. Modish in court circles by the 1580s, and exciting the élite taste for miniature arts, they rapidly became a popular symbol and mocking cliché of self-dramatising infatuation. Romeo and Juliet famously smuggle a sonnet into their dialogue in 1.5 and have much to answer for, but do at least get somewhere thereby ; more usually, sonnets were written (declaimed) in only one (male) voice, because the lady had said 'No' and was not for turning (hence feminist critical suspicion of poems that won't take 'no' for an

---

[24] Baugh, *It Was the Singing* (Toronto and Kingston: Sandberry Press, 2000) ; O'Siadhail, 'Perspectives', in *Hail! Madam Jazz: New and Selected Poems* (Newcastle: Bloodaxe, 1992), the first section of *A Fragile City* (Bloodaxe, 1995), and 'Figures', in *The Gossamer Wall: Poems in Witness to the Holocaust* (Bloodaxe, 2002) ; Harrison, *Selected Poems* (Harmondsworth: Penguin, 1985) ; Soyinka, 'Apollodorus on the Niger', in *Mandela's Earth and other poems* (London: Methuen, 1990). Hill is an astonishing sonneteer, writing individual and paired sonnets as well as sequences ; 'Asmodeus', 'Requiem for the Plantaganet Kings', 'Two Formal Elegies', 'Annunciations', 'Funeral Music', 'Lachrimae', and 'An Apology for the Revival of Christian Architecture in England' are in *Collected Poems* (Harmondsworth: Penguin, 1985).

answer[25]). The major problem, though, was formulaism, worsened by early use in sequences with implicit narratives but tempered (while the taste for miniatures lasted) by a significance granted even to slight variation. Sixteenth-century sonneteers (including Wyatt, Shakespeare, Spenser, Daniel, and Drayton) developed closed worlds of intensely self-interrogating consciousness through iteration ; by the mid-seventeenth century Milton, hardly averse to length but scorning "the troublesome and modern bondage of Rhyming" (N421), could happily write occasional sonnets—'When I consider how my light is spent', 'On the Late Massacre in Piedmont' (N418)—without the least worry that more than one at a time might be called for. The obvious gain in ease of composition (and reading) balances a tendency to become little more than a poetic postcard ; solo sonneteers have since predominated, but there have been fine sequences in every century. Interesting problems also arise from the role of some Elizabethan sonneteers (notably Spenser) in colonial policy, and that the Irish issue is very much among the sonnet's external baggage is plain in reading Yeats, Heaney, and many others.

The showboating difficulties sonnets pose for narrative are eased in the *Onegin stanza*, invented by Pushkin for *Eugene Onegin*. Disciplined by tetrameter, it has cross-, couplet-, and arch-rhymed quatrains + a couplet, in that order, *ababccddeffegg* ; its strictest form specifies three *unstressed* rhymes, with the rest *stressed* (p. 191), *ababeeccciddiff* (vowels indicate unstressed rhymes, consonants stressed ones). It is to this rhyme-scheme Nabokov refers ; his terminology differs but compact sense abounds :

> The *abab* and the *if* part are usually very conspicuous in the meaning, melody, and intonation of any given stanza. This opening pattern (a clean-cut sonorous elegiac quatrain) and the terminal one (a couplet resembling the code of an octave or that of a Shakespearean sonnet) can be compared to patterns on a painted ball or top that are visible at the beginning and at the end of the spin. The main spin-fling process involves *eecciddi*, where a fluent and variable phrasing blurs the contours of the lines so that they are seldom seen as clearly consisting of two couplets and a closed quatrain. The *iddiif* part is more or less distinctly seen as consisting of two tercets in only one third of the

[25] See e.g. Philippa Berry, *Of Chastity and Power: Elizabethan Literature and the Unmarried Queen* (1989; London and New York: Routledge, 1994). Leithauser adumbrated part of the argument in the 11 words + 2 sounds of 'Post-Coitum Tristesse: A Sonnet', in Jarman and Mason, *Rebel Angels*.

> entire number of stanzas in the eight cantos, but even in these cases the closing couplet often stands out so prominently as to cause the Italian form to intergrade with the English one.[26]

Nabokov is considering Pushkin, but illuminates the Onegin stanzas of John Fuller's *The Illusionists* (1980), Seth's *The Golden Gate* (1986, N1994), and Stallworthy's 'The Nutcracker' (1987), where they love a Russian tale.[27]

The *villanelle* has 19 heroic lines, five tercets + quatrain ; the first line repeats as ll. 6, 12, + 18 (notated as a^1), the third as ll. 9, 15, + 19 (a^2), giving a^1ba^2 aba^1 aba^2 aba^1 aba^2 aba^1a^2. Minor variation is allowed in the repeating *burdens* or *refrains*, but only minor, and doubled repetitions produce effects between the tolling of a bell, the insistence of anger or fear, and wry meditation. Originally a dancing folk-form (in Italian *vilano* means a peasant, *villanella* a country-girl), villanelles are (like the repetitive *pantun*) very difficult, depending utterly on their refrains, but manageably short. Good modern examples include Empson's 'Missing Dates', Roethke's 'The Waking', Bishop's 'One Art', and Dylan Thomas's 'Do Not Go Gentle into That Good Night' (N1464, 1500, 1527, 1572) ; Sexton unusually expanded the form to five quatrains + pentain for 'My Friend, My Friend'. Perhaps more than any other form specifying line-repetition, villanelles live or die by what John Hollander calls "one simple phenomenon : repeating something often may make it *more trivial*—because more expected and therefore carrying less information, as an engineer might put it—or, because of shifting or developing context in each stanza preceding, *more important*". For an extreme test try Disch's 'The Rapist's Vilanelle'.[28]

The *sestina* has 39 lines, six sestets + tercet ; the rhyme-words of the first sestet recur in different order as the rhyme-words of every subsequent sestet, *abcdef faebdc cfdabe ecbfad deacfb bdfeca eca* (or *ace*) ; the *b, d,* and *f* rhyme-words must also be used in the tercet, known as the *envoi* (French, 'farewell') or *tornada* (Sicilian, 'turn'). Each stanza is generated from the last by rocking-in, taking in sequence the last, first, penultimate, second, ante-penultimate, and third lines ; thus a stanza

[26] *Eugene Onegin: A Novel in Verse by Aleksandr Pushkin: Translated from the Russian, with a Commentary*, by Vladimir Nabokov (rev. edn, in 4 vols ; London: RKP, 1975), i. 10.

[27] Fuller, *Collected Poems* (London: Chatto, 1996) ; Seth, *The Golden Gate* (London: Faber, 1986) ; 'The Nutcracker' appeared in the *London Review of Books*, 9/16 (17 Sept. 1987), and was collected in *The Guest from the Future* (Manchester: Carcanet, 1995).

[28] Sexton, *Selected Poems* (London: Virago, 1988) ; Hollander, *Rhyme's Reason*, 38 ; Disch, in Jarman and Mason, *Rebel Angels*.

'123456' is followed by '615243', and that by '364125'. Applying this to the sixth (in Italian, *sèsto*) stanza, *bdfeca*, recreates the first, *abcdef*: the form ends with its variations once complete. Sidney famously wrote a double-sestina, 'Ye Goatherd Gods' (N208), intimidating later poets, and seventeenth- and eighteenth-century examples are rare ; since the later nineteenth century the form has regained wide popularity, as Rossetti's 'Sestina (after Dante)', Kipling's 'Sestina of the Tramp-Royal', Pound's 'Sestina: Altaforte', Auden's 'Paysage Moralisé', Hall's 'Sestina', Hecht's 'Sestina d'Inverno' and 'The Book of Yolek' (N1672), Ashbery's 'The Painter' (N1736), and Rumens's 'Rules for Beginners' testify ; Bishop's 'Sestina' is an exemplary poem below. There are also some experimental variants, such as Swinburne's 'Sestina', which uses cross-rhyming end-words and adapts the sequence of repetitions. Difficult to compose, sestinas depend on the chosen end-words as a set and the poet's skill in shaping syntax around them, but can draw great strength from fixity ; then again, Miller Williams in 'The Shrinking Lonesome Sestina' and Ansen in 'A Fit of Something against Something' go brilliantly heterometric, reducing line-length in successive sestets until end-words stand alone, spelling (respectively) "Time [/] goes [/] too [/] fast. [/] Come [/] home." and "*Sestina order*, [/] Austere master, [/] BE GONE!!!"[29]

To the sestina may be added the 65-line *canzone* (Italian, 'song'), five douzaines + pentain using only five end-words. There are many Italian variants but in English a Dantean form is privileged : each douzaine rhymes *abaacaaddaee*, but in successive stanzas the *e*-word becomes the *a*-word, then the *b*-word and so on, with the other rhymes also rotating (12345, 51234, 45123 . . .), until with the fifth douzain the cycle is complete ; the pentain reuses them in order, so the whole is *abaacaaddaee eaeebeeccedd deddaddbbdcc cdcceccaacbb bcbbdbbeebaa abcde* (or *aedcb*). The density of repetition makes *canzoni* wholly dependent on their set of end-words, and wise poets choose at least one with natural variants, as 'day', 'today', 'yesterday', 'dying day' etc. : Auden used 'day', 'love', 'know', 'will', and 'world' in 'Canzone',[30] and for the tremendous 'Samos' (opening 'And' in *The Changing Light at Sandover*, pp. 1, 62, 64), Merrill chose 'sense', 'water', 'fire', 'land', and

[29] Rossetti, Kipling, Pound, Hecht, and Williams in Strand and Boland, *Making of a Poem* ; Auden, *Collected Poems* (London: Faber, 1976) ; Hall and Ansen in Hollander, *Rhyme's Reason* ; Hecht, *Collected Earlier Poems* (Oxford: OUP, 1991); Rumens, *Thinking of Skins: New and Selected Poems* (Newcastle: Bloodaxe, 1993 ; 🖱).

[30] *Collected Poems* (London: Faber, 1976).

'light' (with some clever "leit- [/] Motifs" in variation) to capture a sunlit Aegean glitter and sensory overload.

General forms

Beyond these relatively strict stanza-forms are looser terms, variably defined, which refer to whole poems and impose no finite length : the *ode, ballad, dramatic monologue, verse-letter, epyllion, complaint*, and *country-house poem*. Sonnet sequences are distinct in combining a closed unitary and open general form, but historically linked with *epyllia* and complaints. Note should also be made of musical terms : poetry has always been a kind of singing, and readers should certainly consider whether any poem called or encountered as a 'song' (or *madrigal*) shows, say, musical rather than prosodic measure, which would put quantity (note-length) rather than quality (accent) in charge. Poets' titular uses (after Browning and Eliot) of 'toccata', 'fugue', 'prelude', 'quartet', and even 'symphony' are another matter : readers who understand what such terms mean musically should consider them instance by instance, and others are well advised to look them up if confronted by them, but they have no internal poetic baggage, and as yet only such external baggage as a poet brings to them.

The *ode* (from Greek *'αοιδη* [aoide], 'a song'), is a formal, stately, or grand poem of some length. 'Public' and 'private' odes (for ceremonial occasions or meditative reflection) may be distinguished, but the distinction blurs in mourning and nuptial verse (such as the *epithalamion* [Greek, 'at the bridal chamber'] and *prothalamion*, N195) ; stricter differences inform *Sapphic, Alcaic, Pindaric*, and *Horatian* odes. Sapphic and Alcaic odes, named after Sappho (fl. *c.* 600 BCE[31]) and Alcaeus (fl. *c.* 611–580 BCE), are in highly prescribed and mostly dactylic quatrains : neither adapts well to English, but Sidney, Watts (N589), Tennyson, and Pound (in *Apparuit)* attempted Sapphics, Tennyson and R. L. Stevenson Alcaics. Pindaric odes, after Pindar (522–442 BCE), of three complex stanzas (a metrically identical *strophe* and *antistrophe* + a metrically distinct *epode*[32]), adapt more successfully, as do Horatian odes, after Horace (65–8 CE), a longer form with a less complex and repeating stanza-pattern. There are great Pindaric or Horatian odes by Jonson, Marvell, Dryden, Gray, Wordsworth, Coleridge, and Keats (N337, 486,

31 The non-denominational terms BCE (Before Common Era) and CE (Common Era) replace the Christian BC (Before Christ) and AD (Anno Domini, 'Year of our Lord').

32 Also called the *turn, counter-turn*, and *stand.*

524, 666, 796, 828, 933), but Keats's ode-stanzas are closer to sonnets than classical form, and other Romantics broke the ode's traditional structures without replacing them ; such 'forms' as the *effusion*, an indication by post-/Romantic poets that they feel inspired, are commonly a sort of decayed ode. The ode's decline matches that of public poetry : after Tennyson's great 'Ode on the Death of the Duke of Wellington' (1852) examples of quality are scarce, but in the twentieth century include Tate's 'Ode to the Confederate Dead' and Lowell's answering 'For the Union Dead' (N1417, 1603).

The *ballad* (from Latin *ballare*, to dance) was originally a narrative song, public in address, usually straightforward, often unhappy, and with a refrain. In medieval literature there are closed long-stanza variants collectively distinguished as *ballades* (in *ballade stanzas*), but while originating in public troubadour-verse they became *de facto* a type of refined *lyric* (as in Chaucer), and ceased functioning balladically.[33] More generally, *folk-ballads*, typically anonymous, seemingly simple, and usually in common metre, are distinguished from *literary ballads*, signed poems tending to greater complexity in more original stanzas (if often echoing the heterometric rock of common metre). The disjunction arose with Romanticism, when folk-ballads became print-fashionable ; Wordsworth's and Coleridge's collaborative *Lyrical Ballads* (1802) testifies to their perceived importance, but Anglo-Scottish 'border ballads' (collected by Sir Walter Scott in *Minstrelsy*, 1839, and championed in his fiction) have had more popular influence than anything higher-brow. Despite the popularity of Coleridge's 'Ancient Mariner' literary ballads are often supposed impotent private imitations of public address : a foolishness, as Morrison demonstrated in 'The Ballad of the Yorkshire Ripper' (1985)[34]—one Peter Sutcliffe, who between 1975 and 1981 serially killed thirteen women with DIY tools and was himself later slashed in prison for tearing pictures of topless women from communal tabloid newspapers. He was the first active serial killer in Britain to become a media-sensation, and from the Ripper's journalistic christening to Sutcliffe's prison-hospitalisation, through five years, ten new corpses, and a trial, the case poisoned civic life with appalled incomprehension, panic, suspicions, and dreadful fascination ; nowhere more so than where fear was most justified :

[33] There are some examples in Stillman, *Poet's Manual*.

[34] Published in the *London Review of Books*, and collected in *The Ballad of the Yorkshire Ripper and other poems* (London: Chatto, 1987).

Everyweer in Yorkshire
were a creepin fear an thrill.
At Elland Road° fans chanted   *the home of Leeds Football Club*
'Ripper 12 Police Nil.'

Lasses took up karate,
judo an self-defence,
an jeered at lads in porn shops,
an scrawled stuff in pub Gents,

like: 'Ripper's not a psychopath
but every man in pants.
All you blokes would kill like him
given half a chance.

'Listen to your beer-talk—
"hammer", "poke" and "screw",
"bang" and "score" and "lay" us:
that's what the Ripper does too.'   (pp. 30–1)

Public agreement was limited to declarations that 'If I could get my hands on him I'd . . .' ; when someone did give Sutcliffe 'a taste of his own medicine' it was for ripping paper women, not human flesh—hardly poetic justice, but a kind of justice to the irony of which only poetry could do justice. Morrison, born in Yorkshire but living in London, had to remember the victims' and Sutcliffe's living relatives, while mediating local and national experience/s—in the villanelle of the Yorkshire Ripper ? the limericks ? the sonnets ? The ballad, long accommodating private tragedy to public interest, was his only choice.

Different but equally political sensitivities attend other great modern ballads : Kipling's military *Barrack-Room Ballads* (1892), which privilege accented working-class speech ; *The Ballad of Reading Gaol* (1898), Wilde's witness of capital punishment behind locked doors ; and Dylan's civil-rights song 'The Lonesome Death of Hattie Carroll' (1964), a timely reminder (in its debt to the folk-singer Woodie Guthrie) that an oral tradition remains strong, reinforcing political understandings of the ballad's civility. Causley (N1590), a great balladeer across an exceptional range, adds religious understandings, and a poem like 'Christ at the Cheesewring' profits enormously from the fusion. But there is also a distinct ballad-tradition in *nonsense poetry* and *children's verse*. The famous examples are Victorian, Lear's *Nonsense Songs* (1871) and *Laughable Lyrics* (1877) bracketing Carroll's *The Hunting of the Snark* (1876), but Parker's *Excellent New Medley* is mid-seventeenth century, Quiller-Couch's 'Famous Ballad of the Jubilee

Cup' Edwardian, and the tradition clearly survives in modern children's and humorous verse. Somewhere between the two traditions one should remember the extraordinary suite of ballad-fragments created by Tolkien to emplot the mythic back-stories of *The Lord of the Rings*, and Samuel R. Delaney's memorable novella *The Ballad of Beta-2*.[35]

The *dramatic monologue*, in modern times championed by Browning and liberated by Eliot, has a single speaker throughout, not the poet, whose mind and character are revealed by what s/he does/n't say (and latterly think) ; it privileges printed mimesis of speech, but a listener may also be named or implied, a 'mute interlocutor' before the general audience of readers—so it's productive to ask why someone <u>isn't</u> being interrupted. Dramatic monologues are manipulative, and their speakers tend to strangeness : to Browning's gynocides, Tennyson's time-wasted 'Ulysses' and 'Tithonus' (N992, 1006), and Eliot's dithering Prufrock may be added MacDiarmid's inebriate in *A Drunk Man Looks at a Thistle* ; Lowell's 'Mad Negro Soldier Confined at Munich', abused wife able 'To Speak of the Woe that is in Marriage', and chiller driller in 'Under the Dentist' ; Hill's unimaginably displaced 'Ovid in the Third Reich' ; Snodgrass's suicidal Nazis in *The Fuehrer Bunker* ; Harrison's hallucinating mourner in *V.* ; and the foster-matricide of Gioia's 'The Homecoming'.[36] The attractions of derangement are as obvious in poetry as journalism, but its poetic investigation can be as serious as Browning's in the twelve monologues of *The Ring and the Book* ; compounding and contradicting testimonies from principals and bystanders in a notorious murder-case, rounded by a Papal judgement and a change of plea from the killer, inform a poem as intelligent about human psychopathology as anything since *The Faerie Queene*. But there is no limitation to the odd, however attractive instability may be : Chaucer's speakers in *The Canterbury Tales* are normal enough, 'Mr Sludge, the "Medium" ' a monster only in Browning's eyes, and the "rusty-head sailor with sea-green eyes [/] that they nickname Shabine, the patois for [/] any red nigger" in Walcott's 'The Schooner *Flight*' (N1826; p. 38) is a proudly representative speaker.

The old *calypsonian* of Walcott's 'The Spoiler's Return' is also a notable monologist, and (as with ballads) the orality of monologue should

---

35 Causley, *Collected Poems 1951–2000* (London: Chatto, 2000) ; Parker, in Malcolm, *Origins of English Nonsense* ; A. Quiller-Couch, *Green Bays: Verses and Parodies by* Q (rev. edn, London: OUP, 1930) ; Delaney (New York: Ace, 1965).

36 Hugh MacDiarmid, *Complete Poems* (3 vols, Manchester: Carcanet, 1993–4) ; Robert Lowell, *Collected Poems* (New York: FSG, and London: Faber, 2003) ; Gioia, *The Gods of Winter* (Calstock: Peterloo Poets, 1991).

never be slighted : calypsonians like Walcott's 'Spoiler' do not, in performing cultural commentary, necessarily speak as themselves, but may deploy personae (as Dylan does in songs like 'Idiot Wind'). The fusion or layering of an imperial (and imperious) form with a (post-/African) bardic figure also recalls the work of Babalola : rendering Yoruban folk-tales in vigorous colloquial English, he deploys traditional story-telling formulae and contemporary diction with great success, but when a first-person speaker is added to the mix proper suspicion of a monologist's motives and reliability interacts fascinatingly with the social identity of the tale-teller, as in 'A Tale of the Maize Plant', beginning "I don't know at all, but I wish I knew [/] What clothes the Maize Plant wore when first he came [/] To this Origbo area from Olufe town".[37] With such oral drive, the choice of component-form can be critical. Browning's speakers include sensibly blank versifiers, but his most disturbing murderers rhyme their measures into their madness : 'Porphyria's Lover' (p. 19) speaks in an tetrametric *ababb* pentain made remorseless by the absence of stanza-breaks, the overbearing Duke of 'My Last Duchess' relishes his preeningly heroic couplets, and the hateful monk soliloquises from his Spanish Cloister in cross-rhymed trochaic octets, revealing delusions with every stress (N1009–13). The sonnet-forms into which Lowell packs his abused wife and abusive dentist similarly intensify their respective suffering and sadism, while Snodgrass's Nazis explore insanity and claustrophobia in their ornate stanzas (p. 95)—but heroic couplets were for Chaucer a sturdy vehicle for lengthy tale-telling, Harrison's cross-rhymed heroic quatrains in *V.* invoke Gray's 'Elegy Written in a Country Churchyard' (N669), and Walcott shaped 'The Schooner *Flight*', beyond its constituent monologues, to traverse the Caribbean.

Verse-letters, dramatic monographs to an absent interlocutor, theoretically have the same freedom, but in practice tend strongly to blank verse or heroic couplets. Donne, predictably, tried a variety of tercet- to sestet-forms, but his best-known verse-letters, 'The Storme' and 'The Calme' to Christopher Brooke, and 'To Sir *Henry Wotton*', are in heroic couplets ; later examples clinch the tendency, though the verse-letters constituting Clough's *verse-novels* (p. 62) are in blank octameters. Epistolary novels, thickened if not obsessed by private sentiments, are as good a guide to verse-letters as the freestanding public prose-forms allied to essays, newspapers, and open protest ; even verse-letters written for publication tend more to brooding rumination focused around

[37] In Bassir, *West African Verse*.

their addressee than genuinely public address. Donne's letters to Brooke were (modelled as) genuine communications to a friend, written from experiences of terror and boredom on the high seas ; friendship gives licence, verse-structure discipline, and all may enjoy and profit from results not addressed to them. In the best of the breed—including letters by Jim Powell in exemplary modern blank verse, and Wilmer's 'Letter to J. A. Cuddon' (once his schoolteacher) and 'To Thom Gunn, on his 60th Birthday'—Horatian and other voices mingle in a semi-private form respecting the public sphere,[38] and there is a sense in which poets too weary, disheartened, or cynical to attempt high-strung odes to a deaf public may instead write low-strung letters to friends.

The *epyllion* (a Victorian coinage as a diminutive of 'epic'), also called *minor epic* or (loosely) *Ovidian verse*, tells or applies a myth, typically erotic in representing female sexual agency, from Ovid's *Metamorphoses*, which in the newly accessible original and Golding's 1567 translation had a considerable impact on poets of all persuasions. The best-known *epyllia* are Shakespeare's *Venus and Adonis* and Marlowe's *Hero and Leander*, usually excerpted in splendid isolation but more interesting among their brethren : Beaumont's *Salmacis and Hermaphroditus*, *Willobie His Avisa*, and Daniel's *Complaint of Rosamond* are first-class, Chapman's *Ovids Banquet of Sense* formally extraordinary, and Marston's *The Metamorphosis of Pigmalion's Image* so rude it was publicly burned in 1598.[39] As the overlap of epyllion-writers with sonneteers suggests, the epyllion complements the sonnet-sequence, reversing gender-roles and quelling the narrative stutter induced by the length of sonnets ; as Daniel's title suggests, it also overlaps (especially in the 1590s) with the *(female) complaint*, typically lamenting amorous desertion. 'A Louer's Complaint' followed Shakespeare's sonnets in 1609, its rhyme royal looking intriguingly like half-size Petrarchan sonnets (one quatrain, one tercet), and should be read against them ; an echo of the impulse towards interlocked contrast that produced in quick succession *Venus and Adonis* in sestets and *The Rape of Lucrece* in rhyme royal as contrasting frames for mirrored complaints ending in metamorphosis (Adonis, who won't stay, becomes a flower, and Tarquin, who won't go, midwives a republic). The Renaissance dance of forms within and around forms is fascinatingly apparent in Colin Burrow's fine 'Oxford Shakespeare' *Complete Sonnets and Poems* (2002), an

[38] Powell, 'A Letter', 'Inscriptions', and 'Heights', in *It was Fever* (p. 38) ; Wilmer, *Selected Poems 1965–1993* (Manchester: Carcanet, 1995).

[39] All are found in the anthologies by Donno, Alexander, and Clark.

astonishingly rare collocation of all Shakespeare's non-dramatic verse, but relations are tough to track thereafter. All three clearly survive to the present (though more recent examples, Tennyson's 'Oenone' or Hughes's 'Pygmalion', are rarely called epyllia), but as sonnet-sequences became the exception rather than the norm the charge left the triple relationship ; Ovid remains more visibly influential, and may be tracked in anthologies.[40]

The *country-house poem* draws from a wide range of classical exemplars in expressing thanks to a patron by lauding their estate. It sounds an excuse for ritual hack-work, but not all patrons expect self-censorship and two great poets found in its courtesies occasions of their greatness. Jonson, engaging with the Sidney family, deployed country-house poems written over a decade (including 'To Penshurst', N328) within his mixed sequence *The Forrest* (1616) ; its context, perhaps Jonson's prompt for shaping the sequence was the failure of Philip Sidney's direct line amid other family misfortunes, and the inevitable sense of lost hope and mocked vanity has national resonance. One civil war later, in 1651, Marvell took pains to find himself employed by Lord Fairfax, who had just refused to invade Ireland even if allowed to rule England afterwards ; 'Upon Appleton House' is part admiring thanks, part resignation-letter, and altogether a state-of-the-nation survey of deceptively urbane power. In Fowler's *The Country House Poem*, an anthology often tagged as definitive, 'Penshurst' and 'Appleton House' are items 5 and 56 of 77 listed in order of poets' birth, and the only item later than *c.*1690 is a fragment from Pope's *Odyssey* (1725). One might think the country-house poem found apotheosis in the Civil War and thereafter vanished away ; perhaps it did, though *Augustan* and *Romantic* (p. 294) poems offering prospects of significant buildings (such as Gray's 'of Eton College', N666, and Wordsworth's of 'Tintern Abbey', N765) suggest otherwise—but if so it returned with a vengeance when Yeats seized it from Marvell for his own 'Meditations in Time of Civil War' (collected in *The Tower*, 1928), and Eliot from both for *Burnt Norton* (1935) and *Little Gidding* (1942, N1360). The latter house is at least standing, and the modern possibilities of the form, painfully apparent in the Anglo–Irish civil-war-to-civil-war transmission, have also been more hopefully reworked in Walcott's 'Ruins of a Great House' (collected 1962), considering a former slave- and governor's mansion whose ruination testifies both to terrible wrongs

[40] See the anthologies by Tomlinson, Hoffman and Lasdun, and Ted Hughes's *Tales from Ovid* (1997) now in *Collected Poems* (London: Faber, 2003).

inflicted and positive change. Those interested might also consider the form's relations with a classic modern play, Stoppard's *Arcadia* (1993), and the widespread dramatic, cinematic, and novelistic uses of the country house as a talismanic place.

Book-length forms and genre

Though rarely less than substantial, poems in these general forms do not (saving sonnet-sequences and some dramatic monologues) usually exceed a thousand lines, and most are less than half that. Poets who do reach four-figure territory need other forms of structural division and support, and as anyone writing prose at length discovers, paragraphs alone will not do ; nor yet verse-paragraphs. What verse-paragraphs or stanzas build into, however, is far less predictable than chapters (from Latin *capitulum*, 'heading') in novels : the commonest labels are *cantos* (Italian, 'singings'), which may stand alone (as in *The Rape of the Lock*) or build into *books*[41] (as in *The Faerie Queene*), which may also stand alone (as in *Paradise Lost*) ; more idiosyncratically Carroll's *The Hunting of the Snark* and Causley's *The Tail of the Trinosaur* are in *fits* and *shakes* respectively, while Carson's *The Beauty of the Husband* (N1970) is "a fictional essay in 29 tangos".[42]

There are, in other words, no rules, but what poets decide depends on their needs or desires, and labels (especially if authorial) offer clues. *Verse-autobiographies*, like Wordsworth's *The Prelude* and Walcott's *Another Life*, usually have 'books', like the Bible and Homeric epics in translation ; to versify autobiographically at length perhaps requires a sense of one's life as itself epic (Wordsworth) or resonant with a need for epic dignity (Walcott). Interestingly, longer stanzaic or free-verse works not in books, however autobiographical, rarely bear the label : Bunting's *Briggflatts* (1965, N1421), though formally calling itself 'An Autobiography', is not in any case very biographically informative, but Harrison's *School of Eloquence* sonnet-sequence certainly is, and Shakespeare's *Sonnets* are persistently supposed to be (pp. 316, 322). Verse-letters of sufficient length to need subdivision, though often diaristic and implicitly autobiographical, also tend to use simple numbered 'parts', as Auden did in *New Year Letter* (1940), and Clive James in *Poem of the Year* (1983).[43] Even one of the great poetic autobiographies,

[41] Probably from a Germanic root meaning 'beech', a wood used for rune-tablets.

[42] Martin Gardner, *The Annotated Snark* (1962; rev. edn, Harmondsworth: Penguin, 1974) ; Causley, *The Tail of the Trinosaur: A Story in Rhyme* (Leicester: Brockhampton Press, 1972) ; Carson, *The Beauty of the Husband* (London: Cape, 2001).

[43] Bunting, *Collected Poems* (Oxford: OUP, 1978) ; James, *The Book of My Enemy: Collected Verse 1958–2003* (London: Picador, 2003).

Merrill's *The Changing Light at Sandover* (which has its own highly idiosyncratic structure, p. 64), begins by deprecating its form :

> Admittedly I err by undertaking
> This in its present form. The baldest prose
> Reportage was called for, that would reach
> The widest public in the shortest time.
> Time, it had transpired was of the essence.
> Time, the very attar of the Rose,
> Was running out. We, though, were ancient foes,
> I and the deadline. Also my subject-matter
> Gave me pause—so intimate, so novel.
> Best after all to do it as a novel? (p. 3)

Verse-novels, however, half-embracing their prose-born form, are half-likely to have 'chapters'. There is argument about Byron's *Don Juan* (1818–24), in cantos : a genially discursive mock-epic, it certainly influenced two major continental examples, Pushkin's *Eugene Onegin* (1831), in chapters, and Mickiewicz's *Pan Tadeusz* (1834), in books. Clough preferred epistolary form for *The Bothie of Toper-na-fuisich* (1848) and *Amours de Voyage* (1858), grouping letters in cantos, and both Brownings preferred books, Elizabeth Barrett for a fictional autobiography, *Aurora Leigh* (1857), and Robert for *The Ring and the Book* (1868–9). Modernists tended to find the whole idea of verse-novels self-defeating, but the later-twentieth century saw a revival. Joshi's *The Awakening (A novella in rhyme)* (1993) is undivided ; Tranter's *The Floor of Heaven* (1992), Murray's *Fredy Neptune* (1998), and Walcott's *Tiepolo's Hound* (2000) are in books ; John Fuller's *The Illusionists* (1980), Seth's *The Golden Gate* (1986), Walcott's *Omeros* (1990), Dorothy Porter's *The Monkey's Mask: An Erotic Murder Mystery* (1994), and H. R. F. Keating's *Jack, the Lady Killer* (1999) are in chapters.[44] Walcott's discrimination is suggestive, pointing *Omeros* as a verse-novel (however conscious of Homer) and *Tiepolo's Hound* as a verse-(auto-)biography of himself and the painter Pissarro, but Porter's wildly unusual procedure, grouping irregular lyrics in named sections that function as chapters primarily because that is what crime novels usually have, reinforces wariness about generalisations.

[44] *The Awakening* (New Delhi: UBS Publishers' Distributors, 1993) ; *The Floor of Heaven* (1992; Todmorden: Arc, 2000) ; *Fredy Neptune* (Manchester: Carcanet, 1998) ; *Tiepolo's Hound* (New York: FSG, and London: Faber, 2000) ; *The Monkey's Mask* (London: Serpent's Tail, 1997) ; *Jack, the Lady Killer* (Hexham: Flambard, 1999).

Poets wishing to retain overtly poetic structure at novel-length usually build sequential volumes or individual poems (deploying whatever internal forms) into a larger structure. *Idylls of the King* (written over sixty years) and *The Ring and the Book* (written in five) are both cumulative *cycles*, though Browning certainly trades with the novel and true-crime ; despite their differing scales, both plainly depend on pre-existing stories.[45] Tennyson, working with Arthurian legends, had a widely known body of material providing a chronology and personal relationships he could broadly assume while assembling selected verse-narratives. Browning faced a harder task, as the Roman murder of 1698 he versified was remembered only in Italy, but the 'Old Yellow Book' he bought second-hand nevertheless provided a plot within which his linked monologues were conceived, and which they recreate for readers. Milton similarly had the Bible, but (knowing his contemporaries would follow both plot and strategy) chose to emulate Homeric and Roman *epic* (p. 66) by beginning *in medias res* ('in the middle of things') and flashing-back before catching up and finishing. *The Faerie Queene*, incomplete at six books and two cantos, is a demi-cycle, as the twelve-book schema of virtues that Spenser outlined to Ralegh and the completed books' titles announce. And in especially vivid demonstration, Christopher Logue's ongoing chunks of translation from Homer's *Iliad*—*War Music* (1981), *Kings* (1991), *The Husbands* (1994), their revised collection in *Homer: War Music* (2001), and *All Day Permanent Red: War Music Continued* (2003)[46]—even as fragments map themselves directly against their source, creating imaginations of what a complete Logue translation might be although there is no realistic hope he will ever complete one.

Cycles (like sonnet sequences) are usefully capable of evolving in structure as well as length, and their constituent poems may have individual lives. It is hard to see that the internal order of *The Ring and the Book* could vary much, but that of *Idylls of the King* certainly did during its long growth, and it seems unlikely Harrison's *School of Eloquence* will ever have a single definitive order. Even a final authorial structure may be only one option : when Snodgrass first collected his Nazi monologists in *The Führer Bunker: A Cycle of Poems in Progress* (1977) there were 18 poems by 9 speakers on 12 dates between 1 April and 1 May 1945 ; the single speaker of *Magda Goebbels* (1983) had 6 poems (3 new) on 6 dates (none new) ; 'The Fuehrer Bunker' in *Selected Poems*

---

[45] Conversely, the critical use of sonnet 'cycle' rather than 'sequence' may indicate rejection of any concern with (supposed) narrative.

[46] All published by Faber in London.

1957–1987 (1987) had 15 poems (8 new) by 6 speakers (2 new) on 8 dates (1 new) ; and *The Fuehrer Bunker: The Complete Cycle* (1995) has 87 poems (42 new) by 15 speakers (4 new) and a chorus on 21 dates (8 new).[47] Only 'Magda Goebbels (22 April 1945)' appears in all four collections, and while the three larger collections are chronologically organised, and *The Complete Cycle* is in eight titled sections grouping poems by date, character-sequence remains a necessary mode of reading.

If the cycle is too loose there is always the trilogy. Dante, echoing his beloved *terza rima*, gave poetic trilogism high sanction by building his *Inferno, Purgatorio*, and *Paradiso* into *The Divine Comedy*, but the ideas involved in tripartite structures are either self-evident or highly individual, and two recent examples must suffice. Brathwaite's *Rights of Passage* (1967), *Masks* (1968), and *Islands* (1969), collected as *The Arrivants: A New World Trilogy* (1972), form a complex but coherent exploration of Caribbean culture and history ; the underlying structures mix lyrics and narratives into a greater tale of African diaspora and Caribbean arrival, survival, and success, but reject more obvious epic structures to avoid a classical European poetic form when the most relevant classical European form is slavery.[48] More idiosyncratically, Merrill's 'The Book of Ephraim', 26 sections beginning A–Z, first published as the bulk of *Divine Comedies* (1976), was joined by *Mirabell: Books of Number* (1978), 100 sections numbered 0.0–9.9, and *Scripts for the Pageant* (1980), in sections captioned and beginning with the words 'Yes', 'And', and 'No' ; assembled as *The Changing Light at Sandover* (1982), the form was revealed as fundamentally reworking Dante by mapping the standard semi-circular character-set of the Ouija board, the central prop of a dramatised autobiography featuring Merrill's lover and friends, Auden's ghost (who composes some posthumous poems[49]), assorted familiars and archangels, and an avatar of God. To call this structure a catalogue would be grotesquely unfair—the poem is wonderfully intelligent and very highly wrought, the perfect *canzone* 'Samos' (p. 53) being only a local joy—yet Merrill implicitly shows that any object (and Browning's "Ring" is the radically simple instance) can

---

[47] Brockport, NY: Boa Editions, 1977 ; Winston-Salem, NC: Palaemon Press, 1983 ; New York: Soho Press, 1987 ; Brockport, NY: Boa Editions, 1995. I have been unable to examine another fine-edition pamphlet, *Heinrich Himmler: Platoons and Files* (San Francisco and Cumberland, IA: Pterodactyl Press, 1982), but *Magda Goebbels* is one of the best such I've ever seen, with a stunningly *marbled* cover.

[48] Oxford: OUP, 1973. Brathwaite's *Mother Poem* (1977), *Sun Poem* 1982), and *X/Self* (1987) have also been reworked as a trilogy, *Ancestors* (New York: New Directions, 2001).

[49] See Merrill's remarks in *University of Toronto Quarterly*, 61/3 (1992), 390.

be structurally mapped on a contents-page by sections with almost complete internal freedom to deploy intrinsically unrelated poetic forms : as must be so, for form at this level is a function of the poet's intent.

Beyond form lies *genre* (from French *genre*, 'a type or kind' ; cf. gender, genus), but as poetry *tout court* is commonly labelled a genre alongside 'prose' and 'drama' (itself in verse and prose), and any number of sub- and sub-sub-genres are bandied about, the whole business is problematic. Bluntly, both the term itself (in literary use dating only to the late-nineteenth century), and the 'names' of particular 'genres', are almost universally used without consistency or coherence ; I have argued the case elsewhere, and readers who do not understand what I mean by saying that no essentialist (Platonic) theory of genre is workable are referred to the chapters on genre in *The Drama Handbook* (🖱). The problems are in some ways less severe with poetry (unless performative), but the fundamental outcome is identical : genre cannot be coherently understood as wholly predetermined, nor as any form of receptacle to which texts may be consigned ; it must instead be understood as a loose system based on fluid archetypal assemblages of elements typically presenting together, in which no identity excludes any other. What matters for readers is that genre works through expectation, the presence of one element (a metre, a subject, a style) leading to expectations of another ; if enough elements fit, a generic identity coalesces, but in no way precludes those or other elements from simultaneously or successively generating other (sets of) expectations, and inducing other generic identities. There is, moreover, in poetry a distinct problem where metre and form are involved, for prosodic and/or euphonic expectations are generated, and met or disappointed, with every foot, rhyme, and stanza, quite apart from any expectations narrative may induce or that come with the external baggage of a form.

What matters about genres is therefore the extent to which they are shared by poets and their readers. Some ancient fragment may once have been an essential element of a sacrifice, but if I cannot understand it as such, and find it presented in a very different context, its original generic identity (being unable to raise expectations) is overwritten by others. Nor is this truth extreme : as much could be said of what happens when the *Norton* editors remove one of Shakespeare's songs from the play for which he wrote it, presenting it in a purely poetic context. Overtly thematic anthologies, whether general (poems of love or war) or specific (poems about AIDS or 'for Bosnia'), are partly responsible for our vagueness about genre, and such themes can only helpfully serve as 'genres' if you as a reader are led by their labels to a reasonably specific set of expectations. If not, formal analysis and open-minded consideration of individual poems (if possible in proper context) is a better bet.

The only exceptions are the five modes that were classically distinguished and are now lumped in with genres, the *lyric, epic, satiric, comic*, and *tragic* ; plus *elegy* and *pastoral*. Each of these terms has a long and complex history, beginning (mostly) in classical Greek drama and/or poetry, continuing through Roman adaptation and development of Greek practice and theory, and descending to the present day in continuous, pan-European, and latterly global traditions subject to constant challenge and revision. In brief, 'lyric' is the adjective from 'lyre', a stringed musical instrument, and lyrics—like those of modern songs—would in Greece normally have been musically accompanied ; in early modern use 'lyric poetry' was probably still quite often accompanied, or conceived as singable, but the term now covers most shorter poems, typically expressing (or thought to express) personal emotion, and is defined mostly by a process of exclusion (not any of the other genres, not narrative, not martial . . .). 'Epic' (from Greek *'επικός* [epɪkos], narrative or song), conversely, refers to long narratives collected from oral tradition and literary imitations of them ; the process of imitation, in different cultures at different times, has created tremendous diversity, but the central idea of dealing with group-history and -identity is strong enough to persist in diminutive forms such as the epyllion and compound labels like mock-epic and 'chamber-epic' (as in chamber-orchestra). 'Satire' (from late Latin *satira*, a medley) was until 1605 believed to derive from an earlier medley, the Greek *satyr*, a wood-dwelling half-man-half-goat, and the mistake still causes some confusion : Renaissance 'satires' may simply be a heterogeneous collection, 'things in an anthology', but the (latent) sense of 'purposeful ridicule' dominates thereafter. One does not hear much of 'tragic poetry', nor even 'tragic verse' outside the long association of stage-tragedy with formal language ; 'comic verse' is used as a synonym for *light* or *humorous verse*, but means only 'funny', and has no meaningful connection with classical or Shakespearian comedy unless an individual poet's treatment of a sexual or marital theme signals the invocation of those traditions.

'Elegies' (in Greek and most Romance languages) are songs of lamentation, ritualising grief for individuals or larger losses : Greek literature had specifically elegiac metres, but Greeks also practised graveside ululation ; the English, accustomed to more demure funerals, naturally found pentameter appropriate unless occasion dictated otherwise—compare Gray's 'Ode on the Death of a Favorite Cat, Drowned in a Tub of Goldfishes' (N668), in double-bobbed tetrametric sestets (*aab6ccb6*), with Tennyson's heroic 'Ode on the Death of the Duke of Wellington'. Nowadays any poem can be an elegy (sonnets often have aspirations), but someone or -thing worth mourning at all is probably worth mourning at public length.

'Pastoral', to be useful as an idea, must be understood in more detail. The term, like so many stanza-names, goes back to the Renaissance Italian countryside (a *pastor* is a shepherd), but the genre is usually dated to the *Idylls* of Theocritus (*c.* 310–250 BCE), via the *Eclogues* (poems of pleasant places) and sometimes *Georgics* (poems of instruction) of Virgil ; classical *bucolics* (poems of drunkenness) are also involved. A different but equally important classical root lies in Arcadia, a mountainous district of the Peloponnese to which wealthy Athenians had resort in the summer, a setting that slowly became in literature an archetypal *locus amoenus* ('pleasant place') populated by surprisingly well-dressed and amorously soulful rustics at permanent leisure. In the English Renaissance version, promoted by a famous anthology, *Englands Helicon* (1600, 1614), their names are typically Damon, Clorinda, Phyllis, and the like, and they sing plaintive or jolly songs to one another, often in clever stanza-forms : leisured court-associations are certainly strong—masques, for example, are a good source of pastoral poetry—but (politics aside) the genre is attractive and rewards familiarity. It also features poems in dialogue, which readily makes for qualities of counterpoint and harmony that aesthetically transcend issues of class, but what makes Renaissance pastoral far more than a single historical flowering is that Spenser's *The Shepheardes Calender* (1579, N159), and Marvell's 'Mower' poems (*c.*1650, N482), used pastoral frameworks to much greater social and political purpose by introducing to the sylvan scene self-deprecating or low-ranking figures. Spenser's 'Colin Clout' and Marvell's seasonally working 'Mower', with dramatic help from Shakespeare's Arden (which precludes neither winter nor poverty), enabled the genre to survive as more than a lyric garden, and its modern critical reputation was secured by Empson's *Some Versions of Pastoral* (1935), which yoked Shakespeare to Marvell, Milton, Gay, and Carroll. The extent to which it is in contemporary use (other than occasional invocation, usually ironic) is moot ; the term *urban pastoral* has, however, become quite widespread for poetry of suburban homes and streetscapes, whether as cheery as Betjeman's neglected ironwork, or as glum as Larkin's derelict canals. The connection is what you make of it ; all that matters, in describing Larkin's 'The Whitsun Weddings' (N1652) as an urban–pastoral ode in bobbed heroic stanzas rhyming *ab4abcdecde*, is that you understand what each bit means and how rigorously it means it.

Exemplary Poems

1. John Keats, 'Ode on Melancholy' (May 1819), from *Lamia, Isabella, The Eve of St Agnes and Other Poems* (London: printed for Taylor and Hessey, Fleet Street, 1820), 140–2 (N937). Line-numbers added.

1.

No, no, go not to Lethe, neither twist
  Wolf's-bane, tight-rooted, for its poisonous wine ;
Nor suffer thy pale forehead to be kiss'd
  By nightshade, ruby grape of Proserpine ;
Make not your rosary of yew-berries,
  Nor let the beetle, nor the death-moth be
    Your mournful Psyche, nor the downy owl
A partner in your sorrow's mysteries ;
  For shade to shade will come too drowsily,
    And drown the wakeful anguish of the soul.

2.

But when the melancholy fit shall fall
  Sudden from heaven like a weeping cloud,
That fosters the droop-headed flowers all,
  And hides the green hill in an April shroud ;
Then glut thy sorrow on a morning rose,
  Or on the rainbow of the salt sand-wave,
    Or on the wealth of globed peonies ;
Or if thy mistress some rich anger shows,
  Emprison her soft hand, and let her rave,
    And feed deep, deep upon her peerless eyes.

3.

She dwells with Beauty—Beauty that must die ;
  And Joy, whose hand is ever at his lips
Bidding adieu ; and aching Pleasure nigh,
  Turning to poison while the bee-mouth sips :
Ay, in the very temple of Delight
  Veil'd Melancholy has her sovran shrine,
    Though seen of none save him whose strenuous tongue
Can burst Joy's grape against his palate fine ;
  His soul shall taste the sadness of her might,
    And be among her cloudy trophies hung.

Words and thoughts are rich, but heroic stanzas straightforwardly combine a cross-rhymed quatrain with tercets, *ababcdecde* in stanzas 1–2 but *-cdedce* in 3. The quatrains are always distinct, ll. 4 and 14 ending in semicolons, l. 24 in a colon, but the first (ll. 1–4) is evenly bisected by the semicolon ending l. 2, and the last (ll. 21–4) trisected by the semicolons in ll. 21 and 23 : absolute symmetry is impossible in trisecting a quatrain, but Keats's division here into thirds of 5, 7, and 8 feet creates a smooth progression despite the splitting of l. 23. In a similar pattern, the tercets in stanza 2 (ll. 15–20) are confirmed by the semicolon ending l. 17 (as the preceding quatrain, ll. 11–14, stands whole), but in stanzas 1 and 3 semicolons end ll. 8 and 28, forcing 4 + 2 syntax (*cdec-de* and *cded-ce*) over 3 + 3 rhymes.

The resulting sequence—4 ; 4 ; 2. // 4 ; 3 ; 3. // 4 : 4 ; 2.[50]—is at the service of argument : the logical stages map onto it exactly ('Don't do this ; or this ; because . . . // But when ; then do this ; or this. // Three assertions : two more ; and a consequence.'), but in the first and last stanzas are counterpointed by the underlying 4–3–3 structure. The whole is clarified as argument is pointed and displayed, while the variation of and return (with further variation) to a stanza-form creates an arc and sense of completion. The shortest of Keats's 1819 odes, this might certainly be thought private rather than public in its brevity and sensuous abstraction ; the extent to which it achieves public greatness rides substantially on a clear mastery of form.

2. Elizabeth Bishop, 'Sestina' ; first collected in *Questions of Travel* (1965) ; text from *Complete Poems* (N1520). Line-numbers added.

September rain falls on the house.
In the failing light, the old grandmother
sits in the kitchen with the child
beside the Little Marvel Stove,
reading the jokes from the almanac,
laughing and talking to hide her tears.

She thinks that her equinoctial tears
and the rain that beats on the roof of the house
were both foretold by the almanac,
but only known to a grandmother.
The iron kettle sings on the stove.
She cuts some bread and says to the child,

[50] *Stanza-breaks* are conventionally indicated by a double-solidus (//) (p. 153).

It's time for tea now ; but the child
is watching the teakettle's small hard tears
dance like mad on the hot black stove,
the way the rain must dance on the house.
Tidying up, the old grandmother
hangs up the clever almanac

on its string. Birdlike, the almanac
hovers half-open above the child,
hovers above the old grandmother
and her teacup full of dark brown tears.
She shivers and says she thinks the house
feels chilly, and puts more wood in the stove.

It was to be, says the Marvel Stove.
I know what I know, says the almanac.
With crayons the child draws a rigid house
and a winding pathway. Then the child
puts in a man with buttons like tears
and shows it proudly to the grandmother

But secretly, while the grandmother
busies herself about the stove,
the little moons fall down like tears
from between the pages of the almanac
into the flower bed the child
has carefully placed in the front of the house.

Time to plant tears, says the almanac.
The grandmother sings to the marvellous stove
and the child draws another inscrutable house.

'Sestina' is properly exemplary in its cycle of repetitions, even managing an additional, medial 'child' (l. 27), but distinct in choosing iambic tetrameter. The usual preference for heroic sestinas not only grants an extra 39 feet, but increases the distance between every end-word, and every repetition of an end-word—a wide slalom by comparison with this narrowness of measure. Bishop's decision goes hand-in-hand with its compensation, a large number of triple substitutions : the last line is *de facto* anapæstic tetrameter (with a substitute amphimacer, 'draws anoth-'), and ll. 7, 36, and 38 all but, and the prepositional need for anapæsts shown in these lines ('and the child', 'on the roof', 'in the front', etc.) is widespread ('on the house', 'from the al-', 'on the hot', etc.). Only ll. 1, 3–4, 13, 15, 18, 32–33, and 35 are restricted to eight beats, and one could argue that concentrated medial irregularity in stanzas 4–5 and terminal irregularity in the envoi take 'Sestina' beyond iambics (if not rising tetrametrics) ; but l. 30 is certainly heroic, l. 34 (for my money an anapæst + four iambs) allowably so, and all other lines save the last scannable as iambic tetrameters with up to three anapæstic substitutions. Successively regular lines in the first and last sestets also resist notions of any achieved escape.

Nabokov once remarked (of creating chess-problems) that he "was always ready to sacrifice purity of form to the exigencies of fantastic content, causing form to bulge and burst like a sponge-bag containing a small furious devil".[51] 'Sestina' certainly bulges, but never bursts : it prosodically fights its tetrametric confinement with more vigour than the grandmother and child seem to show amid their kitchen's storm-bound domesticity, but the triple substitutions, however madly dancing, infringe only against metre ; the explicitly finite grip of the sestina-cycle, mapped by the autumn equinox and the grandmother/child contrast onto the inevitabilities of winter and human succession, is untouched. Cascading but never refreshing their rhymes, each stanza is another turn round the same room, and even the fantastical tears of the almanac are for lunar futures as inevitable as the next end-word.

The most fundamental property of the sestina-form is its acute combination of cyclical and linear process, a closed round implying endlessly repeatable identities but never (saving Sidney) delivering more than one. Building from an implicit analogy with human fertility and mortality, Bishop uses every formal property to entrap her subjects and express servitude to time, capping all with a title indifferent to her poem's content but hardly to its form.

[51] *Speak, Memory* (1966; Harmondsworth: Penguin, 1969), 222 (ch. 14.3).

3. Geoffrey Hill, 'September Song', first collected in *King Log* (1968) ; text from *Collected Poems* (Harmondsworth: Penguin, 1985), 67 (N1832). Line-numbers added.

September Song

born 19.6.32—deported 24.9.42

Undesirable you may have been, untouchable
you were not. Not forgotten
or passed over at the proper time. 3

As estimated, you died. Things marched,
sufficient, to that end.
Just so much Zyklon and leather, patented
terror, so many routine cries. 7

(I have made
an elegy for myself it
is true) 10

September fattens on vines. Roses
flake from the wall. The smoke
of harmless fires drifts to my eyes. 13

This is plenty. This is more than enough. 14

Hill's complex poem is intrinsically controversial because of its apposition with the *Sho'ah* (or 'Holocaust', pp. 228–9). The philosopher Adorno, a refugee from Nazism who lived in the US from 1934 to 1960, summarily judged that "Nach Auschwitz ein Gedicht zu schreiben ist barbarisch" (After Auschwitz to write a poem is barbaric)[52] : I disagree, and think it ethically necessary to disagree, but understand the impulse Adorno voiced ; so to approach 'September Song' aesthetically, through form, is not where I would wish to begin. Yet simply to look at the poem is to face a major formal question : whether its careful disposition into 14 lines can mean what it breathtakingly might.

The poem must be said to be in free verse, but iambics are persistently audible and Hill's lines are from the first haunted by heroic measure :

[52] T. Adorno, *Gesammelte Schriften* (Frankfurt am Main: Suhrkamp, 1974), X. 30. Adorno qualified himself to exclude work by survivors in *Negative Dialectics* (New York: Seabury Press, 1973), 362 ; for a summary bibliography of the problem see Young, *Writing and Rewriting*.

"Undesirable you may have been [. . .]" need only stop short to achieve it. Heroic measure is arguably the metre of ll. 3 and 14 (however trochaic the latter's scansion), and is twice prevented only by line-breaks—'an elegy for myself it [/] is true', 'The smoke [/] of harmless fires drifts to my eyes' : the sense of frustration caught by Hill's curtness in ending is partly mediated through such refusals visually to privilege pentameters despite their aural presence. Similarly, while stanzas are highly irregular, all but the last are tercets or a quatrain, and persistent half-rhymes (forgotten/time, marched/patented, end/made, cries/roses) penultimately reach a full-rhyme, cries/eyes.

With 14 lines in quatrain or tercet form and heroic measure in the offing, a ghost of sonnethood emerges. The internal structure, 3.4.(3)3.1, is clearly a possible sonnet-variant, and the full-rhyme of ll. 7 + 13, with the shift of tense from past to present in l. 8 (acting as a turn) and the absence of a full-stop in l. 10, suggest it be read as 3.4 + (3)3.1—two septet-halves providing balance while the need for the curtness of the one-line termination shortens the stanzas after the turn ; shift that isolated verse back to join the first tercet, and you would have a surprisingly clear Petrarchan 4–4–3–3. There is also a theme of love, not only in its negations (undesirable, untouchable), but in Hill's writing an elegy ; his love must be frustrated, and frustrating, its object only being loved as a nameless representative of child-victims all long past love or elegising.

As a sonnet the form is terribly damaged, 114 beats in place of 140, which seems appropriate to the reduced moral circumstances and difficulty in meaning at all that characterise attempts to grapple with the *Sho'ah* (p. 100). And sonnet-identity does not stand alone : avowed as elegy, there are also the title's invocations, underlyingly (given Hill's Anglican faith) of the songs of thankfulness entering the church-round at Harvest, specifically of two poems Hill certainly knew, Yeats's 'September 1913' and Auden's 'September 1, 1939' (N1474).[53] Standing on the brink of world wars, both are deeply disillusioned ; Yeats speaks of adding "prayer to shivering prayer", Auden of a "low dishonest decade" ending as "The unmentionable odour of death [/] Offends the September night". There is also a famous 'September Song' covered by Crosby, Sinatra, and others, a crooning lament for the mutual passing of time : Maxwell Anderson's lyrics were written in 1940 in collaboration with

[53] Excluded by Auden from his *Collected Poems*, but in *The English Auden: Poems, Essays, and Dramatic Writings, 1927–1939* (London: Faber, 1977).

composer Kurt Weill, another refugee from Nazism, and helpless lament is not far from frustrated elegy.

Formal identification as a sonnet cannot be forced, but Hill is a very great sonneteer, and the poem is unquestionably able to mean more (and not simply otherwise) if a sonnet's cohesion and baggage are figured in than if it is supposed a nameless and freestanding invention gesturing roughly at nothing beyond itself.

4. 'Nearing Forty'. (pp. 22–3)

We already know 'Nearing Forty' is (mostly) heroic. It cannot be blank verse because it rhymes, but is printed as a continuous sequence of 32 lines. The first thing therefore is to work out the rhyme-scheme :

abacb	*cddee*	*ffggh*	*hiijj*	*kbklc*	*mjmcb*	*cj*
5	10	15	20	25	30	

Some are less than full-rhymes—for example the half-rhyming sequence gap/deep/seed, *jjk*, ll. 19–21—but it is sensible at first to be ruthless to see if any underlying structural pattern emerges. For that reason I call the gap/deep rhyme (19–20) a couplet, *jj*, and consider the next half-rhyme, "seed" (21), a new rhyme, *k*, picked up by "we'd" (23).

These complicated rhymes could be variously analysed ; of most use would be a principle repeating throughout, and the prime candidate, outside the central sequence of couplets, is overlapping single-rhymed quatrains. This can be seen if the rhyme-scheme is written with each completed structure on a new line but progressing across the page, so rhyme-letters repeated in vertical column denote the same line :

5	10	15	20	25	30	
abac						
acb	*c*					
cb	*cd*					
	ddee	*ffggh*	*hiijj*			
			j	*kbk*		
				kbkl		
				c	*mjm*	
					mjmc	
					mcb	*c*
					cb	*cj*
5	10	15	20	25	30	

The quatrains abutting the central sequence of couplets, *cbcd* and *jkbk,* are weak because the *d*- and *j*-rhymes tend to be subsumed by their couplets, but worth insisting on because there is then only one place, the break at l. 24 between *kbkl* and *cmjm,* where successive structures fail to overlap. Numerically l. 24 is exactly three-quarters of the way through (24/32) ; the only unrhymed line (though with a strong *internal* rhyme, conventional/convectional), it is heavily end-stopped by the second semi-colon (the first is in l. 14, the second *g*-rhyme, midway through the couplets). Syntactically two-thirds of the way through, it is followed by a strong tonal resolution, l. 25 beginning "or you will rise . . .", which marks the last eight lines.

Such analysis clarifies. After initially edging forward, the poem takes a deep breath and drives through the central sequence of couplets, all open (except the first, *dd,* ll. 7–8, and the sixth, *ii,* ll. 17–18) and progressing rapidly until finally spilling out through half-rhymes into the *jjkbkl* sequence (ll. 19–24), which is marked by the return of the *b*-rhyme (rain) and overlapping single-rhymed quatrains, and ended by the unrhymed l. 24. The last eight lines return to the structure of the opening, tying themselves in by using the *b-, c-,* and *j*-rhymes (rain, work, sleep) as well as a positive new *m*-rhyme (elation/imagination). The overlapping quatrains and late return to the *b*- and *c*-rhymes help explain the poem's cohesion and unity, the open couplets its central momentum ; that the quatrains are single-rhymed, two lines in each rhyming with lines elsewhere, explains the internal fluidity, a quality of searching progression or inability to find easy rest or conclusion (cf. the heavy certainty of Eliot's cross-rhymed heroic quatrains in *The Waste Land,* p. 43). This in turn suggests why Walcott gave his last line only seven beats, to mark the ending without betraying his characteristic structure and dominant tone with a cross- or arch-rhymed quatrain (other possible termini).

This nameless form is Walcott's invention in this poem, created from named elements whose combined properties create its properties. Knowledge of the forms, their natures and histories, is something writers, readers, and practical critics cannot afford to be without.

Exercises: formal composition and analysis

1. As with metre, the best way to gain real understanding of stanza-forms is to write, read, and speak them. Common metre or long fives (tetrametric pentains, *ababb10*) offer an easy beginning : pick a small incident, summarise it as baldly as possible in prose, and try to narrate it straightforwardly in a few end-stopped stanzas. Then try again, permitting (or forcing) stanza-enjambment, and read both versions aloud trying to display both the form and any enjambments vocally. Finally, recast the poem in a longer stanza-form, melting two common-metre stanzas into (say) one isometric Sicilian stanza (*abababab*), or two long-fives into one Spenserian stanza, and then read the three versions against one another : what has each form brought to (or subtracted from) the story you set out to tell ?

2. Write a Petrarchan sonnet-octave (*abbaabba*), then, retaining the lines as exactly as possible, recast it successively as *abbaabab, abababba, abababab, aabbaabb, aababbab, abbabbaa*, and *abaababb* : what happens to your content as the internal structures revolve ? Then try successively reducing the intensity of rhyme, with (say) *abcdabcd, abcdcdab*, and *abcddcba*, changing as little as possible beyond the rhyme-word. If you are careful with the initial lines (and clever with punctuation) it is possible to change very few words as you reorder lines, and the sequent results offer an informative tour of a prosodic gearbox.

3. To investigate the relationship between internal and external baggages try to write some bitter or mournful limericks. You will feel an immediate pressure to abandon both triple rhythm and full-rhyme, but the anapæstic skip and trip-coup-let structure must remain, however disguised. By way of example, here is one about Walter Ralegh, who famously laid his cloak over a puddle for Queen Elizabeth I and popularised coffee and tobacco in Britain (ll. 1–2 + 5 are catalectic ; ll. 3–4 have unstressed hyperbeats) : "Sir Walter was handy with cloaks, / And caffeine, and packets of smokes : / Such a mighty romancer / Of insomniac cancer—/ I thank him: and hope that he chokes." It is also interesting to experiment with limericks as a narrative stanza, not least in considering the uses of enjambment within and between stanzas. This fragment from *The Toriad : An Epic in Trimeters* (1989) concerns the IRA bombing of the Conservative Party Conference in 1984 ; 'Her' is Margaret Thatcher, then Prime Minister : "So we entered the middle-decade / disencumbered, 'renewed', 'unafraid' : / then a Brighton hotel / was blown into a shell / and Her brazenness visibly greyed // to a harsher and stonier hue—/ what you might call a gunmetal-blue. / The cost of that bomb / was far more than a tomb / for the unlucky bystanding few." (The use of dactylic words laid over foot-divisions points the sombre way.)

4. To extend formal analysis into critical use, first practise using the terminology efficiently. Flipping through the *Norton Anthology* (or equivalent) at random, try to describe each poem as fully as possible in as few words as you can manage : "Larkin's 'The Whitsun Weddings' is an urban-pastoral ode in bobbed heroic stanzas rhyming *ab4abcdecde*" ; "Donne's 'A Valedicition forbidding mourning' is an ironic reverse-complaint, promising erotic fidelity in nine cross-

rhymed tetrametric quatrains." As you gain confidence try longer or less regular poems : "Pope's *The Rape of the Lock* is a mock-epic in five cantos of 74, 71, 89, 88, and 75 heroic couplets" ; "Eliot's *The Waste Land* is . . ."

5. To train your eyes in reading, take a poem (or excerpt) in stanzas, display the structure and its qualifications, then read aloud as you look. In my exemplary Spenserian stanza, for example, one could use colour (🖱) or shading to articulate the 4–4–1 rhyme-structure and faces for the 5–4 split :

LIKE AS A SHIP, WHOM CRUELL TEMPEST DRIUES
   VPON A ROCKE WITH HORRIBLE DISMAY,
   HER SHATTERED RIBS IN THOUSAND PEECES RIUES,
   AND SPOYLING ALL HER GEARES AND GOODLY RAY,
   DOES MAKE HER SELFE MISFORTUNES PITEOUS PRAY.
   So downe the cliffe the wretched Gyant tumbled;
   His battred ballances in peeces lay,
   His timbered bones all broken rudely rumbled,
So was the high aspyring with huge ruine humbled.

Did you, for example, notice before that the new sentence in l. 6 introduces the *c*-rhyme? *Quod erat demonstrandum* ; visuals help.

Chapter Glossary

alexandrine : in English, an iambic hexameter ; in French a line of 12 beats, however metrically constituted, and the staple form (as iambic pentameter is in English).

arch-rhyme : a rhyme scheme with mirror symmetry, as *abba*; also called *chiasmic rhyme.*

ballad : a narrative poem, commonly of traditional origin, often in quatrains with refrain ; *literary* and *folk* ballads are now distinguished.

blank : of a poem, stanza or other unit, unrhymed.

blank verse : unrhymed iambic pentameter.

burden : or *refrain* ; a line or lines that are repeated.

canto : a numbered section into which longer poems are commonly divided ; cf. *book, chapter.*

closed : of a couplet, with the second line end-stopped ; of form, prescribed.

common metre : also *ballad metre* or *ballad-stanza,* an iambic quatrain of the form *a8b6c8b6.*

complaint : (or *female complaint*) a poem of protest and lament, typically at amorous disappointment, betrayal, or desertion ; in the decades around 1600 deeply caught up with the *epyllion* and sonnet-sequence, not least in Shakespeare.

country-house poem : primarily, a substantial group of seventeenth-century poems describing and usually lauding a landowning patron's house and grounds, but extending to later poems centrally featuring such houses and grounds.

couplet : a stanza or unit of two lines, usually rhyming, often used terminally to summarize or moralize ; a very popular form in the eighteenth century.

cross-rhyme : alternating double-rhymes, as *abab.*

dramatic monologue : a poem cast as a speech by a particular (historical or imaginary) person, usually to a specific auditor. The form is particularly associated with Browning and Tennyson, but remained popular throughout the twentieth century.

elegy : a poem (or other composition) mourning a death or other loss.

end-stopped : of a line or stanza, having a terminal mark of punctuation.

enjamb, enjambment : of lines, couplets, or stanzas, not end-stopped, with sense and/or syntax continuing into the next line, couplet, or stanza.

envoi : a shorter terminal stanza, such as the tercet in villanelles or pentain in *canzoni.*

epic : a classical mode, epics are long narrative poems usually dealing with the heroic or martial exploits of a person, tribe, or race, and are associated with nation-founding scale. Several classical epic devices, including the *epic* *simile, epic catalogue*, and beginning *in medias res*, commonly serve as touchstones in modern epics. There are diminutive forms, notably the *mock-epic* and 'chamber-epic', and a quite distinct Brechtian use of epic to designate a dramaturgical approach and theatrical mode of production.

fourteeners : couplets in iambic heptameter.

genre : in literary use, a late-nineteenth-century coinage now covering all (supposed) methods of distinguishing and grouping (literary) forms, from classical modes to modern thematic anthologising ; more practically, a collective noun for the various sets of conventional or typical expectations readers (or other consumers of art) learn to have ; cf. 'twist'. Coherent theories of poetic genre must partly discount the functions of expectation in prosody.

heroic : of a form, in iambic pentameter.

heterometric : of stanzas, with lines of varying length.

isometric : of stanzas, with lines of constant length.

lyric : a classical mode, lyrics were at first musically accompanied ; the term now covers most short, non-narrative, non-dramatic verse.

mock-epic : a poem comically or satirically dressed in epic conventions for which its subject and/or manner are inappropriate.

octave : the first eight lines of a Petrarchan sonnet.

ode : a formal poem of some dignity or length ; *Alcaic, Sapphic, Pindaric,* and *Horatian* odes are formally distinguished.

open : of form, variable ; of couplets, with the second line enjambed to the first line of the next couplet (or other component unit of form).

ottava rima : a stanza of eight lines, in iambic pentameter, rhyming *abababcc.*

pantun, pantoum : a highly repetitive Malay form, cross-rhymed quatrains successively reusing two lines from each in the next ; once in French vogue, but never in English.

pastoral : a mode or genre, classically and until the Renaissance featuring the leisure-time rusticity of the high-born, on the model of Athenian resort to Arcadia ; once very highly stylised, with designated roles and role-names for amorous play and witty debate, but latterly used as a means of considering class-issues and post-industrial geography ; cf. *urban pastoral.*

pentain : a stanza of five lines.

Petrarchan : of sonnets, having an octave rhyming *abbaabba*, and a sestet rhyming *cdecde* (or a variant thereof).

quatrain : a stanza of four lines ; often used for narrative.

rhyme royal : a stanza of seven lines, in iambic pentameter, rhyming *ababbcc.*

rhyme-scheme : a method of notating the pattern of rhymes in a stanza or poem using the alphabet. The first line, and all subsequent lines that rhyme with it, are *a* ; the next line that does not rhyme, and all subsequent lines that rhyme with it are *b*, and so on. Line-lengths may also be indicated, by placing the number of beats after the letter denoting the line.

satire, satiric : a classical mode, initially meaning a mixed sequence or form, potentially the primary sense as late as the Renaissance ; latterly a loose collective term for all art that mocks or otherwise ridicules (purportedly) to urge correction and reform.

sestet : a stanza or unit of six lines, including ll. 9–14 of Petrarchan sonnets.

Shakespearian : of sonnets, rhyming *ababcdcdefefgg*.

single-rhyme : a rhyme-scheme with only one pair of rhyming lines, as *abcb* or *abac*.

sonnet : until the early seventeenth century, any short lyric poem ; thereafter supposedly and conventionally a poem of 14 lines in iambic pentameter, but variants ranging from 10½–20 lines are recognised. Its traditional use, especially in sequences, is for poems of (frustrated) love and courtship, but since the seventeenth century occasional sonnets on almost every topic imaginable have been written, and there are now long-standing connections with many poetic modes, including the elegiac, satirical, and confessional.

Spenserian : of sonnets, rhyming *ababbcbccdcdee* ; of stanzas, heroic and rhyming *ababbcbccl2*.

stanza : a group of lines displayed on the page by blank lines above and below, typically with a constant structure or rhyme-scheme.

tercet : a stanza or unit of three lines in which one or more does not rhyme with the others.

terza rima : successive tercets rhyming *aba bcb cdc ded* etc.

turn : (or *volta*) a moment of disjunction and/or renewal, creating a shift or development in the sense at a specified point in a form ; in relation to the Pindaric ode, a name for the strophe.

triplet : a stanza or unit of three lines which all rhyme together.

verse : (1) a single line or equivalent stichic unit (as in 'chapter and verse') ; (2) a poet's prosodic and formal craft, or, collectively, versified work (as in 'Shakespeare's verse'), and with reference to drama, metrical lines as distinguished from prose and/or song (as in 'blank verse') ; (3) especially with reference to any nationality, period, or theme before Modernism, a synonym for poetry (as in 'Renaissance verse') ; (4) in post-Romantic apposition with 'poetry', sometimes a mildly stigmatic term for 'supposedly dull craftwork nuts-and-bolts'.

3
Layout

The poems commanded themselves to shape up.

JOHN HOLLANDER, *Types of Shape*, p. xvi.

Layout is intimately bound to *punctuation* and *rhyme* through *lineation* (division into lines), a form of spatial punctuation determining both a principal issue of layout and the *display* of rhyme. Though treated here in separate chapters, all must be integrated once individually understood—yet though it is plainly crucial most people never consider layout as in its own right a feature of written texts. If, for example, you see three printed pages, from a novel, a telephone directory, and a volume of poetry, you need not be close enough to read words to identify each ; page-size and the pattern of black words and white space would tell you at a glance. And if you were fooled—if the novel were columnar, the telephone directory in continuous prose—both would be deeply irritating to read.

Readers (as you see) absorb and react to unexpected layouts, but expected ones are commoner : the headlines + column-format of newspapers ; *alinéa* (new item, new line) for lists and addresses ; itemisation of ingredients in a recipe, followed by instructions ; separate lines for the 'Dear . . .' and 'Yours . . .' that top and tail letters, and so on. Precisely because such formats are familiar, registered by your eyes before you begin to read words, they tend to be noticed automatically, not thought about consciously—and usually fair enough, their whole purpose being to make different kinds of texts equally easy to read by helping readers analyse their sequence of characters correctly, as spaces distinguish each word from the next. Onlywheninterwordspacesorhyphensaremissing, ort he layout incorrect, do you realise how vital they are. In poetry, however, automatic noticing won't do, for common things may be used in uncommon ways.

Layout is more than where words go and spaces are left. There are also whether words are capitalised in Lower-Case, in SMALL CAPS, or

ALL CAPS ; in roman, *italic*, **bold**, black letter,[1] or another distinguishing *face* or *fount* ; whether type-fount and -size are constant ; whether colour, underlining, or *diacritical marks* are used[2] ; whether left and right margins are *justified* (straight-line) or *ragged* ; how title and *epigraph*,[3] if any, are *set*, etc. Decisions about these things in relation to the *metal page* were almost always made by printers, not authors ; since Modernism, however, poets in particular have sought command, telling publishers what they want, and in *post-metal* publishing, normative online submission of texts or *camera-ready copy* has accelerated the process. The collective term for 'basic layout + all these features' is *mise-en-page* (French, 'putting-on-the-page'[4]) : a *text* in the abstract has no *mise-en-page*, but a book must have one, and most people still encounter most texts in books ; nor is computing a release, for to read is to encounter, if not *mise-en-page*, then *mise-en-écran* ('putting-on-screen'), texts on screen no less than paper having to be laid out one way rather than another. Multiple versions can, however, be simultaneously available online, and the ability to download or scan images, with the capacity of inkjet- and laser-printers to handle them, means critics no longer have any technical excuse for failing to confront the significances of *mise-en-page*, in poetry as elsewhere.

A first distinction is whether lines follow directly from one another, as always in blank verse and usually in couplets, or are grouped into stanzas ; a second is whether a line is flush with the left margin (*ekthesis*) or *indented* (*eisthesis*). In poems set as continuous lines, indenting only for verse-paragraphs, the most interesting question is whether (first words of) lines have *initial* capitals. The practice is conventional, but unless a particular word is usually capitalised the only reason to supply

---

[1] Now popular for band-names or places called *Ye Olde . . .*, black letter was standard in all printed books until *c.*1580, and is occasionally used in later poetry as a distinguishing fount : in the first edition of Byron's *Childe Harold's Pilgrimage*, for example, the title was in black letter, in keeping with the terminal -e of "Childe".

[2] Diacritical marks modify letters. Though limited in English the following may be encountered : acute (née) and grave (changèd) accents, modifying vowels or marking stresses ; the circumflex (entrepôt), indicating omitted s ; the diaeresis (naïf), preventing a diphthong, or umlaut (Führer), altering Germanic vowels ; the cedilla (soupçon), softening c ; the *tittle* (frō), indicating omitted n or m, or *macron* (statūs), lengthening vowels ; the *tilde* (Señor), indicating palatalised n ; and the breve (drŏll = 'drol', not 'drowle'), shortening vowels. Other European languages use the caron (č), over- (ė) and under-dot (ạ), over-ring (å), and ogonek (ę) ; classical Greek additionally uses the lenis (’) and asper (‘).

[3] An *epigraph* (from Greek ’επι [epi], 'upon' + *γράφειν* [graphein], 'write') is a short motto, often a quotation, placed between title and text.

[4] Cf. *mise-en-scène*, material production of a playscript—casting, costumes, props, etc.

one is to reinforce lineation : helpful when first encountering poetry, usually redundant thereafter. Printers used to mark the <u>end</u> of every line as well, usually with a comma, whether or not one was needed : editors always remove these as obscuring sense, but often keep initial caps ; poets increasingly use caps only for words usually commanding one, or that they wish to emphasise. In stanzaic poems it is equally optional-conventional to indicate rhyme-schemes eisthetically : up to quatrains it's easy to see rhyme, and so common to set ekthetically ; with more complex stanzas indentation really helps, as in Keats's 'Ode on a Grecian Urn' (N938 ; text from 1820) :

> Thou still unravish'd bride of quietness,
>   Thou foster-child of silence and slow time,
> Sylvan historian, who canst thus express
>   A flowery tale more sweetly than our rhyme :
> What leaf-fring'd legend haunts about thy shape
>   Of deities or mortals, or of both,
>   In Tempe or the dales of Arcady ?
>   What men or gods are these ? What maidens loth ?
> What mad pursuit ? What struggle to escape ?
>   What pipes and timbrels ? What wild ecstasy ?

The *abab-cde-dce* rhyme-scheme is exactly reflected in the eisthesis, *a*- and *c*-lines unindented, *b*- and *d*-lines indented by one unit, and *e*-lines by two. You might expect every new rhyme to be more deeply indented, but even short poems would soon shuffle to the other margin, so indentation is usually reset as soon as any substructure is complete, here between the cross-rhymed quatrain (ll. 1–4) and interlocked tercets (ll. 5–10).

Sonnets, particularly Shakespearian, are a special case. Perhaps because unlinked cross-rhymed quatrains are easy to see and hear, it is usual to print Shakespearian douzaines ekthetically and couplets indented (as in 1609 and N257–69), but the *b*-lines of Petrarchan octaves (*abbaabba*) often are indented, and variations (such as the Sicilian *abababab*) visible at a glance. More radically, blank-lines between component quatrains and tercets (as in 'September Song') *display* substructures but may mask form (cf. 'exploded' diagrams), and general care is needed, for poets can deliberately use eisthesis <u>against</u> rhyme. Alert readers will have noticed that the layout of Keat's 'Ode on Melancholy' in the 1820 edition of *Lamia, Isabella . . .* (p. 68) does not reflect the shifting tercet-form, though many editors silently emend it to display the third-stanza variation. More systematically, Wilbur's arch-rhymed quatrains in 'A Baroque Wall-Fountain in the Villa Sciarra' (N1635) are set thus :

> Under the bronze crown
> Too big for the head of the stone cherub whose feet
> A serpent has begun to eat,
> Sweet water brims a cockle and braids down

The tensions of layout and rhyme make each stanza more ornate than if layout supported rhyme, evoking baroque decoration : presumably Wilbur's point, stanzaic complexity echoing the fountain's. Eisthesis may also (as here) distinguish line-length rather than rhyme, or when heterometrics and rhyme patterns coincide (as in common metre) both.

Medial capitalisation is more complex. It is *deictic* punctuation (p. 106), as are italicisation, small caps, expanded spacing, and other means of local emphasis ; any of these may be combined (as in the biblical 'L O R D'), and practices differ culturally, historically, and generically. In German the Convention is still to capitalise all Nouns ; in Britain the liberal use of caps dried up with the Enlightenment, and has never been restored despite Serious Romantic Efforts, though italic emphasis survives ; and dramatic verse is a special case, not least because in Shakespeare's First Folio and some other Jacobethan play-texts medial capitals suggest (and perhaps record) emphasis in delivery. Shakespearian editors, declaring Folio practice non-authorial and grammatically inconsistent, almost always reduce it to the conventional modern paucity of proper names and words after full-stops—but speak the Folio text of Mark Antony's "Friends, Romans, Countrymen" (🖱) and the coherent value for actors of its discriminating and viciously ironic capitalisation is plain.

Moreover, in EVERY CASE (and *face*, as word-processors make newly apparent in their facility to add caps or toggle faces on and off) deictic punctuation is an overlay, a textual hypersystem, and with intrinsic doubleness (word, FACE) necessarily in play no emphasis can blindly be guaranteed free of interesting criticism (live up to the italics you *nominally* deserve) or instructive irony (oh I'll respect you, my *Lord*, to the italic letter). Even wholly conventional emphasis of titles and names can in its ubiquity become a window on a more authoritarian, scrupulous, and consistent world than our own (as drama-students familiar with status-games will appreciate). Ralph Crane, a scribe who prepared several Folio texts, offers one interesting lesson : his *hand* is identified partly by his observance of a particular Jacobethan convention editors always remove, the parenthesisation of *vocatives*, spoken 'calls' of address like "(Sir)", "(Good Gentleman)", and "(*Paulina*)"—all from *The Winter's Tale*,[5] which excited Crane to 369 parentheses, far more than in any other F-text. Pedantic as he may seem, Crane rightly points readers first to the peremptory commands of (and frightened deference to) Leontes in tyrant-mode, then to the personal apologies he must tender ; the many vocatives are a distinctive feature that should be noted by readers, as (necessarily) by actors, about both of whom Crane thought more helpfully than editors allow. Marvell, equally, rarely retains the interlocking caps and italics of *Miscellaneous Poems* (1681), but why it should be thought helpful to remove either is beyond me ; consider two stanzas from 'The Definition of Love' (N480) explaining why his love is impossible :

VI.

Unleſs the giddy Heaven fall,
And Earth some new Convulſion tear ;
And, us to joyn, the World should all
Be cramp'd into a *Planiſphere.*

VII.

As Lines ſo Loves *oblique* may well
Themſelves in every Angle greet :
But ours ſo truly *Paralel,*
Though infinite can never meet.

One need not with this text be a mathematician to see that the italicised words are critical to the thought. Consulting the *OED* (or annotated editions), one discovers from Blundevil's *Exercises* (1594) that the "Aſtrolabe [. . .] is called of ſome a Planiſpheare, becauſe it is both flat and round, repreſenting the Globe or Spheare, having both his Poles clapt flat together" : the claim is that these lovers can meet only if the north pole kisses the south, as it may (short of apocalypse) only on paper. Stuck with a stubborn globe, Marvell suggests a comparison between meridians of longitude, which "*oblique* may well [/] Themſelves in every Angle greet" at each pole (✳), and the *Parallels* of latitude, "infinite" in their circularities that "can never meet" (⊙). There is an arcane philosophical payoff under Plato's 'Third Man Rule',[6] in that intrinsically latitudinous lovers can never (if Platonically

[5] F1, 'Comedies', 299 ; the italics of "(*Paulina*)" mark a proper name.
[6] Summarily, that universals may not be self-instantiating.

true to themselves) claim the latitude needed for them to meet, but the "*Planiſphere* [. . .] *Paralel*" is italicised for all to see. The roman caps matter less, but their patterning of Heaven-Earth-World and Lines-Loves-Angle is helpful, as all (and 'Convulſion') are for readers-aloud as cues to consider emphasis (or sustenance of tone etc.). Verse first published after 1800 (unless light, regional, or self-consciously *déclassé*) is relatively unlikely ever to have had much deictic punctuation of this kind, but if Shakespeare and Marvell can suffer so badly from editorial slash-and-burn approaches to *mise-en-page*, there are compelling reasons to read early texts (especially with the Web to facilitate access).

Stanza-numbering is a particular issue. In the *Miscellaneous Poems* it is applied to every non-dialogic stanzaic poem, whether in quatrains, sestets, or octets, more as an element of fine display on large pages than a reference system ; it is often retained for 'Upon Appleton House' because of that poem's length, but elsewhere discarded with other deictic punctuation. The matter seems simple, but has lately been very interestingly complicated by Jorie Graham in a group of six 'Self-Portraits' in *The End of Beauty*, in which irregular groups of lines (many single verses, some as long as sonnets) appear beneath Arabic numerals.[7] Helen Vendler has suggested Graham is not numbering lines (which Vendler thinks may be interrupted by a centred numeral on a line of its own), or even irregular stanzas, but has instead created a "long numbered pause" as part of a "sequestering of the pause".[8] The implications for punctuation and especially lineation are considerable (pp. 102, 174), and to read earlier work with the notion of numbered pauses rather than numbered stanzas in mind refreshes a convention that too often goes unheeded.

Another surprisingly consequential issue is whether lines are single-, double-, or more widely spaced, and how many lines are left blank between stanzas. The amount of a page left white is called the *leading*, because in metal type spaces between lines and stanzas are created by bars of lead.[9] Particularly between the early-eighteenth and mid-nineteenth centuries (say, first editions, Gay to Browning) there was an age of great printing in England : some masterpieces—the joke-pages in Sterne's *Tristram Shandy*, the engraved poems of Blake—are acknow-

---

[7] 'Self-Portrait as the Gesture between Them', '. . . as Both Parties', '. . . as Apollo and Daphne', '. . . as Hurry and Delay', '. . . as Demeter and Persephone', and 'Pollock and Canvas', in *The End of Beauty* (New York: Ecco Press, 1987).

[8] Vendler, *Breaking of Style*, 82, 84.

[9] Larger spaces are usually created with wooden blocks, for which the collective term is 'type-furniture'. Computers have made the technique of leading obsolete, but the word is still used.

ledged, though accurate reproductions of their *mises-en-page* are rare. In an age of great printing ordinary books may also be printed very intelligently, and a characteristic feature of most *Augustan* to *Victorian* first-edition poetry is heavy leading, lines double (or wider) spaced, pages elegantly clear to read ; in cheaply bound modern paperbacks with as much text as possible on each page to keep production-costs down, such *mises-en-page* are distant memories. Better inelegant books than no text, and the cheaper the better—but this cheapness costs. Byron's *Don Juan*, for example, was first printed with two stanzas per page ; Penguin print four, the *Norton* (though it includes only a fraction of the poem) four to five, regularly splitting stanzas between pages (N837–62). In looking up a line or two it makes no odds ; if you read nearly 2,000 stanzas cumulative difference is considerable. Reading *Don Juan* in the six-volume first edition (smelling calfskin, feeling each thick page, every stanza spaciously pl/easing the eyes) discovers a more leisurely, considered poem than reading the commercially cramped Penguin text, where constricted economy makes it seem rattlingly comic, less capable of moving seriously[10] : it's cheaper, so more people can afford it, but readers pay a price. Nor is *Don Juan*, however substantial, an extreme case : modern protocols of editing have until very recently ruthlessly deprivileged *mise-en-page*, even when authorial, and rarely acknowledge its loss ; the more fool they, the 'mere layout' they think to discard being only a beginning of what poets do with *mise-en-page* and materialities of text.

In free verse without patterns of rhyme or line-length to display, layout is promoted to carry meaning and nuance it may subjectively express but cannot always communicate. Glancing through the post-1900 pages of the *Norton* one finds many such experiments, including those of Olson, Levertov, and Ammons (N1511, 1677, 1695). Such idiosyncracy puts many (less experienced) readers off, though comic instances may become beloved : cummings's 'r-p-o-p-h-e-s-s-a-g-r', where 'grasshopper' hops about as "PPEGORHRASS" and "gRrEaPsPhOs" until achieving its proper order, or Enright's 'The Typewriter Revolution', imitating a typewritten (not printed) document. Generalisation is unhelpful, a poet's particular strategy demanding particular attention ; all, however, owe Eliot's *The Waste Land* (and Pound's *Cantos*) for

[10] In the same way reading the Bible in an old lectern-bible in church and a modern pocket-paperback are not the same experience : for one you need a table or lectern, will handle pages differently, see headings printed in red, etc. ; to damage such a book would take effort, but small paperbacks may be casually used and maltreated.

legitimising non-standard layout as a central strategy of Modernism, and sections of parts II ("My nerves are bad tonight", N1347) and III ("The river sweats [/] Oil and tar", N1351), where Eliot aggressively displays one-sided conversation and dirges, are as good a guide to what follows as anything. The evolving layout can be seen in the facsimile *drafts* and *typescripts* (TSS) of *The Waste Land*, Eliot's continuing uses of it in 'Coriolan', 'Choruses from "The Rock" ', and 'The Hollow Men' (N1356).[11]

Although the case has never been substantively made for poetry, as it almost has for prose,[12] the impact and idiosyncrasies of typewriters are worth pondering generally. They were certainly agents of Modernism : for Eliot, as for many, production of a typed text was an important stage, and his expression of layout had to use the keys available on a manual typewriter with ratcheted (hence quantised) spacing. cummings is clearly a typewriter-poet, and W. C. Williams's progressively indenting tercet (p. 42), another influential Modernist layout, is also indebted, I suspect, to preset mechanical tabs or a round number of spaces, easy to iterate. The constraints of typewritten and printed pages are different, but close enough that typewriterly features pass readily into print, acquiring authority, influence, and disguise as they go—the running joke of Don Marquis's 'archy' poems, typed by a "vers libre bard" reincarnated as a cockroach and so unable to work the shift-key. In amateur verse (and widely in prose) the TS is tied also to carbon-paper and various kinds of stencil-duplication, and there are similar links in the 1960s–1980s between golfball-, daisywheel, or dot-matrix printing and the photocopier ; at a professional level, for poets like lain Sinclair (in *Lud Heat*, 1975, and *Suicide Bridge*, 1979) and Peter Reading (in *Ukelele Music*, 1985, the ironic *Stet*, 1986, and *Perduta Gente*, 1989) the available/affordable distinguishing faces (caps, bold, italic) became a constant 'typoetic' grammar. Word-processing has broadened the picture enormously, but is no simple liberation : in standard w.p. packages spacing remains quantised, fine printing of poetry (as for *broadsheet* poster-editions) is still often metal-set (or silkscreened), and poets who enthusiastically deploy

---

[11] cummings, *Complete Poems 1913–1962* (New York: Harcourt Brace Jovanovich, 1972) ; Enright, *Collected Poems, 1948–98* (Oxford: OUP, 1998) ; Eliot, *The Waste Land: A Facsimile and Transcript of the Original Drafts, Including the Annotations of Ezra Pound* (London: Faber, 1971) and *Complete Poems and Plays* (London: Faber, 1969) ; see also Leunard, *But I Digress*, plate 8, pp. 200–1.

[12] See Leon Edel, 'A Fierce Legibility', in *The Life of Henry James* (2 vols, Harmondsworth: Penguin, 1977), and Wilfred A. Beeching, *Century of the Typewriter* (1974; Bournemouth: British Typewriter Museum Publishing, 1990).

multi-variant *mise-en-page* may find publishers less keen. Michael Horovitz's 'A Postcard from Ireland (sound-poem score for contraction or extension with improvised or illegible noises)' (1966) was unpublished for twenty-three years and uncollected for twenty-eight, while Brathwaite more or less had to publish *Barabajan Poems 1492–1992* himself.[13] One consequence of the Web, however, is to make available founts once restricted to fine metal pages, and type-designers like Herman Zapf and Sumner Stone have already produced screen-founts to ponder.[14]

Looking back, the typewriterly (post-)Modernist line descending particularly from Eliot is revealed as only a spur from a broader and much older tradition. Even layouts that seem to us self-evident are culturally acquired and transmitted, and to confront MSS and older editions is an education in the variety of what poets, scribes, and printers can do. At the same time certain possibilities are clear : columnar formats, for example, when not simply an economic response to short lines (as with Bishop's 'Jerónimo's House'), have always been able to ask questions about order of reading, as they do in Pollard's 'Harriman Revisited'. An anonymous poem of *c.*1600 begins :

I hold as faythe	What Englands Church allowes
What Romes church saith	My conscience disavowes

Here the use (if not purpose) of equivocal readings in line (⇉) and in column (↓↓) is politically plain, but the possibility is always there with columns, and in medieval MSS there are many such oddities ; 'Hir face, Hir tong, Hir wit', published anonymously in *The Phoenix Nest* (1593) and attributed to Ralegh, has three columns and makes clever sense in all of them. Such poems are not so different in their spacious pleasures from, say, Figueroa's 'Spring has Come', in which six dimetric octets with rotating burdens are printed in two rows of two above and below two in centred single column (2/1/1/2)—a cheerful

13 Marquis, published in newspapers 1916–*c.*1939, and collected as *archy and mehitabel* (1927), *archy's life of mehitabel* (1934), *The Complete archy and mehitabel* (London: Faber, 1998), *archyology* and *archyology II* (Newcastle: Bloodaxe, 1996, 2000) ; Sinclair, now published jointly (London: Vintage, 1995) ; Reading, all in *Collected Poems 2: Poems 1985–1996* (Newcastle: Bloodaxe, 1996) ; 'Stet' (Latin, 'let it stand') is an instruction by a corrector to ignore his or her correction ; Horovitz, *Wordsounds and Sightlines: New and Selected Poems* (London: Sinclair-Stevenson, 1994) ; Brathwaite, Kingston and New York : Savacou North, 1994.

14 Sebastian Carter, *Twentieth Century Type Designers* (1987; new edn, New York: Norton, 1995).

embodiment of cyclicality and interchange that looks like a fat capital 'I'.[15]

Looks like, yes, but is meant to resemble ? In Figueroa's case I doubt it, but in *shape-poetry*, pictorial and verbal representation fuse. The Greeks called shape-poems *technopaignia*, 'games of artifice', the Romans *carmina figurata*, 'figure-poems', crude modernity *concrete poems* ; whichever you prefer they demand attention. Please find the *Norton* and consider for a moment both its texts of the most famous English example, Herbert's 'Eaſter Wings' (N368–9); then turn to the illustrations over*leaf*, which show the poem as it appears in the Jones *manuscript* (MS),[16] and in the first edition of *The Temple. Sacred Poems and Private Ejaculations* (Cambridge: Buck and Daniel, 1633), 34–5.

The corrections to the Jones MS are probably authorial, but the primary hand isn't, so the 'choice' of horizontal layout need not be Herbert's ; moreover, in the licensing-copy for *The Temple* (Bodleian Library MS Tanner 307) both (parts of the) poem/s are also laid out horizontally. But the striking vertical layout in 1633 remains, not something any printer (let alone the official printers to Cambridge University) would do casually, and in metal time-consuming to achieve ; so much so that in the first six Cambridge editions of *The Temple* (1633a, 1633b, 1634, 1635, 1638, 1641), each (as usual) otherwise wholly reset in type, the texts of 'Eaſter Wings' are identical, printed from blocks of type created in 1633, permanently fixed together, and stored in Buck's and Daniel's print-shop for at least eight years—to my knowledge the only such retention of set type over an extended period that can be demonstrated.[17] Vertical *setting* was retained (with increasing variation) into the nineteenth century, but as 'professional' editing took hold was abandoned for horizontal setting with all 20 lines of the 1633 *opening* (two *facing* pages, *recto* and *verso*) under one title ; as late as its 3rd edition (1983), the *Norton* printed 'Eaſter Wings' thus, but from the 4th (1996) printed horizontal and vertical versions—a better solution, but still an editorial shrug of the shoulders.

[15] Bishop, *Complete Poems* ; Pollard, *Shame trees don't grow here . . . but poincianas bloom* (Leeds: Peepal Tree, 1992) ; Anon., Folger Shakespeare Library, Washington, DC, MS V.a.198, fol. 14r (for a full text see Lennard, *But I Digress*, 266–7, or 🖰) ; Ralegh, *Poems* (London: RKP, 1951 [Muses' Library]) ; Figueroa, *The Chase: a collection of poems 1941–1989* (Leeds: Peepal Tree, 1992).

[16] MS Jones B 62, Dr Williams's Library, Gordon Square, London ; with whose permission it is reproduced.

[17] My source for all 'Eaſter Wings' material is Random Cloud, 'FIAT ƒLUX', in R. M. Leod, ed., *Crisis in Editing: Texts of the English Renaissance* (New York: AMS Press, Inc., 1994), 61–172, which includes a stunning rogues' gallery of 18 editions spanning 1838–1978.

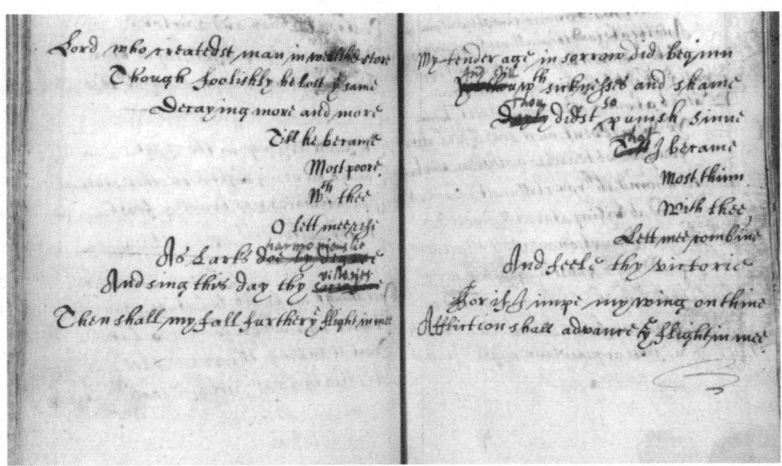

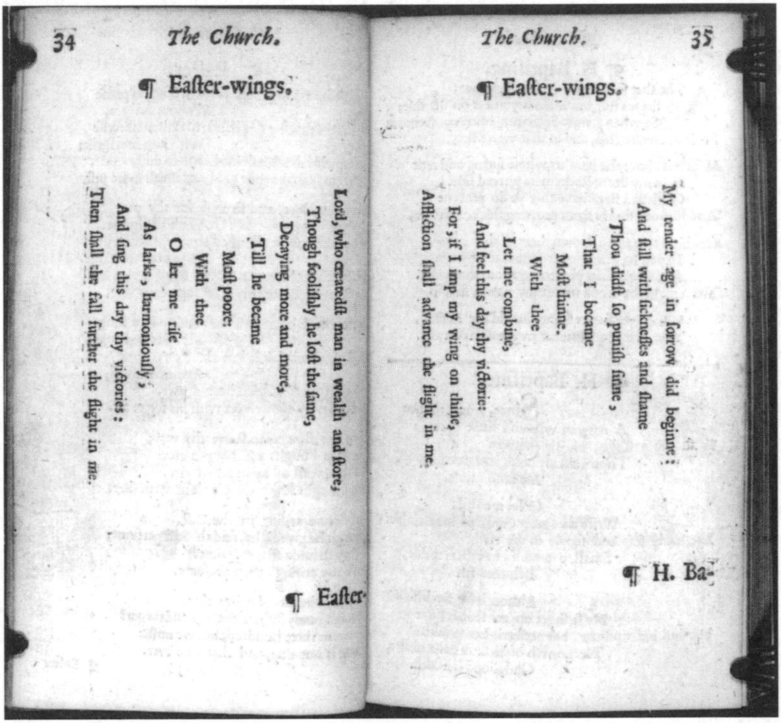

Lord who createdst man in wealth and store
Though foolishly he lost the same
Decaying more and more
Till he became
Most poore
Wth thee
O lett me rise
As Larks harmoniously
And sing this day thy victories
Then shall my fall further the flight in mee

My tender age in sorrow did beginn
And still wth sicknesses and shame
Thou didst so punish sinne
That I became
Most thinn
With thee
Lett mee combine
And feele thy victorie
For if I imp my wing on thine
Affliction shall advance the flight in mee

34 *The Church.*

¶ Easter-wings.

Lord, who createdst man in wealth and store,
Though foolishly he lost the same,
Decaying more and more,
Till he became
Most poore:
With thee
O let me rise
As larks, harmoniously,
And sing this day thy victories:
Then shall the fall further the flight in me.

¶ Easter-

The Church. 35

¶ Easter-wings.

My tender age in sorrow did beginne:
And still with sicknesses and shame
Thou didst so punish sinne,
That I became
Most thinne.
With thee
Let me combine,
And feel this day thy victorie:
For, if I imp my wing on thine,
Affliction shall advance the flight in me.

¶ H. Ba-

Manuscript of George Herbert's 'Easter Wings' (MS. Jones B 62).
Reproduced by kind permission of the Trustees of Dr Williams's Library.

The exact *authority* (author-ity) of 1633 is uncertain : the deathbed *autograph* MS on which it is supposedly based is lost, and the relative authority of the Tanner and Jones MSS insusceptible of proof. At the same time, there was no need to set vertically (measure the lines and page-width), and that the 1633 setting happened without the direction or agreement of Nicholas Ferrar (who supposedly received the deathbed MS and certainly arranged the publication of 1633) is incredible. It might be a private notion of Ferrar's, but it was he to whom Herbert sent his unpublished poems, and editors are in general happy enough with 1633 as *copy-text*. However understandably, they balk only with 'Easter Wings', where layout matters most, and it won't do.

Both MSS and 1633 insist there are two poems called 'Eaſter Wings' ; 1633 marks both titles with the *paraph* or *pilcrow* (¶) whereby it distinguishes elements among its contents, and the *catchword* on p. 34 (isolated lower-right but in my photograph partly lost in the *gutter*), helpfully informing readers(-aloud) of what begins the next page, is "Eaſter". Implicitly, the reading-procedure in 1633 is to see both shapes before you read any words, and between the pages/wings the spine of the book ; then, beginning p. 34, to read the (first) title, rotate the book 90° left, read the vertical lines on that page, rotate 90° right, read the catchword on p. 34 and then the (second) title on p. 35, rotate 90° left, read the second set of vertical lines, rotate 90° right, and via the catchword on p. 35 proceed to the next poem, 'H[oly]. Ba-[ptiſme]', on p. 36. Were 'Eaſter Wings' a single 20-line poem it would in 1633 presumably begin at the 'top' (i.e. right margin) of p. 35 and proceed to the 'bottom' (left margin) of p. 34, with the invocatory "Lord . . ." in its eleventh (not first) line—a delightfully il/logical procedure which 1633 invites, as having once rotated the (small) book 90° left it is very hard (try it!) to imagine anyone not clocking the possibility.

Intentionally or otherwise, 1633 as prime authority, however posthumous, creates uncertainty about how many poems there are, problematises reading ll. 1–20 or 1–10 + 1–10, and provokes a host of shapely questions. The *Norton*, alas, mostly confuses, despite trying to better itself by adding a cropped, gutterless photoquotation of pp. 34–5 of 1633 to its 'normal' text, which is derived from Hutchinson's 1941 Clarendon edition and reproduces the different, more symmetrical x-shape/s Hutchinson gave the poem/s.[18] Herbert borrowed his wing-shape from 'Pterygion' (attributed to Simmias of Rhodes, fl. *c.* 275 BCE), printed vertically in at least one edition of *The Greek Anthology* to which

[18] *The Works of George Herbert* (Oxford: Clarendon Press, 1941).

he had access[19] ; inadvertently, Hutchinson's (and the *Norton*'s) horizontal setting imposes a different shape also used by Simmias, a double-axe-head Herbert also saw and did <u>not</u> borrow. Worse still, the *Norton*'s footnote—"we reproduce the poem almost as it was first published. The stanzas were printed on two pages and arranged to suggest two birds flying upward, wings outspread"—is so misleading and presumptuous one is grateful it doesn't venture to identify an avian species.

What Herbert (or possibly Farrar) was doing was to take his own metaphors visually and literally. A deeply religious man, the dedicatee of Bacon's *Translations of Certain Psalmes* in 1625 and ordained in 1630, Herbert's poems are prayers, offered in *The Temple* ; his book is its own material metaphor for a building dedicated to worship, specifically the beautiful church at Little Gidding (🖱). Entering The *Temple* the reader passes through 'The Church-porch' (comprising 'Perirrhanterium', for sprinkling holy-water before entering, and 'Superliminare', the lintel over the church-door), into 'The Church' (a *running-head* is visible on both pages of the Jones MS and of 1633). In 'The Church' readers see first (looking straight up the aisle, a poem shaped as) 'The Altar' (N367), and about 160 more poetic devotions, including groups dedicated to material structures ('Church-monuments', 'Church-lock and key', 'The Church-floore', 'The Windows' [N373]), the liturgical round ('Good Friday', 'Eaſter', 'Whitſunday', 'Trinity Sunday', 'Chriſtmas', 'Lent'), and particular concepts ('Nature', 'Sinne', 'Affliction', 'Repentance', 'Faith', 'Prayer' [N369–72]). And a little way in is (a/poem/s shaped as) 'Eaſter-wings' (for my money attached, if anywhere, to an intercessant angel sharing *The Temple*'s spine) to carry heavenwards prayers of and for that resurrection of the "Most thinne", "Most poore" body that devout Christians expect. Far from a dangerous oddity to be removed, the extraordinary 1633 layout of what I shall (with Gollum) now call 'Eaſter Wingſes' is an integral part of Herbert's sacred work.

The pictures made by shape-poems are schematic, lacking visual perspective, and subordinate to their constituent words $\left(\frac{\text{WORDS}}{\text{picture}}\right)$; in the early-seventeenth century, when Herbert was writing, a parallel form, the *emblem*, balanced drawing and writing more evenly $\left(\frac{\text{PICTURE}}{\text{WORDS}}\right)$.[20] Emblems explicitly matched an illustration, usually a woodcut, with a poem on the same subject, often moral or political ; collections in

---

[19] *Heroici Poetae Graeci* (Geneva: Fugger, 1556), then in the library of Trinity College, Cambridge, where Herbert was a fellow.

[20] The whole Renaissance was characterised by intense interest in the visual, including major areas of culture (handwriting, printing, political imagery) and minor but intriguing oddities (pictures in false or mirror perspective, decorated page-borders).

emblem books were popular but fell out of use after the Civil War.[21] At the other extreme, where a motto is subordinate to a picture, often symbolic, ($\frac{\text{PICTURE}}{\text{words}}$), are coats-of-arms, sentimentally moral Victorian pictures with pointed titles ('Too Late!'), and forms like posters, printed advertisements, and charity T-shirts. When Picasso and Braque began to paint or collage words into paintings many thought it a radical feature of Cubist technique, but both were working in an old tradition.

There has recently been intensive development of the graphic novel : another story, but an exception must be made. Some poems attract illustrators ; there are in particular editions of *The Rime of the Ancient Mariner*, from David Scott's (1837) to those by Doré (1876), Peake (1949, 1978), and Garrick Palmer (1994), with interesting lessons to offer : where Doré chose to create 42 plates, Peake settled for 8, while the Folio Society edition of Palmer fascinatingly uses light-blue paper, starkening Palmer's woodcuts and inducing a perceptible chill. Hunt Emerson (1989) outdid them all, distributing Coleridge's text into captions and speech-bubbles in a full-length graphic poem-as-novel. His decisions about freehand layout are often *de facto* very impressive critical analysis, as are Martin Rowson's in his graphic *The Waste Land* (1989), and to a lesser extent Art Spiegelman's in his illustrated edition (1994) of March's *The Wild Party* (1926), and Michael C. Caine's in his broadsheet of Harrison's 'The Fire Gap'. The brilliance of these editions is the work of the artists, but they open a new chapter in the history of poetic *mise-en-page*.[22]

In one respect they are unhappily typical, taken by those who haven't read them as comic/s and therefore lightweight. Emerson is funny, and in mocking any claims the *Rime* has to tragedy genuinely comedic, but levity and gravity may coexist ; the real point, underpinned by editorial treatment of Herbert, is that in Anglophone letters the graphic is typically associated with juvenile simplicity, and shape-poetry (or anything resembling it) thought an unimportant-because-amusing game—a situation not helped by the best-known examples after Herbert, Carroll's 'Fury Said to a Mouse' and mirror-stanza, written for children. But 'Easter Wingses' are as serious as Herbert's hopes for his immortal soul, and committed shape-poets, like Riddell,

[21] The best known was *Emblems* (1635), by Francis Quarles (1592–1644).

[22] Scott, Edinburgh: Hill, 1837 ; Doré, London: Doré Gallery, 1876 ; Peake, London: Chatto and Windus, 1949, 1978 ; Palmer, London: Folio Society, 1994. Peake 1949 omitted a plate (Life-in-Death) restored in 1978. See Woof and Hebron, *The Rime of the Ancient Mariner: The Poem and its Illustrators* (Dove Cottage: Wordsworth Trust, 1997). Emerson, London: Knockabout Comics, 1989 ; Rowson, New York: Harper and Row, 1990 ; Spiegelman, New York: Pantheon, 1994 ; Caine, Newcastle: Bloodaxe, 1985.

Swenson, the great John Hollander (N1775), and Manuel Portela (also the Portuguese translator of Blake and Sterne) are more like Herbert than Carroll. Even occasional shape-poems, like Senior's dedicatory gourd-shaped 'Gourd', readily rattle with significance ('calabash', the usual Jamaican term for bottle-gourd trees, is the press that first published Senior and an arts festival). Even those who simply use *mise-en-page* intensely tend to be serious, as Eliot was.[23] cummings, rightly celebrated as a lyric poet, was also tragic and satiric, and deployed typography in all three modes, as his *Complete Poems* shows. Snodgrass, in *The Fuehrer Bunker*, used layout to distinguish monologists : Himmler, obsessed with occult codes, writes grid-poems of 25, 50, or 75 lines, each 30 characters long, arranged in pentains, the initial letters of lines running *abecedarially* (A–Z) once, twice, or thrice per poem ; Speer, trained in architecture, writes stanzas with each line longer or shorter than the last, forming with every 11 lines right-angled triangles that combine in trapezoid shapes and individually embody diminutions into silence and cascadings into speech profoundly typical of Speer (the only senior Nazi to plead guilty at Nuremberg who yet always denied any prior knowledge of his part in the *Sho'ah*—and a man Snodgrass had met).[24] And there is always the simple, demanding occasion, as for Christopher Logue when Homer's Patroclus was mightily berserking outside Troy but :

> Coming behind you through the dust you felt
> —What was it?—felt creation part, and then
>
> [----------------page-turn 29/30]
>
> # APOLLO!
>
> Who had been patient with you
>
> [----------------page-turn 31/32]
>
> Struck.

---

[23] Riddell, *Eclipse: Concrete Poems* (London: Calder and Boyars, 1972) ; Swenson, *Iconographs* (New York: Scribners, 1970) and *The Complete Poems to Solve* (New York: Macmillan, 1993) ; Hollander, *Types of Shape* ; Portela self-published *Cras! Bang! Boom! Clang!* (1991), *Pixel, Pixel* (1992), and *Rimas Fodidas e Outros Textos Escolares* (1994) ; his *Cantigas de Inocencia and da Experiencia* (Lisbon: Antigona, 1994), *Uma Ilha na Lua* (Antigona, 1996), and *A Vida e Opinioes de Tristram Shandy* (Antigona, 1997–8) are 'graphic translations' ; Senior, *Gardening in the Tropics* (Newcastle: Bloodaxe, 1995), p.vii.

[24] See Gitta Sereny, *Albert Speer: His Battle with Truth* (London: Macmillan, 1995), or Edgar's dramatisation, *Albert Speer* (London: Nick Hern Books, 2000).

His Hand came from the east,
And in his wrist lay all eternity;
And every atom of his mythic weight
Was poised between his fist and bent left leg.
Your eyes lurched out. Achilles' helmet rang[25]

—as well they might when the Mouse God comes calling in such wise. To embody a fatally overwhelming divine presence in letters so big that six + *screamer* (!) fill an entire opening is a simple trick, as booming the name is if reading this episode aloud—but both work just fine. Shape-poetry is a sort of game, and fun—but not necessarily funny, and you can never be sure a layout is inertly standard, even if it looks it, until you check for yourself.[26]

Finally, two distinct suggestions. The most enjoyable and best way to learn the ins and outs of line-layout is in practice. Word-processors allow experiment with different founts and leading ; better still, do some hand-press printing, learning to *compose* (set letters and interword spaces) and *impose* (put pages of type on the press) with cold-metal type. Various institutions offer courses in(cluding) hand-presswork, and the opportunity is worth seizing. When you are responsible for every letter and space, and overall balance, the importance of layout becomes clearer than reading can ever make it. Theory also helps : the editorial follies I upbraid arise from a particular theory of text distinguishing substantives ('intentional' words) from accidentals (unavoidable but irrelevant *mise-en-page*), promulgated by Sir Walter Greg in dealing with Shakespearian quartos but as Platonically unworkable as essentialist genre-theory (p. 65). A much more sensible theorisation by Jerome McGann distinguishes *lexical codes* ('text') from *bibliographical codes* (*mise-en-page* + all material issues of paper, binding, etc.), and his *Critique of Modern Textual Bibliography* (1983) is seriously worth understanding.

---

[25] *War Music* (1981 ; London: Faber, 1988), 29–32 ; page-numbers 30 + 31 are omitted.

[26] Shaped layouts also occur in prose, extraordinarily so in Alasdair Gray's *1982 Janine* (Harmondsworth: Penguin, 1985), 177–90. The text develops over several pages multiple columns which widen, narrow, and collide, representing the fracturing mind of a man attempting suicide by overdose ; blank pages represent sleep. Gray designs himself, and *Poor Things* (Harmondsworth: Penguin, 1993) is (among much else) a compendium of layouts.

Exemplary Poems

1. Emily Dickinson, 'I heard a Fly buzz—when I died—' (*c.*1863), published in *Poems* (1896) ; text and textual annotation from R. W. Franklin, ed., *The Poems of Emily Dickinson* (3 vols, Cambridge, MA, and London: Belknap Press, 1998), ii. 587 (N1121).

I heard a Fly buzz—when I died—
The Stillness in the Room
Was like the Stillness in the Air—
Between the Heaves of Storm—

The Eyes around—had wrung them dry—
And Breaths were gathering firm
For that last Onset—when the King
Be witnessed—in the Room—

I willed my Keepsakes—Signed away
What portion of me be
Assignable—and then it was
There interposed a Fly—

With Blue—uncertain—stumbling Buzz—
Between the light—and me—
And then the Windows failed—and then
I could not see to see—

Division [l.] 1 when | [l.] 5 them |

A *mise-en-page* is of a particular printed version, but common metre is common, and there would be no reason to remark Franklin's *mise-en-page* were it not (as his *textual annotation* suggests) for Dickinson's MS practices. Her poems progressed from *foul papers* (worksheets with revisions) to *fair copies*, bound into notebooks known as 'fascicles', or gathered in loose 'sets' ; (variant) fair copies might at any stage be sent as letters, and some poems were revised after fair-copying, generating a second foul-paper-to-fair-copy sequence. This is orderly, and in general (though never intending to publish) Dickinson maintained her archive rigorously, destroying drafts once a fair copy had been made ; however,

> Constraints such as the edges of the paper, the presence of a boss, stains or imperfections, or the overlaps of envelope construction would redirect [Dickinson's] pencil or pen. The shapes of her materials—odds and ends of wrapping paper, advertising flyers, notebook leaves, discarded stationery—gave physical contour to her poems as they went on to paper. A draft of "The mushroom is the elf of

> plants" [. . .] was recorded on the inside of a yellow envelope, set on point with the horizontal measure increasing then diminishing. The poem began at the peak, with only the first word laid down before line breaks began. Altogether, four were required for the first line ["The [/] mushroom [/] is the Elf [/] of plants—"]. The measure expanded until no additional ones were needed, then contracted until three were required by the last line ["And fleeter [/] than a [/] Tare—"]. There are many examples in which two or more copies of the same poem appear on papers of different shapes, yielding different line breaks [. . .] These were working drafts, but the same effect occurs on more formal copies, such as those sent to others and [. . .] in the fascicles. The former was typically on notepaper, the latter on stationery of larger size, yielding different configurations. Once line breaks began, it is not easy to find a manuscript of any poem in Dickinson's hand that exactly matches the physical lineation of the same poem in other copies.
>
> (Franklin, i. 34–5)

Waste not, want not : paper is (and was) expensive, and neither lines nor quatrains are in doubt. Franklin simply displays them, recording the "physical lineation" he eliminates : here there are two, in ll. 1 and 5, and as there is only one MS of 'I heard a Fly buzz' readers know that in Dickinson's autograph ll. 1–8 (or 10) were laid out thus :

> I heard a Fly buzz—when
> I died—
> The Stillness in the Room
> Was like the Stillness in the Air—
> Between the Heaves of Storm—
> The Eyes around—had wrung them
> dry—
> And Breaths were gathering firm
> For that last Onset—when the King
> Be witnessed—in the Room—

And there is the problem, because that is exactly how the MS appears, the *turn-downs*, displaced portions of metrical lines, having 'physical lines' to themselves : as readers can see in the facsimile *Manuscript Books of Emily Dickinson* published under Franklin's supervision in 1981.[27] They can also see that both turn-downs could without undue cramping have been avoided, and that in the penultimate line, almost at the

[27] 2 vols, Cambridge, MA and London: Belknap Press, 1981, i. 591.

bottom of the page, "then" is cramped because a turn-down would displace the last line overleaf. Even in a rough draft like the one Franklin cites of "The mushroom is the elf of plants", ll. 3–5, at the widest portion of the paper, follow the same curious pattern, so that in the very middle "Hat" is followed by space extending across the whole diagonal : "At morning—in a Truffled [/] Hat [/] It stops upon a spot [//] As if it tarried always"; the stanza-break, fractionally wider than line-spacing, also occupies central space. Dickinson could neatly have written out all eight lines simply by using the envelope as a square rather than a diamond—but she didn't, any more than she usually adjusted the size of her hand to the available paper. Franklin, in a lovely phrase, invokes her "regard for boundaries" (i. 11) : those of words, lines, quatrains, and paper are constantly regarded and clashed—as different syntactical possibilities are encouraged to clamber about within and between quatrains, treating all those dashes (every one a boundary to regard) as handy monkey-bars.

This is not universal print-practice—turn-downs are normally right-justified and don't count as lines themselves—but whether to eliminate Dickinson's "physical" line-breaks is unexpectedly difficult. In the first properly edited *Collected Poems*, Johnson's in 1955,[28] they went, and regular quatrains with blank lines between were imposed on most poems in which such structures are audibly present. Franklin is more cautious, correcting errors in transcription (he added the dash after "uncertain" in l. 13), but also standardises lineation. Both editors thus eliminate an unorthodox practice that Dickinson was at some pains to maintain (and none to suppress) throughout her life. They disregard another of her boundaries, in that with 1,700+ short poems to include, none gets a page to itself as it might in its fascicle (and 'I heard a Fly buzz', cramping its penultimate line, does). Moreover, in Johnson the march of quatrains over so many pages made Dickinson seem to march herself, despite her dashes ; a falsely induced sense of unflinching regularity that makes the fascicles a shock. Franklin's print edition, re-endorsing metrical regularity and display, partly pacifies a furore his photographic edition ignited, but the "physical" line-breaks can be reconstructed from his edition, and sometimes should be[29] : it was, during and after all, Dickinson who pointingly put them there.

[28] *The Complete Poems of Emily Dickinson* (3 vols, Cambridge, MA and London: Belknap Press, 1955).

[29] See Martha Nell Smith, 'Dickinson's Manuscripts' and Sharon Cameron, 'Dickinson's Fascicles' in Gudrun Grabher, Roland Hagenbüchle, and Cristianne Miller, eds, *The Emily Dickinson Handbook* (Amherst: U. Massachusetts P., 1998).

Dickinson's handwriting poses two other problems : how to identify dashes (p. 144), and what to do with *litterae notabiliores* ('more noticeable letters'[30])—often larger *minuscule* forms (handwritten 'lower-case') rather than distinct *majuscule* forms (handwritten 'upper-case'), and a judgement-call for transcribers. Her capitalisation is unpredictable and the *duct* of her hand changed with age, so there is room for doubts ; in general Johnson and Franklin agree, and concerned readers can now check for themselves. Franklin does beg a question by noting that Johnson "preserved" Dickinson's capitalisation and punctuation "within the limits of conventional type" (i. 6), while he "follows" them "within the capacity of standard type" (i. 36) : both phrases seem to mean the same thing, my 'normative limits of the metal page', but Franklin, who worked on computers, was not in the same boat as Johnson ; however Dickinson "Signed away [/] What portion of me be [/] assignable", one could now reproduce her capitalisation more accurately, and again, should sometimes do so.

2. 'September Song' (p. 72).

Some aspects of layout (especially "it [/] is true") are necessarily subsumed in and treated under 'Lineation' ; the critical issue remaining is Hill's decision to explode his sonnet with *blank* lines between 'stanzas'. His intent is undoubted : no compositor or publisher would impose such layout of themselves, and Hill's insistence that even the justified prose-poems of *Mercian Hymns* be quoted exactly is widely known (N2050). For readers the primary consequence is to disguise his invocation of sonnet-form, but that is not Hill's primary purpose, which (taking a deep breath) I suggest as graphic representation of his humility in speaking at all, and of the pressing reasons for gladly curt reversion to silence following "This is more than enough."

Grimly humorous, one might say that with the *Sho'ah* it is easiest to keep your feet out of your mouth if you don't have too many feet about ; the visual spareness of 'September Song'—its deficit in articulacy represented by the failure of the black-and-white outline to match that of other sonnets, and 26 'missing' beats—suggest layout as (in Eliot's term) an 'objective correlative' of Hill's difficulty in meaning. To speak of the *Sho'ah* at all is to face epistemological difficulty ; to speak as Hill does is to risk incomprehension, or worse. One acid test is to type 'September Song' as a prose-paragraph (but, if you respect Hill and the

[30] This term usefully covers both handwritten and printed forms ; the singular is *littera notabilior*.

gravity of his subject, don't post or print it) and let your eyes flick between screen and Hill's own layout : which better grasps his meaning and integrity ? Relineations and resettings to display as much as possible of the sonnet-form are equally object lessons in what might be called (in the Brechtian sense) an alienating layout.

3. 'Nearing Forty' (pp. 22–3)

The text of 'Nearing Forty' on pp. 22–3 reproduces closely (though in a different fount, correcting a misprint, and with line-numbers) its *mise-en-page* in Walcott's *Collected Poems 1948–84*, the most recent edition 'seen through the press' by the poet. The 32 lines are ekthetic, without initial capitals, reflecting the single sentence from the capital of "Insomniac" to the full-stop after "weep". There is good leading, as throughout the *Collected Poems*, so each line is clearly seen, metrical and rhyme-schemes readily worked-out, and enjambed syntax easily followed ; if a poet will use these devices, and wants readers to appreciate them, it is good to be kind to those readers' eyes. On the other hand, this *mise-en-page* does not do things it might : there is no eisthesis of rhyme, nor annotation of the unfamiliar, and for many readers a one-sentence block of type marching down its pages is more intimidating than a poem broken into manageable pieces. It is an elegant setting, achieving visual clarity—but that also enhances authority.

Title, dedication, and epigraph are in italics (unused elsewhere), and the latter are indented. This is standard ; yet epigraphs need not be italicised and at five lines this is long to be so ; printed with good leading (where epigraphs are often single-spaced, even if their poem is double-spaced), its attribution, "—S A M U E L J O H N S O N", is nicely set in spaced small caps with an initial rule : all decisions by someone. The point, as of heavy leading and ekthesis in the main text, is probably (besides pleasing the eye) to recall the first edition of the source-text—Johnson's *Preface to Shakespeare*, published in 1765 ; Walcott could by 1969 (and certainly 1985, when the *Collected Poems* appeared) have seen the first-edition *mise-en-page* in various places, including a new paperback facsimile[31] ; intentionally or otherwise, his own elegant, intimidating layout visually alludes to the Johnsonian certainty evident in his epigraph—and as the poem is partly trying to recover some such certainty in the twentieth century, during a spiritual crisis in middle age, these visuals are useful.

---

[31] Menston : Scolar Press, 1969.

Exercises: Laying it out

1. Common metre probably derives from couplet fourteeners, the last three feet of each *a14* line being reset to produce *a8b6c8b6*. Take any short poem in common metre and convert it to fourteeners : ll. 1–8 (or 10) of 'I heard a Fly buzz' (adjusting merely initial caps that become medial) would become :

> I heard a Fly buzz—when I died—the Stillness in the Room
> Was like the Stillness in the Air—between the Heaves of Storm—
>
> The Eyes around—had wrung them dry—and Breaths were gathering firm
> For that last Onset—when the King be witnessed—in the Room—

Looking at the new *mise-en-page*, list features that are but were not displayed ; reverting to 'normal' layout, how do they survive in your awareness when not displayed ? Similar experiments can be tried with other forms—Lear laid out his limericks as quatrains, *a9a9b12a9*, making the *b*-rhyme 'couplet' a *leonine* rhyme in mid-tetrameter (p. 198), and texts of Marvell's 'Horatian Ode' waver between *a8a8b6b6* quatrains, couplet ekthesis, and indenting only the trimeters. Read that poem seriously in all three layouts and prepare as precise a statement as possible of their relative dis/advantages.

2. Marvell's *Miscellaneous Poems* (1681) also uses stanza-numbering, as in 'The Definition of Love' (p. 85); editors often remove it. Try both a complete short poem and a chunk of 'Appleton House' with numbers and without : what are their effects ? would you as editor retain them ? is the choice of Roman or Arabic numerals significant ? Now try the series of 'Self-Portrait' poems by Jorie Graham in *The End of Beauty*. What do you make of them ? Apply the "long numbered pause" to a pauseful poem you know, and see what happens ; try also that lineation without numbers. Again, catalogue effects <u>precisely</u> and fully.

3. Take a modern poem you know well and judiciously apply first emphatic medial capitalisation, then distinguishing italics, then both in joint-harness and counterpoint. Try both versions on people who <u>don't</u> know the poem : given their druthers . . . ?

4. If you have the confidence (not skill) to draw, find a short dramatic monologist whose voice attracts (commands, seduces . . .) you and create an outline storyboard for a graphic edition. Once you have mapped out your panels and organized them in pages, various standard programs will allow you to print the panel-frames and speech-bubbles + text, after which you need only supply artwork. Matchstick figures are fine : as with New Math, the fun is in the working-out.

5. Finally, what Jeremy Maule used to call 'practical practical criticism'. Prepare an edition of 'Easter Wingses', and a statement of the principles governing your handling of its text/s. I have in the past seen a mobile, with each wing multiply reproduced back-to-back with its partner, all to spin above candles in an Eastertide church ; a curious cardboard contraption that required mounting on a 16-RPM gramophone ; and more than one involving rubber-bands. There should be an exhibition.

Chapter Glossary

autograph : of manuscripts, in the author's (as distinct from a scribal) hand.

blank : of physical lines, empty of type ; of type, uninked.

catchword : the first word or syllable of a page printed below the last word of the previous page, as a courtesy to readers(-aloud).

composition : in hand-press printing the process of assembling the individual pieces of type, including inter-word spaces, in the correct order.

display : the presentation or emphasis of elements by layout.

eisthesis : the indentation of a line or lines by one or more spaces from the left margin.

ekthesis : the setting of a line or lines hard to the left margin.

epigraph : a short motto or quotation prefixed to a text.

face : of a type, a particular appearance of the letters and numbers, as roman or *italic* ; thus any given fount of type will have many faces.

fair copy : a carefully copied text without blots or corrections etc.

foul papers : an author's drafts with revisions etc., the precursor of *fair copy*.

fount : (in the USA, 'font') of type, a particular design of the letters and numbers ; each fount will comprise designs for each character in a number of faces.

imposition : in hand-press printing the process of arranging the composed type on the bed of the press ; decisions about leading, ornaments, running-heads, etc. are involved, and two or more pages will have to be imposed together in any book or pamphlet format.

indentation : the setting of a line or lines in from the left margin by one or more spaces.

justified : of text and margins, aligned straight up and down.

leading : the amount of white space left between lines, stanzas, or other units of form, and in the margins.

leaf : a single sheet of paper ; one recto, one verso.

lineation : the organization of a poem into lines.

metal page : my coinage for the archetype, at a given time or in general, of pages printed by metal type ; usually with reference to the typographical and/or design limits of such pages.

mise-en-page : the actual layout of a given poem (or prose text) on a given page.

ragged : of text and margins, not justified.

recto : the front of any leaf ; in books, each right-hand page.

set, setting : arranging type in order to print ; a portion of type so ordered.

shape-poem : one whose text is organised on the page to depict a shape, or otherwise to involve pictorial as well as verbal representation ; also known as *technopaignia, carmina figurate*, and *concrete poems*.

turn-down, -up : also *turn-over, turned line* ; in verse-lines that exceed the measure, that part which is set on the physical line below or above.

verso : the back of any leaf ; in books, each left-hand page.

4
Punctuation

verse, whatever else it may be, is itself a system of *punctuation* ; the usual marks of punctuation themselves are differently employed

T. S. ELIOT, letter to the *TLS*, 27 Sept. 1928

(Where the hurry is stopped) (and held) (but not extinguished) (no)

JORIE GRAHAM, 'Soul Says'[1]

Punctuation is to words as cartilage is to bone, permitting articulation and bearing stress. Like layout it is always there and frequently critical, but rarely thought about ; this, mostly depunctuated, is from *Bleak House* :

> out of the question says the coroner you have heard the boy cant exactly say wont do you know we cant take that in a court of justice gentlemen its terrible depravity put the boy aside

Restore Dickens's wholly conventional punctuation and :

> 'Out of the question,' says the Coroner. 'You have heard the boy. "Can't exactly say" won't do, you know. We can't take *that* in a Court of Justice, gentlemen. It's terrible depravity. Put the boy aside.'[2]

Punctuation-marks and distinguishing cases and faces do a great deal, as lawyers know : because commas are easy fraudulently to insert or delete, some legal documents are written without them (or pronouns, s/he also being vulnerable), making for grim reading but insuring against ambiguity. In poetry, however, it may be precisely a possible ambiguity, uncertainty, or opportunity delicately to shade meaning that makes a particular punctuation attractive.

[1] *Region of Unlikeness* (New York: Ecco Press, 1991), 125.
[2] For commentary see Parkes, *Pause and Effect*, 1.

To understand punctuation profitably one must reject most received analysis. Grammarians will promulgate how one should (not) punctuate, but their best efforts for 500 years have found no valid rule for punctuating English : because there are none. Punctuation is an open system in which all is possible but there are conventional (not regulated) ways of doing most things ; unlike rules, conventions can constructively and aesthetically be ignored or broken. They are more like dress-codes than maths : if $2 + 2 \neq 4$, a rule is broken[3] ; if you marry in red in a consecrated building you may be socially stigmatised—without cultural context, who can say ? Break too many punctuational conventions and you'll be hard to read, their whole point being facility of communication, but to break one or two at a time is very useful, and (especially in literature) there is no 'in/correct' punctuation, only un-, counter-, and conventional punctuation, where conventions are (more or less) straightforwardly employed, or exploited. It can be un/helpful, in/elegant, (more, or less) economic, in/consistent : in poetry such questions matter far more than, unanswerably, whether it is 'correct'.

One underlying problem is flawed analysis of function. Some grammarians argue that all punctuation is *elocutionary*, signalling pauses to guide the voice in reading aloud (cf. breathing and bowing marks in music) ; others, that all punctuation is *syntactic*, indicating grammatically intended sense. All admit some punctuation is *deictic* (or *emphatic*), stressing a word or phrase with cases/faces as well as marks, but soon return to Derby-and-Joaning (Is—Isn't—Is . . .) about elocutionary v. syntactic. The debate is arid : in *c.* 383 the young St Augustine was so astonished to find St Ambrose reading silently that—unwilling to interrupt the marvel he saw and did not hear[4]—he waited for hours to speak, and thereafter knew that punctuation is elocutionary and syntactic, which mode predominates depending on whether you're reading aloud. It works in turn or harness for ear and eye **:** that colon is syntactic**,** and that comma, but when reading aloud you'll pause at both, and quite right too.

Another (interlocking) problem is definition. Dictionaries tend to

[3] cummings titled a collection *is 5*, remarking that poets rejoice "in a purely irresistible truth (to be found, in abbreviated costume, upon the title page of the present volume)" : *Complete Poems*, p. 223.

[4] *Sed cum legebat oculi ducebantur per paginas et cor intellectum rimabatur, vox autem et lingua quiescebant* (But while reading his eyes glanced over the pages and his heart scrutinised the meaning, but his voice and tongue were at rest : *Confessiones*, vi. 3 ; Parkes, p.116 n. 6). The *vox*/*lingua* distinction covers subvocalisation, implying genuinely eyes-only reading, and hence a speed typically 3–4 times higher than vocalised speed ; speed (like spacing) affects attitudes and responses to punctuation.

insist, as grammarians to assume, that punctuation means punctuation-marks—but it is fatal to ignore its deictic and *spatial* forms. The mostly depunctuated passage from Dickens retained interword spaces and acquired spatial punctuation distinguishing it as a quotation ; hadIgivenyouinsteadabitofdickenslookinglikethisyouwouldhavefeltfar lessequitableaboutthewholethingbleakhouseawholelotbleakeranywayn evermindingthefog. Dictionaries also give the game away : 'punctuation' is 'points, marks and c.', but 'to punctuate' is 'to interrupt at intervals'—with whatever : most often, plainly, space.

A third (explanatory) problem is that punctuation often cannot operate identically in different languages. In synthetic languages like Greek and Latin where grammatical meaning is built into words, grammar overrides any but the heaviest intervenient punctuation : *Joe said toBob* and *toBob said Joe* mean Joe talks and Bob listens no matter how punctuated, but in analytical languages punctuation's powers are altered, and there is no synthetic-language equivalent of *Joe said "Bob is a fool"* and *"Joe" said Bob "is a fool"*—case-structure obliging words to change with the speaker. Many grammarians' difficulty has been a compulsive quest for a neoclassical theory of English punctuation, ignoring (as prosodists often do) a basic change altering the whole system.

Cutting across all punctuation is what is called 'modernisation' but is often simply alteration. I demonstrate the evils of its current academic form in quotations, but the practice is old and connected to public authority. Even in Latin a full-stop can determine one meaning over another, and as Augustine remarked (of John 1: 1–2 in the Vulgate[5]), mispunctuating and so misconstruing the Bible can damn you. Nearly a millennium later monks repunctuated the sacred texts they 'copied' to reflect new Thomist orthodoxy,[6] and such exegetical control of texts is the authoritarian master of lawyers' punctuational suspicions. Even well-meaning academic editors are in this tradition, and in consequence even professional readers now rarely see punctuation on other principles than those 'we' suppose normative and superior. The

[5] The verses read (with interword spaces) *in principio erat verbum et verbum erat apud deum et deus erat verbum hoc erat in principio apud deum* : the danger is putting a full-stop one word early (*erat. Verbum*), which would alter the meaning from "In the beginning was the Word, and the Word was with God, and the Word was God. The same was in the beginning with God." to "In the beginning was the Word, and the Word was with God, and God was. The same Word was in the beginning with God.", so impugning the divinity of the Word.

[6] Parkes, 'Punctuation', in Murphy, ed., *Mediaeval Eloquence* (Berkeley: U. California P., 1978).

cost is far greater than individual exploitations : conventions are unstable ; marks passing unscathed through the modernising mill may not have meant in their original context what they seem to mean in their new one. Modernising denies readers (and students charged to understand <u>con</u>text) a contemporary, even authorial construction which may well do a better job of making text informative than the modern, supposedly more helpful constructions editors impose. Unthinking modernisation is declining (McGann blew its rationale apart, p. 96) but not extinct, and deep confusions of pedagogical purpose remain common.[7]

These four problems, spaghettiing through our minds and bookshelves, make for crippling limitations of literary sensibility. Focusing on each clearly in your mind, consider two pages, from a twelfth-century manuscript (beautifully laid out, colour, columns, illumination, but a maximum of 4–5 marks) and a nineteenth-century novel (machine-pressed, maximal text-per-page, little spatial articulation, but up to 19 marks). Certain things become apparent :

(a) punctuation includes marks, spaces and *mise-en-page* ; and
(b) its elocutionary, syntactic, and deictic functions are not mutually exclusive ; because
(c) it is a fuzzy-logical system of conventions not a strict-logical system of rules ; and thus
(d) the meaning of a given punctuator is neither absolute nor historically constant, but always relative and contextually determined ; hence
(e) the difference between twelfth- and nineteenth-century balances of (spatial + deictic punctuation) and (pointing), the MS compensating with *mise-en-page* for a paucity of standard marks, the novel with marks for commercial economy of space.

Propositions (a–d) correspond to the four problems, and though (a + b) are empirically obvious, and (c + d) first-order implications, few critics say anything about any of them. Proposition (e) is the beginning of what can be done with an adequately transfunctional and historicised theory of punctuation.

Classical grammarians said little about marks because most didn't exist and all were the privilege of readers, while the Church Fathers wanted to enforce specific constructions, not explore general or literary

---

[7] Compare some 'Notes on the Text' in editions of Shakespeare, especially where series policy is set out.

practice. Until Victorian times the scale of successive linguistic, cultural, and technological changes made radical rethinking increasingly necessary while neoclassicism and prescription allied to state authority made it impossible. Late Victorian critics and bibliographers, trying to come to grips with the mass-market and machine-presswork, saw that more practical textual taxonomies were needed, but those they formulated, like essentialist genre- and textual theory, have proved unworkable. With Modernism, however, revolting as much against grammatical as social decorum and revalorising space across the arts, thinking and sensibility began to change. Scholars like Simpson, Sparrow, Honan, and Ong began close empirical work, followed eventually, a quarter-century in the making, by Parkes's magisterial *Pause and Effect: An Introduction to the History of Punctuation in the West* (1991)—152 pages of text with 74 plates that utterly surpass two millennia of grammarians. Discriminating between histories of theory and usage ("punctuation should be studied according to the ways it has been used rather than the ways some have thought it ought to be used"), presenting each for the first time complete in outline ("the best way to understand usage is to study it historically"), and generalising only on a firmly empirical basis backed by plates and quotations ("a general introduction, however ambitious, is needed"), Parkes's Herculean labours cleaned the Augean stables and slew all manner of mythical beasts ; in his wake the history of usage has been expanded by Henry, Sutherland, Grafton, and others.[8]

So how does this help? Considering Parkes's lessons, I have devised an eight-level scale within which all punctuation can be assessed :

1. letter-forms punctuating the blank page ; *scriptio continua,* wordswithoutspacesormarksbetweenthem ;
2. interword spaces, including three special varieties : the paragraph-, verse line-, and stanza-break ;
3. punctuation-marks, including *stops, tonal indicators, inverted commas, rules, dis/aggregators, signs of omission, signes de renvoi,* mathematical punctuation, and *special sorts,* with their conventionally associated spaces (which vary within media and cultures) ;
4. words or other units distinguished by fount, face, colour, sign, or position ; deictic emphasis, eisthesis, etc., the detail of the *mise-en-page,* decisions which in cold-metal setting come under composition ;

[8] *Pause and Effect,* p. xi ; other works in the Bibliography.

5. the organisation of the page and opening ; decisions about basic fount and face, margins, etc. ; the principles of the *mise-en-page*, decisions which in cold-metal setting govern composition or come under imposition ;
6. pagination or *foliation* ; the use of the page, leaf, or opening as units, as in new item, new page formats, and graphic novels ; by extension, that regular turning of the page which punctuates our reading of all *codices* + mouse-clicked scrolling and jumping in screen- and web-reading ;
7. the structures of grouped pages : sections, chapters, prolegomena and appendices, apparatus, etc. ; the articulation presented by contents-pages + site-maps ;
8. the MS, TS, codex, scroll or leaf as a complete object punctuating space or a constituent volume in a greater whole, itself a punctuating object.[9]

Functionally, deictic punctuation is concentrated on level 4, but all functions operate at all levels.

Theoretically, levels 1–4 correspond to McGann's lexical codes, and 5–8 to bibliographical codes.

Historically, 1 + 8 are oldest, implicit in the earliest written words ; 5–7 come with the early medieval *codex* (bound book), while 2 + 4 developed only from the eighth century ; 3, created in classical times and boosted under Charlemagne, underwent sustained development only from the twelfth century.

Practically, 1–3 are an authorial province, 4–8 largely determined by scribes, compositors and other printers, editors, and/or publishers, all operating within historically specific technological constraints.

Literarily, the contrast of twelfth- and nineteenth-century pages is revealed as a shift between levels 3 + 4 driven over most of a millennium by *Humanist* pedagogy and the increasing size of editions (a function of 8, because each space costs <u>per copy</u>).

Poetically, for example, *The Waste Land* (and other Modernist departures from minimum-space and/or rigidly orthodox layouts) reverse that shift, which clarifies (among other things) Eliot's acute interest in Dante and Petrarch, whose innovative stanzas challenged scribal and established printed practice ; his relations as a dramatic mono-

[9] This scale was first promulgated under 'Punctuation' in Cuddon, *Dictionary of Literary Terms* (4th edn, 1998) ; mildly reworded in 'Mark, space, axis, function' ; and again here.

> logist with Browning, to which Langbaum pointed[10] ; his practice (visible in MSS and TSS) of revising by eliminating marks ; and his poetic influence as an editor at Faber and, posthumously, in a world where larger destabilisations and post-metal printing have radically confirmed the Modernist discontinuity.

The scale makes possible a (brief) survey of (poetic) punctuation on a proper basis. Volume-structures (levels 7–8) have already been assessed under 'Form', and deictic elements (4) under 'Layout', while line-breaks (2) get their own chapter ; some aspects must be deferred to 'Syntax'. What belongs here are some spatial forms (6, 4–1) and the marks (3).

The **page** (level 6) came under 'Layout', but the new poem, new page convention deserves remark. Pre-Humanist examples are rare, but the fourteenth-century Petrarchan-Dantean development of complex lyric stanzas and the urge to present them clearly (beautifully and usefully) disseminated the convention fast. With the Renaissance growth of printing and explosion of verse come interesting contrasts : Spenser's *Amoretti and Epithalamion* (N190), printed for Ponsonby in 1595, displays each sonnet and stanza on its own page with decorative borders (p. 138), and gives 'Epithalamion' an internal title-page ; Shakespeare's *Sonnets*, pirated (?) by Thorpe in 1609, prints 2+ sonnets per page, and though it does start 'A Louer's Complaint' on a new page, omits it from the main title-page, provides no other, and prints 4+ rhymes royal per page—a mess contributing to the poem's relative obscurity (especially for Shakespeare). What might have been the consequence of a 1609 *Sonnets and A Louer's Complaint* paginated like the *Amoretti and Epithalamion* ? With collections by individual poets now often subsidised or accepted as loss-leaders by large publishers, short individual volumes tend to retain the new-page convention (a natural form for assembled TSS), but in longer *Collected* or *Selected Poems* and anthologies maximal-lines-per-page setting is a powerful norm ; nor has the Web obviated commercial restriction, for linking each poem as a separate web-page takes more time to enter and RAM to sustain than scrollable text without pagination. At the other extreme is the broadsheet poem, where enlargement makes fount-detail and print-quality consequential (cf. televisual and cinematic film-stock) ; it isn't chance that Tolkien's Elvish calligraphy has put 'Bilbo's Song' on more walls than most other poems have managed collectively.

---

[10] *The Poetry of Experience* (New York: Random House/London: Chatto, 1957).

The rhetorical-aural **period** and syntactical-visual **sentence** (levels 3–4, pp. 265–7) are, respectively, classical-Renaissance and modern units "forming the grammatically complete expression of a single thought" (*OED*). The conventional indication of periods with initial capital and terminal full-stop did not develop until the eighth century. In printing or typing it is usual to put (additional) space between periods or sentences, so a normal break has three elements : full-stop/ space/capital. It follows that several intensities can be indicated : full-stop/space, full-stop/capital, etc. e. e. cummings (who printed his name thus) enjoyed this game, and Lisa Prospere used it to vary the burden of 'My.Times.In.Your.Hands'.[11] It is often said complete sentences must comprise subject + in/transitive verb (+ object)[12] : yet one may punctuate as a sentence that which isn't, as in imitations of speech (try Browning's 'Caliban upon Setebos', ll. 24 and 284).

The **paragraph** (level 2), dating from the second century BCE, is the oldest surviving spatial punctuation. A basic unit of printed argument, in fiction it tends also to be a unit of emotion, the tone of last sentences signalling the 'tonic key' of paragraphs and colouring re-readings. This may be true of verse-paragraphs, but is rarely so if they are notably long (like Milton's). The *special sorts* (p. 139) called the *paraph* (¢, ¶, ||) and *paragraphus* or *signum sectionis* (§) indicate paragraphs or sections, and may replace or accompany initial eisthesis (a classical-medieval practice now again useful when e-transfer strips spatial formatting). I use paragraphūs below to distinguish families of marks, and in some footnotes.

The **word** (level 2) is a traditional unit of sense. Word-separation began in Ireland in the later-seventh century, before which all writing was in *scriptio continua* (continuous script), astringoflettersrecordinga stringofsounds. It is unusual to omit word-separation, though Hopkins did with "lionlimb", "yestertempest's", "firedint", and cummings with "deafanddumb", "firstclassprivates", "yellowsonofabitch" (N1169–71, 1394), but common to replace interword-spaces with hyphens and obligatory to promote some to line- or stanza-breaks (pp. 153–4) ; words may also be interrupted by punctuation (try cummings again), or to display rhyme (pp. 196–7). In free verse large interword-spaces are sometimes deployed to offset a word   or words   within a

[11] In Lee, *Roseau Valley*.

[12] An *intransitive* verb does not take a direct object, a *transitive* verb does. "The water exists." It need not exist something, and 'to exist' is intransitive. If "the water fills . . ." it must fill something, and 'to fill' is transitive.

line, as in Clampitt's 'Let the Air Circulate' and Pollard's 'Bridgetown (Summer '78)'.[13]

The punctuation of white space by **letter-forms** (level 1) is taken for granted, but medieval illumination (abstract or thematic) promotes a distinct awareness of letters. The "*Woodden O*" (*Henry V*, Prologue) is famously an icon of the Globe theatre, but 'O' ('Oh') is a notably self-illustrating sound in delivery (say it to a mirror), and Spevack's *Concordance* lists 2,434 others in Shakespeare's canon. Puns involving 'ay/e' and 'eye' may similarly come to rest on the narrowly individual shape of 'I'. Such examples, like the joke-forms of 'look' and 'boobs' with pupilled or nippled 'o's, the use of heart-shaped *jots* above 'i's, the addition of smileys to 'o's or looped *descenders* in signatures, and the advent of txtng suggest the possibility of such *iconicity* should be borne in mind. So do the continuing popularity of fine editions of poetry using drop-caps, elegant founts including *ligatures* ('tied' letters, as æ, fi, fl[14]), and post-metal freedom typographically to enhance individual letters or words. The relevance for artist-poets like Blake, Stevie Smith, Peake, and Walcott is obvious, and a general case for 'Alphabetic Letters as Icons in Literary Texts' has been made by Max Nänny[15] ; *ampersands* and *@pestails* may also be iconic, as well as decorative and/or functional (p. 140). Some rhetorical figures are intrinsically iconic—*chiasmus*, for example, if used (say) as a 'noun-verb/verb-noun' reversal in consecutive lines forms the X-shape for which it is named—and punctuation-marks can readily become so in themselves or as metaphors, especially if accompanied by their names. When Bunting writes in 'Fruits breaking the branches' of "the curl of a comma", Twitchell in 'The Cut' of "the stitches' exactness, [/] row of faint commas", Brodsky in 'Lithuanian Nocturne' of "Folk [. . .] protecting the commas [/] of their candle flames in trembling brackets of hands", Harsent in 'Dumbcake' of "a furious ellipsis [/] where she'd pricked his name", Schultz in 'Star-Gazing' that "The hyphen is a bridge", Pollard in 'Conversation (again?)' of "the spaces [/] between sparse words", France in 'Constellations' of "ampersands [/] like kisses with rucksacks", or Carson in *Beauty*

---

13 Clampitt, *What the Light Was Like* (London: Faber, 1986) ; Pollard, *Shame trees*.

14 Ligatures are created in metal type for ff, fl, fi, ffl, and ffi because the top of 'f' (which juts beyond the body of the type) is otherwise damaged by the next letter ; long-s (ſ) ligatures were also needed, and *scharfes-S* (ß) is long+short-s (ſs). The nameless œ usually derives from Greek -oi- spellings, but in modern texts, like OE *ash* (æ), *thorn* (þ = unvoiced *th*) + *eth* (Đ, ð = voiced *th*), and ME *yogh* (ȝ = *y, gh*), may indicate iconising care.

15 Max Nänny and Olga Fischer, eds, *Form Miming Meaning: Iconicity in Language and Literature* (Amsterdam: Benjamins, 1999).

of the Husband of italics' "dip and slant [/] of mindfulness", the shapes they ask readers to imagine are present on their pages. *Lunulae* (the most eye-catching indicators of parentheses, these curves) are a special case, because the idea of being in parenthesis is of special value while lunulae display enclosure as mirror-crescents (pp. 126–7).[16]

Punctuation-marks (level 3) come in fairly distinct families : *stops*, pointing syntactic completion (with concomitant pauses) ; *tonal indicators* ; *dis/aggregators*, distinguishing and/or displaying distinct sets of words ; *signs of omission* ; *rules* ; *combinate-marks* ; and *signes de renvoi* (with certain *special sorts* and symbols). These families practise inter-marriage (and any mark can prove promiscuous) but usefully articulate the kinds of operation punctuation is standardly expected to perform. A catalogue follows, in which the families are treated in order, separated by rules, and distinguished by a *paragraphus* (§).

---

§ There are four **stops** : the *full-stop*, *colon*, *semi-colon*, and *comma*.

• The **full-stop** (US, *period*, Latin *punctus*, whence 'punctuation') is the heaviest, ending classical periods and modern sentences ; in reading aloud it normally enforces a substantial pause. Even in free verse full-stops are conventional, but Eliot experimentally omitted them in *The Waste Land* (ll. 279–91, N1352), and in *Four Quartets* "the punctuation [. . .] includes the *absence* of punctuation marks, when they are omitted where the reader would expect them"[17] ; others have followed suit (N1695), occasionally or (as in some *L=A=N=G=U=A=G=E* poetry, p. 276) systematically. The 'same mark' occurs as decimal-points and within other stops, tonal indicators, and signs of omission—an object lesson in the relative value of all marks. Full-stops must not be confused with medial points (·) in *hemistichic* lines, as in *Piers the Ploughman* ("In a somer sesun · whan softe was the sonne, [/] I shope me shroudes · as I a shepe were"), even if 'low points' are used and only position distinguishes medial point and full-stop, as in Reading's 'Gula'—"Glutton was going . to get himself shriven, [/] and made for St Michael's . to confess his misdemeanours."[18]

[16] Bunting, *Collected Poems*, 93 ; Twitchell, *Perdido* (London: Faber, 1992), 39 ; Brodsky, *Collected Poems in English* (Manchester: Carcanet, 2001), 215 ; Harsent, *News from the Front* (Oxford: OUP, 1993), 12 ; Schultz, *Aleatory Allegories* (Applecross and Cambridge: Salt, 2000), 49 ; Pollard, *Shame trees*, 70 ; France, *The Simultaneous Dress* (Newcastle: Bloodaxe, 2002), 24 ; Carson, *Beauty of the Husband*, 75.

[17] Sleeve-notes to *Four Quartets* ; quoted Ricks, *Force of Poetry*, 342.

[18] Langland, B-Prologue ll. 1–2 from Skeat (1886) ; Reading, *Work in Regress* (Newcastle: Bloodaxe, 1997), 34.

: The **colon** is the second heaviest stop. In roman, colon/s are the mark/s, but in italics *colon, cola* refer to the part/s of a period or sentence separated by colons : thus three colons give four *cola* (1 **:** 2 **:** 3 **:** 4 **.**). Division into *cola* dates from antiquity, but marking them was a medieval development ; affecting construction and rhythm, it involves both *rhetoric*, 'formal persuasiveness of argument', and *style*, 'how argument is verbally conducted'.[19] The rhetoricians Cicero (106–43 BCE) and Quintilian (*c.*35–*c.*100 CE) suggested good periods had four *cola* **:** Renaissance neoclassicists took Cicero very seriously, making his suggestion a recommendation **:** so (especially *c.*1500–1700) it is worth counting *cola* in periods **:** for there are unlikely to be four by chance. Such tetrapartite periods often express arguments their authors think well-proportioned ; the rhythm in fours is (like quatrains and squares) intrinsically attractive, but as an element of 1580s *Euphuism* (flowery hyper-Ciceronianism, after Lyly's *Euphues*, 1578) may be mocked. The form of colons settled with printing,[20] and in normal modern use its distinctive feature is to imply logical or dependent relationship, like electrical connection in series ; whereas semi-colons usually connect clauses in parallel. The common example is a list—'There are four stops : the *full-stop, colon, semi-colon,* and *comma*'—where commas separate enumerated terms referred by the colon to the preceding clause ; the same function is seen even in sophisticated exploitations. In maths (double) colons express (compound) ratios, 'punctuation : words :: cartilage : bone' (punctuation *is to* words *as* cartilage *is to* bone), and *cola* are associated with argument by analogy.

; The **semi-colon** is the second lightest stop, one of three surviving marks invented by Humanist scholars and printers *c.*1360–1500 (the others are *exclamation-marks* and *lunulae*). Created by Pietro, Cardinal Bembo in 1490s Venice, the upper point of a colon placed above a comma expressly as an intermediate stop, it was disseminated with *Bembine* and *Aldine* founts in sonnets.[21] Extending Ciceronian analysis subdivides *cola* into *semi-cola*—hence the distinction of roman semi-colons, marks, and italic *semi-cola*, parts of a *colon* indicated by

[19] 'Rhetoric' used to mean 'formal rhetorical devices'—parentheses, repetition, etc.—but now (especially in the US) has a looser sense of 'persuasiveness'.

[20] Hopkins used an enlarged form, the 'great colon', as a metrical mark.

[21] The second printed book to use semi-colons was Bembo's Petrarch, and they feature extensively in French Pléiade sonnets (1550s) and English sequences of the 1580s–1590s.

semi-colons. One function is clearer connection in parallel than commas can manage : in the sentence about stops each comma could be a semi-colon—'There are four stops : the *full-stop* ; *colon* ; *semi-colon* ; and *comma.*'—but in short lists with short items it's needless. If the list were longer ; or its items varied in length ; and especially if, as here, some were sufficiently long to have internal commas not signifying a new item : it helps to create *semi-cola*. Their more interesting function is to make syntactical turns, allowing a clause to move away at a tangent ; Henry James is notorious for prose repeatedly using semi-colons thus and can leave readers dizzy, but at his best was a subtle, steely punctuator.[22] Beckett's Watt decried them ("How hideous is the semi-colon."[23]) but used one five words later ; in verse they are essential to *Early Modern* (1500–1700) *periods* and longer *Modern* (post-1700) *sentences* (p. 265), and powerful in short poems or stanzas ; try Keats's 'Ode to a Nightingale' (N935) attending to semi-/colons : you'll be surprised. In classical and modern Greek the same mark is used as a question-mark.

, The **comma** (or, rarely, *virgula*) is the lightest stop, but adding, or omitting, them affects pace tone logic and clarity. Roman comma/s are mark/s, italic *comma/ta* section/s into which *semi-/cola* may be divided, and Cicero's method as a whole is 'analysis *per cola et commata*'. The *solidus* (/) and *dash* (—) are cousins of the comma, and were once called the *virgula suspensiva* and *plana*, 'raised' and 'flat' *virgulae* (cf. French *virgule*, comma) : both are now distinct, but share the comma's single or double (parenthesising) usage. Dashes are treated as *rules* below, but *virgulae suspensivae* are not slashes, as Ralegh reveals in MS :

My boddy in the walls captived
feels not the wounds of spighfull° envy .   *spyful, spiteful*
butt my thralde° minde / of liberty deprived /   *thralled*
fast fettered in her auntient memory /
douth nought beholde butt sorrowes diing face /
such prison earst was so delightfull
as it desirde no other dwellinge place /
Butt tymes effects / and destines dispightfull
haue changed both my keeper and my fare /
loves fire / and bewtis° light I then had store /   *beauty's*

[22] James often changes grammatical subject across semi-colons : "The cat slept on the sofa ; old and lumpy, it was comfortable." This doesn't mean the cat was "old and lumpy". Other great semi-colonisers include Proust and Paul Scott.
[23] *Watt* (London: Calder, 1976), 156.

butt now closs keipt° / as captives wounted are — *close-kept*
y^{to} food / that heat / that light I find no more / — *that*
  Dyspaire bolts vp my dores / and I alone 12
  speake to dead walls / butt thos heare not my mone /.

The terminal double-stop, "/.", with the virgula not subsumed into the full-stop as a comma would be, implies an independence of virgulae, and other disjunctions of expected order are equally apparent. The full-stops ending ll. 2 + 14 divide "My boddy" from "my thralde mind" (2.12 against the 12/2 layout) : ll. 1–2 are without virgulae, and whole swiftness reinforces their assertion of indifference ; ll. 3–14 have multiple virgulae, and choppiness embodies a trapped mind pacing within its skull. The closing couplet is distinguished by the *littera notabilior* of "Dyspaire" but attached to ll. 3–12 by the absence of a full-stop in l. 12 ; "My", "Butt", and "Dyspaire" (ll. 1,8,13) all follow virgulae, while "butt" (l. 3) follows the full-stop : so full-stops (2.12), *litterae notabiliores* (7/5/2), rhyme (4/4/4/2), and layout (12/2) are as multiply at odds as Ralegh and his cell. Printed virgulae have been rare since the 1520s, and editors routinely substitute commas—but Coleridge, a self-confessed 'library cormorant', used them in notebooks, and if most *solidi* you see will be *slashes*, you may yet find one making no slash-sense but readable as a comma (see N1857). The commonest commabuse is *comma-splicing* clauses in loose series where a semi-colon or conjunction (and, but, for, etc.) is needed ; poets rarely offend, but may (like Eliot) omit commas prose would require, especially if coincident with line-breaks. One before an 'and' ending a list—*a, b , and c*—is the *Oxford comma,* because OUP's (but not CUP's) house-style prescribed them. For first-class comma-control try Heaney's 'The Strand at Lough Beg'.[24]

The classical stops were for a millennium most of the punctuation-marks there were, and form a substantial system in themselves. Bembo's semi-colon enriched stopping, but signalled a major expansion of marks between Humanism and Modernism (*c.*1350–1900) which by *c.*1700 almost wholly undid the classical grammatical inheritance to create modern sentences. As late as Milton and Dryden, however, one can see the stops in majestically concerted operation ; this is *Paradise Lost,* IV.268–311 (text from 1667)—a single period within which I have displayed emboldened stops with space :

[24] Ralegh, Hatfield House, Cecil Papers, 144 ; quoted Parkes, *Pause and Effect,* 110 ; Heaney, *Opened Ground: Poems 1966–1996* (London and Boston: Faber, 1998).

Not that faire field
Of *Enna* , where *Proſerpin* gathring flours
Her ſelf a fairer Floure by gloomie *Dis*
Was gatherd , which coſt *Ceres* all that pain
To ſeek her through the world ; nor that ſweet Grove
Of *Daphne* by *Orontes* , and th' inſpir'd
Caſtalian Spring might with this Paradiſe
Of *Eden* ſtrive ; nor that *Nyſeian* ile
Girt with the River *Triton* , where old *Cham* ,
Whom Gentiles *Ammon* call and *Libyan Jove* ,
Hid *Amalthea* and her Florid Son
Young *Bacchus* from his ſtepdame *Rhea's* eye ;
Nor where *Abaſſin* Kings thir iſſue Guard ,
Mount *Amara* , though this by ſom ſuppoſ'd
True Paradiſe under the *Ethiop* Line
By *Nilus* head , encloſ'd with ſhining Rock ,
A whole dayes journey high , but wide remote
From this *Aſſyrian* Garden , where the Fiend
Saw undelighted all delight , all kind
Of living Creatures new to ſight and ſtrange :
Two of far nobler ſhape erect and tall ,
Godlike erect , with native Honour clad
In naked Majeſtie ſeemd Lords of all ,
And worthie ſeemd , for in thir looks Divine
The image of thir glorious Maker ſhon ,
Truth , Wiſdome , Sanctitude ſevere and pure ,
Severe , but in true filial freedom plac't ;
Whence true autoritie in men ; though both
Not equal , as thir ſex not equal ſeemd ;
For contemplation hee and valour formd ,
For ſoftneſs ſhee and ſweet attractive Grace ,
Hee for God only , ſhee for God in him :
His fair large Front and Eye ſublime declar'd
Abſolute rule ; and Hyacinthin Locks
Round from his parted forelock manly hung
Cluſtring , but not beneath his ſhoulders broad :
Shee as a vail down to the ſlender waſte
Her unadorned golden treſſes wore
Diſſheveld , but in wanton ringlets wav'd
As the Vine curles her tendrils , which impli'd
Subjection , but requir'd with gentle ſway ,

> And by her yeilded , by him beſt receivd ,
> Yeilded with coy ſubmiſſion , modeſt pride ,
> And ſweet reluctant amorous delay .

Milton's sexism is as objectionable as his spelling (even for 1667) is idiosyncratic, but his fluent, precise stopping, as erotic as it is dogmatic, demands respect. The syntax seems overwhelming but builds carefully, as one sees by listing *semi-/cola* : 'Not that . . . ; nor that . . . ; nor that . . . ; Nor where . . . : Two . . . ; Whence . . . ; though . . . ; For . . . : His . . . ; and . . . : Shee . . . .' Four arcing *cola* (19½, 12, 4, and 8 lines) represent four subjects (the negative catalogue and Satan's arrival : Adam and Eve : Adam : Eve) with a diminuendo of *semi-cola* (4 : 4 : 2 : 0). There is initial capitalisation of *cola* (somewhat disguised as *cola* 2–4 begin on new lines) but not of *semi-cola*.[25] The period pointedly runs from raped Proserpina to Eve's "wanton ringlets" and (marvellously comma-free after 348 words) "ſweet reluctant amorous delay"—the innocent sexuality of Eden (as Milton affirms in ll. 312–18, a complete 39-word, 7-line period also beginning "Nor . . ."). For detailed work such structural guidance is essential, and even reading fast it's not hard to jot down the major stops :

;;;:;;;:;:.

which tells one enough to make reading much easier ; add the commas :

,,;,;,,,;,,,,,,:,,,,,,,,;;,;,,,:;,:,,,,,,.

and focus tightens, highlighting Satan's serpentine slalom through *semi-cola* 4 + 5 and gendering commanding Adam against commaidenly Eve. For further proof of Milton's adeptness with stops, compare the 1667 text of VIII.1–41, "No [. . .] poem.", with the same passage (usually IX.1–41) in other editions, asking how various 'modernisations' introducing marks Milton couldn't or didn't use do/n't help readers with sense and argument.

:;::;;:;;;;;;. — 1667
.–;.;;:();:;. — N425–6
.;;.;;;;();;. — Oxford Anthology of English Literature (1973)
;–;;;;:––;:. — Complete English Poems (4th edn, London: Dent, 1990)

As in other matters Milton pushes the envelope, but similar demonstrations could be made for most stichic and couplet verse of 1500–1700,

[25] One of the few changes I would make to 1667 would be to lose the automatic initial capitalisation of lines, the better to display *cola*.

including that of Marlowe, Shakespeare, Jonson, Marvell, and Dryden. The punctuation of early editions, even if not authorial, is on principles authors knew, and brings out carefully designed rhetorical structures that modernisation leaves as roadkill in its wake.

---

§ There are two thriving **tonal indicators**, the *question-* and *exclamation-mark* ; one obsolete one, the *percontation-mark* ; and an emergent sub-family, *string-commands* and *emoticons*. The whole idea of printed tone is odd, and all punctuation may be pressed into expressive tonal service ; these marks are distinguished by a primary connection with spoken or emotional tones.

? Systematic use of the **question-mark** (or *punctus interrogativus*) began at the court of Charlemagne, in the late eighth century. That use is, of course, to 'mark questions' and **?** signals their characteristic spoken inflection—but any word can take a question-mark ('Tapirs?'), and Latin has four primary verbs of enquiry (*quaero, inter/rogare, sciscitor,* and *percontor*) as well as presumptive forms (famously, that '*Num* . . .' expects the answer 'no'). 'Interrogations' (demanding 'yes' or 'no') certainly take a *punctus interrogativus*, but whether 'queries' (lookings, searches), 'sciscitations' (repeated enquiries), or 'percontations' (soundings, as of water with a pole) should do so is unclear. English has only two of these verbs (question/query and interrogate) but adds Germanic 'ask' (callings for or upon) while fudging all their distinctions—as the very loose term 'rhetorical questions' shows : are they unanswerable? unanswerable in time? or just unanswered (in time) ? In drama (as in court) the distinction might be life or death, but no conventional means of marking it is available. Question-marks may, however, be doubled or tripled, to indicate bewilderment or surprise. The lower point usually has the value of a full-stop, but need not, and the question-mark can be used medially (see *Paradise Lost* IX.546, N437). In 1754 the Real Academia Española began the practice of inverting question-marks at the beginning (¿What did you say?) ; as European integration proceeds initial inversion may spread, and has uses in TESL.

! The **exclamation-mark** (or *punctus admirativus*) was the earliest Humanist mark. Invented in the 1360s by Iacopo Alpoleio da Urbisaglia (or so he claimed), it may be used medially or in place of a full-stop. Double or triple exclamation-marks are common in comics and letters but tend to make things louder rather than refining sense, as tabloid-journalists' addiction to what they call *screamers* suggests. Even poets as exuberant as Brathwaite and Reading use few exclamations, but they occur frequently in Browning's dramatic monologues (N1010). In Spanish inverted marks are used initially (¡Ouch!).

⸮ The **percontation-mark** (or *punctus percontativus*), the standard Arabic question-mark, indicated 'percontations', questions open to any answer or (more loosely) 'rhetorical questions', in various books of *c.*1575–*c.*1625. This usage seems to have been invented by the translator Anthonie Gilbie or his printer Henry Denham (a pioneer of the semi-colon) : roman examples appear in their *psalms of Dauid* (1581), black letter ones in Turbervile's *Tragicall Tales* (1587).[26] It didn't catch on in print because, being reversed, expensive new type was needed, but was used by scribes including Crane, who worked on Shakespeare's First Folio : so how did compositors set percontation-marks present in their copy but not type-cases? One possibility is that italic or black letter question-marks amid roman type record otherwise unsettable percontation-marks : a strong case can be made for *Measure, for Measure* 1.2 (1623 F1^{r} 🖱), and Spenser's sonnet XLIII in the 1595 *Amoretti* is suggestive. Those that certainly exist, as in the Gilbie–Denham psalter, now can and should be reproduced, and post-metal printing offers the percontation-mark a true second chance.

String-commands and **emoticons** (or *smileys*) evolved in e-mail from *c.*1990 to compensate for an early inability to support deictic punctuation associated with 'plain text'. String-commands follow a computing-language model, are normally indicated by asterisks, and typically end paragraphs or messages with a facial/gestural term qualifying emotional tone : *sigh* *groan* *smirk* etc. Emoticons use marks pictorially, taking a basic colon-eyes + dash-nose + closing-lunula-mouth ':–)' and building hundreds of variants:

:–(	unhappy	:–|	unamused	:–)))))	very happy	(|–)	robotic
8–)	I see you	;–)	wink	!–)	squint	:–0	shocked

The very happy smiley, clearly <u>not</u> 'happy with double chins', reveals an ability to intensify by iteration characteristic of tonal indicators, and ::–) would suggest 'four eyes' or 'seeing double', not the mathematical meaning of '::' in notating congruent ratios. I have yet to see string-commands or emoticons in professional poetry, but will ; their rapid

[26] See Parkes, *Pause and Effect*, plates 34–5.

development among e-mailers denied rich text is eloquent testimony to Parkes's superb rule-of-thumb definition of punctuation as "the 'pragmatics' of the written medium".[27]

---

§ The **dis/aggregators** comprise two linked sub-families, *brackets* and *slashes*, and a distinct sub-family, *inverted commas*. Their function is to display a/word/s as mutually exclusive alternatives or (distinct) units with 'individual status' of some kind. Maths jargon usefully distinguishes the opening *bra* from the closing *ket*.

< > **Angled brackets** are rare in poetry, but used (sometimes with ~~strikethrough~~ ⟨crossing-out⟩) to show textual variants. Where colour and underline are unavailable they may distinguish *eddresses* ⟨bloggs@xyz.edu⟩ and URLs ⟨http://. . .⟩.

{ } **Braces** ('curly' brackets) most often appear in poetry as a solo ket indicating triplets among couplets (N599) and are worth remembering as a mark which may be hand-added to texts (as in exams). They were once used rather inventively, as in this couplet from a twelfth-century copy of a Latin poem with medial as well as terminal rhyme :

<table>
<tr><td>Miles ad arma fre</td><td rowspan="2">} mit</td><td>vita fraus Hectora d</td><td rowspan="2">} emit[28]</td></tr>
<tr><td>Vrbem pugna pre</td><td>troia sub hoste tr</td></tr>
</table>

Such layouts disappeared as Humanist *mises-en-page* developed to display all text more clearly, and would have been very awkward (and expensive) on the metal page.

[ ] **Crotchets** ('square' brackets) developed during the fifteenth century. Their principal use is to indicate something changed or inserted by an editor, not shading meaning but signalling a new author (cf. inverted commas). Anthologists may crotchet titles they supply (as Hoover does in *PostModern American Poetry*), but for poets normal function is a point of departure : Browning crotcheted the first and last paragraphs of 'Caliban upon Setebos' to distinguish thought from speech, and Hill his helpful, peppery self-editorialisation in *The Triumph of Love* :

---

[27] Parkes, *Pause and Effect*, 2.

[28] Parkes, *Pause and Effect*, 99 ; see also 238, plate 45.

The intellectual
beauty of Bradwardine's thesis rests
in what it springs from: the Creator's grace
praecedentem tempore et natura ['Strewth!!!
'already present in time as in nature'?—ED]
and in what it returns to—our arrival
at a necessary salvation.

Those inclined to sympathise with the screamers might remember that "'Strewth" (as its apostrophe signals) contracts 'God's truth', and go carefully. Equally, in Finkel's *The Wake of the* Electron, the bizarre story of a yachtsman's disappearance in 1969, absent crotchets are telling : "All epigraphs and interpolations set in **bold** represent the actual words of Donald Crowhurst [. . .]. All voices other than Crowhurst's are set in *ordinary italics*" : so matters are clear but the vocal medley (like Crowhurst's mind) uninterrupted by crotchety nit-picking. Editorial *ellipses* (. . .) were oddly exempt from the general rule that emendations should be crotcheted, and in older criticism one cannot safely identify ellipsis in quotation as authorial without checking ; they have grown steadily commoner in poetry as elsewhere since *c.*1780, and critical practice (including mine) is now usually to crotchet editorial ellipses. ⌈*Broken* crotchets⌉ may be used in editing dramatic verse to indicate relative textual authority.[29]

() **Lunulae** ('round' brackets), the 'little moons', were the second of the Humanist marks.[30] As a rhetorical figure *parentheses* (one clause intercluded within another) date to antiquity ; the practice of marking them ⌈initially like this, then⟩ with lunulae was invented by Colluccio Salutati in the 1390s, and marking with commas or dashes is later still. There is thus a distinction between lunulae, the marks, and parentheses, bra + contents + ket. As the primary means of dis/aggregation within texts since *c.*1500, lunulae feature in many conventions : most are found in poetry, including the display of relative and conditional clauses, vocatives (p. 85), references, concessions, comparisons, qualifications, omissions, absence, attributions of speech, stage-directions, turn-ups and -downs, page-numbers, and *lemmata* (short quotations

[29] Hill, *The Triumph of Love* (Harmondsworth : Penguin, 1998), 67 ; Finkel, *The Wake of the* Electron (New York: Atheneum, 1987), p. ix.

[30] Sometimes called *parentheses*, but parentheses then indicate parentheses ; printers refer to 'parens'. *Lunula/e*, coined by Erasmus in 1531, is gaining currency. I draw freely here on my *But I Digress*, where readers can see many conventional and exploitative uses.

for exegesis). Some conventions thrive, some come and go : lunulae always distinguish their contents but how they do so depends on context. Grammarians argue parentheses are subordinate, irrelevant, or clumsy, but poets never mean 'Skip this bit if you like', rarely mean 'Oops', and often mean 'Pay special attention' ; in satire parentheses intensify words-behind-the-back or throwaway condemnations.

The point is illustrated by two forgotten Jacobethan conventions : the display of *sententiae*, wise saws or epigrams, in arguments by authority ('It's in *x* so it must be the truth'), and of comparisons in arguments by analogy ('*a* is like *b*'). These correspond to parenthetical references in empirical and academic argument, and are just as critical : a continuity which means printed parentheses track (among other things) the evolution of argument. When Webster (or his printers) had Antonio say in *The Dutchesse of Malfy* (Q1623, B2^r) :

> It then doth follow want of action
> Breeds all blacke male-contents, and their cloſe rearing
> (Like mothes in cloath) doe hurt for want of wearing.

he pointed delivery by displaying (not subordinating) the analogy of idle malcontents and moth-eaten clothes. Similarly, in Donne's 'Ecclogue. 1613. *December* 26' (1633, pp. 124–5) :

> So are thoſe Courts, whoſe Princes animate,
>   Not onely all their houſe, but all their State,
> Let no man thinke, becauſe he is full, he hath all,
> Kings (as their patterne, God) are liberall
> Not onely in fulneſſe, but capacitie,
>   Enlarging narrow men, to feele and ſee
> And comprehend the bleſſings they beſtow.

both the critical analogy with God and an irregular ekthesis of its line (embodying a freedom to qualify patterns) are literally pointed out. A century later, Pope, apologising for his satirical vocation in 'Epiſtle VII. To Dr. ARBUTHNOT' (N627 ; text from *Works*, 1735, ii. 56), revealed a new sense of kings (or at least George II) and argument :

>   'Tis ſung, when *Midas'* Ears began to ſpring,
> (Midas, a ſacred Perſon and a King)
> His very Miniſter who ſpy'd them firſt,
> (Some ſay his *Queen) was forc'd to ſpeak, or burſt.
> And is not mine, my Friend, a ſorer caſe,
> When ev'ry Coxcomb perks them in my face ?
>
> *The Story is told by ſome of his Barber, by *Chaucer* of his Queen. See the Wife of Bath's Tale in *Dryden's* Fables.

Both in the individual 1734 edition and 1735 *Works* the text appears thus, footnote snug and the line after "in my face ?" on a new page, overtly displaying the satirical parentheses (note Midas losing his italics) and careful factual explanation (quite unrelated to Queen Caroline's and Minister Walpole's current difficulties with an asinine king).[31] Half-a-century later again Cowper reversed Pope's attitudes in *The Task* (N697 ; text from 1785, p. 62) :

> The pulpit therefore (and I name it, fill'd
> With ſolemn awe, that bids me well beware
> With what intent I touch that holy thing)
> The pulpit (when the ſat'riſt has at laſt,
> Strutting and vap'ring in an empty ſchool,
> Spent all his force and made no proſelyte)
> I ſay the pulpit (in the ſober uſe
> Of its legitimate peculiar pow'rs)
> Muſt ſtand acknowledg'd, while the world ſhall ſtand,
> The moſt important and effectual guard,
> Support and ornament of virtue's cauſe.

Beyond anticipating the Bellman's "What I tell you three times is true" in *The Hunting of the Snark*, Cowper's lunulae (subsuming commas one might expect) practise an iterative qualification empowering his argument as responsibly rather than satirically drawn. And a modern assemblage of examples :

> But the bullets cried with laughter,
> the shells were overcome with mirth,
> plunging their heads in steel and earth—
> (the air commented in a whisper).
>
> (Douglas, 'Gallantry', N1622)

> Horsfall of Ottiwells°, if the bugger could, *a mill-owner*
> d've° liked to (exact words recorded) *ride* *would have*
> *up to my saddle-girths in Luddite blood.*
>
> (Harrison, 'The Rhubarbarians')

[31] Cf. Finkel, 'King Midas Has Asses' Ears', in *Selected Shorter Poems* (New York: Atheneum, 1987).

> The workers on the derricks live in terror.
> You can't stroll out across the sea at night.
> Professor Walrus writes (see *Drowned in Error*):
> 'The lemon sole are taught to shoot on sight.'
>
> (Fenton, 'This Octopus Exploits Women')

> The roaring
> of the wind, he° wrote (hyperbole again, but *Keats*
> never mind) would be his wife, the stars
> seen through the window would be his children.
>
> (Clampitt, 'The Elgin Marbles')

makes very plain the continuing dependence of poetic argument (whether grimly ironic, bitterly factual, mockingly absurd, or slyly concessive) on lunulae : a tradition no reader of poetry should ignore, and the visible destruction of which is a mortal sin of modernisation.[32]

The intrinsic iconicity of lunulae invites them to figure all manner of curving things. In lineated isolation a ket can be a moon, as in cummings's 'Post Impressions I' :

> (ta-te-ta
> in a parenthesis!said the moon
>)

More conventional pairs can be arms, as in Thomson's *The Seasons* (text from 1730, p. 71) :

> The daw,
> The rook, and magpie, to the grey-grown oaks
> (That the calm village, in their verdant arms,
> Sheltering, embrace) direct their lazy flight; (Summer, ll. 223–6)

or fonts and elliptical basins, as in Walcott's 'The Star-Apple Kingdom' :

---

[32] Douglas, *Complete Poems* (1978; Oxford: OUP, 1987), 99 ; Harrison, *Selected Poems*, 160 (Horsfall was assassinated by Luddites in April 1812 ; Harrison quotes him from E. P. Thompson, *The Making of the English Working Class* (1963 ; rev. edn, Harmondsworth: Pelican, 1968), 612—but slips in with a repersonalised pronoun an italicised tribute to Thompson, who wrote that Horsfall "had boasted that he wished to 'ride up to his saddle-girths' in Luddite blood") ; Fenton, *The Memory of War and Children in Exile : Poems 1968–1983* (Harmondsworth: Penguin, 1983), 103 ; Clampitt, *What the Light Was Like*, 56.

> Before the coruscating façades of cathedrals
> from Santiago to Caracas, where the penitential archbishops
> washed the feet of paupers (a parenthetical moment
> that made the Caribbean a baptismal font,
> turned butterflies to stone, and whitened like doves
> the buzzards circling municipal garbage),
> the Caribbean was borne like an elliptical basin
> in the hands of acolytes, and a people were absolved
> of a history which they did not commit;

Body-parts (especially lips) are common referents—Fletcher's "Come Wench a kisse between each point ; kisse close ; [/] It is a sweet Parenthesis." ; John Fuller's "That soft inevitable kiss [/] Anonymous and unrestricted [/] Upon the lips' parenthesis"—but genuine resemblance is not needed, as Simpson showed "In that same (hoovered) room". cummings and Walcott, in naming the figure when using the mark, join a tradition stretching back through Byron's *Don Juan* VI. lvi ("Kind reader! pass [/] This long parenthesis") to Barnes's 'Elegy II' ("*Euer prolonging out myne endleſſe clauſes* [/] *With iffs Parentheſis*") and the earliest English uses of the mark.[33]

Given such diversity, the significance of lunulae must be inferred in context, but they always create a disjunction between one status of text, equivalent to a tonic key, and another. For examples to ponder, try Marvell's 'Bermudas' (N476), where a "(perhaps)" is exquisitely shaded ; Coleridge's 'Dejection' ll. 11–12 (N828), where lunulae figure 'the new moon in the old moon's arms' ; and *The Waste Land* ll. 24–30 (N1344), a parenthesised main verb that "deepens the meaning of Puttenham's definition of a parenthesis as 'your first figure of tollerable disorder' ".[34] Roethke's 'I Knew a Woman' (N1500) incorporates lunulae into its heroic stanza-form, *ababcc(c)* ; 'September Song' is considered below.

/ The **(forward) slash** or *solidus*, once the *virgula suspensiva*, is related to the comma and dash (a divorced member of this sub-family ; pp. 116, 136). It now mostly does humble but important duty to indicate line- and stanza-breaks, and dis/aggregate such alternatives as

[33] cummings, *Complete Poems*, 89 ; Walcott, *Collected Poems*, 387 ; Fletcher, *The Elder Brother* 1637, H2v ; Fuller, *Collected Poems*, 224 ; Simpson, 'Poems of Passage: Father of the Bride', *London Review of Books*, 11/1 (5/1/1989), 15 ; Barnes, *Parthenophil and Parthenophe* 1593, Liv. See Lock, 'Those Lips : On Cowper (*Ekphrasis* in Parentheses)', in Østermark-Johansen, ed., *Angles on the English Speaking World* 3 (2003).

[34] Ricks, *Force of Poetry*, 309.

s/he, and plural/s (if lunulae are not preferred). Linguistics, where in /pairs/ it displays phonemes, and URLs (http://. . .) have made its capacities familiar, and it is found, conventionally and un/, in free-verse poems like Di Prima's 'The Loba Addresses the Goddess / or The Poet as Priestess Addresses the Loba-Goddess' and Cruz's 'Areyto'.[35]

| The **vertical slash** is handy when forward slashes are otherwise engaged, as for foot-divisions (which are not line-breaks) in discussing 'Metre' (p. 3). It is rare as an authorial mark in verse except in Hopkins, who used it to mark *caesurae* (mid-line breaks, p. 155),[36] but Hill's last four volumes (a sequence[37]) deploy assorted slashes in intriguing ways. *Canaan* (1996) and *The Triumph of Love* (1998) do not use vertical ones, but in the latter dashes become frequent and intrusive (p. 123), and *Speech! Speech!* (2000) erupts :

> Júst as únjust. I know the game,
> for and against. Poetics of self-rule.
> Why nót twist Luther | self-parodist?
> Justified self-accusation at list price.
> CAPITALS | STAGE DIRECTIONS AND OTHER
> FORMS OF SUBPOENA. *Italics* | words
> with which Í—*sometimes*—surprise *myself*. (117, p. 59)

The association with metrical accents implies the superscript slashes derive from Hopkins's idiosyncratic prosodic notation, and most can be read as caesurae ; but not all :

> These public claims | these besieged privities |
> like, when to act entitled to a laugh;
> like, kick yourself for courage, doubling up
> as your dead stand-in; like to go under
> only to be | insensately revived. (67, p. 34)

The first line invites a reading of the slashes as (inverted) commas that the last line precludes. Overall, however, the slashes in *Speech! Speech!* go with a decrease in dashes, and *The Orchards of Syon* (2002) is marked in many ways by a greater balance :

---

[35] Both in Hoover, *PostModern American Poetry*.

[36] Some texts omit them, some use full-size marks (N1171), some a superscript form.

[37] All Harmondsworth : Penguin, 1996–2002 as specified.

I'm not driving |
fortunately. How slowly it all goes
hurtling to oblivion. Line after line
solidly fractured *without*
effort and without discord—COLERIDGE; the eye
of Imagination passive and a seer. (XXX, p. 30)

Blancoed halyards,
guy-ropes, fresh cordage, stress-tested wires,
tug to attention; new and ascendant
flags thrapping the wind. Memory
hyperactive—poised on time—that word
gyroscope | spinning for my balance | *gnōthi*
seauton sounds like adult fun, a trip
to Olympus, or, it could be, Ithaca,
glittery cold Cornell, Château-Thierry's
Chirico-vista'd mausoleum. (XXXVII, p. 37)

The transliterated Greek phrase is a famous oracular tag meaning 'know thyself', and though (after these quotations) the claim might surprise, these late volumes of Hill's, produced by his standards very rapidly, are in general and apparently by relaxed design much more accessible than his earlier lyrics. Unconventional use of an uncommon mark may seem to thwart such purpose, but readers cope with much that frets critics : thinking (precisely in these quotations) of the persistent, playful self-reference, I read the slashes as initially marking a Hopkins-caesura but becoming a free addition to Hill's punctuational repertoire that can be funny ("I'm not driving | [/] fortunately."), graphic ("| these besieged privities |"), or elegant ("| spinning for my balance |"). Certainly they leave "Line after line [/] solidly fractured *without* [/] *effort and without discord*" ; are "stress-tested" and "tug to attention" ; I also like them as "new and ascendant [/] flags thrapping the wind", and in practical critical terms any greater articulation is welcome (especially if adaptable as notation for analysis or verse-speaking). There is also a case for considering them as acting in conjunction with another punctuator (mark or space) to emphasise or inflect its meaning, as dashes do in the combinate-marks (p. 138).

\ The **backslash** has mathematical and computing uses, again making it more widely known than used in literature. In drama it now indicates overlaps of speech ; this practical convention may transfer to poems in dialogue or otherwise choric.

“ ”

Inverted commas or *quotation-marks* (preferred in the US but misleadingly privileging one function) may be single or double, and simple strokes (′,″) or raised commas inverted to open a quotation or speech (‘, “) but not inverted to close it (’,”). If two varieties are used within a text it is possible to distinguish what each does : commonly, double inverted commas signal direct speech and accurate quotation, while single ones are *scare quotes* (in speech signalled tonally and with waggling fingers) doubting the ‘value’ of a word or phrase. House-styles differ, but clarity and consistency (in <u>that</u> order) matter more than what each variety happens to mean in a particular case.[38] If a poem or stanza is all in direct speech inverted commas may be used (as in Lowell’s dramatic monologues) but usually aren’t (as in Browning’s), and omission can be a technique in its own right : *The Waste Land* ll. 111–38 (N1347) has a series of questions in inverted commas (presumably spoken aloud) but answers without (presumably <u>thought</u>) ; alter this and the waste land of an unhappy marriage will be signally changed.

Eliot’s discriminating non-/use was new but poetic exploitations of speech are old. Like French *guillemets* (« »), inverted commas developed from the *diple*, a *nota* (marginal-mark) used in theology to make lemmata refindable (cf. marginal pencilling). Sixteenth-century printers made them punctuation-marks by using them within the type-measure, still to indicate quotation but increasingly for simple emphasis (cf. lunulae, italics), including the display of *sententiae*—as in Shakespeare’s *Rape of Lucrece*, stanza 13 (text from 1594 B3ʳ) :

> This earthly ſaint, adored by this devil,
> Little ſuſpecteth the falſe worſhipper ;
> "For unſtained thoughts do ſeldom dream on evil ;
> "Birds never limed no ſecret buſhes fear .

Extending this, English printers began to indicate direct speech as well as quotations, and there are numerous seventeenth-century prose examples. In this extended function inverted commas came (by the eighteenth century and in the novel) to be supported by *alinéa*, the convention of giving each speaker a new line, but in poetry, where lineation has other values, speech proved trickier, as witness Marlowe’s *Hero and Leander* (1598 C2ʳ, N246) :

[38] *House* or *in-house* style are standing-orders in a printshop, habitual ways of doing particular things. Compare a play in two editions, and you’ll see printing conventions differ between publishers—whether stage-directions are italicised or bracketed, for instance.

A dwarfiſh beldame beares me companie,
That hops about the chamber where I lie,
And ſpends the night (that might be better ſpent)
In vaine diſcourse, and apiſh merriment.
Come thither ; As ſhe ſpake this, her toong tript,
For vnawares *(Come thither)* from her ſlipt,
And ſodainly her former colour chang'd,
And here and there her eies through anger rang'd.

and Swift's wonderful 'Verses on the Death of Dr. *Swift*, D.S.P.D.' (1731, ll. 225–42, N583) :

  My female Friends, whoſe tender Hearts
Have better learn'd to act their Parts,
Receive the News in *doleful Dumps*,
" The Dean is dead, (*and what is Trumps?*)
" Then Lord have Mercy on his Soul.
" (Ladies I'll venture for the *Vole*.°) *all the tricks*
" Six Deans they ſay muſt bear the Pall.
" (I wiſh I knew what *King* to call.)
" Madam, your huſband will attend
" The Funeral of ſo good a friend.
" No Madam, 'tis a ſhocking ſight,
" And he's engaged° To-morrow Night! *busy*
" My Lady *Club* wou'd take it ill,
" If he ſhou'd fail her at *Quadrill*°. *a game at cards*
" He lov'd the Dean. (*I lead a Heart*.)
" But deareſt Friends, they ſay, muſt part.
" His Time was come, he ran his Race ;
" We hope he's in a better place.

Both poets manage the available resources marvellously well, and to modernise is to destroy (not clarify) particular textures : "*(Come thither)*" links Hero's Freudian slip to "the night (that might be better ſpent)" in a way unmatched by 'Come thither', and if all four of Swift's "female Friends" may speak (most social card-games being four-handers) how many do is tellingly moot. Austen similarly blurred speakers (as unmodernised Penguin Classics editions show), and the exact combination of conventions that is now the English way of indicating direct speech, distinguishing paragraph-breaks within speech from changes of speaker etc., dates only from 1857 (and Brontë's MSS of *Villette*). Other (combinations of) conventions prevail elsewhere—German uses „low commas" to open, raised ones to close ; Franco-Irish *alinéa* + initial rule is as widely known as *Ulysses*—but beyond historical and national variation poetry remains a far less stable environment than prose for speech and quotation. Most poetic functions of inverted commas (including quotation, qualification, and direct speech) do, however, reflect the mark's history. The simple double-mark (″) is a sign for 'ditto' that can turn up poetically, as in Over's 'Mouthwash'.[39]

---

§ The **signs of omission** are the *apostrophe, suspension-mark*, and *ellipsis*. Rules may also mark omission, as in coy eighteenth-century names, 'Mr P—', swearwords, 'd—d', and orthodox Jewish references to 'G–d' ; so may lunulae (see Shakespeare's sonnet 126), space within the measure, and *asterisks* (normally a *signe de renvoi*), but none <u>necessarily</u> do so. Etymologically related to astronomical eclipse and geometrical ellipse, grammatical ellipsis has never been theoretically formalised in English despite the example of the 1611 Bible, which italicises words supplied in translation (i.e. elided in Hebrew) ; Qur'anic studies have a formal theory of *ijaz*, ellipses in classical Arabic. But lack of theory does not mean lack of practice, and even a simple English sentence—'He rose, went to the door, and left.'—is densely elliptic : it says, but doesn't, 'He rose *and then he* went to the door *and then he opened it and then he went through the doorway* and *so* left *the room*.' Viewed thus, ellipsis is a necessity if conversations (let alone poems) are ever to finish—but in poetry, with the general instability of English grammar, high potency of punctuation and word-order to affect meaning, and line- and stanza-breaks in play, both marked and spatial ellipsis can be put to remarkable use, as 'September Song' shows. More generally one might note the evident relations of punctuation-marks to grammatical ellipsis (as also in the comma-splice), deepening a sense of the relations between marks and (many kinds of) space.[40]

’

The **apostrophe** is the same mark as a closing (un)inverted comma, used (i) with/out 's', to indicate possession (the ship's bell ; the ships' bells) ; and (ii) to display elision (it's = it is, I'll = I will, etc.).[41] Words ending in -s take possessive 's (Jones's, Dickens's) unless they end in <u>two</u> s-sounds (usually biblical or classical names, as Jesus and

---

[39] *A Little Bit of Bread and No Cheese* (Manchester: Carcanet, 2001).

[40] An invaluable history of English literary usage, Henry's *In Ellipsis* . . ., is forthcoming.

[41] Grammatically, possession is the *genitive* case (mine), as opposed to the *nominative* (I) for subjects, and *accusative* (me) for objects.

Moses, Narcissus and Ulysses) ; lax modern practice has spawned the *butcher's apostrophe,* applied randomly to plurals in -s. Elisional apostrophes indicate initial and terminal *suspension* and medial *contraction* (runnin' o'er 'em). Contraction has a special place in poetry, but before Modernism was (oddly) restricted to prosodic elision (typically in the weakly form'd past tense[42]) and time-honoured poeticisms (n/e'er, e'en, etc.). Modern use admits *enclitic* apostrophes (contracting one word into another, as will in I'll), but some poets don't contract elisions ("it 's", not "it's"), which affects pronunciation but not meaning and is commonest in dialect or regionally accented poetry : Harrison in particular uses the 'floating s' to reconcile iambs with his Leeds accent (N1873), and an isolated "d've" (woul**d** ha**ve**) occurs in 'The Rhubarbarians' (p. 125). In Lallans, the lowland Scots of Dunbar (N86), Henryson, Burns (N747), Goodsir Smith, and some MacDiarmid, the heavy use of elisional and enclitic apostrophes has been condemned for representing Scots as inferior English ; newer work and some recent editions of older Lallans poetry follow the style-sheet formulated by the Edinburgh Makars Club in 1947 to avoid "the vile, truckling apostrophe".[43]

• The **suspension-mark** (or, more loosely, 'abbreviation-mark') indicates words shortened by suspension of terminal letters, as 'etc.' for 'et cetera'. Properly speaking it should not be used after contractions (medial omissions)—thus 'ed**.**' but 'eds', 'vol**.**' but 'vols', 'Rev**.**' but 'Revd' and 'Fr'—but often is, as 'Dr**.**', 'Mr**.**', 'Rd**.**' etc. 'St' and 'St**.**' are both proper for 'street', only 'St' for 'Saint', but in English discrimination by position (St Mark, Mark St) generally makes exact notation unnecessary.

• • • Three suspension-marks form an **ellipsis**, indicating (i) that words have been omitted from a quotation (when it should be crotcheted, p. 123) ; or (ii) an interruption (in drama more usually marked by a terminal dash) ; or, commonly in poetry, (iii) a trailing-off into silence (N1696) or some variant thereof. The distinction of ellipses from dashes or multiple short rules is recent, and though many ways of

[42] Weak verbs form pasts in -ed (walk/ed), strong ones change their radical vowel (run, ran).

[43] An unnamed American quoted by MacDiarmid in a letter to the *Scotsman*, 28 Aug. 1968, and reprinted in *Lines Review*, 27 (Nov. 1968) ; see also Goodsir Smith's 'Preface' to his *Collected Poems 1941–1975* (London: Calder, 1975 [The Scottish Library]).

marking omission are found from the late-sixteenth century, conventional discrimination comes only with Modernism. Its value was doubted as late as 1901, when *The Inheritors*, a collaborative novel by Hueffer (a.k.a. Ford) and Conrad, was "received by the English critics with a paean of abuse for the number of dots it contained",[44] and to the best of my knowledge there is not one ellipsis in the whole of James's fiction. Poets have known better since Eliot (at Pound's behest) revised a fatly cross-rhymed quatrain in *The Waste Land* (*Facsimile and Transcript*, p. 46) :

> —Bestows one final patronising kiss,
> And gropes his way, finding the stairs unlit;
> And at the corner where the stable is,
> Delays only to urinate, and spit.

into the most famous of poetic trailings-away (ll. 247–8, N1351) :

> Bestows one final patronising kiss,
> And gropes his way, finding the stairs unlit . . .

Indication of omission expands into expression of shabby post-coital descent into the night. Poets may also, like scholars, distinguish 'internal' ellipsis from a 'terminal' four-dot form comprising ellipsis + full-stop, as Lowell did 'To Speak of the Woe That is In Marriage' :

> Oh the monotonous meanness of his lust **. . . .**
> It's the injustice **. . .** he is so unjust—
> whiskey-blind, swaggering home at five.

The distinction has clear value in speech, as does the contrast of ellipses and dash. More complexly, poets have since *c.*1960 been able to follow the dramatic examples of Beckett and Pinter in distinguishing ellipses of 2–5 suspension-marks to notate variant pauses in delivery—a system of value only if sharply observed, but potentially remarkable.[45] Outside

[44] F. M. Ford, *Joseph Conrad: A Personal Remembrance* (London: Duckworth, 1924), 149 ; cf. "We both desired to get into situations, at any rate when any one was speaking, the sort of indefiniteness that is characteristic of all human conversations, and particularly of all English conversations that are almost always conducted entirely by means of allusions and unfinished sentences" (p. 135 ; both quoted in Henry, *In Ellipsis . . .*).

[45] "Silences never worried Beckett [. . .] he would read the script, and I have a memory of him saying: 'Billie, will you bring your pencil over here and look at page 2, speech 4, fifth word. Will you make those three dots, two dots.' [¶] Looking through the script of *Play* as I'm writing this, I can see [. . .] only one speech with dots, and I've crossed one dot out with my pencil. 'The strain . . .' it says, 'to get it moving, momentum coming.' [. . .] If this sounds like Pseuds' Corner, I can't help it. I knew

speech, narrative finds few occasions for interword ellipsis, but section-breaks marked by rules, (large) centred asterisks, or other symbols (as in my Preface) are in effect decorated ellipses, and that possibility should be considered, especially in fine editions.

---

§ The family of **rules** currently comprises the *hyphen*, the slightly longer *en-rule*, the *dash* (commonly, as in this book, an *em-rule*), and such longer brethren as a setter cares to assemble, culminating in rules as long as a page is wide or high, and simple or decorated *borders*. Actual lengths will vary between founts and with the size of type, but an 'em' is by definition the body-width of the fount (equal to that of a lower-case 'm', the widest letter), and an 'en' is by definition half the body-width (equal to that of a lower-case 'n').

- The **hyphen** has no spaces on either side, and yokes two words or halves of a word broken by lineation. On the metal page en-rules were commonly used for hyphens, but a somewhat shorter, fatter rule is now usual. The use at line-ends is patently helpful but not in itself interesting ; yoking words is a fascinating resource English inherits from German. Compound nouns are conventionally hyphenated only when adjectival—the twentieth century, twentieth-century poets—but convention wavers when a first-element is itself adjectival (late(-) twentieth) unless the compound is sufficiently distinct to bid for wordhood (the well-meaning late twentieth century) ; extended use humorously or emphatically forces phrases into adjectival service (the well-meaning-late-twentieth-century blues). House-styles interfere, but poets may obsess on hyphenation : 33 lines of Keats's 'To Autumn' yield in 1820 *bosom-friend, thatch-eaves, cottage-trees, o'er-brimm'd, soft-lifted, half-reap'd, cyder-press, soft-dying, stubble-plains, full-grown,*

exactly what Beckett wanted. In my script I find I've drawn a little arch over the dot. [. . .] if I were a musician I'd have put a crotchet here instead of a quaver." : Billie Whitelaw, . . . *Who He?* (London : Hodder, 1995), 77–8. Cf. "I've had two full-length plays produced in London. The first ran a week, the second a year. Of course, there are differences between [them]. In *The Birthday Party* I employed a certain amount of dashes in the text, between phrases. In *The Caretaker* I cut out the dashes and used dots instead. So that instead of, say: 'Look, dash, who, dash, I, dash, dash, dash,' the text would read: 'Look, dot, dot, dot, who, dot, dot, dot, I dot, dot, dot.' So it's possible to deduce from this that dots are more popular than dashes, and that's why *The Caretaker* had a longer run than *The Birthday Party*. The fact that in neither case could you hear the dots and dashes in performance is beside the point. You can't fool the critics for long. They can tell a dot from a dash a mile off, even if they can hear neither." : Pinter, 'Writing for the Theatre' (1962) in *Plays 1* (1976; London: Faber, 1996), pp. vii–viii.

Hedge-crickets, red-breast, and *garden-croft* ; in the *Norton* (N939) "Hedge crickets" and "redbreast" are dehyphenated in opposite directions, while 'o'erbrimmed' and 'cider press' meet similar fates elsewhere. Clearly, some first elements are common qualifiers (*half-, over-, full-*), but *cottage-trees* and *soft-dying* can only mean as they do in this form. Hopkins (intensively) and Eliot (judiciously) were also hyphenators (it's 'Ash-Wednesday', not 'Ash Wednesday') ; the best living compound-welder is Hill : N1831–36 yield *stone-angel, stone-wearing, hot-beds, bay-mouth, Thunder-heads, comings-on, apple-branches, Eel-swarms, half-bricks, classroom-floorboards, phone-calls, moss-green, soft-thudding, half-effaced, bird-dung,* and *martyr-laurels*.

– The **en-rule** is now commonly used in professional printing (and occasionally in word-processed documents) to link numbers (page and date spans) and in expressions such as 'the London–Edinburgh journey', 'the Jamaica–Antigua match'. It is slightly longer (and often thinner) than most hyphens, and can be produced on most standard computer-keyboards by using Control + the hyphen on the numeric keypad. Some publishers use it, with a space on either side, for a dash.

— The **dash** is normally used in script, typescript, and word-processing (but not print) with spaces on either side. In typed and word-processed documents it may be variously represented by single em- or double en-rules (the latter becoming less common with auto-formatting) ; in print an unspaced em-rule is usual, but spaced en-rules are also used. The dash's Latin name is the *virgula plana*, the 'flat virgula' as against the 'raised' *virgula suspensiva* (solidus) ; both are varieties of comma, and—like commas—dashes are used in pairs to create *dash'd-off* parentheses, or singly in (infinite) sequence—to chop sentences up—and change subjects—to anything—even dragons—without the inconvenience of grammatical stops.[46] This can suggest breathlessness or clipped delivery (as with Dickens's Mr Jingle in *The Pickwick Papers*), or be simple laziness, substituting dashes for every other mark and sacrificing subtlety and range to worthless ease (as too often in Shelley). The eighteenth century was unreasoningly fond of the dash used in this careless way, and it has since been popular in letters, probably because it is felt to make writing less formal, more like speech between friends. In strongly felt speech a dash may have breath-breaking force, as Browning knew in 'The Worst of It' ("For I was true at

[46] It is better to write 'dash'd off' than 'dashed off', to avoid confusion.

least—oh, true enough !" : text from *Dramatis Personæ*), and dashes abound, solo, paired, or *combinate*, in his monologues. Unsurprisingly, given his recent epiphany of slashes, Hill has most fully realised what the mark can do—by *beginning* with it :

TO THE HIGH COURT OF PARLIAMENT
November 1994

—who could outbalance poised
                                        Marvell ; balk the strength
of Gillray's unrelenting, unreconciling mind ;
grandees risen from scavenge; to whom Milton
                                        addressed his ideal censure :   (*Canaan*, p. 72)

Syntactically, the title completes the first line ; graphically the dash leaps from nowhere into perfect demonstration (with medial line-break and eisthesis) of what it might mean to "outbalance poised [/ tab tab tab] Marvell", famously Horatian and urbane—and from 1659–78 a Member of Parliament for Hull as well as an active satirist. Yet, even so, Marvell was a private citizen intrinsically incapable (as poetry and the vicious, principled caricatures of parliamentarians by maddened Gillray may be incapable) of matching the public civil and governmental balance a national parliament must and could achieve : But didn't in 1644, when Milton published *Areopagitica ; A Speech* [. . .] *For the Liberty of* VNLICENC'D *PRINTING, To the* PARLIAMENT *of* ENGLAND; nor 350 years later in 1994, when fifteen years of overt cronyism and greedy denationalisations had packed both chambers with more "grandees risen from scavenge" than they usually boast. A variant form, the *swung dash* (~), is used in some dictionaries to indicate the headword in illustrative quotations ; Dickinson's famous dashes and their possible variants are considered with 'I heard a Fly buzz—' below.

Longer rules can be fun, as in Sterne's *Tristram Shandy* (a stupendous shaggy-dog story) where four lengths of dash—the ¼- , ½-, ¾-, and inch———represent meditative or wool-gathering pauses of different durations/qualities ; some rules continue for several lines, or pages, as the narrator pauses or nods off. Poetry rarely offers space for this kind of thing, but post-Modernist poetry is almost as likely to deploy variant rules as variant eisthesis ; see Spicer's 'Phonemics', Rothenberg's 'Cokboy', Sobin's 'Eleven Rock Poems', and Padgett's 'Big Bluejay Composition'.[47]

---

[47] All in Hoover, *PostModern American Poetry*.

Borders, implicitly promoted by Humanist concerns with beautifully clear display, were once not uncommon, as in Spenser's *Amoretti and Epithalamion* (p. 121), but went the way of all 'unnecessary' *mise-en-page* with the Enlightenment and machine-press and survived only in facsimiles and fine editions. Studded rules (——♦—— etc.) are used decoratively in collections, especially by American publishers. The rectangular stanzas of Over's '*Wunderkammern*' are boxed with rules, as are some entries in Elson's posthumously edited notebooks, some of Raworth's untitled 'catacoustics' and individual words in his 'Unease' ; full borders remain rare (they were usually woodcut), but may return to the post-metal page.[48]

---

§ Three of the **combinate-marks** have been christened by Nicholson Baker the *commash* (**,—**), *semi-colash* (**;—**), and *colash* (**:—**),[49] to which may be added the *periodash* (**.—**), *question-* and *exclamation-markash* (**?—, !—**), and *lunulashes* (**—()—**). Their history, as Baker laments, is inadequately researched, but (like emoticons) they clearly represent a compensation : though found in some eighteenth-century books their real province is machine-press books of *c.*1800–1920, and their mass die-back (but not quite extinction) coincides with Modernist revalorisation of space. The single dash as pause or disjunction is clearly the basic term which each prefixed mark (or occasionally suffixed, in *reverse commashes* **—,** etc.) colours or qualifies according to its nature. Something of their capacities can be seen in Barrett Browning's 'Lady Geraldine's Courtship' (text from 1856) :

'Quite low-born, self-educated! somewhat gifted though by nature,
And we make a point of asking him,—of being very kind.
You may speak, he does not hear you! and, besides, he writes no satire,—
All these serpents kept by charmers leave the natural sting behind.'

(XI)

'The live air that waves the lilies waves the slender jet of water
Like a holy thought sent feebly up from soul of fasting saint:
Whereby lies a marble Silence, sleeping (Lough the sculptor wrought her),
So asleep she is forgetting to say Hush!—a fancy quaint.

(XXIX)

---

48 Over, *Bread and No Cheese* ; Elson, *A Responsibility to Awe* (Manchester: Carcanet, 2001) ; Raworth, *Collected Poems* (Manchester: Carcanet, 2003).

49 'The History of Punctuation', in *The Size of Thoughts* (London: Chatto, 1996), 82.

'Not so quickly,' she retorted.—'I confess, where'er you go, you
Find for things, names—shows for actions, and pure gold for honour clear:

(XXXIV)

Ever, evermore the while in a slow silence she kept smiling,
But the tears ran over lightly from her eyes and tenderly:—
'Dost thou, Bertram, truly love me? Is no woman far above me
Found more worthy of thy poet-heart than such a one as *I*?'

(Conclusion VIII)

Seen in concert with one another and individual marks, it is clear combinate-marks can be fairly straightforwardly functional, as the exclamation-markash (XXIX) and periodash (XXXIV) are, though the latter embodies slowing, or can catch closely at revealing rhythms of speech, as the commashes (XI) do. Articulation is enriched, and as combinate-marks pepper nineteenth-century poetry (including Browning, Tennyson, Meredith . . .) and prose (Thackeray, Trollope, Eliot, Dickens . . .), besides extending at least to the prose of Woolf, Nabokov, and Updike, one might expect them to have been more widely mourned. The peculiar twentieth-century combination of late-metal-page Modernism (pro-space), editing (anti-*mise-en-page*), and devalued rigour (anti-detail) is probably responsible, and neither scholarship nor the Web have made facsimiles of Victorian work available as they have Renaissance works. Things may change, and combinate-marks have been idiosyncratically revived by Bidart[50] ; those interested in the nineteenth-century at large or its verse in particular should in any case familiarise themselves with what the combinate-marks can do.

---

§ **Signes de renvoi** ('signs of sending back') are "any sign used to associate matter in the text with material added in the margin".[51] The commonest are superscript arabic numerals keyed to foot- or end-notes (as in this book) ; the *degree-sign* (°), *asterisk* (*), *obelus* or *dagger* (†), *double-obelus* (‡), *paraph* (¢, ¶, or ||), *pilcrow* (¶), *paragraphus* or *section-mark* (§), and various other *special sorts* of type also serve as *indices* (the plural of *index*). Some have particular meanings or associations : the

[50] *In the Western Night: Collected Poems 1965–90* (New York: FSG, 1990).
[51] Parkes, *Pause and Effect*, 307.

forms of the paraph derive from upper-case C for *capitulum* (a heading, whence chapter) ; the paragraphus was the *signum sectionis*, formed from two Ss ; the obelus was a nota indicating a scribe's belief that a passage in the copy was corrupt. An obelus following a name indicates death, and crossed-swords death in battle.

& The **ampersand** is an sign for 'and'. There was another form, the *Tironian* sign *7* (invented by Tiro, a freedman of Cicero's), used for *et* (and), while & was used for 'et' in words (as &ernity, b&ter—txtrs, *plus ça change*). When & took over as *et* (from which it is formed—*et* & **&**) it became known as 'and *per se* and', whence 'ampersand'. It serves to disambiguate (or hierarchise) in lists (*a* & *b* and *x* & *y*), but in Renaissance printing most often saved space (within the measure) or filled it, especially in its *swash* (decorative) forms (*&*). Modern use shows both decorative and aggressively functional aspects.

@ The **apestail** (Dutch, *aapestartje*) is used in commerce for 'at [. . .] each', and for 'are playing at' in American journalism (Yankees@Boston). Its principal use now is in *eddresses* and for the letters 'at' in txtng (c@food). All these may turn up in poetry any time soon.

£$€ and other **currency-symbols** have as much to do with poetry as any profession or art, and are found in poems about their normal business, as are ©, ™, and the like (sometimes with satirical intent, as in Raworth's 'And His Share of the Loot, if I Know Shorty Fleming'). Various mathematical notations, including the operators (+/ –/×/÷), infinity (∞), square-root (√), *n*-ary summation (Σ), approximates (≈) and greater/less than or equal to (≤, ≥) may also be seen.[52]

---

§ The **foot**- (or other) **note** and its associated indices is a form of punctuation in its own right.[53] In some poems with authorial notes but no indices, such as *The Waste Land*, it seems desirable to keep notes and text separate—as Eliot did, having supplied notes under protest to prevent his publishers including 'Gerontion' to make up a full book (level 8), and they are usually printed as endnotes (7) : but the *Norton* and other anthologies incorporate Eliot's notes into their own footnotes (5 or 6). Other poems pose other problems. Should Pope's footnotes

52 See Cajori, *A History of Mathematical Notation* (Chicago: Open Court, 1928).

53 especially if the reader obeys a *signe de renvoi* and reads the footnote before continuing the text proper, and in academic work (see Grafton, *The Footnote*).

(p. 124) or Byron's be preserved in annotated editions within the 'poetic' section of each page ? or relegated to small-print ? and if so, what of their indices ? Coleridge's *marginalia* to *The Rime of the Ancient Mariner*, added to the 1802 text in 1817, have no indices and are often omitted, but footnote-text can be integral to a poem (see Harrison's 'The Heartless Art', N1879) though it is commoner to exploit foot- or endnotes intensively in prose, often comically, as in Swift's *A Tale of a Tub* and Nabokov's *Pale Fire*. Factual endnotes or acknowledgements may retrospectively qualify sense, and though such data is usually not associated by any mark with the poem to which it refers is nevertheless a potential form of that poem's punctuation.

——(. . . |☺| . . .)——

The full sense of what is possible with punctuation has been tragicomically demonstrated by the novelist Jonathan Safran Foer, who had already shown himself no mean user of the colon, line-break, and justification by dedicating his novel *Everything is Illuminated* :[54]

Simply and impossibly:
FOR MY FAMILY

His web- and wingding masterpiece, though, is 'A Primer for the Punctuation of Heart Disease',[55] in which he sets out 18 new marks or uses of marks :

- □ the silence mark
- ■ the willed silence mark
- ?? the insistent question mark
- ¡ the unexclamation point, indicating a whisper
- ¡¡ the extraunexclamation point, indicating whispers too quiet to be heard
- !! the extraexclamation point (not used in Foer's family)
- ~ the pedal point, indicating dissolution into suggestive silence
- ↓ the low point, accompanying or replacing statements of dejection
- ❄ the snowflake, indicating a unique familial phrase
- ☺ the corroboration mark
- :: the reversible colon, allowing clauses to be dependent or refer forwards + backwards
- ← the backup, indicating an attempt to start over more honestly

[54] London: Hamish Hamilton, 2002.

[55] *New Yorker*, 10 June 2002, pp. 82–5 ; see also Foer's 'About the Typefaces Not Used in This Edition', in *the Guardian*, 7 Dec. 2002.

{ } should-have brackets, indicating words that should have been spoken

✂ 🕸 the severed web, a Barely Tolerable Substitute approximating to 'I love you'

→|← a nameless Barely Tolerable Substitute approximating to 'I love you'

👂 □ a nameless Barely Tolerable Substitute approximating to 'I love you'

🔒 a nameless Barely Tolerable Substitute approximating to 'I love you'

✕✈ a nameless Barely Tolerable Substitute approximating to 'I love you'

Together, Foer explains, these make possible the following conversation with his father :

"Are you hearing static?
"{I'm crying into the phone.}"
"Jonathan?"
"□"
"Jonathan~"
"■"
"??"
"I::not myself~"
"{A child's sadness is a parent's sadness.}"
"{A parent's sadness is a child's sadness.}"
"←"
"I'm probably just tired¡"
"{I never told you this, because I thought it might hurt you, but in my dreams it was *you*. Not me. *You* were pulling the weeds from my chest.}"
"{I want to love and be loved.}"
"☺"
"☺"
"↓"
"↓"
"🔒"
"☺"
"□↔□↔□"
"↓"
"↓"
"▶▶| ○ |◀◀"
"□ + □ → ■"
"☺"
"👂□"
"⌦⌫"
"◎□❖●◆●¡¤♦⊙●"
"■"
"{I love you.}"
"{I love you. So much.}"

Not since Victor Borge's famous "Phonetic Punctuation" in the 1950s (making all marks audible in speech) has quite so much pointed fun been had. Traditionalists may balk at calling Foer's conversation a poem, but it demonstrates beyond doubt the relative, freeform, exploitative, conventional, expressive, and intense values that any and all things serving as punctuation can and do have, in poetry as elsewhere.

Exemplary Poems

1. 'The Flea' (pp. 14–15)

Major stops divide the nine-line stanzas (three couplets + triplet) into clear and variant patterns (2 ; 2 ; 5 . // 2 . 2 ; 2 . 3 // 2 ? 2 ? 2 ; 1 ; 2 .) mapping an increasing complexity of argument. All make good syntactical sense, but the last stanza needs consideration :

Cruell and ſodaine, hast thou ſince
Purpled thy naile, in blood of innocence ?
Wherein could this flea guilty bee,
Except in that drop which it ſuckt from thee ?
Yet thou triumph'ſt, and ſaiſt that thou
Find'ſt not thy ſelfe, nor mee the weaker now ;
'Tis true, then learne how falſe, feares bee ;
Juſt ſo much honor, when thou yeeld'ſt to mee,
Will waſt, as this flea's death tooke life from thee.

The parallel question-marks easily pass unnoticed as carrying full-stop weight, but what would it mean for the lady to answer either with a firm 'No' ?—that she didn't kill the flea ? wasn't cruel and sudden ? that it was guilty of more than biting her ? Lines 19–20 are an interrogation, demanding 'yes' or 'no' and so loaded that in conceding the self-evident (Yes, I killed it) the lady must admit cruelty, abruption, and slaughter of innocence ; ll. 21–22 are a percontation dismissing any objection the lady might make (though no one needs more reason than being bitten to kill a flea). The questions jointly form a sciscitation : the marks are medial, the whole stanza one period, and the last semi-colon raises the stakes. Closing couplets, as (moralising) summaries, are often (implicitly) preceded by a colon, and within the triplet a colon might be expected to end l. 25, especially given the dependent syntax of ll. 26–27, declaring what the lady will "learne" and the promised retribution of "when [not if] thou yeeld'ſt", "will [not shall] waſt". One could argue a semi-colon diminishes the threat of retribution by allowing ll. 26–7 an independence lessening their promise of justice for the flea's death—but the period of three *semi-cola* ('Did you ? why did you? you triumph ; true triumph, false fears ; you'll learn.') is given impetus by its 2 ? 2 ⸮ 2 ; 1 ; 2 form that would not survive a colon and enhances the articulation ; not a threat, but a promise.

Editors usually leave these major stops alone, but commas are more liable to be changed, probably because they clearly mix syntactic and elocutionary functions :

Marke but this flea, and marke in this,
How little that which thou deny'ſt me is ;
It ſuck'd me first, and now ſucks thee,
And in this flea, our two bloods mingled bee ;

The comma after "flea" (1) passes syntactic muster, but the one after "this" divides verb ("marke") from direct object ("that which thou deny'ſt"). The comma after "flea" (4) also interposes, between object ("flea") and subject ("our two bloods") : reversed order might be held to justify it syntactically—'our bloods are mingled in this flea'; 'in this flea, our bloods are mingled'—but no such practice can be demonstrated in Donne's hand or Marriot's printshop, and elocutionary reading seems preferable.[56] But of what kind ? The syntactic increments of comma, semi-/colon, and full-stop are clear, but elocutionary increments (pause one beat for a comma, two for a semi-colon etc.) are unworkable (try it!), and readers-aloud always have greater freedom of elocutionary than silent readers of syntactic interpretation. Other 1633 commas—"mariage bed, and mariage temple" (13), "Let not to that, ſelfe murder added bee" (17), "thy ſelfe, nor mee" (24), "how falſe, feares bee" (25)—suggest a usage I call the 'emphatic comma' (found in Shakespeare's Folio), cueing emphasis on the following word. One might then represent these lines with italics rather than commas—'marriage bed *and* marriage temple', '*ſelfe* murder', 'thy ſelfe *nor* mee', 'how falſe *feares* bee'—and this makes good sense of ll. 1 + 4 : '*How* little', '*our* two bloods'.

2. 'I heard a Fly buzz—when I died—' (p. 97)

Dickinson's poetry is usually printed with the many dashes identical, but the fascicles suggest she distinguished several varieties. Certainty is impossible—there is, for example, a problem distinguishing dashes from free-floating cross-strokes of 't's—but while a hand may stretch if someone is writing fast, duct is unlikely to change once a hand is settled, and there are instances where Dickinson's normal dash (very short and low) is accompanied by a longer rule.[57] There are also slight changes in the angle of dashes, but these are within normal variation. 'I heard a Fly buzz' is unaffected (though the penultimate dash was omitted by Johnson), but if putatively significant variations were

[56] On Donne's hand see Roth-Schwartz, 'Colon and Semi-Colon in Donne's Prose Letters: Practice and Principle', in *Early Modern Literary Studies*, 3/1 (1997) and online—but this piece is ignorant of Parkes, and exhibits deep confusions.

[57] See e.g. 'It Always felt to me—a wrong' (Johnson 597, *Manuscript Books* 551, l. 7.).

reproduced in a printed edition it would substantially alter some poems, and perhaps her poetry as a whole.[58]

The general issue of Dickinson's punctuation is urgent in every poem. There are commas and exclamation-marks (as in 'The only Ghost I ever saw', Johnson 274, *Manuscript Books* 247–48), question-marks ('Knows how to forget!', J433, *MB* 425, 1220–21), and full-stops ('We talked as Girls do—', J586, *MB* 427–28), but overall her repertoire is minimal, relying on dashes, capitalisation, and line- + stanza-breaks. Dickinson's extraordinary language and perceptions would make her compelling with any punctuation, but the intense, unexpected play of two variables (capitals, dashes) within the largely fixed form (if not always display, pp. 97–9) of lines and quatrains adds a memorable style and to a considerable degree enables the language and perceptions. As deictic punctuation the caps are syntactically inert, and dashes are precisely not stops, leaving questions of syntax permanently open. In the opening lines :

I heard a Fly buzz—when I died—
The Stillness in the Room
Was like the Stillness in the Air—
Between the Heaves of Storm—

The Eyes around—had wrung them dry—

one can see the pattern of the effect with "—when I died—" and "—[/] Between the Heaves of Storm—", which can both be referred backwards or forwards :

I heard a fly buzz. When I died the stillness in the room was like the stillness in the air between the heaves of storm. The eyes around had wrung them dry . . .

I heard a fly buzz when I died. The stillness in the room was like the stillness in the air. Between the heaves of storm the eyes around had wrung them dry . . .

This applies to most dash'd-off phrases, and possibilities rise exponentially as a poem proceeds. Links between Dickinson's poetic and epistolary composition suggests a source for her dash-practice in the lax punctuation of letters in her grand/parents' generations : she retains a vigorous colloquialism but replaces lazy indistinction with principled dissolution. Isolated phrases have values and glint as they could not

[58] On the difficulties in transcribing Dickinson see McGann, *Black Riders*, 26–41.

readily do in runs of conventional syntax, and Dickinson is an outstanding example of a poet whose distinctive personal style turns on deeply unconventional, deeply coherent punctuation.

3. 'September Song' (p. 72)

The most important punctuation is spatial (pp. 73, 100), the poem's display of its maimed identity. Stops articulate simple sentences, but in ll. 8–10 something deeply unusual happens:

(I have made
an elegy for myself it
is true)

Line-breaks are critical, but work in conjunction with the lunulae and the absent comma one might expect after "myself" + absent full-stop one does expect after "true". The result of the absences and lineation is a principled ambiguity : *I have made an elegy for myself it is true* might only mean 'it's true my elegy is for myself'—as all funeral-rites and obsequies are for the survivors—but in Hill's punctuation also means 'yes, my elegy is for myself (as elegies must be) but is nevertheless a true elegy', one to stand up against Adorno's pre-emptive declaration of its barbarity (p. 73). The lunulae parenthesise the only 'I' in the poem, a sign of Hill's refusal to allow inevitable self-mourning to displace the victim he honours, and display with that 'I' the shift from the past ("I have made") to the present ("it [/] is true"), locating it in the only place it could have happened (the poet's perception) and can continue to happen (the poem as it is read). Hill learned what lunulae could do primarily from Eliot, for whom in 'The Hollow Men', 'Ash-Wednesday', and *Four Quartets* they registered and charted what unbelief, conversion, and settled faith could mean to individuals ; he follows Eliot here with a parenthesis as morally alert to reticence as inclusion.

Two small changes between first publication (*Stand* 8.4, 1967) and collection in *King Log* (1968) should be noted : "Zyklon", the gas of the *Sho'ah*, was originally "zyklon", an error (the stuff was patented) "which too much lowered its hateful rank" ; and in the "italicised sub-heading (dedication? epigraph? sub-title?)" ("*born 19.6.32—deported 24.9.42*") Hill changed "a bureaucrat's semi-colon [to] a stone-mason's dash" [59] : the sonnet as headstone.

[59] Ricks, *Force of Poetry*, 298, 302.

4. 'Nearing Forty' (pp. 22–3)

The first oddity is the crotcheted dedication, "[*for John Figueroa*]". It may simply be house-style : it's common to place dedications within lunulae, withdrawing them from the sequence 'title—epigraph—poem' (and when poets read, dedications may be omitted or spoken aside), but crotchets, stronger and rarer, pose a different question. Lowell, whom Walcott knew, wrote 'The Quaker Graveyard in Nantucket' (N1592) "(FOR WARREN WINSLOW, DEAD AT SEA)", and the poem is partly about such drownings ; 'Skunk Hour' (N1601), modelled on one of her poems, is "*(For Elizabeth Bishop)*" ; but 'The March 1' is "[FOR DWIGHT MACDONALD]". This may be variant house-styles, but 'The March' is about an anti-Vietnam demonstration, and crotchets may dissociate MacDonald from Lowell's political opinions to preserve the gift of dedication. If the crotchets in 'Nearing Forty' are Walcott's, therefore, he may intend them to prevent easy identification of Figueroa (1920–99), a distinguished Jamaican educator, cricket historian, poet, and critic, with the "you" the poem addresses. If the dedication were unguarded one might straightforwardly read it as saying Figueroa's "life bled for [/] the household truth", and so on ; with crotchets in place that is less possible. On the other hand, published drafts (pp. 333–4) show the poem was dedicated early in its composition, and suggest Figueroa's implicit presence throughout.

The second oddity is the ellipsis ending the epigraph. In the 'Preface to Shakespeare' Johnson's sentence and paragraph end with "truth.", so the apparent value of the ellipsis, that words are omitted, is misleading. The other value, an uncertain trailing-away of voice, produces a cadence false to Johnson's full-stop after "truth", and alien to his elegant eighteenth-century prose and moral certainty—so the ellipsis can be read as ironising elegant certainty and undermining "the stability of truth".

The poem proper comprises one 32-line sentence of three *semi-cola* (semi-colons in ll. 14, after "rainspout", and 24, after "convectional") ; there are 32 *commata*, and the identical number of lines and *commata* (though the two are often at odds) is probably serendipitous, but interesting given the balanced feel of the poem. Each semi-colon clearly performs its 'turn' rather than 'listing' function : the first comes after water flowing downwards, the second after water evaporating upwards, so these turns (like the corners of a coat-hanger) are what allows the thought developing away from the initial "early-rising rain" (2) to be modulated back towards the terminal "lightly falling rain" (30). Each also marks emotional resolution, turns towards the upbeat ("; glad" +

"; [/] or you will rise"), mapping the poem's emotional cycle onto the underlying water-cycle of rain, evaporation, and more rain. Each *semi-colon* is shorter than the last (13½ lines, 10½, 8), and the number of commas in each (13, 10, 6) decreases disproportionally because there are more in the first five lines (2, 1, 2, 1, 1) than the last five (0, 1, 1, 2, 0), reflecting development from a troubled, alert opening to a more accepting, restful close. The terminal full-stop, conventional as it is, carries weight after such a long sentence (and short last line), bringing the poem to a definite and balanced end at a point of achieved complexity. Walcott's willingness to have a full-stop (by no means compulsory) reads against the ellipsis which replaced the full-stop in the epigraph and undermined the stability of Johnson's "truth". There are also two hyphens : one creates "early-rising" (2) because 'early rising rain' would be ambiguous, the other splits "gutter- [/] ing" (13–14) between lines (p. 24).

Exercises: Pointing it out

1. Given the way punctuation is/n't taught it is hard to learn to see punctuation-marks as faithfully as words—hence my use of spaces before some stops and tonal indicators. As with other kinds of perception only practice establishes habit : begin by choosing a few short poems of different kinds and dates, print versions with the marks enlarged or otherwise displayed, and analyse the repertoire in use ; you might also display space with colour.

2. It is an object lesson in differing understandings to ask students 'wholly to depunctuate' a poem and compare results. The exercise can be done individually by creating progressively depunctuated copies, removing families of marks in order, deictic punctuation, stanza- and line-breaks, interword-spaces : line them up and compare the articulation lost at each stage.

3. If you can work with someone, each depunctuate a poem the other doesn't know (sonnets are good), hand over the result, and each try to repunctuate ; then compare results with originals. How do your and poets' understandings of punctuating compare ? The exercise can be interestingly varied by choosing a highly spatial and highly marked poem, and instead of depunctuating, repunctuate by substituting marks for space and space for marks : how close and communicable an equivalence can you find ?

4. Choose an Early Modern poem or chunk of dramatic verse (Shakespeare is good) and compare the original with as many modernised editions as you can find, analysing and characterising the changes made in each. How many distinct operations does modernisation involve in each case (from changes of basic fount upwards) ? and how do the modernising practices of distinct periods relate to the *Zeitgeist* of each and to senses of authority ?

5. Read chosen poems aloud and try to deliver the punctuation. Borge-style noises are fun, but in verse-speaking the issue of audible punctuation is serious : Burton (again) had an astonishing ability to display stanza-forms with his voice, but shading stops is tough. To begin you might try Heaney's 'The Strand at Lough Beg', first exaggerating the presence and absence of commas with extended or minimised pauses, then scaling down the exaggeration until you reach a level that combines aural display with smooth delivery.

Chapter Glossary?

apostrophe : the mark ', used with or without 's' to indicate possession (the genitive case), or the elision of a letter.

braces : curly brackets, marked '{ }' ; a single brace is conventionally used to indicate a triplet within couplet-rhyme.

brackets : a generic term covering angle-brackets, braces, crotchets, and lunulae ; all may be used singly, but crotchets and lunulae normally pair to create parentheses isolating a word or phrase.

colon/s : the second-heaviest stop, marked ':' ; conventionally implies a completion of the immediate sense and a logical or dependent relationship between *cola*.

colon, cola : the part(s) into which a period is divided by colons.

comma/s : the fourth and lightest stop, marked ',' ; conventionally implies the completion of a sub-clause or clause, and used in pairs to create parentheses.

comma(ta) : the part(s) into which a period (or smaller unit of syntax) is divided by commas.

crotchets : square brackets, marked '[ ]' ; conventionally used to distinguish editorial comments and emendations from authorial prose.

dash : a rule and variety of comma, marked '—' ; conventionally used, in script, typescript, and word-processing (though not in print) singly with a space on either side, simultaneously to distinguish and link a sequence of clauses, and in pairs to create parentheses.

deictic : of punctuation, used to emphasize a word or phrase ; distinguished from spatial, elocutionary, and syntactic punctuation.

dis/aggregators : the family of brackets, slashes, and inverted commas, which group or isolate a/word/s.

ellipsis : the omission of a word or words, and the indication of such omission with three suspension-marks, '. . .'.

elocutionary : of punctuation, indicating speech-derived pauses ; distinguished from spatial, deictic, and syntactic punctuation.

em-rule : in printing, —, a rule as long as a lower-case 'm' ; often used for the dash.

emoticon : a tonal indicator resembling a face created with punctuation-marks.

en-rule : in printing, a rule (–) as long as a lower-case 'n' ; slightly longer than the hyphen and used for dates and page-ranges etc. (9–13, London–Birmingham train).

exclamation-mark : a tonal indicator, usually of rising pitch and volume, used (instead of a full-stop) to indicate exclamations, marked '!'; may be used both medially and terminally.

full-stop : (or in the USA, *period*) the heaviest stop, marked '.' **;** conventionally required at the end of a period or sentence.

hyphen : used to join two words into one, or to join the parts of a word split between lines, marked '-'.

iconicity : here, the capacity of a mark, letter, or word to become an icon, as lunulae of lips, O of a mouth etc.

inverted commas : one of the dis/aggregators, used to indicate direct speech and quotations, marked " " or ″ ″ ; may also be single (' ', ′ ′) ; as *scare quotes* indicate a suspension of sense, or distrust of a word. Conventions of use vary historically and culturally ; the modern English set of conventions dates only from 1857.

lunula/e : round brackets, marked '( )' ; historically used in many conventions, including the indication of stage-directions, attributions of speech, comparisons, quotations, *sententae*, and other cruces of argument ; commonly used to indicate both subordination and emphasis ; invented by Colluccio Salutati (1331–1406) in *c.*1399.

nota/e : marks made or printed in the margins of texts ; distinguished from punctuation within the text.

paragraph : the division of stichic verse or continuous prose into groups of lines, marked by the indentation of the first or (modern business-style) a blank line ; a unit of argument and emotion ; the oldest surviving form of Western spatial punctuation.

parenthesis : in rhetoric, one clause intercluded within another ; such clauses may in written texts be marked with paired commas, dashes, or lunulae, and the parenthesis comprises the opening mark, alphanumeric contents, and closing mark.

percontation-mark : an archaic tonal indicator of percontations (questions open to any answer), marked '⸮'.

period : a classical, rhetorically defined unit of syntax and argument, composed of *cola* and *commata* ; closer to the modern paragraph than the modern sentence ; latterly, and in the USA, a full-stop.

punctuation : a variety of marks, spaces, and other signs (such as distinguishing type-faces or founts) placed within the text to articulate, dis/ambiguate, or otherwise refine and/or display the sense.

question-mark : a tonal indicator, usually of rising pitch, used (instead of a full-stop) to indicate questions, marked '?' ; may be used both medially and terminally.

semi-colon/s : the third heaviest stop, marked ';' ; conventionally implies completion of the immediate sense, and <u>either</u> a development in the sense between *semi-cola* <u>or</u> the itemization of each *semi-colon* ; invented by Pietro Bembo (1470–1547) in Venice in the 1490s explicitly as a stop intermediate between the colon and the comma.

semi-colon, semi-cola : the part/s of a sentence between semi-colons, and/or between a semi-colon and a heavier stop.

sentence : in modern use, the largest unit of syntax, composed of one or more clauses, and normally containing at least one grammatical subject, one in/transitive verb, and if appropriate an object ; typographically, sentences begin with a capital letter and end with a full-stop.

Punctuation

signe/s de renvoi : 'sign/s of sending back' ; any mark/s used (typically as an index) to associate matter in the text with added material (including *marginalia* and *foot-* or *endnotes*).

slash/es : a sub-family of dis/aggregators comprising the forward slash (or *solidus*), marked '/', used singly to indicate alternatives (as 's/he') and line-breaks, and doubly (//) to indicate stanza-breaks ; the vertical slash, marked '|' (or in superscript '$^{|}$'), which may indicate foot-division or caesurae ; and the backslash, marked '\'.

spatial : of punctuation, deploying space rather than a mark or face etc. ; distinguished from deictic, elocutionary, and syntactic punctuation.

stops : a family of punctuation-marks comprising the comma, semi-colon, colon, and full-stop, syntactically indicating some degree of completion of sense, and elocutionarily suggesting a pause or emphasis.

suspension-mark/s : a single suspension-mark (.) indicates the suspension of one or more letters (as in etc., ed.) ; three suspension-marks, usually spaced (. . .) indicate an *ellipsis*.

syntactic : of punctuation, indicating construction of sense ; distinguished from deictic, elocutionary, and spatial punctuation.

virgula/e : the medieval family of commas, including the *virgula suspensiva* (now the solidus) and *virgula plana* (now the dash).

5
Lineation

in simple, shining lines, in pages stretched
DEREK WALCOTT, 'Nearing Forty'

Christopher Ricks once offered this rule-of-thumb : that whereas prose must go to the end of the line, in poetry it's an option—that is, poetry uses one additional form of punctuation, the line-break, a moment of spatial

organisation different from every mark and other space. It's a bald way to tell poetry from prose—a distinction less obvious than it seems : some prose is metrical or rhymed, some poetry blank free verse—but holds good as hairy ones fail, covering *prose-poems*, those always exercising the option, with stichic, stanzaic, and free verse. It is thus important to indicate *lineation* (division into lines) in poetry you quote : in *indented* quotations all layout should be reproduced ; in *embedded* quotations (usually set off by inverted commas within prose) line-breaks are represented by a crotcheted forward slash [/], stanza-breaks (blank lines) by a double-slash [//]. There is no agreed way of indicating eisthesis in transcription, and simple rhyme-display can be ignored, but consequential layout may be indicated by a brief note following the slash, as '[/ tab]', '[/ centred line]', etc.

In regular metres and forms there are clear constraints on how line-breaks can be used, though division of a line into halves is always possible with medial line-breaks (as when speakers change mid-line in verse-drama). Equally, the freedom of free verse has much to do with using line-breaks at will, but there are at every line-break questions of what words frame it and whether the line is end-stopped (line-break reinforced by a punctuation-mark) or enjambed (line-break as punctuation in its own right). Both affect a line-break's value, and (as with lunulae) meaning is determined by context ; in enjambment across stanza-breaks (the frequency of which depends on the stanza) stakes will be as higher as stanza-breaks are heavier. These lines are from Heaney's 'The Strand at Lough Beg', dedicated to his cousin Colum McCartney, murdered in the Northern Irish 'Troubles' while driving :

> What blazed ahead of you ? A faked road block ?
> The red lamp swung, the sudden brakes and stalling
> Engine, voices, heads hooded and the cold-nosed gun ?
>
> What BLAZED | aHEAD | of YOU ? | a FAKED | ROAD BLOCK ?
> The RED | LAMP SWUNG, | the SUD- | den BRAKES | and STAL- | ling
> ENgine, | VOIces, HEADS HOOD- | ed and | the COLD-| NOSED GUN ?

"stalling" creates an unstressed hyperbeat ; "Engine, voices," both invert the iambic metre : so after "the sudden brakes" the impetus of rising rhythm is lost until "the cold-nosed gun". But metre does not work alone, for the line-break—"and stalling [/] Engine,"—makes the falling rhythm cough or stutter, miming the treacherous car-engine ; the effect is reinforced by commas after "Engine" and "voices", making it as impossible for rhythm to take off as it was for McCartney to drive safely away. What Heaney achieves cannot be described without reference to the lineation separating "stalling" from "Engine".

As with other punctuation, a good way to see how lineation matters is to do without. Here is the first paragraph of Tennyson's dramatic monologue 'Tithonus' (N1006) set as prose[1] :

> The woods decay, the woods decay and fall, the vapours weep their burthen to the ground, man comes and tills the field and lies beneath, and after many a summer dies the swan. Me only cruel immortality consumes : I wither slowly in thine arms, here at the quiet limit of the world, a white-haired shadow roaming like a dream the ever-silent spaces of the East, far-folded mists, and gleaming halls of morn.

Some blank-verse lines signal their metrical integrity, but display lineation and all is clearer :

> The woods decay, the woods decay and fall,
> The vapours weep their burthen to the ground,
> Man comes and tills the field and lies beneath,
> And after many a summer dies the swan.
> Me only cruel immortality

---

[1] Tithonus loved and was beloved of Aurora, Goddess of Dawn. Granted immortal life, he forgot to ask for eternal youth : hopelessly infirm, he now wishes only to die.

Consumes : I wither slowly in thine arms,
Here at the quiet limit of the world,
A white-haired shadow roaming like a dream
The ever-silent spaces of the East,
Far-folded mists, and gleaming halls of morn.

Each of ll. 1–4 is self-contained, end-stopped, and a parallel clause. The full-stop after "swan", coinciding with a line-break and completing a sentence and blank quatrain, is followed, in strong contrast, by the first enjambed line—but syntax requires only one word from l. 6. One's ear has adjusted to end-stopped lines, so "immortality [/] Consumes :" effectively mimics Tithonus's unending life, forcing readers to carry on when they expected to be able to stop, and stressing "Consumes" in its endless present tense. End-stopping returns for two lines, then enjambment again, delicately creating in "dream [/] The ever-silent spaces" an odd half-silence as the reading voice wants to stop but is forced to continue (never silent). The value of this second enjambment is more ghostly (or dream-like) because syntax requires all of both lines, and there is no equivalent to the early pause enforced in l. 6 by the semi-colon. The last line metrically echoes the first, a comma after the second foot producing a distinctly broken rhythm to end the paragraph audibly as it ends syntactically.

The medial pauses created by the semi-colon in l. 6 and commas in ll. 1 + 10 are called *caesurae* (from Latin, *caedo*, to cut). Some people argue that all lines have a natural caesura whether or not enforced by punctuation ; I think this true only of lines longer than a tetrameter. Up to eight beats, the line can be (though need not be) whole ; unpunctuated pentameters tend to split 4–6 or 6–4, and unpunctuated longer lines almost always split somewhere in the middle, like a tree-branch grown too long. Common metre (*a8b6c8b6*) probably originated as a heptametric couplet (*a14a14*) that became a single-rhymed quatrain when the last three feet of each line broke off at an 8–6 caesura to become *b*-rhyme trimeters ; short metre (*a6b6c8b6*) similarly derives from poulter's measure (*a12a14*). In unpunctuated lines caesurae naturally occur roughly in the middle, but poets can force them back- or forwards with punctuation, as Tennyson did with his semi-colon after "Consumes", producing a 2–8 split. Arguably, Heaney's "Engine, voices, heads hooded and the cold-nosed gun?" has two caesurae, commas creating a 2–2–6 split, but many critics use caesura only of a single distinctive break, and would call what Heaney's commas create 'pauses' (or equivalent). *In extremis*, multiple caesurae can all but destroy a line's identity, and in verse-drama pose a real problem for actors : try observing the punctuation and respecting the metrical integrity while saying Lear's "Neuer, neuer, neuer, neuer, neuer." or Ferdinand's "Couer her face : Mine eyes dazell : ſhe di'd yong." (in *The Dutcheſſe of Malfy*).

In any regular form caesurae can be delicately manipulated. One principal effect, much used in blank verse, is obtained by having caesurae in the same place in successive lines, giving a sequence such as 6–4 / 6–4 / 6–4. If there is punctuation at caesurae and lines are enjambed, the two post-cæsural feet of each line + the three pre-caesural feet of the next create lines of the right length (– 4/6 – 4/6 – 4/6). Eyes see printed lines, but ears begin to hear caesura-to-caesura lines in counterpoint, sense reading against layout to create a feeling of never reaching a finish, the end of each line in mid-clause and the end of each *clause* (p. 264) in mid-line. Such *rocking lineation* is a common engine of Shakespeare's blank-verse speeches, and the closed couplet with which he often ends a way of braking its momentum.

A good example comes in *The Prelude*, of which (in full form) there are two texts : *1805*, the first complete version, and *1850*, published posthumously. This is I.412–27 in *1805*, Wordsworth remembering a childhood evening when he 'borrowed' a boat, rowed onto Ullswater (in the English Lake District), and became frightened by a mountain which from a new perspective suddenly loomed over him (the verse-paragraph ends with l. 427) :

With trembling hands I turned
And through the silent water stole my way
Back to the cavern of the willow-tree.
There, in her mooring-place, I left my bark
And through the meadows homeward went with grave
And serious thoughts ; and after I had seen
That spectacle, for many days my brain
Worked with a dim and undetermined sense
Of unknown modes of being. In my thoughts
There was a darkness—call it solitude
Or blank desertion—no familiar shapes
Of hourly objects, images of trees,
Of sea or sky, no colours of green fields,
But huge and mighty forms that do not live
Like living men moved slowly through my mind
By day, and were the trouble of my dreams.

In most good verse there is a swirling relationship between clauses, grammatical units, and lines, poetic units ; variations produced by clauses shorter or longer than a line are instrumental in preventing dullness. Wordsworth wrote great blank verse in this manner, and the first part of this, to "modes of being." (1. 420), is a fair sample : read it aloud, punching through enjambed line-breaks and pausing appropriately at punctuation-marks, and you will hear (and see) patternings of clause against line. But after the full-stop in l. 420 Wordsworth begins to do something more muscular with rocking lineation. A medial full-stop creates the heaviest possible caesura, demanding a substantial pause by splitting l. 420 7–3 ; l. 421, split 5–5, also has a heavy caesura forced by a dash. The first counterpoint-line has only eight beats, –3/5– ("In my thoughts [/] There was a darkness—"), but its isolating caesurae are heavy, metrical brevity appropriate to its meaning, and l. 422 is again split 5–5 by a dash, creating a full-length counterpoint-line, –5/5– ("—call it solitude [/] Or blank desertion—"), as a dash'd-off parenthesis. Line 423 is also split 5–5, creating a second full-length counterpoint-line ("—no familiar shapes [/] Of hourly objects,"). As all three counterpoint-lines begin and end in mid-iamb they become <u>trochaic</u> pentameters :

> IN my | THOUGHTS / there | WAS a | DARKness—
> CALL it | SOLi- | TUDE / or | BLANK de- | SERtion—
> NO fa- | MILiar | SHAPES / of | HOURly | OBjects,

To hear this falling rhythm emerge from blank verse creates aural interference, a metrical disturbance analogous to the mental disturbance the lines report. Admirable craftsmanship continues as the energy of rocking lineation is harnessed : the caesura in l. 423 is weaker than its predecessors, forced only by a comma ; another comma end-stops the line, and in l. 424, also end-stopped with a comma, the caesura moves back a beat to split the line 4–6. The welter of short clauses bleeds off momentum, as an eddy detracts from a current ; there is steady backward movement of caesurae, successive lines from 420 splitting 7.3 / 5–5 / 5–5 / 5,5 / 4,6 : the weight of the caesura lessening from full-stop to dash to comma as it retreats. In the last three lines, 425–7, Wordsworth reaps the profit of his labour, producing a huge clause enjambed through two line-breaks : in reading aloud the length of breath required is unexpected, and one wants to stop after "forms", "live", and "men", and even then must go beyond "mind" to gasp out "By day" and gratefully, finally, reach a comma and draw breath. Effectively 22 beats without pause (natural pauses coincide with and are negated by enjambment), this long clause interrupts the movement of the caesura as the "huge and mighty forms" interrupt the tenor of Wordsworth's days, but l. 427 splits 2–8, completing the retreat (1–9 is very rare) and bringing the verse-paragraph to an aurally satisfying close.

What such structuring achieves can be judged by comparison with *1850* (N783), with which Wordsworth had been fiddling for forty-five years :

With trembling oars I turned,
And through the silent water stole my way
Back to the covert of the willow tree ;
There in her mooring place I left my bark,—
And through the meadows homewards went, in grave
And serious mood ; but after I had seen
That spectacle, for many days, my brain
Worked with a dim and undetermined sense
Of unknown modes of being ; o'er my thoughts
There hung a darkness, call it solitude
Or blank desertion. No familiar shapes
Remained, no pleasant images of trees,
Of sea or sky, no colors of green fields ;
But huge and mighty forms, that do not live
Like living men, moved slowly through the mind
By day, and were a trouble to my dreams.

Stops and a commash are added, lessening ambiguities and eliminating difficulties of reading aloud ; rocking lineation is eliminated and phrasing made more conventional, allowing clichés distorted in *1805* ("a trouble to" rather than "the trouble of", for example). Lines 393–400 in *1850* might be thought syntactically clearer than ll. 420–7 in *1805*, but to my mind (and ears) the stopping in *1850* is generally much less coherent than in *1805*, and *1850* infinitely poorer as poetry : Wordsworth would have done better to leave well alone.

Heaney, Tennyson, and Wordsworth variously suggest what can be done with heroic lines, the spine of canonical verse from Chaucer to Arnold (*c.*1380–1900) ; with other kinds of line come different problems and opportunities. One obvious possibility is rather than having lines simply follow one another, to set them *antiphonally* against one another : the basic models are classical dialogue-poems, call-and-response structures in the Christian liturgy, and hymns with *versicle* + chorus. Sacred lyrics like Herbert's are frequently antiphonal, and eisthetic display of rhyme and stanza-construction in secular lyrics readily creates a similarly 'doubled' voice, as in Christina Rossetti's early observation 'On Albina' :

> The roses lingered in her cheeks,
>   When fair Albina fainted ;
> Oh! gentle Reader, could it be
>   That fair Albina painted ?

The cross-pairings of sense (ll. 1–2 ; 3–4), eisthesis (ll. 1 + 3, 2 + 4), and rhyme (ll. 2 + 4) give even a slight verse in common metre sturdily memorable construction, and equivalent effects are normative in lyric stanzas.

Marvell pointed one way of developing antiphony in 'An Horatian Ode' by choosing a 4–4–3–3 (rather than 4–3–4–3) form (N486; text from 1681, Bodleian MS Eng.Poet.d.49) :

> He nothing common did, or mean,
> Upon that memorable Scene ;
>   But with his keener eye
>   The axes edge did trye.
> Nor call'd the Gods with vulgar spight
> To vindicate his helplesse right ;
>   But bow'd his comely head
>   Downe, as upon a bed.

Charles I's gracious and fearless behaviour at his execution in 1649 (which Marvell witnessed) was widely bruited, and Marvell honoured it despite his political opposition to Charles : the antiphonal trimetric couplets, reinforced by their parallel "But" beginnings and the intervening "Nor", grant Charles a cutting brevity of his own. Morality and politics momently fuse, and the commentary on a dead King and subsequently Cromwell as successive ruler make possible the final double-edged judgement of the poem :

> Besides the force it° has to fright *Cromwell's sword*
> The spirits of the shady night ;
>   The same Arts that did gaine
>   A Pow'r must it maintaine.

Elegy and proverbial warning, the ending on a trimetric couplet is predictable but acquires from its identity as a *semi-colon*, antiphonal apposition to 'shady spirits' (like Charles's ?), and compaction a caustic force longer lines would lose : live by the sword, die by the sword.

The antiphonal voice can expand to become the major or only voice of a poem, and in doing so is typically embodied in short lines that refuse the fullness of heroic sound, pitching themselves as a counter-voice to a heroic normality present only by implication. Emerson's 'Ode' (N943) of 1847 ends with an interesting example :

> The Cossack eats Poland,
> Like stolen fruit ;
> Her last noble is ruined,
> Her last poet mute :
> Straight, into double band
> The victors divide ;
> Half for freedom strike and stand;—
> The astonished Muse finds thousands at her side.

Alienated observation of Russian imperial counter-insurgency (after the Polish uprising of 1831–2) fills the short lines, but the celebratory greeting of renewed uprising (in 1846) is heroic (with an initial hyper-beat), and with it scorn evaporates. The same implicit contrast underlies Vendler's acute observation that "Heaney, writing *North* [1975], found himself looking to the 'thin' music of poetry written in the Irish language for a positive alternative body to the broad (and colonizing) placidities of the English pentameter"[2]—and the famous 'Bog People' poems from *North*, including 'Bog Queen', 'The Grauballe Man', and 'Punishment' (p. 167) are in short two- and three-stress lines quite distinct from the tetrameters and heroics of earlier work like 'Digging' (N1899) and 'Death of a Naturalist'.

At the other extreme, antiphonal structure can be reduced to the bob-line, commonly comic, but capable of many moods in *echo verse* (where the last syllable/s of a line 'reply' to themselves with a shifted meaning, as 'wholly/*Holy*'). The best-known echo-verse is Herbert's 'Heaven', where God (or Church) do the replying, but such sacred use is uncommon (Herbert was imitating his brother Herbert of Cherbury's 'Echo in a Church' and 'Echo to a Rock') ; more suggestive are Webster's *Dutcheſſe of Malfy* 5.3, where the echo warns from the duchess's grave, and the famous terminal bobs ("nevermore!") of Poe's 'The Raven' (N977), which come close to echo through the density of rhymes. Bobs are capable of melancholy in their own right, as in Betjeman's 'I. M. Walter Ramsden', beginning :

2 Vendler, *The Breaking of Style*, 3.

Dr. Ramsden cannot read *The Times* obituary to-day
  He's dead.
Let monographs on silk worms by other people be
  Thrown away
  Unread
For he who best could understand and criticize them, he
  Lies clay
  In bed.

The extreme heterometric contrast and tolling rhymes of the double-bobs offset the comedic manner initially generated by the pathos (and bathos) of "He's dead". More subtly, and far more terrifyingly, Snodgrass used rhyming trimetric bobs to clip the pronouncements of Magda Goebbels giving poison to her six children in the ruinous heart of Hitler's Berlin :

Open wide, now, little bird ;
I who sang you your first word
Soothe away every sound you've heard
    Except your Leader's voice.
Close your eyes, now ; take your death.
Once we slapped you to take breath.
Vengeance is mine, the Lord God saith
    And cancels each last choice.

Much is carried by the triple rhymes, but the counter-pronouncements of the trimeters ("Except", "cancels"), confirmed by their own terminating alliteration and rhymes ("Leader's voice", "last choice"), convey the method in the madness with appalling brevity.[3]

The logical opposite of a bob, an extended line, doesn't seem to have a name, but can be called a *pronged* line. *Prongs* are commonest as terminal alexandrines, as in the Spenserian stanza, the trimetric sestets (*ababcc12*) of Jonson's 'Ode to Himself' (N336), and the complex stanzas of Berryman's 'Homage to Mistress Bradstreet' (N1546 ; usually *a10b10c6b8d10d10b6a12*) and Holmes's 'The Chambered Nautilus' (N974 ; *a10a6b6b10b10c6c12*). This last looks like rhyme royal (heroic *ababbcc*) with couplets substituted for cross-rhyme (*aabbbcc*) + triple bob + prong (*aa6b6bbc6c12*)—suggesting inspiration by Wordsworth, who borrowed pronged rhyme royal (*ababbcc12*) from the prologue to Milton's 'On the Morning of Christ's Nativity' for 'Resolution and

[3] Betjeman, *Collected Poems*, 197 ; Snodgrass, *The Fuehrer Bunker*, 185.

Independence' (N394, 790), and created pronged tetrametric octets (*ababccdd12*) for 'Ode to Duty' as well as heterometrically pronged sestets (tetrametric *ababc10c12*) for 'Beggars'. Medial prongs are rarer, but occur in some couplet verse, providing (like inset triplets) an emphatic variation ; here is Dryden getting excited by 'Lucretius, The Fourth Book. *Concerning the Nature of Love*' (text from *Sylvæ*, 1685, omitting two swash braces and turn-downs) :

> Which never wou'd thoſe wretched Lovers do,
> But that the common heats of Love they know ;
> The pleaſure therefore muſt be ſhar'd in common too. (p. 92)
>
> Hence Families ſuch different figures take,
> And represent their Anceſtors in face, and Hair, and make.
> Becauſe of the ſame Seed, the voice, and hair,
> And ſhape, and face, and other members are,
> And the ſame antique mould the likeneſs does prepare. (p. 93)

The first and third prongs ("The pleaſure [. . .]" + "And the ſame [. . .]") are alexandrines, but "And repreſent [. . .]" is a whopping fourteener made odder by the 'quadruplet' it technically prevents but cannot make invisible (Hair/hair/are/prepare). In the last prong there is a touch of versifying convenience, but the first (its medial caesura creating even halves with "muſt" as the grammatical *copula*) more than carries the satirical weight of its bulking tautology ("ſhar'd in common too"), and the fourteener may embody differing 'lines of descent'. Medial prongs are prescribed in short metre (trimetric, *abc8b*), used for hymns like Hatch's 'Breathe on me, Breath of God', and found in complex stanza-forms like that of Donne's 'The Indifferent' (heroic, *a8b12b14ac8c8cdd*), where identifying ll. 2–3 as a poulter's measure (*b12b14*) pronged into a miniature version of itself (*a8 . . . a10*) is helpful in considering tone. Where measure is established, however temporarily, prongs can manifest in free verse, as in Herd's 'Ophelia's Confession' :

> It was far too pretty, but I had to improvise
> and I was a poet, far more than him,
> who threw out every word he ever thought
> as if that might have kept his sorry life afloat.[4]

[4] *Dead Redhead* (Newcastle: Bloodaxe, 2001).

The Shakespearian heroics intimated in the title are approximated in the first two lines and achieved in the third, but promptly subverted by the alexandrine, a failed effort to swim embodied in its subjunctive mood, brief extension "afloat", and definite termination.

Long lines are used in their own right, but have never been favoured in the Petrarchan manner. In post-medieval English, after the demise of the fourteener and poulter's measure (rare after *c.*1600), they almost always have to be read against the heroic lines they conspicuously aren't (pp. 36–7) : adoption of a long line is not necessarily anti-heroic, but is usually (co)un(ter)-heroic, searching for a quality heroics wouldn't allow. Blake's fourteeners (as in *The Book of Thel*) accommodate his prophetic voice and style, and Kipling's in some of the *Barrack-Room Ballads* (including 'Danny Deever', 'Mandalay', 'The Men that Fought at Minden', and 'Cholera Camp') allow regionally class-specific speech to attain moral pungency.[5] Clough's verse-novel octameters are chattily intimate ; Poe's paeonic tetrameters (in 'The Raven') and Browning's trochaic sesquiheptameters (in 'A Toccata of Galuppi's') are tumblingly musical. As these examples suggest, the nineteenth century saw the long line return from exile : add a few long-line poems by Tennyson ('Locksley Hall' etc.) and many by Swinburne and Dowson, and it is clear there was growing dissatisfaction with heroics—probably related to their imperial inflation by Victorian pride and jingoism. Stages of reaction can be seen : in Dowson's 'Non sum qualis eram bonae sub regno Cynarae' (N1211)—a Horatian tag meaning roughly 'I'm not as I was in good Cynara's day'—a bobbed alexandrine sestet is enough to convey wearied decadence :

> All night upon mine heart I felt her warm heart beat,
> Night-long within mine arms in love and sleep she lay ;
> Surely the kisses of her bought red mouth were sweet ;
> But I was desolate and sick of an old passion,
>   When I awoke and found the dawn was grey :
> I have been faithful to thee, Cynara! in my fashion.

For Swinburne, however, reaction was fiercer, and his 'Hymn to Proserpine [/] (After the Proclamation in Rome of the Christian faith)' is in anapæstic hexameters with free catalexis and iambic substitution : hardly the Anglican way of addressing Christ :

[5] Those surprised by praise of Kipling might consult his *Complete Barrack-Room Ballads* (London: Methuen, 1973).

Thou hast conquered, O pale Galilean ; the world has grown grey
from thy breath ;
We have drunken of things Lethean, and fed on the fullness of death.
Laurel is green for a season, and love is sweet for a day ;
But love grows bitter with treason, and laurel outlives not May.
Sleep, shall we sleep after all ? for the world is not sweet in the end ;
For the old faiths loosen and fall, the new years ruin and rend.

Given the medial and terminal rhymes and very evenly central caesurae, this could be called cross-rhymed trimetric quatrains laid out as couplets, but the long lines acquire an identity of their own that takes them beyond the comic trip of anapæsts to a bitter fluency, rhyming and verbal richness thrown against the colourless Christianity they condemn. More reasonable, but similarly overgoing the galumph of fourteeners to find in them a space for defiance, is the rebuke of Kipling's generic 'Tommy' (or British soldier ; N1181) :

We aren't no thin red 'eroes, nor we aren't no blackguards too,
But single men in barricks, most remarkable like you ;
An' if sometimes our conduck isn't all your fancy paints,
Why, single men in barricks don't grow into plaster saints ;

As these examples show, neoclassical long lines (mostly duple hex- to octameters, triple tetra- to hexameters, and quadruple tri- or tetrameters) have qualities, and poets still resort to them on occasion ; mostly comic.[6] The sustained Modernist reaction against heroics—"(To break the pentameter, that was the first heave)", as Pound has it in *Canto* LXXXI—took in the end a decisively different form, most closely anticipated not by any published Victorian poets just mentioned, but in Britain by Hopkins (1844–89), unpublished until 1920, and in America by Whitman (1819–92), furiously condemned from 1855. Coming to grips with them requires going back to a medieval Northern European conception of the poetic line, and forward to a new conceptual poetics of the line, neither based on neoclassical feet in any number.

Milton wasn't joking when he complained of the "troublesome and <u>modern</u> bondage of Rhyming" (N421). Rhyme is now sufficient in many minds to define poetry, and manages to lock down the neoclassical foot-based line as a primary unit defined by spatial display + aural position—but no classical poetry rhymes, and 'Petrarchan' rhyming

[6] Eliot's 'Macavity the Mystery Cat', for example, is in deutero-paeonic (uxuu) tetrameters and sesquitrimeters (14 or 16 beats).

exploded from Sicily across Europe precisely because it was enchantingly new. In the older cultures across which Humanism with its new and neoclassical burdens flooded, neither rhyme nor classical prosody were necessarily normative ; Germanic cultures had traditions related to earlier Greek models than those the Romans adopted, refined, and passed on. Old English (*c.* 500–1066) used *alliterating hemistiches*, half-lines bound by repeated sounds and rhythmic patterns ; *Beowulf* (N2) begins :

Hwæt wē Gār-Dena   in geārdagum,
þēodcyninga   þrym gefrūnon,   [þ = unvoiced 'th']
hū ðā æþelingas   ellen fremedon.[7]   [ð = voiced 'th']

This manner of composition originated in *oral formulaism*, a bardic technique in which a stock of hemistiches covering typical places, times, and actions is learned and freely drawn on in live performance ; ask the bard for the same tale two days in a row and you'd get the same narrative, but not in exactly the same (hemi + hemi) stich combinations. A similar practice explains *stock epithets* in Homeric epic (strong-thewed Achilles, the wine-dark sea, etc.), prefabricated units occurring many times in a narrative. Conventions of alliterative and rhythmic linkage are complex, but in adapted form clearly underlie the *Middle-English* (1066–1500) line of Langland's *Piers the Ploughman* (N71), where medial points usually indicate hemistiches (p. 114) ; similarly, *Sir Gawayne and the Grene Knyght* begins :

Siþen þe sege and þe assaut watz sesed at Troye,
þe borȝ brittened and brent to brondeȝ and askez,   [ȝ = 'gh' or 'y']
þe tulk þat þe trammes of tresoun þer wroȝt
Watz tried for his tricherie, þe trewest on erþe :[8]

Though medial points are not used, hemistichic construction is always audible, and in the fourth line becomes explicit with the comma ; each stanza, however, ends with a rhyming tail (or *wheel*)—"Where were and wrake and wonder [/] Bi syþez hatz wont þerinne, [/] and oft boþe blysse and blunder [/] Ful skete hatz skyfted synne."[9]—and this

[7] In Heaney's translation, "So. The Spear-Danes in days gone by [/] and the kings who ruled them had courage and greatness. [/] We have heard of those princes' heroic campaigns." : *Beowulf* (London: Faber, 1999).

[8] In Tolkien's translation, "When the siege and the assault had ceased at Troy, [/] and the fortress fell in flame to firebrands and ashes, [/] the traitor who the contrivance of treason there fashioned [/] was tried for his treachery, the most true upon earth—" : *Sir Gawain and the Green Knight, Pearl, and Sir Orfeo* (London: Allen and Unwin, 1975).

[9] "where strange things, strife and sadness, [/] at whiles in the land did fare, [/] and each other grief and gladness [/] oft fast have followed there." : ibid.

proto-metrical rhyming line (derived from Petrarchan lyric) came, via the *London School* of Chaucer and Gower, to dominate, while the long alliterative line was remembered only via Langland. *Sir Gawayne* and the other poems attributed to the anonymous *Gawain-poet* ('Patience', 'Pearl' [N75], and 'Cleanness' or 'Purity') survived in a single MS (BM Cotton Nero A.x), were unpublished until 1839 and 1864 respectively, and now tend to be labelled as the centrepiece of a short-lived late-fourteenth-century (or *Ricardian*) *alliterative revival*.

Early English Alliterative Poems (1864) was the first publication of the Early English Texts Society, based in Oxford—where Hopkins read classics at Balliol 1863–6. His interests in Anglo-Saxon (learned at Oxford) and Welsh (learned at St Beuno's in 1874) are often remarked, but the extraordinary verse that began to erupt from him with 'The Wreck of the *Deutschland*' in 1876 points in mixing alliteration and rhyme to the 'Gawain poet' :

> I did say yes
> O at lightning and lashed rod ;
> Thou heardst me truer than tongue confess
> Thy terror, O Christ, O God ;
> Thou knowest the walls, altar and hour and night :
> The swoon of a heart that the sweep and the hurl of thee trod
> Hard down with a horror of height :
> And the midriff astrain with leaning of, laced with fire of stress.
>
> (stanza 2, ll. 9–16)

Faced with conservative rejection, Hopkins concocted the elaborate theory of *sprung rhythm* to explain his verse in neoclassical feet, but what he had created was a free adaptation of the Middle-English line : there can be as many un/stressed beats as Hopkins wanted, but alliteration is *de rigueur* and hemistichic structure usually audible, within a single line ("Hard down [·] with a horror of height") or across two ("I did say yes [/] O at lightning and lashed rod"). The pattern plays out throughout his brief career : when additional beats distend lines almost beyond recognition, as in 'That Nature is a Heraclitean Fire and of the comfort of the Resurrection' (N1171), superscript slashes appear to mark the hemistichic division :

> Cloud-puffball, torn tufts, tossed pillows | flaunt forth, then chevy on an air-
> built thoroughfare : heaven-roysterers, in gay gangs, | they throng ; they glitter in marches.

Conversely, the pared-down style promotes hemistiches to full lines, adding rhyme :

Márgarét, áre you grieving
Over Goldengrove unleaving ?

(N1168, 'Spring and Fall', ll. 1–2)

Both thought and thew now bolder
Are told by Nature : Tower ;

('Morning, Midday, and Evening Sacrifice', ll. 9–10)

One <u>can</u> set about trying to scan such lines as Hopkins earnestly advised and notated, but it is better to forget feet, accept with Auden that in free verse "you need an infallible ear to determine where the lines should end" (Nlxxix), and stop asking if Hopkins could count, concentrating instead on how he could hear. The music of such verse, lacking neoclassical prosodic structures, is fairly subjective, and more responsive to regional accent and personal tone than is usual with metrical lines—but whatever the qualities of one's own voice, to read lines aloud with a consistent approach to where stresses fall (and where rapidity demotes or promotes their frequency) is, in a while, to hear the beat of their music.

Once Hopkins reached a wider public after 1920 his influence became (and still is) enormous. Close imitation is rare, because it tends rapidly to *pastiche*, mocking a style as *parody* mocks a work, but the short Hopkins line, stripped of alliterative ornamentation, is often heard and has amalgamated with the short (two- or three-stress) line of Gaelic poetry. That line was known to Hopkins and independently to Yeats, widely publicised in his work from the 1890s ; Heaney's antiphonal anti-heroics in *North*, looking mostly to Yeats, have enough alliteration and hyphenation to suggest Hopkins's presence also : "It blows her nipples [/] to amber beads, [/] it shakes the frail rigging [/] of her ribs. [/. . .] Under which at first [/] she was a barked sapling [/] that is dug up [/] oak-bone, brain-firkin : [/. . .] her blindfold a soiled bandage" ('Punishment', N1900). The "thin" sound Vendler remarked (p. 160) is clearly audible in the two-stress lines, but hemistichic antiphony, pared to the bone, remains the basic articulation. Hopkins's long line is less easily stripped down but has also flourished, as in Eliot : consider the opening of 'The Dry Salvages' :

I do not know much about gods ; but I think that the river
Is a strong brown god—sullen, untamed, and intractable,
Patient to some degree, at first recognised as a frontier ;
Useful, untrustworthy, as a conveyor of commerce ;
Then only a problem confronting the builder of bridges.

The problem once solved, the brown god is almost forgotten
By the dwellers in cities—ever, however, implacable,
Keeping his seasons and rages, destroyer, reminder
Of what men choose to forget. Unhonoured, unpropitiated
By worshippers of the machine, but waiting, watching and waiting.

One isn't quite supposed to look for something as 'crude' as alliteration in high Modernists, but it is repeatedly explicit here, from the delicacies of 'strong/sullen' and 'untamed/intractable' to the overt 'conveyor of commerce', 'builder of bridges', double 'un-'s, and massed terminal 'w's. Medial cæsurae are forced in every line but one, and the play of rocking lineation around the double march of hemistiches structurally sets the tempo of Eliot's Mississippi music. The same line appears in his dramatic verse, in short-form for choruses and some monologues, and in a relatively spare long-form for dialogue : this is from Act 3 of *The Confidential Clerk* :

LUCASTA. I'm sorry to come back. It's an anti-climax.
  But there seems to be nobody to answer the door.
  I've just let someone in. It's the Mrs Guzzard
  Whom you are expecting. She looks rather formidable.
SIR CLAUDE. It's Parkman's day off. But where's the parlourmaid?
LUCASTA. I thought I heard someone singing in the pantry.
LADY ELIZABETH. Oh, I forgot. It's Gertrude's quiet hour.
  I've been giving her lessons in recollection.
  But she shouldn't be singing.
LUCASTA. Well, what shall I do?

(*Complete Poems*, 504)

Such loosely stressed, lightly echoing, and far from unstructured lines ("Whom you are expecting. She looks rather formidable.") are in the mainstream of free verse, and perhaps the form most free-versifiers first grope towards. But Auden's warning about the need for an "infallible ear" was well taken, and deafer attempts at free hemistiches, in short- or long-line layouts, often provoke public scorn at 'pretentious, craftless' (late or post-)Modernist verse.

Whitman's poetics were more original, but correspondingly lack the structure Hopkins took from alliterating hemistiches. From a famously self-centred and expressive beginning in 'Song of Myself' ("I celebrate myself, and sing myself, [/] And what I assume you shall assume", N1060) to the foundation of a distinctly American poetics in 'Crossing Brooklyn Ferry' ("Ah, what can ever be more stately and admirable to me than mast-hemm'd Manhattan? [/] River and sunset and scallop-edg'd waves of flood-tide ?", N1066) and throughout the *Leaves of Grass*, Whitman simultaneously inscribed himself and a perception of the New World free from most neoclassical constraints. Critical attempts to describe what he did are (to say the least) conflicting, but many American and some British poets have been explicit about debts to and respect for Whitman's music : Creeley, for example, introduced a selection with a moving tribute to Whitman having taught him that it "is, paradoxically, the personal which makes the common",[10] and among Whitman's great virtues is that no word or expression can be prosodically excluded. His sensuality and ambivalent sexuality dismayed or offended early readers, but are necessarily generous and inclusive, seeking sensation in experience and requiring an active concrete world as a screen for projected response. In his poetic music all modernity, however decadent, rebarbative to traditionalists, truly machine-ugly, or plain functional can find a place without displacing the ictūs of iambs and incurring an ironised frame by failing to meet inherited and long-hollowed heroic expectations.

The most interesting descriptions of Whitman's lines follow W. C. Williams in characterising them (and the poems, work, life) spatially, as *areas* within which expression occurs and is notated. Notions of sequence, left-to-right or top-to-bottom, are challenged and poems become sets of co-ordinates rather than narrative progressions : such dissolution–resolution and precipitation of personality on the page is one great thread of twentieth-century poetry, from American *Confessionalist* and L=A=N=G=U=A=G=E work to European late Modernism and beyond. Implicitly rejecting the (real and supposed) embodiment of narrowness, rigidity, and hidebound sequentiality in neoclassical lines, area poetics rejects a British inheritance (though not all European ones), and resonates with other trans-Atlantic discriminations. In English, for example, to be 'sincere' (probably from Latin *sine* + *cera*, 'without wax') one must reveal homogeneous density (be gold all through), be profoundly (deeply) consistent—all vertical metaphors ; only in the US does one 'go the extra mile', horizontally, and only in American terms can Hunter Thompson's gonzo warning about Nixon, that 'deep, deep down, he's shallow', be more than paradox. As geography and politics intertwine there is a sense of areas informing a republican and democratising poetics, conscientiously welcoming all people and phenomena, but for that reason also readily bereft and anxious about

[10] *Whitman Selected by Robert Creeley* (Harmondsworth: Penguin, 1973 [Poet to Poet]), 7.

technique; like Hopkins with 'sprung rhythm', Williams tried to theorise himself neoclassically but his *variable foot* has similarly confusing and unnecessary results (feet in mouth, not metre). The whole point was freedom from artificial constraint, and only familiarity with a wide range of poets can make audible and visible the conventions of sound and typography that accreted as the linear freedom of free verse was tested in practice (though pre-set typewriter tabs and Microsoft proprietary bundles remain a useful guide to what has been done, if not what it means). Much easier to see, and more generally helpful, are the clear counter-currents to Whitman's looseness that can be identified, often the provision of a nominated 'rule' or 'aim' by way of compensation for all that freedom.

Imagists of the 1910s–1920s, for example, such as H.D. (Hilda Doolittle) and briefly the energetic Pound, believed lines should be a clear image and poems written by stacking such lines together; this is from H.D.'s 'Wine Bowl' (N1313):

> I will cut round the rim of the crater,
> some simple,
> familiar thing,
> vine-leaves
> or the sea-swallow's wing;
> I will work at each separate part
> till my mind is worn out
> and my heart:

The variable intervals and degrees of rhyme, and freedoms of line-length, work well for eye and ear—always a good sign—but however possible it is to write poetry like this, making Imagism a rule is like arguing a car is best driven, always, in one gear. Poets soon made freer with their resources, but the austere clarity of Imagist lines influenced early Stevens:[11]

> An old man sits
> In the shadow of a pine tree
> In China.
> He sees larkspur,
> Blue and white,
> At the edge of the shadow,
> Move in the wind. ('Six Significant Landscapes', I)

> The jar was gray and bare.
> It did not give of bird or bush,
> Like nothing else in Tennessee. ('Anecdote of the Jar', N1260)

[11] *Collected Poems* (1954; London: Faber, 1955).

These are from *Harmonium* (1923), and the short clear line dropped out of Stevens's later work. For W. C. Williams, however, trained and working as a physician and deeply concerned with specifics ("no ideas but in things", he said in *Paterson*), the short line was a necessity in early work like 'The Red Wheelbarrow' (N1274) and the progressively indented tercet of 'Asphodel, That Greeny Flower' (N1276)—sometimes called the *triadic* or *step-down line*, but more like three short lines than one long one. Snodgrass, in his excellent *De/Compositions: 101 good poems gone wrong*, instructively relineates one of Williams's best-loved pieces, 'Poem' (N1275), beginning (original on the left) :

As the cat climbed over the top of	As the cat climbed over the top of [. . .][12]

Williams's lines—however seemingly fragmentary—are shown to be in balance with themselves and one another, making for a memorability and impact the 'decomposed' version entirely lacks. Setting himself against Eliot's dominance and insisting on 'The Poem as a Field of Action',[13] Williams was an influential figure for Zukovsky, Olson, Creeley, Levertov, and Lowell—himself the influential teacher of Sexton and Plath, who came terribly to a form of the short line in her *Ariel* poems during the year before her suicide :

White
Godiva, I unpeel——
Dead hands, dead stringencies. ('Ariel', N1842)

Soon, soon the flesh
The grave cave ate will be
At home on me ('Lady Lazarus', N1843)

Words dry and riderless,
The indefatigable hoof-taps.
While
From the bottom of the pool, fixed stars
Govern a life.[14] ('Words')

Though lines can flex or lengthen at will, the persistently spare meas-

[12] *De/Compositions*, 208–9.
[13] In Gioia, Mason, and Schoerke, *American Poetics*.
[14] *Collected Poems* (London and Boston: Faber, 1981), 239, 244, 270.

ure embodies diminution and isolation ; in the disturbing 'Cut' it catches at a mental pathology that found increasingly bloodless expression in imagery as Plath's capacity to suicide ripened. In poems that endure and command readers, as these do, persistently short lines can carry an expressive burden regardless of content, but as a versifying habit, weakly derived from Hopkins or Williams, may testify only to voices too small for the world they find themselves in.

The uncertainty of Imagism, leaving what constituted a 'clear image' to the discretion of poets, limited the effect of their manifesto, and poets have variously promulgated other, stricter principles of free-verse lineation—grammatical, phrasal, stichic, antiphonal, quasi-stanzaic, and relating to breath-length or visual identity within the *mise-en-page*. All must be inferred and judged in context, any may be discarded in any particular poem : what matters is how those a poet chooses to observe are combined and the effect of reliance on them (itself usually a function of the voice the poet achieves). Though always open to parody and condemnation by the overly traditional, free lineation within an area has real capacities, splendidly exemplified by Hollander in the friendliest of pastiches :

And to be able to wander, free
(in a wide field, as it were)
verse can amble about
on a kind of nature walk
the lines following no
usual path, for
then the poem might seem
to have wandered into
another kind of meter's backyard
but
sometimes
seeming
to map out the syntax,
sometimes
seeming to do almost the
opposite,
this kind of meandering verse can
even
oddly
come upon a flower
of familiar rhythm

a sight for sore
ears, or encounter
a bit later
on,
once again a patch of
trochees growing somewhere
(like an old song)
and
take one by the
stem
and
break
it
off

(*Rhyme's Reason*, 29–30)

The fun cannot disguise the genuine pleasures of exemplifying meaning in lineation and layout, nor the expressive power such nimble technique can harness ; yet Hollander's very success is a warning, for unless conventions are self-referentially instantiated in content there may be no way of recognising them. Drawing on Frost's famous remark that he'd "as soon write free verse as play tennis with the net down", one might say that in netless tennis net-cords and errors must be as apparent to spectators (readers) as players (poets with themselves) : and back one comes to Auden's "infallible ears", a scarce commodity.

Much has been made since the 1980s of the *New Formalism*, a supposed reversion to metrical and rhyming verse, but the label is overstated ; formalism never went away. Both in the US and UK (late) Modernist poetry has included and paralleled entirely formal poetry, as any general anthology confirms : cummings, Auden, Eliot, Betjeman, Moore, Lowell, Roethke, Bishop, Merrill, Larkin, Hecht, Harrison, Hill, Walcott, Heaney, Porter, and a hundred more rhyme and/or lineate for received form some if not all of the time, and while the continuation of tradition is welcome, it needs no special remark unless one has deluded beliefs about its demise. A considerable (if flexible) formalism of alliteration, rhythm, and rhyme is also present in the long lines of Dylan's verses and the sometimes even longer lines of Afro-American *rap*, Trinidadian calypso, and other (quasi-)improvisatory popular forms engaged in running social and political commentary ; the same might be said of Berryman's *Dream Songs* (N1548) and the highly varied lyrics of the *New York* poets Ashbery, O'Hara, Koch, and Schuyler.[15] These and other poetic forms using collaged quotations or *found* text, relying on juxtaposition and casting the poet as *de facto* editor and/or versifier, may oddly approach a sort of printed (or in performance genuinely oral) formulaism, drawing from a stock of pre-assembled 'hemistiches' a running record of lived experience ; the poets who have commanded audiences and/or readerships by doing so have marked bardic qualities.

The great modern critic of the line has been Helen Vendler, notably in *The Breaking of Style: Hopkins, Heaney, Graham* (1995). Hopkins and Heaney have several times passed in review here, but Graham remains, and (having approached Hopkins as prosodist and Heaney as grammarian) it is she upon whom Vendler brought most fully to bear her understanding :

> Lineation (like prosody and grammar) is a feature of style that often goes unnoticed. It, too, has existential meaning—and as Graham passes from short antiphonal lines to numbered long lines to square 'areas' of long-lined long sentences, her sense of the poet's task, which changes from volume to volume, is carried precisely (if not solely) by these stylistic changes.[16]

The course Vendler charts—through Graham's short-lined *Erosion* (1983), numbered long- (lined or paused, p. 86) *The End of Beauty* (1987), and long- (lined + sentenced) *Region of Unlikeness* (1991) and *Materialism* (1993)—can be conveniently followed in *The Dream of the Unified Field: Selected Poems 1974–1994* : and the voyage has continued.[17] Graham maintained long (lines and sentences) in *The Errancy* (1997), and 'Thinking' deserves mention as a perfect, very accessible example of post-Modernist self-reflexivity combined with straightforward natural observation—a crow taking flight + Graham's awareness of herself as observing (hence transforming) and interpreting (hence transforming) crow and flight. Long sentences twist round first and second takes, third thoughts, and jumping associations, but give way when focus tightens :

> The wire he's on wobbly and his grip not firm.
> Lifting each forked clawgrip again and again.
> Every bit of wind toying with his hive of black balance.

---

[15] Berryman, New York: FSG, 1969/London: Faber, 1990; others, Ford, *The New York Poets*.

[16] *Breaking of Style*, 6.

[17] All Hopewell: Ecco Press, as dated ; Carcanet also publish *Unified Field*.

Every now and then a passing car underneath causing a quick
rearrangement.
The phonelines from six houses, and the powerlines from three
grouped-up above me—some first rung of sky—him not comfortable,
nature silted-in [. . .] (p. 40)

and the long sentences resume to reach for the bird's flight and poem's crystallisation. A similar antiphony of line-groups plays through the sequence of 'Guardian Angel' poems,[18] including the wonderful 'The Guardian Angel of the Private Life', beginning "All this was written on the next day's list." and ending, some 80 lines and not enough full-stops later :

that nothing distract, that nothing but the possible be let
to filter through—
the possible and then the finely filamented hope, the filigree,
without the distractions of wonder—
oh tiny golden spore just filtering in to touch the good idea,
which taking form begins to twist,
coursing for bottom-footing, palpating for edge-hold, limit,
now finally about to
rise, about to go into the other room—and yet
not having done so, not yet—the
intake—before the credo, before the plan—
right at the homesickness—before this list you hold
in your exhausted hand. Oh put it down. (p. 22)

The volume's blurb suggests it is a place where "angels are overheard muttering warnings", but the poems are immanent with the distractable and refracted human mind, and it is a very cinematic angel who can (relatively, at least) snap "Oh put it down"—the thought ? the list ? or something altogether else necessarily interrupting the poem ? Alice Fulton has proposed a taxonomy 'Of Formal, Free, and Fractal Verse',[19] using Mandelbrot's mathematical concept of *self-similarity*, a pattern structurally repeated at multiple scales : artificial examples include, say, a portrait in pixel-miniatures of the portrait in pixel-micro-miniatures . . . and so on, but the more interesting natural examples include coast-lines and water-courses. Applied to Graham's constantly recursive considerations—(of the many roads that might not have been taken, or

[18] 'The Guardian Angel of the Little Utopia', '[. . .] of Self-Knowledge', '[. . .] of the Private Life', '[. . .] of Not Feeling', '[. . .] of Point-of-View', and '[. . .] of the Swarm'.

[19] In Gioia, Mason, and Schoerke, *American Poetics*.

might still not be taken, and (with the road that is in every moment of the body, and so the mind (and poem) being taken) are being not taken)—one might say the fractal spirallings of these poems are in full engagement with the indispensably rich and oppressive multiplicity of the modern world to a modern mind : as Plath's shrunken lines came to betoken a dried life she could not endure.

In *Swarm* (2000), however, Graham abandoned long (lines + sentences), and the blurb's helpful gloss on the title explains why : 'To "swarm" is to leave an originating organism—a hive, a home country, a stable sense of one's body, a stable hierarchy of values—in an attempt, by coming apart, to found a new form that will hold'. This is the beginning of 'Probity', whom (or which) one may (not) take to be a person like 'Daphne', 'Eve', and the speaker of 'Eurydice on History' :

Moves us   no end

like a wall   no end

you see a thing or two

doing the   rounds

you see

as far as it goes

the "universal"

lord how narrow

and its fist open

shopkeepers   chosen wombs

I have shown up sweet lord

have put my hand out

have looked for a long while

have run a hand along

looked for a symbol at the door

a long while

devices   prejudices

have felt for the wounds

have tired eyes (pp. 93–4)

Nineteen lines, separated from those that follow by a centred asterisk, constitute a verse-paragraph within which internally antiphonal hemistichic lines come and go with short lines that may follow or be antiphonally set. Double-spaced, they occupy more than a page and (especially in the fine Ecco Press editions Graham favours) white expanses left on wide pages by short lines and heavy leading catch at a weary endurance (other than but not unlike Beckett's) ; in the sixteen poems called 'Underneath [+ a parenthetical qualifier]'[20] the voice becomes a speech of female poverty and suffering, breeding and dying, as those however 'underneath' do in our world. As one of several selections '*from* The Reformation Notebook' puts it :

[20] In order, 'Underneath (9)', '[. . .] (Upland)', '[. . .] (Sibylline)', '[. . .] (Always)', '[. . .] (Calypso)', '[. . .] (7)', '[. . .] (1)', '[. . .] (2)', '[. . .] (3)', '[. . .] (8)', '[. . .] (Libation)', '[. . .] (Eurydice)', '[. . .] (with Chorus)', '[. . .] (11)', '[. . .] (Spezzato)', and '[. . .] (13)'.

> Locations are omitted.
>
> Uncertain readings are inserted silently.
>
> Abbreviations silently expanded.
>
> *
>
> A "he" referring to God may be capitalized
>
> or not.
>
> *
>
> (is crying now)   show me
>
> *
>
> is crying now   (what's wrong)   (p. 3)

From lines that are almost found text, sentences ten thousand editors have written and will write (but tweaked—the second is a gem), Graham turns to simple hemistiches made resonant by lunulae and space, complex by an intervening asterisk, and troubling by *anaphora* (lines beginning identically) and repeated call and response across the cæsurae (↓↓ + ⇉) set <u>against</u> the chiasmic lunulae (X). So doing she registers mismatched hearing and audibility among callers and respondents, agents and patients, first and third world—a lineation as sacredly broken as Hopkins's, and as politically nuanced as Heaney's. Most recently, in *Never* (2002) the style/s of *The Errancy* have returned, with spatial austerity in relative abeyance, and where Graham will next take her lineal quest and sensibility is one of the great evolving stories of twenty-first century poetry.

Finally there is the *prose-poem*, fitting itself to the full page-measure or a designated lesser measure within which determined lines are lost to the flow of prose. Consciously 'poetic' prose, at least as old as Tyndale's biblical translations, was boosted by Romantic and Aesthetic attitudes, and prose paragraphs by Wordsworth, Beddoes, de Quincey, and Wilde may be called prose-poems ; the real story begins with hyperstrict eighteenth-century French neoclassicism, promulgating elaborate rules distinguishing poetry and prose that incited the wilful paradoxicality announced in the label 'prose-poem'. Descending to the nineteenth century baggaged with oil-and-water incompatibilities and anti-neoclassical rebellion, the prose-poem came to Baudelaire (*Le Spleen de*

Paris, 1869), Rimbaud (*Illuminations*, 1872–6), and the Symbolists Mallarmé, Gide, and Valéry as a ready-made 'objective correlative' of self-conscious alienation from received understandings, delighting in indeterminacy and the sense of truth that comes from flouting convention. In their wake it remained a respected part of French poetry, and leaped from them, and the Cubist Cendrars, to W. C. Williams, from whom an American tradition descends to Bly, Ashbery, Bernstein, and others. The multiply hybrid work of Stein (N1248) is also influential, and in her clearly shows a Baudelairean connection with those who (however successful) feel themselves irredeemably out-of-joint with the dominant world, and determine to live as their unconventional selves at any cost.

A remark by Clive Scott about Rimbaud, identifying in his prose-poetry intertwinings of "the lyric process of undergoing oneself and the more properly novelistic business of mapping out a behaviour",[21] suggests the range of applications the form can have, and its hallmark paradoxicality has been a specific attraction to an age of fierce contradiction. The lines of Ginsberg's *Howl* (1956) (N1708), for example, though often described (on Ginsberg's cue) as dilations of Whitman's line, can be read as paragraphs of a prose-poem :

> I saw the best minds of my generation destroyed by madness, starving hysterical naked,
> dragging themselves through the negro streets at dawn looking for an angry fix,
> angelheaded hipsters burning for the ancient heavenly connection to the starry dynamo in the machinery of night,
> who poverty and tatters and hollow-eyed and high sat up smoking in the supernatural darkness of cold-water flats floating across the tops of cities contemplating jazz,
> who bared their brains to Heaven under the El [. . .]
> Peyote solidities of halls, backyard green tree cemetery dawns, wine drunkenness over the rooftops, storefront boroughs of teahead joyride neon blinking traffic light, sun and moon and tree vibrations in the roaring winter dusks of Brooklyn, ashcan rantings and kind king light of mind,
> who chained themselves to subways [. . .]

Many more lines begin "who", itemising how "the best minds of my generation" suffered and failed. A typography of deliberative lineation

[21] Quoted in *The New Princeton Encyclopedia*, 978a.

half-remains, but right-justification is specific to prose and (as the title *Howl* suggests) emotions are too chaotic for a regular metre or stanza ; had Ginsberg tried for a closed form the power of his poem would be less. It isn't an option poets could take very often, but it is an option—though there is a warning in the wilful opposition that came to be for Ginsberg more routine pose than response to reality.

The British situation is different. Eliot (the seminal Modernist) drew on Baudelaire, Rimbaud, and Valéry as much as or more than Williams, but published only one prose-poem, 'Hysteria', in *Prufrock and other Observations* (1917),[22] perhaps recognising that his (desire for) social and theological conservatism sat badly with the form's baggage. Auden, a more openly alienated figure, felt the form's attractions more substantially, and (arguably) used it four times : for parts 1–2 of *The Orators: An English Study* (1931) ; for 'Caliban to the Audience', the final section of *The Sea and the Mirror: A Commentary on Shakespeare's* The Tempest (1942–4) ; in the quasi-dramatic *The Age of Anxiety: A Baroque Eclogue* (1944–6) ; and for *Dichtung und Wahrheit (An Unwritten Poem)* (1959).[23] In all but *Age of Anxiety* prose passages are extended, and tend to be read simply as prose juxtaposed with poetry, not prose-poems, while in *Age of Anxiety* shorter passages pass as amplified stage-directions ; Auden's recourse to prose-poetry and its resonance for his self-understanding are generally ignored, and mainstream British prose-poetry is rare.

It has, however, had two great champions in the counter-culture, Ivor Cutler and Viv Stanshall. Cutler is an illustrator and composer as well as a poet, whose bizarre, funny, and lugubrious observations, sometimes called poems, sometimes stories, have appeared in volumes like *Glasgow dreamer* and *Life in a Scotch Sitting Room, vol. 2* ; he records his work, and is best known through broadcasts on BBC Radios 1 and 3 by John Peel and Andy Kershaw. Stanshall was once famous through the Bonzo Dog Doo Dah Band, late 1960s musical counterparts of the Monty Pythons, and was a genuine eccentric, self-damagingly himself at all costs ; post-Modernism might label him a 'performance artist', making his life his work, but his primary mode was social parody and amid various post-Bonzo projects was a stunning sequence of prose-poems in soap-operatic form, again broadcast by Peel in 1975–9, 1988, and 1991–5 (when Stanshall died). They were collected on two albums, *Sir Henry at Rawlinson End* (1978, filmed 1980), and *Sir Henry at*

---

[22] Two others, 'Introspection' and 'The Engine', were published in *Inventions of the March Hare: Poems 1909–1917* (New York and London: Harcourt Brace, 1996).

[23] 'The Orators' in *The English Auden*, all others in *Collected Poems*.

Ndidi's Kraal (1983) ; some scripts were published. Though cited as influences by Stephen Fry and other comics of his generation, these too go largely unrecognised as prose-poetry, probably because they are so funny, rude (Sir Henry's aged servant 'Scrotum, the wrinkled retainer' being a choice example), and unashamedly populist in mocking post-imperial dufferishness and magazine-fiction clichés—but Stanshall's life and death are comparable to Baudelaire's, and for a man profoundly English yet alienated from the mainstream of his culture the comedic-satiric prose-poem was a perfect form.[24]

There is one other major example, Hill's *Mercian Hymns* (1971 ; N1833, 2050), 30 prose poems focused on and through the eighth-century Mercian King Offa, each of one to four paragraphs justified right with all lines after the first indented (a *hanging indent*). In the original volume (Deutsch, 1971), lacking page-numbers, poems numbered I–XXX are followed by a 'List of Hymns' providing titles (many repeated), and a four-page 'Acknowledgements' including notes that in their tricksy admixture of helpful fact and off-beam remarks recall Eliot's notorious notes to *The Waste Land*. In the Penguin *Collected Poems* and Houghton *New and Collected Poems* titles appear on the general prefatory contents-pages, and Penguin print the notes separately in a terminal collection of 'Notes and Acknowledgements' ; Houghton wholly omit the notes (though other volumes' 'acknowledgements' appear)—an omission I assume Hill authorised, as in granting permissions for *Mercian Hymns* he requires lineation and right-justification to be exactly reproduced, and would not suffer sub-editorial curtailment without protest. The lines of *Mercian Hymns* look like prose, with many words hyphenated around line-breaks, but Hill insists lineation matters, so larger structures must matter also ; yet he has in one edition stripped his poem/s of an addendum in less than poetic (but not unartistic) prose offering an interesting connection, and in two allowed conventional arrangements to suppress what was at first creative oddity. One consequence is the loss of a humour dryly open in the notes :

> IV : 'I was invested in mother-earth'. To the best of my recollection, the expression 'to invest in mother-earth' was the felicitous (and correct) definition of 'yird' given by Mr Michael Hordern in the programme *Call My Bluff* televised on BBC 2 on Thursday January 29th 1970. [. . .]

---

[24] *Life in a Scotch Sitting Room, vol. 2* (first recorded 1978 ; Revola, 2002 ; first pub. 1984 ; London: Mandarin, 1998) ; *Glasgow dreamer* (London: Mandarin, 1990) ; *Rawlinson End* (Charisma Records, 1978) ; *Ndidi's Kraal* (Charisma, 1983) ; *Sir Henry at Rawlinson End and other spots* (n.p.: Eel Pie, 1980 ; 🖰)

> XVIII : 'for consolation and philosophy' : the allusion is to the title of Boethius' great meditation, though it is doubtless an excess of scruple to point this out. [. . .]
>
> XXV : [. . .] 'quick forge' : see W. Shakespeare, *Henry V*, V, Chorus, 23. The phrase requires acknowledgement but the source has no bearing on the poem.
>
> 'wire' : I seem not to have been strictly accurate. (pp. [43–5])

Readers wandering (through unnumbered pages) from notes to poems and back are more likely to hear the rich humour(s) of Hill's diction (as Cope did in the wonderful parody 'Duffa Rex'[25]) ; to which most seem sadly deaf. A different humour attends a spatial moment in hymn VII, when one boy loses another's toy plane through floorboards :

> Ceolred let it spin through a hole
> in the classroom floorboards, softly, into the
> rat droppings and coins.

Interword spacing is increased to maintain justification, but "rat" would easily fit into the line above and there is no hyphen to compound "rat droppings", as there could (or should) be—so the point, I imagine, is that wide interword-spaces visually represent gaps ; "rat droppings and coins" are literally below "the classroom floorboards". It's hardly hysterical, but prose-poems <u>are</u> playful, and Hill's general decision to use the form allows him to use unusual words in a language full of vocal and conversational humours ; one might also hear notes of disaffection with an Englishness he supposedly embraces. The critical point, however, may be precisely that prose-poetry in English lacks a history—which matters because the *Hymns* are about English history. Hill in effect found a form which for (British) readers had only internal baggage, and used it to examine a swathe of history from eighth to twentieth centuries : any form with external baggage would snag on some bits of history, tangling with subjects ; the prose-poem allowed him to attend to all periods without unintentionally privileging or complicating any ("the source has no bearing on the poem"). In using it, however, Hill has greatly increased its baggage : he hasn't returned to the form and while there have been occasional borrowings—Harsent in 'Bedtime Story' and Gravender in 'The Book of James' have imitated his style, and Harsent used his layout for 'The Curator' and 'The Old Curiosity Shop'[26]—whether more sustained uses will follow Hill's remains

[25] *Making Cocoa for Kingsley Amis* (London: Faber, 1996), 51.

[26] Gravender, *Tabla Book of New Verse 2004* ; Harsent, *News from the Front* and *A Bird's Idea of Flight* (London: Faber, 1998).

moot ; as the future of lines and line-breaks, however defined or conceived, does not.

Exemplary Poems

1. 'Ode on Melancholy' (p. 68)

Keats's lines rest securely within the heroic tradition, stanza-enjambment is avoided, and the driving syntax is that of sentences (not periods), so despite the dialectic argument ; eisthetic display of rhyme, quatrain + tercets stanza-structure ; and structural counterpoint of *semi-cola* with tercets, lines are persistently stichic rather than truly antiphonal. But within the strict observance of form a game of enjambment is played out, and can be notated using a Wingding arrow (→|) to indicate enjambed line-breaks, the normal slash (/) to indicate end-stopped line-breaks, and showing <u>medial</u> punctuation only :

, , , →| , , / →| , / / , →| , →| / / /   →| / / / / / / / , / , /   — / , →| ; / / , →| / →| / / /

The virtual disappearance of enjambment from the second stanza marks the catalogue of alternatives in the tercets, ll. 15–20 beginning 'Then / Or / Or / Or / Emprison / And', but Keats plays off it on either side, driving coiling imperatives in the first stanza and reflective assertions in the last with enjambments throughout. He carefully gives impulsion to the itemising middle stanza with an initial enjambment, and ends all stanzas with three end-stopped lines, in the first a *cde* and in the last a *dce* tercet (ll. 7–10 + 27–30) sounding the full heroic measure those stanzas otherwise avoid, and in the middle a *cde* tercet whose last two lines are broken with commas to vary the monotony with which itemising pentameters threaten the music. Read aloud, observing line-breaks and punctuation with tonal and temporal care, and you can plainly hear the metre Keats rides, sense the form within which he rides it, and feel the punctuation with which he curbs it : synthesise all three (as helpful display does) and you have the measure of his lines, the course/s taken.

2. 'Sestina' (pp. 69–70)

The intense demands of the (tetrametric) sestina foreclose on lineation as much as diction and syntax, and Bishop's anapæstic drummings in its grip were considered under 'Form'. With 39 end-words (+ 3 medial ones) prepositioned on the page, the play of enjambment becomes a primary resource, less against lines than stanzas. Mapping the full-stops within sestets + tercet is revealing ; (→) indicates stanza-enjambment, (//) an end-stopped stanza :

1.5. // 4.1.1 → 4.2 → ½.3½.2. // 1.1.1½.2½ → 6. // 1.2.

The importance of sixfold variation, the dynamics introduced by medial full-stops and one-line sentences—"September rain falls on the house." (1), "The iron kettle sings on the stove." (11), "*It was to be,* says the Marvel Stove. [/] *I know what I know,* says the almanac." (25–6), "*Time to plant tears,* says the almanac." (37)—and of the long 8½-line antepenultimate sentence are all suggested, and reading aloud discovers how they work within the music. The frequency of anapæstic substitutions and use of tetrameter (rather than heroics) means lines can be allowed to sound whole without worrying about the inflation heroics can induce, but in shortening the measure (even when anapæstically re-distended) lessens the capacity of individual lines : sestinas derive from a dance-form, and in Bishop's dance of generations handing-on and whirling round matter more than individual or stately display.

One might argue that ll. 8, 36, and 38–9 ("And the rain that beats on the roof of the house" ; "has carefully placed at the front of the house." ; "The grandmother sings to the marvellous stove [/] and the child draws another inscrutable house.") are prongs : three have triple substitutions, the last is an anapæstic tetrameter. The first seems simply emphatic, a tripping mimesis of rain dancing on rooves that imposes itself on the poem as sound does on the domestic scene, old and young sheltering in a warm kitchen. The others (two ending with "house") occur in the last four lines, separated only by the last pronouncement of the almanac, and as well as individually pronging the last sestet to end the 8½-line sentence, and double-pronging the tercet, they collectively prong the poem. Given the cycle/s of the form, it might be an effect like the thickened base of a pot spinning on a wheel, but the maximal extensions of line as form forecloses (and time takes its course) might equally be eloquent with protest, or futility. Yet the only iamb in ll. 38–9 is the first foot of 38 (The GRAND) ; thereafter seven tripping anapæsts in a row fuse acceptance with liveliness, and the last lines can as well be read antiphonally within the tercet, against the need "*to plant tears*", as following from it. In either case the "marvellous stove" and "inscrutable house" are at some odds with planting tears, and edge it away from any thought of dragon's teeth or fields ploughed with salt towards safer kitchen husbandry of herbs and vegetables ; without that balance in the envoi the whole spinning edifice could fall tonally flat, and with it the relatively suppressed identity of lines returns to its own.

3. 'Nearing Forty' (pp. 22–3)

The pairing of catalectic and hypermetric lines was mentioned under 'Metre', and the short final line under 'Form' and 'Punctuation' (pp. 24–5, 75, 148). The poem begins by alternating end-stopped and enjambed lines, turns to repeated enjambment, and returns to rough alternation favouring enjambment over endstopping : this pattern matches and interlocks with the quatrains-to-couplets-to-quatrains form and lighter punctuation of the last *semi-colon.*

A greater problem is posed by ll. 12 ("in simple, shining lines, in pages stretched") and 25 ("or you will rise and set your lines to work"). Stretching through the poem is a sequence of words with poetic meanings (metred, metaphor, etc.) to which these "lines" belong ; together they map one primary concern, writing poetry, onto another, the water-cycle. The "lines" are principally poetic, but become falling rain, wrinkled age, and the arrows whereby geographers illustrate the water-cycle. Repeating "lines" pushes it towards the status of "rain" and "work", used thrice, and both "lines" are described positively with qualification, as "simple, shining" and "set [. . .] to work [/] with sadder joy". In Walcott's idea of what it is to be a poet, crafting lines is clearly of prime importance for a poem to work.

It isn't then surprising that Walcott's senses of lineation and interplay between clause and line (32 *commata*, 32 lines) is very fine : one reason 'Nearing Forty' is such a pleasure to read aloud. Lines like "by the bleak modesty of middle age" (7) and "ambition as a searing meteor" (16), enjambed both into and out of, are not grammatical units, but their visual display and aural integrity as pentameters enable them to contribute far more to the poem than the same words in the same order could add to a paragraph of prose.

Exercises : Lining words up

1. Poems in sestets or shorter stanzas often trade (as 'Sestina' does) on the fall of full-stops to vary unitary form, and decisions about full-stopped cæsurae become critical. It's always instructive to consider lines, stanzas, and sentences carefully, best done by preparing texts to isolate each by presenting stanzas, then sentences, as single lines ; the sentence-by-sentence layout can then have stanza-breaks added. Good candidates include Larkin's 'An Arundel Tomb' (N1650), where line- and stanza-enjambment plays beautifully against tetrameters, and Pugh's startling 'Official briefing for ministers on the recent violence in the capital' (p. 247) and 'Paradise for the children'.[27]

2. Iambic tetrameters, consciously short of heroism, can bounce, as Swift's do in his 'Verses on the Death of Dr. Swift' (pp. 39–40, 131) ; equally, they can be limpid, as Marvell's are in 'The Garden' (N484) and Tennyson's in 'In Memoriam A.H.H.' (N996). Choosing 20 or so lines from each, compare closely : how are rhythm and pace controlled ? how do lines vary ? and how are tetrametrics harnessed to such differing ends ?

3. A superb modern control of tetrametrics is shown by Snodgrass in 'April Inventory',[28] a poem deeply dependent on antiphonal calm and detachment but also on statements of fact (and fancy) that acquire implacability from the very calmness of voice and metre. Chart end-stopping, enjambments, and medial marks (as for Keats, p. 182), then sentences and stanzas (as in 1 above) : how do these elements combine to generate the tone audible throughout?

4. Relineating stanzaic poems to display other components has an interesting reverse-form, relineating free verse to see if stanza-forms can be achieved. The opening of Tomlinson's 'The Picture of J.T. in a Prospect of Stone' (N1746), for example, can be recast from its short tercets (or triadic line) in the iambic tetrameters of its model, Marvell's 'The Picture of Little T.C. in a Prospect of Flowers' (N481) :

What should one
wish a child
and that, one's own
emerging
from between
the stone lips
of a sheep-stile
that divides
village graves
and village green?

What should one wish a child and that,
one's own emerging from between
the stone lips of a sheep-stile that
divides village graves and village green?

The cross-rhymed quatrain is not in Marvell's stanza (*abaccbd4d10*), but points to a greater regularity that one might suspect from Tomlinson's original layout,

[27] *Selected Poems* (Bridgend: Seren, 1990).
[28] *Selected Poems 1957–87* (New York: Soho, 1987).

and it's worth knowing that the first sentence flows iambically <u>and</u> in syntactic units until the clustered trochees of "divides village graves and village green"—not least in seeing how the tercets accommodates that cluster as the quatrain does not. Moreover, the poem is wholly divisible into tetrameters with startling results, implying that Tomlinson meant to summon Marvell's line as much as his observations of T.C. Try that relineation and compare both versions with Marvell's poem : how could one best describe the incomplete but vital presence of tetrameters in Tomlinson's original ? and what happens if Marvell's complex stanza is fragmented into Tomlinson's tercets ?

5. Complex stanzas, iso- and heterometric, are less habitual a choice than they once were, but remain a valuable poetic currency—Vendler has noted, for example, Plath's clever stanza-form/s in 'Electra on Azalea Path'.[29] Good stanzas work both to bind and showcase their individual lines, as Marvell's (in 4 above) has two *a*-, two *b*- and two *c*-rhymes (*abaccb*) before its closing heterometric bob + prong *d*-rhyme couplet. Design a stanza with some effect in mind, then write some to see if your design works.

[29] *Coming of Age as a Poet*, 121, 166.

Chapter Glossary

alliterative revival : a handy but inaccurate term for the mid–late fourteenth-century work of (especially) Langland and the Gawain-poet, distinguished from the 'London School' by alliterating hemistiches derived from OE verse and notably public political concerns.

antiphonal : 'sounded against', a/line/s responding to an/other/s ; originally exactly that, choric call-and-response within the liturgy, but by extension (i) a mode (composed or imposed) of verse-lines which creates or displays a bipolar pattern (not a simple sequence, as in blank verse), & (ii) a quality of voice associated with such lines as protesting or refusing a dominant or demanding position.

area : a term promoted in American poetics by W. C. Williams to refute an implicitly narrow, unyielding, hidebound, and rigidly sequential quality associated with neoclassicism ; lines, poems, poetic practices, and poets' lives may all be recharacterised as areas rather than progressions.

caesura, -ae : the medial pause/s in a line ; if there is no punctuation it will tend not to occur in lines shorter than a tetrameter, and to occur approximately centrally in tetrametric or longer lines ; it may be forced towards the beginning or the end of a line by punctuation.

end-stopped : of a line or stanza, having a terminal mark of punctuation.

enjamb/ed, enjambment : of lines, couplets, or stanzas, not end-stopped, with sense and/or syntax continuing into the next line, couplet, or stanza.

hemistich : a half-line, used in pairs typically bound by alliteration and/or rhythm ; verse in such lines is hemistichic.

Imagists : a school of poetry in the 1910s–1920s, advocating poetry written in short lines each containing a clear image ; Pound & H.D. were leading members.

lineation : the organization of a poem into lines.

line-break : the turn of one line into the next, notated as '/'.

oral formulaism : a mode of bardic composition in pre- or early literate cultures in which a large stock of hemistiches are learned, and variously combined (according to various rules) in performance.

prong, pronged line : my coinage for a line longer than a normative measure ; the opposite of a bob.

prose-poem : one written and printed as prose, without the use of line-breaks and often with a justified right margin.

rocking lineation : the effect of counterpoint (cæsura-to-cæsura) lines created by placing cæsurae in the same position in two or more successive lines.

stanza-break : the physical (and syntactical) space (and pause) between stanzas, marked in transcription with a double slash, '//'.

triadic line : a name for the progressively indented tercet created by W. C. Williams, insisting on its identity as one long line rather than three short ones ; also called the 'step-down line'.

6
Rhyme

To be a *critic*, ah,
How deeper & more scientific.
JOHN BERRYMAN, 'Olympus'[1]

Poetry was spoken before it was written, and rhyme, the coincidence of sounds, has prehistoric origins in ritual, celebration, and memory training. Most Westerners learn nursery rhymes or children's chants, and know a fair number of simple rhymes giving information (red sky at night, shepherd's delight) or advice (if you can't beat 'em, join 'em). Its systematic use in poetry, however, is surprisingly recent, spreading from Troubadour and Sicilian Verse in the early fourteenth century to dominate Western lyric verse until Modernism and beyond.

Rhyme is another form of punctuation closely bound to lineation and layout, helping on the page and in performance audibly to organise the relations of words. Its role is clear if lineation and layout are subtracted—as in the rhymed prose of Nashe's *Pierce Penileſſe his Supplication to the Diuell* (text from 1592, omitting an illuminated cap. and changing black letter to roman) :

> Hauing ſpent manie yeres in ſtudying how to liue, and liude a long time without money ; hauing tyred my youth with follie, and ſurfetted my minde with vanitie, I began at length to looke backe to repentaunce, & addreſſe my endevors to proſperitie : But all in vaine, I sate vp late, and rose early, contended with the colde, and conuerſed with ſcarcitie ; for all my labours turned to loſſe, my vulgar Muse was despised and neglected, my paines not regarded or ſlightly rewarded, and I my ſelfe (in prime of my beſt wit) layde open to pouertie.

[1] *Collected Poems 1937–71* (New York: FSG, 1989; London: Faber, 1990), 180.

The capitalised medial "But" midway notwithstanding, this is a single Ciceronian period (pp. 265–7), with two *cola* each of two *semi-cola* whose last words are "money", "prosperitie", "ſcarcitie", and "pouertie". All rhyme, the first and second pairing in one sense, money–prosperity, the third and fourth in its opposite, scarcity–poverty, reflecting the central division marked by colon + capitalised "But". In the second *semi-colon* the first and second *commata* join in (follie, vanitie), and in the third so does the third *comma* (early). In such a system, rhyme-sound leads you to expect a punctuation-mark, and rhyme + punctuation-mark together signal completion of a unit. The same is true in verse when rhyme and lineation coincide ; doubly so if both coincide with punctuation, as in closed couplets. Rhyme signals closure to ears as clearly as any mark or space can to eyes, and in more open forms links forged by rhyme are a principal means of elaborating or ironising sense and controlling pace.

Vision is now our primary sense, and for many to hear clearly how rhyme works in a poem means seeing a *rhyme-scheme*. The conventional method indicates with letters which lines rhyme with which : the rhyme-word ending the first line, and all lines that rhyme with it, are *a*; the second rhyme-word and all lines that rhyme with it are *b*, and so on, making couplets *aabb*, cross-rhymed quatrains *abab* etc. Unrhymed lines in rhyming stanzas can be notated within this system, or designated by *x, y* etc. : thus variant stanzas in Berryman's 'Homage to Mistress Bradstreet' with ll. 3 + 7 unrhymed might be notated as *abcbddea* or *abxbccya*, and successive tercets rhyming *abb cdd eff* as *xaa xbb xcc*. Successive *x*-lines may not rhyme.

I have so far assumed that rhyme is binary (two words do or don't) and attended only to *end-rhyme* (of words ending lines)—which is clearly inadequate, but worth assuming when <u>first</u> working out rhyme-schemes, in case (as in 'Nearing Forty') sophisticated variation conceals a simpler structure. There is also a problem notating rhyme-schemes to show variance : one can use vowels and consonants (as Nabokov did, p. 51), cases (*aa* as one kind of rhyme, *aA* another), or faces (a*a*, **a**a)—but there is no standard system. If working intensively on a poem with variant rhymes it's worth devising a notation to show them in abstract, and the only requirement then is to be clear. The underlying problem is that English terminology of rhyme is plentiful, but lacks (by comparison with French, German, and Italian) systematic organisation. Confusion and complexity can be faced down, however, using two axes of analysis : the kind of rhyme (such as *full-*, *half-*, *para-*, and *auto*-rhyme) ; and its position (*end-, internal, medial*, and *initial* rhyme) : beyond which lie *alliteration* and *assonance*.

Full- (or *perfect*) *rhyme* occurs when two or more words or phrases share the same last stressed vowel + all following sounds. If the stressed vowel is in the last syllable, so both halves of the rhyme are stressed (CAT/BAT, aBOARD/igNORED, disbeLIEF/TeneRIFE), rhyme is *stressed* (or *masculine*) ; if the stressed vowel is followed by one or more unstressed syllables (WILlow/BILlow, RAPidly/VAPidly) rhyme is *unstressed* (or *feminine*). Any number of unstressed beats may follow the stressed vowel, but with more than two rhyme tends to sound comic, and comedy soon becomes silliness—but may remain funny, especially if half the rhyme is made of monosyllables whose stresses are slightly wrenched, as Gilbert's 'lot o' news/hypotenuse' (N1144) or Byron's 'merry in/heroine' (N858). Such silly rhyming is *hudibrastic*, from its prevalence in Butler's *Hudibras* (1663–80), but a rhyming phrase (rather than word) is more neutrally called *mosaic rhyme*.

The only kind of rhyme stricter than full-rhyme is *rime riche* ('rich rhyme'), where sounds before the last stressed vowel must also be identical (hence its other name, *identical rhyme*). *Homographs*, spelt identically, as well/well (not ill/of water), *homophones*, pronounced identically, as 'there/their' or 'Underground/under ground', and polysyllables differing by a letter, as 'd/evolutionary', are all *rimes riches*.

There are many kinds of *imperfect rhyme*, beginning with *half-* (or *near* or *slant*) *rhyme*, where either the stressed vowel or following sounds differ. If consonants differ, it's *vowel-rhyme* (bite/fire, courage/bunker) ; if vowels, *pararhyme* (lust/lost, honour/winter), favoured by Owen and Yeats and commoner in their wake, but found in all periods. While full-rhymes chime, or confirm sense, half-rhymes tend dissonantly to question sense (but only tend, as Copus reminds by ending 'Topsell's Beasts' with *child/homeward*). Mary Evelyn used successive pararhymes to ironise advice for suitors in 'A Voyage to Marryland' :

Then Bracelets for her Wrists bespeak,
(Unless her Heart-strings you will break)
With Diamond *Croche*° for Breast and Bum, *a miniature bishop's crozier*
Till to hang more on there's no room.[2]

Here dissonance is mild and as intrinsically comic as "Bum", but pararhyme can be severe, as Yeats showed ending 'The Circus Animals'

[2] Copus, *In Defence of Adultery* (Newcastle: Bloodaxe, 2003), 45 ; Evelyn, Stevenson and Davidson, *Early Modern Women Poets*, 475.

Desertion' (N1207), one poem in which he reclaimed *ottava rima* from Byronic comedy (p. 47) :

> These masterful images because complete
> Grew in pure mind, but out of what began ?
> A mound of refuse or the sweepings of a street,
> Old kettles, old bottles, and a broken can,
> Old iron, old bones, old rags, that raving slut
> Who keeps the till. Now that my ladder's gone,
> I must lie down where all the ladders start,
> In the foul rag-and-bone shop of the heart.

The opening cross-rhyme seems perfect for a quatrain (complete/street, began/can) but slides into pararhyme as the sestet completes (slut, gone) and emphasises its dissonant end-rhymes with repetitions and rhymes within ll. 4–6 ; when full-rhyme returns in the couplet (start/heart) it sounds too neat and can no longer please.

Beyond half-rhyme are more radical forms of imperfection, like *eye-* (or *printers'*) *rhyme*, where words only look as if they rhyme : commonest are *-ough* endings (cough/bough/dough/enough) and combinations like 'picturesque/queue'. Unless deliberately comic the jilt of an eye-rhyme may be severe (A miner, he made little dough / and died with rotted lungs a-cough). Simpler omission can also be satiric, as in Byron's 'Epitaph' with terminal rule :

> Posterity will ne'er survey
>   A nobler grave than this :
> Here lie the bones of Castlereagh :
>   Stop, traveller,——.

Or a non-rhyme may be supplied, as in Cope's 'Verse for a Birthday Card' :

> Many happy returns and good luck.
> When it comes to a present, I'm stuck.
> If you weren't far away
> On your own special day,
> I could give you a really nice glass of lager.

And there are a variety of *spelling rhymes*, where one or another trick is pulled to amuse :

If all the trains at Clapham Jctn
Were suddenly to cease to fctn
The people waiting in the stn
Would never reach their destintn. (Anon.)

The alkaloid natives of Pollux
Engage in the strangest of frollux—
  They each get their kicks
  Chewing alkali sticks,
Which makes them, of course, alkihollux. (Edith Ogutsch)

When I've a syllable de trop,
  I cut it off, without apol. :
This verbal sacrifice, I know,
  May irritate the schol. ;
But all must praise my dev'lish cunn.
Who realize that Time is Mon.[3]

(Harry Graham, 'Poetical Economy')

The aim is comedy, but (as with Byron, who loathed Castlereagh with a passion, and perhaps to some extent Graham) there can be a sharper point also.

Great care is needed with imperfect rhymes, for pronunciation varies historically and regionally, and rhymes vary with it. The traditional 'move/love' and 'prove/love' could be called eye-pararhymes, but probably used to be full-rhymes ; for Wordsworth, born in Cumberland, 'water/matter' was full-rhyme, but to readers born in southern England it was and is pararhyme. These considerations weigh : 'water/matter' is from Harrison's 'Them and [Uz]'[4] (N1873), describing how at 12 his English teacher stopped him reading Keats aloud because his Leeds accent outraged the *King's English*[5] of the poem. Keats was a Cockney whose speech was not 'King's English' ; his poetry is accentless, but to prevent a child with an accent from reading it aloud is to suppress regional variation and impose élite language. Similar issues are raised by ethnic variations in accent, and attend 'Nearing Forty'.

Participle endings allow an odd variation : if stressed they would be

---

[3] Cope, *Making Cocoa for Kingsley Amis*, 33 ; others in Cohen, *Comic and Curious Verse* (Graham, 203), *More Comic and Curious Verse* (Byron, 280), and *Yet More Comic and Curious Verse* (Anon., 316 ; Ogutsch, 327). In McGann's ed., the Byron is 343, IV. 279.

[4] "[Uz]" = 'us' as 'uhz', common in northern England ; 'uss' is common in the south ; 🖱.

[5] Or *Queen's* or *BBC English* : in either case, supposed grammatical correctness + elegance in a Home Counties accent, such as BBC radio newsreaders used always to have.

full-rhymes, but usually aren't and can be stacked as rhyme-words whose stressed stems are blank and unstressed endings identical, as in Shakespeare's sonnet 87 and Whitman's 'Patroling Barnegat':

Wild, wild the storm, and the sea high running,
Steady the roar of the gale, with incessant undertone muttering,
Shouts of demoniac laughter fitfully piercing and pealing,
Waves, air, midnight, their savagest trinity lashing,
Out in the shadows there milk-white combs careering,
On beachy slush and sand spirts of snow fierce slanting,
Where through the murk the easterly death-wind breasting,
Through cutting swirl and spray watchful and firm advancing,
(That in the distance! is that a wreck? is the red signal flaring ?)
Slush and sand of the beach tireless till daylight wending,
Steadily, slowly, through hoarse roar never remitting,
Along the midnight edge by those milk-white combs careering,
A group of dim, weird forms, struggling, the night confronting,
That savage trinity warily watching.[6]

Arguably none of these end-words except the repeated "careering" rhyme at all, to give *abcdefghijkelm* ; or is it *aaaaaaaaaaaaaa*, with additional *a*-rhymes in ll. 3, 8 + 13 (piercing, cutting, struggling) ? Up to a point which notation you prefer doesn't matter : any account of the poem must notice the tolling participles, patently a principle of construction. Their chime amid otherwise varied words and images becomes a threnody of wind in wires and rigging ; I also suspect the wave-pattern of the ragged right margin is intentional, a back-and-forth contrast with the identical last letters of each line. Even odder is the octave of Hopkins's Petrarchan sonnet 'The Windhover' (N1166), an intense study of a wild falcon : *a*-rhymes are stressed and *b*-rhymes unstressed—but set stress aside and the rhymes rhyme :

I caught this morning morning's minion, king
dom of daylight's dauphin, dapple-dawn-drawn Falcon, in his riding
Of the rolling level underneath him steady air, and striding
High there, how he rung upon the rein of a wimpling wing
In his ecstasy ! then off, off forth on swing
As a skate's heel sweeps smooth on a bow-bend : the hurl and gliding
Rebuffed the big wind. My heart in hiding
Stirred for a bird,—the achieve of, the mastery of the thing !

[6] *Complete Poetry and Collected Prose* (New York: Library of America, 1982), 402 (3N775).

End-rhyme is almost the least sound-effect Hopkins uses here, but amid the symphony it helps keep order. The *a*-rhymes pair in meaning, 'king-/wing' because the bird's mastery of air makes it regal ; 'wing/swing' because it banks ; and 'swing/thing' because "thing" is both the falcon's anatomy and colouring, and the intense but common beauty of its circling movement. The *b*-rhymes also pair, 'riding/striding' catching at the falcon's activity in flight and 'gliding/hiding' contrasting its freedom with the watcher's breathtaken constraint. The octave-structure these pairings reflect and enforce allows a complex of sounds to be deployed effectively, and it's intriguing that Whitman and Hopkins should both have used such *wrenched monorhyme* to evoke natural phenomena (storms, falcons) : as iterative maths is used to describe such natural fractals as coastlines and river-courses (p. 175). One might think a complicated equation would be needed to generate a curve like a coastline, but a simple process endlessly repeated does the business, mathematically, poetically, and in nature.

Perhaps the most intrinsically interesting kind of rhyme is represented by Whitman's "careering", *autorhyme,* of a word with itself. In one sense repetition isn't rhyme at all (it's also called *null rhyme*), in another the most perfect rhyme possible : either way it can have remarkable effects and force readers-aloud to accommodate it. Shakespeare was a master of autorhyme (see *Titus* 3.2.1–33 ; *John* 2.2.4–15 ; *Othello* 4.2.72–82), and its value is plain in *Macbeth* 2.2.24–31, when he tells his wife he has "done the deed" and of the grooms, drugged by the Lady, whom he passed entering and leaving the room where he murdered Duncan :

MACB. One cry'd God bleſſe vs, and Amen the other,
As they had ſeene me with theſe Hangmans hands :
Liſtning their feare, I could not ſay Amen,
When they did say God bleſſe vs.
LADY. Conſider it not ſo deepely.
MAC. But wherefore could not I pronounce Amen ?
I had moſt need of Bleſſing, and Amen ſtuck in my throat.
(F1, 1623)

Editors usually reject the final line as a prong and relineate ("and Amen [/] Stuck in my throat"). Either way, "Amen" could not stick in the reader's throat as in Macbeth's if the word didn't end ll. 29 + 26 as well ; there is also a medial use in l. 24. Macbeth's insistent repetition of 'Amen' contrasts with his previous inability to say it at all : one 'Amen' marks the end of a prayer ; repeated use in murderous dialogue, followed by a question-mark (which implies rising pitch), and immediately rhyming (trying and failing to answer the "Amen ?"), is profoundly disturbing. This murder without an Amen was an unhallowed end ; these uselessly late, volleyed Amens mark a terrible beginning.

Eliot was also a fine autorhymer (see *The Waste Land*, ll. 25–9, 62–3, 162–3, 347–56, and 414–21), and (like falling rhythm) autorhyme is always to be pondered. As a formal requirement in sestinas and villanelles it is critical to those forms ; even in Lear's limericks (p. 8), where first and last lines often form autorhyme, it provokes attention. It can also frame stanzas or whole poems : France's clever sonnet 'On First Looking into Raymond Chandler' (taking off from Keats's 'On First Looking into Chapman's Homer', N905[7]), approximately Petrarchan, uses its second and fourth sentences to generate a pronoun autorhyme as the *a* of the arch-rhyme : "I [/] grew up with Humphrey Bogart, Hollywood. [/ . . . /] Then, browsing a second-hand bookstall, I [/] saw this faded green and cream Penguin." (ll. 1–5). Even more delicately, her 'No Man's Land' seems blank save for the sibilance of plurals, but the first line ("Where is the country she's exploring : it has no borders.") and the last ("And was blood [/] really that red, the colour they use to mark borders."), subtly linked by missing question-marks, use autorhyme to anchor the poem's movement. Copus adapted the device to equally good effect in 'Kim's Clothes', repeating-reversing in the second stanza the first and last lines of the first—"The summer you died and your mother sent me your clothes", "holding them up to the light, the soft tubes of their arms"—to enclose her elegy in an arch of autorhyme.[8]

One other kind of rhyme commands attention, *broken rhyme*, when a word is split across a line-break to facilitate rhyme (as "gutter- [/] ing" in 'Nearing Forty'). As open impropriety, forcing rhyme by damaging a word, effects tends to be comic or grotesque (cf. wrenched accents) : badly handled, it annoys ; well-handled, it can be devastating. In Merrill's mocking 'Snow Jobs' every *ababbcbc* stanza easily maintains the same *a*-, *b*-, and *c*-rhymes until :

Like blizzards on a screen the scan-
dals thickened at a fearful rate,
Followed by laughter from a can
And hot air from the candidate.[9]

[7] See Vendler, *Coming of Age as a Poet*.

[8] France, *Red* (Newcastle: Bloodaxe, 1992), 58, and *The Gentleness of the Very Tall* (Newcastle: Bloodaxe, 1994), 37 ; Copus, *In Defence of Adultery*, 56.

[9] *A Scattering of Salts* (New York: Knopf, 1995), 23.

This works because "scan-" is a word in its own right, appropriate to scanning the TV news and the scanning beam of TV pictures, but is also picked up retrospectively by the telling inversion of "laughter from a can" (as opposed to the cliché 'canned laughter') and the *embedded* but unneeded rhyme of "<u>can</u>didate". Such embedded rhymes can be displayed as broken-rhymes in performance to complete a rhyme, and the remnant of the word is usually tacked on with comic bathos—as memorably in the long lines of Lehrer's song 'Smut' : "a dirty novel I can't shut if it's uncut and unsubt- le", "I thrill to any book like *Fanny Hill*, and I suppose I always will if it is swill and really fil- thy".

As these examples show, the other way rhyme can vary is by position. With end-rhyme the first variable is whether it produces couplets, each rhyme-word paired as quickly as possible, or separates rhyme-words by one or more lines, as in single-, cross- and arch-rhyme : the effects of each common arrangement and of chain-rhyme were considered under 'Form' (pp. 43–4), but it should be noted generally that a line whose end-word rhymes with an earlier end-word both extends a poem (which may speed it along) and looks backward (which may slow it down). Tension between these pulls of a rhyme can control pace, as can rhyme that is *accelerated* or *delayed* by comparison with others in the poem : the *a*-rhyme in the *abbcac* sestets of Larkin's 'An Arundel Tomb', for example, is delayed by comparison with the couplet-*b*- and cross-*c*-rhymes, giving the poem power and gravitas. Conversely, Plath's notorious 'Daddy' (N1840) repeatedly returns to the same rhyme-sound (do/shoe/Achoo), but in clumps, never a settled pattern : the poem is so disturbing partly because rhyme never allows a steady pace but forces the reading voice to spurt and tumble. Such *free rhyme* became common in the twentieth century, perhaps because the modern world was felt to be so rapidly changing, unsettled, and adrift, that to use more regular rhyme about anything modern was necessarily to counterpoint form and content—but in that case a First World War sonnet like Owen's 'Anthem for Doomed Youth' poses serious questions (pp. 17–18); as do Betjeman, Auden, Larkin, and the regular rhymers of 'New Formalism', including Merrill, Harrison, Fenton, Gioia, and Morrison (N1716, 1872, 1961, 1972). Harrison in particular has written little (if any) verse that isn't rhymed (and metred), but is the last poet one could accuse of being stilted or artificial, or of burking the modern world ; his consistent combination of strictly observed rhyming forms with topical subjects and colloquial language (pp. 206–10) challenges anyone who thinks regular full-rhyme inapposite in modern poetry.

All free-rhymers owe a debt to Eliot, who used free rhyme brilliantly : in 'The Love Song of J. Alfred Prufrock' (N1340), for example, there is this verse-paragraph :

> And indeed there will be time
> To wonder, "Do I dare?" and, "Do I dare?"
> Time to turn back and descend the stair,
> With a bald spot in the middle of my hair—
> (They will say: "How his hair is growing thin!")[10]
> My morning coat, my collar mounting firmly to the chin,
> My necktie rich and modest, but asserted by a simple pin—
> (They will say: "But how his arms and legs are thin!")
> Do I dare
> Disturb the universe?
> In a minute there is time
> For decisions and revisions which a minute will reverse.

The rhyme (schematically *abbbccccbdad*) is working hard : after the apparently unrhymed "time" there is first a sequence of three successive rhymes (dare/stair/hair), then one of four (thin/chin/pin/thin), which force pace and pitch upwards as the reading voice tries to control the hysteria incipient in Prufrock's hammering neurosis. The last of the four is also the first, " 'thin!')" (41, 44), and begins a process of recursive autorhymes as "dare" (45) answers back to "dare?" (38), and "time" (47) to "time" (37) : neurosis subsiding into indecision. The autorhyming of ll. 45/38 + 47/37 sends the poem arching back over its own tracks, and within ll. 46–8 a more compact complementary pattern of arch- and autorhymes emerges as "revisions" (48) looks back to "decisions" (48), "minute" (48) further back to "minute" (47), and (the perfect last word for Prufrock) "reverse" (48) back further still to "universe" (46). Wheels spin wildly going nowhere ; rhyme shows Eliot in absolute control of the skidding acceleration and braking that convey the tenacity of Prufrock's neurosis.

Eliot goes beyond free end-rhyme to *internal* rhyme. The strictest form is *leonine* rhyme, the word before a cæsura rhyming with the end-word : it is popular in the third line of common metre, making *abcb* into *ab*(*cc*)*b*, as in Causley's 'Christ at the Cheesewring' (p. 56) :

[10] Norton, following the American *Collected Poems*, use crotchets around ll. 41 + 44 (and elsewhere) ; I restore the lunulae of every other edition.

As I walked on the wicked moor
Where seven smashed stones lie
I met a man with a skin of tan
And an emerald in his eye.

The stressed leonine MAN/TAN chimes audibly and (like syncopated beats in music) hurries narrative along, scooping up the pararhyme with "skin", countering any drag the otherwise unrhymed *c*-line might impart,[11] and providing impetus put to good use in a story as strange as an emerald eye. Leonine rhyme also sweetens refrains in such Elizabethan roundelays as Shakespeare's 'Under the Greenwood Tree' (N273), but occasional or imperfect forms can go unnoticed to claustrophobic effect, as in Betjeman's 'Death in Leamington' (N1460) and Allnut's 'convent'.[12] Systematic leonine rhyme is now restricted to songs and comic verse : occurrence in every line is rare, but use in alternating lines common ; the form *(aa)b(cc)b* is a double-tercet laid out as a quatrain, as in Eliot's 'Bustopher Jones' and 'Skimbleshanks' :

He's the cat that we greet as he walks down the street
In his coat of fastidious black :
No commonplace mousers have such well-cut trousers
Or such an impeccable back. (*Complete Poems*, 230)

There's a whisper down the line at 11.39
When the Night Mail's ready to depart,
saying 'Skimble where is Skimble has he gone to hunt the thimble ?
We must find him or the train can't start.' (p. 232)

'Mungojerrie and Rumpelteazer' intermittently pulls the same trick with *(ab)(ab)* lines that form a cross-rhymed quatrain laid out as a couplet with *medial* as well as end-rhymes :

They had an extensive reputation. They made their home in Victoria Grove—
That was merely their centre of operation, for they were incurably given to rove.
(p. 218)

Eliot was metrically very clever in mixing rising feet throughout *Old Possum's Book of Practical Cats*, but leonine and medial rhymes guide stress and provide impetus pulling readers through rhythms that can

[11] It is helped by anapæsts substituted for iambs in ll. 3 ('with a SKIN') + 4 ('And an EM-').

[12] *Beginning the Avocado* (London: Virago, 1983), and in France, *Sixty Women Poets*.

become quite choppy (especially in 'Mungojerrie and Rumpelteazer'). He occasionally used another form of internal rhyme, *(ab)a*, pairing the word before a cæsura with the end-word of the next line, as in 'The Naming of Cats' :

> First of all, there's the name that the family use daily.
> Such as Peter, Augustus, Alonzo or James,
> Such as Victor or Jonathan, George or Bill Bailey—
> All of them sensible everyday names. (p. 209)

'name/James' is a pararhyme, and 'Jonathan/names' a vowel-rhyme, but with such strong end-rhymes variation is welcome. This delayed medial-terminal rhyme is sometimes called 'cross-rhyme' ; it's rare outside comic verse but a reversed form, *a*(*ab*)*c*, has been modulated into simple good-humour by Lykiard in another cat-poem, 'Appreciation After Breakfast' :

> Pressed hard in sheer soft pleasure, singers with tight-shut eyes,
> wiseguys drunk
> and shameless with dribbling chins,[13]

Used with a light touch in early stanzas ("these [/] thinnest", "raising [/] fluffed-up tails"), the chime across a line-break works beautifully here with the unexpected "wiseguys", and later in embedded form, "furred [/] urgency" : a light subject, but much more than light verse.

There is *initial* rhyme, but it's an odd business. As autorhyme, repeated beginnings, it is generated by *anaphora*, as in Psalms ; the effect is often to induce a form of chanting, and hence affirmation, but can become touching or disturbing, as in *Jubilate Agno* (N678) :

> For I will consider my Cat Jeoffry.
> For he is the servant of the Living God duly and daily serving him.
> For at the first glance of the glory of God in the East he
> worships in his way.
> For is this done by wreathing his body seven times round with
> elegant quickness.
> For then he leaps up to catch the musk, wch is the blessing of
> God upon his prayer.
> For he rolls upon prank to work it in.[14]

Smart's formulaic openings signal imitation of the Psalms, but are part

[13] *Cat Kin* (1985; rev. edn, London: Sinclair-Stevenson, 1994), 41.
[14] (1939; London: Hart-Davis, 1954), 115–16.

of his own ritual and register his willingness to see God's hand and mercy in all creation, certainly in Jeoffry. It is also possible fully to rhyme first rather than last words (When I try it / then you can see / first-word rhymes are / tough to hear, can / burst the rhythm, / rough-up syntax, / and still not sound / grand or pleasant.) but it's extremely awkward to do, enforces falling rhythm, and has never found a champion. Words with identical beginnings (often prefixes, as 'un-' or dis-') might also be called initial rhymes, but the consonance always precedes the last stressed vowels (even if the prefix acquires stress), and is not heard as rhyme.

Looser forms of internal rhyme must be judged in context, and can be described with terms already covered. They generally bind or tighten sense, and can wrap the oddest lines in unifying wreaths of sound, as Thompson famously managed in 'The Hound of Heaven' :

> To all swift things for swiftness did I sue ;
>   Clung to the whistling mane of every wind.
>   But whether they swept, smoothly fleet,
>   The long savannahs of the blue ;
>   Or whether, Thunder-driven,
>   They clanged his chariot 'thwart a heaven,
> Plashy with flying lightnings round the spurn o'their feet :—
>   Fear wist not to evade as Love wist to pursue.
>   Still with unhurrying chase,
>   And unperturbèd pace,
>   Deliberate speed, majestic instancy,
>   Came on the following Feet,
>   And a Voice above their beat—
>   'Naught shelters thee, who wilt not shelter Me.'[15]

The poem moves at terrific pace despite wandering eisthesis and leaping oddities of sense, partly for metrical reasons but also through constant completion of this and that rhyme, of all kinds in all positions. Besides full-, wrenched, para-, and auto- end-rhymes (sue/blue/pursue, instancy/Me, -driven/heaven, feet/Feet), there are leonine rhymes (to/pursue, thee/Me), medial auto-, para-, and vowel rhymes (wist/wist, whether/Thunder, flying/lightnings), mosaic *rime riche* (shelters thee/shelter Me), and a host that combine types (swift/swiftness, wind/driven, unhurrying/unperturbèd, unperturbèd/speed, . . .). As bizarre as it is pious (it helped inspire *The Hound of the Baskervilles*) Thompson's

[15] *The Poems of Francis Thompson* (1913; London: OUP, 1937).

intoxicating near-nonsense had extraordinary effects on people—Field Marshal Wavell (a fine anthologist) "repeated the words of this greatest of all lyrics under fire, on a rough Channel crossing, in pain of body or mind"[16]—but now seems closer to the decadence of Swinburne than sacred verse. Modernist austerity foreclosed on such heavy rhyming as on neoclassical long lines (pp. 163–4), and it's now rare in printed verse that intends gravity, though not serious song (think of Dylan) or *rap* lyrics ; the closer poetry is to performance the less snooty poets are about rhyme.

Beyond internal rhyme are *alliteration*, proximate use of the same consonant/s, and *assonance*, of the same vowel/s—which, when not principles of versification (as in Ricardian poetry and Hopkins, pp. 165–6), can be oddly derided or thought childish. Not so : both are basic to alphabetical languages, and have rich possibilities in English, where enormously disparate vocabulary (pp. 222–5) and shameless grammar make <u>all</u> systemic repetitions welcome guides :

> Each phrase in literature is built of sounds, as each phrase in music consists of notes. One sound suggests, echoes, demands, and harmonises with another ; and the art of rightly using these concordances is the final art in literature. It used to be a piece of good advice to all young writers to avoid alliteration ; and the advice was sound in as much as it prevented daubing. None the less for that was it abominable nonsense, and the mere raving of those blindest of the blind who will not see. The beauty of the contents of a phrase, or of a sentence, depends implicitly upon alliteration and upon assonance. The vowel demands to be repeated ; the consonant demands to be repeated ; and both cry aloud to be perpetually varied. You may follow the adventures of a letter through any passage that has particularly pleased you ; find it, perhaps, denied a while to tantalise the ear; find it fired again at you in a whole broadside ; or find it pass into congenerous sounds, one liquid or labial melting away into another. And you will find another, much stranger circumstance. Literature is written by and for two senses : a sort of internal ear, quick to perceive 'unheard melodies' ; and the eye, which directs the pen and deciphers the printed phrase.[17]

Thus R. L. Stevenson, and those who (like Churchill in *The Prophecy of*

---

[16] *Other Men's Flowers*, 25.

[17] Stevenson, 'On Some Technical Elements of Style in Literature', in *Essays in the Art of Writing* (London: Chatto, 1905), 30–2.

Famine) "often, but without success, have prayed [/] For apt Alliteration's artful aid" find that the problem lies with the author, not the device.[18] On the principle of understanding something by doing without, you can find a crazy display of abandon and awkward disavowal with anti-assonant wording in a long work of fiction, *La Disparition* (1969), an instructional oddity put into Anglo-Saxon by Adair as *A Void* (1994) ; I don't think it took him all 25 annual rounds to do his translation, but it wouldn't astonish if it had, for Adair had at all costs to avoid using **e**, as Perec did in the original : imitating him even for a few lines is exhausting, frustrating, and interesting as one struggles to keep the letter out (even harder in English without 'the' + 'have' than in French, where 'le' + 'les' go, but 'la' + most present tenses of 'avoir' remain available).[19] It's a crazy but not stupid game, for denial of a sound is a potent tease—one Brecht put to remarkable use in 'Die Moritat von Mackie Messer' ('The Ballad of Mack the Knife') : opening *Die Dreigroschenoper* (*Threepenny Opera*) with a Berlin street-song he loaded lyrics with the gutturally rolled Berlin 'r', repeatedly hawked in delivery as Mackie's crimes are described, until the last verse, where its absence allows a singer to shift tone stunningly (as in Lemper's memorable recording[20]).

There is also a condition called 'colour hearing', in which letters have for an individual a specific and constant colour ; for anyone familiar with his prose it is no surprise to discover that Nabokov saw alphabetical rainbows :

> V is a kind of pale, transparent pink : I think it's called, technically, quartz pink [. . .] N, on the other hand, is a greyish-yellow oatmeal color. But a funny thing happens : my wife has this gift of seeing letters in color, too, but her colors are completely different. There are, perhaps, two or three letters where we coincide [. . .]. It turned out [. . .] that my son [. . .] sees letters in colors, too [. . .] and we discovered that in one case, one letter which he sees as purple, or perhaps mauve, is pink to me and blue to my wife. This is the letter M. So the combination of pink and blue makes lilac in his case. Which is as if genes were painting in aquarelle.[21]

[18] 'Assonance' did not then have its modern sense : 'alliteration' covered vowels and consonants, so Churchill wasn't making a foolish mistake.

[19] Perec, *La Disparition* (Paris: Editions Denoël, 1969) ; trans. Adair, as *A Void* (London: Harvill, 1994).

[20] *Ute Lemper sings Kurt Weill* (Decca CD 425 204–2, 1988).

[21] *Strong Opinions* (1973; London: Weidenfeld, 1974), 17.

What did the openings of *Lolita* or *Pale Fire* look like to Nabokov as he wrote them ? What part might colour-clashes have played in choosing words ? Secret shade-harmonies might play over repetitions audible to all. How widespread it is is uncertain, but a surprising number of writers, if asked, admit to some sense of letters as coloured, and the possibility is worth bearing in mind (especially as colour returns to the post-metal page).

The axes of type (from *rime riches* through full- and half-rhyme to mosaic and eye-rhyme) and position (from accelerated initial through medial to delayed terminal) give bearings on any rhyme, but it is possible by establishing an alternative pattern to avoid rhyme without abandoning it. In iambic metres an unstressed end-rhyme will almost always be an unstressed hyperbeat,[22] but stressed rhyme can be carried by normal terminal stress, without hyperbeats ; the reverse is true in trochaic metres. A stressed hyperbeat, however, will (if rhymed) be a stressed rhyme, and an unstressed hyperbeat, unstressed rhyme. To hear rhyme is also to hear stress, and in the version of *terza rima* devised for the heroic 'Dante' passage in part II of *Little Gidding* (ll. 80–151; N1362, 2041) Eliot showed (by alternating lines with normal terminal stress and unstressed hyperbeats) that to hear stress is as if to hear rhyme :

> And last, the rending pain of re-enactment
>   Of all that you have done, and been ; the shame
>   Of motives late revealed, and the awareness
> Of things ill done and done to others' harm
>   Which once you took for exercise of virtue.
>   Then fools' approval stings and honour stains.
> From wrong to wrong the exasperated spirit
>   Proceeds, unless restored by that refining fire
>   Where you must move in measure like a dancer.

Eliot is sombrely listing "gifts reserved for age", and chose heroics. He needed (for complex reasons) to allude to Dante, so wanted *terza rima,* but not constant chain-rhyme sweetening the pain he had to express. For the same reason he couldn't risk unstressed rhymes becoming hudibrastic, but wanted sadly cadenced trochaic and amphibrachic words creating unstressed endings. His unorthodox answer, using end-

[22] The only other possibility is for it to be catalectic, omitting the last beat.

ings instead of rhyme, is brilliantly successful and the passage is famous for painful honesty and gravely beautiful sound. Poets learned the lesson. Cohen's 'Suzanne Takes You Down' (better known as 'Suzanne') relies to fine effect on one stressed rhyme in each stanza (blind/mind) amid persistently unstressed endings :

> Jesus was a sailor
> when he walked upon the water
> and he spent a long time watching
> from a lonely wooden tower
> and when he knew for certain
> only drowning men could see him
> he said All men will be sailors then
> until the sea shall free them,[23]

In performance Cohen exaggerates persistently unstressed endings with falling *pitch contours* (vocal curves from one pitch to another) in trochees (SAIlor, WAter) and mosaic half-rhymes (SEE him, FREE them)—which brings out rhyme but subordinates it to cadence. Such endings characterise his songs, and are partly responsible for his reputation as a melancholic. Conversely, upbeat songs prefer stressed full-rhyme—consider the chorus of Connell's 'Red Flag', an international Socialist anthem (written for 'The White Cockade' but usually sung to 'Tannenbaum') : "Then raise the scarlet standard high. [/] Within its shade we'll live and die, [/] Though cowards flinch and traitors sneer, [/] We'll keep the red flag flying here."

Some critics make much of whether a rhyme is *semantic*, of words with cognate meanings, and/or *thematic*, of words resonant with a principal theme of the work. Both qualities are desirable but basic : those who 'just try to make it rhyme' (as Dylan is accused of doing, and Jim Morrison too often did) soon fall flat, go splat, and that's that. Certain traditional rhymes, notably love/prove and death/breath, carry a semantic charge, and the art of the clerihew (p. 41) lies as much in semantic or thematic rhyme as in the unlikeliness of a name and heterometrics, so both need watching for—but impeccably semantic and thematic rhyme did McGonagall no good at all : this, unsurprisingly, is 'Wreck of the Steamer "Stella" ' :

[23] *Selected Poems 1956–1968* (New York: Viking, 1968), 209.

'Twas in the month of March and in the year of 1899,
Which will be remembered for a very long time ;
The wreck of the steamer 'Stella' that was wrecked on the Casquet Rocks,
By losing her bearings in a fog, and received some terrible shocks.

The 'Stella' was bound for the Channel Islands on a holiday trip,
And a number of passengers were resolved not to let the chance slip ;

and so on for 15 interminable stanzas, and scores of other cheerfully chuntered disaster-epics. Tin-ears, unflagging enthusiasm for pedestrian sentiment, and repeatedly stating the obvious have as much to do with McGonagall's celebrated badness as clunking rhymes—but they are semantic (horribly so in 'trip/slip'). Even deftly used, though, the point may be as much a set-up as anything else, as in Jamie's 'The Barometer', where following the semantic and thematic pararhyme 'waiting/tutting' comes this sequence :

I catch myself biting
dead skin from my lips.
I have played with my gloves all day.

I ought just to jump
and meet Hades half way.

The semantic vowel-rhyme 'biting/lips' seems complete until 'lips' finds a cross-pararhyme with 'jump'. In the mosaic pararhyme 'all day/half way', day/way is semantic, all/half *counter-semantic* (pairing opposites), but 'lips/jump' is stubbornly unsemantic, and packs an unpleasant shock boosting subjunctive resentment ("ought just to", not 'will') in the last lines. Such delicate local control is a primary virtue, but even more interesting is to see rhyme play out in the long term of a career than the shorter term of a poem.[24]

I have mentioned Harrison as an inveterate rhymer and creator, in *A Cold Coming* (1991), of the most brutal rhymes I know, stressed and unstressed (p. 40). Responding to a Gulf-War photograph by Kenneth Jarecke showing one of many Iraqi casualties from the bombing at Mutla Gap, a soldier incinerated whole and upright at the wheel of the truck in which he was fleeing Kuwait, the poem imagines that Iraqi's speech :

[24] McGonagall, *Collected Poems* (1934; Edinburgh: Birlinn, 1992), 132 (2nd series) ; Jamie, *Mr and Mrs Scotland are Dead: Poems 1980–1994* (Newcastle: Bloodaxe, 2002), 19.

Don't look away! I know it's hard
to keep regarding one so charred,

so disfigured by unfriendly fire
and think it once burned with desire.

Though fire has flayed off half my features
they once were like my fellow-creatures',

till some screen-gazing crop-haired boy
from Iowa or Illinois,

equipped by ingenious technophile
put paid to my paternal smile

and made the face you see today
an armature half-patched with clay,

an icon framed, a looking glass
for devotees of 'kicking ass',

a mirror that returns the gaze
of victors on their victory days

and in the end stares out the watcher
who ducks behind his headline : GOTCHA !

or behind the flag-bedecked page 1
of the true to bold-type-setting SUN ![25]

The last couplets now need annotation they didn't at the time,[26] but that doesn't affect the sequence that begins with savagely stressed full-rhyme for two short sentences (hard/charred, fire/desire), sets stress at ironically musical odds as the next long sentence conditionally begins (features/creatures, boy/Illinois, technophile/smile), returns to stressed full-rhyme as a reminder (today/clay), veers and sneers around a northern full-rhyme and southern pararhyme (glass/ass), and slams through the last complex sequence with a stressed-unstressed-stressed hat trick

[25] *The Gaze of the Gorgon* (London: Faber, 1992), 51–2 ; 'A Cold Coming' appeared in *the Guardian*, 18 Mar 1991 ; then (+ photograph + 'Initial Illumination') as a pamphlet (Newcastle: Bloodaxe, 1991).

[26] *The Sun*, a tabloid paper owned by Rupert Murdoch, strongly supported the Conservatives, in power during the Falklands and Gulf Wars ; notorious for triumphal or alarmist headlines with screamers, and topless 'page-three girls', it frequently prints cut-out Union Jacks so readers can display their patriotism in war and football alike. Its response to sinking the cruiser *General Belgrano* with the loss of 700+ Argentine lives was 'GOTCHA!' Murdoch's News International also owns *The Times*, and forced in the mid-1980s a move of London newspapers from Fleet Street to Wapping, resulting in a workforce cut by 90+ per cent and more profits (needed for BSkyB). Once, the sun was supposed never to set on the British Empire.

(gaze/days, watcher/GOTCHA!, 1/SUN!). By choosing tetrametric couplets for such a narrative (a kind of dramatic monologue) Harrison made rhyme his major challenge, and (given his subject) raised the political stakes through the roof ; his complete success is best judged by reading the whole poem aloud to an audience, but even these lines read aloud allow you to hear that far from being obstacles he must somehow overcome, the all-too-regular rhymes are like sticks of bombs Harrison himself drops with shame and anger. Time has not lessened their acute relevance.

Harrison could not have let himself go with such rhymes (and some in *A Cold Coming* are bitterer still) had he not long since practised and mastered rhyme's vagaries, understanding restraint as well as insistence. His great dramatic monologue *V.* as the last of his *Selected Poems* offers an interesting case.[27] Damned for colloquial obscenity by (supposed) readers who failed to see its relations with Gray's 'Elegy in a Country Churchyard', *V.* achieves among many successes a rhyme to ponder, first as the speaker surveys graffitoed headstones :

> The language of this graveyard ranges from
> a bit of Latin for a former Mayor
> or those who laid their lives down at the Somme,
> the hymnal fragments and the gilded prayer,
>
> how people 'fell asleep in the Good Lord',
> brief chisellable bits from the good book
> and rhymes whatever length they could afford,
> to CUNT, PISS, SHIT and (mostly) FUCK! (*Selected Poems*, 237)

and again in (imaginary) conversation with the aerosolling yob, vandaliser of the poet's parents' grave, whose speech is picked out by italics :

> 'Listen, cunt!' *I* said, 'before you start your jeering
> the reason why I want this in a book
> 's to give ungrateful cunts like you a hearing!'
> *A book, yer stupid cunt, 's not worth a fuck!* (p. 242)

[27] *V.* was added to the 2nd edition of *Selected Poems* (Harmondsworth: Penguin, 1987). There is an excellent edition (Newcastle: Bloodaxe, 1989) with material relating to its broadcast by Channel 4 TV : newspaper comments and the ignorance of politicians attacking *V.* for 'obscenity', must be seen to be believed. Interestingly, the C4 log shows most hostile calls came before or during broadcast ; a substantial majority of calls, including most after broadcast, were strongly supportive.

One point is phonetic—in a Leeds accent, especially a thick working-class one, 'book' and 'fuck' are closer to full-rhyme than in most British accents. The importance of accent to the rhyme can be judged in contrasting uses by France (also a North-Easterner by birth and residence, but unaccented on the page) in her sequence of prostitution-poems, 'On the Game' : ending 'The John Sonnets. 4' a 'john' (or customer) slaps down a vile full-rhyme :

> Who'd want a wife who's common as muck?
> There's one you love and the other you fuck.

and beginning 'Sexual Politics' a narrator counters Jong's famously 'zipless fuck' with a warning pararhyme :

> She is a woman who knows when a fuck
> has zips. And this, sweetheart, is it. First mistake :[28]

The contrast of full- and pararhymes is central to the thematic dissonances France achieves, but in Harrison's 'book/fuck' both effects are present, folded within the issue of accent—a rhyme encapsulating primary themes of his verse yet one he had been holding off throughout his career. Earlier in the *Selected Poems* one finds 'fuck' rhymed with "*Brooke*" ('The Curtain Catullus') and "luck" ('Palladas 63. On a Temple of Fortune turned into a tavern') ; 'book' with "duck" ('Palladas 37') ; and 'books' with "Puck's" ('Aqua Mortis') and "looks" ('A Good Read', 'Bringing Up'). Amid the clashing registers of *V.* it's easy to miss the consummation of the rhyme, reinforced by the autorhyme of "book", but it matters intensely, contrasting the (supposedly) sexless mental activity of reading with the most flatly physical of terms for (supposedly) mindless sexual activity, and perfectly coupling two great passions of Harrison's life and work, book-learning and what might properly be called fuck-learning. As for Byron,[29] sex is talismanic for Harrison, and changes to the sexual life he might have had as a working-class Yorkshireman are among the consequences of his education out of his natal class and culture. Since *V.* he has avoided repeating the pure rhyme (though 'books/fucks' has turned up tragically in 'The Act'

[28] *Storyville* (Newcastle: Bloodaxe, 1997), 77, 65.

[29] "I had such projects for the Don—but the *Cant* is so much stronger than *Cunt*—now a days—that the benefit of experience in a man who had well weighed the worth of both monosyllables—must be lost to despairing posterity": *Selected Letters and Journals* (London: John Murray, 1982), 220.

and satirically in 'Deathwatch Danceathon'[30]) ; its unexpected equation of generating love, babies, and learning in a vandalised urban churchyard haunted by Gray's 'Elegy' is (despite the obscenity that makes it a rhyme of a length few poets could afford) among the subtlest of Harrison's rebukes to a characteristic British contempt for bookishness.

Like lineation, rhyme is so taken for granted readers assume they notice it ; not so. Read *Paradise Lost* straight and you'll probably agree it is, as blank verse should be, unrhymed ; read just end-words and rhymes appear like rabbits out of a hat ; take any ten lines and ask which of 70+ words rhyme with any others. Here is Eve's last unfallen parting from Adam :

> Thus ſaying, from her Huſbands hand her hand
> Soft ſhe withdrew, and like a Wood-Nymph light
> *Oread* or *Dryad*°, or of *Delia's*° Traine, *kinds of nymph ; goddess of hunting*
> Betook her to the Groves, but *Delia's* ſelf
> In gate ſurpaſſ'd and Goddeſs-like deport,
> Though not as ſhee with Bow and Quiver armd,
> But with such Gardning Tools as Art yet rude,
> Guiltleſſe of fire had formd, or Angels brought,
> To *Pales* or *Pomona*°, thus adornd, *goddesses of pastures and fruit*
> Likeſt ſhe seemd, *Pomona* when ſhe fled
> *Vertumnus*°, or to *Ceres*° in her Prime, *god of seasons ; goddess of agriculture*
> Yet Virgin of *Proſerpina* from *Jove*. (N433; 1667, VIII. 385–96)

Some of the rhymes are : husband/hand, hand/hand, hand/and, Oread/dryad, like/Betook, Delia's/Delia's, groves/bow, withdrew/bow, gate/deport, goddess-/guiltless, rude/fled, *Pomona/Pomona, Pales/Ceres* ; and ll. 389–94 (deport/armd/rude/brought/adornd/fled) form a double tercet (*abcabc*) driving syntax through its complex comparisons. Sound- and rhyme-patterning of this density is a norm in *Paradise Lost*, and integral to what and how it means.

Milton's denunciation of rhyme does not show him a poet of his word, and his complaints should (like Blake's, Pound's, Flint's, and others) be taken with a lot of salt ; or, better, set against Levi's observation in 'Rhyming on the Counterattack', that the rhyming poet :

> is committed to ending a verse not with the word dictated by discursive logic but with another, strange word, which must be drawn from the few that end 'in the right way'. And so he is compelled to

---

[30] *Gaze of the Gorgon*, 21 ; *Laureate's Block* (Harmondsworth: Penguin, 2000), 11.

> deviate, to leave the path that is easier because it is predictable ; now, reading what is predictable bores us and so does not inform us. The restriction of rhyme obliges the poet to resort to the unpredictable : compels him to invent, to 'find' ; and to enrich his lexicon with unusual terms ; to bend his syntax ; in short, innovate. (p. 113)

Just so ; <u>and</u> a juicy pleasure in mouth and ear. The constraint of closed rhyming forms may well be shrugged off, like that of neoclassical metre, but the occurrence from time to time of rhyme, free or licensed to bind so lines' designs agree to dance, and sound once found is bound ably to intensify (and how!) the flow to show the consonance of words absurd or hard as maybe, makes sense (as Levi ever-cleverly presents) that only bores or fools ignore.

Exemplary Poems

1. 'I heard a Fly buzz—when I died—' (p. 97)

Dickinson was an inveterate pararhymer, and dissonance is a major feature of her work. Here, two of four end-rhymes are pararhymes (Room/Storm, firm/Room) and one at best a very loose vowel-rhyme (be/Fly) ; only in the last stanza does full-rhyme sound (me/see)—a reversal of what one might expect, associating dissonant half-rhymes with continuance and full-rhyme with a supercession of death. The reversal is mapped in the cluster of delayed autorhymes—"buzz" (ll. 1 + 13), "Room" (ll. 2 + 8), and "me" (ll. 10 + 14)—and by the internal half-rhymes giving way to accelerated full- and autorhyme—"I heard [. . .] I died" (1), "Between [. . .] Storm" (4), "Eyes [. . .] dry" (5), "last Onset" (7), "willed my [. . .] Signed away" (9), "Blue [. . .] Buzz" (13), "me be" (10), "And then [. . .] and then" (15), "not see to see—" (16) : the last chime of failing sight and life. The aural finality of the mosaic vowel- + autorhyme[31] is countered by the terminal dash, but prevented from escalating into the hysteria closely proximate rhymes can induce (as in 'Prufrock') by a subtle link between "I <u>wi</u>l<u>led</u>" (9) and "<u>Wi</u>ndows fai<u>led</u>" (15), distending the making of dispositions into the progressive collapse that brings the poem to a (potentially) serene termination.

Chain-rhyme pairs stanzas, creating a central division of statement ("I heard") and resolution ("I willed") marked by initial mosaic auto- + pararhyme, but the confident (even triumphant) resignation of "when the King [/] Be witnessed—in the Room" (ending the first pair) is carried

[31] Cf. Hopkins, 'Carrion Comfort', ending "wrestling with (my God!) my God."

into the calm business of dying (in the second). "Room/Storm" seems counter-semantic by contrast with quasi-semantic "firm/Room", but the arch-autorhyme of "Room" promotes the chain-pararhyme of "Storm/firm", sowing suspicion this may be the truly semantic rhyme, pointing the unstoppable "Heaves of Storm" and the frailty of flesh. The semantic chain-rhyme 'be/me' (ll. 10 + 14) is also unsettlingly trumped by the unsemantic non-rhyme 'Fly/see' (12 + 16), completing what "I heard a Fly" began.

2. 'Anthem for Doomed Youth' (p. 18)

MS drafts (🖱) show the poem's sonnet-form, Shakespearian octave + double-tercet sestet (*ababcdcdeffegg*) was complete in second draft ; a rhyme-scheme revision had to respect :

What passing-bells for you who die in herds ?
  —Only the monstrous anger of the guns !
  —Only the stuttering rifles' rattled words
Can patter out your hasty orisons. (2nd draft)

What passing-bells for these who die as cattle ?
  —Only the monstrous anger of the guns !
  Only the stuttering rifles' rapid rattle
Can patter out their hasty orisons. (final draft)

Arguing for rhyme as a stimulus to revision, N. S. Thompson makes some interesting points :

> the more direct and colloquial phrase to 'die as cattle' [. . .] left [Owen] with a difficult rhyme [. . .]. He was thus forced out of the 'poetic' and inappropriate metaphor of rifle shots as 'words' towards the concrete and active 'rattle'. [. . .] The impersonal 'cattle' is exactly what the context demands rather than the cliché 'herds' because it brings the reader more closely to the implied metaphor of butchery without making it obvious. The benefits of 'rattle' range from the actual use of rattles for communication on the Western Front to the tension between play and death in games of war, with the macabre suggestion of being taunted by a rattle (which in this case brings with it death). The change also supports the revision of 'you/your' to 'these/their' where the distancing lends sympathy rather than diminishes it as it suggests the panoramic scale of the slaughter.[32]

[32] 'Form and Function', in *P.N. Review*, 295 (May–June 2003), 42–6, p. 45.

I suspect it was vice versa, the existing "rattled" in l. 3 suggesting itself as the rhyme enabling "die as cattle" (which appeared in third draft), but about cattle/rattle and pronominal changes Thompson is spot on, and the availability of multiple drafts invites further investigation.

In its earliest complete form ('Anthem for Dead Youth') the structure was very loosely 7 + 7, but thereafter form rapidly clarified and settled :

fast/guns/mouths/burials/none/wail/shells
lost/eyes/candles/wreaths/palls/minds/blinds (BL MS 43721, fo.54a)

herds/guns/words/orisons
bells/choirs/shells/shires
all/eyes/goodbyes/pall/minds/blinds (BL MS 43721, fo.55a)

cattle/guns/rattle/orisons
asphodels/choirs/shells/shires
all/eyes/goodbyes/pall/minds/blinds (BL MS 43721, fo.56a)

cattle/guns/rattle/orisons
bells/choirs/shells/shires
all/eyes/goodbyes/pall/minds/blinds (BL MS 43720, fo.17a)

The quality of revision is evident in the *b*-pararhyme, guns/orisons, allowing the unstressed full-rhyme cattle/rattle to sound freely. Owen may have been prompted by Hamlet, who in Q2 pairs "awry" and "orizons" ending "To be, or not to be" (F has "away"), but the rhyme is utterly his own, trenchantly counter-semantic yet wrenched toward appalling semanticism, monstrous volleys over massed corpses. The brief appearance in l. 5 of "asphodels" is unexpected, and the third draft—a nearly fair-copy cancelled by a diagonal stroke—is very close to the fourth save in l. 5 :

No chants for them, nor wreaths, nor asphodels (3rd draft)

No ~~music for all their~~ no nor
mockeries for them ; ~~from~~ prayers ~~or~~ bells ;
now (4th draft, omitting two braces)

Clearly the line gave trouble, but in the final version ("No mockeries now for them ; no prayers or bells ;"), with the dactyl "mockeries" interfering at the beginning and "prayers" compressed to a monosyllable, rhythm is much stronger than in the third draft, where only the amphimacer "asphodels" resists over-regularity. The simplicity of bells/shells also offsets the rather less simple choirs/shires better than the counter-semantic asphodels/shells, and the octave as a whole becomes as bleakly flowerless as the battlefields in Owen's mind's eye.

In the sestet conversely, though the adjective for "minds" (l. 13) gave trouble (becoming "patient" only in fourth draft), "flowers", "tenderness", "minds" themselves, and all of l. 14 ("And each slow dusk a drawing-down of blinds") were achieved in first draft. Most of ll. 9–12 was also there, and all but a few words finalised in second draft—as one might expect from the sestet's greater tranquillity, elegiac rather than angry tone, and memorial sentiment. This odd reversal, calm sestet waiting on effortfully wrought octave, registers circumstances of the poem's composition in hospital, and must be deferred to 'Biography' (p. 326).

Yet why did Owen want rhyme at all ? His partly paradoxical choice of sonnet-form (p. 18), once made, more-or-less obligated him to rhyme—yet more distorted models were available to him, and in first draft the 14 lines were far from Petrarchan, reaching full-rhyme only in the couplet. For readers today applying formality to the charnel-house of the trenches seems bizarre, but Owen's poetic preferences weren't unusual among the poets of the First and Second World Wars (as anthologies show), and if partly a matter of his generation and the canonical poetry he knew, there is throughout his work a sense of form expressing a desire for order that trench-life made impossible in reality. As an expression of order, rhyme is part of that desire, and here, in its insistent equations of guns with orisons, shells with bells, eyes with goodbyes, all with pall, and minds with blinds, it poses (against the supposed order of military explanations and patriotic ignorance) an alternative interpretation of mass-slaughter that has better withstood the tests of time than less highly-wrought protest.

3. 'Sestina' (pp. 69–70)

Despite Swinburne's rhyming sestinas the form's *donné* (given basis) is substituting repetition for rhyme, and audible full- or half-rhymes are liable to disrupt the prescribed autorhyme. But cycling brings each autorhymed word in turn into proximity across a stanza-break and otherwise keeps them at least 3 and usually 6–8 lines apart, which can over-isolate. Bishop controls this with delicate consonance supporting each end-word in every line :

> September rain falls on the house.
> In the failing light, the old grandmother
> sits in the kitchen with the child

beside the Little Marvel Stove,
reading the jokes from the almanac,
laughing and talking to hide her tears.

on its string. Birdlike, the almanac
hovers half-open above the child,
hovers above the old grandmother
and her teacup full of dark brown tears.
She shivers and says she thinks the house
feels chilly, and puts more wood in the stove.

Ranging from simple alliteration ("Marvel Stove") and assonance (kitchen/child) to stronger vowel- and para-rhymes (wood/stove, Birdlike/almanac), these consonances leave no end-word unattended. They rise into openly leonine rhyme in ll. 12 ("She cuts some bread and says to the child") and (if rhyme is allowed to dictate the cæsura) 35 ("into the flower bed the child"), but apart from such incidental full-rhymes as the distant medial 'bread/bed' in these lines, 'up/teacup' in ll. 17/22, and 'be/the' in l. 25, no further—full-rhyme not being the sestina's way. It's easy amid fierce structural autorhyming to miss these delicately supportive effects, but their meticulous density shows Bishop's sense of their importance.

4. 'Nearing Forty' (pp. 22–3)

Like many Caribbean writers, Walcott (a St Lucian) is endlessly capable of poetry with beautiful, effectively patterned sound. This may reflect early and sustained exposure to a culture with far more oral artistry than is now usual in the UK or US (cf. dub poets, rappers, and MCs), but will also have been honed by poetic labour and work as a playwright. Whatever the reason, sound and rhyme are principal facts in 'Nearing Forty'.

How, though, does Walcott's spoken accent, founded on Lucian[33] but affected by long residences elsewhere, correlate with accents you or I as readers bring to the poem ? It can be spoken in any accent and readers need not imitate Lucian to understand it ; equally, to hear Walcott or any Lucian speak offers access to phonetic and rhythmic patterns that may emphasise or reveal meanings other accents elide. Words containing 'th', '-ing', '-sion', and '-tion' are particularly affected, as are pitch

[33] The accents of islands differ, but a Lucian accent is closer to a Jamaican or Trinidadian accent than any non-Caribbean accent.

and cadence, features audible in Caribbean speech.[34] In particular "ambition" and "elation" (ll. 16, 26) sound different if imagined with medial -bi- + -la- higher-pitched and '-tion' more stressed than in my own speech, and in l. 28 "imagination" : in 'The Schooner *Flight*' (N1825), Walcott wrote "I had no nation now but the imagination",[35] a pun equally thematic in 'Nearing Forty'.

Just how thematic is revealed by the major problem of pronunciation : "clerk" in l. 29. In Received Standard English it is 'clark', a semantic pararhyme with "work" (l. 31), but in Caribbean (and other) accents can move towards 'clurk', a full-rhyme—and work matters in this poem. Walcott's pronunciation is closer to 'clark', but the recording[36] is rather formal, and authorial instance cannot settle the matter ; voices vary with time and circumstance, and always between readers. The decision (or deliberate fudge) between 'clark' and 'clurk' that a speaking voice must make for "clerk" chooses between identities, one assimilated to Englishness, another refusing colonial imposition in favour of West Indian independence assimilated to work (and imagi/nations). These issues recur under 'Diction', 'History', and 'Biography', but nowhere more sharply posed than by the unstable rhyming of "clerk".

Internal rhyme, alliteration, and assonance generally elaborate the structure of overlapping quatrains and couplets. A complete rhyme-scheme is difficult to make clear, but what Walcott is about may be seen from the rhyme-words in ll. 1–7 (before the first couplet) :

> Insomniac since four hearing this narrow,
> rigidly metred, early-rising rain
> recounting, as its coolness numbs the marrow,
> that I am nearing forty nearer the weak
> vision thickening to a frosted pane.
> nearer the day when I may judge my work
> by the bleak modesty of middle age

Using cases to indicate half-rhyme (so *aa* is full-rhyme, *Aa, aA,* + *AA* half-rhymes) one could begin to notate this as *abc/dBe/Bc/bAf/EBe/gEgF/-fh* (or, sticking to end-rhymes, not *abacbcd*, but *abacbCd* : a first quatrain with a full-rhyme, *abac*, but a second and third, *acbC* + *cbCd*, already weakening to half-rhymes). Fuller notation shows the pattern-

[34] In reggae, rap, and dub songs phonetic features are for complex reasons often exaggerated.

[35] Beginning § 3, 'Shabine Leaves the Republic', *Selected Poems*, 350.

[36] *Derek Walcott reads a selection of his work* [from] Collected Poems 1948–84 *and* Omeros (Argo/Polygram, 1994; cat. no. 522–222–4).

ing of sound round end-rhymes, neither mere ornament nor fully weight-bearing, and points thematically important pararhymes, "rain"/"vision" (ll. 2 + 5) and the sequence 'weak/work/bleak' (*fFf*), where the expected end-rhyme is unexpectedly pararhyme, but a full-rhyme comes three words later and meanings are as closely related as sounds. But even this tithe of rhymes overstretches a notation that misses, for example, the rolling vowel- to pararhyme 'four/forty/day'—alluding to the biblical flood, when it rained for forty days and nights, and helping to explain the connections between nearing forty, listening to rain, and wondering what of one's work, if any, is worth preserving (and capable of being preserved).

As well as this general aural method, there are specific effects. The first involves the central couplets : 'middle age/average', 'bled for/metaphor', 'wretched/stretched', 'gutter-/sputter', 'foresaw/meteor', 'settle/kettle', 'gap/deep'. Except for the last, a pararhyme, they look like full-rhymes, but in each case something is wrong, usually stress.[37] Thus "average" is not 'AVER-AGE' (a spondee) but 'AV-er-age' (a dactyl), so 'middle age/average', is an eye full-rhyme pronounced as a pararhyme. Stress and enjambment affect 'BLED for/METaphor', because one needs to speak it not as "bled for [pause /] the household truth" (emphasising rhyme with "metaphor"), but as "bled [pause] for [/] the household truth" (blurring rhyme). 'wretched/stretched' mixes stressed and unstressed rhyme ; 'gutter-/sputter' is broken, and "gutter-" can hardly be lingered over long enough for the rhyme to be enjoyed ; and 'foresaw/meteor' is like 'middle age/average', "foresaw" a spondee and "meteor" not 'MEATY-OAR' but the dactylic 'MEET-i-er'. Like the enjambments, these skewed rhymes diminish the itemising certainty which so attracted eighteenth-century poets (including Dr Johnson) to heroic couplets, and make the extended central use of couplets compatible with the searching progression of the overlapping single-rhymed quatrains fore-and-aft. Only with the closed full-rhyme 'settle/kettle' does an unperturbed couplet emerge—a moment's rest with a hot drink—and it is immediately succeeded by an open half-rhyme, 'gap/deep'.

The second effect concerns "call conventional for convectional" (24). The leonine half-rhyme ruefully matches greenhorn with more seasoned perceptions, and "convectional" is either the only unrhymed end-word, giving emotional weight a technical polysyllable would not normally have, or a half-rhyme with 'settle/kettle' : the poem settling

[37] My scansion doesn't reflect Lucian pronunciation, but wouldn't be affected by it.

for understanding imaginative convection as neither more nor less useful than steam from a kettle-spout.

The third effect involves the autorhymes "rain" (ll. 2, 22, 30) and "work" (ll. 6, 25, 31) : pair them (2–6, 22–25, 30–31) and it's clear the interval between these key-words successively reduces until they lie snugly alongside one another, no longer at insomniac odds. The final pairing is part of the last quatrain, 'clerk/rain/work/weep' (*cbcj* or *Cbcj*), which links "clerk" to "work" (ll. '1' + '3'), while "work" and "weep" (3 + 4) alliterate ; rain weeps (2 + 4) as clerks work (1 + 3), and the central pair of autorhymes "rain" and "work" (2 + 3) isolates "clerk" and "weep" (1 + 4) : a weeping clerk, or resigned poet, to record the working rain. Everything becomes multiply cross-matched, like sudden emergence from complex hand-movements of a completed cat's cradle whose angled strings find in one another the perfect length and tension to allow the whole creation to be passed on.

Finally, the most distant full-rhymes are the *j*-sequence, "deep", "sleep", + "weep" (ll. 20, 27, 32). Interval again reduces, but is not eliminated : the reaching-back of l. 32 for its full-rhyme ties what could be a loose end into the weave of the poem ; the slow chime of "weep" (for which ears know there are full-rhymes even if eyes take a moment to find them) sustains the ending, confirming a peaceful resolution and (as a distant chime, not an alarm-clock couplet) allows deep sleep to continue beneath working, weeping, and now "lightly falling" rain.

Exercises: Rhyme-time

1. Like metre and form, rhyme is best understood in practice. Choose a word you like, systematically list multiple rhymes of every kind from full- to eye-, and then try deploying them in simple couplets, tercets, or quatrains. Keep as much else as possible (tone, metre, etc.) fixed in successive attempts : how do pressures on and effects of the rhyme(-type) vary?

2. Alliteration and assonance are also best learned in practice. After *La Disparition* Perec deployed all his unused **e**s in *Les Revenentes*, using no other vowel, and the game | is very instructive : try to write ten words without one | **a**, and as many again without &c, as logically follows in turn, | yet keep sense at your command and fend off all | straining and wrenching it, and learn the hard way that | all vowels bar one are in English hard to do | without. Versifying with restricted vowel-choice really is tough, even at minimal length, but teaches ears a lot that is tougher still to learn in other ways. Then try consonants !

3. Despite problems with notation, it is worth working out a complete rhyme-scheme at least once. Choose a short poem (sonnets are good) and map as completely as possible all sound relations, using colours as well as cases and/or faces. However well you thought you knew it, rhymes and other aural links that surprise you will emerge : how do discoveries affect your sense of the poem ? and how can one best relate the totalities of its sound/s and meaning/s ?

4. Unless otherwise indicated, words on the page are usually accentless, but many poets (and readers) have strongly regional voices. Choose two poems, one deploying full-rhymes and one half-rhymes, written by poets known to have accents other than your own ; chart what happens to the rhymes in your own voice and in (as nearly as you can) the poet's voice, and assess the consequences for meaning and implication.

5. The order of a rhyme may matter. In Shakespeare's *Sonnets*, for example, 'heart' precedes 'part' in 47 and 122 (and 'hearts' precedes 'parts' in 31), but 'part' precedes 'heart' in 23, 53, and 62 ; each precedes the other in 46. Contrariwise, 'heart' precedes 'art' in 24 and 125, but 'art' never precedes 'heart'. Look closely at sonnets 23, 24, 31, 46, 47, 53, 62, 122 and 125, and analyses the whys and wherefores of this rhyming leapfrog.

Chapter Glossary

accelerated : of rhyme, occurring relatively more proximately than others in a given poem ; thus ll. 3–4 of limericks produce metrically accelerated rhyme, and couplets are accelerated by comparison with cross- or arch-rhyme. The opposite is delayed rhyme.

alliteration : the repeated use of the same consonant/s in two or more proximate words.

arch-rhyme : mirror symmetry, as *abba*.

assonance : the repeated use of the same vowel/s in two or more proximate words.

autorhyme : a word rhymed with itself (my coinage) ; sometimes called 'null' rhyme.

broken rhyme : a word split between lines to facilitate a rhyme, as 'rent'/'vent- // ricle'.

chain-rhyme : systematic carrying-over from one stanza or component unit of form to the next of one or more rhyme-sounds, as in *terza rima* and Spenserian sonnets.

counter-semantic rhyme : between words with opposite or antagonistic meanings, as 'tall/small' or 'fear/leer'.

cross-rhyme : alternating double-rhymes, as *abab*.

delayed : of rhyme, occurring relatively more distantly than others in a given poem ; thus the cross-rhymes of Shakespearian sonnets are delayed by comparison with the couplet. The opposite is accelerated rhyme.

embedded rhyme : between a word and part of another word, as 'pit/ hospitality'.

end-rhyme : between words ending lines.

eye-rhyme : (or *printers' rhyme*) between words which, having endings spelt identically, look as if they rhyme, but are not so pronounced, as 'though/rough'.

free rhyme : deployed without specific interlinear pattern ; free end-rhyme is also sometimes called 'occasional' or 'random' rhyme.

full-rhyme : (or *perfect rhyme*) between words whose last stressed vowel and all following sounds are identical.

half-rhyme : (or *near* or *slant rhyme*) between words whose last stressed vowel <u>or</u> all following sounds are identical, but not both ; includes vowel- and pararhyme.

homographs : words with different meanings spelt identically.

homophones : words with different meanings pronounced identically.

imperfect rhyme : all kinds other than *rime riche* and full-rhyme.

initial : of rhyme, between words beginning lines.

internal rhyme : within a line, between two medial or a medial and the end-word, or between medial + medial or medial + end-words in different lines ; includes leonine rhyme.

leonine rhyme : between the word preceding the cæsura and the end-word of the same line.

medial : of rhyme, between medial words in successive lines.

monorhyme : when all lines rhyme, as *aaaa*.

mosaic rhyme : between a word and phrase, or between phrases.

pararhyme : between words whose last stressed vowels differ but following sounds are identical.

rhyme : the coincidence of sounds.

rhyme-scheme : an alphabetic method of notating rhyme-pattern in a stanza or poem ; line-lengths may be indicated, by placing the number of beats after the letter denoting the line.

rime riche : (or *identical rhyme*) between words whose sounds before <u>and</u> after the last stressed vowel are identical, as rhyming homophones.

semantic rhyme : between words with related or cognate meanings, as 'jeer/sneer' or 'love/give'.

single-rhymed : of a quatrain or other short unit of form, having only one pair of rhyming lines, (as *abcb* or *abac*) ; the pattern of non-rhyming lines thereby created.

spelling rhymes : between words deliberately (and usually comically) misspelt or abbreviated to create the rhyme, as 'hisses/Mrs' or 'devilry/S.O.B'.

stressed : of endings, with one or more stressed hypermetrical beats ; of rhymes, with the stressed vowel in the last beat.

thematic : of rhyme, puns etc., between or involving words whose meanings are engaged to the major theme/s of the work.

unstressed : of endings, with one or more unstressed hypermetrical beats ; of rhymes, with one or more unstressed beats following the last stressed vowel.

vowel-rhyme : between words whose last stressed vowels are identical but following sounds differ.

wrenched monorhyme : between unstressed participle endings (my coinage).

7
Diction

I prod our English : cough me up a word
JOHN BERRYMAN, 'Sonnets to Chris', 66.9[1]

Diction (from Latin *dicere*, to say) began by meaning 'a word', and evolved to mean the "manner in which anything is expressed in words" (*OED2*) ; in practical criticism it may be most simply and usefully defined as 'the choice of words (including the reason/s for and consequence/s of that choice)'.

The problem and opportunity is that English has the largest recorded vocabulary of any language. The *Oxford English Dictionary* (1884–1928; 2nd edn, 20 vols, 1989 + supplements—*OED2*) lists 300,000+ words in 620,000+ forms and combinations : it records few words coined after 1976 and is far from complete, but includes many archaic words and senses, and *etymology* (words' derivations)—so use *OED2* rather than a lesser dictionary, for poets often use older senses. There are also Joseph Wright's *English Dialect Dictionary* (6 vols, 1898–1905), with *c*.100,000 entries (many not in *OED2*), and substantial recent dictionaries of Lallans and of American, Australian, Canadian, Jamaican, New Zealand, South African, and West Indian English that collectively add 40,000+ words and far more senses. Still more recent computer-dictionaries and data-bases drawing on a recorded *corpus* of language (or many *corpora*) are able far more comprehensively and rapidly than print-dictionaries to include variant forms, phrases, and (very) new language, and if all are counted the recorded words of English run into millions. No one knows them all, and no *active* vocabulary (words I use) is as large as a *passive* vocabulary (words I know). That is a first constraint on diction—you can't say what you don't know how to say—but writers' active vocabulary is often large : Shakespeare's was *c*. 30,000 words, and

[1] *Collected Poems 1937–1971*, 103.

Winston Churchill's supposedly *c.* 65,000—barely 5 and 10 per cent respectively of *OED2*,[2] but enough to mean that in reading either everyone needs the dictionary.

Poetry tends to use words intensively, not simply extensively, and poetic diction for all its richnesses is in some ways more constrained than other dictions. Before a poem begins there is in theory complete freedom of choice, but some kinds of word (notably scientific polysyllables) are rare in verse, and any chosen metre, form, and rhyme will sharply limit the choices available. The *discourse* of a poem[3]—the sum of its choices of words, the particular diction it achieves (and discourse is to diction as scansion is to prosody, pp. 9–10)—may rule out (or in) slang, archaisms, or any other specified *lexical set*. A dramatic monologue, for example, should use words its supposed speaker would use, whose age, gender, class, and occupation narrow a poet's choices. The perception of what kinds of language are (supposedly) un/poetic is also influential, and requirements of literal truth, emotional honesty, or moral probity may mean that in the whole language only one word will do—or none, in which case a *coinage* may be needed, or a borrowing from another language. A voice under strain may also need a non-word, a grunt or howl—Shakespeare's dramatic poetry is full of such noises—or even silence, and the unsaid may need equal consideration.

One reason English has such a large vocabulary is that (alone among modern European languages) it combines two major etymological groups, the word-hoard of *Germanic* (or *Teutonic*) tongues, such as German and Dutch (with many concrete monosyllables), and the vocabulary of *Romance* languages (derived from Latin), such as Spanish and French (with many abstract polysyllables). There is thus often a choice between words differently derived which share meaning but are not true *synonyms* (with the same meaning) : consider canine/dog-like, uterus/womb, infant/baby, armament/weapon, even 'Fahrenheit' (a German scientist's name) and 'centigrade' (Latin, '100 steps'). Since the great Renaissance additions to English vocabulary, choice between Germanic and Romance words has been very real, not only for poets :

---

2 Shakespeare's vocabulary was a much larger percentage of the language then extant.

3 *Discourse* (cf. 'discursive') has many meanings : most strictly a form of prose argument (this book is *A Discourse of Poetic Craft*), it now usually means something much wider involving social circulation of words. My analogy 'discourse : diction :: scansion : prosody' is of more use in practical criticism than elsewhere, but personal choice is involved in most uses.

'four-letter words' are of Germanic origin (though some say 'Pardon my French') while polite or medical equivalents are Romance ; copulate/ fuck is a good example, and using the wrong one in the wrong company (whichever way round) is likely to embarrass.

Sometimes parallel to, sometimes criss-crossing the patterning of Romance against Germanic vocabulary is patterning of shorter words against longer. Varieties and interactions are infinite, in everyday conversation as well as poetry, but it is a matter to which poets attend, and in poetry is likely to be more considered and weightier. Here is the first stanza of Vaughan's 'The Water-fall' (N452 ; text from *Silex Scintillans*, 1655, omitting a drop-cap.) :

With what deep murmurs through time's ſilent ſtealth,
Doth thy tranſparent, cool, and watry wealth,
    Here flowing fall,
    And chide, and call,
As if his liquid, looſe Retinue ſtaid
Lingring, and were of this ſteep place afraid,
    The common paſs,
    Where, clear as glaſs,
    All muſt deſcend
    Not to an end :
But quickned by this deep and rocky grave,
Riſe to a longer courſe more bright and brave.

Vaughan was deeply religious, and 'The Water-fall' explores the soul's approach to and passage through death. In the last four lines Vaughan's hopes of eternal life are physically embodied in verse, as the dimeters (ll. 7–10) about descending and ending give way to the last pentameters (ll. 11–12) about being "quickned" ('quick' meaning alive, as in 'the quick and the dead') by the grave. Readers alerted by these longer lines about "a longer courſe" may notice that use of short against long lines is anticipated in the diction : "deep" (Germanic) against "murmur" (Romance), "ſilent" (R) against "ſtealth" (G), "tranſparent" (R) against "cool" (G), "liquid, looſe" (RG) against "Retinue" (R), "Lingring" (G) against "ſteep place afraid" (GRG). The point isn't rigid patterning (one word is Romance so the next must be Germanic) which would hobble the verse, but a play-off between the sounds and associations of words, and the differing effects on scansion and vocal pitch of a polysyllable and a sequence of monosyllables. Disturb the bisyllable, six monosyllables, bisyllable of "Lingring, and were of this ſteep place afraid", and the line will be less able to hold its place in the stanza ;

transpose "watry" (2) and "liquid" (5), and more than alliteration is lost ; replace "clear as glaſs" (8) with 'vitreous', and with metre, meaning, and rhyme preserved, line and stanza would be lessened, for neither at that point wants a Latinate polysyllable. The stanza's movement begins with the play-off of words, and Vaughan uses the momentum they generate to reach into motion a larger play-off of lines.

Another reason for the size of English is that it seizes words from every language its speakers hear. Between 1580 and 1630 words entered English from 50+ languages ranging from Amerindian tongues (tomahawk, wigwam) to Malay (orang-utan), since when many more have contributed : verandah is Hindi, almanac Arabic, sushi Japanese, laager Afrikaans, kitsch German, boomerang Aboriginal, tae kwon do Korean, and so on. All but 'kitsch', unsurprisingly, are *nouns*, and most stay that way, but some (like boomerang) also become *verbs* and develop multiple forms[4]—a trick English pulls with its own nouns (consider dogging, hounding, rabbiting, parroting, badgering, beavering, ratting, crowing, ferreting, and swanning, as well as spidery handwriting, waspish attitudes, catty remarks, sheepish looks, or mulish behaviour). Absorption into the mother-tongue can be judged in part by whether a word retains italics : *Lebensraum*, 'living room', a desire for and/or policy of territorial expansion, usually keeps them and refers specifically to Hitler's Eastward expansions of the Third Reich ; *Zeitgeist*, 'spirit of the age', may not take italics (it often loses its German capital) and is generally applied ; coup d'état, an illegal change of government, led by the individually absorbed 'coup', now usually doesn't, but *état* (French, 'state') keeps its acute accent. Plurals are tricky—but slapdash modern usage flattens everything into simple –s forms anyway (oxes for oxen, referendums for referenda, stigmas for stigmata, radiuses for radii, etc.). In general, though, this insouciance of English in plugging words into its own flexible analytical grammar is a great strength.

For poets it all makes the language at once sweetshop and minefield. When Loy's 'Mexican Desert' begins with "The belching ghost-wail of the locomotive" heading into a "jazz band sunset" there is as much

---

[4] Words are traditionally analysed in 9 categories : *nouns*, names of persons, places, or things (cat) ; *pronouns*, substitutes for nouns (he, it, who) ; *adjectives*, qualifying nouns (small, tabby) ; *verbs*, expressing a state or action (be, purr) ; *adverbs*, qualifying verbs, adjectives, other adverbs, or whole sentences (very, so, loudly) ; *articles* (a, an, the) ; *prepositions*, relating pro/nouns to the rest of the sentence (at, on, with) ; *conjunctions*, linking words or word-groups (and, but, if) ; and grammatically independent *interjections* (oh, damn). Thus 'The tabby cat slept soundly on its sofa but snored, alas.' gives the sequence 'article adjective noun verb adverb preposition pronoun noun conjunction verb interjection'.

aural dissonance as pleasure in the juxtapositioning of Old-English 'belch' and 'ghost', Middle-English 'wail', industrial Latin 'locomotive', Afro-American 'jazz', and Germanic 'sunset' ; whether poetic synthesis is achieved is moot. Much surer-footed, Loy's later 'Hot Cross Bum', beginning "Beyond a hell-vermilion [/] curtain of neon [/] lies the Bowery", ends with a mingling of words as multi-ethnic as New York itself :

> Aptest attainer
> to apex of Chimera
>
> Inamorato
> of incognito ignis fatuus
>
> fatuitous
> possessor of thoroughfare
>
> O rare behaviour
>
> a folly-wise scab of Metropolis
> pounding with caressive jollity[5]

Here "ignis fatuus", literally 'foolish fire' and admitted to the *OED* as a freestanding English noun, has only inappropriate alternatives (neither 'marshlight' nor 'werelight' go with the Bowery, nor 'will o' the wisp'[6] or 'Jack a Lantern' with anonymous sex) but should perhaps be in the plural, properly *ignes fatui*, and picks that up with "fatuitous" (concealing 'fortuitous' ?) ; the whole mélange (including an *allusion* to "O rare Ben Jonson", the text on his gravestone in Westminster Abbey) follows a more consistent path than it seems. Other poems conscious of a mingled or multiple subject may also show unusually heterogeneous diction, as Hill's trans-historical *Mercian Hymns* (pp. 180–2) and Muldoon's *Madoc: A Mystery* (a tribute to Coleridge's and Southey's 'Pantisocracy') do on a grand scale. But it may be a game, or just for pleasure in words : Raworth's 'Sixty Words I've Never Used Before' attaches each to a date between 1937 (when he was conceived) and 1996 (when I assume the poem was written), and sends readers to a dictionary for an entertaining round of working out how each dated word ("1937 astragal [/] 1938 constat [/] 1939 gony [/] 1940 keck [/] 1941 olid") relates to the life they oddly chart—but without an *OED* Raworth's humour is pretty much unavailable.[7]

---

[5] *The Last Lunar Baedeker* (1982; Manchester: Carcanet, 1985), 17, 187, 198.

[6] Which *OED2* wonderfully defines as figuratively covering anything that "deludes or misleads by means of fugitive appearances".

[7] Muldoon, *Poems 1968–1998* (London: Faber, 2001) ; Raworth, *Collected Poems*, 524.

Dialect and the incredibly rich regional diversity of English is another matter. With MacDiarmid's *A Drunk Man Looks at a Thistle* readers know immediately that they are dealing with Lallans (p. 133), and glossing is usually provided :

I amna fou sae muckle° as tired—deid dune°.	*drunk as much ; exhausted*
It's gey° and hard work coupan° gless for gless	*very ; upending*
Wi° Cruivie and Gilsanquhar and the like,	*with*
And I'm no° juist as bauld° as aince° I was.	*not ; bold ; once*
The elbuck fankles° in the course o time,	*elbow becomes clumsy*
The sheckle's no sae souple°, and the thrapple°	*wrist ; supple ; gullet*
Grows deif° and dour° : nae langer up and down	*unimpressionable ; stiff*
Gleg° as a squirrel speils° the Adam's apple.[8]	*lively ; climbs*

Whether acknowledged as a language or labelled a dialect of Scots or English, this is sufficiently distinct to enable use of all that Lallans provides without alienating readers (who if not speakers of Lallans need help anyway) ; it is also fully political in embodying a lowland Scots identity, as MacDiarmid's titular thistle is a Scottish emblem and drunkenness a (supposed) national pastime. The same politics applies to Black American dialect and *idiom* (characteristic turns of phrase etc.) in poets like Paul Dunbar (N1223)—however controversial the politics of free people using 'plantation' dialect at all—and to *patois*, *creoles*, and *nation language* in Caribbean poetry. When Bunting translates *Son los pasariellos del mal pelo exidos*, an unascribed epigraph to *Briggflatts* (N1421), as "The spuggies are fledged" matters are less clear : "spuggies" is a Northumbrian form of a word occurring in Northern English dialects and Scottish but little-known elsewhere ; in using it Bunting exemplified his regional identity and poetic music, but also provided a note ("*Spuggies* : little sparrows") not all editions carry, nor all readers find.[9] Bunting himself thought "Notes are a confession of failure, not a palliation of it, still less a reproach to the reader, but may allay some small irritations", and it's easy to snort agreement—but why, if 'spuggies' was richly familiar to him, should its use be deemed a failure ? and what, exactly, fails ? Not politics : the quotation is from the thirteenth-

[8] Respelled with MacDiarmid's permission by J. C. Weston (Amherst: U. Massachusetts P., 1971).

[9] "The Northumbrian tongue travel has not taken from me sometimes sounds strange to men used to the koiné [common tongue] or to Americans who may not know how much Northumberland differs from the Saxon south of England. Southrons would maul the music of many lines in Briggflatts" : *Collected Poems*, 148 ; other quotations, pp. 38, 148, 147.

century Spanish *Libro de Alexandre*, or 'Book of Alexander [the Great]', an episode in which informs part III of *Briggflatts* ; dialect translation of such an arcane source speaks to prejudicial (Southern English) assumptions that Northumbrian accent and dialect imply rural ignorance and limitation. There is a challenge to readers, but 'failure' is too harsh for a helpful gloss, and if such limitations are accepted what is to stop demands that poetry always be written for the laziest readers ? Moreover, what (if anything) is the difference between Bunting's "spuggies" and, say, Stickney's "math" in 'Age in Youth' :

> In the rude math her torn shoe mows
> Juices of trod grass and crushed stalk
> Mix with a soiled and earthy dew,
> With a smear of petals gray as chalk.[10]

Easily taken as a misprint for 'path', 'math' (from OE *mæþ*) is that which has been mown ; as *OED2* notes, it is "*obs.* exc. *dial.*" (obsolete except [in] dialect)—but survives unrecognised in 'aftermath'. Stickney's apolitical use is exact, sending me to the dictionary to kick myself for not making the connection. Rare words, whatever their reason for rarity, and whether truly rare or in limited geographical or occupational uses, always make readers work ; rightly.

A different aspect of problem-and-opportunity comes into focus in translations of whole poems, for despite its huge vocabulary there are things English won't easily do. Lacking a grammatical form for reflexive verbs, for example, their deliberate abuse is hard to catch,[11] and the more engaged language is with moral and political pressure, the harder a translation. The outstanding recent example is Celan's tremendous *Sho'ah*[12] poem 'Todesfuge', of which there are many translations : the

---

[10] Parini, *Columbia Anthology*, 294.

[11] An epigraph to Hill's *Collected Poems* is Péguy's *Quand le monde moderne avilit, mettons que c'est alors qu'il travaille de sa partie* : with no direct object *avilir*, 'to tarnish', should be reflexive (*s'avilit*) ; not so, it creates a grammatical frisson hard to translate. The nearest I can come is 'When the modern world smirches, let's say that then it warms to its work'.

[12] The first word used for events in Germany from 1933, by Jews from *c.* 1936, was Hebrew *churban* (Yiddish *churbm*), often in *der driter churbm*, 'the third *churbm*', after destruction of the First and Second Temples. By 1940 a group of Jewish scholars in Palestine felt events did not allow a term implying comparability and imposing Deuteronomic interpretation, that Nazis were God's agents, and chose Hebrew *Sho'ah*, 'destruction' or 'catastrophe', with biblical roots but in broader secular use. 'Holocaust' came into English use in 1956–8, and became increasingly standard and restricted in meaning (earlier holocausts were denied the word) until Lanzmann's film *Shoah* (1986) opened debate—as well it might : 'holocaust', from the Septuagint,

best-known is probably by Hamburger, who calls it 'Death Fugue', but the best is by Felstiner in the course of his unusual, brilliant biography, *Paul Celan: Poet, Survivor, Jew.*[13] He calls it 'Deathfugue', registering the grammatical difficulty of *Todesfuge* in German and attempting in a strange spondee some equivalent of "the accentual (and atrocious) symmetry of *Tó-des fú-ge*" (pp. 32–3). "Deutschland", a word that occurs in Celan's verse only in 'Todesfuge', doesn't become 'Germany' ; knowing it has been "drilled into everyone by Nazism's 'Deutschland, Deutschland, über Alles' " (p. 36), Felstiner lets it stand, preserving in "he writes when it grows dark to Deutschland" the rhythm and alliterative shock of Celan's "der schreibt wenn es dunkelt nach Deutschland" (cf. Hamburger's "he writes when dusk falls to Germany"). More radically, Celan's "der Tod ist ein Meister aus Deutschland", repeated four times, progressively reverts to German—"this Death is a master from Deutschland", "Death is a master aus Deutschland", "Death is ein Meister aus Deutschland", "der Tod ist ein Meister aus Deutschland"—to stop it lapsing into familiarity : "In this gradual reversion, unavailable to German readers, we re-enter the darkness of deathbringing speech" (p. 40). Another phrase, "dein goldenes Haar Margarete [/] dein aschenes Haar Sulamith", is also translated once ("your golden hair Margareta [/] your ashen hair Shulamith") but repeated as the last lines of the poem stands identically in Celan's German and translation—as *Sulamite, Shulamith* can only do : it is a *hapax legomenon*, a word found only once in the surviving records of a language, in the Song of Solomon 6: 13. Probably a variant of 'Shunnamite', 'inhabitant of Shunem', it might mean anything ; as the name or quality of the 'dark but comely' beloved whose praises Solomon so extravagantly and (in most readings) vainly sang, it has come to signify a dark-complexioned, usually Jewish, beauty, especially as a mistress, but for those who know its origin may carry a sense of a woman besieged. In Celan's dreadful contrast of golden Nordic blonde and ashy Jewish brunette, in the mind of the Deathmaster and within/without the camp where gold was taken and ash created, there stir meanings nor English nor German can

is "A sacrifice wholly consumed by fire ; a whole burnt offering" (*Sh. OED*). Gentile etymology and Christian associations pose problems, particularly in 'sacrifice' : Jews (and others) were 'sacrificed', Nazis wielded knife and fire ; but 'sacrificed' to whom in hope of what ? The long complicity of Christian churches with anti-Semitism makes any Christian term dubious. See Young, *Writing and Rewriting*, 85–9.

[13] New Haven and London: Yale UP, 1995 ; the translations that structure the biography are gathered and augmented in *Selected Poems and Prose of Paul Celan* (New York and London: Norton, 2001). Hamburger, *Poems of Paul Celan* (1972; New York: Anvil Press, 1988).

encompass alone, but that Felstiner, following Celan's recourse to Hebrew roots, has been able to gift between tongues.

Conversely, shadows of unspeakability wrap Hill's *"born 19.6.32—deported 24.9.42"* in 'September Song', for despite the correspondence of *"9"* with 'September' one cannot really <u>say</u> it : comparing the difficulty with trying to speak the title of Larkin's 'MCMXIV' (N1653), which means but is not the same as '1914', Ricks comments (in a critical lightning-bolt) that "Larkin uses roman numerals for a departed honour ; Hill uses modern numerals for a new dishonour."[14] Not all numerals are so unspeakable, but like other non-alphabetic symbols with verbal equivalents (including punctuation-marks) all carry the possibility for poets in need. If silence is a primary concern, though, matters are likely to pass swiftly beyond diction to layout and white space, or illustration—as Stevie Smith's haunting drawing of an unspeaking woman restates and completes 'Not Waving but Drowning'.[15]

These are sombre considerations, but diction need not be solemn (it need not be anything). Consider Herrick's little poem 'Upon Julia's Breaſts' (N358, and see 359 ; text from *Hesperides*, 1648, omitting a drop-cap.) :

> Diſplay thy breaſts, my *Julia*, there let me
> Behold that circummortal purity :
> Betweene whoſe glories, there my lips Ile lay,
> Raviſht, in that faire *Via Lactea*.

This could easily be paraphrased as offensive wolf-whistle ('tits out for the lad'), but coinage of the slightly absurd "circummortal" and a horrible pun on *"Via Lactea"* (Milky Way) make for loving jest rather than leering insult. Eliot did something similar beginning the solemn-sounding 'Mr. Eliot's Sunday Morning Service' with "Polyphiloprogenitive", which he invented to mean 'liking to have lots of children' : it's a learned joke, but it <u>is</u> a joke, for poets are not quite supposed to fill entire tetrameters with single words, especially ones that don't exist. One step more and Mary Poppins is singing "Supercalifragilisticexpialidocious".

Invented words are particularly odd : if they don't catch on or (like *supercali . . .*) remain tied to their source, they are *nonce words* (invented

[14] *Force of Poetry*, 302.

[15] *Selected Poems* (Harmondsworth: Penguin, 1978) ; also sans drawing N1440.

for a specific occasion), often comic ; if they do catch on they become *neologisms*, and cease to be recognised in their original sources as new. Since the nineteenth century there has developed a critical attitude that poets should make do with words that exist, and that coinages are appropriate only in comic verse, like Carroll's wonderful *portmanteau* words (combining existing words) in 'Jabberwocky' (N1135)—but among the reasons English has such a large vocabulary is that poets once happily invented words if no existing one meant what they wanted. In Renaissance poetry especially neologisms abound that one would not wish to lack—including 'discourteously' ('Greensleeves', so Henry VIII ?), 'sunburnt' (Sidney), 'attune', 'display', 'scorched', 'graceful' (Spenser), 'waggles' (Nashe), 'chirrup' (Marlowe), and 'lifelong' (Browne), all helpfully marked in Norbrook's and Woudhuysen's *Penguin Book of Renaissance Verse*. But new words now are often restricted to scientific or colloquial use, though some, particularly *acronyms* (NIMBY, Not In My Back Yard ; DINKY, Dual Income No Kids Yet) and coinages by dub-poets and rappers (the portmanteau 'contagerous', 'contagious + dangerous', to describe AIDS), gain wider usage, as 'scuba', 'laser', and 'ginormous' ('self-contained underwater breathing apparatus', 'light amplified by the stimulated emission of radiation', 'giant + enormous') did long ago.

A concentrated test of neologisms is provided by Hollander's 'Adam's Task' (N1776), which takes as epigraph Genesis 2: 20, "And Adam gave names to all cattle, and to the fowl of the air, and to every beast of the field". Hollander names 19 imaginary animals : paw-paw-paw, glurd, spotted glurd, whitestap, implex, awagabu, verdle, McFleery's pomma, grawl, flisket, kabasch, comma-eared mashawk, pambler, rivarn, greater wherret, lesser wherret, sproal, zant, lily-eater. What sort of animal is each ? Your imagination is as good as mine, but 'paw-paw-paw' to 'awagabu', in the first stanza, are (I think) cattle ; 'verdle' to 'comma-eared mashawk', in the third, fowls of the air ; 'pambler' to 'lily-eater', in the fifth, beasts of the field. Ponder what led Hollander to these coinages, and why you dis/like each ; with all sounds available he could easily have produced an irritating mess, but managed a fine *jeu d'esprit*. Deliberate *archaism* of diction has similar potential for awkwardness : it can inform forgery, as in Chatterton's *Poems, Supposed to have been written at Bristol, by Thomas Rowley* (1777), but Coleridge revised 'Rime of the Ancient Mariner' to scrap its fake-medievalism in 1798, and T. E. Brown, despite fine lyric and narrative verse, is remembered only for one line of 'My Garden'—"A garden is a lovesome thing, God wot !"—whence 'godwottery', kitsch garden-decorations (gnomes etc.) or affectedly archaic language.

One reason Hollander succeeds is that readers mentally triangulate from what they have already read sets of expectations about the sorts of thing likely to be said next, and how they are likely to be said—collectively, the *register* of a text. In classical antiquity register was straightforward. Cicero distinguished three styles of composition, the low, intermediate, and grand, and ordered their use by theme : low style (*parva*) for the everyday and base, matters of fact, financial affairs, and comedy ; intermediate style (*modica*) for middling and mixed matters ; high style (*magna*) when lives were in the balance or great eloquence needed, and for tragedy. But as Auerbach showed in a remarkable essay, '*Sermo Humilis*', "in the Christian context humble everyday things, money matters or a cup of cold water, lose their baseness and become compatible with the lofty style ; and conversely [. . .] the highest mysteries of the faith may be set forth in the simple words of the lowly style which everyone can understand".[16] Augustine, worrying at Cicero, accepted a threefold division but related styles to an author's (Christian) purpose (to teach, condemn/praise, and persuade[17]), not theme or subject-matter, and so opened the way theoretically to justify more or less any diction a writer thought might work. In modern practice almost all command multiple spoken registers (distinct ways in which you speak to friends, parents, teachers, uniformed officials et al.), but written register is not so readily flexible—and however unstable the theory, practice is as sharp as catching a pretentious word in conversation. *Decorum* still has some teeth.

Register is instructively clear in humour. Mortimer Collins's 'Salad', a marvellous pastiche of Swinburne beginning "O cool in the summer is salad", turns high style on low matter :

> Take endive . . . like love it is bitter ;
>   Take beet . . . for like love it is red ;
> Crisp leaf of the lettuce shall glitter,
>   And cress from the rivulet's bed ;
> Anchovies foam-born, like the Lady
>   Whose beauty has maddened this bard ;
> And olives, from groves that are shady ;
>   And eggs—boil 'em hard.

"Anchovies foam-born, like the Lady" earns a giggle, and the wrenched

[16] *Literary Language*, 37.
[17] *docere, vituperare sive laudare, flectere : De Doctrina Christiana* 19.

accent of an-chó-vies next to the vowel-rhyme of "foam-born" is a good dig at Swinburne's elaborate sound, but the last line works through a cruder (if still funny) drop in register. J. K. Stephen's 'A Sonnet', on the other hand, goes straight for the Romantic jugular :

> Two voices are there : one is of the deep ;
> It learns the storm-cloud's thunderous melody,
> Now roars, now murmurs with the changing sea,
> Now bird-like pipes, now closes soft in sleep :
> And one is of an old half-witted sheep
> Which bleats articulate monotony,
> And indicates that two and one are three,
> That grass is green, lakes damp, and mountains steep :
> And, Wordsworth, both are thine : at certain times
> Forth from the heart of thy melodious rhymes,
> The form and pressure of high thoughts will burst :
> At other times—good Lord ! I'd rather be
> Quite unacquainted with the ABC
> Than write such hopeless rubbish as thy worst.[18]

Stephen's ear for Wordsworthian voices is sharp enough to make Romanticists wince (as well they might : Wordsworth did infamously write in 'The Thorn' "I've measured it from side to side : [/] 'Tis three feet long and two feet wide"[19]), but if inspired as criticism, his game is comedy and his mode pastiche. The octave gives an excellent sample of registers, and the interplay of pentametric lines and iambic rhythm with mono- and polysyllabic words can be seen shifting between quatrains, but repeating that pattern in the tercets, with a slight elevation of his own diction ("thy worst" ?[20]), lets Wordsworth off with only a buffet.

With parody, more tightly directed, blows may be shrewder. In late December 1817 a banker called Horace Smith wrote a sonnet he called 'On a Stupendous Leg of Granite, Discovered Standing by Itself in the Deserts of Egypt, with the Inscription Inserted Below'. It begins :

---

[18] 'Salad' and 'A Sonnet' : Jerrold and Leonard, *Century of Parody*, 286, 376.

[19] Wordsworth revised ll. 32–33 for *Miscellaneous Poems* (1820), to read "Though but of compass small, and bare [/] To thirsty suns and parching air"—but the original was allowed to stand from 1798, through 4 editions of *Lyrical Ballads* to the first collected *Poems* (1815).

[20] *Thou, thee, thy, thine* are intimate forms of second person singular (cf. French *tu*, German *du*) : Shakespeare distinguished them from the formal singular + plural *you, your, yours* (see Hotspur's parting from Kate in *1 Henry IV* 2.3), but by *c*.1800 *thy* was consciously archaic.

In Egypt's sandy silence, all alone,
Stands a gigantic Leg, which far off throws
The only shadow that the desert knows.
'I am great Ozymandias,' saith the stone,

Smith was staying with Shelley, who discovering what his guest was about made his own attempt, which he called less simply 'Ozymandias' (N870), rather more famously beginning :

I met a traveller from an antique land,
Who said—'Two vast and trunkless legs of stone
Stand in the desart . . . Near them, on the sand
Half-sunk a shattered visage lies, whose frown[21]

If an object lesson in titling and pararhyme, Shelley's success turns on inflation. Smith's problem (one of them, anyway) is that "gigantic Leg", which "all alone" simply cannot in its monosyllabic curtness bear the awe it supposedly provokes ; Shelley's solution, "vast and trunkless legs", risks absurdity in coining 'trunkless' (cf. 'legless', 'truncated') but with the (wrongly) plural "legs" comes triumphantly through ; "lifeless" (l. 7) and "boundless" (l. 13) join "trunkless" in a lexical set restraining the vigorous reverence with which Shelley re-animates fragmented majesty. And restraint is needed : "antique land" (l. 1) shoots past, but peered at reveals more sound than sense ; "shattered visage" (l. 4) and "sneer of cold command" (l. 5) teeter towards melodramatic cliché ; sheer intoxication with 'Ozymandias' (an ancient Greek corruption of a Pharaonic title, 'User-ma-Ra') banishes common sense—as polysyllabic South American volcanoes do in Turner's 'Romance' ("Chimborazo, Cotopaxi [/] Had taken my speech away. [/. . .] O shining Popocatapetl [/] It was thy magic hour"[22]). How vulnerable Shelley left himself for all his success is indicated by Nemerov's 'Ozymandias II', beginning "I met a guy I used to know, who said : [/] 'You take your '57 Karnak, now [. . .]' " and never ceasing a mercilessly admiring deflation of Shelley's grandiosity.[23]

The general contrast between Shelley's and Nemerov's dictions is that of high refined and low *demotic* registers, but four words in 'Ozymandias II' pose other questions : the '57 Karnak (an imaginary model named for the great Egyptian temple-complex) has "rubber boobs for

[21] Both texts quoted from Davenport, 'Ozymandias'.
[22] First published in *The Hunter and Other Poems* (1916) and very widely anthologised.
[23] *Collected Poems*, 457.

bumpers" and is "owned by a nigger now [/] Likelier'n not" but "that fucking car still runs" ; there is also an interjection, "Jeezus". All four questionable words are within inverted commas, spoken by the "guy I used to know", not the poet, let alone Nemerov *in propria persona*, and no British student I've asked has found any unacceptably offensive in context : "boobs" is humorous and "fucking" a standard demotic intensifier, expected in speech ; "Jeezus" is taken in the same spirit, with a tweak of American accent ; and "nigger", a word that usually raises immediate hackles and open protest, seems sufficiently protected in this context by a sense of truth to a particular speaker's idiom (backed by the specifically American-demotic "likelier'n not"). In America and some Commonwealth countries neither obscenity nor profanity have become as normative as in Britain, and "nigger" (despite its partial reclamation as 'nigga/z' in rap) is famously still 'the N-word', unspeakable even in court : so British readers may underestimate the risks Nemerov ran, and 'politically correct' ones be so offended that they compulsively conflate the demotic with prejudice and reject the poem wholesale. Strongly gendered approaches, sensitive to masculine bias in obscenity, may also react to "fucking" as more than a venial sin.

Such conflations are unhelpful. The problem with obscenity may indeed be misogyny, if, for example, 'cunt' is used to mean 'woman'—and there is a proper political and ideological concern with sexism, as with racism ; but taste in obscenity and blasphemy may also reflect formal censorship or middle-class nicety, and varies historically. Before the *Lady Chatterley* trial in 1960 most obscene material could not legally be published in Britain, but the level of censorship that prevailed *c.*1850–1960 was unprecedented. Though one couldn't publish overt obscenities, Jacobethans were far more bothered by blasphemy than sex : after 1606 'God' could not be printed as an oath in play-texts, but nobody minded Hamlet's "Country matters". The Restoration, thoroughly bawdy, produced in Rochester the most systematically obscene poet on record, habitually even-handed in obscenity (misanthropic not misogynistic) and genuinely challenging. In 'A Ramble in St James's Park', "rows of mandrakes tall did rise [/] Whose lewd tops fucked the very skies"[24]—forcing us to recognise that if we are all too used, since Freud, to almost anything as a metaphor <u>for</u> sex (fountain-pens, popping corks . . .), we have become unused to sex <u>as</u> a metaphor : confronted not simply with a striking idea, tall plants 'fucking the skies' as

[24] Vieth, ed., *Complete Poems* (New Haven and London : Yale UP, 1968)—the first complete *unexpurgated* edition—p. 40.

they grow, but with tall mandrakes (human legs below ground and plant bodies above) doing that same thing, the modern mind balks. In the end, I suspect, most of the obscenity relates outward to politics, as Rochester's raging attack on his own impotence in 'The Imperfect Enjoyment' (N551) reflects his alcoholism and relates a topos in classical bucolics to his own hopeless position at court as an aristocrat of a kind whose day was largely done. There is also a lesson about the limits of propriety : in *Poems on Several Occasions* (1680) the text of 'The Maim'd Debauchee' includes this stanza :

> Nor ſhall our *Love-fits Cloris* be forgot,
> When each the well-look'd *Link-Boy* ſtrove t'enjoy
> And the beſt Kiſs, was the deciding *Lot*,
> Whether the *Boy* uſ'd you, or I the *Boy*.

Surviving MSS show even this first printing is *euphemistic*, substituting "uſ'd" for another verb. Subsequent editions, even if generally including (in *bowdlerised*[25] form) Rochester's poems of heterosexual promiscuity, simply omitted this casual admission of bisexual practice, or confined it to end-notes, but in Vieth's edition Rochester's first impulse was restored with "Whether the boy fucked you, or I the boy" (N550). Barbara Everett, analysing 'The Sense of Nothing' in Rochester, commented after quoting 1680 that "It could hardly be said that this [stanza] gets worse when Vieth reads ["fucked"]. In fact a strong case could be made for feeling that the verse undoubtedly gets better in the more brutal transposition"[26]—and that those who found 'used' less offensive than 'fucked' were peculiarly misguided.

Lewd or slyly explicit verses continued to be written openly in the eighteenth century—Gay's 'Work for a Cooper', like much of Swift, holds its own with *Tom Jones* or *Fanny Hill*—but later in the century several factors began to foreclose on freedom of diction. Most important were probably growth of the middle classes with bourgeois standards of gentility to uphold and display, and Enlightenment rationalisations of language represented by standardised *orthography* (spelling) and the emergence of 'Received Standard' English. Governments also lurched rightward after the French Revolution in 1789, and didn't lurch back until well after the Napoleonic Wars ended in 1815.

---

[25] Thomas Bowdler (1754–1825) produced the *Family Shakespeare* (10 vols, 1818), with all rude, lewd, or otherwise dubious words replaced or cut : "God" always becomes "Heaven", Lear's "Aye, every inch a king" is cut from 22 lines to 7, Doll Tearsheet vanishes altogether.

[26] *Poets in Their Time*, 104.

Both factors inform the nineteenth-century political renewal of Non-Conformity, sidelined since 1660, and from the 1870s Neo-Puritanism was a dominant force. John Fowles once sweepingly claimed that "in the nineteenth century [. . .] not a single novel, play or poem of literary distinction [. . .] ever goes beyond the sensuality of a kiss"[27] : patently not right (Byron, Browning, Dobson . . .), but not so wrong. The period 1885–1967, during which all male homosexuality, irrespective of age, consent, and privacy, was in Britain a criminal offence punishable by two years' hard labour, was anticipated by sharp restrictions of what it was legally, socially, and literarily acceptable to say, and by *c.*1900 adult ignorance of sexuality was being manufactured on an unprecedented scale. The scars ran deep—think of the lurid fussing over Eliot's rumoured '[Colombo and Bolo verses]', only published in 1996, or Larkin's "Sexual intercourse began [/] In nineteen sixty-three [/] (Which was rather late for me)" in 'Annus Mirabilis'[28]—and still have not wholly healed.

But things have changed, especially since 1980. In November 2002 the *Guardian* offered the following tart definition on the front-page of its review-section :

> **fuck** /fʌk/ *v. formerly coarse slang* **1** Mild expression of exasperation or surprise, equiv. cripes, crickey, blimey, damn, darn, dash it all. **2** *n.* Negligible amount of concern (esp. in. I couldn't give a) **3** Conversational device favoured by Brit. middle classes to obscure speaker's social background (as in Didn't you think the Pinter series on BBC4 was fucking brilliant?) **4** Non-specific verbal punctuation device favoured by C21 Brit. children. equiv. umm, errr **5 fucking** *ppl a. and adv.* Adjective reinforcing adverb, cf. very, exceedingly, rather jolly.[29]

Britain has come a long way since Tynan shocked a nation in November 1965 by saying 'fuck' on BBC Radio, and the brouhaha in November 1984 over the broadcast of Harrison's *V.* (p. 208)—as forceful a demonstration as Rochester's of how obscenity can have value. But the poetic journey is full of pitfalls : when Larkin, in 'This Be The Verse' (N1657), wrote "They fuck you up, your mum and dad" he

---

[27] *The French Lieutenant's Woman* (1969; London: Triad, 1977), 231.

[28] Eliot, *March Hare* ; Larkin, *Collected Poems* (London: Faber, 1988), 167.

[29] 21 Nov. 2002 (🖱) ; punctuation corrected. See Sheidlower, *The F Word* (New York: Random House, 1995), a dictionary whose primary entries for 'fuck' as noun, verb, adjective, and interjection cover pp. 90–122.

meant every letter of rueful expletive and bitter pun ; no politer word would do.[30] Katie Campbell's 'Intimations of Immortality II', however, despite managing to get 'fucked' three times in the first two lines, doesn't stand up to Wordsworth's 'Ode. Intimations of Immortality from Recollections of Early Childhood' (N796) as Nemerov does to Shelley, and is left by misjudged obscenity as a squib.[31]

If 'fuck' has entered ordinary social and poetic usage, 'cunt' remains more difficult as a resource, distinctly rude and 'politically incorrect' (despite attempts at reclamation). It was probably repeated use of 'cunt' as a man-to-man insult that got *V.* into trouble rather than its (more radical) rhyme of 'book/fuck' (p. 209), but Harrison had shown long before that he knew what he was about. 'Doodlebugs', remembering adolescent sexual doodling, ends far from obscenely with "a boy's true bent [/] for adult exploration, the slow discovery [/] of cunt as coastline, then as continent", while a bitter *School of Eloquence* sonnet, 'Next Door II', identifies in new, audible neighbours a true obscenity : "He beat her, blacked her eye. [/] Through walls I heard each blow, each *Cunt! Cunt! Cunt!*" Some years after *V.*, in 'The Pomegranates of Patmos', Harrison set explicit lyrics of sex against Reagan's millenarian beliefs in apocalypse, but while most readers of the *London Review of Books* (where it appeared) seemed happy enough, as good a poet as Szirtes was moved to protest : "My brother, my bright twin, Prochorus, [/] For Patmos read Pathos throughout : [/] Now Harrison's fucking in chorus, [/] You'll fuck along with him no doubt". Harrison seems to have taken the point : his most explicit poem since, 'Fig on the Tyne', is less profane. Updike learned a similar lesson between the early 1970s, when 'Cunts' tried to get through the shock of the word by repeated use, and mid-1980s, when 'Klimt and Schiele Confront the Cunt' uses it only in the title. France also shows restraint, avoiding in her intensely erotic 'Taking Me from Behind' any word more explicit than "coupling" (of train-carriages), but matching the bitter obscenity of Larkin in the single expletive of 'Weighing the Heart' ("*The bed's a fucking mess.*"), and turning in 'Airhead' to the demotic with tremendous force :

---

[30] Similar decisions are <u>sometimes</u> appropriate in criticism : the activity of typist and young man in *The Waste Land,* say (p. 32), might fairly be called (even in exams) "a lonely fuck" rather than "lonely copulation", for what they are doing has no love in it, a deal of aggression, and no true joining, which is what 'copulation' (from Latin *copulare,* to fasten together) means. But care is needed, from critics as from poets.

[31] Larkin, *Collected Poems,* 188 ; Campbell, *Let Us Leave Them Believing* (London: Methuen, 1991).

I knew one once. He was that far gone
he took it as a compliment, padding
his brain's blank spaces with psychedelic
graphics, cool as seraphic cadillacs, sweet
as angel cunt.
[. . .]
                                        The air inside
his head smelled

of farm, of fire, of fuck. He hummed
the mantra *love* over and over.

Even so, she bolsters demotic obscenity with the paradoxical quasi-blasphemy of "angel cunt" and some fierce monosyllabic alliteration. By comparison with older female poets who have written about sex—Bishop in 'Four Poems', Stevenson intermittently in the book-length *Correspondences*, Downie in 'She Played the Trumpet in My Bed [/] *(for Dr Bowdler)*', Adcock in 'Against Coupling', 'Kissing', and 'Coupling', Boland in 'Daphne with her Thighs in Bark'—parameters of poetic language have shifted for France, born in 1958. A cultural contrast is also clear between her work and that of, say, the slightly older Guyanan-British poets Nichols and Agard, whose sensual 'Fat Black Woman' and 'Limbo Dancer' poems, if fairly explicit, never deploy obscenity ; cultural restraint might also be seen in sexual poems avoiding *indecorum* by closer contemporaries, including Schnackenberg's 'Love Letter', Peacock's 'Have You Ever Faked an Orgasm?' and 'The Return', Wicks's 'Rain Dance' and 'Human Geometry', Kay's 'Close Shave', and Bhatt's 'Shérdi' and 'Jane to Tarzan'.[32]

Very occasionally a degree of restraint may itself be troubling. Muldoon's irregular sonnet 'October 1950', named for the month of his conception, begins :

---

[32] Harrison, *Selected Poems*, 20, 130 ; 'The Pomegranates of Patmos' appeared in *LRB* 11/11 (1 June 1989), 12, and is collected in *Gaze of the Gorgon* ; Szirtes's poem, also 'The Pomegranates of Patmos', appeared as a letter in *LRB* 11/13 (6 July 1989), 4 ; 'Fig on the Tyne' is in *Laureate's Block* ; Updike, *Collected Poems 1953–1993* (1993; Harmondsworth: Penguin, 1995) ; France, *Gentleness of the Very Tall*, 50 ; Bishop, *Collected Poems* ; Stevenson, *Collected Poems 1955–1995* (Oxford: OUP, 1996) ; Downie, *Collected Poems* (Newcastle: Bloodaxe, 1995) ; Adcock, *Poems 1960–2000* (Newcastle: Bloodaxe, 2000) ; Boland, *Collected Poems* (Manchester: Carcanet, 1995) ; Nichols, *The Fat Black Woman's Poems* and *Lazy Thoughts of a Lazy Woman* (London: Virago, 1984, 1989) ; Agard, *Limbo Dancer in Dark Glasses* (1983), in *Weblines* (Newcastle: Bloodaxe, 2000) ; Schnackenberg, *The Lamplit Answer* (1982 ; London: Hutchinson, 1986) ; Peacock in Jarman and Mason, *Rebel Angels* ; Wicks, *The Clever Daughter* (London: Faber, 1996) ; Kay and Bhatt, 'Shérdi', in France, *Sixty Women Poets* ; Bhatt, 'Jane', *Augatora* (Manchester: Carcanet, 2000).

Whatever it is, it all comes down to this ;
My father's cock
Between my mother's thighs.

As with Larkin, there is a flat truth all might acknowledge—or not, as Muldoon can hardly be suggesting that he was conceived through intercrural intercourse. Is the gendered asymmetry (and inaccuracy) of cock/thighs respectful ? observant of taboo ? an invitation to Freudian theory ? Muldoon's poem is fierce, sad, and plaintive, commanding respect but never (after this beginning) resting easy ; had he been more equally explicit he would raise other questions, not fewer. Similar doubt invades Berryman's 'Sonnet to Chris. 67', when after tenderly evoking sexual intimacy ("your weaving [/] Thighs agile to me") he reaches "your face bright and dark, back, as we screw [/] Our lives together" : 'screw' is (to my ear) a meaner, more misogynistic verb than 'fuck', a supposed euphemism that like 'use' reveals an absence of care, and despite retrospectively soothing enjambment ("screw [/. . .] together") remains an off-note. Far easier to assess, and still regrettably common, is overt censorship : in the 3rd edition of the *Norton* (1983), ll. 19 and 33 of cummings's 'i sing of Olaf glad and big' (3N1042) were printed as "I will not kiss your f.ing flag" and "there is some s. I will not eat' ; in the 4th (1996),"fucking" and "shit" appeared in full (4N1284), and it matters. I doubt many users of the *Norton* needed protection from those words, or hesitated to infer them from "f.ing" and "s." : so on whose behalf did the 1983 editors bowdlerise ? Pressure from particular US state boards of education, backed by power as potential mass-purchasers, is the probable explanation, but allowing a sentiment while suppressing its honest expression suggests some real confusions of value, poetic and otherwise.[33]

Racial abuse, however, like misogynistic obscenity, is not a matter of taste but ideology. Feminist writers stress connections between obscene misogyny and violence against women that Harrison's abusive neighbour embodies, and since revelation of the *Sho'ah* in 1945 the appalling ends to which beliefs and assumptions embodied in group abuse can lead have been hideously plain. This doesn't mean terms of abuse can never find a place in poetry, but does mean their unguarded use will be contemptible and offensive, and any use, however guarded, probably unacceptable to some—even if, for example, it's clearly not a poet using a term personally, but a sexist or racist character within a poem (as in

[33] Muldoon, *Poems 1968–1998*, 76 (also in Levin, *Penguin Book of the Sonnet*) ; Berryman, *Collected Poems*, 104.

'Ozymandias II'). An obvious issue is the gender, race, or nationality of the poet : if a black poet uses 'nigger' it is different than for a brown, yellow, or white poet to use the word. A reader's skin-colour may affect how they judge any particular instance, but however any reader feels, premises of judgement are affected by a poet's skin-colour : Nemerov took a greater risk in 'Ozymandias II' than Walcott in 'Blues' and 'The Schooner *Flight*' (N1826), the Jamaican Mervyn Morris in 'Responses' and 'Afro-Saxon', or the Afro-Americans Reginald Shepherd in 'Desire and the Slave Trade' and Rita Dove in 'Nigger Song : An Odyssey', 'Nothing Down', and 'Crab-Boil'. The same is true of Jewish and gentile poets and anti-Semitic terms : in some, notably Pound, the vile prejudice is incontestable ; in others, notably Eliot, evidence points both ways, and it is horribly easy to find oneself condemning or reprieving in a way itself partial and prejudiced, making no distinction between using a racially abusive term and active moral collusion with genocide. Such issues are emotive, and difficult to think about clearly : but unless distinctions are made one may wind up committing racist nonsense by accusing a black poet who uses 'nigger' of prejudice, or confusing the positions adopted by Hill (British gentile) in 'Ovid in the Third Reich', Gershon (British Jewish) in 'I was not there', and Pagis (Bukowina-born Israeli survivor) in 'Written in Pencil in the Sealed Railway-Car'.[34]

As a brief example of how abusive terms may find their value consider the opening of Layton's 'For My Brother Jesus' :

> My father had terrible words for you
> —whoreson, bastard, *meshumad* ;
> and my mother loosed Yiddish curses
> on your name and the devil's spawn
> on their way to church
> that scraped the frosted horsebuns
> from the wintry Montreal street
> to fling clattering into our passageway

A "*meshumad*" is apostate from Judaism, implicitly a turncoat or betrayer ; the three insults together reverse the old Christian calumny against the Jews as 'killers of Christ'. But what matters is that these lines appear beneath the astonishing title 'For My Brother Jesus' : even

[34] Walcott, *Collected Poems* ; Morris, *Shadowboxing* (London and Port of Spain: New Beacon, 1979) ; Shepherd, *Angel, Interrupted* (Pittsburgh: U. Pittsburgh Press, 1996) ; Dove, *Selected Poems* (New York: Vintage, 1993), *Grace Notes* (New York: Norton, 1991) ; Hill, *Collected Poems*; Gershon, *Collected Poems* (London: Papermac, 1990) ; Pagis, *Selected Poems* (trans. Mitchell, Manchester: Carcanet, 1972).

before speaking them Layton calls the abuses in l. 2 "terrible words" and makes it clear they were spoken by another ; then that they were provoked, aimed less at Jesus or Christian belief than at those who, claiming to be Christians, throw "horsebuns" into someone's doorway simply because that someone is Jewish. The poem's discourse can contain the destructive energies of its second line—the only words in the passage to be isolated and contained by punctuation-marks ; note also Layton's subsequent choice of "frosted horsebuns", a homelier and gentler term appropriate to remembered childhood. Line 2 is enough at one time, and the poem avoids the disillusionment 'shit' could generate (as when Shepherd in 'Jouissance' writes of "sudden snow that patched over cracks [/] on Halsted Street, freeze-dried dog shit and lost [//] single gloves"). What emerges is an unexpected perspective, humbling in its restraint and moving in its compassion : the amplitude of these emotions would be less if the insults, offensive in themselves, were bowdlerised away.[35]

Another interesting category is scientific diction, alarmingly excluded not only from poetry but almost all mass-media and common conversation. Some words mellow into acceptability (astronomer, polystyrene), abbreviations admit famous chemicals (PVC, DNA, LSD[36]), and there are good mnemonic and cautionary verses,[37] but in general scientific words are fiercely policed and serious transgression as rare as genuine expertise in both art and science. Even as great a polymath as Nabokov, six years a Research Fellow in the Museum of Comparative Zoology at Harvard, writing in 'A Discovery' of a butterfly says only "I found it and I named it, being versed [/] in taxonomic Latin" ; the name he gave, *Lycæides sublivens* Nabokov, mentioned in his afterword 'On a Book entitled *Lolita*' and naturally iambic, is unmentioned in the poem devoted to its bearer. Nabokov did hymn his pleasure in science :

> My needles have teased out its sculptured sex ;
> corroded tissues could no longer hide
> that priceless mote now dimpling the convex
> and limpid teardrop on a lighted slide.[38]

[35] Layton, *A Wild Peculiar Joy: Selected Poems 1945–82* (Toronto: McClelland and Stewart, 1982), 154 (3N1157) ; Shepherd, *Angel, Interrupted*, 52.

[36] Polyvinyl chloride, deoxyribonucleic acid, and lysergic acid diethylamide.

[37] My father, who liked Harry Graham's *Ruthless Rhymes for Heartless Homes*, wrote this one : "Johnny finding life a bore [/] drank some H_2SO_4. [/] Johnny's father, an M.D., [/] gave him $CaCO_3$; [/] now he's neutralised, it's true, [/] but he's full of CO_2".

[38] *Poems* (New York: Doubleday, 1959), 15 ; also in *The Annotated Lolita* (New York and Toronto: McGraw-Hill, 1970), 328.

and thought of his butterfly "Wide open on its pin (though fast asleep)". The commoner reaction is Dickinson's :

> I pull a flower from the woods—
> A monster with a glass
> Computes the stamens in a breath—
> And has her in a 'class'!
>
> Whereas I took the Butterfly—
> Aforetime in my hat—
> He sits erect in 'Cabinets'—
> The Clover bells forgot
>
> (" 'Arcturus' is his other name", Johnson 70)

Her first stanza provides a motto, "It's very mean of Science [/] To go and interfere!", and *A Quark for Mister Mark : 101 Poems about Science* (2000) confirms that even when science is positively the matter in poetic hand its terminology is usually thought beyond the poetic pale.

It is, of course, hard for the uninitiated. Muldoon did manage to get into his long poem 'Yarrow' "a sprig of *Achillea millefolium*, as it's classed. [/ centred rule /] *Achillea millefolium* : with its bedraggled, feathery leaf", "my precious *Bufo bufo*", and "the larva [. . .] of *Pieris* [/] *brassicae*"—but presuming by analogy with *Bufo bufo*, the common toad, he wrote in 'Incantata' of "a sherbet-green *Ranus ranus* [/] plonked down in Trinity" ; alas, the common frog is *Rana temporaria*, and Muldoon later made the change at some cost to rhyme and metre. His 'Author's Note' is pithy :

> Other than to correct such factual errors as my having written 'painfully' for 'painstakingly,' 'bathyscope' for 'bathysphere,' '*Ranus ranus*' for '*Rana temporaria*,' 'jardonelle' for 'jargonelle,' and 'aureoles' for 'areolae,' I have made scarcely any changes in the texts of the poems, since I'm fairly certain that, after a shortish time, the person through whom a poem was written is no more entitled to make revisions than any other reader.

"scarcely any changes" cannot be taken at face-value from the author of 'Errata' ("For 'ludic' read 'lucid.' [. . .] For 'ode' read 'code.' "), and an author's right to revise must be deferred to 'Biography' (p. 319), but of the given examples all but first and (perhaps) fourth are errors of scientific nomenclature. Implicitly these errors are "factual", as science is, and so command revision as artistic second thoughts should not : I'm not sure I agree, but the belief interestingly glosses the reluctance of poets to sully their work with scientific language.[39]

Yet as in many things interdisciplinary connections are breaking into hoarded privacies and discourses, and as there have been very good recent scientific plays, so scientific poems are appearing in greater numbers from more scientifically-minded poets. Most impressively and sadly, Rebecca Elson worked as an astronomer, and even in her lyric poems, dominated by personal life and latterly the cancer that killed her at 39, uses words like "geodesic" ('Explaining Relativity'), "calculus" ('Carnal Knowledge'), and "murine [. . .] synapses" ('OncoMouse, Kitchen Mouse') with exact force. The posthumously published 'Extracts from the Notebook' shows in poems she didn't (or couldn't) publish a more sustained use of scientific language carrying thought at once scientific and poetic : 'Simulations of the Universe I' has "particles which could be dust [/] Or stars, it makes no difference" and "hyperbolae [/] The magnetism of each mutual centre [/] When sufficient time has elapsed" ; 'Origins' has "seeds of galaxies [/] Shaken in the dark soil of space" ; and an untitled entry for 9 February 1994 "a storm of galaxies [/] Like snowflakes in the vortex of a streetlamp". Comparably, Burnside, a risk analyst, has written in a prose-poem of "citrinous velvet dust like jars of myrrh" ('Home'), and in lyrics of "Virgin and angel curving [/] into the centripetus" (Annunciation'), "spaces curled on themselves, [/] salted and purged from the sea [/] like ammonites between the stones and yews" ('The Fishermen's Graveyard in Autumn'), and "beetles, their polychrome eyes [/] still functional, deep in extinction" ('Killed in Action'). At higher levels of structure Paterson organised 'The Scale of Intensity' on the 12 steps of the Beaufort Scale, and Copus sections of 'Playing it by Ear' as public-health assessments of noise-pollution in decibels ; she also called sections of *In Defence of Adultery* 'Fission and Fusion' and 'Astronomy and Perception', and as the daughter of an inventor (to whom she gives special thanks) shows in poems like 'Home Physics' and 'Lamb's Electronic Antibiotic' a familiarity with science less specific than Elson's but no less robust. Fulton's mathematical poetics of fractals have been mentioned (p. 175), and though never scientifically trained a strong scientific

[39] *Poems 1968–1998*, pp. xv, 348, 369, 381, 338. The original reading of 'Incantata' is in *The Annals of Chile* (London and Boston: Faber, 1994), 23. "bathyscope" doesn't exist, and was probably an error for bathyscaphe = bathysphere, a deep-sea exploration-vessel ; "jardonelle" doesn't exist, but 'jargonelles' were an Elizabethan variety of pear ; "aureoles" covers various kinds of halo, but not 'areolae', pigmented areas of skin surrounding a nipple.

understanding and vocabulary can be seen in poems like 'A Foreplay' and 'Southbound In A Northbound Lane'. All these poets might invoke the spirit (if not style) of the physician-poet W. C. Williams, observant, descriptive, and accurate ; though less widely known outside the US, they might also light candles for Ammons, holding a B.Sc. rather than BA, and Merrill, whose *Changing Light at Sandover* includes fairly technical material about genetics and radiation, and is an attempt poetically to fuse modern biology + ecology with Dantean theology + cosmology. E-language is also beginning to appear poetically (as in Shcherbina's 'Ru.net'), and while specifically scientific poetry of high calibre will probably always be rare, it seems likely that the extreme exclusion of science so evident in the canon is now passing into history, where it belongs.[40]

As a reader (certainly as a practical critic) one must first be concerned with any poem in itself, so the primary question, once hard words are sorted and some sense of lexical set/s established, is whether and how the poem commands its particular discourse. Sorting can in itself be enormously informative : verb tenses, noun groups, colours and textures, mono- and polysyllables, each or all may emerge as dominating particular poems. As a given poet becomes familiar a sense of characteristic diction will emerge—Hill's struggles with probity, Dickinson's cadent polysyllables, Hopkins's dappling hyphenations—playing over individual poems and sequences. In *The Breaking of Style* Vendler was able to chart Heaney's political and philosophical evolution as a poet through successive predominance in groups of poems of nouns and adjectives, verbs and adverbs, reflecting awarenesses of im/materiality and in/action. Browning's diction is also remarkably rich, partly because dramatic monologue led him to occupational vocabularies and a wider range of registers than one might imagine from his formality : read him seriously, looking up <u>every</u> word you don't know, and two enormous lexical sets appear, concerning clothing, and plants. The haberdashery agrees with his many Italian Renaissance settings (painters like Mantegna and Raphael were obsessed with textures of cloth), but the botany, including many common names of plants with associated herb and medicinal lore, is an interest his speakers get from him,

[40] Elson, *A Responsibility to Awe*, 13, 21, 58, 70, 87, 90–1 ; Burnside, *Common Knowledge* (London: Secker, 1991), 4, 27, 32, 54 ; Paterson, *Quark for Mister Mark* ; Copus, *Adultery* ; Fulton, *Sensual Math* (New York: Norton, 1995) ; Shcherbina, *Life Without: Selected Poetry and Prose 1992–2003* (trans. Dugdale, Newcastle: Bloodaxe, 2003).

and he got from natural curiosity and attentive readings of Shakespeare, also thoroughly plant-minded.

Such discoveries are a pleasure, but a quest for words can equally attract the satirist. Writing to his wife of their dead daughter, John Shade (in Nabokov's poem-novel *Pale Fire*) recalls :

> Sometimes I'd help her with a Latin text,
> Or she'd be reading in her bedroom, next
> To my fluorescent lair, and you would be
> In your own study, twice removed from me,
> And I would hear both voices now and then :
> 'Mother, what's *grimpen* ?' 'What is what ?' 'Grim Pen.'
> Pause, and your guarded scholium. Then again :
> 'Mother, what's *chthonic* ?' That, too, you'd explain,
> Appending : 'Would you like a tangerine ?'
> 'No. Yes. And what does *sempiternal* mean ?'
> You'd hesitate. And lustily I'd roar
> The answer from my desk through the closed door.
>
> It does not matter what it was she read
> (some phony modern poem that was said
> In English Lit to be a document
> 'Engazhay and compelling'—what this meant
> Nobody cared) ;[41]

The poem is never named, but the memorable words occur in Eliot's *Four Quartets* ('East Coker' II, 'The Dry Salvages' V, 'Little Gidding' I), and Nabokov's dislike of Eliot is notorious. He might have been kinder about 'grimpen', invented by Conan Doyle for the "Great Grimpen Mire" in *The Hound of the Baskervilles* and attesting (like Macavity as the "Napoleon of Crime") to the intriguing presence in Eliot's work of Sherlock Holmes. But 'chthonic', awkward and arcane, is a dubious late Victorian coinage from Greek for "of or pertaining to the underworld", while the older 'sempiternal' smacks of tautology (*semper*, always + *aeturnus*, eternal) and if labelled "*poet[ic]* and *rhet[orical]*" sounds anything but in Eliot's use. Nabokov's general dismissal is easily set aside (Shade's target should have been whoever said '*engagé* and compelling'[42]), but his ear for misjudgement is sharp, and Eliot <u>is</u> sometimes guilty of irritable reaching after words that "strain, [/] Crack and sometimes break, under the burden, [/] Under the tension, slip, slide, perish,

[41] *Pale Fire* (1962; Harmondsworth: Penguin, 1973), 39–40 ; 'chthonic' is misspelled.
[42] Applied to poetry, *engagé* usually means 'overtly presenting ideological beliefs'.

[/] Decay with imprecision, will not stay in place, [/] Will not stay still." ('Burnt Norton' V). Eric Griffiths calls *Four Quartets* (1935–42) the 'first great post-*OED* poem', and tracking Eliot's diction through *OED1* (but allowing one's eyes to wander other definitions near each word) leaves no doubt that Eliot was browsing its pages as he wrote—a sometimes too rich resource for his diction.

Wariness of sempiternal indigestibilities (or just over-egging the pudding) keeps poets to plainer diction, as do poetic credos involving popular comprehensibility or prescriptions of low style. I have so far been concerned only with primary senses of words, but with surface-plainness at a premium, attention turns to poetry's characteristic activation of secondary and tertiary senses. Sometimes non-primary senses are allowed to accumulate and retroactively detonated, as strikingly in Atwood's 'You Fit into Me', where "hook" and "eye" apparently mean a clothes-fastening but become fish-hooks and open eyes. Less nauseatingly, but no less disturbingly, Hopkins in 'Carrion Comfort' (N1169) realises with shock he is "wrestling with (my God!) my God.", and readings of 'my God' as blasphemous oath, statement of fact, and devotional vocative jostle harshly. In another register, Pugh's 'Official briefing for ministers on the recent violence in the capital' tells of a "disaffected itinerant" who confronted "certain persons with a licence to trade [/] on church premises" and "began vandalising their property, [/] (mainly currency and pigeons)", slowly allowing readers to twig that this briefing dates from when Jesus "began to cast out them that sold and bought in the temple, and overthrew the tables of the money-changers, and the seats of them that sold doves" (Mark 11: 15).[43]

Non-primary senses can be punning, and puns, especially *thematic* ones connected to the subject of a work, often express arguments by analogy (p. 124). Who laughs at Hamlet's "A little more then kin, and leſſe then kinde", despite his kin/kind and friendly/sort puns ? Of course such puns can also be comic, and in Renaissance poetry erotic as well. A famous example is Donne's 'A Valediction forbidding mourning' (N306), where, telling his wife not to weep because he must depart, he invokes a pair of dividers (text from 1633) :

Our two ſoules therefore, which are one,
  Though I must goe, endure not yet
A breach, but an expanſion,
  Like gold to ayery thinneſſe beate.

[43] Atwood, *Eating Fire: Selected Poetry 1965–1995* (London: Virago, 1998; also 3N1375) ; Pugh, *Selected Poems*, 26.

If they be two, they are two ſo
  As ſtiffe twin compaſſes are two,
Thy ſoule the fixt foot, makes no show
  To move, but doth, if the'other doe.

And though it in the center ſit,
  Yet when the other far doth rome,
It leanes, and hearkens after it,
  And growes erect, as that comes home.

The apparent point is to insist that however far apart he and she are they remain joined, as dividers remain joined at the hinge even when the points are wide apart ; the fixed point does not seem to move when the dividers are rotated to move the other, but in fact rotates in place in consequence of their unity. The implicit joke is the notion that as dividers close they return to a vertical position—which Donne calls "erect" by way of promising he will 'grow erect' when he comes home as she will 'erect' her legs in the air. Once the bawdy is seen 'ſtiffe' (l. 26) ceases to mean only metallic rigidity, and "comes" (l. 32) may not be innocent. Further back in the poem, "layetie" (l. 8) (often modernised as 'laity') is revealed as bawdy, because the 'layetie' lie with one another as Catholic clergy do not ; hence also the spelling of "rome" (puns and argument alike are destroyed by modernisation.) The poem as a whole carries a terrific erotic charge, as in part a promise by the poet to his love that he will be faithful and abstinent while he is away, knows what he's missing, and will return to her.

Even more extended is the punning of a mock-epic such as Pope's 'The Rape of the Lock' (N604), where sustained mismatch in register between grand senses and trivial subjects is a basic method. Pope wrote it in response to a feud created when Lord Petre cut off, without permission, a lock of Miss Arabella Fermor's hair ; exaggerating all gravity, presenting a 'rape' of a lock as an epic with a vast machinery of sylphs and stars, Pope ridiculed the pride that alone was wounded. To tread the line of gentle mockery—pointed enough to work, rounded enough not to offend further—requires judicious diction, and Pope's performance is a lexical *tour de force* ; yet even so some worry about his devaluation of the word 'rape' (the practical and legal meaning of which remains subject to acute juridical debate).

Such dictions depend on words having multiple senses, and despite its huge vocabulary many English words have an astonishing range of meaning. The longer a word the less likely it is to be *polysemic* ; those with the biggest array tend to be simple monosyllables which are verbs, adjectives, and nouns : examples include 'cast' (a stone, in bronze, of a play), 'rose' (in the world/air/morning, a colour, a flower), and 'hand' (give to, of cards, attached to arms, a sailor). One consequence is that words to look up are not only those you don't know, but also familiar polysemic words to make sure you consider all relevant meanings. Jonson was a master of such words : his sequence *The Forrest* (1616) begins "Some act of *Loue's* bound to reherſe, [/] I thought to binde him, in my verſe" : look up "bound" in the *OED* and 23 meanings apply, from 'leap', through 'boundary' and 'tied', to 'setting off' ('bound for somewhere'), and such archaic senses as "Of persons : Dressed". One could read the first line as 'Being obliged to rehearse some act of love' ; 'On the way to rehearse some act of love' ; 'To rehearse some act of physical love' ; 'To rehearse some act showing limits of love'—or any of a dozen possibilities. Such dense meaning is extraordinary, but so was Jonson ; only careful scrutiny of his poem, the sequence, and the *OED* allows any meaning of 'bound' to be ruled out. Nor need one wish to rule out : I think Jonson meant most of these things, and his virtuoso (but perhaps not so virtuous) opening is a good guide to a remarkable sequence.

Eventually, diction cumulatively becomes imagery via *syntax*, the relations of words. There may be a sequence of words whose primary meanings vary, but secondary meanings join existing lexical sets or form a new set : in Snodgrass's terrifying 'Magda Goebbels' (p. 161) she says, as she gives her children poison, "Take this on your tongue ; this do [/] Remembering your mother who [/] So loved her Leader", hideously echoing ritual words of Christian Communion and the liturgical phrase "who so loved". In 'September Song' (p. 72) the simple phrase "Not [. . .] passed over" just as dreadfully summons and inverts the Jewish feast of Passover, confronting it a few lines later with "Zyklon"—in capitalised form (p. 146) no longer polysemic (as it was when it meant 'cyclone') but bound for ever to the obscenity of the *Sho'ah*. It may also be a matter of a repeated word, like "duſt" in Herbert's 'Church Monuments', used six times (+ "duſty") for the multiple applicability of its single meaning—dust to dust, in an hourglass, worthless, and so on ; or of a single weighty word, an image in its own right : in Marvell's 'The Definition of Love' "*Planiſphere*" must be fully understood if the rest is to make sense : one word is the key (p. 85). In such cases issues of diction, and particular issues of discourse in a specified poem, fuse with other matters at stake in that poem—but a poem is nothing if not words, and diction can never safely be ignored.

The comedians Peter Cook and Dudley Moore had a sketch in which Pete recounted childhood Saturdays spent 'getting a medical certificate' to allow use of the 'big dictionary' in a public library and looking up the 'rudest word in the world', mispronounced as 'bastárd'. 'What does it mean?' asks Dud. "A child born out of wedlock." "Urgh. What's a wedlock, Pete?" "Well, it's this big metal thing . . .". W, of course, was in a different volume ; a new medical certificate would be needed. I lost count long ago of students claiming to have read a text who prove ignorant of primary meanings—even when footnotes provide glossing. I use my *OED* almost every working day, and if it remains an expensive resource, online editions of scores of dictionaries, conveniently linked at sites like RefDesk, mean there is almost no excuse for not finding out what a poet has in lexicographical fact said. For those who don't ignorant misprisions cluster as thickly as comprehension in every poem they read.

Exemplary Poems

1. 'The Flea' (pp. 14–15)

The poem shows Donne's customary vigour and exactitude of diction. The flea-variant of the *carpe diem* topos needs no more excuse than the intimate access fleas enjoy, but Donne knew a particular spice it acquires in French, where *puce* is a flea, *pucelle* a virgin, and *pucelage* maidenhead, which probably influenced his first stanza. There is also the consequence of long-s in "ſuck'd" and "ſucks" (3) : Donne must have been aware of the lurking obscenity and probably meant it, here and in 'Elegie [VIII. The Comparison]' ("Are not your kiſſes then as filthy, and more, [/] As a worme ſucking an invenom'd ſore ?")—but not every 'suck' hides the pun, initial long-s wasn't always used in handwriting and no autograph MS survives ; I have no doubt myself, but those who dislike the idea have half-a-case to make. The metrically necessary "w'are" (14), like all such contractions in 1633, shows the pressure Donne applied to words and his innovative use of apostrophes (sometimes qualifying an interword-space rather than marking elision) to give readers metrical help.

One oddly surprising thing also needs attention—oddly, because Donne's compulsive fusions of sacred and erotic are a standard critical observation but haven't been much noticed in 'The Flea'. They are perhaps more obvious in primarily sacred poems deploying sexual imagery (as, famously, 'Holy Sonnet [XIV]', "Batter my heart, three perſon'd God", N320), but just as important in primarily erotic poems deploying religious imagery, as 'The Flea' does with increasing intensity. The sacred is explicitly summoned in l. 6 ("ſinne"), and if taken seriously the repetition-development of "two bloods" as "one" (ll. 4, 8) suggests Incarnation, divine and mortal bloods mingling in Jesus—a thought picked up in the second stanza : "Oh ſtay, three lives in one flea spare". 'Three in one' is Trinitarian in any context, and the stanza also has a "mariage bed", "mariage temple", and "cloiſterd" (a wicked pun, given the celibate life of the cloistered). The Trinity returns in its closing triplet :

> Though uſe make you apt to kill mee,
> Let not to that, ſelfe murder added bee,
> And ſacrilege, three ſinnes in killing three.

There is a widely remarked pun on "kill", which like 'die' could refer to orgasm, but if that line and "ſelfe murder" in the next are easily understood from the mixing of his and her blood in the flea, "ſacrilege" is less simple : even as blasphemous jest it requires the flea to become in part a figure of Christ—and <u>that</u> is confirmed when the third stanza begins with the flea's death violently shedding its (and his, and her) blood as a prelude to judgement.

It is important to understand exactly what happens to provoke the exclamation "Cruell and ſodaine, hast thou ſince [/] Purpled thy naile, in blood of innocence ?" Fleas are tough : fingertip-pressure cannot kill them, so nails are needed and when a full flea bursts, the blood in its stomach jets out. Sexually, Donne forces in the closing triplet an equation between blood forced from the flea onto a finger-nail and blood that will be forced from the woman's hymen when he deflowers her (with his 'nail' ?) ; the underlying Christian figure forces an additional comparison, with Christ's blood spilt by iron nails to 'stream in the firmament' (as Marlowe has it in *Doctor Faustus*). The last line—"Will waſt, as this flea's death tooke life from thee"—openly invites comparison with the god 'who died that we might live', and retrospectively confirms the religious reading as an integral part of Donne's design.

How one then reads the whole poem is another matter. "Batter my heart" famously ends by imploring God's violently redemptive intervention :

> breake that knot againe,
> Take mee to you, imprison mee, for I
> Except you'enthrall mee, never shall be free,
> Nor ever chaſt, except you raviſh mee.

God, that is, must *carpe diem*, seize the day, or Donne's soul will be lost. Syntactically, the "knot" that must be broken binds Donne to his and

God's enemy, Lucifer, but knots have long been associated with marriage (human and divine) ; Shakespeare's Mariana called maidenhead her "Vntide [. . .] virgin knot"[44] (*Pericles*, Q1609 G1^{v}). 'The Flea' projects a similar sacramental desire to be ravished onto the woman, which helps to explain how Donne could achieve judgement of real force in pronouncing that defloration by him will teach her a thing or two she needs to know. But the risk is substantial, and critical reluctance to annotate this reading probably as protective as it is blind—and none the less misguided for that : one either has sympathetic faith with Donne's poetics of the erotic and sacred, trying fully to imagine in what he tried fully to say, or hasn't, finding him intolerably sexist and conceited (as Dr Johnson did and many feminists do). If the latter, fine ; if the former, one must turn to biography, for repeated conjunctions of the erotic and sacred encompass as much as inhabit any individual poem. Either way, individual words first raise the question.

2. 'Ode to Melancholy' (p. 68)

Richness of diction is a Keatsian trademark, and his propensity for hyphenated compounds (p. 135) is evident. "Wolf's-bane" (l. 2) (a generic name for aconites, including wild monkshood, *Aconitum napellus*) + "yew-berries" (l. 5) are standard, "tight-rooted" (l. 2) + "droop-headed" (l. 13) ordinary enough—but "death-moth" (l. 6) seems to be Keats's own contraction of 'death's-head moth' (*OED2* has no other citations), "sand-wave" (l. 16) may also be a coinage (but has become a technical term in physical geography), and "bee-mouth" (l. 24) is curious. The number of hyphenations decreases in each stanza (4, 2, 1), partly because "death-moth" and "bee-mouth" belong to a bird + insect lexical set restricted to the first and third stanzas ("beetle", l. 6, "owl", l. 7), while the others belong to a flower set ("nightshade [. . .] grape", l. 4, "flowers", l. 13, "rose", l. 15, "peonies", l. 17, "grape", l. 28) that begins strongly with three poisons in five lines but fades into abstraction, and is represented in the last 13 lines only by the repeated "grape". Such patternings, like internal rhymes in the last lines of each stanza (shade/shade + drown/soul, ll. 9–10, hand/rave + deep/deep/eyes, ll. 19–20, taste/might + among/hung, ll. 29–30), keep the richness palatable.

Capitalised words repay thought. In the first stanza "Lethe", "Proserpine", and "Psyche" are unimpeachably classical ; there are none in the second stanza ; in the third "Beauty", "Joy" (twice), "Pleasure", "Delight", and "Melancholy" are personified abstractions, a late class-

[44] *OED2* cites this use of 'untied' as "Wrongly used for 'unloosed' ".

ical development that flowered in medieval allegory and on which many Romantics (fascinated by the medieval) seized. Despite the weirdness of personified 'Melancholy' (literally 'black bile', one of four supposed bodily humours in early physiology), most readers are happy to accept it, partly because Keats sets it up persuasively with the more concrete place and persons and natural observations of stanzas 1–2 ; if the whole poem asked *ab initio* for acceptance of a "temple of Delight" populated by glimpsed and posed abstractions, it would probably be less forthcoming. The curious "bee-mouth" looks, amid these abstractions, like a welcome detail, an uncommon compound summoning a common sight that embodies both an image of utter sensory fullness (drinking nectar within a flower) and buzzing, iterative work.

As Empson pointed out in *Seven Types of Ambiguity* this kind of doubleness is a basic method of the poem : "Keats often used ambiguities of this type to convey a dissolution of normal experience into intensity of sensation. [. . .] in the *Ode to Melancholy* it pounds together the sensations of joy and sorrow till they combine into sexuality". In exemplary detail he says of ll. 11–14 (the "melancholy fit" as "April shroud") :

> *Weeping* produces the flowers of joy which are themselves sorrowful ; the *hill* is *green* as young, fresh and springing, or with age, mould and geology ; *April* is both rainy and part of springtime ; and the *shroud*, an anticipation of death that has its own energy and beauty, either is itself the fact that the old *hill* is hidden under *green*, or is itself the grey mist, the greyness of falling rain, which is reviving that verdure.[45]

Just so, and the gloss on "green" is an excellence instance of why even familiar words (that so easily slide past) reward scrutiny, and simple monosyllables pack a polysemic punch. One might add that "shroud" is also part of a religious lexical set ("rosary", l. 5, "mysteries", 8, "soul", 10, "heaven", 12, "rainbow", 16, "temple", 25, "veil'd" + "shrine", 26, "soul", 29) that does what it can to complicate the sexual fusion of joy and sorrow.

Finally, four words stand out to my ear : "anguish" (l. 10), "Emprison" + "rave" (l. 19), and "burst" (l. 28). All come late in their stanzas and concentrate argument : the emotive power of "anguish" and violent action of "burst" are unproblematic, but a 'richly angry mistress' who found her hand 'emprisoned' and her complaint aesthetically enjoyed as 'raving' might have even richer and angrier things

[45] Empson, W., *Seven Types of Ambiguity* (1930; London: Hogarth Press, 1984), 214–16.

to say about it. In any case "rave" is awkward, for if the sense of enthusiastic rather than deranged speech developed in the first half of the eighteenth century that sense was (as it remains) in a lower register than the rest of the poem, and the pejorative sense remains strong. The problem is compounded by the infelicities of 'feeding deep' on "peerless eyes" (20), where the primary gastronomic meaning of "feed", gluttonous gloss of "deep", and visual sense of 'peer' are all unwanted, and it doesn't seem accidental that the compound awkwardness is in the only lines whose sentiment (and hence, in this poem, argument) are properly objectionable. If one wanted to attack the poem, the granting of primary meaning to sensuality rather than sense in the crooning vowels of "feed deep, deep upon her peerless eyes" would be the place to begin.

3. 'Anthem for Doomed Youth' (p. 18)

Both octave and sestet begin with one-line questions they devote themselves to answering : both first lines must therefore be substantial, and are :

> What passing-bells for these who die as cattle? (1)
>
> What candles may be held to speed them all? (9)

After the murderous hurly-burly of the octave the space and "candles" are a welcome relief, so "speed" is a strong touch ; the sonnet as a whole, though, is in constant diminuendo from its instant density of opening. "What passing-bells for these [. . .]" and already a complex of things is assumed, from multiple deaths to Anglican traditions in English villages where the gender and age of a person dying in the parish are announced by church-bells ; four words more and the problem is clear, the shambles of youth 'dying as cattle' overwhelming all belfries and bell-ringers, and indifference to human death as in a slaughterhouse is the central moral and aesthetic problem to be confronted. For some lines afterwards concentration is sustained by ordinary words (mostly adjectives) in more than ordinary contexts—"monstrous anger" (2), "stuttering rifles' " (3), "hasty orisons" (4), "mockeries" (5), "shrill demented choirs" (7)—but with the "bugles calling for them from sad shires" (8) some equivalent of the passing-bells that could not be properly rung is admitted, and thereafter, "speed" notwithstanding, all is more ordinary. Under other circumstances "holy glimmers" (11) might be amazing, but Owen attributes them generically to "boys" ; "girls' brows" have a similarly conventional "pallor", but the idea of such pallor as "their pall", a cloth draped over a coffin or hearse, verges on absurdity. In the octave it might pass, but the more placid sestet provides less camouflage for a line that might be by Brooke (so often reviled for not seeing the wickedness and folly of a war that killed him while waxing pastorally patriotic). Matters are rescued in the couplet with 'flowering tenderness' in "patient minds" (far from the demanding question of l. 1) and the "drawing-down of blinds" subtly echoing "passing-bells".

Overall, diction is (like metre, pp. 18–20) constrained. The few words that now need glossing (passing-bells, orisons, pall) were better-known in 1917, and beyond any aesthetic purpose of verbal, metrical, and formal constraint Owen may have been thinking about a reading-public just beginning to understand something of the horror men suffered in the trenches, and to suspect that even in victory there would be only loss. To address them, inducing sympathetic rather than defensive anger, would require care, not what the English once jeeringly called *inkhorn terms* ; nor could the powers of traditional poeticism and cliché be scorned. Not all Owen's diction is so plain : some early poems are pastoral or quasi-romantic and a few (such as 'Greater Love' and 'The Promisers') sound like Swinburne, but there are war-poems ('The Letter', 'The Chances', 'Inspection') that follow Kipling's expressive use of regional accent and sub-bourgeois speech, investing idiomatic diction with great value. It is with these that the charged common language of 'Anthem for Doomed Youth' is in sympathy, as much in what it avoids as in the plain-man's speech it favours.

4. 'Nearing Forty' (pp. 22–3)

As it was impossible to discuss all 322 syllables under 'Metre', so it is to discuss all 218 words, though something could be said about most (and many have already been considered). Most worth noticing is the patterning of diction, which takes several forms.

Throughout the poem Romance and Germanic words are strikingly balanced, each of these pairs combining the etymologies : 'Insomniac/four', 'recounting/coolness', 'weak vision', 'bleak modesty', 'fireless/average', 'household/metaphor', 'parallel/ wretched', 'pages stretched', 'occasional insight', 'foresaw ambition', 'searing meteor', 'vision narrower', 'louvre's gap', 'cynicism/seed', 'sadder joy', 'steadier elation', 'imagination ebbs', 'water clerk'. I don't suppose Walcott consulted a dictionary as he wrote, but was guided by his (fine) ear and a sense of etymology those who deal in words and often consult dictionaries acquire : balance in sound, concreteness or abstraction of meaning, and association of words makes each individually more striking and effective, and contributes to the remarkable general balance of the poem. It also strongly contrasts with predominantly Romance diction in the epigraph, where 'irregular', 'combination', 'fanciful', 'invention', 'delight', 'novelty', 'common', 'satiety', 'quest', 'pleasures', 'sudden', 'exhausted', 'repose', and 'stability' are all Latinate. Dr Johnson, having compiled his dictionary, knew what he did, and a taste for these words involves his neoclassicism and authority ; the diction of 'Nearing Forty', like other aspects of the poem, pits against that authority a less easily abstract truth, not abandoning Johnson's truth (for the argument of the poem follows that of the epigraph), but adding to it the counterbalance of a more painfully realised and personal truth.

Of several overlapping lexical sets, the most important concern water and fire. The water-set, in order, is 'rain', 'coolness', 'fireless', 'bled' (blood is wet), 'bleaching', 'rainspout', 'damp', 'wheezing' (of steam), 'kettle' (containing water), 'rain', 'convectional', 'ebbs', 'water', 'rain', 'weep' ; the fire-set is 'dawn', 'fireless', 'bled' (in the system of humours blood is hot), 'searing', 'meteor' (a 'firedrake'), 'match', 'dry', 'kettle' (heated with fire). Fire and water begin in natural opposition, joining only to create bleakness ("dawn, fireless") and suffering ("bled"), but in the central *semi-colon* are brought together by a "damp match" and "the dry wheezing of a dented kettle" : images that realise "household" truths, after which fire-words are subsumed into emotional renewal ('joy', 'elation', 'sleep')—allowing rain, once "rigidly metred, early-rising", to return, weeping but working and only "lightly falling". Also worth pondering is Walcott's retention of rain as tears, which a lesser poet might have used early, as the last word, when its emotional impact commingles with upbeat resolution.

A third set orients the poem in time : 'four', 'early-rising', 'day', 'dawn', 'foresaw', 'then', 'year's', 'night', 'sleep', 'moon'. Awake before dawn (l. 8), the 'poet' enters morning and makes a hot drink (ll. 17–18) ; a second movement in time takes him from remembered schooldays (l. 23) to a second rising and work (l. 25) "until the night when you can really sleep" (l. 27) ; by the end it is again night but with a new moon (implying a previous dark of the moon to go with insomniac lack of inspiration). Night to night is one of the poem's cycles, like those of water and emotion, unobtrusively vital in pacing it to a point of rest.

A set concerning the business of poetry—'metred', 'vision', 'work', 'style', 'metaphor', 'lines', 'pages', 'ambition', 'vision', 'leaves' (of paper), 'conventional', 'lines', 'work', 'imagination', 'conventional', 'clerk', 'work'—was mentioned under 'Lineation', and the autorhyming of "work" under 'Rhyme'. As well as "lines" (ll. 12, 25), two other words are repeated, "vision" (ll. 5, 19) and "conventional" (ll. 24, 29) ; to which may be added "narrow" and "narrower" (ll. 1, 19). Repetition gives subtle but significant emphasis : vision (not mere sight) is essential, for without it there is nothing to say, but the narrowing of vision with age, and the realisation that it was always narrower than youthful hope imagined, must be accepted : as age's slow recognition of (predominant) convention must be grown into ; one might as well resent the conventionality of rain, and ignore its role in sustaining life. A poetry that shirks quotidian reality and rainy days may be fine poetry such as the young will always write, but is unlikely to be of moral probity or toughness, or steadfastly and durably true.

Other sets can be picked out. Terms of judgement reward attention ('hearing', 'recounting', 'judge', 'just', 'truth', 'gauges', 'measuring', 'weighs') and affect images, making a louvre's slats bar the window ; so does the set concerning diminution and incapacity ('numbs', 'weak', 'bled', 'bleaching', 'fumble', 'wheezing', 'thin', 'end', 'ebbs', 'weep'). Alliterative patterns within lines ('rigidly/rising/rain', 'modesty/ middle', 'false/fireless') or widely separated ('fireless—average/foresaw—ambition', 'glad—sputter/ gauges—seasons'), also help bind the poem : but as with any great poem every careful reading will notice something new.

More complex phrases will be considered under 'Syntax', but five two-word combinations are best considered here. First, "false dawn" (l. 8), sometimes hyphenated, is a compound noun referring to a first spill of light over the horizon before true dawn, when the leading edge of the sun's disc becomes visible—but this unhyphenated use, metrically a spondee following a pyrrhic ('as a FALSE DAWN'), by stressing "false" partially restores its meaning of 'cheating, untrue'. As it is raining, the rising sun obscured by clouds, this disturbing flicker of a dawn with no sun (following a night with no moon) deepens the poem's early bleakness.

The second and third combinations are related. "household truth" (l. 10) fuses the domestic and metaphysical : immediately following the poem's most agonised moment, the 'home truth' of "which would be just" (l. 9), it is a marker to which, as to rain, the poem returns with the values of convention and work. The same thought is embodied in a "damp match" (l. 17) which still serves to light gas ; a common domestic object also matches damp with damp, a potential realised when rain at last becomes external weeping to match internal sadness.

The fourth combination is "prodigious cynicism" (l. 21), a troubling phrase. Cynics are "disposed to rail or find fault [. . .] to deny and sneer at the sincerity and goodness of human motives and actions" (*OED*) ; "prodigious"—which can mean 'ominous, abnormal, or amazing' and is here best caught by *OED*'s sense 4, "of extraordinary size, extent, power, or amount"—has in a context of remembered childhood and "seed" (l. 21) associations with the 'Prodigal Son' of Luke 15: 11–32. Implications of bountiful dispensation and lavished forgiveness are sharply at odds with the wizened closure and trammelled denial of generosity implicit in "cynicism". The paradoxicality of finding the words side by side isn't a problem to solve, or somehow bypass, but a wonderfully economic register of tensions that tauten the poem's arc and find resolution in the equally but untroublingly paradoxical "sadder joy but steadier elation", and the practical response to rain durably balanced emotions make possible.

The final term is "water clerk" (29), defined in *OED2* (under **"Water . . . 29**. special comb[inations]") as "an employee of a ship's chandler" ; citations are offered from an 1898 *Barbados Freight Report* and Theroux's *Saint Jack* (1973). A chandler supplies ships with nautical stores and provisions : water clerks meet by boat incoming ships, secure business for the chandler employing them, and liaise between captain and chandler while the ship is docked. It's a dogsbody sort of job (in American slang, a 'gofer'[46]), and so appropriate at this late stage of the poem, cohering with acceptance of quotidian work and controlled farewell to youthful ambitions—but that doesn't explain what this particular water clerk is up to :

> or you will rise and set your lines to work
> with sadder joy but steadier elation,
> until the night when you can really sleep,
> measuring how imagination
> ebbs, conventional as any water clerk
> who weighs the force of lightly falling rain,
> which, as the new moon moves it, does its work
> even when it seems to weep.

In this odd context, "weighs" most obviously means "To consider [. . .] in order to assess [. . .] value or importance ; to ponder, estimate, examine, take due account of ; to balance in the mind with a view to choice or preference" *(OED v.*[1], 12) ; the lines might then imply that water clerks (like poets) must still go on working in the rain, and may, as they

[46] One who 'goes for' this or that, fetching and carrying for someone else.

(wait to) meet ships, consider it. The "lightly falling rain" and lack of wind it implies might affect when a ship will arrive. Clerks are usually office-workers (like poets), and presumably some water clerks, whose job involves paperwork and boating, relish getting out and about whatever the weather, while others prefer to keep dry ; some no doubt complain and some are stoical : this one "weighs", suggesting care and dutiful practicality. The lines remain unusual, and most readers would need recourse to a dictionary ; but this sense of 'weigh' offers adequate sense.

There is, however, more to it, for 'to weigh' is very polysemic. The commonest literal meaning, "To ascertain the exact heaviness of (an object or substance) by balancing it in a pair of scales" (*OED v.*[1], 7) isn't applicable to "lightly falling rain" (though water clerks might weigh out provisions), but an archaic meaning, "To bear, carry, hold up" (*v.*[1], I) and the specific sense "To raise up, exalt" (*v.*[1], 4b) are : water clerks must bear rain and hold up under it, as the "I" in 'Nearing Forty' commends the "you" for doing ; the movement of the poem is from 'bearing' "early-rising rain", unhappily insomniac, to exalting "lightly falling rain, [/] which [. . .] does its work". Obsolete secondary senses do not press upon the poem as the primary sense of 'weigh' does, but for a reader aware of them they insinuate themselves persistently into the poem's fabric ; so does a nautical meaning, "To heave up (a ship's anchor) from the ground, before sailing" (*v.*[1], 5). Though in no way required to make sense of the lines, this would add 'weigh' to the same lexical set as "measuring", "ebbs", "water clerk", and "work" (ll. 28–31) ; the clerk's job ends as the reprovisioned ship weighs anchor, sailing with the ebb tide for a new destination while the clerk awaits another ship to begin the cycle of chandler's work anew. The implications (like those of the new moon) are of renewal and rededication, and the little constellation of secondary meanings and connections centred on the water clerk's world ballasts the poem's end, making its balance possible.

Exercises: Words and wordplay

1. To help your sense of diction develop take a short poem or two and look up <u>every</u> word, tagging each by part of speech and language of origin. What patterns are formed by parts of speech and etymological groups ? how do they relate ? Highlighting or on-screen displays can be helpful in analysis.

2. Repeat, but this time identifying <u>all</u> secondary senses + their inter-relations and with primary senses. How many are relevant ? do any detract from the poem ?

3. Identify a sequence of near-synonyms with differing etymologies (as, understand/comprehend, wood-working/carpentry, cliff/precipice, etc.) and write two short poems in identical form on the same subject, using all the Romance words in one, and all the Germanic words in the other ; then write a third drawing freely on either group. How do they compare? If you can identify a third near-synonym derived from another language (gestalt, xyloturgy, *khud*), what are the effects of introducing it ?

4. Take a canonical poem using arcane words that most people will have to look up (try Eliot or Hill), and one that is demotic in diction (try Kipling or Paul Dunbar), and consider carefully what choices the poets had. Were simpler or more refined synonyms available ? What would be lost if the arcane or demotic words were replaced ? Are the respective difficulties and vulgarities earned ? carried off ? or, in the end, demerits ?

5. If a group-discussion is possible, and especially if different religious and ethnic cultures are represented, it is very informative to have a frank exchange about what words (if any) individuals consider beyond the poetic pale. Where someone does have a strong or absolute objection, try to establish <u>exactly</u> why that is so, distinguishing grounds of blasphemy, profanity, obscenity, ideology, and taste. If others object to the objection, let them be equally exact in their grounds of argument. In summary, consider whether and how poetry can be an open meeting-place, and what restrictions (if any) should apply to its diction. People often think they know what they and others think ; you may be surprised.

Chapter Glossary

active : of an individual's vocabulary, that part which is actually used.

bowdlerise : to cut or replace with euphemisms anything thought 'improper' ; an eponym from Thomas Bowdler (1754–1825), editor of the *Family Shakespeare* (1818).

coinage : of a word, a neologism or nonce-word ; often used possessively, to indicate the coiner. Implicitly, new words are 'struck' or 'minted' rather than 'made' or 'invented'.

creole : (from Spanish *criollo,* a slave born in slavery ; ultimately probably from Latin *creare,* to create) a noun and adjective for people, cultures, and languages of mixed European and/or African and/or Amerindian heritage ; of a language the word typically implies 'formerly a pidgin tongue, now the sole or native language'. It is now sometimes spelled 'kweyol'.

decorum : (from Latin *decorus,* seemly) appropriateness, consistency, and civility of register, style, etc. in artistic compositions ; the opposite is indecorum.

demotic : (Greek, 'popular') of a word, register, or style, of the common people, often with an implication of vulgarity.

dialect : now usually a regional form of a dominant language, implying different words and/or syntax rather than simply accent.

diction : the choice of words (including the reasons for and consequences of that choice).

discourse : here, the diction of a particular poem, the relations between the words it actually uses. (A specialised use of an ambiguous and polysemic term.)

etymology : the derivation and history of a particular word, or the general study of how words evolve.

Germanic : of languages, belonging to a particular group of Indo-European languages, including modern German and Dutch, and Old English ; of modern English words, deriving from one of these languages.

idiom : generally, a language or dialect, the tongue and expressions of an area or group ; most specifically, a turn of phrase etc. habitual to native speakers but whose meaning is not readily predictable from the meanings of constituent words (go get 'em, tiger ; well I never).

lexical set : any set of words specified by a given criterion.

nation language : a politically correct term for Caribbean creoles and/or patois, usually deployed with ideological purpose (and sometimes adopted in Black American poetics).

neologism : a new word.

orthography : conventionally correct or proper spelling, and its study.

passive : of an individual's vocabulary, the whole range of words that is known.

patois : (? from Old French *patoier,* to handle roughly) loosely, a dialect ;

specifically, West Indian creoles drawing on English, French, or Spanish + African and/or Amerindian languages. It is now sometimes spelled 'patwa'.

polysemic : of words, having many senses and/or distinct meanings.

portmanteau : a word created by merging two or more existing words.

register : generally, the chosen level or pitch of style + diction + decorum in a text, assessed as e.g. 'high' or 'demotic' ; in printing register refers to the exactitude of repositioning the paper when multiple impressions are needed (as for colour + B&W), or both sides of a leaf bear text.

8
Syntax

the braided syntax
of a zeal ignited somewhere to the east,
concealed in hovels, quarreled over,
portaged westward : a basket weave, a
fishing net

AMY CLAMPITT, 'Westward'[1]

English syntax and its historical development are complex. Linguists and grammarians deal at length with auxiliary and phrasal verbs, dangling modifiers, and lost inflections, and a full treatment of syntax may require all these and more—yet poetic syntax has additional licence and must be more complex still. This tends to discourage readers not specifically interested in linguistics, but to grasp and use the basic points requires little specialised knowledge.

Simply enough, if *grammar* is what you can do in a language, rules for constructing sentences that guarantee comprehensibility, *syntax* is what you have done. There is incorrect grammar—*Me hit he* muddles cases—but not really 'incorrect' syntax. Like punctuation, it may be clear or unclear, cogent or vague, verbose or spare, etc. (p. 106), and affects (shades of) meaning. This is partly because the analytical nature of English affects the importance of word-order. In Latin, *Nero interfecit Agrippinam* and *Agrippinam interfecit Nero* both mean 'Nero killed Agrippina', because the cases ensure *Nero* does the killing and *Agrippinam* the dying—but *Nero killed Agrippina* and *Agrippina killed Nero* don't mean the same thing, and to keep 'Agrippina' as first word but still dying requires a passive construction, 'Agrippina was killed by Nero'. Meaning is then preserved, but the emotional impact of *active* and *passive voices* is not identical—compare 'He loves me' with 'I am loved by him'—and it matters : the hard-headed publishers Mills and

[1] *Collected Poems* (New York: Knopf, 1997), 301.

Boon direct authors to attend carefully to this, because active voice for a swooning heroine (or passive for an energetic hero) disturbs the sexist stereotypes on which their mass-market romances trade. A different example is 'split infinitives', the possibility (given a two-word form in English) of placing a word between 'to' and the verb. Grammarians and other pedants say one 'should' avoid doing this, and 'to boldly go', from a voiceover in the original *Star Trek,* is famous as a solecism. Certainly, infinitive forms create a link between 'to' and verb which should not be broken without reason, or the breaker realising it is being broken, but what matters isn't that *only to believe* and *to believe only* are 'correct', and *to only believe* 'incorrect', but that they don't mean the same thing. In *only to believe* 'only' governs 'to believe' ; in *to believe only* it governs what is believed ; *to only believe* is ambiguous. Thus syntax can be exploited to shade, vary, or otherwise affect meaning, and there's no point calling cummings's magnificently split infinitive "to in any way (however slightly or insinuatingly) insult" a 'mistake'.[2]

The terminology commonly used to discuss syntax is imprecise, but indispensable. *Clause* (from Latin *clausula,* the close of a period) is a generic term for units bigger than a word or phrase but (usually) smaller than a *sentence*—itself, as Ernest Gowers admitted, "not easy to define"[3] and in practice usually no more than 'the words occurring between one full-stop and the next'. A sentence may have only one clause ('I sat down.'), but most combine them ('I sat down, stretching my legs, and . . .') ; a complex sentence may have many *sub*-clauses (giving syntactically unnecessary information) in sequential *commata* or hierarchised *semi-/cola* each of which may itself be subdivided. As in that sentence this commonly involves prepositions, relative pronouns, conjunctions, and perhaps parentheses (one clause intercluded within another) indicated by commas, dashes, or lunulae. Such syntactical architecture is very flexible and there are an infinite number of possible sentences—but particular centuries show trends, habits, or conventions of syntax which careful readers discover. Compare the prose of a seventeenth-century writer such as Browne with that of eighteenth-century Johnson, early nineteenth-century Austen, and late nineteenth-century Conrad, and you can see and hear syntactic construction changing in length and rhythm[4] ; in poetry traditional

---

[2] *The Enormous Room* (Harmondsworth: Penguin, 1971), 108.

[3] *The Complete Plain Words* (1954; Harmondsworth: Pelican, 1962), 259.

[4] Prose is more commonly and thoroughly modernised than readers are aware : Austen doesn't always distinguish in/direct speech, and prose written before *c.* 1700 suffers badly.

prosody and form may disguise syntax, but there too it has changed a good deal since Shakespeare's day.

There has in particular been one major conceptual change that all readers of older work need to understand, the evolution of the modern, grammatically defined *sentence* and the decline of the classical, rhetorically defined *period*. Broadly speaking, the grounds on which a sentence is grammatically defined derive from linguistics and use such elements as subject, object, and verb ; only one of each is required for a grammatical sentence, and complete sentences are typographically signalled by initial capital letters and terminal full-stops. Many critics and translators seem to think this has always been what a 'sentence' is, but while the word (in various forms) dates to classical antiquity, its linguistic definition is much more recent, some elements being formulated only in the twentieth century—and one must beware what exactly the word means in earlier work. I referred (under 'Rhyme') to the first 'unit' of *Pierce Penileſſe* as a period, not a sentence, and the distinction is clear if the punctuation of the first edition of 1592 (p. 189) is compared with that of a modernised edition. The first edition has only one full-stop, at the very end, and is marked as a single unit. The integrity of that unit, and that it finishes when it does, have nothing to do with linguistic completion of minimal grammatical sense and everything to do with rhythmic completion of maximal rhetorical sense : the full-stop does not mark the end of a complete grammatical unit but of a complete unit of argument, a period of time, thought, and speech more like a modern paragraph than a modern sentence. Each *colon* of a period may be grammatically self-sufficient, as able to stand alone as a modern sentence, or only a clause, but all are linked in argument and so by colons. The modernised edition is very different :

> Having spent many years in studying how to live, and lived a long time without money ; having tired my youth with folly, and surfeited my mind with vanity, I began at length to look back to repentance and address my endeavours to prosperity. But all in vain. I sat up late and rose early, contended with the cold, and conversed with scarcity ; for all my labours turned to loss, my vulgar muse was despised and neglected, my pains not regarded or slightly rewarded, and I myself, in prime of my best wit, laid open to poverty.

The modernising editor divides Nashe's single period into three sentences, making the argument a sequence of statements rather than one complex statement ; structure is lost, and rhyme no longer displayed. Where Nashe's period angles and bolts *commata* and *cola* into a single structure, the editor's sentences lay clauses end to end and inject arbitrary full-stops.[5]

The same issue affects Shakespeare, sometimes seriously. In the Folio *Measure, for Measure* (F4^{v})[6] one speech of Isabella's is printed like this :

> *Iſab.* Could great men thunder
> As *Ioue* himſelfe do's, *Ioue* would neuer be quiet,
> For euery pelting petty Officer
> Would vſe his heauen for thunder ;
> Nothing but thunder : Mercifull heauen,
> Thou rather with thy ſharpe and ſulpherous bolt
> Splits the vn-wedgable and gnarled Oke,
> Then the ſoft Mertill : But man, proud man,
> Dreſt in a little briefe authoritie,
> Moſt ignorant of what he's moſt aſſur'd,
> (His glaſsie Eſſence) like an angry Ape
> Plaies ſuch phantaſtique tricks before high heauen,
> As makes the Angels weepe : who with our ſpleenes,
> Would all themſelues laugh mortall.

The copy-text for this passage was almost certainly prepared by Ralph Crane, a professional scribe, and while the punctuation is probably not Shakespeare's, it is patently clear and consistent.[7] There are four *cola,* the third beginning with a capitalised "But" : the first and third are about man's usurpation and abuse of divine authority (vectored from earth to heaven), while the second and fourth are about the behaviour of God and his angels (from heaven to earth). The syntax is like an 'M', moving from fallen mankind to divine justice, back and forth ; one period constituting one speech and one argument—but this is done away with by modernising editors. Here is the Arden 2 version (1965) :

> *Isab.*   Could great men thunder
> As Jove himself does, Jove would ne'er be quiet,
> For every pelting petty officer
> Would use his heaven for thunder; nothing but thunder.

---

[5] *Pierce Penniless* [. . .] *and Selected Writings,* ed. Wells (London: Arnold, 1964), 26. The middle 'sentence' must be read as "But [it was] all in vain.", a reader supplying subject and verb, to be syntactically complete ; it therefore seem to apply to what precedes ("I began [. . .] to prosperity.") rather than, as in 1592, what follows ("I sate [. . .] with scarcitie").

[6] The unexpected titular comma is in F, and probably indicates a stress on "*for*".

[7] And theatrical, intended to help actors : try reading 1623 and 1965 aloud yourself, and asking friends to sight-read them. Which generally produces better delivery ?

> Merciful Heaven,
> Thou rather with thy sharp and sulphurous bolt
> Splits the unwedgeable and gnarled oak,
> Than the soft myrtle. But man, proud man,
> Dress'd in a little brief authority,
> Most ignorant of what he's most assured—
> His glassy essence—like an angry ape
> Plays such fantastic tricks before high heaven
> As makes the angels weep; who, with our spleens,
> Would all themselves laugh mortall.[8] (2.2.111–24)

The words are unchanged, but even without distracting relineation and substitution of dashes for lunulae,[9] readers are hard-pressed to derive from this the balanced movement of Isabella's argument in F (earth—heaven—earth—heaven), because her four movements are broken into three sentences. The pattern of repunctuation is different in detail from that in Nashe, but similarly destroys the structure of a period, and to my mind makes it harder to read despite supposedly 'helpful' modernisation : the periodic syntax relating *colon* to *colon* is lost, and with it Isabella's patterned coherence of speech and argument. Reducing and distorting syntax reduces and distorts meaning, and modernised editions of prose, poetry, and drama predating *c.*1700 are almost always syntactically vandalised.

To read any syntax elements must be related—referents of *relative* clauses worked out, *main* clauses linked up,[10] parallelism of *cola* observed, etc.—yet reading poetry may involve clear understanding, not elimination, of deliberate ambiguity. In writing a sentence scores of choices are made, about word-order within sub-/clauses and the order of clauses themselves ; in poetry these must make a sentence do as a poet wants in conveying (shade of) meaning, and conform to

---

[8] Lever, ed., *Measure for Measure* (London: Methuen, 1965).

[9] Which has consequences : "—[/] His glassy essence—" must be read as a parenthesis, and so a relative clause in apposition to "what" in the line above ; the grammatical subject of "Plays" is then "man, proud man", and actors must (impossibly) link subject to verb across two sub-clauses, a parenthesis, and a simile. Lunulae were and are used in various conventions to emphasise, and need not be read as parenthesising (cf. italics, underline). Here they point a morally critical analogy of man mirroring (not aping) God, and in F "(His glaſsie Eſſence)" is the grammatical subject of "Plaies", which makes sense much easier to speak by shortening the pitch contour. Riverside, New Cambridge, Oxford, and Everyman editions of *Measure* differ mildly from Arden 2, but all enforce the same (wrong) reading.

[10] Relative clauses gives extra information. In *The man, who was tall, came in* "who was tall" relates to "The man". "The man" and "came in" are main clauses, "who was tall" a sub-clause.

requirements of metre, lineation, rhyme, diction, and form. The complexity of these requirements, and the intense awareness of language poetry generates, allows poets to use syntax in ways that would be out-of-place in ordinary speech or writing.

It does not do, however, to forget conventions of syntax, nor to break or ignore them heedlessly : the makers of *Star Trek* intended to excite admiration for Captain Kirk and his crew, not become famous for a solecism. Poets must also consider before breaking with convention whether consequences have been foreseen, there is a profit on the breakage, and cost can be borne before profit is reaped. The great test-case is *Paradise Lost*, famously Latinate in placing adjectives after nouns and ignoring the supposedly ideal sequence subject–verb–object. The beginning of Book IX (N425 ; text from 1667) bristles with examples :

No more of talk where God or Angel Gueſt
With Man, as with his Friend, familiar uſ'd
To ſit indulgent, and with him partake
Rural repaſt, permitting him the while
Venial diſcourse unblam'd : I now muſt change
Thoſe Notes to Tragic ; foul diſtruſt, and breach
Diſloyal on the part of man, revolt
And diſobedience ; On the part of Heav'n
Now alienated, diſtance and diſtaſte,
Anger and juſt rebuke, and judgement giv'n,
That brought into this World a world of woe,
Sinne and her ſhadow Death, and Miſerie
Deaths Harbinger :

Why Milton wrote thus is a good question : he read and wrote Latin, so it may have sounded less odd to his than modern ears, and as Virgil's *Aeneid* was a principal model he may have thought Latinate sound appropriate to epic. His blindness is relevant, in that he could not see his text but had it read to him, and presumably thought more aurally than visually. In any case he has paid a heavy price, for the difficulty of construing his syntax puts many people off *Paradise Lost*, but clearly got a good return on expenditure. The *semicolon* in ll. 6–8 would more conventionally be ordered as 'foul distrust and disloyal breach, revolt and disobedience on the part of man' ; Milton instead created stress on "foul diſtruſt, and breach" (l. 6) and "And diſobedience" (l. 8) by isolating them within lines ; produced the finely emphatic and symmetrical line "Diſloyal on the part of man, revolt" (l. 7) ; obtained as successive end-words the mutually reinforcing "breach" (l. 6) and "revolt" (l. 7), the latter a half-rhyme with "gueſt" (l. 1) and "diſtaſte" (l. 9) ; inserted between "diſtruſt" and "diſloyal" and "diſloyal" and "diſobedience", line-breaks heightening contrast between these human qualities and Heaven's "diſtance and diſtaſte" (l. 9), and so on. Whether such effects make the difficulty of reading worthwhile is a question for each reader, and readers come to opposing judgements : what cannot be argued is that Milton didn't know what he was doing.

Paradise Lost offers many lessons in how syntax can be profitable ; the commonest is to *delay* a word to the end of a sentence or clause, as "diſobedience"—used in the first line of book I—is delayed to the end of its *semi-colon* for emphasis. Similar technique marks a text of Dickinson's "Safe in their Alabaster Chambers"(N1111 ; J216a, F124B) :

Safe in their Alabaster Chambers—
Untouched by Morning
And untouched by Noon—
Sleep the meek members of the Resurrection—
Rafters of satin,
And Roof of stone.

Light laughs the breeze
In her Castle above them—
Babbles the Bee in a stolid Ear,
Pipe the Sweet Birds in ignorant cadence—
Ah, what sagacity perished here!

If l. 7 were 'the breeze laughs light' there would be no incentive to construe it as anything but a poetic description ; as it is, it also means the breeze is created by the laughter of light. Lines 4, 9, and 10 each begin with a verb conventionally placed in the middle (ll. 9, 10) or at the end (l. 4) : at the beginning of its line "Sleep" immediately follows "Noon", to which it is opposed ; symmetry (reinforced by capitals) pits "Sleep" against "Resurrection" ; and the sequence of rhymes is preserved, 'Noon/Resurrection/satin/ stone'—the last two created by milder inversions, "Rafters of satin" and "Roof of Stone". "Babbles the Bee", separating alliterating words and giving initial stress to "Babbles", sounds better than 'the Bee Babbles' :

BABBles the | BEE in a | STOLid | EAR,

makes sense as two dactyls + trochee + stressed hyperbeat, triple feet creating a babble, the trochee and hyperbeat lessening that babble to offer metrical support to "Stolid". But in :

The BEE | BABBles | in a | STOLid | EAR,

iamb + trochee + pyrrhic + trochee + stressed hyperbeat does nothing to support sense, and metrically cannot decide if it rises or falls. Line 10 is odder, and perhaps prompted as much by l. 9 as its own requirements, but a metrical case can be made :

PIPE the | SWEET BIRDS | in IG- | norant CA- | dence—

is logical, moving from a trochee, through a spondee, to an iamb and anapæst ; it isolates "Sweet Birds" as a spondee and plays the shift from falling to rising rhythm against "ignorant", and the cadence of "Cadence" against lengthening rising rhythm. But 'The Sweet Birds Pipe . . .' would be two iambs, or iamb + spondee, and either way metre would weaken. The syntactical oddity of Dickinson's overwhelming preference for the dash is considered with "I heard a Fly buzz" (p. 145), but one consequence of her technique is that most of her poems are short, for such sequentially itemising syntax cannot be long extended without becoming self-defeating, nothing—more—important—because—everything—is—equally—stressed. A version of the problem mars Shelley's 'Hymn to Intellectual Beauty' (N864), the tendency of which to gush (or mush) is related to its 21 dashes and slipshod syntax.

Conversely, the *epic catalogue* and *epic simile* deliberately create an overwhelming list or extended comparison, within which syntax of individual clauses, *cola*, and sentences is clear but the whole invokes the unimaginable or unknowable. Homer devoted 300 lines in book II of the *Iliad* to itemising commanders, identities, and ship-strengths of units comprising the Greek forces at Troy, embodying massive force in verbal extent, and Milton followed suit : the first *colon* of the Miltonic period on p. 118 combines catalogue and multiple (negative) similes to insist on the eternal tragedy of Satan's arrival in Eden, and the opening of book IX on p. 268 repeatedly deploys catalogues (count 'and's) to beef up its sombre turning of attention to the Fall. Much as the sublime is supposed to be more than one can take in, so epic catalogues and similes push syntax to the boundaries of comprehension, and their real test (beyond the awe and wonder they should induce) is in regathering the syntactical thread once an epic digression is over. In corresponding mock-epic forms, the conclusion/return may also be the point of detonation, where an inflated comparison bursts and some kind of 'common sense' returns with a less grandiloquent and typically more muscular syntax.

These considerations apply as much to prose as poetry (though inversions are rarer in prose), but poetic syntax must relate to form, for clearly line-length and stanza-size powerfully condition how syntax can/not be extended. In stanzaic poetry the general condition is coiling of syntax within stanzas and the need to end-stop a stanza or fashion enjambment across the stanza-break. Some stanzas, notably the Spenserian, are difficult to enjamb[11] ; in others enjambment can be brilliantly effective, as in Hope's 'Imperial Adam' (N1482), or MacNeice's 'The Sunlight on the Garden' (N1485) :

> The earth compels,
> We are dying, Egypt, dying
>
> And not expecting pardon,
> Hardened in heart anew,

The line before the stanza-break quotes (substituting "We are" for 'I am') a line from Shakespeare's *Antony, and Cleopatra*[12] (4.15.41) which is end-stopped in F, well-known as a complete quotation in its own right, and ends with the appropriately final "dying" : so MacNeice's unexpected continuation, "dying [//] And not expecting pardon, [/] Hardened [. . .] anew" (which refers back to the first stanza) is made shockingly strong.

In couplets syntax is an aspect of form, making the distinction of open and closed types. Open couplets are examined in relation to sequence of 'Nearing Forty' (p. 283) ; for closed ones, consider the opening of Dryden's 'Absalom and Achitophel' (N501 ; text from 1681), a period (among the most elegant in the language) satirising the promiscuous Charles II :

> In pious times, e'r Prieſt-craft did begin,
> Before *Polygamy* was made a ſin ;
> When man, on many, multiply'd his kind,
> E'r one to one was, curſedly, confind :
> When Nature prompted, and no law deny'd
> Promiſcuous uſe of Concubine and Bride ;
> Then, *Iſrael's* Monarch, after Heaven's own heart,
> His vigorous warmth did, variouſly, impart
> To Wives and Slaves : And, wide as his Command,
> Scatter'd his Maker's Image through the Land.

[11] Byron managed it in Cantos 3 and 4 of *Childe Harold's Pilgrimage* ; the effect is strange, and Byron shifted to couplets or *ottava rima* (much easier to enjamb).

[12] Another titular comma from F, which calls it *The Tragedie of Antony, and Cleopatra.*

The measured closure of the first three couplets is plain ; all are complete *semi-cola,* and throughout the poem most couplets are end-stopped with a semi-colon or heavier mark, a predominant rigidity wherein Dryden could build up great power. Here l. 1 sets a syntactic pattern, "In [. . .] e'r", which the first two parallel couplets reiterate and amplify : lines begin 'In/Before', 'When/E'r', the end-stopping makes each a satiric shaft, and the exquisite, comma'd isolation of "cursedly" (l. 4), like that of "variously" (l. 8), is needle-sharp. The third couplet seems set to follow, l. 5 like l. 3 beginning "When", but internal enjambment after "deny'd" gives swingeing emphasis to the key-word "Promiſcuous", and the need to read ll. 5–6 together begins to generate not pace—ll. 6 and 7 are end-stopped and Dryden is after power, not speed—but mercilessness. "Then", beginning l. 7, signals the attack proper, and an end-stopping comma forces attention to the phrase "after Heaven's own heart", the point of Dryden's shaft : when God said "Be fruitful, and multiply" (Genesis 1: 28 ; 8: 17) it was no charter for royal lechery. The metrical arc between "vigorous" and "variously" in l. 8 is the arrow in flight, and the opening of the fourth couplet as the syntax overflows l. 8 and penetrates l. 9 is the head sinking into flesh, its barbs the plural "Wives" and "Slaves" whose bodies were commandeered by royal lust ; the short fifth *semi-colon* salts the wound with the impiety of "Scattered"[13] and a chastening comparison of Monarch and Maker. What happens involves lineation, but also syntax : structuring word-order to make sense conform to or breach couplet-boundaries, ordering sense-structure to place words that matter where they will count ; controlled elegance of construction make the indictment of inelegant and uncontrolled sexuality far more damning. Yet as any commentary on the poem will rapidly tell you (N501 n. 5), Dryden wrote it in response to a fierce political dispute between Charles and the Whig faction (led by Shaftesbury) about succession,[14] and Dryden sided with the King. As the poem's biblical allegory unfolds, venial sins in David (Charles) come to seem much less serious than political ambitions in Achitophel (Shaftesbury) ; in retrospect readers realise that the exquisite syntax of the opening, making it locally sharper, also restrains its satire. The very elegance of the lines enforces suave good humour, and Dryden makes readers laugh, not wince, at profligate Charles ; his later portrait of grasping Shaftesbury did real damage. In both aspects

[13] One may "plough the fields and scatter" corn—but hardly heirs to the throne.

[14] Charles had only illegitimate children ; Shaftesbury and the Whigs wanted him to exclude from succession his brother James, a Catholic, in favour of a son, the Duke of Monmouth.

of control Dryden depended on mastery of syntax, nowhere more so than this beautifully balanced and double-edged opening.

In comparison, here are ll. 1–9 of Browning's 'The Bishop Orders His Tomb at Saint Praxed's Church' (N1014 ; text from 1845), a dramatic monologue in blank verse spoken on his deathbed by a bishop, in "[ROME, 15—.]" :

> VANITY, saith the preacher, vanity !
> Draw round my bed : is Anselm keeping back ?
> Nephews—sons mine . . . ah God, I know not! Well—
> She, men would have to be your mother once,
> Old Gandolf envied me, so fair she was !
> What's done is done, and she is dead beside,
> Dead long ago, and I am bishop since,
> And as she died so must we die ourselves,
> And thence ye may perceive the world's a dream.

In a manner alien to Dryden Browning sought a printed mimesis of the speaking voice, and people rarely speak in proper sentences when well, let alone when dying. He also sought to use mimed voice to reveal character, and whatever his failings this bishop has character to reveal. His first line misquotes Ecclesiastes 1: 2, "Vanity of vanities, saith the Preacher, vanity of vanities; all is vanity", ironically setting up his main interest, rich decoration of the tomb he will shortly inhabit ; his second, a worried exhortation of those attending him, establishes the poem's other pole. Each is a complete sentence, and with them neatly and rapidly out of the way Browning could begin to depict character—with an euphemism ("Nephews", which any bishop may have), a pause, a correction ("sons mine", which a Catholic bishop probably shouldn't have), a longer pause, and a blasphemy followed by fudging evasion of the issue ("I know not") worse than admission of unchastity. "Nephews [. . .] not !" is grammatically hopeless, but its syntax splendidly catches dying self-exculpation and ingrained dishonesty not even imminent death can obviate. The next sentence, "Well—[/] She, men would have to be your mother once, [/] Old Gandolf envied me, so fair she was !", is grammatically as bad : until the middle line is construed as 'the woman on whom men once believed I had fathered you' meaning is unclear, but make that construction, allowing lack of clarity as integral to the memorial drift of a dying mind, and to the Bishop's sins may be added geriatric cupidity (as he remembers the beauty of the woman with whom he broke his vows) and unlessened pride (as he remembers the envy of Gandolf, his predecessor as Bishop). There are implications about Gandolf, and the quality of episcopal succession at St Praxed's : so Browning has again enhanced meaning by word-order. The next much longer sentence (ll. 6–9) is far more grammatical, moving from difficult confession and fragmented memory to comfort in practical, then pious, platitudes, but syntax is still hard at work. "she is dead [. . .] and I am bishop", like the thought of Gandolf's envy and recovering grammar, signal renewing confidence and self-aggrandisement[15] ; glissading pronouns, from "as she died" to "so must we die" to "thence ye may", reduce any acknowledgement that only the bishop is dying obsessed with funereal vanities, and needs, far more than his healthy sons, to "perceive the world's a dream". In later monologues, particularly 'Mr Sludge, "the Medium" ', Browning made this revelatory syntax a fine art, and the scope of his skill is evident here.

The contrast between Dryden's third-person narrative voice and Browning's first-person expressive voice, despite common heroics, suggests the range of pressures syntax can come under, and of ends it can be made to serve. Browning's willingness to deploy overtly ungrammatical syntax in service of expression taught a lesson Modernists (especially Eliot) took to heart, and many poets have since deployed such syntax to many ends. cummings used highly original distortions (misusing parts of speech) satirically, as in 'anyone lived in a pretty how town' (N1396), and in the elegiac 'my father moved through dooms of love' ; he also wickedly rolled clichés together to satirise mindless patriotism in ' "next to of course god america i' (N1394). Eliot eerily evoked psychological alienation by thinning syntax in *The Hollow Men* (N1356), Corso used manic syntactical comedy aimed at the neat divisions of suburban domesticity in 'Marriage' (N1807), and Baraka angrily attacked self-assumed white superiority in 'It's Nation Time'.[16] In Berryman's *Dream Songs* (N1548) sense can usually be made, but compressions and fragmentations record irrationalities of the id and mutual interruptions by the protagonist, Henry, and one Mr Bones, a superego-voice, to build a polyphonic personal history and national hymn. And dramatic monologists remain, as always since Browning, capable of pretty much anything, in word as in deed.

Such powerful distortions of 'normative' (non-poetic, straightforward) syntax are of necessity strong medicine, and more delicate

[15] Cf. Barabas in Marlowe's *Jew of Malta* 4.1.43–4, who, admitting fornication, comments "But that was in another country, [/] And besides, the wench is dead."

[16] Most easily found at 3N1358.

means will often be wanted. In Dunn's 'The Penny Gibbet', for example, considering the scene before an execution, a particular habit of syntax offers a primary clue. Sense seems straightforward, but on reflection one realises everything is referred to via *synecdoche* (part for whole, as 'counting heads') or *metonymy* (attribute for whole, as 'addressing the bench')—an earlier execution didn't kill a person, but "strangled breath", and "there are other throats [/] Brought here to weight the frosted ropes today" ; a beggar stands not by soldiers and gibbet but "by the guarded carpentry". As obliquities pile up the poem combines fierce attention with sliding evasion, like a film of the scene that managed to imply everything while showing only off-centre details (the shadow of the gibbet, the feet of waiting spectators). The analogy with camera-work is interesting : just as cinematography is distinct from script and delivery, so a poet's choice of syntactical pans, zooms, close-ups, and jump-cuts needs to be distinguished from content and form.

Enlarging the scale again there are practices like those of Graham in 'The Guardian Angel of the Private Life' (p. 175) where constant recursions of syntax, ever worrying at its precisions and apprehensions, coiling back on itself as a condition of progress, embody with astonishing power a rare degree of philosophical and linguistic awareness whose motto is Heaney's lines in 'Terminus' : "Is it any wonder when I thought [/] I would have second thoughts ?"[17] But Graham is further down a different road : Heaney's lines, as grammatical as ambiguous, cover the political and social self as well as the philosophical mind, and he is, like Graham, notably polylingual, but Graham's work is more deeply possessed by a specifically linguistic uncertainty that has been one of the great currents of (post-)modern thought.

This is a complex matter, but the crunch-point, bluntly, is that much twentieth-century philosophy and, from the 1950s–1960s, literary theory, was centrally engaged with linguistics, developing a far-reaching hypothesis that language was anterior to thought. Everything must be expressed in language, and is determined by language ; language is learned ; the self, constituted in language, is structured beyond its control by pre-existing meanings ; and so on. One powerful symptom of the adoption of this hypothesis in academic literary criticism and by avant-garde writers is disavowal of intentionality (p. 319) and the 'false consciousness of the self' implicit in the idea of poems as personal and intentional expressions or commentaries ; instead, poems

[17] Dunn, *Dante's Drum-kit* (London: Faber, 1993), 56 ; Heaney, *Opened Ground*, 295.

are one form of language writing itself through the (supposedly) irrelevant medium of an individual—and for those holding such views the use of clear syntax to convey intended meaning is intrinsically problematical. Drawing on and surpassing techniques like Burroughs's 'cut-and-paste' disruptions of narrative and syntax, some consciously post-Modernist poets almost seek to prevent meaning, or force it always to be arbitrary : in particular American *L=A=N=G=U=A=G=E* poets, including Andrews, Hejinian, Perelman, and Silliman, cultivate the mathematical, seek randomness, and rejoice in extreme difficulty of interpretation in opposition to (more traditional) assumptions about poetry embodied in 'New Formalism'. Their ideas about indeterminacy of meaning and freedoms of language, and the textures of wordscapes they invite readers to explore or spectators-auditors to experience in performance or installation, can be exhilarating or tedious : but particular poems are, if at their best experience-able, almost by definition unteachable without extensive theoretical induction. While L=A=N=G=U=A=G=E poems are in theory neither susceptible to close reading nor intended to repay it, in practice chunks may be reasonably construable and display obvious thematic links, but there will also be sequences of words and lines offering little if any discernible meaning beyond the dictionary-definitions of individual words. What happens then is entirely up to you.

Such thinking is less mainstream outside America, but by no means unknown. In Britain the most interesting living figure is probably J. H. Prynne, whose work is sometimes called 'late Modernist'. Though always unusual, most of his earlier poems do yield meaning to enquiry, and some, notably 'Sketch for a Financial Theory of the Self', have become celebrated ; work from the 1980s and after, however, becomes more *post-Modernist*, and though a potent discipline of form is almost always apparent, extended coherence of syntax is rare. Drew Milne similarly defies sensible quotation, though some of his titles and dedications ('In Memoriam Joseph Beuys', 'A Modest Preposition [/] *for the people of East Timor*') announce themes or areas of investigation ; his academic interests in Beckett and Raworth suggest other means of approach, but advanced literary (and in Milne's case Marxist) theory and linguistic philosophy are essential. The combination of political intent with unfathomable sense is dangerous, and a poem like Nicholas Johnson's 'The Margarete-Sulamith Cycles of Anselm Kiefer', playing spelling and layout games with lines from Celan's 'Todesfuge' (p. 229) amid allusions to Kiefer's paintings, seems offensively amoral, and unworthy of attention ; the problem of his moral agency is a matter for those who care to familiarise themselves with the necessary theory.[18]

Since Joyce's *Ulysses* (the last 40 pages of which represent the drifting thoughts of Molly Bloom and contain no marks of punctuation) syntax has been more radically and productively destabilised in prose fiction, for in poetry lineation creates *de facto* syntactical units even when no other indication of syntax is provided. Such destabilized syntax is not a tool to dismiss, given the brilliance of Eliot's and cummings's uses, but seems to me of limited value in poetry, because close reading is by definition to (among other things) construe, and unless the writer is generating words and word-order randomly (as in so-called 'computer poetry'[19]) syntax will be implicit in the act of writing. If no syntactical construction is indicated readers will seek implicit syntax, and failing that, create some—for without syntax words are only words, and might as well remain in alphabetical sequence in the dictionary.

Exemplary Poems

1. 'The Flea' (pp. 14–15)

Donne's characteristic force of argument usually derives from formally contained energy of syntax, and is clearly generated here. Throughout the poem clarity of increasingly complex argument is sustained by syntax coiled tightly within lines and couplets, and builds in a triadic pattern (three couplets + triplet per stanza, three stanzas) that embodies the Trinity the diction repeatedly invokes (p. 251). Verbs of existence (is, bee, are) and common action (said, wooe, doe, spare, met) are syntactically delayed to fall in rhyme-positions, while key prepositions (How, Yet, Where, Though, Wherein) and conjunctions (And), are commonly initial, so each couplet sounds as a unit and plainly adds a link to the chain of argument . For all the fantastical wit and alarming theology, neither immediate demands of meaning nor the general need for clarity are ever forgotten (though metrical regularity is sacrificed, p. 16).

The only genuine difficulty in construing syntax comes in the third stanza, as Donne reaches his astonishing conclusion :

---

[18] Prynne, *Poems* (1999 ; Newcastle: Bloodaxe, 2005) ; Milne, *The Damage: New and Selected Poems* (Cambridge and Applecross: Salt, 2001) ; Johnson, *Show* (Buckfastleigh: Etruscan, 2001).

[19] See Nemerov, 'Speculative Equations: Poems, Poets, Computers' and 'Computer Poetry' in *Reflexions on Poetry and Poetics* (New Brunswick: Rutgers UP, 1972).

Cruell and ſodaine, hast thou ſince
Purpled thy naile, in blood of innocence ?
Wherein could this flea guilty bee,
Except in that drop which it ſuckt from thee ?
Yet thou triumph'ſt, and ſaiſt that thou
Find'ſt not thy ſelfe, nor mee the weaker now ;
'Tis true, then learne how falſe, feares bee ;
Juſt ſo much honor, when thou yeeld'ſt to mee,
Will waſt, as this flea's death tooke life from thee.

The first two couplets are clear, but if the third is clear in local meaning, the bad argument it reports is intrinsically unclear. The woman 'triumphs' in killing the flea (using her nail to shed its blood), and presumably supposes she has crushed Donne's erotic argument, but her meaning is as uncertain as the nature of the 'weakness' to which she refers : vulnerability to a superior force (the flea to her, humans to God) ? or weakness of the flesh to urgings of desire, such as leads Donne to proposition her and might lead her to fall ? Either way, killing the flea is (in terms of the arguments Donne has advanced) a crudity, a response but not an answer, and the complexity of the final triplet begins with his apparent acceptance of her point (" 'Tis true") and immediate reversal of it ("then learne how falſe, feares bee").

The nature of "feares" is as uncertain as that of 'weakness'—of death ? defloration ?—but the uncertainties are parallel (vulnerability/death, desire/sex), so "then" has both logical (therefore) and temporal (next) force. One reading would be that as the woman is happy to triumph in the blood of the flea, so she will be happy to triumph in her own hymeneal blood (as all Christians are happy to triumph in the blood of the lamb) ; another, that as she claims (by nail-shed blood) to have proven neither herself nor Donne the weaker, her fears of his 'nail' shedding her blood must equally be groundless (as human fear of Christ Crucified would be). In both cases the equations of 'nailing' fleas, virgins, and Christ create considerable unease, and the developing uncertainty about the larger argument is one of the things that make the reading voice slow, but the surface and local clarity is enough to force readers onwards, delivering them into the final two lines and up to Donne's judgement :

Juſt ſo much honor, when thou yeeld'ſt to mee,
Will waſt, as this flea's death tooke life from thee.

If taken as an adjective qualifying "honor", "Juſt" has its quantitative sense ; if taken as an adverb attaching to "Will waſt", it has more than quantitative implications : either way, legal and theological senses of the word are sufficiently active to colour meaning. Steel grammar—"when", not if, "thou yeeld'ſt", "Juſt ſo much honor [. . ./] Will", future determinative, not shall, "waſt"—holds a complete argument by analogy in tremendous balance : only a soulless flea, but its life ; a woman, but only her (supposed) honour. If the woman was right to value her honour, and will be right to believe defloration a dishonour, she will have to acknowledge her sin in killing the flea ; if she was right to kill the flea, her hymen will prove equally worthless to the force that spills its blood. To attempt any paraphrase of these two lines is to discover what astonishing force and density of syntax Donne achieves ; whatever theological, psychological, sexual, and moral difficulties the poem presents, its triumph is utterly to do with deployments of syntax (and hence punctuation) within formal parameters.

2. 'Ode on Melancholy' (p. 68)

Given the richness of diction and imagery one might expect greater complexity of syntax, but it is a part of Keats's skill to drive a clear line of sense through such richness. Local advantage is taken of delayed verbs (for rhyme) and initial prepositions and conjunctions (for emphasis and clarity), and beyond these a simple dialectical pattern is played out, 'nor' dominating the first stanza, 'or' the second, and 'and' the third. The itemising nature of the first two stanzas (Don't do that, nor that . . . But do this, or this . . .) makes for short components mapped on to the couplets and tercets, and while the syntax expands in parallel it cannot become overly complex. With 'and' in the third stanza, the limitation is lifted :

> She dwells with Beauty—Beauty that must die ;
>   And Joy, whose hand is ever at his lips
> Bidding adieu ; and aching Pleasure nigh,
>   Turning to poison while the bee-mouth sips :
> Ay, in the very temple of Delight
>   Veil'd Melancholy has her sovran shrine,
>   Though seen of none save him whose strenuous tongue
> Can burst Joy's grape against his palate fine ;
>   His soul shall taste the sadness of her might,
>   And be among her cloudy trophies hung.

The difficulty is the sense (Beauty that constantly "must" but never does die, Joy ever leaving but never gone) and not really syntactical—but awkward uncertainty attends "aching Pleasure" (or given the comma after "nigh" something else ?) "Turning to poison while the bee-mouth sips" : what, exactly, poisons whom and when ? Impossible present participles (aching, turning) are consistent with the allegorical ever-now the stanza establishes, and a general sense of Dead Sea fruits turning to ashes in the mouth (loathing what one achieves even in achieving it) is clear enough—but uncertainties affecting basic syntactical decisions (including the subject of the main verb) reflect a serious underlying problem with the logic of allegory. That problem was not of Keats's making, and has defeated far greater allegorists than he (including Spenser and Bunyan), but while he can skim over it in such a brief lyric as this, the basic problems of formulation it causes within a quatrain indicate he had no real strategy for coping with the ontological and epistemological paradoxes of allegory.

Metaphysically, things worsen with personification of Melancholy (excess of black bile) as a "sovran" deity and a need to "burst Joy's grape" with a "strenuous tongue" to see even her "Veil'd" appearance. Sensually, they jumble when a soul tastes the sadness of might, and theologically become alarming (not to say pagan) when it becomes a temple-trophy of some kind. But syntactically nothing is hard to follow, and the images Keats assembles speak a psychological truth about human emotions and thought before logical weakness in some component-images catches up. The variant rhyme-scheme of the final stanza, in tension with invariant eisthesis and so a form of cross-bracing, helps sustain syntax, but could not do so were it not itself clear and forceful, line by line, tercet by tercet, and quatrain by quatrain.

3. 'I heard a Fly buzz—when I died—' (p. 97)

The predominant effect of Dickinson's punctuation on syntax, uncertainty of construing successive dash'd off phrases backward or forward, has been discussed (p. 145). Her frequent construction of phrases as freestanding clauses promotes the effect : of 19 here, 6 begin with prepositions (including two 'between's and two 'when's), 5 with 'and', 2 with 'I', 2 with 'the', and 1 with an auxiliary verb ("had"), producing phrases that like more promiscuous atoms happily bind to or sit alongside almost anything else. At the same time the metrical drive of iambics and tetrametrics is strong, boosted by reliance on the dash (and consequent absence of stops) and the poem as a whole, like most of Dickinson's, so short that it is usually taken in a swift gulp. On an incomprehensible, syntactically straightforward base of reporting in the past tense the events of one's own deathbed, the poem establishes what is in effect a timeless present within which the usual linearity of syntax is in part suspended.

There is, however, a counter-pattern. Although beginning in the past ("I heard"), Dickinson reverts to a more distant past ("had wrung") which becomes dynamic ("were gathering"), looks to the future ("when the King"), and regains the initial past with the reappearance of the fly before continuing to a moment of cessation—in miniature, the pattern of classical epic, beginning *in medias res* and proceeding by flashback, reversion, and continuance. Slight as it is in such miniature form, this structure gives the poem a comprehensible general form within which the dash'd-off phrases can safely bombinate.

Considering her syntactical-punctuational practice at large, as well as its deployment in this poem, one might say her constant isolation of words and phrases produces a needle-sharp rat-a-tatting emphasis that brings every component and observation into clear focus. Dickinson often uses this effect to deconstruct and itemize the miseries and hypocrisies of the very masculine (and increasingly scientific) world in which she had to live, but could turn it on herself to give flights of language, imagination, and fantasy telling clarity, detail, and articulation. However odd a given poem may be if considered whole, the syntactical force of each isolated, often clarion phrase (with the accumulating, disciplined observations of metre and form) is sufficient to persuade readers that oddity is to be profitably accepted and worried at ; were individual phrases syntactically woollier, the whole could not stand firm.

4. 'Nearing Forty' (pp. 22–3)

As a single sentence, or modern period of one very complex *colon* articulated as three *semi-cola,* the poem requires of readers an extended act of syntactical construction only re-reading can clarify, but richly rewards that effort. Not surprisingly, many sub-clauses must be identified before the high road of main clauses can be trodden ; one way is to pick out words crucial to the main syntax, often prepositions and conjunctions beginning *commata*. Treated thus the first *semi-colon* becomes : "Insomniac since four, hearing [. . .] that I am nearing forty [. . .] when I may judge [. . .] which would be just, because [. . .] ;". The pattern of compact moments of syntactical reorientation inter-spaced with longer, elaborative developments (the qualities of rain, weakening vision, judgement, the reasons for its justice) is an alternative to formal analysis as an explanation of how the poem moves forward. The compact moments are stress points of syntax, and (in true testimony to

Walcott's craft) aurally linked : four/forty, hearing/nearing, when—judge/which—just. It is notable that as the period begins to build, complex syntax to grow, the natural visual stress on first words of a line is employed to help readers construe by promoting important small words : "that" (l. 4), "by" (l. 7), "as" (l. 8), "which" (l. 9), "that" (l. 11), "in" (l. 12). Taken together, these considerations partly account for the impact of "which would be just" (l. 9) : as well as being fraught with the pain of confessional honesty, it is syntactically self-contained to set it against elaborative clauses about coolness, weak vision, and bleak modesty ; the simplicity of "which" is strained by the emotional freight it gathers into itself as a relative pronoun, strain a reader must register.

A similar pattern emerges from the second *semi-colon* : "glad [. . .] you who [. . .] will fumble [. . .] and [. . .] settle [. . .] then [. . .] recall. which [. . .] ;". The elaborations are of what is settled for and what recalled, and syntactical complexity is again made easier to follow by the linear positioning of "will" (l. 17), "for" (ll. 18, 19), "then" (l. 20), and "which" (l. 23). This central section is syntactically compressed in the frequency with which words needed for full construction must be inferred from earlier uses : in l. 17, for example, one must read "will fumble [. . .] and [. . . will] settle" ; in l. 19 "[and . . . settle] for vision" ; in l. 20 "[and] then [. . . you will] recall" ; in l. 22 "[recall how . . . prodigious cynicism] gauges our seasons". These syntactical eddies are appropriate to meditative, rueful memory, as more sequential syntax was in the first *semi-colon* to the painful and bleak business of enumerative judgement.

The last and shortest *semi-colon* returns to sequentiality, "who" (l. 30) referring only to the "water clerk" (l. 29). The greater simplicity of construction, aided by easier flow of lines (only ll. 29 + 31 have medial punctuation) and the momentum of more strongly rising metre, underpins emotional resolution and a sense of restored balance that enable the poem to close.

Although many possible relations between the 218 words are precluded by grammar, lineation, and punctuation, the syntax of such a period is multiply complex, and the approach I take above only one of many possibles. The largest syntactical divisions, into *semi-cola,* were considered under 'Punctuation' (pp. 147–8), and one could take an extremely robust view, picking out only first and last words of each—"Insomniac [. . .] rainspout ; glad [. . .] conventional ; or [. . .] weep"—which (in further testimony to Walcott's craft) is as terse a summary of the poem's thought as can be imagined. How exactly you respond to syntax is up to you : the only things ruled out absolutely are to ignore it or think it happens of its own accord.

Two further points are worth noticing here : the manipulation of syntax and enjambment in open couplets, and the complex phrases of ll. 10–14 (elaborating on "the household truth") and ll. 28–32 (imagination, the water clerk, and the moon).

The first couplet (ll. 7–8) is end-stopped by the comma after "average" ; the penultimate one (ll. 17–18) by the comma after "kettle" ; the last (ll. 19–20) is different, a half-rhyme ('gap/deep') with the first line end-stopped and the second out-rhyming, with 'sleep' and 'weep' (ll. 27, 32) (p. 218) : but the second to fifth (ll. 9–16) are open, and all internally as well as externally enjambed (including the extraordinary "gutter- [/] ing"). The momentum this imparts helps prevent the poem miring in self-judgement, and is worth looking at closely :

                                        fireless and average,
which would be just, because your life bled for
the household truth, the style past metaphor
that finds its parallel however wretched
in simple, shining lines, in pages stretched
plain as a bleaching bedsheet under a guttering rainspout; glad for the sputter
of occasional insight, you who foresaw
ambition as a searing meteor
will fumble a damp match and, smiling, settle
for the dry wheezing of a dented kettle, for vision

This is no rocking lineation, but a spurt of syntax (like rainwater from a gutter's spout) that begins after the phrase I find myself obliged to read most slowly and with greatest pain : "which would be just". Having forced itself to that admission, the poem urgently needs to explain it and achieves explanation with the idea of "household truth" : that itself then requires explanation in terms of writing. "however wretched" qualifies "parallel", and in prose would probably be indicated by commas : 'finds its parallel, however wretched, in simple': by omitting commas Walcott preserves the openness of the couplet and maintains pace because the voice must take the words as if a hyphenated compound noun ('parallel-however-wretched'), which makes them a stronger parallel to "household truth". Conversely, ", shining lines," *is* isolated by commas, which slow the voice to allow time for admiration, but internal syntactical parallelism in l. 12 ("in [. . .] in [. . .]") keeps things moving because too long a pause after "lines," would endanger the necessary construction "finds its parallel [. . .] in pages stretched". The extraordinary final clause of the *semi-colon,* "in pages [. . .] rainspout", again batters through two line-breaks, but is marked by a pulsing rhythm and *plosive* diction[20] (all Ps and Bs) that disturb momentum : yet with syntax straightforward (in what other order would you place these words ?) it isn't difficult to make it to the semi-colon. That mark is a strong pause, but in the middle of a line can't be too long : the reader, like the poem, cannot afford to puddle under the rainspout, but must go on. The "searing meteor" is no more than a shooting star, l. 16 enjambed both in to and out of, but its blaze, burning out as a candle gutters, marks the last open couplet, and again there are absent commas. In prose one would read : "you, who foresaw ambition as a searing meteor, will fumble", and as before the absent commas, keeping the couplet open, act to compound, making the subject not simply "you" but 'you-who-foresaw-ambition-as-a-searing-meteor'. If isolated by commas the qualification of "you" could be left behind ; thus compounded it must be carried on to create potent contrast between subject and the verbs "fumble" and "settle". And again absence of commas is later matched by a presence, around ", smiling,", braking momentum as the sequence of open couplets ends, allowing time for a smile but making it, in isolation, inward and sad. The subtle, highly effective control Walcott effects in these lines by playing lineation, enjambment, and syntax off against one another is very close to the poem's heart.

In ll. 10–14, it may seem "the style past metaphor" is contradictorily illustrated by a metaphor, the "bleaching bedsheet". A metaphor is a "figure of speech in which a name or descriptive term is transferred to some object to which it is not properly applicable" (*OED*) : but "in [. . .] in" (l. 12) suggests a "parallel", not a metaphor. Is "the style past metaphor" an explanation of "the household truth" ? or a second thing for which "your life bled" ? "the style [. . .] that finds its parallel [. . .] in simple [. . .] lines" could be a way of being that finds expression in more direct writing, as the poem itself eventually finds in the simpler syntax of the third *semi-colon* ; but is the bed-sheet outside, actually being bleached by rain ? or bleaching and wearing thin with age, and "under a gutter- [/] ing rain-spout" because, like the spouting poet lying under it, it is in a room past the window of which rainwater from the gutter is

[20] *Plosive* means that in articulation the vocal tract is completely closed, then opened, producing a small explosion of breath/sound—as in English with Ps and Bs. See Crystal, *Encyclopedia of Language*, 152–68.

falling ? For me, the latter makes more satisfying sense, but syntax allows either and the ambiguity is arguably one of the poem's few weaknesses.

Finally, there are the last and very moving lines :

> or you will rise and set your lines to work
> with sadder joy but steadier elation,
> until the night when you can really sleep,
> measuring how imagination
> ebbs, conventional as any water clerk
> who weighs the force of lightly falling rain,
> which, as the new moon moves it, does its work
> even when it seems to weep.

More missing commas (after "clerk" and "work") declare their absence, so that at this very last moment the working is not confidently final—'does its work, even when [. . .]'—but soundlessly and efficiently compounded with weeping. There is also a slight problem, for if "conventional [. . .] rain" (ll. 29–30) is taken as a sub-clause (which the commas that <u>are</u> present indicate), the main clause must run from "ebbs" (l. 29) to "which" (l. 31) ; and "which", "it", and "its" (l. 31) must then refer to "imagination" (l. 28). In one way that reading makes good sense, for if "imagination [/] ebbs" it is being imagined as a tide, and the moon does move the tides ; moreover, at the new (as at the full) moon, the tide will be a spring tide, flooding higher than the neap tides that occur near the first and last quarters. Yet tides do not (to me at least) readily "seem to weep", so "it" (l. 32) would more satisfactorily be taken to refer to the "lightly falling rain" ; "its" (l. 31) and "it" (l. 32), despite being in the same clause, would then have different referents—at which point a grammarian or anyone guided by the MLA handbook would reach for a red pencil. As with the bedsheet there is ambiguity here, a degree of torque in the syntactical structure which brings together falling rain and ebbing tide ; like the poet the reader must surrender to the movement and pass beyond a restrictive logic of rules to faith in the boundless cycle, believing that what goes out with the tide will come in with the rain.

Exercises: Stringing words together

1. It is important, in the first place, to know the nine parts of speech. Taking two or three short poems (perhaps written in different centuries, or by the same poet in distinct phases or styles) identify each and every word grammatically and catalogue the syntactical certainties and ambiguities their poetic order generates. The exercise may seem basic, but results can be both profound and unexpected (as Vendler showed in demonstrating Heaney's shifting preference, volume by volume, for the dominance of nouns, adjectives, and verbs).

2. Syntax should be studied with the voice as well as eye, and the easiest test of any syntax is to seek to read it aloud comprehensibly for auditors. In poetry metrics and lineation must be handled simultaneously, but as both commonly indicate stresses necessary for clear delivery this is help rather than hindrance. It is worth practising both with lyrics and verse drama, for successful playwrights tend to know exactly what they are doing, and the extent to which complex ideas can be clearly conveyed if key words (often small prepositions) are stressed needs to be heard to be believed. For an object lesson, take any complex speech from mid- or late Shakespeare (Angelo in Act 2 of *Measure*, Hermione in Act 3 of *Winter's Tale*), in the Folio text, and experiment with delivery, attending to initial and terminal words however apparently unimportant and unexceptional. Then try delivering a verse-paragraph from *Paradise Lost* : how unspeakable is Milton ? and how much of any difficulty is syntactical ?

3. Verb tense is commonly critical, and too often missed. Take any poem of reasonable length and identify the tense of every verb : you'll be surprised. As a model, try Tennyson's 'Ulysses' (N992), apparently dealing determinedly with the future, but as Christopher Ricks memorably pointed out, rising into the future tense only once : where ? and what happens to the tenses surrounding that point ? Dramatic monologues are generally good to look at this way, but tense can be equally vital in lyric verse, as 'September Song' shows (p. 146).

4. To consider the interactions of form and syntax, take passages in blank verse and couplets and relineate them to display syntactical units (*comma, colon,* period ; *comma,* clause, *semi-/colon,* sentence). Compare the various new versions as visual clues to sense and oral/aural cues for delivery, and on returning to the original you should find your sense of the interplay between progression of sense and iteration of form enhanced. The same exercise may profitably be undertaken between two poems in regular quatrains, one habitually end-stopping and the other habitually enjambing stanzas. With practice one learns to analyse the interplay in any given poem in a single *sotto voce* sight-reading (handy in exams).

5. For anyone intending to write about the poetry they read a primary concern should be their own syntax. There are few student essays from which 20–35 per cent of the words cannot be removed without losing anything substantive, and besides the appalling costs in trees and reading-time, such verbosity is a severe handicap in closed exams and word-limited coursework and in the age of the PC unacceptable and unnecessary : practise editing yourself, duplicating a recent

essay and reworking it to see how much more compactly (cogently, tellingly, lucidly) you could have said what you did ; when you swear not one more word can go, stop, save, sleep, return, duplicate, start again, and before long you'll have, say, 1,200, 1,000, and 800 word versions of the same thing. Identify what you have done to compress matters at each stage (e.g. passive to active switches, elimination of adjectives, adverbs, and phrasal scaffolding, revision of verb and noun choices), and feed that knowledge back into your habits of composition : sooner than you think you'll be able to compose in first draft what you now achieve only in third or fourth. Practise with punctuation is needed (p. 149), but that is simply the left hand to syntax's right, and the ability to say something with maximal force and density but within specific parameters is both a common demand of the marketplace and a constant training in one's ability to read.

Chapter Glossary

active : of an individual's vocabulary, that part which is actually used.

clause : a word with no fully agreed definition, but used to mean units of syntax larger than a word or phrase and smaller than a sentence. It is possible, however, for a sentence to have only one clause. Sub-, relative, and main clauses are (among others) distinguished.

delayed : of a verb, withheld from its 'normal' place in the syntax to fall in a significant formal position (as the end of a sentence or line).

epic catalogue : a formal (as much as long) catalogue of something, typically intended (in epic as elsewhere) enumeratively to express a large number or high degree. The seminal example is Homer's 300+ line catalogue of ships and commanders in book II of the *Iliad.*

epic simile : a simile endowing a subject with glory and/or significance by comparing it (usually at elaborate and digressive length) to a incident, person, or topos from classical epic ; a favourite resource of Milton's in *Paradise Lost.*

grammar : the rules governing the cases of words and the 'permissible' syntax of any given language.

L=A=N=G=U=A=G=E poetry : a highly theorised poetics and method of poetic composition that emerged in New York and San Francisco in the early 1970s.

main clause(s) : those dealing directly with or continuing the principal action of a sentence ; distinguished from sub-clauses.

metonymy : a rhetorical figure in which an attribute of something is substituted for the thing itself (as 'the stage' for 'the acting profession').

passive : of an individual's vocabulary, the whole range of words that is known.

period : a classical rhetorically defined unit of syntax and argument, composed of *cola* and *commata* ; closer to the modern paragraph than the modern sentence ; latterly and in the USA, a full-stop.

plosive : of letters, requiring for their pronunciation that the vocal tract be closed and then opened, producing a small explosion of breath/sound.

relative clause : one that gives additional but syntactically inessential information about a subject, verb, or object ; commonly signalled by 'who', 'which', or 'that'.

sentence : in modern use, the largest unit of syntax, composed of one or more clauses and normally containing at least one grammatical subject, one transitive or intransitive verb, and if appropriate an object ; typographically, sentences begin with a capital letter and end with a full-stop.

sub-clause : any that is not a main clause, including all relative clauses, parenthetical clauses, etc.

synecdoche : a rhetorical figure in which a part of something is named instead of the whole (as 'counting heads').

syntax : the relations between words and clauses (of whatever kind) within a period or sentence.

9
History

> Both isms and periods are mentioned in this book, since they do have a certain utility, but they are mentioned sparingly and with strong reserves : [. . .] most seem to be post hoc, approximate labels, fortuitous in origin and often misleading in application.
>
> PATRICK O'BRIAN, *Pablo Ruiz Picasso: A Biography*

> And, after all, it is to them we return.
> Their triumph is to rise and be our hosts :
> lords of unquiet or of quiet sojourn,
> those muddy-hued and midge-tormented ghosts.
>
> GEOFFREY HILL, 'An Apology for the Revival of Christian Architecture in England', i. 1–4[1]

The role of historical knowledge in practical criticism has always been uncertain. The book in which I. A. Richards first theorised the discipline, *Practical Criticism* (1929), reports an experiment, giving students poems for comment without identifying author, date, or title. Richards wanted responses to what was on the page, rather than to a name or date, and so far as it goes this is sensible : Eliot, for example, is reputedly 'difficult' ; give a class a passage ascribed to him and many students seem unable to respond because 'Eliot's too hard' ; given the same passage unascribed, they respond to what they do understand and ask questions about what they don't. 'Shakespeare' has the same effect : 'If it's by Shakespeare it must be perfect'—as if he wrote from earliest youth with the greatness of adult vision, and never a bad day or mistake. This is nonsense, but Shakespeare's position in the canon, and the unthinking praise of him known as *bardolatry*, make his name deeply inhibiting.

The impulse that prompted Richards to try to exclude historical

[1] O'Brian (1976; London and New York: Norton, 1994), 78 ; Hill, *Collected Poems*, 152.

assumptions has been greatly extended in the theoretical criticisms derived from Marx, Freud, Barthes, Derrida, and feminist thinkers. Each theoretical model (Marxism, psychoanalysis, structuralism, deconstruction) seeks in one or another way for a general theory of poetics, a way of reading and understanding as applicable to *Beowulf* as to *The Waste Land*, as helpful about Chaucer as about Dryden or Pope—and anything so general must reduce the importance of immediate historical contexts in which authors lived and works were written.[2] Some things apply as much to the unknown author of *Beowulf* in the first millenium CE as to Eliot in the twentieth century—both were white, male, formally innovative Christian poets given to alliteration—but others differentiate them, including differences between times, and it is not obvious that a better understanding of either can be achieved by the principled dismissal of historical facts.

Nor is it obviously possible so to dismiss history, and the last quarter of the twentieth century saw a double debate : among literary critics the issue tended to be the 'relevance' of history to texts and possibility of reading ahistorically ; among historians, the 'relevance' of literary texts to history and possibility of objective history. Older historians tend implicitly to claim 'objective' status, and write as if simply revealing natural relations of facts ; the problem for historians has been a new understanding that histories, like fictions, inevitably assume, construct, and rhetorise, and *value-free* history is not possible.[3] And history, proverbially 'written by the winners', usually has higher stakes than fiction : in 1980s Germany, central issues in the *Historikerstreit* ('battle of historians') were how to write of Germany's defeat, and Nazi history. Which ways of writing German history help defeat neo-Nazism ? or un/intentionally collude with it ? The issue is vital because many neo-Nazis are apologists for Auschwitz, attempting to warp history by editing evidence and abusing method to deny the *Sho'ah* (p. 228). To these politically perverted 'historians' the debate about the reliability and rhetoric of history books was a golden opportunity for disinformation, and what began as timely academic house-cleaning became in the mass media political dynamite.

[2] Marxism does not dismiss history, but Marxist critics often seem most interested in the Marxist theory of history, and tend to flatten particularities.

[3] The extreme version is that 'history' is texts ; whatever 'actually happened', events are only available through, and masked by, texts that supposedly report but rhetorically construct them. This can seem counter to common sense—things do happen—but it is patently true that the vast bulk of 'historical facts' one 'knows' are learned from 'texts'.

In literature moral stakes are rarely so intense, but Salman Rushdie (against whom, for writing *The Satanic Verses*, a capital *fatwa* was issued by the late Ayatollah Khomeini) is a sharp warning, and in many texts historical and moral issues must not be ignored. In English literature the most difficult issue is probably complicity of canonical texts with imperialism : whether one knows Spenser helped administer and enforce Elizabeth I's brutal Irish policy, or wonders why Forster's *A Passage to India* has been reprinted more than sixty times since the first paperback in 1936, connections between literature and (post-)imperial politics are not easily dismissed. In this light history and (in the broad sense) politics are closely intertwined, and readings ignorant of history as political as informed ones : the question is only whether ignorance results from blindness, censorship, or wilfully averting one's eyes.

One might also ask why it should ever be thought desirable to exclude history. Much literature is about specific historical events, and can make little sense if one subtracts that history. Take Marvell's great poem 'An Horatian Ode, Upon Cromwell's Return from Ireland' (N486), for which the *Norton* editors provide 24 notes, more than half explicit provisions of historical fact : if one knows nothing of the English Civil War, execution of Charles I, part played by Cromwell, bloody campaign he fought in Ireland, and political events catalysed by his return to the centre stage of post-regicide politics, what sense can one make of it ? If there is that in it which is in all poems, what and where is the interest or delight of this particular poem if historical specificities are stripped away to leave it as a bald universal truth ? Why read this poem and not another equally stripped to that same truth ?

Nor need history be centrally explicit to matter. Browning's 'My Last Duchess' (N1012) was probably prompted (as the *Norton* editors note) by the lives of Alfonso II d'Este, a sixteenth-century duke of Ferrara, and his first wife, whom he probably had murdered ; one needn't know these names to enjoy the poem, but if one knows nothing of arranged marriage or the existence and function of marriage-brokers, of Renaissance attitudes to art or Italian and aristocratic pride, the extent to which it can be understood is limited. In Browning's duke's willingness to have his wife murdered because she smiled at someone else, and admit her murder to a marriage-broker with whom he is negotiating for a second wife, is a portrait of masculine pride and uxoricidal violence which is not historically limited : one has only to read newspapers to find accounts of men who kill women for much the same vile unreasons. But Browning's portrait is set in a particular history, and contains words and references made meaningless if the poem is abstracted from it ; he could have chosen a different setting and speaker, but this historical Italian setting and aristocratic speaker were what he employed his craft to realise, and his possible reasons offer good ways into the poem.

In any case, all poems are written at a particular historical moment, and one way of approaching them (as all art) is location in history. The *Norton Anthology*, like many, is organised chronologically, from 'Caedmon's Hymn' (N1) to the work of Greg Williamson, born in 1964 (N2023). Riffle its pages : each topic already discussed, from 'Metre' to 'Syntax', has its own history, and intertwining histories makes Caedmon's work differ from Williamson's. An ability to discern a difference in Dryden's handling of heroic couplets in the last quarter of the seventeenth century, and Pope's in the first half of the eighteenth, is only acquired through extensive and intensive reading—but it doesn't take a reading superstar to notice that spelling, diction, syntax, form, etc. in Chaucer differ from those in Auden, and the dimmest historical awareness will (despite modernised texts) place Chaucer's "At night was come into that hostelrye [/] Wel nine and twenty in a compaignye" (N20) as written much earlier than Auden's "Watch, then, the band of rivals as they climb up and down [/] Their steep stone gennels in twos and threes" (N1477). And that is a mere beginning : most students study poetry drawn from periods between the late-medieval world of Chaucer and the present, and as literary periods are understood through known examples, historical sense refines. Since the mid-twentieth-century work of Christopher Hill on English Civil War literature, the academy has conceded the self-expression, commentary, and investigation embodied in literature as resources for historians. Conversely, to understand Metaphysical poetry, relating characteristic themes to characteristic forms, is more difficult, probably impossible, without some knowledge of political and social history, including subjects as diverse as patronage, printing, religious belief, and sexual mores ; to pretend there is no relation between the Enlightenment and the closed-couplet lucidity of Augustan verse, or between the social and poetic fluidities of the twentieth century, is wilfully perverse.

Then again, the patchwork of labels for periods of English literature is certainly inadequate. The commonest are regnal, as *Ricardian* (1377–99), *Elizabethan* (1558–1603), *Jacobean* (1603–25), the hybrid *Jacobethan* (1558–1625), *Caroline* (1625–49), *Commonwealth* (1649–60), *Restoration* (1660–*c.*1700), *Victorian* (1837–1901), and *Edwardian* (1901–10) ; to which may be added three dynastic terms, *Tudor* (1485–1603), *Stuart* (1603–1714), and *Hanoverian* (1714–1901). *Georgian*, important in architecture, can confuse in literature : a particular set of Georges may be meant (I–IV = 1714–1830, V–VI = 1910–52), but more often it designates a group of primarily pastoral poets in the 1910s (p. 300). These are supplemented by looser terms designating literary groups, styles, or milieux, and potentially referring not to all literature within their dates but only to that meeting certain (unspecified) criteria, notably *Metaphysical* (predominantly poetry, *c.*1580–*c.*1650), *Cavalier* (Royalist poetry of the Civil War), *Augustan* (*c.*1700–*c.*1760), *Romantic* (*c.*1789–*c.*1830), and *Modernist* (*c.*1914–*c.*1960). Others have been proposed, such as *Antiquarian* to cover eighteenth-century work from Pope's adaptations of Chaucer to Percy's *Reliques*, Chatterton's forgeries, and Coleridge's first, deliberately archaic text of 'The Rime of the Ancient Mariner', and one can always fall back on increments (post-Restoration, proto-Romantic) or the general historical labels of 'Renaissance' or *Early Modern* and *Modern*—but gaps and overlaps remain.

As they should : Marvell is called the 'last Metaphysical', and poems like 'The Definition of Love' support the claim, but tetrametric couplets preferred in other, longer poems point him as proto-Augustan. Neither label will do alone—and a sense of Marvell as (*inter alia*) transitional is helpful. Others also fall on cusps—Hardy the Victorian novelist and Modernist poet—and even those who seem squarely labelled (Augustan Pope, Romantic Wordsworth) are not thereby summed up (Antiquarian Pope, Victorian Wordsworth) : as with other schemes of classification, the sensible thing isn't outright rejection but constant awareness of limitation and contingency. It helps to know something of a label's provenance : that Dr Johnson coined (with hostile intent) the literary use of 'Metaphysical' is widely known, but fewer people realise 'Romantic' only came into use as a literary designation at the end of the nineteenth century, and to Wordsworth himself would have been meaningless. The general difficulty is apparent in the twentieth century, too recent to have been digested, where 'Modernist', 'late Modernist', and 'post-Modernist' play catch-as-catch-can with an array of artistic manifestos (Dadaist, Futurist, Surrealist) and looser groupings (*Bloomsbury*, the *Movement*, the *Beats*, the *New York School*), some *termini a quo* (post-1918/1945/1968/1989) and decade or event identities (war poets, poetry of the 1930s), and a clutch of (supposedly) distinctive generalisations (post-colonial, magic realist, neo-formalist) : if we are spared, everything will be much clearer next century (including the periodicity of American and other literatures in English, still far from agreed)—but by then the problem will be labelling what happened in this twenty-first century.

There is one body of historical knowledge to which all readers must have constant recourse in reading older literature : earlier senses of words that have changed meaning between being written and read. An obvious example is 'gay', now almost always with the primary meaning '(male) homosexual', which until the mid-twentieth century simply meant 'cheerful'. When Dickens described someone as 'gay' or having a 'gay time' he didn't mean they were homosexual, and a reader who thinks he did is demonstrably misreading (and confused[4]). Another example which gives trouble is 'silly', which once meant—and in some places still does—'feeble ; defenceless ; deserving of pity' (as 'silly sheep'), but the modern sense ('foolish, trifling') developed in Shakespeare's day (and works), and has eclipsed the older, wider meaning. 'Officious', conversely, was then simply how any officer (including civil office-holders) did and should behave ; the pejorative modern sense ('interfering ; over-assertive of authority') was just emerging (the *OED*'s earliest citation is 1602), but gained little ground until the later seventeenth century. The *OED*'s inclusion of these older senses, and dating of all senses by earliest and latest quotations, are why it is <u>the</u> dictionary to consult.

There is also the meaning given to a particular word, form, or technique by previous uses. One can't write a sonnet without knowing what one is—which implies knowledge of existing sonnets, of how and what they are, the form's capacities and history, which bear upon a new act of writing. And within the sonnet (or any form) may be dozens of techniques or words learned from a poem : all bear upon the meaning. I've mentioned Yeats's 'Leda and the Swan' as using form ironically (pp. 33, 47, and 50), forcing association of courtship and rape despite their antipathy. If intentional, such invocations of a style (or tradition or individual work) are *allusions*, and in some poets allusion is a central and vital procedure : books have been devoted to one poet's reception and invocatory use of another, and canonical giants (especially Shakespeare and Milton) offer in themselves a way of approaching most of their successors. Literary relations need not be matters of intent : a poet may forget where they first encountered a phrase or technique, and a reader recognise what the poet did not ; neither ignorant writing nor ignorant reading alters the existence of that phrase or technique in the two poems, or a relationship in time between them—which can enrich reading of the older poem as much as the newer. The web of relations between one text and others, allusive and unintended, is now called

[4] There are characters readers may reasonably believe gay, but 'gay' doesn't convey that.

intertextuality, and many critics seem happy to imagine it cancels history, as if texts and books did not in reading constantly declare themselves fashioned by different minds formed in different ages and places. Eliot, unsurprisingly, saw more clearly, and elegantly made the point in 'Tradition and the Individual Talent' by saying that the past is altered by the present as much as the present by the past : in both kinds of operation it is as well to know something of present and past, whose interaction makes history.

A knowledge of how words shift sense is a beginning, histories of forms a next step, and there is no limit to the growth and refinement of one's sense of literary history. I use my *OED* almost every day, and many oddities in history continue to intrigue me : why, for example, Marvell could use iambic tetrameter gravely, while fifty years after his death it had become predominantly comic ; why the triple rhymes of *ottava rima*, far from comic in the hands of Fayrfax, are richly so in those of Byron ; or why long triple metres had such a vogue in the later nineteenth century. Among the answers will be historical facts and processes : as among the reasons that made Dryden write 'Absalom and Achitophel' as he did (pp. 271–3) were developing Augustan passions for clarity and exactitude of language and for satire, satisfyingly reconciled in the heroic couplet ; and among those that made Browning write 'The Bishop Orders His Tomb at St Praxed's' as he did (pp. 273–4) were a Romantic legacy of interest in mental pathology, and the remarkable development of vocal *mise-en-page*, which began in the eighteenth century and culminated in his own legacy to Eliot.

There is, though, an obvious limit to the history that can be brought to bear on a poem, especially in an exam : what a reader knows. Acquiring a sense of history and literary developments and influences takes time, and continues throughout one's reading life—but you can cultivate or ignore it ; try to bring knowledge to bear on a poem, or bash ahead not giving a hoot for accuracy ; care about your reading of a poem, even in an exam, or treat it as a chore. The exploration of history, political, social, cultural, or literary, is pursued in many ways beyond my scope : knowledge of fashion, for example, can be invaluable in reading poetry of the Renaissance, and a museum with old clothing (like the V. and A. in London) a revelation.[5] It's a general pursuit, with consequences far beyond reading, but as a reader I always find it worth cultivating a sense of history, for as much as vision and

[5] As an example, find out what a farthingale was and read Donne's 'Elegy XIX' (N312).

hearing it enhances my enjoyment and understanding of the poems (and prose) I read.

Exemplary Poems

1. 'Ode on Melancholy' (p. 68)

Keats has almost *ab initio* been read as the most ahistorical poet in the canon. Byron, incensed by disparagement of Pope in 'Sleep and Poetry', decried his passionate style—"such writing is a sort of mental masturbation—he is always f—gg—g his *Imagination* [. . .] viciously soliciting his own ideas into a state, which is neither poetry nor anything else but a Bedlam vision produced by raw pork and opium"[6]—and politer versions of that view (Keats as inward, isolated from even his own times, and hence timelessly true) remained dominant ; so much so that in 1979 McGann remarked Keats as "a poet for whom historical analysis—by the virtually unanimous decision of Western literary critics—has no relevance whatsoever". The only substantial exception was in formal studies, Ridley in the 1930s and Zillman in the 1960s considering Keats as a critical figure in the sonnet tradition.[7]

McGann, however, was not approving : his essay 'Keats and the Historical Method in Literary Criticism', demonstrating the rich possibilities of a historical approach, sparked a major reassessment evident in the essays gathered by Roe in *Keats and History* (1995). The 'Ode on Melancholy' has yet to receive attention in this debate, but two of McGann's major points—that many features of Keats's thought and work require the historical context of Romanticism to be understood fully, and that the publishers of *Lamia, Isabella* . . . (Taylor and Hessey) were deliberately cautious, excluding poems they thought topically controversial—apply as much to 'Melancholy' as to the 1819 odes that have been substantially re-examined. So too does the argument of Watkins's *Keats's Poetry and the Politics of the Imagination* (1989), placing Keats's great flowering of 1816–20 firmly in the post-Napoleonic context of intense anxiety and rising public violence so evident in Shelley's 'England in 1819' (N871).[8]

[6] Byron, letter to Murray, 9 Nov. 1820, in Marchand, ed., *Byron's Letters and Journals* (12 vols, London: Murray, 1973–81), vii. 225. I could not check the (bowdlerising ?) transcription of "f[ri]gg[in]g" as the Murray Archive is in transit to the National Library of Scotland.

[7] McGann, *Beauty of Inflections*, 26 ; Ridley, *Keats' Craftsmanship* (1933; London: Methuen, 1963) ; Zillman, *John Keats and the Sonnet Tradition* (New York: Octagon, 1970).

[8] Roe, ed., (Cambridge: CUP, 1995 ; Watkins, Rutherford, NJ: Fairleigh Dickinson UP, 1989).

In keeping with Taylor's and Hessey's caution, a product of politically hostile reviews of the *Poems* (1817) and *Endymion* (1818), nothing in 'Melancholy' demands historical reading ; but the poem is very much of its late Romantic time, and besides its historical specificity of formal experimentation, features such as the awkward and reverential personification of Melancholy (p. 253) would be surprising in an earlier poet. The inwardness of its subject, less concrete than a nightingale, urn, or even (pictured) autumnal scene, seemingly debars topical immediacy, but invites biographical consideration in relation to Keats's hostile reception (Shelley thought vicious reviewing a factor in his early death) and his difficult relationship with Fanny Brawne : a primary implication, after all, is that (despite relative youth) the poet knows something about melancholy not everyone knows, and such knowledge is commonly learned the hard way. Beyond personal reasons for melancholy, moreover, events of 1819 were depressing for Keats, as for Hunt, Shelley, and other literary radicals : they culminated in August in the infamous Peterloo Massacre (driving Keats to a rare explicitly political passage in his letter to George Keats of 17–27 September), to which the ode 'To Autumn' may be in part a response ; a tense, disheartening foreboding was evident in London well before May. This context also illuminates a specific aspect of the poem's textual history, the cancelled first stanza preserved in MS and usually quoted in annotated editions :

> Though you should build a bark of dead men's bones,
> And rear a phantom gibbet for a mast,
> Stitch creeds together for a sail, with groans,
> To fill it out, blood-stained and aghast ;
> Although your rudder be a dragon's tail
> Long-severed, yet still hard with agony,
> Your cordage large uprootings from the skull
> Of bald Medusa, certes you would fail
> To find the Melancholy—whether she
> Dreameth in any isle of Lethe dull.

Editors tend to note a connection with imagery in Burton's *Anatomy of Melancholy* (1621), but naval detail (bark, mast, sails, rudder, cordage) and the driving metaphor of ingenious building and rigging, recalling the 'phantom bark' in *Rime of the Ancient Mariner*, also point to the tremendous public awareness of the Royal Navy during Keats's life. Throughout the French Revolutionary and Napoleonic Wars (1793–1801, 1803–15) Britain's primary effort was at sea, and Captains' reports of naval actions were extensively reprinted in newspapers, with commentaries of one or another kind ; the age's single greatest national experience of inseparable joy and grief came with news of Nelson's death and crushing victory at Trafalgar in 1805, which arrived a week before Keats's tenth birthday after months of high alarm at the prospect of invasion ; and destitute naval veterans, many amputees, remained common, in London as elsewhere, for a generation after 1815. As in Austen, also long supposed to have written in splendid isolation from events, such awareness is neither casual nor sentimental, but bespeaks informed understanding of national marine dependence and naval indebtedness.

The 'Ode' clearly remains at a greater distance from history (however defined) than, say, elegies, verse-biographies, and occasional sonnets, but distancing was explicitly imposed on the whole of the 1820 volume, and must be reframed as only one, wilfully spun aspect of Keats's composing mind, to which his more topical work must be added. The poem can be more explicitly restored to historical and biographical specificity in assessments of its lexicon, poetic imaginary, and dialectical argument, and it would be a very conservative reader who now insisted on Keats as "a poet for whom historical analysis [. . .] has no relevance whatsoever" ; the lesson is that such an assertion about *any* poet is better taken as a clear signal of critical opportunity than as anything resembling the truth.

2. 'Anthem for Doomed Youth' (p. 18)

Owen, conversely, comes in a period wrapper that for most readers defines who he was and why he matters. As a 'poet of the First World War', supposedly writing in its trench-heart and killed with sanctifying irony a week before the Armistice in November 1918, a tragic identity is imposed before a word he wrote has been read. Many of his poems were in fact written during his extensive hospitalisation and convalescence in Britain between June 1917 and August 1918, as recollections rather than immediate reports, and I will come to this under 'Biography' ; here my concern is with the limitations of the larger history that tends to be imposed.

One consideration is the almost exclusive concentration in anthologies and selections on the 'War Poems' (pp. 35–86 in Day Lewis's edition of the *Collected Poems*) at the expense of all others (pp. 89–143). Whatever his importance as a trench moralist, various aspects of Owen's 'War Poems', including form and diction, are more easily understood in company with lyrics and pastorals that link him as much to overtly *Georgian* contemporaries (including Edward Thomas, another trench-poet, and John Drinkwater)[9] as to the (supposedly) distinct group of 'war-poets' (including Sassoon, Rosenberg, and Gurney). The modes of poetic expression Owen admired and understood sufficiently to employ were not those of Modernism, but of the pre-Modernist canon and the Georgians ; however important his poetic witness of insane and inept military horror, it cannot be understood as *sui generis* a product of trench-experience. The 'Anthem', whatever its anthemic qualities as a testament to 'the horror of war', is also a sonnet, and the formal paradoxes attending such sonnet-content can only be satisfied historically ; the diction and sentiment of the sestet, comparable to Brooke's pastoral nostalgias or Tolkien's trench-escaping imaginations of Middle Earth (and subsequently Hobbiton), equally insist on a broader context than latter-day constructions of poetic protest against the general stupidity and grotesque inhumanity of the Western Front.

A second concern is the monolithic construction of trench-experience as continuous and unremitting horror that tends to be produced by magpie introductions and annotations to 'the poetry of the First World War'. Other theatres (including Gallipoli) with other experiences of horror tend to be forgotten ; so too is the epigrammatic truth that warfare is 99 per cent boredom and 1 per cent sheer terror, although it is necessary to explain just how and why a trench-dweller could be writing such poems as Owen's. There has also been a great deal of extremely interesting work on individual experiences of the First World War, notably Lyn Macdonald's social histories based on interviews with surviving veterans and a continuing sequence of military-historical investigations into how such slaughter could be tolerated, most recently centring on effects for commanders of wireless isolation (then a very new phenomenon). Even within more simplistic and received views of the First World War as the originary horror of the twentieth century, quite basic facts are not conveyed.

Throughout the UK and Commonwealth, as well as some parts of the USA, for example, one finds public memorials naming the local dead of

[9] The label 'Georgian', coined by Edward Marsh (1872–1953) in 1911 in reaction against lingering Victorianism and established in a series of anthologies from 1911 to 1922, now tends to be derogatory, indicating (supposedly) vapid and nostalgic formalist pastoralism properly swept aside by Modernism and ignored in favour of the agonised truths of trench-poets. Considering such Georgians as Lawrence, Graves, de la Mare, Masefield, and Sassoon, and the range of Owen's and Thomas's work, this simply will not do as even the bones of an account.

the two World Wars ; in Britain these typically take the form of columns or plaques, and simple observation shows (i) that there are more names for the First than for the Second World War, and (ii) that names for the First are more repetitive, a family often being represented many times. One implication, easily confirmed, is that the British death-toll in the First World War (commonly given as 450,000–500,000) was indeed significantly higher than that in Second (commonly *c.* 350,000) ; military death-tolls are even more discrepant, as civilian casualties in the Second World War (*c.* 80,000–100,000, most from bombing) were massively greater than in the First. One explanation, easily arrived at, is that annihilation of whole regiments, as at the Somme and Passchendaele, is unmatched in the Second World War, where the memorialised deaths (when specified) are of an airman here, a soldier there, a sailor in this or that sea. But the critical underlying fact—that throughout the First World War the predominant pattern of British regimental recruiting was county-based, so that even a company's annihilation might in ten minutes deprive a given area of all men born between 1890 and 1900—is little understood : yet it, more than anything, makes forceful sense of the repeating family names in the lists of the dead, and of the "bugles calling [. . .] from sad shires" for the massed dead of Owen's 'Anthem'.

The 'War Poets' in general, Owen in particular, and this 'Anthem' in especial, are object lessons in how a crude history, limitingly applied, can cripplingly impede subtle or nuanced reading of so complex a thing as a poem. Yet who would wish to divorce the 'Anthem' from history, or contend it was not shaped by the compellingly violent hands of history as much as the victimised and voluntary hands of Owen ?

3. 'September Song' (p. 72)

With the *Sho'ah*, more than any other history, a spotlight automatically comes up on each person confronting it as an interpreter ; that will be considered under 'Biography'. There is also, uniquely, the absolute difficulty bleakly posed in the designation of Auschwitz as the 'black sun' to rival the 'white sun' of Hiroshima : it is no more possible to find meaning in the heart of the *Sho'ah* than in a nuclear inferno—tragedy, narrative force, and lyric pity alike are as atomised and negated as the matter of victims' bodies. This is partly what informed Adorno's denunciation of all poetry attempting the *Sho'ah*, and equally informs Hill's deployments of damaged and attenuated form and of warding lineation and lunulae (pp. 73, 100, and 146). Yet if Hill's responses are necessarily formal and personal, the problem is anything but.

For philosophies of history and practices of historiography alike, the ideologically and sociopathologically driven, highly organised, and industrially scaled extermination of *c.* 7 million people, including *c.* 6 million European Jews, overwhelmingly within the four years 1941–5 and primarily at four purpose-built deathcamps in southern Poland, poses a problem neither has overcome. How could the Renaissance and Enlightenment deliver this logistical and unimaginable horror ? how can any notion of history as progress survive such convulsive abandonment of civility, community, and common humanity ? and how, in the face of its own, distinctive self-recording of its machine facilitation (so many train-timetables, so many orders in triplicate for patented Zyklon gas, so many individual assignments to genocide), can historians of the *Sho'ah* practise their craft ? Particularly since the 1970s, this compound of problems has been central to a series of debates driving the re-emergence of the historian-as-self-conscious-interpreter, a distinct presence within his or her own pages who does not pretend to neutrality or omniscience and is permitted to express human emotions. But when Hill was writing poems (including 'September Song') specifically in response to the *Sho'ah,* in the late 1950s and 1960s, the historians' debates had barely begun to be framed, and in some ways 'September Song' (one culmination of Hill's *Sho'ah* poetry and clearly displaying a sharply moral consciousness of the needs for self-admission and self-occlusion) could be thought to have been ahead of history : though not, of course, of the events from the reception of which history is made.

The poem's own fierce and extended reception (including my responses here) suggests it is indeed so understood by a significant body of readers. One may dislike this or that among its manœuvres, yet in managing to utter a response to the *Sho'ah,* with as many safeguards and delicacies as utterance can bear yet also a trenchant human sorrow rooted in the continuance of living plenty, 'September Song' did not simply promise but delivered the possibility of speech. Before the 1980s most Anglophone poets who turned in any way to the *Sho'ah* did so in desperation (the famous example is Plath, but Berryman, Jarrell, and Sexton were also suicides after "representing themselves literarily in light of the Holocaust"[10]) ; Hill alone seemed able poetically to confront, respond, and survive knowledge of the horror. Beneath Adorno's cry of guilt and despair has always lurked Nietzsche's dire warning that "Wer mit Ungeheuern kämpft, mag zusehn, dass er nicht dabei zum

[10] Young, *Writing and Rewriting the Holocaust,* 127.

Ungeheuer wird. Und wenn du lange in einem Abgrund blickst, blickt der Abgrund auch in dich hinein." ('He who fights with Monsters might take care lest he thereby become a Monster. And if you gaze for long into an Abyss, the Abyss gazes also into you.') Hill had taken such care, and not only been able to gaze into the abyss for a long moment, but also to record that moment with poetic integrity.

'September Song', that is, is not only of and in history ; in a respectable sense, with immense moral effort, it made and makes history. From the hovering time of a present September to the grim precision of two typical events (*"born 19.6.32—deported 24.9.42"*) whose conjunction is at once common and a synecdoche of unimaginable horror, and in returning to the present tense and tension of its final line, the poem is fundamentally concerned with a morally adequate apprehension in this present of that past. It is in effect a tomb of the unknown child ; a crafted memorial of one anonymous, curtailed life whose loss representatively structures the present in which it is commemorated with honourable survival. Hill's commitment to confronting and examining history, intense and personal as it must be, is a civil and public commitment to an intellectual community of citizen-readers, and no living poet has a better claim on our historical imaginations and responsibilities.

4. 'Nearing Forty' (pp. 22–3)

The title suggests closer involvement with biography than history at large, and lyric inwardness excludes the historical concerns courted by satirical and narrative poetry. That in no way lessens the importance of locating Walcott as a Caribbean poet whose island and people have suffered a violent history, often at British hands, but does focus that importance on Walcott as an individual, and I will come to it under 'Biography'. The recent publication of some drafts of the poem, making available an aspect of its textual history, is directly connected with the death of John Figueroa, its dedicatee, and also belongs under 'Biography', but less personal history is explicitly and complicatedly invoked in two ways : by the epigraph, and a particular intertextual association of "water clerk" (29).

The epigraphic quotation comes from the seventh paragraph of the *Preface* to Dr Johnson's great edition of Shakespeare, published in 1765 ; the poem seeks to follow it from "irregular combination" to "stability" while testing Johnson's certainty by pitting it (and its prose cadences) against poetic justice, harsh self-judgement, and a "household truth" acknowledged as a form of diminishment. Literary judgements and understandings of the eighteenth century are under reappraisal, and older models, concentrated on the intellectual predominance of reason and linguistic predominance of elegance, look ideologically simplified : but tastes for reason and elegance must be embodied in any new models, and are well exemplified by Johnson. His ability to declare without qualification that "the pleasures of sudden wonder are soon exhausted and the mind can only repose on the stability of truth" is characteristic of his thinking, and came more easily in the fairly stable and self-assured mid-eighteenth century than it would have done in the mid-seventeenth, when England was racked by civil war, or mid-twentieth. We do not yet have the benefits of hindsight, but there is no doubting the twentieth century was deeply unsettled politically, socially, and culturally, and that this was manifest to Walcott when he wrote. These twentieth-century problems aren't what 'Nearing Forty' is 'about', but they are a background of failures and uncertainties against which Walcott's ability to write of "judg[ing] my work [/] by the bleak modesty of middle age [/] as a false dawn" makes deeper and fuller sense, as the successes and certainties of the eighteenth century illuminate Johnson's willingness to make absolute pronouncements.

The details of eighteenth- and twentieth-century histories and perceptions of history are complex, but an epigraph is not a complicated way of invoking a historical comparison : any epigraph might do so. What does complicate things is the point in the *Preface* from which the epigraph is taken : Johnson is elaborating on Jonson's claim (N343) that Shakespeare "was not of an age, but for all time", that his truths were universal and ahistorical :

> Nothing can pleaſe many, and pleaſe long, but juſt repreſentations of general nature. Particular manners can be known to few, and therefore few only can judge how nearly they are copied. The irregular combinations of fanciful invention may delight a-while, by that novelty of which the common ſatiety of life ſends us all in queſt ; but the pleaſures of ſudden wonder are ſoon exhauſted, and the mind can only repoſe on the ſtability of truth.
>
> *Shakeſpeare* is above all writers, at leaſt above all modern writers, the poet of nature ; the poet that holds up to his readers a faithful mirrour of manners and of life. His characters are not modified by the cuſtoms of particular places, unpractiſed by the reſt of the world ; by the peculiarities of ſtudies or profeſſions, which can operate but upon ſmall numbers ; or by the accidents of tranſient faſhions or temporary opinions : they are the genuine progeny of common humanity, ſuch as

> the world will always ſupply, and obſervation will always find. His perſons act and ſpeak by the influence of thoſe general paſſions and principles by which all minds are agitated, and the whole ſyſtem of life is continued in motion. In the writings of other poets a character is too often an individual ; in thoſe of *Shakeſpeare* it is commonly a ſpecies.
>
> It is from this wide extenſion of deſign that ſo much inſtruction is derived. It is this which fills the plays of *Shakeſpeare* with practical axioms and domeſtick wiſdom. It was ſaid of *Euripides*, that every verſe was a precept ; and it may be ſaid of *Shakeſpeare*, that from his works may be collected a ſyſtem of civil and œconomical prudence. Yet his real power is not ſhewn in the ſplendour of particular paſſages, but by the progreſs of his fable, and, the tenour of his dialogue ; and he that tries to recommend him by ſelect quotations, will ſucceed like the pedant in *Hierocles*, who, when he offered his houſe to ſale, carried a brick in his pocket as a ſpecimen.

Only the extract Walcott quotes must be considered, but the ellipsis ending the epigraph points out (*inter alia*) that there is more than is quoted, and it is clear 'Nearing Forty' draws more than its epigraph from this passage : the excellence Johnson attributes to Shakespeare is very close to the praise Walcott's poem gives to "your life" (9). Most crucial is the relation between Johnson's "domestick wisdom" and "œconomical prudence"[11] and Walcott's "household truth", but beyond this striking echo is the whole movement of Johnson's argument towards Shakespeare's practical value rather than rhetorical splendour, and the equivalent movement in Walcott's poem towards endorsement of quotidian and water-clerkly work. It is not "fanciful invention" or the "searing meteor" which endures, but the workaday world ; if the natures of fancy and work changed between Shakespeare's time and Johnson's, and again between Johnson's and Walcott's, the truth of a distinction between them did not. Walcott's poem squares up to his own ageing, to the passing of young fancies, recognising bleaker truths ; in that painful transition it is a comfort to know that what he discovers, and must acknowledge, is a timeless truth, discovered and acknowledged by great precursors. But the epigraphic truth that transcends history is taken from the literary history that preserves Johnson to make his *Preface* available, two centuries later, to Walcott. Moreover,

[11] Johnson is probably using "œconomical" in the *OED*'s sense "1. Pertaining to a household or its management", and "prudence" in sense "2. Wisdom; knowledge of or skill in a matter. Cf. JURISPRUDENCE" ; "civil and œconomical prudence" implies that from Shakespeare may be learned all that is necessary for wise management of state and household alike.

it is a fragment of history that reaches back to a still older history in Shakespeare, and its value to Walcott is precisely historical endorsement, a truth verified by Johnson, and through him by Shakespeare. You may think this a paradox ; it may equally be understood as a loop of opening and closing historical perspectives, a history cycle to accompany cycles of water and emotion : as the knowledge that one's predicament is age-old may at one moment be comforting, yet at another seem a lessening of self.

The intertextual spark that connects with "water clerk" is not formally acknowledged in the same way as the epigraph, and the term is not a quotation as such, but so far as Walcott's intent is held to matter, I think it highly likely he was aware of his reference and the word constitutes an allusion. In first attempting to understand the presence of this "water clerk [/] who weighs the force of lightly falling rain" (pp. 258–9), I mentioned that *OED2* offered illustrative quotations from 1898 and 1973. These, from obscure sources, are cited as the earliest and latest uses known to the editors ; beyond harbour-life the term is not common—encountering it I had to hunt for the meaning—but in the *OED* offices are ten further recorded usages,[12] all from the same high-canonical text : Joseph Conrad's *Lord Jim* (1900).

Conrad's name is an interesting one to encounter investigating Walcott, for a score of specific issues, from miscegenation to the sight of a schooner under sail, run persistently through the works of both, and Conrad's novel of lost honour, analysing Jim's self-esteem, ambition, and decline, is immediately suggestive of links with the poem. Conrad (1857–1924) was 43 when *Lord Jim* was published, and offers perspectives on life and ambition from just beyond the rubicon Walcott's poem contemplates and fears. More specifically, the novel has three extended references to water-clerking in general or Jim's in particular, and each serves to focus textual links, bringing to the poem's end a degree of darkness that greatly deepens the complexity of its balance. The connection begins with the novel's opening paragraphs :

> He was an inch, perhaps two, under six feet, powerfully built, and he advanced straight at you with a slight stoop of the shoulders, head forward, and a fixed from-under stare which made you think of a charging bull. His voice was deep, loud, and his manner displayed a kind of dogged self-assertion which had nothing aggressive in it. It seemed a necessity, and it was directed apparently as much at himself as at anybody else. He was spotlessly neat, apparelled in immaculate white

[12] I am indebted to Dr Philip Durkin of the *OED* staff for searching them out.

from shoes to hat, and in the various Eastern ports where he got his living as ship-chandler's water-clerk he was very popular.

A water-clerk need not pass an examination in anything under the sun, but he must have Ability in the abstract and demonstrate it practically. His work consisted in racing under sail, steam, or oars against other water-clerks for any ship about to anchor, greeting her captain cheerily, forcing upon him a card—the business card of the ship-chandler—and on his first visit on shore piloting him firmly but without ostentation to a vast, cavern-like shop which is full of things that are eaten and drunk on board ship ; where you can get everything to make her sea-worthy and beautiful, from a set of chain-hooks for her cable to a book of gold-leaf for the carvings of her stern ; and where her commander is received like a brother by a ship-chandler he has never seen before. There is a cool parlour, easy chairs, bottles, cigars, writing implements, a copy of harbour regulations, and a warmth of welcome that melts the salt of a three months' passage out of a seaman's heart. The connexion thus begun is kept up, as long as the ship remains in harbour, by the daily visits of the water-clerk. To the captain he is faithful like a friend and attentive like a son, with the patience of Job, the unselfish devotion of a woman, and the jollity of a boon companion. Later on the bill is sent in. It is a beautiful and humane occupation. Therefore good water-clerks are scarce. When a water-clerk who possesses Ability in the abstract has also the advantage of having been brought up to the sea, he is worth to his employer a lot of money and some humouring. Jim had always good wages and as much humouring as would have bought the fidelity of a fiend. Nevertheless, with black ingratitude he would throw up the job suddenly and depart. To his employers the reasons he gave were obviously inadequate. They said 'Confounded fool!' as soon as his back was turned. This was their criticism of his exquisite sensibility.

To the white men in the waterside business and to the captains of ships he was just Jim—nothing more. He had, of course, another name, but he was anxious that it should not be pronounced. His incognito, which had as many holes as a sieve, was not meant to hide a personality but a fact. When the fact broke through the incognito he would leave suddenly the seaport where he happened to be at the time and go to another—generally farther east. He kept to seaports because he was a seaman in exile from the sea, and had Ability in the abstract, which is good for no other work but that of a water-clerk. He retreated in good order towards the rising sun, and the fact followed him casually but inevitably. Thus in the course of years he was known

> successively in Bombay, in Calcutta, in Rangoon, in Penang, in Batavia—and in each of these halting-places was just Jim the water-clerk. Afterwards, when his keen perception of the Intolerable drove him away for good from seaports and white men, even into the virgin forests, the Malays of the jungle village, where he had elected to conceal his deplorable faculty, added a word to the monosyllable of his incognito. They called him Tuan Jim : as one might say—Lord Jim.[13]

The *OED*'s citations, functionally informative, left the water clerk an impersonal figure ; the echo of Conrad suggests identification with a particular water clerk, Jim, and briefly gives Walcott's figure a gendered identity and history : a past he flees, a fate he lives, and a destiny he approaches. A principal consequence of such intertextuality is often to make readers conscious of the rhetorised, self-dramatising aspects of a work, and here self-dramatising affects the poem's presentation of "you" (and implicitly "I") as happily buckling down to clerkly work. The casting of Conrad's tale as a tragedy, his presentation of Jim's potential heroism and nobility, living a life coloured with exotic names and shadows, momentarily sneaks back into the poem a high romantic world and imagined destiny ("ambition as a searing meteor") that seemed to have been transcended. Yet Conrad was as aware of the problems of youthful ambition, ageing, and a "keen perception of the Intolerable" as Walcott shows himself to be ; each subsequent return in *Lord Jim* to the matter of water-clerking is more sombre and jagged. Both are narrated by Marlow, whose voice is at odds with the third-person of the opening ; the first is in chapter 13, by which time readers have learned the "fact" from which Jim flees, that as chief mate of the *Patna* he once behaved as a coward, abandoning ship with other officers while hands and passengers were still aboard :

> [Jim] was then working for De Jongh, on my recommendation. Water-clerk. 'My representative afloat', as De Jongh called him. You can't imagine a mode of life more barren of consolation, less capable of being invested with a spark of glamour—unless it be the business of an insurance canvasser. [. . .] I don't know how Jim's soul accommodated itself to the new conditions of his life—I was kept too busy in getting him something to do that would keep body and soul together—but I am pretty certain his adventurous fancy was suffering all the pangs of starvation. It had certainly nothing to feed upon in this new calling. It was distressing to see him at it, though he tackled it with a stubborn

[13] Joseph Conrad, *Lord Jim* (Harmondsworth: Penguin, 1949), ch. 1 (pp. 9–10).

> serenity for which I must give him full credit. I kept my eye on his shabby plodding with a sort of notion that it was a punishment for the heroics of his fancy—an expiation for his craving after more glamour than he could carry. He had loved too well to imagine himself a glorious racehorse, and now he was condemned to toil without honour like a costermonger's donkey. He did it very well. He shut himself in, put his head down, said never a word. Very well ; very well indeed—except for certain fantastic and violent outbreaks, on the deplorable occasions when the irrepressible *Patna* case cropped up. (ch. 13, pp. 116–17)

The complex lexical echoes uniting Conrad's text with Johnson's and Walcott's—fanciful, fancy, imagine, imagination, sudden wonder, violent outbreaks, searing meteor, steadier elation, stubborn serenity—underpin a common theme of learning to settle for the workaday without the consolation of what was perhaps always overreaching fantasy and is in any case lost. Johnson dismisses the fantasy, Conrad has Marlow suppose Jim grieves for it, and Walcott inherits both to complicate his own need for resolution. Conrad's sense of Jim's fallen position is, however, dynamic, and in the contrast between the first exposition of water-clerking (its skill) and this exposition (its menial diminishment) intertextuality truly begins to bite. Walcott's poem seeks, in banal terms, 'to look on the bright side', finding in the image of the working water clerk a source of consolation ; Conrad's novel tends to tragedy, and Marlow's recharacterisation of water-clerking as "barren of consolation" is a step on that road. As such it is an intertextual current counter to the movement of 'Nearing Forty' at the moment when they connect, an undertow beneath the crest of Walcott's ending.

The novel's final return to the subject of water-clerking throws intertextuality into relief. Marlow is recounting the reactions of one Egstrom, a chandler who had employed Jim, to Jim's abrupt and unexplained decision to quit his job in the middle of a working day:

> ' "When I understood what he was up to, my arms fell—so ! Can't get a man like that every day, you know, sir ; a regular devil for sailing a boat ; ready to go out miles to sea to meet ships in any sort of weather. More than once a captain would come in here full of it, and the first thing he would say would be, 'That's a reckless sort of lunatic you've got for water-clerk, Egstrom. I was feeling my way in at daylight under short canvas when there comes flying out of the mist right under my forefront a boat half under water, sprays going over the masthead, two frightened niggers on the bottom boards, a yelling fiend at the tiller, Hey ! hey ! Ship ahoy ! ahoy ! Captain ! Hey ! hey ! Egstrom and Blake's

> man first to speak to you ! Hey ! hey ! Egstrom and Blake ! Hallo ! hey ! whoop ! Kick the niggers—out reefs—a squall on at the time—shoots ahead whooping and yelling to me to make sail and he would give me a lead in—more like a demon than a man. Never saw a boat handled like that in all my life. Couldn't have been drunk—was he ? Such a quiet, soft-spoken chap, too—blush like a girl when he came on board. . . .' I tell you, Captain Marlow, nobody had a chance against us with a strange ship when Jim was out. The other ship-chandlers just keep their old customers, and . . ."
>
> 'Egstrom appeared overcome with emotion.
>
> ' "Why, sir—it seems as though he wouldn't mind going a hundred miles out to sea in an old shoe to nab a ship for the firm." '
>
> (ch. 18, pp. 148–9)

"conventional as <u>any</u> water clerk" . . . ? On this account, there was in Jim's water-clerking a degree of élan sufficient to proclaim desperation. Not just any water clerk, but a regular devil, a fiend of a water clerk, careless of all weathers ; hardly one "who weighs the force of lightly falling rain", however that phrase is read. With this the oddity of Walcott's words is partly explained : "water clerk" creates the intertextual invocation of Jim's decline from first mate towards an obscure death, but the preceding qualification of the clerk as "conventional" keeps apart a water clerk of Jim's recklessness and the one imagined in the poem. One distinct complication is the presence in Conrad's third passage of the reiterated "niggers"—which (however one may point out that it is in reported speech, it would in 1900 have been acceptable, and all the rest of it) is now redolent with offence. Egstrom's story (and more largely Marlow's and Conrad's) is structured around Jim's class-conscious self-estimation by professional and racial criteria, his need to demonstrate personal courage and social standing ; though Conrad may in *Lord Jim* as a whole criticise the imperial honour-codes by which Jim lives and is hounded, the historical fact and consequences of those codes for many colonial subjects (including Walcott) remain, intransigent and unpalatable. To follow this strand of the intertextuality, however, would lead beyond history at large and towards more personal territory, and I will return to it under 'Biography' (pp. 330–4).

I knew 'Nearing Forty' well (I thought) before being prompted by writing this book to go beyond the *OED's* definition of 'water clerk' and discover the connection with Conrad. More than any other detail it has unsettled my sense of the poem, and now seems to stand to the poem's end as Johnson does to its beginning, Conrad's text silently triangulating itself with Johnson's and Walcott's. The impossibility for Jim of settling to the diminished, quotidian world of water-clerking, and the instability 'truth' repeatedly creates in his life, opens to the reader's eyes the deep pit yawning beneath the final balance of 'Nearing Forty'.

Beyond the intertextual the most important histories in the poem are the literary histories of component forms and images. The iambic pentameter, sonorous, flexible, strong, and deeply traditional, affords the 'poet'—the speaker/writer who is but is not Walcott (p. 331)—the prosodic space to be lyrical while containing and marshalling emotion, and supports the quest for harmonious acceptance of the truth the epigraph proclaims. Closed heroic couplets were predominant in Johnson's day, corresponding as a form with the moral self-certainty expressed in his oracular prose, and Walcott's central sequence of couplets alludes to the history behind the epigraph ; moral self-certainty was also a part of the age's imperialism and a reason so many eighteenth-century British merchants could in all conscience be slave-traders. Walcott's position as a post-independence West Indian and descendant of slaves gives him a very different perspective from that of imperial slavemasters, and he qualifies his allusion to the poetry of their age—his couplets are open, their rhymes skewed, and the poem must break out of them to find rest. Troubled and disturbed by its Johnsonian and Conradian intertextualities, the poem turns at the very last to the picture of the new moon controlling lines of falling rain, and implicitly summoning renewed poetry. Thus Walcott invokes a symbol of the poetic muse in self-benediction ; both symbol and benediction are utterly traditional, but historically the moon was invoked poetically far more in the Renaissance (before Johnson) and Romantic poetry (after Johnson) than in Augustan poetry. It marks a moment when Walcott passes beyond Johnson and Conrad, or returns them to the old histories to which they belong ; the lunatic hope his new moon expresses for the future is a final answer to the dead certainties of the Johnsonian epigraph and 'reckless lunacy' of Lord Jim.

Exercises

Considering the greater scope of history, the value of craft-exercises is moot. That said, it is unquestionably worth taking a short poem with historical content that interests you and doing one full round of proper contextual research. Go beyond handy annotation and dig out from a good library as many professional historians' accounts of the relevant events as you can find ; quarry their notes, and track down any recorded eyewitnesses ; for later periods add journalism where relevant : and consider as fully as possible the poetic witness with which you began against these other voices. A poetic angle of incidence is rarely that of respondents or commentators in other modes of language, and only some detailed experience of comparing poetic and non-poetic apprehensions of an historical event will enable the development of your historical sense of any given poem.

It might also be said here that however dull rote-learning, it is a basic necessity to have firmly in one's head some measure by which historical sequence can be established. The modularisation of much secondary and tertiary education, and the revulsion since the 1960s at obligatory memorisation, have left many British students knowing something of, say, the Civil War, the Industrial Revolution, and Luddism, but little certainty as to which came first. The same problem is evident in American and Commonwealth students. Old-fashioned as it is, for the poetic canon a British regnal list from Richard II (1377–99) to Elizabeth II (1952–) takes very little time to learn, and ever after provides (much as a yardstick in archaeological photographs) a measure by which other data can be properly scaled and related. It is also worth habitually attaching a date to every work, and dates to every author, that you read ; even very competent students are often unable to identify the years of birth and death of canonical luminaries with whose works they are reasonably familiar—and so, however smart and hardworking, are unable in written exams to display any creditable degree of historical accuracy, and may pay a heavy price. The mistake is easy to avoid, but requires distributed attention throughout one's study and cannot readily be crammed ; regular quizzing of and by fellow-students (Chaucer's dates ? T. S. Eliot's ? During which years could Milton, Browne, Marvell, and Dryden have met ?) is a painless way of setting about the task, especially if it has hitherto been neglected and a beginning must be made.

Chapter Glossary

allusion : most generally, "a covert, passing, or indirect reference" (*Sh. OED*) ; in literature, usually an intentional but undeclared reference within a text to another text (the quotidian stuff of intertextuality) or to a historical event, person, belief etc.

Antiquarian : a proposed 'school' of eighteenth-century English literature, encompassing such phenomena as Augustan Chaucerianism, the Ossian and Rowley forgeries, and early Romantic medievalism.

Augustan : of literature, that of the later-seventeenth and first half of the eighteenth centuries. The boundaries are ragged, but in schemata 'Augustan' follows 'Restoration' and is followed (after a gap) by 'Romantic'. In self-congratulatory use before 1700, the term derives from the 'Golden Age' of Roman literature during the reign of Augustus (27 BCE–14 CE) and is intrinsically imperialistic ; the most obvious formal feature of Augustan poetry is the prevalence of closed heroic couplets.

bardolatry : the worship of Shakespeare.

Beats : an abbreviation for 'the Beat Generation' designating an influential group of mainly West-Coast American writers, including Ginsberg, Kerouac, Burroughs, and Corso, who matured in the 1950s and were gurus to the 1960s. The San Francisco poets (including Snyder and Ferlinghetti) may also be meant.

Bloomsbury : a tag for the loosely affiliated writers and intellectuals living in that area of London around 1914–18, most notably the Woolfs, Strachey, Keynes, and Forster.

Commonwealth : of literature, (i) that produced during the interregnum of 1649–60, or (ii) with reference to post-1945, the literatures of the nations of the British Commonwealth.

Edwardian : in literature, usually of the reign of Edward VII (1901–10), and typically with the double-implication of a post-Victorian relaxation and a last, pre-war ignorance and carelessness of impending catastrophe.

Georgian : of literature (as very much distinct from architecture), usually with reference to a group of writers, mostly poets, published by Edward Marsh in successive volumes called *The Georgian Anthology* issued between 1912 and 1921 ; implicitly indicating a pastoralism and nostalgia made irrelevant by the First World War and Modernism.

Hanoverian : of literature, written under a Hanoverian monarch (Georges I, 1714–27 ; II, 1727–60 ; III, 1760–1820 ; and IV, 1820–30 ; William IV, 1830–7 ; Victoria, 1837–1901).

Historikerstreit : (German, 'the battle of historians') ; a sharp debate beginning in 1986–7 initially about whether it was acceptable to argue that the story of the Wehrmacht's defence of Germany's Eastern Front in 1944–5 deserved to be told as a tragedy. The principal figures involved were Ernst Nolte, Andreas Hillgruber, and Jürgen Habermas.

intertextuality : generally, the relations between texts ; more specifically, the aspects of a given text which derive meaning from relations with an/other text/s.

Metaphysical : of poetry, that of the later-sixteenth and first half of the seventeenth centuries ; characterised (and in Dr Johnson's hostile use, weakened) by complex stanza forms and arguments, and by elaborate comparisons (or conceits).

Movement : a term derived from a 1954 *Spectator* article for a (supposed) movement in some British literature, especially poetry, towards level-headed and often formalist sceptical empiricism ; those dubbed poets of the Movement include Davie, Enright, Gunn, Jennings, and Larkin.

New York School : used since the 1960s to designate a group of poets closely linked to the New York School of painting who emerged together in the 1950s ; the core-members of the group are O'Hara, Ashbery, Koch, and Schuyler.

Restoration : of literature, of the period following the Restoration of Charles II in 1660 ; the later boundary is ragged, varying between *c.*1690 (when poetry may be thought already Augustan) and 1737 (when the Licensing Act imposes a discontinuity on dramatic practice).

Romantic : of literature, that of the later-eighteenth and first half of the nineteenth centuries ; the Romantic movement was in part a reaction against the Enlightenment, and its poetry is characteristically vigorous, formally innovative, and concerned amid rich diction and imagery with nature, aesthetics, and subjective emotion. Romanticism has troubling relations with nationalism and Napoleon, and the parallels with Modernism one full century later are striking.

Stuart : of literature, written under a Stuart monarch (James VI and I, 1603–25 ; Charles I, 1625–49 ; Charles II, 1660–85 ; James VII and II, 1685–88 ; William III and Mary II, 1688–1702 ; Anne, 1702–14).

Tudor : of literature, written under a Tudor monarch (Henry VII, 1485–1509 ; Henry VIII, 1509–47 ; Edward VI, 1547–53 ; Mary I, 1553–58 ; Elizabeth I, 1558–1603).

'value-free' : history: history supposedly written objectively, without ideological selection or emphasis of material ; presently regarded as a chimera.

Victorian : of literature, written during the reign of Victoria (1837–1901) ; used in schemata of literary history to fill the gap between the Romantics and Modernists.

10
Biography

I saw history through the sea-washed eyes
of our choleric, ginger-haired headmaster
DEREK WALCOTT, *Another Life* 11.III.1–2

Critics and theorists dismissive of history at large think equally little of authorial biography. Vital irrelevance is often proclaimed, seminally by Wimsatt and Beardsley :

> The poem is not the critic's own and not the author's (it is detached from the author at birth and goes about the world beyond his [*sic*] power to intend about it or control it). The poem belongs to the public. It is embodied in language, the peculiar possession of the public, and it is about the human being, an object of public knowledge. What is said about the poem is subject to the same scrutiny as any statement in linguistics or in the general science of psychology.[1]

These claims are as much for critical objectivity as against authorial subjectivity ; the extreme version is that readers should ignore identity, experience, and intention of authors, a view most associated with Barthes (who in 1968 wrote 'The death of the author'). At the same time a different question was posed by Foucault : 'What is an author?' (1969) examined the cultural and commercial functions of ascribing texts, and asked how they affect readers.[2]

A sound basic point is being made : Wimsatt, Beardsley, Barthes, and Foucault were reacting against ingrained habits of *expressionist* criticism (not the same thing as in art history or drama), which regards a poem as expressing the intention of its author and as determined and limited by that intention. At worst such biographically driven criticism

[1] 'The Intentional Fallacy' (1946) in e.g. Lodge, ed., *20th Century Literary Criticism.*
[2] Barthes and Foucault in e.g. Lodge, ed., *Modern Criticism* and Walder, ed., *Literature in the Modern World*. Barthes was echoing Nietzsche's "Gott ist tot".

speculatively and without scruple relates minute details of texts to spurious reconstructions of lives : a good example is the endless pursuit of who the 'lovely boy' and 'dark lady' of Shakespeare's sonnets 'really' were, as if knowing that (supposing we could) would 'solve' the literary problems posed by the dense complexity of Shakespeare's sequence. Perhaps the saddest critical work I know is A. L. Rowse's *Shakespeare's Sonnets: The Problems Solved*[3] : a good historian and in many ways an admirable man, Rowse was at sea with literary criticism, and impatiently believed his prose versions and brisk historical identifications fulfilled his risible subtitle. But even watered-down expressionism will not do, for an underlying principle is fundamentally in error : whatever one's beliefs about Rushdie and *The Satanic Verses*, events have shown clearly that what an author intends readers to understand, and what readers do understand, are not necessarily the same ; and it is not good enough, when they diverge, for the author to say 'But what I meant was . . .'. What is true of intention in this extreme case is true in all, and no work can have its meaning fixed or in any way limited by intention.

However, to the *intentional fallacy* must be added the *intentional-fallacy fallacy* (as A. D. Nuttall happily dubbed it). Properly stated, the intentional fallacy is the erroneous belief that the meaning of artwork is limited by the intention of its creator/s ; which neither says nor implies such intention is irrelevant. The intentional-fallacy fallacy is the erroneous belief that the intentional fallacy is to believe intention relevant, and concomitant belief that it shouldn't be considered—as if one could write a sonnet or novel without intending to do so and shaping it accordingly. Being mildly unkind, I suspect many critics with bold theoretical views would not want to meet the authors about whom they pronounce, but run a mile to save themselves the embarrassment of telling Shakespeare, Tennyson, or (God help them) Milton that their intent and intensive efforts of creation are irrelevant to the works that resulted.

There is thus a good and necessary question as to how one identifies an author's intentions. Titles, epigraphs, or annotations may state or imply intent ; other writings may illuminate it. If an author is alive one might ask, but without going so far as to think they might lie, it would be naïve to take answers at face value : many reasons, including sheer complexity of 'intention', make its full statement impossible. If the author is (long) dead, intention becomes even more difficult to

[3] 1964; 2nd edn, London: Macmillan, 1973.

discover and interpret, even if a diary or letters are available. Absolute knowledge of intent cannot be obtained ; such knowledge as can be had obligates caution.

It is also plainly true that art is not autobiography. However much some works may be given special validity by autobiographical status, a sense that they must have special truth-value because an author is 'writing from experience' or 'dealing in facts' that 'really happened', *Othello* in its greatness does not make us believe Shakespeare was black, nor that he killed his wife, nor even that he must to write it so well have wanted to kill his wife. The play is a fiction, imaginatively as well as professionally wrought, and were it anything else our interest in it would be quite different. In drama generally, an author presents an argument or view in distinct voices ; one role may to a greater extent than others be a mouthpiece, but role and author are never simple equivalents. Novels have dialogue as well as narration, and again the views of characters and narrators (especially unreliable ones) cannot be easily attributed to authors. So too in poetry, and a poem need not be a dramatic monologue (supposedly spoken by a distinct individual) for there to be an appreciable gap between a poet (as history and biography might reveal them) and the *persona* who appears to write (or speak) a particular poem. Critics make this distinction variously : some refer to the persona, others distinguish the *poet* (William Wordsworth, 1770–1850) from the *'poet'*, a rhetorical persona inferred from a given poem (the 'individual' designated by 'I' in *The Prelude*). Wordsworth wandered a great deal, sometimes alone, but the 'I' who "wandered lonely as a cloud" is not only (or even chiefly) the Wordsworth who on given days had the experience and first thought and wrote the line. Dickinson made the point in a letter to Thomas Higginson : "When I state myself, as the Representative of the Verse—it does not mean—me—but a supposed person"[4] ; how exactly you signal that "supposed person" doesn't much matter, but that you do signal it, and remember it in reading, is vital.

The genuine complexity of the issues is doubled into relief in drama, where in much criticism (and more teaching) performative roles such as 'Lady Macbeth' (a series of speeches, many in verse, given by highly variant performers in productions over 400 years) are reified as novelistic characters whose minds and personal attributes can be discretely considered ('what is the character of Lady Macbeth ?'). These

[4] Johnson and Ward, eds, *The Letters of Emily Dickinson* (3 vols, Cambridge, MA: Harvard UP, 1958), 268.

suppositious biographical entities are then related to an equally supposed biography of the offending playwright (Shakespeare being Scottish and misogynistic to appeal to James VI and I). Throughout the nineteenth century a view that Shakespeare was unhappy when his father died and so wrote *Hamlet* was perfectly respectable ; even twentieth-century Greg, allegedly dry-as-dust factual and a bibliographical scholar rather than critic, once saw fit to write at length about where Theocritus was sitting and what passed by his window while writing his first 'Idyll'. It is now a very funny passage, and was always the purest tosh—yet a work that sounds the apogee of projected authorial fantasy, Cowden Clarke's tales collected as *The Girlhood of Shakespeare's Heroines*,[5] turns out to be as interesting in practice as it is misguided in dramatic theory. It is more revealing of Clarke's assumptions about the shape of lives and nature of psychology than of Shakespeare's, but energy and intelligence were brought to the task, as well as thoroughgoing knowledge of the Shakespearian canon (she had edited a *Concordance*) and a lively sense of history versed in current scholarship. In calling her stories 'tales' Clarke explicitly presents them as fiction, but they resonate with the post-Stanislavskian systems or methods of acting that expect those 'realising' roles to equip themselves with densely imagined biographies of 'characters' as they have 'become' through the lifetime that in naturalistic reading (but by no means all reading, and certainly not all acting) implicitly precedes every entrance. Any which way, no Shakespearian can afford to ignore the force of imagination that made Clarke, like Dr Johnson (p. 304) and many more recent commentators on page and stage, want to fill in and act out the biographical blanks—nor anyone interested in drama since Ibsen.

Poetry is (usually) less ontologically and epistemologically complex than drama (though it has a far stronger relationship with performance than most prose), but is not fundamentally different in the necessary processes of triangulation. Authors write at particular moments with individual intent, from whom and from which (compoundedly) their poems are in their nature but to varying degrees offset ; readers read at similar moments and for various reasons texts embedded in books' materiality and history : in one or another fashion, a voice is heard. Just as all poems are written at a particular historical moment, so they are written by particular persons, whose nationality, age, education, experiences etc. will partly determine what (kinds of) poems they can and do write. And just as with a quotidian contemporary document

[5] London: Bickers and Son, 1879.

one necessary part of any professional reading is knowing who wrote it, and allowing for any formal constraints and authorial spin, so biographical knowledge of a poet (more or less resonant with one's own experiences and life) is a very useful approach to the nexus of a poem. From the evident attractions for readers, when available, of audiotapes, photographs, and film, or best of all live performance, as from the peculiar void felt in encountering a work by 'Anon.', it is clear that biographical data stimulates reading ; if it is terrain strewn with pitfalls, so much the better for our alertness. For all the difficulties and potential abuse of biographical criticism, equally severe problems beset the arguments of those who wish to ignore biography, not least why the manifest difficulties with authorial intention should ever be thought to justify the wholesale ditching of biographical enquiry.

The most powerful current argument to that effect, identified with post-Modernism and drawing on Derrida, is that 'intention' (and pretty much all forms of individual agency) is illusory, and any personal apprehension or communal belief to the contrary a delusion. There are structures (including human animals and language) and forces (psychological, historical, socio-cultural, economic, genetic, divine) that in passing animate structures (a human animal says something) ; the animal may believe it has 'voluntarily' done something by intent, but this is a misunderstanding by an incidental plaything of inhuman forces. Some version of this neo-determinist philosophy informs Muldoon's contention that "I have made scarcely any changes in the texts of the poems, since I'm fairly certain that, after a shortish time, the person through whom a poem was written is no more entitled to make revisions than any other reader" (p. 243) ; others underlie the deliberate incomprehensibility (lack of clear intent) of L=A=N=G=U=A=G=E poetry and some post-Beckettian work, practitioners of which may deny their own intent in creating it, or admit only to unavoidable shards and traces of a 'weak intent' remaining despite their best efforts (pp. 275–6). Whatever its philosophical merit there are practical issues : some poets do forgo copyright (and so royalties), but few decline praise for published work, and most claims of 'weak intent' are closer to moral evasion of others' reality than substantive abnegation of one's own. In any case, theories of personal inefficacy and irrelevance clearly relate to post-1945 tastes for ahistoricity and a slate cleaned by the deaths of God, all grand narratives, hopes of liberal progress, and the author ; as those tastes continue to wane, biographical agency will reclaim a central place in highbrow criticism.

Note should be made of performance poetry, particularly American 'slam' contests and their supporting culture. Within that culture and its net-extensions is both a theory and practice of shareware and freeware exchange applied to forms of intellectual property, and an awareness of what a poem 'going about the world' beyond anyone's power 'to intend about it or control it' might mean to make Wimsatt sit up in his grave. Like blogged poetry, this needs the general context of what is happening to identity on the Web ; another story. For the broad reaches of mainstream canonical poetry, the counter-case is best made with examples.

Consider first Coleridge's 'Rime of the Ancient Mariner' (N812). Given the supernatural story no one would suppose the poem autobiographical, and knowing that in *Lyrical Ballads* (1798) a part of Coleridge's intention was to revive balladic poetry, if interesting, is secondary. Shockingly primary is knowing that when he wrote it Coleridge had never been to sea, and though he'd lived in harbour-towns does not seem ever to have been aboard ship : his powerful evocation of sea-life was wholly generated from reading sea-stories. When I discovered this (from Lowes's *The Road to Xanadu*[6]) I could barely credit it, and reread the poem with astonished admiration for the fertile coherence of Coleridge's imagination : I also realised that if Coleridge had had first-hand experience of a long voyage he would have written a very different poem. To know he was imagining everything in the poem, rather than remembering and adding imagination, shows how the poem is shaped, and how Coleridge could eliminate any discontinuity between the (apparently) unusual (killing an albatross[7]) and the supernatural (consequences of that killing). The poem's illustrators (p. 94), especially Peake, are also interesting to consider in light of their own biographies, and the insights it gave or denied them into a visual fabric commensurate with Coleridge's textual one.

The importance of biography, like that of history, can range from the immediate and self-evident to the broad and general influence of background, as Clare's rural life stands behind his rural poems (N893). But even if a poem is explicitly written in response to a particular experience, as Tennyson's 'In Memoriam A.H.H.' (N996) repeatedly declares itself the product of grief for Arthur Hallam, the nature of the response is not always straightforward. Tennyson's great sequence was written over some seventeen years ; poems vary in length but all use arch-

[6] Subtitled *A Study in the Ways of the Imagination* (1927; London: Picador, 1978).

[7] A common practice among sailors in albatross latitudes (more probably with a baited hook than a cross-bow) long after Coleridge had made it superstitiously reviled by passengers. Long-line fishing now kills them by the hundred.

rhymed quatrains in iambic tetrameter, and continuity of form is part of the poem's concern with unremitting grief. Look through the selection in the *Norton* and its importance is apparent : arch-rhyme *(abba)* makes each stanza self-contained, ending in closure that looks backward ; in many lines symmetry of rhyme is reflected in a central cæsura splitting the line 2–2. Both are prosodic expressions of the rocking movement of grief, back and forth ; continuity of form expresses persistence of grief : or should it be vice versa ? Tennyson's grief was remarkably prolonged, and he wrote the earliest 'In Memoriam' poems within days of hearing Hallam was dead ; his form, with its grieving rock of lines and rhyme, is from the first fully achieved : so did Tennyson instinctively divine a form he would need for the extended grief he was entering, or did the form seized in his first grief entrap him ? Prosody and form give 'In Memoriam' a curtness that contains grief, preventing dissipation ; had Tennyson written instead, say, a heroic elegy, trumpeting his painful loss, grief might have been cathartically purged so much the sooner. Tennyson's form and psychic history are entwined ; if one was cause and one effect it isn't in the least obvious which is which.

More cheerily, if still often dead, the cast of Merrill's *The Changing Light at Sandover* (p. 64) can hardly be understood without his biography. Auden (1907–73) is not posthumously composing at Merrill's ouija board simply as a great poet who died during the poem's composition, nor Maya Deren (1917–61) simply as a film-maker famously interested in divine possession : both were friends of Merrill's, a sociable man whose inherited wealth (as a scion of Merrill Lynch) made him something of a patron as well as a poet. Readers must negotiate with themselves how fictive, deluded, or revelatory Merrill's supernatural and sometimes flat-out divine narrative is, and what status capitalised parts of it that are (supposedly) poeticised transcripts of ouija-board dialogue with shades and angels should enjoy ; the whole is in the largest sense a response to Dante and all a 'divine comedy' might now be, but a major part of its mechanics is a constantly intelligent and amusing discourse about (auto)biography as art and craft. The primary drive is the need for new arrivals (living or dead) to account for themselves ; the flywheel is Merrill's tolerant, sometimes gossipy, sometimes wasp-tongued interest in the days of his own and others' lives. Here, Marius (Bewley) is an accomplishedly dead friend of the recently dead Mary (Jackson, 1890–1975), whose son David (D) was Merrill's permanent partner in life and at the ouija board ; Maria (Mitsotáki, 1907–74) is a friend of Merrill's who had died the previous year :

Marius: EACH TO HIS OWN MARY & I
ARE OFF TO SEE HER VIRGIN NAMESAKE WHY
DO PEOPLE BOTHER ALWAYS SUCH A CRUSH
She holds court? TRAFFIC COURT Mary: BYE BYE
And starts to leave, but D has broken down.
NO TEARS O DARLING STOP HIS TEARS DON'T CRY
Mama, your last words—YES YES & YOUR FIRST ONES
Was it awful? Did it hurt to die?
I LOOKED DOWN AT YOUR POOR OLD WRINKLED FACE
THOUGHT OF MY BABY LEARNING HOW TO TALK
MARIA LOANED ME HER VOICE MINE TOO WEAK
She goes.—Maria, is that *done*? ENFANTS
ALL THINGS ARE DONE HERE IF U HAVE TECHNIQUE

(*Mirabell : Book 0.5*)

The truths and jokes of overlapping births and deaths, the passions in posthumous chat, trade as much on biography as in fiction ; ironic distance, after all, means something to be distanced from. Nor is the wisdom dependent on literal truth, or belief in communication with revenants, for it lies in the memorable snapshot of maternal and filial love before exhibiting practical understanding of real value. One minatory and unpleasant line of sub-Freudian criticism implies pathological links between Merrill's wealth, poetic prolixity, and homosexuality—a character-assassination by inference that is a striking abuse of biographical method ; it is true, though, that he did not have to sing for his supper, nor yet his Greek villa, and that is as much an enabling fact for his great poem as Clare's impoverished rural labour was for his astonishing poetic work. The sheer scale of *The Changing Light at Sandover*, the living time its massy composition (and the '1001 nights at the ouija board' it reports) necessarily represent, bespeaks subsidy—but so does work on any scale in any medium, and the strings attached are usually more numerous and irksome if the source is public.

Somewhere short of Tennyson's and Merrill's extremes is Harrison, who pro/claims a powerful identity, regional and personal. His establishment on the English stage is deeply tied up with use of a specifically Northern English accent and lexicon, and in poetry with the broadcast of *V.* in 1984 : a film-presentation of the poem with Harrison in the Beeston graveyard it haunts, where his parents lie under a vandalised tombstone that was his *donnée*. His other best-known poems are almost all Meredithean sonnets from *The School of Eloquence*, and close readings, whatever the theoretical stance of the critic, assume primary (not exclusive) relations with Harrison's working-class childhood and transformative education. No moment is necessarily 'true' in a simple sense (it happened just this way), but moral and political coherence in Harrison's work depends on general 'truthfulness', verisimilar representation of 'how it was' and seemed ; to discover he really grew up in Southern bourgeois wealth would liquefy everything. Hence, in part, the fate his work suffers in its popularity, taught as straight autobiography ; as if *V.* were not also a formal response to Gray's 'Elegy' (p. 208), traditions of *doppelgänger* fiction,[8] and Browning's development of a mute interlocutor in dramatic monologues (p. 57). These intellectual influences and filters are themselves framed within the dynamic of Harrison's poetry, matters he finds germane and helpful, that his parents and childhood peers have probably never heard of, made available to him precisely by the alienating education that is his most recurrent theme.

Other examples abound, as varied in nature and importance as the lives and works of poets. The course of Donne's poetry from secular to sacred has a powerful analogue in his career, culminating in appointment as Dean of St Paul's (though caution is necessary, p. 324) ; Milton's 'When I Consider How My Light Is Spent' (N418) must puzzle those unwilling to remember his blindness, a handicap that like his political career as a Republican plays interestingly against *Paradise Lost* ; Smart's *Jubilate Agno* (N678) is movingly illuminated by knowledge of his confinement to an asylum ; Hopkins's 'No Worst, There Is None' (N1169), like Roethke's 'In a Dark Time' (N1501), is deepened by knowledge of the battles with mania and despair its maker faced. The Eliot of *Ash-Wednesday* and *Four Quartets* can no more be intelligently understood without reference to his Christian conversion than the Dylan of *Saved* and *Shot of Love* ; it matters that Wordsworth was a walker, racking up more miles in a week than most of us now manage in a lifetime ; that any parent before 1900 could expect to bury some children, as a score of great poets did ; even, simply, that Pope was self-consciously short, Byron lame, and Spender as uncomfortably tall as he was thin.

The exemplary poems continue the argument and post cautions ; the bottom line is that a biographical approach remains a standard professional operating procedure, besides being a resource few readers will forgo. If a poem matters, so too does the life that created it.

---

[8] Involving a 'secret sharer', a left-hand dream-dwelling double (cf. *Jekyll and Hyde*).

Biography

Exemplary Poems

1. 'The Flea' (pp. 14–15)

Donne (1572–1631) is, in biographical as other matters, a study in temptation. Many facts about his life are known,[9] but few (despite surviving work and letters, often problematic as evidence) that are poetically or sexually intimate. There was a *Life* as early as 1640, thanks to Henry Wotton (1568–1639) and Izaak Walton (1593–1683), both personal friends, and ever since the facts have fallen (or been cast) into two groups : a lesser one concerning youth and intemperate marriage (unsanctioned and a severe blow to his career), and a greater one concerning fifteen or so years as an active preacher in London and at court, during most of which he was Dean of St Paul's. This fits the poles of his verse, erotic and sacred ; the temptation is to impose a simple and oh-so-convenient poetic chronology of sexual youth and pious age, when few of Donne's poems and almost no lyrics can be dated more precisely than a forty-year span, and the relative chronologies (this poem later than that) are largely speculation.

It is easy, that is, to assume 'The Flea' is a poem of Donne's youth in the 1590s, but it and his 'Hymn to God the Father' (N321), typically supposed much later, might for all we know have been written on consecutive days in any year between 1597, when he met his future wife, Anne More, on whose name his hymn puns, and 1631, when he died. Of course it 'makes sense' to assume an archetypal career from wildness to piety, but it does not follow that wild poems predate pious ones ; Donne's whole potency is admixtures of the sacred and erotic, and extended parallelism of composition with a running overlap is as likely as a simple phase one, phase two schema. That possibility implies repeated conjunctions and juxtapositions of the figures addressed in erotic intimacy with both Donne's uxoriousness and his self-racking devotion to God : desire and devotion hand-in-hand, whether strolling or grappling.

A host of questions then arise that the assumption of a simple 'wild oats–marriage–piety' chronology forestalls ; in particular, whether the erotic poems might all have been for Donne primarily marital, reflecting sexual and spiritual fixation with his wife. Raised in Roman Catholicism, whose priests must be celibate, he ended as a widowed Anglican priest ; granting only that his sexual experience

[9] By far the best recent summary is David Colclough's article in the new *Oxford Dictionary of National Biography* (Oxford: OUP, 2004;).

with Anne More was to him a felicity tantamount to earthly grace—more bluntly, that he knew his greatest spiritual happiness in sexual union with his wife—it makes sense to think of the problems that experience might occasion a man of Donne's spiritual intensity and theological bent. The 'Hymn to God the Father' (N321) in particular asks to be read as describing such problems, worrying that closeness to his wife must part him from God ("When thou haſt done, thou haſt not done, [/] For, I have more."), and his other famously rueful pun in a letter to his wife ('John Donne. Anne Donne. Un-done') need not refer only to the earthly career revelation of their clandestine marriage cost him. A poem like "Batter my heart" (p. 250) is also helped by the thought that what Donne wanted God to do was to ravish him as he had been ravished by his wife, with a force taking him through seeming ruination to utmost felicity. Most generally, Christopher Ricks once began an essay with the memorable assertion that "Donne's poems, whether or not they are personal memories, record a dislike of having come",[10] and his case is deepened by the idea that what soured Donne's post-coital sadness was not simple religious revulsion at having again surrendered to fallen desire, but conflict between a sense of coital grace and returning post-coital awareness of theological contradictions. For a contemporary poet of Puritan leanings, such as Spenser, affirming the compatibility of licit sexual desire with a sacred calling (priests can marry) and not himself ordained, such an explanation could carry little force ; for Donne, given his particular biography and *œuvre*, it can, and does.

In 'The Flea', troubling religious dimensions are illuminated by considering the Christian conception of Christ's marriage to his church, and supposing Donne took literally the sexual implications of what most suppose metaphysical metaphor. Such an approach could produce a reading in which God speaks seductively to humanity, figuring the flea as a type of Christ (p. 251) ; is rejected with supposedly judicious murder (nailing the flea) ; and responds with promissory judgement—which need neither displace nor override readings as a *carpe diem* exercise or witty tale of a chat-up gone wrong, for its whole thrust is that Donne's secular and sacred impulses cannot be neatly separated, nor his poems profitably polarised.

---

[10] 'John Donne: 'Farewell to Love', in *Essays in Appreciation*, 19.

2. 'Anthem for Doomed Youth' (p. 18)

Wordsworth famously wrote that "Poetry is the spontaneous overflow of powerful feelings : it takes its origin from emotion recollected in tranquillity".[11] Owen's 'Anthem', however powerfully associated with and evoking the Western Front, was written at Craiglockhart War Hospital, Edinburgh, in September–October 1917, and powerfully exemplifies the kind of composition Wordsworth reported. It was also written with encouragement from Sassoon, a fellow-patient as well as fellow-poet whose confidence and support helped Owen, and is a poem of convalescence from wounds received in May. In November he was discharged, but spent a year recuperating before returning to active service in France in September 1918.[12]

The progress of the 'Anthem' is recorded in surviving drafts, and rapid completion of the grieving sestet with its traditional consolations, dictating the form, followed by struggle with the needed explanatory and emotive octave (p. 214), turns out to make excellent biographical sense : the sestet-material was Owen's present, the octave-material a hated and fearful recollection. Had he written it in the trenches, as he did some poems, with horror all about and the English shires impossibly far away, it would be quite other than it is.

Owen's friendship with Sassoon at Craiglockhart has been (as one might expect) extensively studied and fictionally reconstructed, notably by Barker in *Regeneration* (1991, filmed 1997), but remains a nexus of ambiguities. Far surer is a datum provided in the *Norton*'s only annotation (courtesy, I imagine, of editor Jon Stallworthy, Owen's biographer and editor), that Owen "was probably responding" to an "anonymous prefatory note" in *Poems of Today* (1916), which he owned, that talked of "the bugle-call of Endeavour, and the passing-bells of Death" (N1386 n.1) by way of endorsing the ignorant sentiment that *dulce et decorum est pro patria mori*, as Brooke (1887–1915) had just done. A degree of animus towards patriotism ignorant of what was happening in France was understandably common among trench-veterans, and certainly played its part in the complexities of Owen's thought (as angry and traumatised as Sassoon's but less mutinous) : but that is evident in the general history. What isn't is the immediate context of the words Owen took from the *Poems of Today* note—an

[11] Preface to *Lyrical Ballads* (1802), in Gill, ed., *William Wordsworth* (Oxford: OUP, 1984), 611.

[12] The standard biography is Jon Stallworthy, *Wilfred Owen* (London: OUP/Chatto, 1974), supplemented by Dominic Hibberd, *Owen the Poet* (Athens: U. Georgia P., 1975) and *Wilfred Owen: A New Biography* (London: Weidenfeld, 2002).

explanation that the anthology is not thematically divided : "There is no arbitrary isolation of one theme from another ; they mingle and interpenetrate throughout, to the music of Pan's flute, and of Love's viol, and the bugle-call of Endeavour, and the passing-bells of Death."

Owen's recasting of the bugle-calls as sad substitutes for the passing-bells is a shrewd blow at the sentiment in this rhetoric : even so, that sentiment accompanies the borrowed words. It is not rejected wholesale, any more than the poem rejects service and sacrifice while deploring their devaluation and impossibility in the hell of the trenches, or than Owen himself rejected them when he returned to France, and to his death. It therefore seems likely that Owen's recollection of the passage in the note, if partly in reproof, brought with it an endorsement of mingled and interpenetrating organisation—a very helpful frame within which to consider the major problem the poem presents, its contradictory relations of content and form as an agonised, regular, protesting Georgian sonnet (pp. 19, 300). It would make sense of this overdetermined poetic identity if there were in and behind it a sense of experiment, of attempting forced mutual engagement of divided content with inapposite form and antagonistic themes, and the exact biographical connection between the poem and a passage suggesting the values of such a clash is a solid gain in understanding.

Owen called his poem an 'Anthem', and its emblematic place as a premier anti-war poem has made it as much like a protest or rock anthem (all together now . . .) as a "song of praise and gladness" or one "adopted by a nation to express patriotism or loyalty" (*Sh. OED*). To restore it to a life filled with cross- and counter-currents—patriotism, duty, readiness of sacrifice, camaraderie and loyalty as well as fear, loathing, angry protest, horror, and numbness—is to understand more clearly the contradictory structuring of the poem, but also makes the title a problem : for how can a sonnet be an anthem ? and are—is ?—the "Doomed Youth" for whom Owen wrote it really the many who have <u>already</u> 'gone to their doom' ? or the more singular youth who saw them do it and already knew he would do so again, quite probably joining them ? Biography here has a frontier with prophecy as well as with history, a personal apprehension (in every sense) predicated on acceptance of future suffering as well as protest ; Owen, after all, was <u>not</u> wholly of Sassoon's mind, and remained closer to Georgian values than he. One might even argue that the real greatness of the 'Anthem', an underlying reason for its popularity, is precisely that much as it mourns the manner of mass-death in the trenches, and its consequences at home, it does <u>not</u>, ever, denounce the war itself as wrong, nor imply (as Sassoon often does) that it is no more than bloody farce rendering all ideas of honour and sacrifice gross delusions. The Georgian connections of its form and some diction, the echoes of Brooke (p. 255), do indeed bespeak a connection to a people who and a time that endorsed the war, Owen (in some measure) among them.

Given the weight of history on 'poetry of the First World War', biographical particularity about individual poets is a necessary counterweight, and in many cases—Sassoon, Owen, Graves, Rosenberg, Thomas, and Gurney—rapidly poses very interesting questions. Without it no real justice can be done to a poem wrought not by the 'crucible of history', but by an individual in that crucible ; with it, in this case, even a generalisation as illuminating as Wordsworth's about emotion and tranquillity is still more illuminatingly challenged.

3. 'Sestina' (pp. 69–70)

Bishop was famous within her lifetime (1911–79) as a poet (and of particular importance to some feminists), so her biographies are well documented.[13] Understanding the correlations with her poetry is another matter, but it is clear the situation in 'Sestina'—a child and grandmother emblematically together in a house, with no sign of the parents—mirrors Bishop's own. Her father died the year she was born, her mother never recovered, and from 1915 to 1917, and intermittently until 1923, she lived with her maternal grandparents in Great Village, Nova Scotia : if any specific house, child, and grandmother are meant in or by 'Sestina', they are these ones, though aspects of Bishop's paternal grandparents and elderly Aunt Maude, with whom she also lived as a child, are also to be expected.

Facts are one thing, tone another. In an autobiographical story about Nova Scotia, 'In the Village' (1953), Bishop wrote :

> [. . .] The child is visiting the blacksmith.
>
> In the blacksmith's shop things hang up in the shadows and shadows hang up in the things, and there are black and glistening piles of dust in each corner. A tub of night-black water stands by the forge. The horseshoes sail through the dark like bloody little moons and follow each other like bloody little moons to drown in the black water, hissing, protesting.[14]

[13] There is a biography by Brett Millier, *Elizabeth Bishop* (Berkeley and London: U. California P., 1993), and many critical studies are firmly biographical (and psychological). There is a convenient summary chronology by Neil Astley in Anderson and Shapcott, eds, *Elizabeth Bishop: Poet of the Periphery* (Newcastle: Bloodaxe, 2002).

[14] *Collected Prose* (1984; London: Chatto, 1994), 253.

The story predates the poem, but the memorable moons register ambivalently in both : despite the prose diction (black, night-black, dark, bloody little) the shop is fascinating, the patient horse being shod reassuring ; a mix like the poem's saturation with gloom and domestic security. But the world of the forge (and horse) is excluded from the kitchen-world of the poem, inviting gendered readings (p. 346), and knowing the moons as almanacs and planted tears in 'Sestina' it's a surprise to find them being quenched as red-hot horseshoes—though a stove hot enough to make waterdrops "dance like mad" thickens the connection.

Clearly, 'Sestina' is autobiographically underpinned ; the sensibility that managed to report what it reports was one that knew whereof it spoke, and a desire poetically to capture and evoke the long-term trauma of the losses and psychic damage Bishop suffered is implicit in her success. Biographical investigation also sharpens a sense of what was discarded to achieve that poetic success ; it can, locating the poem firmly in the 'Elsewhere' section of *Questions of Travel* (1965)—that is, poems not in 'Brazil', where Bishop lived from 1951 to 1971—insist on an immediate context removed from equinoctial gales in Nova Scotia by more than 70° of latitude. But that is equally true of other poems in 'Elsewhere' (including those like 'Manners', 'First Death in Nova Scotia', and 'Sunday, 4 A.M.' that do admit the grandfather and horse), and most of those to whom I've taught 'Sestina' find it memorable not as an autobiographical snapshot, but in the eerie combination of apparently particular people with only generic identities (the child, the grandmother), a recurrent and cyclical situation (the seasons and years of earthbound human lives), and a slow tornado of a form in which apprehensions of pasts and futures are flung out by individual words (failing, almanac, plant) and extended through the sestina's swirling iterations. Despite its fairly overt autobiography, 'Sestina' is not in the end a poem that trades on such truth ; some of its pity, but very little of its power, would be lost were it obviously quite unconnected with Bishop's own childhood experience. Suspicious as the old idea of personal experience being transmuted into art may be, it is an alchemy poetry can and does achieve.

4. 'September Song' (p. 72)

Poetry of the *Sho'ah* is under the same, almost unendurable moral and linguistic pressure as all documentation of the events that term designates, and few British poets attempted it as early as Hill. Ricks notes that Hill, born in 1932, was 13 when he and Britain heard shocked reports of unimaginable atrocity that began with Richard Dimbleby's BBC broadcasts from Belsen, and suggests it caught Hill at a special moment : "he belongs to the generation whose awakening to the atrocity of adult life was an awakening to this unparalleled atrocity".[15]

'Born in 1932' points a piece of biographical information the *Norton* editors supply, that Hill was born on 18 June, one day before his imagined victim (*"born 19.6.32—deported 24.9.42"*). This implies he doesn't simply mourn a child whose murder he representatively imagines, but ponders the chance that placed his own birth safely in England, and another child's the next day fatally in Germany or a country that Germany had, by 1942, invaded. No responsibility for the murder, let alone the *Sho'ah*, can lie at Hill's door, but as a human (and a communicant Anglican) he found himself possessed by the guilt of being safe (his first collection in 1959 was *For the Unfallen)*, and as a poet needed to express commingled senses of gratitude, pity, horror, and anger fuelled by imagination of the child's death <u>and</u> knowledge of his own life. He had to incorporate himself into the poem, but needed to do so in a way that did not displace from its centre the child who died, for that would be to slide from expression of pity to impression of self-pity. One way he found of doing this was to place 'I' in parenthesis (p. 146) ; another was the oblique relation of the subtitle to his own birthday, unstated in the poem but readily available to any reader who cares to investigate—a form of incorporated signature acknowledging his responsibilities in and for his poem.

5. 'Nearing Forty' (pp. 22–3)

As a Lucian creole, spiritually tenter-hooked between European and African inheritances but offered by politics and history a chance of an independent Lucian and West Indian identity painted by both continents, Walcott is of necessity deeply autobiographical in his work. At the largest scale his preoccupation was expressed in a verse-autobiography, *Another Life* (1972), but lesser levels are attested by recurrent Lucian place-names (the Roseau Valley, Castries, Gros Ilet) and protagonists like Shabine in 'The Schooner *Flight*' (from *The Star-apple Kingdom*, 1979) who share Walcott's mixed racial and cultural inheritances. The

[15] *The Force of Poetry*, 287. There is no biography of Hill, but biographical data is variously given in Robinson, ed., *Geoffrey Hill: Essays on his Work* (Milton Keynes and Philadelphia: Open UP, 1985), Bloom, ed., *Geoffrey Hill* (New York: Chelsea House, 1986), and the 60th birthday issue of *Agenda*, 30/1–2, (spring–summer 1992).

'I' of a Walcott poem (even of *Another Life*) cannot be simplistically identified with Walcott himself, as if the poem were an interview—even here there is a 'poet' as well as Walcott the poet—but neither can it be pretended or hoped that there is no connection.

The autobiography of 'Nearing Forty' begins with its title : it was first published in *The Gulf* in 1969, the year before Walcott's fortieth birthday, and so does express one aspect of his response to (as the cliché has it) mid-life crisis, moments at which one recognises oneself as middle-aged, more than half of one's life already lived. This may be obvious, but everything would be changed if Walcott had written the poem aged 20, or 80. Two canonical poems that vividly evoke the experience of age, Tennyson's 'Tithonus' (N1006) and Eliot's 'Love Song of J. Alfred Prufrock' (N1340), were written by poets in their twenties,[16] and knowledge of the discrepancy between what they could then have known and what they imagined presses on readings of those poems. It is equally important to know no such oddity attends 'Nearing Forty', and that the poem could draw as much on experience as on imagination.

The epigraph and literary histories implicit in the poem are biographical testimonies of another sort : to education and wide reading. It was an imperial and colonial education, politically compromised, but by Western standards thorough and classically grounded, granting access to a rich tradition of letters Walcott began by imitating and has now joined. Most astonishingly, in *Omeros* (1990, N1827) he fused Aegean and Caribbean archipelagos, mapping Homer's *Iliad* onto Lucian fishermen and staring down objections from less imaginative classical scholars ; he restated his point in a creolised Homeric drama, *The Odyssey*, premiered by the Royal Shakespeare Company in 1992. For a West Indian of Walcott's age a journey from St Lucia to Stratford is not easy : in a *South Bank Show*, Walcott remarked that while his own experience of colonialism was largely benign,[17] he was of a generation of West Indian poets who hesitated to write 'mango' or 'breadfruit' because they were conscious these tropical trees lacked the literary dignity of an oak in Shakespeare's Warwickshire. The remark reveals how

[16] Strictly, a young Tennyson wrote 'Tithon' and an older one revised it as 'Tithonus'.

[17] A text of the interview appears in Daryl C. Cumber, ed., *New World Adams: Conversations with contemporary West Indian Writers* (1992; 2nd edn Leeds: Peepal Tree, 2004). Walcott specifically mentions memories of a village policeman whose hat schoolboys would steal but who was more-or-less polite even so, then Martiniquan gendarmes and 'South American cops', but is at pains throughout to stress he spoke specifically of personal experience, knowing the horrors in the historical record and that many had quite other experiences.

even a poet of the greatest talent, if of colonial birth, can be as intimidated as enriched by induction into an imperial mother tongue and literature ; in Walcott's generation, which faced and celebrated independence, intimidation met a nascent nationalism demanding to know why a mango was not as good as any oak. The work of younger West Indians and black writers in the UK and USA—singers, poets, and rappers—tends to show that nationalism more overtly than Walcott's : poetically neither better nor worse, but reflecting generational attitudes. Other poems of Walcott's deal with these matters explicitly, but they are relevant to 'Nearing Forty', in the background they provide to his severe self-judgement, and because the poem is unobtrusively but suggestively West Indian.

To a British reader the obvious Caribbean references are the dedication to John Figueroa (1920–99), a distinguished West Indian ; "year's end rain"; and "louvre's gap". The noises of rain, domestic architecture suggested by its audibility, the louvres, a bedsheet but no blanket, all suggest a tropical rainy season, still warm, agriculturally essential but often emotionally oppressive. But one Jamaican reader[18] finds the poem insidiously British, full of talk about weather and fears of a persistent dampness that is anything but West Indian. For this reader, who left the Caribbean to pursue education, the distinction of happy memories of youth and a present rainy melancholia spoke of an island childhood, when it seemed and usually was sunny, and time as an adult in Britain, always feeling cold and often getting wet in endless, miserable rain—yet longing to return to the Caribbean is qualified by the same desires that force departure, the appreciation that though paradisal it is constricting. Walcott had by the late 1960s sufficient experience of travel for this reaction to be germane, yet had not himself then left the Caribbean anything like as decisively as he did in the late 1970s.

In considering a poem biographically it helps to consider the poet's career volume by volume, and where volumes are personally shaped to make them a primary context. Some indication of how 'Nearing Forty' parallels other poems in *The Gulf* is given by Lloyd Brown ; to deal with the problem of the poetic 'I' that is and is not Walcott, he refers to "Walcott's poet" :

> In [. . .] *The Gulf*, Walcott's poet is marked by an even greater sense of isolation [. . .] paralleled by the divisions, or gulfs, which the poet himself perceives in the world [. . .] The poet's personal sense of alienation and separation is [. . .] a private extension of the divisions which

18 Dr Francis Ingledew of Fairleigh Dickinson University, to whom I am indebted.

> he sees in the world of the 1960's : the Vietnamese War ('Postcards'), racial violence in the United States ('Blues'), and the civil war in Nigeria ('Negatives'). The gulf is everywhere, compelling our awareness of the very real divisions which mock our most passionate attempts at unity or intimacy [. . .]. The Caribbean landscape itself reflects the human gulf. [. . .] And the prospects for the future are not reassuring: 'The Gulf, your gulf, is daily widening.'[19]

I would count 'Nearing Forty', ruthlessly self-judgemental but fighting to reach personal accommodation with ageing, literary accommodation with precursors in the imperial canon, among "our most passionate attempts at unity or intimacy" : but attempts would not be needed were it not for gulfs between its "I" and "you", and (severely) between the younger "I", a greenhorn schoolchild, callow but passionately hopeful, and the older "I" whose passions are withered by sleepless knowledge. What unity can bridge the gulfs between nations if nations themselves are internally divided ? if citizens feel divided from their former selves ? Yet Walcott found his life, genes, culture, nation, and times made him painfully aware of such gulfs echoing on many scales, and that is in part what 'Nearing Forty' reports.

This barely begins investigation biography might prompt or assist ; even attention paid to Walcott since 1992 as a Nobel Laureate has only begun to deal with this aspect of his work—he is still alive and has, like us all, a right to privacy. After an author's death such materials as letters and diaries are fair game, and some authors destroy them or interdict use for a time by leaving them to libraries under binding conditions. These wishes should be respected, but it is natural, if work matters to a reader, to want to know more of the person behind the words and deepen understanding of the mind that arranged them.[20] In the case of 'Nearing Forty' unusual insight is granted by Walcott's donation of some MS drafts for publication in a memorial issue of *Caribbean Quarterly, At Home the Green Remains: Caribbean Writing in Honour of John Figueroa*.[21] As well as providing cancelled readings and sight of the rhyme-scheme evolving, they show the dedication to have happened well before composition was complete, and suggest Figueroa was for Walcott explicitly the exemplary "you" through considering whom he

[19] *West Indian Poetry* (1978; 2nd edn, London: Heinemann, 1984), 129–30.

[20] There is a biography, King's *Derek Walcott* (Oxford: Oxford UP, 2000), but if invaluable for facts, readers should still begin with *Another Life*, and continue with Walcott's Nobel address, *The Antilles: Fragments of Epic Memory* (New York and London: FSG/Faber, 1992).

[21] 49/1–2 (March–June 2003), 56–8.

finds resolve. This doesn't mean 'you' is simply a pronoun for 'John Figueroa', but attests to his importance to Walcott, not only as a teacher in the 1950s but as a moral exemplar two decades later, in the heart of his life and very middle of one of his great poems. The memorial volume includes a full text of 'Nearing Forty', and in this new context (where 'you' is most purely Figueroa), surrounded by memoirs that grant a personal sense of Figueroa as father and friend, mentor and resource, the usual tables are turned and the poem acquires additional identity as a resource for Figueroa's biographers.

Finally, one should note the poem's paradox, that (like Coleridge's 'Dejection', N828) it refutes its own content. Walcott did <u>not</u> settle for the quotidian, imagination has not ebbed, and his career since writing 'Nearing Forty' has been triumphant.[22] He shares with Heaney a chair in poetry at Boston once held by Lowell, as a Nobel Laureate with the best verse-autobiography since Wordsworth and most popular long poem since Tennyson under his belt ; as a dramatist commissioned by and performed in theatres around the world. It doesn't mean 'Nearing Forty' isn't 'true', but does ask questions the poem invites and cannot answer.

[22] See Parini, ed., *World Writers in English* (2 vols, New York and London: Scribner's Sons, 2004), ii. 721–45.

Exercises

As with history, specific biographical exercises are moot, but it never hurts to familiarise yourself as widely as possible with canonical lives (the *Dictionary of National Biography* and *Oxford Companion to English Literature* cover most) and, where possible, look at still photographs, film, or video and/or audio-tapes. Knowledge of an individual accent or manner of speech can help with more than metre and rhyme ; knowledge of appearance, education, and family-life enables sharper reflection on the apprehending sensibility behind the poems. Handwriting and habits of composition can mesh with overt features of poetic work. For a substantial majority of published poets at least some information is as available as a web-search, and as an enquiring reader of a given poem one never knows what biographical datum will help to bring it more fully into one's own life.

Chapter Glossary

expressionist : of criticism, believing the meaning of a text to express and to be determined by the author's intentions. (The term has other meanings in art history and theatre studies.)

intentional fallacy : the erroneous belief that the meaning of an artwork can be limited by the intent of its creator/s.

intentional-fallacy fallacy : the erroneous belief that the intention of artists is irrelevant to the meaning of their work (i.e. that the intentional fallacy is to believe intention relevant).

persona : an alternative for 'poet'.

poet : as distinct from 'poet', the actual historical person ; the author.

'poet' : as distinct from poet (without single inverted commas), the supposed writer or speaker of a given text ; the rhetorical construct designated by 'I' or me. Also referred to as the 'persona'.

11
Gender

SWEENEY: I knew a man once did a girl in.
Any man might do a girl in
Any man has to, needs to, wants to
Once in a lifetime, do a girl in

T. S. ELIOT, 'Fragment of an Agon'

Every woman adores a Fascist

SYLVIA PLATH, 'Daddy'

All of reality in late capitalist culture lusts to become an image for its own security.

DONNA HARAWAY, 'Teddy Bear Patriarchy'[1]

As biography is an aspect of history, so gender is of biography ; it is also much more, and while historically and biographically oriented criticisms were strongly challenged in the theory-minded 1970s–1990s, gender studies have steadily grown in importance since Modernism. *Feminist* critics point to inequalities and iniquities of the canon, dominated by male writers selected by male critics ; to female voices, experience, and history suppressed or excluded by male-forged criteria of excellence ; and to the need for a positive, separate consideration of women's writing while including it generally in teaching and research.

The charges cannot be denied : to examine the contents of any non-feminist anthology, or scan poetry shelves in library or bookshop, is to see how persistently and systematically the work of women is under-represented. The *Norton*'s brief, including American and living poets, is wider than some, and the editors (two of whom are women, in cogent testimony to Norton's sensibilities), clearly have a view on representing

[1] Eliot, *Complete Poems*, 124 ; Plath, *Collected Poems*, 223 ; Haraway, quoted in Epstein and Straub, eds, *Body Guards*, 284.

women. Of 339 named poets, 73 are female, ranging from Askew (N140) in the sixteenth century to Greenlaw (N2015) in the twentieth, and no century is allowed to seem a male preserve. Even so, only just over 21 per cent of the poets included are women, and few besides Dickinson are generously represented, so the percentage of poems would be smaller ; there are to my mind also more surprising female omissions (Mary Coleridge, Vita Sackville-West, Loy, Townsend Warner, Gershon, Nichols, Angelou, Kumin, Louise Bennett) than male ones (Masefield, Finkel, John N. Morris, Parini). Yet given the state of other prestigious anthologies, the *Norton* is much to be commended.

Less prejudiced anthologisation is one answer to *phallocracy*, rule of the *phallus*,[2] but as many women who might have written were prevented or discouraged from doing so, and much unpublished work by women is lost, it will never be possible wholly to redress the balance for past centuries ; yet much work by women can be recovered from libraries, periodicals, and private collections. There are anthologies of women's writing from the seventeenth and eighteenth centuries to challenge critical orthodoxies and platitudes, enrich understandings of literary history, and convey the suffering to which women have been subjected. More anthologies and studies will follow, and as more women gain access to the power structures of society and academia balances are redressed.

On this almost all can agree, and there is widespread acceptance of a need for alternatives to the once ubiquitous use of 'men' and 'his' as equivalents of 'people' and 'her', but some theories feminist critics advance about the nature of fe/male writing are controversial, and as hotly disputed by women as men. In particular, critics such as Julia Kristeva (b.1941) and Luce Irigaray (b.1939), founding work on Freudian-Lacanian theories of language and gender acquisition, and Mary Daly (b.1928), a feminist theologian best known for *Gyn/Ecology*,[3] raise radical questions about gendered language. That wo/men write about different subjects, have differing emotional concerns, and analyse with differing priorities is plain enough ; recent magnetic resonance imaging of electrical patterns in fe/male brains doing the same task suggest some differences are neuroanatomical : but do wo/men write differently in the sense of employing language in a fundamentally distinct way ? are there male and female languages ? and to end

[2] A phallus is not a penis but its ideological counterpart : 'she wears the trousers' credits the female partner in a relationship with a phallus, but doesn't imply she has a penis.

[3] *Gyn/Ecology: The Metaethics of Radical Feminism* (Boston: Beacon Press, 1978).

patriarchal oppression, must women develop a new language, because the old language (say, English as it now is) is saturated with inalienable maleness encoding misogynistic structures ? On these issues there is no consensus, and the views feminists take on them relate closely to wider gender-political views—whether, for example, they are *liberal* or *separatist*, seeking co-operation with men or spurning it.

These kinds of question assume a binary opposition of anatomical *sex* rather than overlaps of cultural *gender*. Almost everybody is, genetically and anatomically, *male* or *female* at birth and acquires in growing up both *masculine* and *feminine* characteristics ; individuals' combination of masculinity and femininity—personal, sexual, vocational, professional—constitutes their gender. In consequence, though the oppression of women and women's writing is the largest concern of gender studies, its power as a discipline is not identical with that of feminism : gay and lesbian writing is also being recovered and explored, and representation or concealment of homoeroticism in canonical works re-thought. The legacies of Freud and early sexologists, particularly Ellis, and the work of Foucault on histories of sexuality, open up to debate an enormous area of the human psyche, awareness of which substantially challenges traditional reading, complementing and qualifying the challenge of feminism/s. What are the consequences for reading of the simple but bizarre fact that while (in Britain) practice of male homosexuality was from 1885 to 1967 a statutory crime, lesbianism has never been criminalised[4] and rarely fulminated against ? What qualities[5] are typical of male characters created by lesbian authors, or female ones by gay authors ? Can study of the writings of oppressed or liberated women and homosexuals teach us about how and why they continue to be oppressed or became liberated, or how others are likely to be persecuted ? What can we learn about the persecutors, who as much as the persecuted are all among us ? There are signs of emergent *masculinism*, a movement focusing on oppression of men, often by men : the commonest theme of first plays by men is bullying, undoubtedly as endemic in Britain as the binge alcoholism that puts a million male drunks on the street in competitive groups every Friday and Saturday night. Male–male violence will not be lessened by any masculinism less powerful or resilient than feminism has proved itself, and will have to reach a long way beyond the study of

[4] Queen Victoria was so incredulous at a paragraph on lesbianism in the 1885 bill criminalising private homosexual acts that she refused to sign it until the paragraph was deleted.

[5] See Parker and Willhardt, *Cross-Gendered Verse*.

poetry, but as a man desiring reform of maleness I find literature, especially poetry uncovered by feminist and gender critics, a necessary study.

Gender criticism is complex and variable, but it remains hard to escape dealing with issues in polarised terms. The shift from 'male v. female' to 'feminine and masculine' is away from polarity (black/white) towards a fluid scale (greys), but polarity creeps back in other ways (rigid/fluid ; straight/gay ; butch/femme ; anal/oral) ; such oppositions may prompt thought, but the more sharply they are polarised the less helpful they are likely to be, and it is worth examining how flexibly (or otherwise) a critic's categories are conceived and applied. The discipline is recent, still in its exploratory stages, so it is no surprise that there is little consensus ; with so many ideas in the air this flexibility test is a helpful rule-of-thumb.

Problematically, the mode of analytical thinking in which practical criticism is grounded is felt by some feminists to be patriarchal. The obvious target is use of *feminine* and *masculine* to describe rhymes and line-endings, imputing heavy tread to masculine and a pittering pat to feminine ones.[6] This sexist language is changing—I prefer to write of stressed and unstressed hyperbeats or rhyme—and not (as in any language with full-blown grammatical gender) obviously part of a systematic sexism inscribed through technical terms. A spondee is in English neither masculine nor feminine, <u>the</u> not *le* or *la*, and may be applied as neutrally by man as woman, to 'female' as much as 'macho'. Still, the force of the accusation that practical criticism is intrinsically patriarchal lies less in specifics than in contrasting a supposedly male analytical, divisive mode with a supposedly female fluid, unifying mode. There is some truth in that contrast, particularly in its development by French feminists into an *écriture féminine*, a mode that finds new ways of writing femininity and the female body into texts ; used as a critical (rather than creative[7]) tool it produces very limited results. Applying the flexibility test suggests this is partly because it tends to be applied very rigidly, and to drift away from masculine and feminine aspects of writing (which is interesting) towards predetermined opposition of male and female authors (which usually isn't).

---

[6] Cf. Suckling, 'A Ballad upon a Wedding', ll. 43–5 : "Her feet beneath her petticoat, [/] Like little mice, stole in and Out [/] As if they feared the light" (N410).

[7] The best *écritures féminines* I know are the brilliant essays by Cixous, particularly 'The Laugh of the Medusa' and 'Coming to Writing', but it does not seem chance that her primary subject is her own experience rather than a text. For the best translations (preserving puns, *d'hommicile fixe* becoming 'perMANent address') see Cixous, *Coming to Writing*.

One specific argument with which I disagree is gendered punctuation—that Dickinson's use of dashes is in some way feminine, as the popularity of dashes among recent female poets confirms. As argument it doesn't stand up, not only because Dickinson's dashes may have been falsely transcribed and standardised (p. 144) and there is every likelihood more recent poets are imitating Dickinson rather than demonstrating femininity ; until other probable influences on Dickinson's punctuation—who taught her, her religious life and education (a primary influence on individual practices of punctuation), the mores of her culture and times—are discounted, it is foolish to think her dashes and femininity essentially related.

It is of course true that a poem may seem overtly by a fe/male writer, in ways that will have to do with the sex and gender of the reader as well as of the poet, but that seeming is usually an effect of the whole poem, commonly lost in analytical dismemberment. As a result, it is tricky to point to specific features of the poem that make it seem fe/male ; rather, one winds up discussing content, subject, and approach as embodied in the whole work. There is nothing wrong with that—but such discussions easily lose their edge and become impressionistic. An instructive example for me was a question in a 1993 Cambridge examination paper, asking candidates to compare an anonymous poem of 1740, 'Epitaph on a Child Killed by a Procured Abortion', with Brooks's 1945 poem 'The Mother', beginning "Abortions will not let you forget." The 70+ answers I marked showed two pronounced traits : an assumption that both poems were honestly autobiographical (the anonymous author was the woman who had the abortion, Brooks was writing of her own multiple abortions) ; and an absolute refusal to express a personal moral opinion, pro-life, pro-choice, or uncertain, about the actual abortions supposed to be reported. Assumption of autobiography, identification of 'poet' with poet, if emotionally understandable, is foolish, and in answers to other questions candidates mostly showed themselves aware of that ; the intensity of abortion as a topic imploded their critical intelligence. Refusal to express personal opinions is probably tied to being instructed at school never to use 'I' in practical criticism : it is not to be used often, and as a teacher I understand what prompts prohibition—but it's nonsense all the same (p. 355). The emotional and critical response to these poems of any candidate who has from experience or belief acquired strong views about abortion will be thereby affected ; exam discipline requires candidates to respond without polemic, but constructing a written response from which personal morality and emotion have been excluded is misguided. To point to a poetic intensity created by metre or rhyme does not require self-identication, but a written answer as a whole is a personal as well as critical document, and the best answers were those in which examinees had been willing to *inscribe* themselves, to write as individuals answers acknowledging that the poems drew passionate as well as watchful reactions. Some of these more forthright folk were men, some women ; all acknowledged their own sex as one ground of their response (only women can have abortions), and personal in/experience/s of abortion another. In these (and all) matters the *politics of representation*, the ways in which each gender writes and reads itself and other genders, are inescapable, and best acknowledged.

The study of gender in literature should thus include how gender affects reading, and foreground the identity (including sex and gender) of readers as much as authors. An important way forward for gender-conscious study of poetry is inclusion within practical critical responses of the critic's gender beside a continuing search for the ways in which texts and language may be intrinsically or intentionally gendered. Amid the debate it would be nice to find truly common ground, and such statistical and linguistic facts as are known are set out in *The Cambridge Encyclopedia of Language*. Having discussed Japanese, where there are differentiated male, female, and sex-neutral forms of speech, it says :

> In English, the situation is less clear. There are no grammatical forms, lexical items, or patterns of pronunciation that are used exclusively by one sex, but there are several differences in frequency. For example, among the words and phrases that women are supposed to use more often are such emotive adjectives as *super* and *lovely*, exclamations such as *Goodness me* and *Oh dear*, and intensifiers such as *so* or *such* (e.g. *It was* so *busy*). This use of intensifiers has been noted in several languages, including German, French, and Russian.
>
> More important are the strategies adopted by the two sexes in cross-sex conversation. Women have been found to ask more questions, make more use of positive and encouraging 'noises' (such as *mhm*), use a wider intonational range and a more marked rhythmical stress, and make greater use of the pronouns *you* and *we*. By contrast, men are much more likely to interrupt (more than three times as much, in some studies), to dispute what has been said, to ignore or respond poorly to what has been said, to introduce more new topics into the conversation, and to make more declarations of fact or opinion.
>
> Most interpretations of these differences refer to the contrasting

> social roles of the sexes in modern society. Men are seen to reflect in their conversational dominance the power they have traditionally received from society ; women, likewise, exercise the supporting role that they have been taught to adopt—in this case, helping the conversation along and providing men with opportunities to express this dominance. The situation is undoubtedly more complex than this, as neither sex is linguistically homogeneous, and considerable variation exists when real contexts of use are studied. The danger, as some commentators have pointed out, is that in the process of criticizing old sexual stereotypes, researchers are in danger of creating new ones.[8]

The factors that sustain such linguistic differences in speech and cross-sex conversation may inhibit them in poetry, often an intense and private mode of engagement with language—but it is reasonable to expect <u>some</u> relationship between characteristic patterns of an individual's social speech and poetry, so it is worth asking whether such features are reflected in male and female poetries. Readers must decide for themselves ; my own belief is that there is evidence in the work of Dickinson, Bishop, Miles, Brooks, Levertov, Rich, Plath, and Clampitt (N1110, 1515, 1586, 1609, 1677, 1791, 1836), of good listening (and good looking), unexpectedly and pleasingly free of opinionated assertion, that is a significant factor in generating a readerly sense of work by a woman.

There is also, patently, differentiation of subject-matter and points of view that reflects common gender-differences in male and female biographies, and is probably clearest in the relations of a poetic voice to its domestic *roomscape* (indoor 'landscape') and to the public sphere. Patriarchal and misogynistic constructions of the female body in poetry often involve architecture, imagining women as temples for worship, fortresses for conquest, or palaces for decoration, and political misogynies seek to control women by domestic and functional imprisonment, as the Nazis did in asserting women's 'proper' concerns as 'Kinder, Küche, Kirche' (children, kitchen, church). One consequence of such oppression is that common female experience of domesticity is very different from male, as much imprisonment as shelter ; in the same way female entry into the public spheres of society, especially authority and political power, has to be fought for and negotiated in ways few men experience. These pressures influence characteristically feminine conceptions of space, and—drawing power from

[8] Crystal, *Cambridge Encyclopedia of Language*, 21.

traditional male imaginations and representations of virginity as determinative of moral value, of sexual intercourse as penetration and conquest, and of the womb as a space within the female body men seek to occupy and control—make issues of space as acute for many women in private self-imaginings as in daily life and political consciousness. Domestic and architectural imagery in Dickinson and Plath closely relates to images of self-as-woman, threats of claustrophobic entrapment within bodies, dress, roles, and dwellings, and agoraphobic or suicidal liberation. The same themes are equally keyed to individual elements of poetic craft—Dickinson's dashes and quatrains, Plath's rhyme and metre—and the possibilities of understanding how their femininity and poetry co-operate are among the great enrichments of reading that gender studies has begun to offer. It also offers consideration of how Eliot's or Hardy's heterosexual and Auden's or Crane's homosexual masculinity exists in their poetries, and has posed fascinating questions about (for example) the sexual orientation of Marvell,[9] while equally demanding to know who put the curse on Tennyson's 'Lady of Shalott' (N984). As a reader of poetry I find issues here which can disrupt as thoroughly as a cow in a china shop poems I thought I knew ; as a teacher of practical criticism I can report no detectable gender bias in the enthusiasm, comprehension, or ability of students to perform the close reading and writing that is required to begin to answer those questions.

Exemplary Poems

1. 'I heard a Fly buzz—when I died—' (p. 97)

As the pre-eminent female poet of the nineteenth century (overwhelmingly so in American terms), Dickinson has been central to much feminist and gender-conscious criticism. Extreme and naïve positions have been as common as median and sophisticated ones, and mapping them offers a record of recent feminist literary scholarship and criticism.[10]

---

[9] Perhaps the only really interesting candidate for 'outing' in the mainstream canon, as a celibate gay (cf. Stephen Fry). The usual objection is 'To His Coy Mistress', but poet ≠ 'poet', and homosexuality would make potent sense of other poems (including 'The Definition of Love' and 'The Picture of Little T.C.') and of qualities in Marvell's life. The interested might begin with Aubrey's statement in *Brief Lives* that Marvell, a drinker fond of his claret, was never drunk in company—radically unusual behaviour for the time.

[10] See Ackmann on 'Biographical Studies' and Dickie on 'Feminist Conceptions', in Grabher et al., eds, *Emily Dickinson Handbook* (p. 99).

Given biographical issues of Dickinson's relative seclusion and retirement, yet constant epistolary engagement with wide circles of relatives and friends, terms such as 'entrapment', 'repression', 'imprisonment', and 'enclosure' are common in criticism. Underlying them is often a conflict between 'patience' (in 'life') and 'agency' (in 'writing'), which reflects the age-old sexism of a private female and public male sphere,[11] and in Dickinson's poems of death becomes acute. Here, is the "supposed person" (p. 317) whose moment of death specifies a time ("when I died") active or passive ? and is it a woman ? If so, the tableau (common in nineteenth-century melodrama) the poem presents is striking : a poem within the head of a woman, motionless on her deathbed with (ungendered) "Eyes around". When she 'wills' and 'signs away' she must act and speak : within the moment ? or prior to the deathbed assemblage ? Either way, everything fails within the poem, which in all its seeming passivity and patience is an utterance whose perspectives command startled attention.

The genderless fly sharpens this with precision. Potential associations range from those who wouldn't hurt one, through the 'fly scene' in Shakespeare's *Titus Andronicus*, to (most obviously) the fat flies that lay their eggs on corpses and have a nose for them—of which the unrefrigerated nineteenth century was altogether aware. As partly in Shakespeare, it is the fly's agency that is critical : its buzz—metonymic of self-propelled intrusion though later coloured by adjectives ("Blue—uncertain—stumbling") that project the dying life onto the intrusive, unaffected energy of the fly—is the poem's primary axis, only moving object, and immediate agent of terminal darkness. In the light of Dickinson's and many nineteenth-century female lives, profoundly subject to industrial and imperial extensions of patriarchal control and imaginative determination, this tableau plus fly, highlighting passivity and action, illness and uncontrollability, speaks directly to Dickinson's politics of representation and to repressive (even pathological) levels of sexism constraining her life.

The whole is substantially underpinned by biographical reading, but despite assumption of a self-referential 'I', and even the clear statement that the death occurs in a "Room", there is nothing absolutely to deny, say, that the speaker is a soldier mortally wounded in one of the Civil

[11] The earliest articulated version is the Greek theatrical opposition of the unseen, female-controlled world of the *oikos* and seen, male-controlled world of the *polis*.

War battles reported before its composition in *c.*1863—the middle year of the single bloodiest and most modern war before 1914–18—and such possibilities should be weighed with any other gendered interpretation.

2. 'Sestina' (pp. 69–70)

There are better excuses for assuming biography with Bishop than Dickinson (p. 328), and the insistent presence of "the grandmother" (matched by the absence of any grand/father or mother) squares with, for example, the Cheshire dialect that terms an illegitimate child a 'granny reardun' (granny-reared-one) ; the poem in large measure exemplifies the association of the feminine, nurturing and cyclically self-continuing, with kitchen-centred domesticity, and seems fair game for feminist criticism. Yet in years of teaching it, and marking many practical criticisms, what stands out is an unwarrantable assumption of gender : Bishop writes unfailingly of "the child", neither sex nor gender ever determined, and criticism that assumes a central grandmother–granddaughter relationship goes persistently astray.

With biography in mind this is unsettling, and clearly one of many aspects that insist on the poem's detachment. Written in Brazil about the far north, in a sundered present about an old memory, and not (in the end) trading on autobiographical truth for poetic power (p. 329), 'Sestina' does make a domestic grandmother central, and excludes a grandfather whom other writings suggest as an equally important childhood presence and source of sustenance. But it carefully does not wholly foreclose on the male, any more than a grandmother (whose daughter was unable to care for her child) would reject a grandson but take a granddaughter.

In many ways the missing term is 'family'. Gender-consciousness (like most political consciousness) cuts across family identities, and draws power from the very common experience of concerted and/or punitive family opposition to an individual member's desire in career or lifestyle ; it is equally true that blood remains, for better or worse, thicker than water, and that family loyalties will often so comprehensively brush aside other identities and discriminations that they are barely registered. Most crucially, it must never be supposed, even if Bishop is thought an essentially feminine writer of an essentially feminine poem, that she cannot or does not write in a way that is resonantly comprehensible by men.

3. 'Nearing Forty' (pp. 22–3)

A majority (of both sexes) of those to whom I have shown 'Nearing Forty' without ascription have felt it is a masculine poem, unlikely to be the work of a woman, but there has been little consensus about which if any of its features may be singled out as producing this conviction.

At the broadest level is a suggestion that the *donnée*, the notion of self-assessment as one approaches 40, is more a male preoccupation and habit, perhaps through such factors as exclusion of women from professional careers (in which 40 is a traditional watershed) or imposition of social value based on biological status rather than age-hierarchised achievement—but there are obvious points in rebuttal : 40 is also traditionally associated with female menopause and loss of youthfulness, and nearing 40 may (especially for women taught self-value as sexual allure and reproductive capacity) provoke acute anxiety as well as sometimes painful and distressing physical changes. Similarly, 40-something husbands notoriously need to demonstrate that they can still attract and 'satisfy' a woman younger than their wives, to bolster virility they fear to be waning with age ; one reader[12] found 'Nearing Forty' humorously to express deeply felt anxiety about paternity, reproduction, and ageing in a specifically male body. The imagery of water in forceful cyclical movement, drumming down and convecting up, contrasts sharply with anxieties about false dawns or dry wheezings that signal entrapment in the failing life-lines of his poetry. The force that symbolically attends the poem's resolution and self-comfort is the moon, traditionally female and associated with renewal : the lunar cycle becomes the paradigm of all cycles, and menstrual connotations identify the course of the poem as from linear male anxiety attending inability to bear children and fear of death to cyclical female comfort promising continued creativity.

In the middle ground is a case that sparsity of domestic detail (bed-sheet, kettle) and exclusion of detailed observation and other people by self-preoccupied rhetoric, are indicative of a masculine (presumably male) author. Without knowledge of Walcott's domesticity, this cannot be confirmed or refuted : the poem doesn't for me suffer from absence of the details it lacks, but I accept there may be, as some critics allege,[13]

[12] Dr Hugh Stevens, now of University College London, to whom I am indebted.

[13] See Fido, 'Macho Attitudes', in Walder, ed., *Literature in the Modern World*.

evidence in Walcott's work as a whole of a masculinity reflecting his age in domestic chauvinism as much as celebration of West Indian independence. The literary origins of "household truth" in philosophically "domestick wisdom" (p. 305) lessen the extent to which it can place truth in a domestic setting, implicitly feminine in contrast to a masculine public sphere. And if, with bedsheet, kettle, blinds, and water clerk, "household truth" rebukes with simple domesticity and commerce an adolescent fantasy of "ambition as a searing meteor" that seems stereotypically masculine, neither the 'poet's' present nor memories seem to include women, nor acknowledge their influence. Other poems of Walcott's, however, certainly do so, and I am not persuaded his (putative) sexism is poetically damaging : it is for example possible to read 'Nearing Forty' as a love-poem, the "you" to whom it is addressed a feminine figure ; even, if biography is wanted, as Margaret Maillard, Walcott's second wife, with whom (after an explosive start and brief first marriage in the 1950s) he was productively settled in Trinidad throughout the 1960s, living largely by journalism and struggling with the Trinidad Theatre Workshop to establish modern drama in the Caribbean. I don't particularly read it like that, but the poem's willingness to co-operate with such a reading makes me cautious about believing it narrowly masculine.

Most precise is the contention that the phrase "as greenhorns at school" (23) is not one a woman would use. As I find the 'poet' masculine, and know no female use to cite in refutation, I agree this is possible : "greenhorns" is more an American than British term (though "school", unless Walcott means 'university', is British), but while America is very conservative about gender roles, I find it hard to believe there has recently been overt pressure on women not to say "greenhorns", or employ it in phrases. "greenhorns at school" also seems to me as poetic as colloquial, and any female poet who wanted to use it would surely do so. But it derives (although some female animals have horns) specifically from the horns of young oxen (which gives it a male slant), and the *OED*'s citations are relentlessly male and masculine ; it is also a term which in schoolroom context has a particularly masculine flavour, so it seems reasonable to identify it as a source for the sense of 'Nearing Forty' as a masculine poem.

Technical features of the poem do not seem much influenced by Walcott's maleness or masculinity. More men than women have written heroic lines, but far more men's poetry has been recorded in all forms. The epigraph invokes the very masculine Johnson, but he is widely influential, and female poets have certainly engaged with his legacy—few as deeply as Walcott, but Walcott's engagement with canonical precursors is a primary cause of his greatness, so the standard is high. Layout is essentially conventional, punctuation supple, and delicacy of rhyme a tribute to West Indian culture rather than sex or gender. Skills of craft, once learned, are instruments of creative expression, and the pain of ageing common to all.

Exercises

The biggest practical problem faced by many school-students and undergraduates is an inability frankly to discuss issues of sexuality and gender in a way that relates theoretical or abstract understandings to personal and anecdotal experience. My own parents were both medical doctors, and far more unmentionable things than sexuality were common currency at our dinner table, but I have learned as an adult that (especially in the US, more conservative by far than Europe in its social mores) others' sensibilities are more constrained. The question shouldn't matter here more than elsewhere, but over the last century or so literary studies have broadly come in the secular West to take the place of Classics and Divinity in providing a forum for humane discussion of personal and moral issues.

Applications of theory, however sophisticated, cannot substitute for self-interrogation. I judge things to have significantly improved in the last decade or so, and that some of the major Anglophone hangups about sexual forthrightness (most obvious in the UK and US) have passed into history ; the problem is neither unabated nor solved. Literature is not in itself any kind of solution : but if you cannot, as a member of a group discussing a poem, contemplate and articulate thoughts about sex and gender ; or cannot articulate them on paper ; your level of inhibition is professionally incapacitating and may prove consequential.

Many poets, from Donne to Larkin, Elizabeth I to Elizabeth Bishop, prominently present among their conundra of entwined lives and poems questions of sex and sexuality, gender relations and politics of representation. Poetry, moreover, has a sneaky habit of being literally minded, as Donne's literal-mindedness about fleas and hymens, Larkin's about parental fuckings-up, and Bishop's about the little-moon shapes in almanacs and of horseshoes need to be taken literally : and in sexual matters the post-Victorian mind may yet balk at the implications. Perhaps the only exercise that really matters is that of awareness : unless you regularly put gender on the agenda, and pursue it as seriously as any other aspect of literary study, you will never be in a position honourably to decide on its limitations.

Chapter Glossary

écriture féminine : in some feminist theory, language that is gendered feminine and written from the female body.

feminine : here, the aspect of gender roles reflecting cultural definitions of women.

feminism/s : collective term/s for beliefs and action intended to assert the rights of women, and to liberate them from oppression by men and the patriarchy.

gender : cultural femininity and masculinity, as distinct from biological femaleness and maleness.

inscribe, inscription : here, the process by which the critic includes him- or herself as an individual within his or her writing. In this sense inscription used to be proscribed in practical criticism, but (used judiciously) is now widely encouraged.

masculine : here, the aspect of gender roles reflecting cultural definitions of men.

masculinism : an emergent set of beliefs and actions intended to liberate men from oppression by other men, particularly peer pressure, bullying, and the patriarchal imposition of emotionally repressive gender stereotyping.

phallus : the representation of abstract patriarchal power (which may be wielded by masculinised women) as distinct from the anatomical penis.

politics of representation : how women and men, femininity and masculinity, are represented by an author or in a text, and how those representations are received by a/reader/s.

roomscape : my coinage for the domestic 'landscape', to which responses are often gendered.

12
Exams and Written Work

The school and undergraduate students for whom this book is primarily intended have chosen to study literature, and I hope for their sakes practical criticism of poetry is a pleasure as well as study, exercise, and preparation—if not they have chosen amiss. Writing it has been a pleasure as well as a job, and I hope I have managed to convey something of my joy in poetry, rather than simply providing an introduction and revision crammer ; but the book must be those as well, which is why I end with a chapter on exams (and some comments on coursework) ; the hardest-working students are ill-prepared if they have not thought about the nature and structure of the test an exam represents.

This is particularly true of exams in practical criticism, for there is deep contradiction between things those exams require. On one hand candidates are asked to read a text, on its own or against others, with the greatest sensitivity and in the greatest detail ; on the other, to write an account of their reading that reveals sensitivity and detail cogently, and amounts to an argument ; there is a time-limit, usually of one hour (in a three-hour, three-question paper). Reading and writing compete for available time : if writing is to be done adequately, reading must be restricted ; if reading is to be done adequately, writing must be restricted : the steel of the test is neither 'Can you read?' nor 'Can you write?', but 'How well can you combine them?' It is this that makes practical criticism relevant beyond English studies, for the balancing act a successful candidate will have managed is of use in many callings.

The need for balance is one reason for mastering technical vocabulary : however off-putting it seems, it is very compact and enables you to say far more in the time available than is otherwise possible. Try to paraphrase 'the poem is in blank verse' or 'in the sonnet's third line the fourth foot is inverted' without using technical terms and you'll see what I mean. Technicalities are also a means of focusing attention :

they are not exhaustive, but cover many things that can be done ; knowing them alerts you to what may be.[1] This won't happen automatically, and one way of beginning your analytical reading in exams (and your critical writing) is to make as complete and short a technical description of a poem as you can : faced with 'Leda and the Swan' (N1200) you need only get as far as 'Petrarchan sonnet', and far from being faced with a blank page to fill you have an embarrassment of things to remark : metrical conformity and deviation, exploitations of rhyme and layout, tensions of form and content, manipulation of syntax and diction etc. Some may be relatively isolated technical matters—the stress afforded to an individual word by a distinguishing foot, for example—but many are connected with and underpin the largest moral issues the poem raises. Yeats's choice of sonnet-form, invoking its traditional associations with courtship and frustrated love, is connected to questions of Leda's complicity and Zeus's responsibility ; that in turn reconnects to smaller details, such as the questioning stress on "Did" in the inverted first foot of the penultimate line, "Did she put on his knowledge with his power [/] Before the indifferent beak could let her drop?"

It is better to have more things to say than time allows than to be groping for material—waffle always reads like waffle—but it poses a problem : what to use available time to say? Right determination of that question is fundamental to the balance that structures a good answer, and while there is no universal 'right determination', solid guidelines will set you on your way. Different people behave differently in exams, and need different routines and methods to enable them to do their best : this is only one—but one I can vouch for.

As best you can, clear your mind of preconceptions and let the poem come to you. Read it carefully, and don't hesitate to mouth the words, so that you can mentally hear the sounds : one reading at that pace may enable you to notice more than three swifter unvocalised readings. Be able to review in your head the possible technical elements represented by my chapter titles (invent a mnemonic if that helps), and ask yourself which are most striking or doing most work in this particular poem. If something appears of little importance—layout is wholly conventional, for example— eliminate it from consideration and move on. If something is clearly complex and would take a great deal of time to sort out—highly disturbed metre, or sprawlingly open form—note it as

[1] For poets, the elements may prompt thoughts in composition, but may prove more useful as a way of learning to revise and polish work—a troubleshooting kit.

something that could be mentioned in one sentence ('Metre, like layout, is disturbed.') and move on. Take care in judging—if every line is end-stopped it may mean lineation doesn't matter much, or be a carefully contrived effect—but judge nevertheless ; within a few minutes you will have a list of three or four elements which are, in this poem, hard at work, and must be partly responsible for its totality, content and effects. It is worth spending a minute or two pondering relations between elements, and then decide in which order your written work should tackle them.

To determine this order yourself is important : it shows you are not simply giving an 'account' of the poem in which it determines the structure. One self-interested reason for avoiding first line to last line accounts is that if you get timing wrong, truncation (1, 2, 3, 4, 5, 6, eek 10) will be glaringly obvious ; a thematic plan (providing, of course, you watch timing closely enough to add a conclusion after your last analytical paragraph) will show nothing amiss even if you don't have time to include all you would like. Accounts, plodding through lines in order, are also more likely to run short of time, and in any case square you up to a poem, rather than allowing you to grasp an interestingly loose end and begin to pull, or dive into the heart of things.[2]

You now have a plan which might note a specific form, unusual punctuation, a succession of half-rhymes, and a subject-matter of historical importance ; or, blank verse with metrical oddities, a layout which splits a line into two half-lines, and a sequence of words with related secondary meanings. As you begin to write about what you can see and hear in the poem, and how you respond, technical identification, explanation, and relation of elements will serve to structure what you write and peg your responses to the text (essential for preventing waffle) ; when you end one paragraph you will know what is due up in the next, so that you don't have to stare into space while you think about it. It also enables you to judge your timing, so that you can measure time left against matters remaining.

A few other points. Plans are important, but stay flexible : if, halfway through writing, you realise you have missed something that matters,

---

[2] To practise thematic organisation, try taking two poems that are too long for exam conditions, allow yourself to become thoroughly familiar with them, and then try to write about them with a stringent word- or time-limit. A pair I find useful for this exercise is Causley's 'Christ at the Cheesewring' and Morrison's 'Whinny Moor' (in *Ballad of the Yorkshire Ripper*) : Causley is riddling, Morrison loquacious, and their mutual engagement so immediate and powerful (both concern preternatural meetings with strange men on moors) that potential thematics leap out and any double-account is clearly impossible.

readjust and include it, acknowledging if necessary (because you're going to contradict something you've already written, for example) that the process of writing has affected your earlier reading. This is an occasion when 'I' can properly be used, and most examiners will be more impressed by clear evidence that *you* are thinking and responding than by your completing a neat plan that strove to be anonymous and ignored something important. It is also an occasion when you might risk a rueful joke, acknowledging your change of mind : humour is tricky, and flippancy *always* to be avoided, but too many scripts show the handicaps of candidates checking their sense of humour at the exam-room door ; earnest responses to comic passages—which examiners may set *as* comic—easily commit howlers and become painful to read. Be careful—but if something strikes you as funny (or sad, offensive . . .) don't be afraid to acknowledge your response, assess it, and put it to critical use.

No plan is good enough if it doesn't go somewhere, and arguments need conclusions : otherwise technical points become simply dots you are asking the examiner to join up for you. The examiner won't : make sure you do. You are being asked for a critical response founded on technical analysis, not simply technical description—an essay, not a blueprint.

In all exams write legibly and with clarity—nothing is more irritating, with a pile of scripts to get through, than words or sentences that have to be puzzled over. Think about this : if your writing is large, with descenders of 'g's and 'y's looping far below the line, write on alternate lines ; if you quote more than a line, leave blank lines above and below the quotation, and indent it slightly ; ensure full-stops, capital letters, and other punctuation are clear ; and if you have time left at the end, proof-read your answers, rewriting illegible words above the line or in the margin and re-punctuating as needed. (Remember your hand worsens as you tire, so proof-read essays in the reverse order of writing.)

A word about rubrics that require you to compare and contrast two or more poems. This clearly puts even greater pressure on available time but the same technique will serve, save that instead of simply asking which technical elements are doing most work in each poem, you must select elements relatively doing the most work that are common to both. The discussion of each element then offers you a point of connection, a bridge between poems ; as those points build up, your judgement of the poems in relation to one another will be enabled and strengthened. It follows (unless it is a very straightforward comparison) that you will probably not know what to say in the concluding paragraph of your argument until you reach it ; judging time is incorporated into writing time. This can make it frightening to begin to write, for you are setting off in the dark, but it is better to do so than tack a preconceived conclusion lamely onto an argument to which it is inappropriate or contradictory. If an element is crucial in one poem but absent or very minor in the other, give it a paragraph to itself, but remember to comment, at least briefly, on the absence as well as the importance, and if you think the two poems have nothing in common, think again : examiners may be bloody-minded (it's actually very rare) but not irresponsible.

Examiners also hate failing people (though few students give them credit for this), but cannot give marks for what is not actually in front of them. The commonest reason for low marks is a short script, and in practical criticism (unless you've blown the timing, which is your problem) it is one thing that is fairly unforgivable, because every poem has some kind of metre, form, syntax, diction, and all the rest—there is always something more you can say.

The first edition of this book ended with three timed (one hour) responses to 'Nearing Forty' produced by first-year students of mine in 1994–5. These now appear, with other such work, on the website, and students facing exams are strongly urged to read them : having read the book, especially the sections on exemplary poems, you are in a position to mark essays on them yourself, judging what their authors have included and what you can see them to have omitted, by choice or in haste or forgetfulness. It is rarely possible for students (or parents) to be able in this way to put themselves into their (children's) examiners' shoes, and it can be a revelation.

Many of the things one can learn about critical writing will equally apply to assessed coursework or long essays, but those have additional requirements about presentation with which very many students, even using word-processors, have apparent difficulty, so this edition ends with a summary checklist about the presentation of written work. Clear and accurate presentation matters, and it is worse than foolish for the hard work of reading to be squandered in careless writing ; be habitually as accurate in writing as practical criticism and poetry demand you be in reading, and all manner of things shall be well.

Some readers thought I should say more about coursework and the general business of writing essays, but taken seriously that would be another and quite different book ; and besides, where practical criticism is concerned, timed and word-limited essays are more or less the same thing (give or take writers' cramp). The compressed economy necessary in closed exams will serve you well in most writing, just as the exercises with your own syntax (pp. 286–7), undertaken at leisure, will improve both your coursework and your first-draft performance in exams. Similarly, the standards and protocols set out in the boxes on the following pages may seem appropriate only for coursework : but if accurate and exact reference is your established habit, you will find it can to a surprising degree be maintained even under time-pressure (and attracts examiners' favour). So I will add only that I have over the years seen many talented students sell themselves short by becoming significantly better readers than writers, and would therefore remind all students to practise their writing. Command of technical vocabulary in particular is never easy in crisp and readable prose, and must be consciously worked on ; but once sufficiently attained, it is a bedrock that will support all else.

Additional material on exams will occasionally be posted on the website.

The Presentation of Written Work

Main text should be double-spaced on A4 (UK) or quarto (US) paper, with margins of 1″/2.5 cm. Pages should be consistently numbered with arabic numerals in the centre of the footer. Titles of plays and books should be in italics (or with single underline[3]), and titles of texts that are items within a book within inverted commas—thus Shakespeare's *Sonnets* or Sonnets, but 'A Louer's Complaint'. If following the style of this book, the inverted commas round titles should be single whereas inverted commas round precise quotations should be double ; in all other cases they should be single, with double for quotations within quotations. The important point is to use the system chosen consistently.

Short quotations (< 2 lines of verse or 25–30 words of prose) should be "embedded in your text within double inverted commas" ; longer quotations, preceded by a colon :

> should be indented from both margins, single-spaced with an additional single space above and below without inverted commas around them.

Embedded quotations of verse should indicate lineation by a forward slash (/) with a space on either side ; indented quotations of verse (including verse-drama) should reproduce lineation ; that of prose need not be noted if there is no reason to do so. Unless your prose is very supple and accurate, it is inadvisable to wrap syntax around indented quotations ; begin a new sentence when you revert to your own voice.

All direct quotations must be absolutely accurate in words and punctuation. An obvious typo in the original can be corrected [within crotchets], or add [*sic*], meaning 'thus', to make clear it is not your typo. Any other changes you make—e.g. replacing a pronoun with a proper name—must be crotcheted. The only exceptions, ever, to this rule have been suspension marks and single or double forward slashes indicating line- and stanza-breaks, but many scholars now crotchet these as well ; crotcheted or not, you must use suspension marks if you omit word/s from a quotation ("Insomniac since four, hearing", or "Insomniac [. . .] hearing", but never "Insomniac hearing"), and you must indicate line- and stanza-breaks in embedded quotations.

The first time you quote from a source you must give a full reference in a foot- or endnote, using a superscript or parenthesised index—[1] or (1) ; notes are usually single-spaced. The most complete form is:

> Author, *Title* (Place of publication: Publisher, date), page reference.

Some style-manuals prescribe more limited forms (publishers are typically omitted) ; if in doubt the full form is safest. If there is an editor and no author as such, the editor's name replaces the author's and is followed by 'ed.' If there is both an author and an editor put the author before and the editor after the title :

> William Wordsworth, *Poetical Works*, ed. E. de Selincourt and H. Darbishire (5 vols, Oxford: Oxford University Press, 1940–9), IV. 279.

[3] An old printers' convention: single underline = *italics* ; double underline = SMALL CAPITALS; triple underline = LARGE CAPITALS ; wavy underline = **bold**.

In the page reference—IV. 279—the roman numeral indicates a volume, and the arabic page-number follows a full-stop : after a volume-number the abbreviation 'p(p).' is not required. If you are using a modern edition of an old work it is helpful to include the date of first publication before that of the edition :

> Robert Browning, *Men and Women* (1855; ed. J. W. Harper, London and Melbourne: Dent, 1975 [Everyman]), p. 87.

All necessary information is usually on the title- or copyright-pages ; as here, a series identity (Everyman) can be included at the end of the bibliographical parenthesis.

For an article in a periodical, the form is :

> Author, 'Title', *Name of Periodical*, volume-number (date): page reference.

If the periodical uses roman numerals for volumes so may you ; again, 'pp.' is omitted. For an essay in a collection the form is slightly different :

> Author, 'Title', in Editor, *Title* (Place: Publisher, date), page reference.

The plural 'eds' and 'vols' are contractions, not suspensions, and so take no following suspension-mark. An italicised title embedded in another italicised title reverts to roman type (*Browning's* Men and Women *: A Study*). Subsequent references to a source may be shortened to author and/or (short) title + page-reference and given in parenthesis immediately after a quotation—e.g. (Empson, p. 56), (*Men and Women*, p. 56). <u>Never</u> use a short title in assessable work unless you have previously given the reference in full.

When quoting repeatedly from the same source indicate in an initial note which edition you're using and follow each subsequent quotation with a parenthesised line or page reference, e.g. (ll. 23–4), (pp. 65–74).

If you have access to a scanner or the Web, consider photoquotations. For most texts they will not be needed, but if you are using a facsimile, for example, you should probably let your examiner see exactly what you see ; illustrations may also be useful. (Be aware, however, if you have a word-limit, that in computer word-counts an entire photoquotation will register as one word, and photoquoted text must be hand-counted.) The sources of photoquotations should be given as for any other quotation, and any reduction/enlargement specified.

Your bibliography should list in alphabetical order all works you quote or cite, and whatever other works you have substantially used. The form is the same as in foot- or endnotes, but place authors' initials or first names after their surnames to obtain neat alphabetical listing and use capitals for surnames. Bibliographical entries should be internally single-spaced, but have a space between each entry. It may help the appearance and clarity of bibliographies to use a hanging indent (where every line after the first is indented). If your bibliography is long (more than, say, 20 items) you may divide it into sections, usually 'Primary'/'Secondary' works.

Bibliographies are typically excluded from word-limits because they substantially duplicate data given in notes ; everything else, including all notes, captions, and quotations, is typically included, but <u>always</u> check a particular institution's rules.

Glossary and Index of Technical Terms

Page-references follow the entry or sub-entry in parenthesis.

abecedarian : arranged alphabetically, a-b-c-d . . . (95)

accelerated : of rhyme, occurring relatively more proximately than others in a given poem ; thus ll. 3–4 of limericks produce metrically accelerated rhyme, and couplets are accelerated by comparison with cross- or arch-rhyme. The opposite is delayed rhyme. (197)

accent : the emphasis or stress placed on a beat. (1)

accentual-syllabic : the kind of prosody principally used in English. (2)

accusative : in grammar the case for the object of a verb. (132)

acronym : a word formed from the initial letters of other words, as 'scuba' or 'snafu'. (231)

active : of an individual's vocabulary, that part which is actually used (222) ; in grammar, a mood, the opposite of passive. (263)

adjective : one of the 9 parts of speech, a word qualifying a noun. Most can be used *attributively* (the blue water) or *predicatively* (the water is blue) ; some inflect to indicate the *comparative* and *superlative* ('elder', 'eldest') ; a few agree with gender ('blond/e', 'naïf'/'naïve'). (225)

adverb : one of the 9 parts of speech, a word qualifying a verb, adjective, other adverb, or whole sentence. (225)

Alcaic : of an ode, of a particular and highly prescribed form ; largely dactylic, Alcaics are very rare in English. (54)

Aldine : of type, designed by Aldus Manutius (*c.*1450–1515). (115)

alexandrine : in English, an iambic hexameter ; in French a line of 12 beats, however metrically constituted, and the staple form (as iambic pentameter in English). (34, 48, 161–2)

alinéa : the convention by which a new item is given a new line, for example, in prose dialogue each new speaker. (81, 132)

alliteration : the repeated use of the same consonant/s in two or more proximate words. (165, 191, 202–3)

alliterative revival : a handy but inaccurate term for the mid–late fourteenth-century work of (especially) Langland and the Gawain-poet, distinguished from the 'London School' by alliterating hemistiches derived from OE verse and notably public political concerns. (166)

allusion : most generally, "a covert, passing, or indirect reference" (*Sh.OED*) ; in literature, usually an intentional but undeclared reference within a text to another text (the quotidian stuff of intertextuality) or to a historical event, person, belief etc. (226, 295)

ampersand : the mark '&', meaning 'and'. (113, 140)

amphibrach : a foot of three beats, the first and last unstressed, the middle stressed (uxu). (3, 4, 18, 28)

amphimacer : a foot of three beats, the first and last stressed, the middle unstressed (xux). (3, 4)

analytical : of a language, distributing meaning into many words, and hence dependent on prepositions and word-order, having no inflections etc. (2, 107)

anapæst, anapæstic : a foot of three beats, two unstressed and the last stressed (uux) ; the metre produced by such feet. (3, 4)

anaphora : a rhetorical figure involving the repetition of a word or phrase in successive units, typically *cola* in periods, clauses in sentences, sentences in paragraphs, and lines in verse ; sometimes specifically associated with the Psalms, where it is common. (200)

angled brackets : marked '⟨ ⟩' ; used in maths and for conjectural words in critical editions but rare in poetry. (122)

antibacchius : a foot of three beats, the first and second stressed, the last unstressed (xxu). (3)

antiphonal : 'sounded against', a/line/s responding to an/other/s ; originally exactly that, choric call-and-response within the liturgy, but by extension (i) a mode (composed or imposed) of verse-lines which creates or displays a bipolar pattern (not a simple sequence, as in blank verse), and (ii) a quality of voice associated with such lines as protesting or refusing a dominant or demanding position. (158–60)

Antiquarian : a proposed 'school' of eighteenth-century English literature, encompassing such phenomena as Augustan Chaucerianism, the Ossian and Rowley forgeries, and early Romantic medievalism. (294)

antispast : a foot of four beats, the first and fourth unstressed, the second and third stressed (uxxu). (3)

antistrophe : (or counter-turn), the second stanza of a Pindaric ode. (54)

apestail : the mark '@', meaning 'at' or 'at . . . each'. (113, 140)

apostrophe : the mark ', used with or without 's' to indicate possession (the genitive case), or the elision of a letter. (3, 132–3)

archaism : the deliberate use of outmoded or obsolete diction. (231–2)

arch-rhyme : mirror symmetry, as *abba* ; also called *chiasmic rhyme* (44)

area : a term promoted in American poetics by W. C. Williams to reject an implicitly narrow, unyielding, hidebound, and rigidly sequential quality associated with neoclassicism ; lines, poems, poetic practices, and poets' lives may all be recharacterised as areas rather than progressions. (169–70)

article : one of the 9 parts of speech, the definite article 'the' + indefinite articles 'a' + 'an'. (225)

ascender : see *descender*.

ash : the Anglo-Saxon ligature 'æ'. (113, 165)

assonance : the repeated use of the same vowel/s in two or more proximate words. (202–3)

asterisk : a *signe de renvoi*, marked '*'(132, 139)

Augustan : of literature, that of the later-seventeenth and first half of the eighteenth centuries. The boundaries are ragged, but in schemata 'Augustan' follows 'Restoration' and is followed (after a gap) by 'Romantic'. In self-congratulatory use before 1700, the term derives from the 'Golden Age' of Roman literature during the reign of Augustus (27 BCE–14 CE) and is intrinsically imperialistic ; the most obvious formal feature of Augustan poetry is the prevalence of closed heroic couplets. (87, 294)

authority : the provenance of a text ; specifically, the extent to which it embodies, or may be supposed to embody, the creative intent of its author free from scribal, compositorial, or editorial interference ; a quality claimed by editors as peculiar to their own editions. (92)

autograph : of manuscripts, in the author's (as distinct from a scribal) hand. (14, 92)

autorhyme : a word rhymed with itself (my coinage) ; sometimes called 'null' rhyme. (191, 195–6)

bacchius : a foot of three beats, the first unstressed and the last two stressed (uxx). (3)

ballad : a narrative poem, commonly of traditional origin, often in quatrains with refrain ; *literary* and *folk* ballads are now distinguished. (9, 54–7)

ballade : a form of poem (or song) used by troubadours, and in medieval Romance-language and English poetry a type of lyric with specified repetitions ; see *ro(u)ndeau, ro(u)ndel, roundelay*. Their typical stanza-forms are sometimes referred to as 'ballade stanzas'. (55)

ballad-stanza : see *common metre*.

bardolatry : the worship of Shakespeare. (290)

BBC English : used to denote a combination of Queen's (or King's) English with a plummy or Home Counties accent, such as BBC newsreaders used to have, particularly on the radio. (193)

BCE : Before Common Era, a non-denominational equivalent of BC [Before Christ]. (54)

beat : a word or syllable/s bearing stress (x) or unstress (u). (1–2)

Beats : an abbreviation for 'the Beat Generation' designating an influential group of mainly West-Coast American writers, including Ginsberg, Kerouac, Burroughs, and Corso, who matured in the 1950s and were gurus to the 1960s. The San Francisco poets (including Snyder and Ferlinghetti) may also be meant. (294)

Bembine : of type, designed by Pietro Bembo (1470–1547). (115)

bibliographical code : in McGann's theorization of text, everything a *lexical code* (text) acquires when given material form, from fount-size and identity to binding and price. (xvii, 96, 110)

black letter : the proper name of the old, gothic-style fount of type ; replaced as a basic fount by roman and italic in the late sixteenth century, it is now used mostly for formal invitations and mock-antique commercialism. (82, 121)

blank : of a poem, stanza or other unit, unrhymed (36) ; of physical lines, empty of type. (100) ; of type, uninked.

blank verse : unrhymed iambic pentameter. (36–8, 117–20, 153–8)

Bloomsbury : a tag for the loosely affiliated writers and intellectuals living in that area of London around 1914–18, most notably the Woolfs, Strachey, Keynes, and Forster. (294)

bob-lines/bobs : in a given stanza form, a line or lines which are markedly shorter than the others. (46, 160–1)

book : in longer poems, a constituent section marked by a heading ; cf. *canto, chapter*. (61)

border : rules or decoration around a word, paragraph, or page. (135, 138)

bowdlerise : to cut or replace with euphemisms anything thought 'improper' ; an eponym from Thomas Bowdler (1754–1825), editor of the *Family Shakespeare* (1818). (236)

bra : mathematical term for an opening bracket. (122)

braces : curly brackets, marked '{ }' ; a single brace is conventionally used to indicate a triplet within couplet-rhyme. (41, 122)

brackets : a generic term covering angle-brackets, braces, crotchets, and lunulae ; all may be used singly, but crotchets and lunulae normally pair to create parentheses isolating a word or phrase. (122–7)

broadsheet : of printed materials, on a paper of a particular size, usually implying that it has not been folded (e.g. a poster). (88, 111)

broken crotchets : incomplete 'square' brackets, marked '⌈⌉'. (123)

broken-rhyme : a word split between lines to facilitate a rhyme, as 'rent'/'vent-[/] ricle'. (196–7)

bucolics : poems (primarily classical) of well-lubricated cheer, or outright drunkenness. (67)

burden : or refrain ; a line or lines that are repeated. (52)

butcher's apostrophe : one that is misapplied, typically to a simple plural ; more generally, the rash of such apostrophes generated by ignorance of their conventional uses. (133)

cadence : a fall, in tone, pitch, etc. (8)

caesura/e : the medial pause/s in a line ; if there is no punctuation it will tend not to occur in lines shorter than a tetrameter, and to occur approximately centrally in tetrametric or longer lines ; it may be forced towards the beginning or the end of a line by punctuation. (128, 155–8)

calypso : a Trinidadian (then generally West Indian) popular form resembling a ballad in public conception, social or political commentary, and festival or occasional performance. Connections with the nymph who detained Ulysses, or with *calapé* (Central American Spanish, 'a fricassee of turtle-meat in the shell'), are suspected, but etymology is unknown. (57–8)

camera-ready copy : hard copy (or its exact e-files) that can be used as a master in photographic printing-processes. (82)

canon : originally the 'authorised' books of the bible, as distinct from the apocrypha ; more generally, the body of work that is at any given time (and in a specified culture) taught and valorised. (12)

canto : a numbered section into which longer poems are commonly divided ; cf. *book, chapter*. (61)

***canzone, canzoni* :** an Italian Renaissance form of 65 lines comprising five douzaines and a pentain envoi using only five end-words ; in the Dantean variant preferred in English, each douzaine rhymes *abaacaaddaee* and each end-word must serve in turn as each rhyme-letter. (48, 53–4)

Caroline : of literature, dating to the reign of Charles I (1625–49). (293)

catalectic : of a line, missing one or more beats. (7)

catchword : the first word or syllable of a page printed below the last word of the previous page, as a courtesy to readers(-aloud). (92)

caudate sonnet : one with a 'tail', typically of one or more tercets. (49)

Cavalier : of literature, applied to the poetry of Thomas Carew (1594–1640), Richard Lovelace (1618–57/8), and Sir John Suckling, all courtiers to Charles I and leading Royalists during the Civil War ; Robert Herrick, though never a courtier, is also usually labelled as a 'Cavalier poet'. (293)

CE : or Common Era, a non-denominational equivalent of AD [Anno Domini]. (54)

chain-rhyme : systematic carrying-over from one stanza or component unit of form to the next of one or more rhyme-sounds, as in *terza rima* and Spenserian sonnets. (42, 49, 204)

chiasmus, chiasmic : a 'diagonal', or mirror-symmetrical, arrangement of words, clauses etc.; of rhyme, arch-rhymed. (44, 113)

children's verse : light verse written for (not by) children. (56)

choriamb : a foot of four beats, the first and fourth stressed, the second and third unstressed (xuux). (3)

cinquain : properly, in English, a syllabic form invented by Adelaide Crapsey, *a2b4c6d8e2* ; in older French and some modern English use, any pentain. (45)

clause : a word with no fully agreed definition, but used to mean units of syntax larger than a word or phrase and smaller than a sentence. It is possible however for a sentence to have only one clause. *Sub-*, *relative,* and *main* clauses are (among others) distinguished. (156, 264)

clerihew : a quatrain of two couplets (*aabb*), preferably with the couplets of unequal length, and possibly with each line of a different length ; the first line is usually someone's name ; so called after its inventor, Edmund Clerihew Bentley (1875–1956). (41)

closed : of a couplet, with the second line end-stopped (38) ; of form, prescribed.

codex, codices : the bound form of the book, as distinct from scrolls. (xiv, 110)

coinage : of a word, a neologism or nonce-word ; often used possessively, to indicate the coiner. Implicitly, new words are 'struck' or 'minted' rather than 'made' or 'invented'. (xxiv, 223, 231)

colash : a *combinate-mark*, ':—'. (138)

colon/s : the second-heaviest stop, marked ':' ; conventionally implies a completion of the immediate sense and a logical or dependent relationship between *cola*. (115)

colon, cola **:** the part(s) of a sentence between colons, and/or between a colon and a full-stop. (115, 119, 265–7)

combinate-marks : those combining a dash with another mark ; the periodash, colash, semi-colash, commash, exclamation-markash, question-markash, and lunulashes are recognised, but others may be found or created. (114, 138–9)

comedy, comic : a classical mode, comedies dealt with ordinary people, social life, and marriage ; applied to verse, 'comic' has tended to the much broader meaning of 'humorous'. (66)

comma/s **:** the fourth and lightest stop, marked ',' ; conventionally implies the completion of a sub-clause or clause ; used in pairs to create parentheses. (116–17)

comma/ta : part/s into which a period (or smaller unit of syntax) is divided by commas. (116–17)

commash : a combinate-mark, ',—'. (138)

comma-splice : the improper use of a comma to join clauses where a semicolon or comma + conjunction (and, for, etc.) are required ; the result is 'parataxis', and the offending clauses 'paratactic'. (117)

common metre : also ballad-metre, or *ballad-stanza ;* an iambic quatrain of the form *a8b6c8b6*. (43)

Commonwealth : of literature, (i) that produced during the interregnum of 1649–60, or (ii) since 1945, those of the nations of the British Commonwealth. (294)

complaint : (or female complaint) a poem of protest and lament, typically at amorous disappointment, betrayal, or desertion ; in the decades around 1600 deeply caught up with the *epyllion* and sonnet-sequence, not least in Shakespeare. (54, 59–60)

composition : in hand-press printing the process of assembling the individual pieces of type, including inter-word spaces, in the correct order. (96, 109)

concrete poem/poetry : see *shape-poem*.

confessional/ist : of poetry or verse, apparently written *in propria persona*, with an 'I' unequivocally designating the real poet ; as a movement, Confessionalism was strongest in the mid-twentieth century, with Lowell, Berryman, early Snodgrass, and Plath. (169)

conjunction : one of the 9 parts of speech, a word co-ordinating ('and', 'but', 'or') or subordinating ('if', 'although', 'because') two (groups of) words ; simple ('if') and compound ('provided that') conjunctions are distinguished. (225)

contraction : a word shortened by medial elision, as 'can't' for 'cannot'. (132)

copula : in grammar (and logic) a word joining subject and predicate in a proposition, typically one or another form of 'to be' or 'to have'. (162)

copy-text : in editing, the 'text' chosen as an exemplar for a new edition, to be followed unless specifically emended ; 'text' is usually taken to exclude *bibliographical codes*, whether it would be possible to follow them or not. (92)

corpus, corpora : in linguistics and lexicography, a recorded body of words and/or phrases in a given language which can be used for reference and research ; now usually a computer-generated and searchable database. (222)

counter-semantic rhyme : between words with opposite or antagonistic meanings, as 'tall/small' or 'fear/leer'. (206)

counter-turn : another name for the antistrophe of a Pindaric ode. (54)

country-house poem : primarily, one of a substantial group of seventeenth-century poems describing and usually lauding a landowning patron's house and grounds, but extending to later poems centrally featuring such houses and grounds. (54, 60–1)

couplet : a stanza or unit of two lines, usually rhyming, often used terminally to summarize or moralise ; a very popular form in the eighteenth century. (38–41)

couplet enjambment : (or external enjambment) that between successive couplets. (38)

couplet-rhyme : a rhyme scheme in couplets, as *aabb*. (44)

creole : (from Spanish *criollo*, a slave born in slavery ; ultimately probably from Latin *creare*, to create) a noun and adjective for people, cultures and languages of mixed European and/or African and/or Amerindian heritage ; of a language the word typically implies 'formerly a pidgin tongue, now the sole or native language'. It is now sometimes spelled 'kweyol'. See also *nation language, patois*. (227)

cross-rhyme : alternating double-rhymes, as *abab*. (43)

crotchets : square brackets, marked '[ ]' ; conventionally used to distinguish editorial comments and emendations from authorial prose. (9, 122–3, 147)

curly : of brackets, a common term for braces. (122)

curtal sonnet : an abbreviation of the form devised by Hopkins, comprising a sestet and 4½-line quatrain. (49)

dactyl, dactylic : a foot of three beats, the first stressed, the second and third unstressed (xuu) ; the metre produced by such feet. (3, 28)

dagger : see *obelus*.

dash : a rule and variety of comma, marked '—'; conventionally used, in script, typescript, and word-processing (though not in print) singly with a space on either side, simultaneously to distinguish and link a sequence of clauses, and in pairs to create parentheses. (116, 135, 136–7)

decorum : (from Latin *decorus*, seemly) appropriateness, consistency, and civility of register, style, etc. in artistic compositions ; the opposite is indecorum. (232, 239)

degree-sign : a *signe de renvoi*, marked '°'. (139)

deictic : of punctuation, used to emphasize a word or phrase ; distinguished from *spatial, elocutionary*, and *syntactic* punctuation. (84, 106, 121)

delayed : of rhyme, occurring relatively more distantly than others in a given poem ; thus the cross-rhymes of Shakespearian sonnets are delayed by comparison with the couplet. The opposite is accelerated rhyme. (197) Of a verb, withheld from its 'normal' place in the syntax to fall in a significant formal position (as the end of a sentence or line). (269)

demotic : (Greek, 'popular') of a word, register, or style, of the common people, often with an implication of vulgarity. (234)

descender : that part of a letter below the line, as the tails of 'g', 'y' etc. : the part above the x-height, as in 'd', 'b' etc., is the *ascender*. (113)

diacritical mark/ing/s : signs attached to a letter to vary its value, such as the diaeresis, macron, breve etc. (82)

dialect : now usually a regional form of a dominant language, implying different words and/or syntax rather than simply accent. (222, 227–8)

diamb : a foot of four beats, the first and third unstressed, the second and forth stressed (uxux). (3)

diction : the choice of words (including the reasons for and consequences at that choice). (222)

dimeter : a line of two feet. (4)

diple : a medieval nota from which inverted commas and *guillemets* subsequently developed. (130)

dis/aggregators : the family of brackets, slashes, and inverted commas, which group or isolate a/word/s. (109, 122–32)

discourse : here, the diction of a particular poem, the relations between the words it actually uses (a specialised use of an ambiguous and polysemic term). (223)

display : the presentation or emphasis of elements by layout. (81, 83)

dispondee : a foot of four beats, all stressed (xxxx). (3)

distinguishing : of a foot, type-face, or fount, different from that normally used. (5)

ditrochee : a foot of four beats, the first and third stressed, the second and fourth unstressed (xuxu). (3)

***donnée* :** the given image, fact, etc. from which a poem or other work proceeds. (214, 322)

douzaine : a stanza of twelve lines. (48, 53)

draft : a working version of a poem still being composed or revised. (88)

dramatic monologue : a poem cast as a speech by a particular (historical or imaginary) person, usually to a specific auditor. The form is particularly associated with Browning and Tennyson, but remained popular throughout the twentieth century. (54, 57–8, 208–9)

drop-cap[ital]. : an initial letter in a larger fount that 'drops' below its own line. (3)

duct : of a hand, the typical manner in which characters follow one another. (100)

duple : of a foot, having two beats ; the rhythm produced by such feet. (7)

Early Modern : of the period 1500–1700. (294)

echo verse : that in which the last syllables/s of (particular) lines are repeated as an echo, often with a shifted or changed meaning. (160)

eclogue : poems of pleasant places, usually classical (Virgil's are famous) but associated with Renaissance pastoral. (67)

écriture féminine : in some feminist theory, language that is gendered feminine and written from the female body. (340)

eddress : my coinage for e-mail addresses, name@domain.functiontag.country. (140)

Edwardian : in literature, usually of the reign of Edward VII (1901–10), and typically with the double-implication of a post-Victorian relaxation and a last, pre-war ignorance and carelessness of impending catastrophe. (293)

effusion : a form wholly without prescription, ideally spontaneous. (55)

eisthesis : the indentation of a line or lines by one or more spaces from the left margin. (82–4)

ekthesis : the setting of a line or lines hard to the left margin. (82)

elegy : a poem (or other composition) mourning a death or other loss. (66–7)

elision : omission, as of one or more letters from a word (usually indicated with an apostrophe) ; the verb is 'to elide'. (2, 132)

ellipsis : the omission of a word or words, and the indication of such omission with three *suspension-marks*, '. . .'. (123, 132, 133–4, 147)

elocutionary : of punctuation, indicating speech-derived pauses ; distinguished from *spatial, deictic* and *syntactic* punctuation. (106)

embedded : of quotations, designated by inverted commas within continuous prose (153) ; of rhyme, between a word and part of another word, as 'pit/hospitality' (197).

emblem : a small picture, usually a woodcut, with an accompanying poem ; often moral or allegorical, emblems were in vogue and collected in emblem books between the later-sixteenth century and the Civil War. (93–4)

emoticon : a tonal indicator resembling a face created with punctuation-marks. (121–2)

emphatic : of punctuation, deictic. (106)

em-rule : in printing,—, a rule as long as a lower-case 'm' ; often used for the dash. (135, 136)

enclitic : of apostrophes, demoting a contracted word into part of another word, as 'not' in 'weren't'. (133)

end-note : one appearing at the end of the text ; distinguished from the *footnote*. (140–1)

end-rhyme : between words ending lines. (190)

end-stopped : of a line or stanza, having a terminal mark of punctuation. (34, 153)

enjamb/ed, enjambment : of lines, couplets, or stanzas, not end-stopped, with sense and/or syntax continuing into the next line, couplet, or stanza. (34, 153)

en-rule : in printing, a rule (–) as long as a lower-case 'n' ; slightly longer than the hyphen and used for dates and page-ranges etc. (9–13, London–Birmingham train). (136)

envoi : a shorter terminal stanza, such as the tercet in villanelles or pentain in *canzoni*. (52)

e-page : my coinage for the archetype of pages designed to be read on screen and incorporating features that cannot be supported in print. See also *metal page*. (xv)

epic : a classical mode, epics are long narrative poems usually dealing with the heroic or martial exploits of a person, tribe, or race, and are associated with nation-founding scale. Several classical epic devices, including the *epic catalogue*, *epic simile*, and beginning *in medias res*, commonly serve as touchstones in modern epics. There are diminutive forms, notably the mock-epic and 'chamber-epic', and a quite distinct Brechtian use of epic to designate a dramaturgical approach and theatrical mode of production. (66)

epic catalogue : a formal (as much as long) catalogue of something, typically intended (in epic as elsewhere) enumeratively to express a large number or high degree. The seminal example is Homer's 300+ line catalogue of ships and commanders in book II of the *Iliad*. (270)

epic simile : one endowing a subject with glory and/or significance by comparing it (usually at elaborate and digressive length) to an incident, person, or topos from classical epic ; a favourite resource of Milton's in *Paradise Lost*. (270)

epigraph : a short motto or quotation prefixed to a text. (82)

epithalamion : a poem celebrating a wedding. (54)

epitrite : a foot of four beats, only one unstressed ; called first (uxxx), second (xuxx), third (xxux), and fourth (xxxu) epitrites according to the position of the unstressed beat. (3)

epode : (or stand) the third and final stanza of a Pindaric Ode. (54)

epyllion : (or 'minor epic' or 'Ovidian verse') a narrative poem of some length, usually telling an Ovidian story : the plural is *epyllia*. (54, 59–60, 66)

eth : the Anglo-Saxon letter **Đ, ð** (= voiced *th*). (113, 165)

etymology : the derivation and history of a particular word, or the general study of how words evolve. (222)

euphemism : a word used as a (supposedly) polite substitute, as 'little boys' room' for 'toilet' or 'enhanced interrogative techniques' for 'torture'. (236)

Euphuism, Euphuistic : (in) the manner of Lyly's *Euphues* (1578) ; excessively flowery, hyper-Ciceronian, preening etc. (cf. Wilde's Aestheticism). (115)

exclamation-mark : a tonal indicator, usually of rising pitch and volume, used (instead of a full-stop) to indicate exclamations, marked '!' ; may be used both medially and terminally. (120–1)

exclamation-markash : a *combinate-mark*, '!—'. (138)

expressionist : of criticism, believing the meaning of a text to express and be determined by the author's intentions. (The term has other meanings in art history and theatre studies.) (315–16)

external : of enjambment, between successive couplets. (38)

eye-rhyme : (or printers' rhyme) between words which, having endings spelt identically, look as if they rhyme, but are not so pronounced, as 'though/rough'. (192)

face : of a type, a particular appearance of the letters and numbers, as roman or *italic* ; thus any given fount of type will have many faces. (5, 82)

facing : of pages, in the same opening. (90)

fair copy : a carefully copied text without blots or corrections etc. (97)

falling rhythm : that produced by feet with unstressed beats following stressed beats. (6–7)

female : of the female sex. (339)

feminine : the aspect of gender roles reflecting cultural definitions of women (339) ; of an ending, with one or more unstressed hypermetrical beats (7) ; of a rhyme, unstressed (191).

feminism/s : collective term for beliefs and action intended to assert the rights of women, and to liberate them from oppression by men and the patriarchy. (337–40)

fit : an archaic equivalent of *canto*, perhaps from Old Norse or German words meaning a hem or piece of marker-yarn ; in regular use until Byron's day, it is now specifically and comically associated with Carroll's *The Hunting of the Snark*, subtitled *An Agony in Eight Fits*. (61)

foliation : the division of a book into leaves (back-to-back pages) ; in early editions foliation rather than pagination may be used for references, typically in the form [letter] + [number] + [r/v], as 'B2^{r}', indicating gathering B, leaf 2, recto. (110)

folk : of a ballad, traditional and of popular origin. (55)

font : see *fount*.

foot : a prosodic unit of stressed and/or unstressed beats, the component of a line. (3)

footnote : one appearing at the bottom of a page ; distinguished from an *end-note*. (140–1)

foul papers : an author's drafts with revisions etc., the precursor of fair copy. (97)

found : of text or other elements of an art-work, quoted, having been seen or otherwise encountered by chance ; typical sources include advertising text, public signs, reported speeches etc. ; not usually used of deliberate literary quotation. (174)

fount : (or in the USA, 'font') of type, a particular design of the letters and numbers ; each fount will comprise designs for each character in a number of faces. (5, 82)

fourteeners : couplets in iambic heptameter. (40, 162)

free rhyme : deployed without specific interlinear pattern ; free end-rhyme is also sometimes called 'occasional' or 'random' rhyme. (197–8)

free verse : poetry in which the metre varies. (10)

full-rhyme : (or *perfect rhyme*) between words whose last stressed vowel and all following sounds are identical. (190, 191)

full-stop : (or in the USA, *period*) the heaviest stop, marked '.' ; conventionally required at the end of a period or sentence. (112, 114)

Gawain-poet : the usual term for the anonymous master believed to have written the four poems preserved in MS Bodley Cotton Nero A.x, *Sir Gawayne and the Grene Knyght, Clenene∬e, Patience*, and *Pearl*. (166)

gender : cultural femininity and masculinity, as distinct from biological femaleness and maleness. (339)

genitive : in grammar the case for possession and origin. (132)

genre : in literary use, a late-nineteenth-century coinage now covering all (supposed) methods of distinguishing and grouping (literary) forms, from classical modes to modern thematic anthologising ; more practically, a collective noun for the various sets of conventional or typical expectations readers (or other consumers of art) learn to have ; cf. 'twist'. Coherent theories of poetic genre must partly discount the functions of expectation in prosody. (65–6)

Georgian : of literature (as very much distinct from architecture), usually with reference to a group of writers, mostly poets, published by Edward Marsh in successive volumes called *The Georgian Anthology* issued between 1912 and 1921 ; implicitly indicating a pastoralism and nostalgia made irrelevant by the First World War and Modernism. (293)

georgic : poems of instruction, usually classical (Virgil's are famous) ; before Addison's essay 'On the Georgic' (1697) the dominant theme in classical georgics, lauding simple country living, was often taken as the defining element, and georgics remain critically associated with pastoral (from which Addison specifically distinguished them). (67)

Germanic : of languages, belonging to a particular group of Indo-European languages, including modern German and Dutch, and Old English ; of modern English words, deriving from one of these languages. (223–5)

grammar : the rules governing the cases of words and the 'permissible' syntax of any given language. (263)

great colon : a larger-fount colon used by Hopkins in prosodic notation. (115)

***guillemets* :** the French equivalent of inverted commas, marked '« »'. (130)

gutter : in books, the inside of the spine, between facing pages ; in graphic novels and comics, the space between sequential panels. (92)

haiku : a Japanese form, of three lines, the first and last of five syllables, the second of seven, ideally with a turn between the first and second, or second and third lines ; see *renga* (42)

half-metre : a single-rhymed quatrain *(abcb)* in iambic trimeter ; see also *common, long,* and *short metre*. (43)

half-rhyme : (or near or slant rhyme) between words whose last stressed vowel or all following sounds are identical, but not both ; includes vowel- and pararhyme. (190, 191–2)

hand : of an individual, their characteristic handwriting. (84, 99)

hanging indent : a paragraph-layout in which all lines after the first are indented. (180)

Hanoverian : of literature, written under a Hanoverian monarch (Georges I, 1714–27 ; II, 1727–60 ; III, 1760–1820 ; and IV, 1820–30 ; William IV, 1830–37 ; Victoria, 1837–1901). (293)

***hapax legomenon* :** (Greek, 'a thing said once') a word or expression found only once in the surviving records of a language, and which is therefore *de facto* untranslatable. The plural is *hapax legomena*. (229)

hemistich : a half-line, used in pairs typically bound by alliteration and/or rhythm ; verse in such lines is hemistichic. (114, 165–6)

heptameter : a line of seven feet. (4)

heptet : a stanza of seven lines. (46)

heroic : of a form, in iambic pentameter. (33, 37, 158)

heterometric : of stanzas, with lines of varying length. (36, 40)

hexameter : a line of six feet. (4, 34)

***Historikerstreit* :** German, 'the battle of historians' ; a sharp debate beginning in 1986–7 initially about whether it was acceptable to argue that the story of the Wehrmacht's defence of Germany's Eastern Front in 1944–5 deserved to be told as a tragedy. The principal figures involved were Ernst Nolte, Andreas Hillgruber, and Jürgen Habermas. (291)

homographs : words with different meanings spelt identically. (191)

homophones : words with different meanings pronounced identically. (191)

Horatian : of an ode, in a shortish but repeated unit of form. (54–5)

house style : the set of printing conventions observed by a given publishing house. (130)

hudibrastic : of rhyme, comically strained or foolish, often because mosaic ; the term derives from Samuel Butler's (1613–80) long comic poem *Hudibras* (1663–80). (191)

Humanism : the great pan-European cultural movement of the fourteenth to seventeenth centuries, associated with the Renaissance rediscovery and transmission northwards from Italy of classical texts, artwork, and thought ; derived from the students of *litterae humaniores*, 'more humane letters', classical literary, political, and historical writing, as distinct from the theological disputes of medieval Scholasticism. (110, 117)

humorous verse : a synonym for light and comic verse. (66)

hyperbeats : those in a line which are surplus to the metre ; *stressed* and *unstressed* hyperbeats are politically corrected *masculine* and *feminine* endings. (7)

hypermetric : of a line in a given metre, with one or more hyperbeats. (7)

hyphen : used to join two words into one, or to join the parts of a word split between lines, marked '-'. (135–6)

iamb, iambic : a foot of two beats, an unstressed followed by a stressed (ux) ; the metre produced by such feet. (3, 4)

iconicity : here, the capacity of a mark, letter, or word to become an icon, as lunulae of lips, O of a mouth etc. (113–14)

ictus : the stressed beat of a foot ; the plural is ictūs (ik-toos). (3)

identical rhyme : *rime riche.* (191)

idiom : generally, a language or dialect, the tongue and expressions of an area or group ; most specifically, a turn of phrase etc. habitual to native speakers but whose meaning is not readily predictable from the meanings of its constituent words (go get 'em, tiger ; well I never). (227)

Imagists : a school of poetry in the 1910s–1920s, advocating poetry written in short lines each containing a clear image ; Pound and H.D. were leading members. (170)

imperfect rhyme : all kinds other than *rime riche* and full-rhyme. (191–2)

imposition : in hand-press printing the process of arranging the composed type on the bed of the press ; decisions about leading, ornaments, running-heads, etc. are involved, and two or more pages will have to be imposed together in any book or pamphlet format. (96, 110)

in-house style : an alternative for 'house style'. (130)

indecorum : see *decorum.*

indentation : the setting of a line or lines in from the left margin by one or more spaces. (82)

indented quotations : those set off as distinct paragraphs, typically by indentation and/or a smaller fount + space above and below. (153)

index : in printing (as well as the usual sense of a listing of subjects in a book with page references), a numeral or other *signe de renvoi* used to indicate a footnote : the plural is indices. (139)

initial : at or near the beginning of lines, stanzas, etc. ; of rhyme, between words beginning lines (191, 200–1).

inkhorn terms : a hostile Renaissance epithet for (over-)learned coinages, usually from Greek or Latin. (255)

inscribe, inscription : here, the process by which the writer includes him- or herself as an individual within his or her writing. In this sense inscription used to be proscribed in practical criticism, but (used judiciously) is now encouraged. (341–2)

intentional fallacy : the erroneous belief that the meaning of an artwork can be limited by the intent of its creator/s. (316)

intentional-fallacy fallacy : the erroneous belief that the intention of artists is irrelevant to the meaning of their work (i.e. that the intentional fallacy is to believe intention relevant). (316)

interjection : one of the 9 parts of speech, an exclamation or other word grammatically independent of the sentence in which it occurs. (225)

internal : of enjambment, between the first and second lines of a couplet (38) ; of rhyme, within a line, between two medial or a medial and the end-word, or between medial + medial or medial + end-words in different lines ; includes leonine rhyme (74, 198–202).

intertextuality : generally, the relations between texts ; more specifically, the aspects of a given text which derive meaning from relations with an/other text/s. (295–6)

intransitive : of a verb, not requiring an object. (112)

inverted : of a foot, the reverse of that normally used in a given line. (5)

inverted commas : one of the dis/aggregators, used to indicate direct speech and quotations, marked " " or ″ ″ ; may also be single (' ', ′ ′) ; as *scare quotes* indicate a suspension of sense, or distrust of a word. Conventions of use vary historically and culturally ; the modern English set of conventions dates only from 1857. (109, 130–2)

ionic (a) majore : a foot of four beats, the first two stressed, the last two unstressed (xxuu). (3)

ionic (a) minore : a foot of four beats, the first two unstressed, the last two stressed (uuxx). (3)

isometric : of stanzas, with lines of constant length. (36)

italic : of a fount, with angled characters (such as *these*). (xxiv, 82)

Jacobean : of literature, dating to the reign of James VI and I (1603–25) ; especially with reference to drama, there is often a contrast with Elizabethan implying greater darkness, more complex and unpleasant violence, and decadence from the 'golden' 1580s–90s. (293)

Jacobethan : a portmanteau of Elizabethan and Jacobean, hence, strictly, of the period 1558–1625, but in use often subsuming Caroline (1625–49). (36, 293)

jot : the dot forming the upper part of lower-case 'i' and 'j' ; a proverbially small thing, as in 'jot or tittle'. (113)

justified : of text and margins, aligned straight up and down. (82)

ket : mathematical term for a closing bracket. (122)

King's English : see *Queen's English*.

L=A=N=G=U=A=G=E poetry : a highly theorised poetics and method of poetic composition that emerged in New York and San Francisco in the early 1970s. (114, 169, 276)

leading : the amount of white space left between lines, stanzas, or other units of form, and in the margins. (86)

leaf : a single sheet of paper ; one recto, one verso. (90)

lemma/ta : short quotations (originally biblical) presented for exegesis in another text. (123–4, 130)

leonine rhyme : between the word preceding the cæsura and the end-word of the same line. (102, 198–9)

lexical code : in McGann's theorisation of text, the alphanumeric string + punctuation constituting a text in the abstract, lacking *bibliographical codes*. (96, 110)

lexical set : any set of words specified by a given criterion. (223)

lexicon : the vocabulary of a particular trade, activity, or profession. (xxiv, 245)

liberal : of feminisms, here used to designate those which are in theory willing to co-operate with men. (339)

ligature : tied letters, as æ, ﬁ, ﬂ etc. (113)

light verse : a synonym for *humorous* and comic verse. (66)

limerick : an anapæstic pentain, of the form *a9a9b6b6a9* ; one or more lines are commonly catalectic. (8, 45, 76)

line : a single sequence of characters read from left to right. (2, 153)

lineation : the organization of a poem into lines. (81, 153)

line-break : the turn of one line into the next ; notated as '/' (99, 153)

literary : of a ballad, composed by a known author, often of recent date. (55)

***littera/e notabilior/es* :** 'more noticeable letter/s' ; a generic term for enlarged *minuscule*, *majuscule*, and *upper-case* forms. (100, 117)

London School : in Ricardian poetry, Chaucer and Gower as distinct from the 'alliterative revivalists'. (166)

long five : my coinage for an iambic pentain, of the form *a8b8a8b8b10*. (45)

long metre : a single-rhymed quatrain (*abcb*) in iambic tetrameter ; see also *common*, *half-*, and *short metre*. (43)

long-s : a distinct form of the letter, 'ſ', used initially and medially until the mid–late eighteenth century ; 's' was used terminally, and the upper-case form was always 'S'. (xvi, 250)

lower-case : of letters, not capitals or small capitals, small. (5, 81)

lunula/e : round brackets, marked '( )' ; historically used in many conventions, including the indication of stage-directions, attributions of speech, comparisons, quotations, *sententiae*, and other cruces of argument ; commonly used to indicate both subordination and emphasis ; invented by Colluccio Salutati (1331–1406) *c.*1399. (114, 123–7, 132, 146)

lunulash/es : the *combinate-mark/s* '—(' and ')—'. (138)

lyric : a classical mode, lyrics were at first musically accompanied ; the term now covers most short, non-narrative, non-dramatic verse. (55, 66)

macron : a bar placed over a vowel, usually to lengthen its sound (ū = oo). The same mark serves as a *tittle*, indicating omitted nasals. (5, 82)

madrigal : a short lyric, originally pastoral and maternal, typically set to music for several voices ; a very popular Tudor form. (54)

main clause/s : those dealing directly with or continuing the principal action of a sentence ; distinguished from sub-clauses. (267)

majuscule : in handwriting, a capital ('upper-case') letter or equivalent. (100)

male : of the male sex. (339)

manuscript : a handwritten document ; abbreviated to MS/S. (14, 90)

marbled : of paper, multicoloured, typically in finely detailed whorls and traceries of contrasting colours ; marbled paper is used decoratively, but there is a famous marbled page within the text of Sterne's *Tristram Shandy*. (64)

marginalium, -ia : a portion of text placed in the margin (of another text). (141)

masculine : the aspect of gender roles reflecting cultural definitions of men (339) ; of an ending, with one or more stressed hypermetrical beats (7) ; of a rhyme, stressed (191).

masculinism : an emergent set of beliefs and actions intended to liberate men from oppression by other men, particularly peer pressure, bullying, and the patriarchal imposition of emotionally repressive gender stereotyping. (339)

medial : at or near the middle of lines, stanzas, etc. ; of rhyme, between medial words in successive lines. (191, 199–200)

Meredithian : of sonnets, having 16 lines in the rhyme scheme *abab cdcd efef ghgh*. (49)

metal page : my coinage for the archetype, at a given time or in general, of pages printed by metal type ; usually with reference to the typographical and/or design limits of such pages. (xiv, 82, 122)

Metaphysical : of poetry, that of the later-sixteenth and first half of the seventeenth centuries ; characterised (and in Dr Johnson's hostile use, weakened) by complex stanza forms and arguments, and by elaborate comparisons (or conceits). (294)

metonymy : a rhetorical figure in which an attribute of something is substituted for the thing itself (as 'the stage' for 'the acting profession'). (275)

metre : the rhythmic pattern of beats. (3)

Middle English : the English language of the years 1066–*c.*1500. (165)

minuscule : in handwriting, a small ('lower-case') letter or equivalent. (xvi, 100)

***mise-en-écran* :** the actual layout of a given poem (or prose text) on a given screen. (82)

***mise-en-page* :** the actual layout of a given poem (or prose text) on a given page. (82, 86, 97–9, 109–10)

mock-epic : a poem comically or satirically dressed in epic conventions for which its subject and/or manner are inappropriate. (39, 66, 248)

Modern : of the period since 1700. (94)

Modernism : a pan-European and world movement, principally in the arts in the last third of the nineteenth and first half of the twentieth centuries, characterised by (i) rejection of inherited Renaissance paradigms (perspective, tonality, neoclassical prosody, hierarchical grammar) in favour of Cubism, abstraction, atonality, free verse etc. ; (ii) revalorisations of space (often deriving from oriental art) ; and (iii) uneasy coincidence in time (and perhaps worse) with Fascism. Clearly a successor-movement to Romanticism, and deeply predicated on industrial technology while rejecting its constraints, Modernism radically reversed some processes evident in language and art since early Humanism. Though delayed in English drama until Beckett, and still restricted in its British stage-influence, poetic and prosaic Modernists (Pound, Eliot, Woolf, Joyce, et al.) were hugely influential from the 1910s ; writers after 1950 are sometimes called late Modernist, usually to avoid post-Modernist. (88–9, 109–10, 189, 294)

molossus : a foot of three beats, all stressed (xxx). (3)

monometer : a line of one foot. (4, 41)

monorhyme : when all lines rhyme, as *aaaa*. (43)

mosaic-rhyme : between a word and phrase, or between phrases. (191)

Movement : a term derived from a 1954 *Spectator* article for a (supposed) movement in some British literature, especially poetry, towards level-headed and often formalist sceptical empiricism ; those dubbed poets of the Movement include Davie, Enright, Gunn, Jennings, and Larkin. (294)

nation language : a politically correct term for Caribbean creoles and/or patois, usually deployed with ideological purpose (and sometimes adopted in Black American poetics). (227)

near rhyme : half-rhyme. (191)

neoclassical : of prosody, etc., derived from Greek and/or Latin writings. (2)

neologism : a new word. (231–2)

New Formalism : a late twentieth-century term for a supposed movement of reversion from free to metrical and rhyming verse. (173)

New York School : used since the 1960s to designate a group of poets closely linked to the New York School of painting who emerged together in the 1950s ; the core-members of the group are O'Hara, Ashbery, Koch, and Schuyler. (174, 294)

nominative : in grammar the case for the subject of a verb. (132)

nonce-word : one invented for a particular occasion or purpose. (230–1)

nonsense poetry : a kind of light verse typically featuring absurd or whimsical events and coinages. (56–7)

nota/e : marks made or printed in the margins of texts ; distinguished from punctuation within the text. (130)

noun : one of the 9 parts of speech, a word naming a person, place, or thing. Most inflect to indicate plurals (cow/s, erratum/errata) and the genitive case (cow's legs, cows' field) ; proper nouns, usually capitalised (George, Paris), are sometimes distinguished (as in the rules of Scrabble) from common nouns (cat, table). (225)

null rhyme : see *autorhyme.*

obelus : also **dagger** ; a *signe de renvoi*, marked '†' ; may also be double, when marked '‡'. (139)

objective correlative : a term popularised by T. S. Eliot in a famous 1919 essay on *Hamlet* : "The only way of expressing emotion in the form of art is by finding an 'objective correlative' ; in other words, a set of objects, a situation, a chain of events which shall be the formula of that *particular* emotion ; such that when the external facts, which must terminate in sensory experience, are given, the emotion is immediately invoked." (100)

octameter : a line of eight feet. (4)

octave : the first eight lines of a Petrarchan sonnet. (44, 46)

octet : a stanza of eight lines. (47)

ode : a formal poem of some dignity and length ; *Alcaic, Sapphic, Pindaric,* and *Horatian* odes are formally distinguished. (54–5)

Old English : Anglo-Saxon, *c.* 500–1066. (1, 165–6)

(Omar) Khayyam stanza : see *rubai/yat.*

Onegin stanza : of 14 lines, in iambic tetrameter, having the rhyme scheme *ababccddeffegg* ; further prescription about stressed and unstressed rhymes may be made. (44, 48, 51–2)

open : of form, variable (23) ; of couplets, with the second line enjambed to the first line of the next couplet (or other component unit of form). (38, 75)

opening : two facing pages in a book. (90)

oral formulaism : a mode of bardic composition in pre- or early literate cultures in which a large stock of hemistiches are learned, and variously combined (according to various rules) in performance. (165)

orthography : conventionally correct or proper spelling, and its study. (236)

ottava rima **:** a stanza of eight lines, in iambic pentameter, rhyming *abababcc.* (47–8, 192)

Oxford comma : one preceding the 'and' introducing the final item in a list. (117)

paeon : a foot of four beats, only one stressed ; called first (xuuu), second (uxuu), third (uuxu), and fourth (uuux) paeons according to the position of the stressed beat. (3)

pantun, pantoum : a highly repetitive Malay form, cross-rhymed quatrains successively reusing two lines from each in the next ; once in French vogue, but never in English. (44–5, 52)

paragraph : the division of stichic verse or continuous prose into groups of lines, marked by the indentation of the first or (modern business-style) a blank line ; a unit of argument and emotion ; the oldest surviving form of Western spatial punctuation. (112)

paragraphus : or section-mark ; used to indicate a paragraph or section, marked '§' (112, 139)

paraph : used to indicate a paragraph or section, marked '¢', '¶', or '||'. (92, 112, 139)

pararhyme : between words whose last stressed vowels differ but following sounds are identical. (190, 191–2)

parenthesis : in rhetoric, one clause intercluded within another ; such clauses may in written texts be marked with paired commas, dashes, or lunulae, and the parenthesis comprises the opening mark, alphanumeric contents, and closing mark. (123–4, 267)

parody : a work mocking or otherwise sending up another specific work. (167, 233–4)

passive : of an individual's vocabulary, the whole range of words that is known. (222) ; in grammar, a mood, the opposite of active. (263)

pastiche : a work mocking or otherwise sending up a style. (167, 233–4)

pastoral : a mode or genre, classically and until the Renaissance featuring the leisure-time rusticity of the high-born, on the model of Athenian resort to Arcadia ; once very highly stylised, with designated roles and role-names for amorous play and witty debate, but latterly used as a means of considering class-issues and post-industrial geography ; cf. urban pastoral. (67–8)

patois : (? from Old French *patoier*, to handle roughly) loosely, a dialect ; specifically, West Indian creoles drawing on English, French, or Spanish + African and/or Amerindian languages. It is now sometimes spelled 'patwa'. See also *creole, nation language*. (227)

pentain : an stanza of five lines. (45)

pentameter : a line of five feet. (3–4, 5)

percontation-mark : an archaic tonal indicator of percontations (questions open to any answer), marked '⸮'. (120, 121)

perfect rhyme : full-rhyme. (191)

period : a classical, rhetorically defined unit of syntax and argument, composed of *cola* and *commata* ; closer to the modern paragraph than the modern sentence (122–5) ; latterly and in the USA, a full-stop. (112, 114, 265–7)

periodash : a *combinate-mark*, '.—'. (138)

permissions : agreements to permit quotation of copyright material. (xv)

persona : an alternative for *'poet'*. (317–18)

Petrarchan : of sonnets, having an octave rhyming *abbaabba*, and a sestet rhyming *cdecde* (or a variant thereof). (48–9)

phallocracy : the rule of the phallus, by the phallus, for those with phalloi. The French term *phallocrat* translates as '(male) chauvinist pig'. (338)

phallus : the representation of abstract patriarchal power (which may be wielded by masculinised women) as distinct from the anatomical penis. (338)

photoquotation : a quotation reproduced photographically from a specific copy of a specific edition of a text, and therefore not in any way altered by the quoter. On the metal-page, photoquotation implicitly guaranteed a level and degree of fidelity otherwise impossible ; on e-pages digital photographs, while still purporting such fidelity, may have been spliced or morphed. (xvii, 92)

pilcrow : a *special sort*, '¶', marking paragraphs or sections ; one form of *paraph.* (92, 139)

Pindaric : of an ode, having three stanzas of a specified form, called the 'strophe' and 'antistrophe' (metrically and formally identical), and the 'epode' (metrically and formally distinct). (48, 54–5)

pitch contour : the movement in pitch from one note to a higher or lower note ; the curve(s) of sound in the voice, or required by a text. (205, 267)

plosive : of letters, requiring for their pronunciation that the vocal tract be closed and then opened, producing a small explosion of breath/sound. (284)

poet : as distinct from 'poet', the actual historical person ; the author. (317–18)

'poet' : as distinct from poet (without single inverted commas), the supposed writer or speaker of a given text ; the rhetorical construct designated by 'I' or 'me'. Also referred to as the 'persona'. (317–18)

poetise/r, poetising : derogatory terms for enthusiastic but lame vapourings ; cf. versification (37).

politics of representation : how women and men, femininity and masculinity, are represented by an author or in a text, and how those representations are received by a/reader/s. (342)

polysemic : of words, having many senses and/or distinct meanings. (248–9)

portmanteau : a word created by merging two or more existing words. (231)

post-metal : of printing, books etc., my coinage for the current age of printing by primarily digital methods bypassing metal type ; see *metal page.* (82, 111)

post-Modernism : a term with many definitions, often used as a buzz-word without regard to any of them ; there are variant forms of capitalisation and hyphenation. I always spell it (unless quoting) with hyphen + 'M' and mean primarily 'coming after and having absorbed Modernism' ; other rigorous definitions, centred on the ways in which IT has restructured data-storage and — articulation have been advanced by the French philosophers Jean Baudrillard (b.1929) and Jean-François Lyotard (b.1924), and the American Marxist Fredric Jameson (b.1934), for whom 'post-Modernism' is famously "the cultural logic of late capitalism". (276, 294)

poulter's measure : an iambic couplet of the form *a12a14.* (40)

printers' rhyme : eye-rhyme. (192)

preposition : one of the 9 parts of speech, a word relating a pro/noun to the rest of the sentence ; simple (at, on, by) and compound (away from, because of) prepositions are distinguished. (225)

proceleusmatic : a foot of four beats, all unstressed (uuuu). (3)

prong, pronged line : my coinage for a line longer than a normative measure ; the opposite of a *bob.* (161–3, 183–4)

pronoun : one of the 9 parts of speech, a word replacing a noun. Personal pronouns (I, you, he, she, they), have accusative (me, him, etc.) and genitive (my, your, etc.) cases, as well as reflexive forms (myself, yourself, etc.) ; 'who' also has cases (whom, whose). Other pronouns, such as relative (which, that), interrogative (what), and demonstrative (this) ones, do not inflect. (225)

prose-poem : one written and printed as prose, without the use of metrical lineation and often with a justified right margin. (153, 177–82)

prosody : the study and notation of metre. (1)

prothalamion : a poem anticipating the celebration of a forthcoming wedding. (54)

punctuation : a variety of marks, spaces, and other signs (such as distinguishing type-faces or founts) placed within the text to articulate, dis/ambiguate, or otherwise refine and/or display the sense. (81, 104–11)

pyrrhic : a foot of two unstressed beats (uu). (3, 4, 5, 11–12)

quadruple : of a foot, having four beats ; the rhythm produced by such feet. (3)

qualitative : of metres, based on patterns of stress or accent. (1)

quantitative : of metres, based on vowel length. (1)

quatrain : a stanza of four lines ; often used for narrative. (34–5, 42–5)

Queen's English : (or King's English) terms used since the sixteenth century to denote an ideologically and grammatically desirable standard of speech and writing, English 'as it should be spoken'. Compare 'BBC English', and the German equivalent, *Hochdeutsch* (or 'high German'). (193)

question-mark : a tonal indicator, usually of rising pitch, used (instead of a full-stop) to indicate questions, marked '?' ; may be used both medially and terminally. (120)

question-markash : a *combinate-mark*, '?—'. (138)

quotation-marks : the common but misleading term for *inverted commas* ; often abbreviated to 'quotes', though in many dictionaries this remains the verb. (130)

ragged : of texts and margins, not *justified*. (82)

rap : an improvised form of song, originally Afro-American, likely to be both lyrically expressive, quasi-narrative, and politically aroused ; rhyme, assonance, and alliteration are all used heavily. (202)

recto : the front of any leaf ; in books, each right-hand page. (90)

refrain : see *burden*.

register : generally, the chosen level or pitch of style + diction + decorum in a text, assessed as e.g. 'high' or 'demotic' ; in printing register refers to the exactitude of repositioning the paper when multiple impressions are needed (as for colour + B&W), or both sides of a leaf bear text. (232–6)

relative clause : one that gives additional but syntactically inessential information about a subject, verb, or object ; commonly signalled by 'who', 'which', or 'that'. (267)

renga : sequences of haiku linked by 14-syllable couplets. (42)

Restoration : of literature, of the period following the Restoration of Charles II in 1660 ; the later boundary is ragged, varying between *c.*1690 (when poetry may be thought already Augustan) and 1737 (when the Licensing Act imposes a discontinuity on dramatic practice). (293)

rhetoric : originally the formal rhetorical devices used in any text, such as parentheses, repetition, etc., but now (especially in the USA) merely 'the persuasiveness of a text'. (115)

rhyme : the coincidence of sounds. (81, 164–5, 189)

rhyme royal : a stanza of seven lines, in iambic pentameter, rhyming *ababbcc*. (46)

rhyme-scheme : an alphabetic method of notating rhyme-pattern in a stanza or poem ; line-lengths may be indicated, by placing the number of beats after the letter denoting the line. (33, 190)

Ricardian : of the reign of Richard II (1377–99) ; a historical term used in literature (following J. A. Burrow) for the intense period which saw most of the work of Langland, Chaucer, Gower, and the Gawain-poet. (166, 293)

rime riche **:** (or identical rhyme) between words whose sounds before <u>and</u> after the last stressed vowel are identical, as rhyming *homophones*. (191)

rising rhythm : that produced by feet with stressed beats following unstressed beats. (5)

rocking lineation : the effect of counterpoint (caesura-to-caesura) lines created by placing caesurae in the same position in two or more successive lines. (156–8)

roman : of a fount, with ordinary upright characters (such as these). (5, 82)

Romance : of languages, deriving from Latin ; of modern English words, deriving from Latin or a Romance language. (223–5)

Romantic : of literature, that of the later-eighteenth and first half of the nineteenth centuries ; the Romantic movement was in part a reaction against the Enlightenment, and its poetry is characteristically vigorous, formally innovative, and concerned amid rich diction and imagery with nature, aesthetics, and subjective emotion. Romanticism has troubling relations with nationalism and Napoleon, and the parallels with Modernism one full century later are striking. (294)

roomscape : my coinage for the domestic 'landscape', to which responses are often gendered. (343)

round : of brackets, a common term for lunulae (66)

ro(u)ndeau, ro(u)ndel, roundelay : medieval lyric forms with prescribed line-repetitions, primarily of French origin. Using capital letters to indicate lines that repeat entire, the rondeau is of 10 lines + bobbed burden, *abbaabC // abbaC*, or 15 + bobs, *aabba // aabC // aabbaC* ; the rondel usually of 13 or 14, typically *ABbaabABabbaAB* or *ABabbaABababAB* ; the (Chaucerian) roundel of ten, *Abb // abA // abbA* ; and the roundelay (or rondelet) of seven, *AbAabbA*. All burdens are likely to be bobbed, and may have to echo (a specific part of) the first line, a feature maintained in the later Swinburnian roundel, *abaB // bab // abaB*. In Elizabethan and critical use 'roundelay' commonly covers any short song with a burden, such as those in *As You Like It*. (48)

rubai/yat : a Persian quatrain-form, *aaba*, overwhelmingly associated, via Fitzgerald's translation, with *The Rubaiyat of Omar Khayyam* ; popular with mid–late Victorians. (44)

rules : in printing, horizontal lines longer than a dash, such as those separating footnotes from the main text. (109, 132, 135–7)

running-head : a title or identifying phrase printed at the top of each page, often in italics or small caps ; running-heads may differ on rectos and versos. (93)

Sapphic : of an ode, of a particular and highly prescribed form ; largely dactylic, Sapphics are very rare in English. (54)

satire, satiric : a classical mode, initially meaning a mixed sequence or form, potentially the primary sense as late as the Renaissance ; latterly a loose collective term for all art that mocks or otherwise ridicules (purportedly) to urge correction and reform. (66)

scanning : the process of working out the scansion. (9–12, 15–17)

scansion : the individual metrical pattern of a particular line or poem. (9–12, 15–17)

scare quotes : inverted commas, usually single, indicating a suspension of sense, or distrust of a word. (xvii, 130)

scharfes-s : (or Eszett) the German ligature 'ß', a long-s + short-s combination. (113)

screamer : journalese for an exclamation-mark. (96, 121)

***scriptio continua* :** text without word-separation, standard until the late-seventh century, thereafter passing into disuse. (109, 112)

self-similar/ity : a mathematical term coined by Benoit Mandelbrot (the seminal theorist of fractals) for patterns repeating on all scales ; used in some recent poetics to describe verse which in its recursions and repetitions is neither formal nor free. (175)

semantic rhyme : between words with related or cognate meanings, as 'jeer/sneer' or 'love/give'. (205–6)

semi-colash : a *combinate-mark*, ';—'. (138)

semi-colon/s : the third heaviest stop, marked ';' ; conventionally implies completion of the immediate sense, and <u>either</u> a development in the sense between *semi-cola* <u>or</u> the itemization of each *semi-colon* ; invented by Pietro Bembo (1470–1547) in Venice in the 1490s explicitly as a stop intermediate between the colon and the comma. (115–16)

***semi-colon, semi-cola* :** the part/s of a sentence between semicolons, and/or between a semicolon and a heavier stop. (115–16, 119)

sentence : in modern use, the largest unit of syntax, composed of one or more clauses and normally containing at least one grammatical subject, one in/transitive verb, and if appropriate an object ; typographically, sentences begin with a capital letter and end with a full-stop. (112, 265–7)

separatist : of feminisms, desiring and recommending the isolation of women from men. (339)

sesqui- : (from Latin, 'semi', half, and 'que', and) may be prefixed to any line-length to indicate 'and-a-half' ; thus 'trimeter', a line of 3 feet, and 'sequitrimeter', of 3½ feet. (7)

sestet : a stanza or unit of six lines, including ll. 9–14 of Petrarchan sonnets. (45–6)

sestina : a poem of 39 lines in six sestets and a tercet envoi, each ending with one of six words in the sequence *abcdef faebdc cfdabe ecb fad deacfb bdfeca eca* (or *ace*), all six terminal words to be used in the *envoi*. (46, 48, 52–3, 69–71)

set, setting : arranging type in order to print ; a portion of type so ordered. (82, 90)

sex : biological, anatomical, and chromosomal maleness or femaleness, as distinct from culturally acquired gender. (339)

shake : an equivalent of *canto* used by Charles Causley, primarily to allude to *fit* but perhaps also from the sense in cooperage, 'a cask-stave'. (61)

Shakespearian : of sonnets, rhyming *ababcdcdefefgg*. (49)

shape-poem : one whose text is organized on the page to depict a shape, or otherwise to involve pictorial as well as verbal representation ; also known as *technopaignia, carmina figurata*, and 'concrete poems'. (90–3)

***Sho'ah* :** the Hebrew word for what is usually referred to in English as 'the Holocaust'. (72, 228–9, 291)

short metre : an iambic quatrain of the form *a6b6c8b6* ; see also *common, half-*, and *long* metre. (43)

short-s : the normal modern form 's'; before the mid-late eighteenth century *long-s* was used initially and medially, short-s terminally. (xvi)

Sicilian stanza : a cross-rhymed octet, *abababab*. (46)

***signe/s de renvoi* :** 'sign/s of sending back' ; any mark/s used (typically as an index) to associate matter in the text with added material (including marginalia and foot- or endnotes). (109, 139–40)

signs of omission : a family of punctuation-marks (including the apostrophe and suspension-marks) indicating that a/letter/s, a/word/s, or larger units have been omitted. (109, 132–5, 192)

***signum sectionis* :** the section-mark or paragraphus, '§', formed from the initial letters 'ss'. (112, 139)

single-rhyme : (as *abcb* or *abac*) of a quatrain or other short unit of form, having only one pair of rhyming lines the pattern of non- rhyming lines thereby created. (43)

Skeltonics : an accentual form devised for satirical and railing verse by John Skelton (?1460–1529). (2)

slant rhyme : half-rhyme. (191)

slash/es : a sub-family of dis/aggregators comprising the forward slash (or *solidus*), marked '/', used singly to indicate alternatives (as 's/he') and line-breaks, and doubly (//) to indicate stanza-breaks ; the vertical slash, marked '|' (or in superscript 'ᑊ'), which may indicate foot-division or caesurae ; and the backslash, marked '\'. (117, 127–9, 153)

small capitals : smaller upper-case letters, such as THESE. (5, 81)

smiley : a small schematic face, ☺ ; also the commonest form of emoticon, a face created from punctuation-marks, ':—)'. (113, 121–2)

solidus : the forward slash, '/' ; the plural is solidi. (9, 69, 116, 127–8)

sonnet : until the early seventeenth century, any short lyric poem ; thereafter supposedly and conventionally a poem of 14 lines in iambic pentameter, but variants ranging from 10½–20 lines are recognised. Its traditional use, especially in sequences, is for poems of (frustrated) love and courtship, but since the seventeenth century occasional sonnets on almost every topic imaginable have been written, and there are now long-standing connections with many poetic modes, including the elegiac, satirical, and confessional. See also *caudate, curtal, Meredithian, Petrarchan, Shakespearian,* and *Spenserian.* (33, 35–6, 48–51, 72–3, 83–4, 115)

spatial : of punctuation, deploying space rather than a mark or face etc. ; distinguished from *deictic, elocutionary,* and *syntactic* punctuation. (107)

special sorts : in a fount of type, non-alphanumeric characters that are rarely used. (109, 139–40)

spelling-rhymes : between words deliberately (and usually comically) misspelt or abbreviated to create the rhyme, as 'hisses/Mrs' or 'devilry/S.O.B'. (192–3)

Spenserian : of sonnets, rhyming *ababbcbccdcdee* ; of stanzas, heroic and rhyming *ababbcbcc12*. (34, 45, 47, 49, 76)

spondee : a foot of two stressed beats (xx). (3, 4, 5)

sprung rhythm : coined by G. M. Hopkins to describe his metrical practice (actually a stress scansion derived from OE and ME verse) in (misleading) neoclassical terms. (13, 166)

square : of brackets, a common term for crotchets. (122–3)

stand : another name for the epode of a *Pindaric* ode. (54)

stanza : a group of lines displayed on the page by blank lines above and below, typically with a constant structure or rhyme-scheme. (16, 33)

stanza-break : the physical (and syntactical) space (and pause) between stanzas, marked in transcription with a double slash, '//'. (69, 99, 153)

step-down line : see *triadic line.*

stichic : of verse, not stanzaic; a sequence of individual lines. (33)

stock epithet : an adjective repeatedly used with a particular name, as 'strong-thewed', 'the bold', 'pious', etc. ; a feature of oral formulaism, but extending to literary epic. (165)

stops : a family of punctuation-marks comprising the comma, semicolon, colon, and full-stop, syntactically indicating some degree of completion of sense, and elocutionarily suggesting a pause or emphasis. (109, 114–20)

stressed : of beats, spoken emphatically, often with the voice pitched slightly higher than for an unstressed beat (1) ; of endings, with one or more stressed hypermetrical beats (7) ; of rhymes, with the stressed vowel in the last beat. (191).

string-command : a form of tonal indicator adapted from computer-languages, typically a word denoting an expression or gesture marked with asterisks, as *sigh*. (120, 121–2)

strophe : (or *turn*) the first stanza of a *Pindaric* ode. (54)

Stuart : of literature, written under a Stuart monarch (James VI and I, 1603–25 ; Charles I, 1625–49 ; Charles II, 1660–85 ; James VII and II, 1685–88 ; William III and Mary II, 1688–1702 ; Anne, 1702–14). (293)

style : here, the verbal manner in which an argument is conducted. (115)

sub-clause : any that is not a main clause, including all relative clauses, parenthetical clauses, etc. (264)

substitute foot : any foot used as a replacement for one of the regular feet in a given line ; includes inverted and distinguishing feet. (5)

suspension : a word shortened by terminal elision, as 'ed.' for 'editor'. (133)

suspension-mark/s : a single suspension-mark (.) indicates the suspension of one or more letters (an in etc., ed.) ; three suspension-marks, usually spaced, indicate an ellipsis. (133–4)

swash : of a character or fount, embellished for display. (140)

swung dash : (or *tilde*), a *special sort*, marked '~'. (137)

syllabic : of verse, with a prescribed number of syllables per line. (2)

synecdoche : a rhetorical figure in which a part of something is named instead of the whole (as 'counting heads'). (275)

synonyms : different words with the same meaning. (223)

syntactic : of punctuation, indicating construction of sense ; distinguished from *deictic, elocutionary,* and *spatial* punctuation. (106)

syntax : the relations between words and clauses (of whatever kind) within a period or sentence. (249, 263)

synthetic : of a language, concentrating meaning into few words, and hence having inflected endings, prefixes etc. (1, 107)

Tennysonian stanza : an arch-rhymed quatrain in iambic tetrameter, so called for its use by Tennyson for *In Memoriam A.H.H.* (44)

tercet : a stanza or unit of three lines in which one or more does not rhyme with the others. (41–2)

terminal : at or near the end of lines, stanzas etc.

***terza rima* :** successive tercets rhyming *aba bcb cdc ded* etc. (41–2, 204)

tetrameter : a line of four feet. (3–4, 5)

Teutonic : of languages or words, Germanic. (223–5)

text : literally 'something woven' ; in apposition to *mise-en-page,* the sequence of words, marks, and spaces that must be disposed on paper, lexical codes awaiting bibliographic realisation. (82)

textual annotation and **collation :** notes indicating textual variation or other difficulty ; collation is the process of comparing editions of a text. (97)

thematic : of rhyme, puns etc., between or involving words whose meanings are engaged to the major theme/s of the work. (205–6)

thorn : the Anglo-Saxon letter **Þ þ** (= unvoiced *th*). (113, 165)

tilde : a curved bar placed over a letter to indicate palatalisation, usually of a nasal, as in 'señor' (= senyor, not senor) ; also, the swung dash. (82)

Tironian : of signs of abbreviation, invented by Tiro, a freedman of Cicero's who devised an early system of shorthand. (140)

tittle : a bar placed over a letter to indicate an omitted following nasal (imaginatiō = imagination) (as in 'jot or tittle'). The same sign serves as a *macron* to lengthen vowels. (82)

tonal indicators : a family of punctuation-marks and notae (including question- and exclamation-marks and emoticons) that attempt to direct printed tone. (109, 120–2)

***tornada* :** the envoi of a sestina or *canzone* ; by extension any such envoi. (52)

tragedy, tragic : a classical mode, tragedies dealt with the lives and fates of individuals, usually of high social or political rank ; long-regarded as the highest or noblest mode in literary and dramatic art. (66)

transitive : of a verb, requiring an object. (112)

triadic line : a name for the progressively indented tercet created by W. C. Williams, insisting on its identity as one long line rather than three short ones ; also called the 'step-down line'. (42, 171)

tribrach : a foot of three beats, all unstressed (uuu). (3, 28)

trimeter : a line of three feet. (3)

triolet : an octet repeating line 1 as ll. 4 + 7, and line 2 as l. 8. (46)

triple : of a foot, having three beats ; the rhythm produced by such feet. (3, 7–8)

triplet : a stanza or unit of three lines which all rhyme together. (41)

trochee, trochaic : a foot of two beats, a stressed followed by an unstressed (xu) ; the metre produced by such feet. (3, 4, 6–7)

Tudor : of literature, written under a Tudor monarch (Henry VII, 1485–1509 ; Henry VIII, 1509–47 ; Edward VI, 1547–53 ; Mary I, 1553–58 ; Elizabeth I, 1558–1603). (293)

turn : a moment of disjunction and/or renewal, creating a shift or development of the sense at a specified point in a form (42, 49) ; in relation to the Pindaric ode, another name for the strophe (54).

turn-down, -up : also *turn-over, turned line* ; in verse-lines that exceed the measure, that part which is set on the physical line below or above.

typescript : originally a document produced on a typewriter ; now a generic term for keyboard fair-copy, usually loose or cheaply bound, often photocopied, as distinct from published copies ; abbreviated to TS/S. (88)

u : notation for an unstressed beat. (3)

unstressed : of beats, spoken unemphatically, often more rapidly and with the voice pitched slightly lower than for a stressed beat (2) ; of endings, with one or more unstressed hypermetrical beats (7) ; of rhymes, with one or more unstressed beats following the last stressed vowel (191).

upper-case : of letters, capitals. (5)

urban pastoral : a loose but suggestive generic label for modern poetry of suburban domesticity and streetscapes, industrial sociology, and civil recreation. (67–8)

'value-free' history : history supposedly written objectively, without ideological selection or emphasis of material ; presently regarded as a chimæra. (291)

variable foot : a term coined by W. C. Williams, supposedly the basis of his scansion but in practice a confusing way of loosely describing his free verse in neoclassical terms ; cf. Hopkins's *sprung rhythm.* (170)

verb : one of the 9 parts of speech, a word expressing a state or action. English verbs have present and past tenses (run, ran), moods (indicative for statements + questions, imperative for commands, subjunctive for wishes, demands, and hypothetical conditions), voices (active or passive), and aspects (progressive or perfective) for continuation or completion. They also have finite and non-finite forms, including the infinitive (to go) and present and past participles (going, gone). Main verbs are used alone (I go) and auxiliary verbs used in support (I can go, I dare not go) ; tenses other than the present (I go) and past (I went), including the future (I will go), past perfect (I have gone), pluperfect (I had gone), and subjunctive (I would have gone) are usually formed periphrastically, with auxiliary verbs. (225)

verse : (1) a single line or equivalent stichic unit (as in 'chapter and verse') ; (2) a poet's prosodic and formal craft, or, collectively, versified work (as in 'Shakespeare's verse'), and with reference to drama, metrical lines as distinguished from prose and/or song (as in 'blank verse') ; (3) especially with reference to any nationality, period, or theme, a synonym for poetry (as in 'Renaissance verse') ; (4) in post-Romantic apposition with 'poetry', sometimes a mildly stigmatic term for 'supposedly dull craftwork nuts-and-bolts'. (36–7)

verse-autobiography : an autobiography in verse ; the term is rarely used of work before Wordsworth's seminal *The Prelude* (despite the widespread assumption of autobiography in reading, say, Shakespeare's *Sonnets*), and is not always applied even to poems declaring themselves autobiographical (Bunting's *Briggflatts*, for example), but has been sustained by the practices of Merrill, Walcott, Harrison, and others. (61–2)

verse-letter : a semi-public letter, effectively a dramatic monograph, usually to a private friend ; blank verse or heroic couplets are the favoured measures. (54, 58–9, 61)

verse-novel : granting 'novel' to mean a print-specific long prose form emerging roughly with Defoe, a novel in verse ; the term is not normally used of works earlier than *Don Juan*, but the form has been regularly pursued. (62)

verse-paragraphs : the divisions of a long poem in a constant, stichic form, indicated (like prose paragraphs) by indenting the first line of each. (38, 61, 112)

versicle : sometimes simply 'a little verse' or 'a single line', but more correctly a biblical or psalmic verse or other short phrase spoken or sung antiphonally within the liturgy, and latterly the short verse of a hymn with a chorus. (158)

versification : (1) the art and craft of casting words into a metrically and/or otherwise prescribed form ; (2) latterly, a derogatory term for craftwork that is (supposedly) mechanically correct but uninspired or (sub-)second-rate, the culprit being a versifier. (37)

verso : the back of any leaf ; in books, each left-hand page. (90)

Victorian : of literature, written during the reign of Victoria (1837–1901) ; used in schemata of literary history to fill the gap between the Romantics and Modernists. (87, 109, 293)

villanelle : nineteen lines in iambic pentameter, of the form *aba aba aba aba aba abaa*, with ll. 1, 6, 12, and 18 a refrain, and ll. 3, 9, 15, and 19 a second refrain. (41, 48, 52)

virgula/e : the mediaeval family of commas, including the *virgula suspensiva* (now the solidus) and *virgula plana* (now the dash). (117)

***virgula/e plana/e* :** a mediaeval form of comma, later the dash. (117)

***virgula/e suspensiva/e* :** a medieval form of comma, later the solidus (117–18, 127)

vocative/s : direct addresses to some one by name or title, in Renaissance books conventionally within lunulae ; in the singular, in grammar, the case for giving and going, typically replaced in English by the preposition 'to'. (85)

volta : see *turn*.

vowel-rhyme : between words whose last stressed vowels are identical but following sounds differ. (191)

wheel : a short rhyming sub-stanza attached to a longer group of alliterative lines, especially in *Sir Gawayne and the Grene Knyght* ; 'bob-and-wheel' is also used, the 'bob' here being a short line used as a bridge between the alliterative and rhyming lines. (165)

word : a single unit of sense. (112–13)

word-separation : the practice of using spaces between words, invented in Ireland in the late-seventh century CE. (112)

wrenched accent : occurs when the requirements of metrical stress prevail over the natural stress of a word or words. (10)

wrenched monorhyme : between unstressed participle endings (my coinage). (193–5)

x : notation for a stressed beat. (3)

yogh : the Middle English letter ȝ (= *y*, *gh*). (113, 165)

Select Bibliography and Further Reading

A : General

Brogan, T. V. F., ed., *The New Princeton Handbook of Poetic Terms* (Princeton: Princeton University Press, 1994; ISBN 0–691–03672–1).

Brower, Reuben A., 'The Discovery of Design', in *The Fields of Light: An Experiment in Critical Reading* (1951; London, Oxford, and New York: Oxford University Press, 1962; ISBN 0–31–322653–9).

Chisholm, Alison, *A Practical Poetry Course* (London: Allison and Busby, 1994; ISBN 0–490–0114–3).

Ciardi, John, *How Does A Poem Mean?* (Boston: Houghton Mifflin, 1959; ISBN 0–39–518605–6).

Cuddon, J. A., *A Dictionary of Literary Terms* (1976; 4th edn, rev. Claire Preston, Oxford: Blackwell, 1998; Harmondsworth: Penguin, 1999; ISBN 0–14–051363–9).

Deutsch, Babette, *Poetry Handbook: A Dictionary of Terms* (1957; 4th edn, 1974; New York: Harper Perennial, 1995; ISBN 0–06–463548–1).

Fenton, James, *An Introduction to English Poetry* (2002; Harmondsworth: Penguin, 2003; ISBN 0–141–00439–8).

Fowler, Roger, ed., *A Dictionary of Modern Critical Terms* (London and Boston: Routledge and Kegan Paul, 1973; ISBN 0–7100–7544–8).

Gioia, Dana, Mason, Robert, & Schoerke, Meg, eds, *Twentieth-Century American Poetics: Poets on the Art of Poetry* (New York and London: McGraw-Hill, 2004; ISBN 0–07–241472–3).

Hamilton, Ian, ed., *The Oxford Companion to Twentieth-Century Poetry* (Oxford and New York: Oxford University Press, 1994; ISBN 0–19–866147–9).

Hawthorn, Jeremy, *A Concise Glossary of Contemporary Literary Theory* (1992; 3rd edn, London: Arnold, 1998; ISBN 0–340–69222–7).

Hyland, Paul, *Getting into Poetry* (Newcastle-upon-Tyne: Bloodaxe Books, 1992 [Bloodaxe Poetry Handbooks, 1]; ISBN 1–85224–118–7).

Padel, Ruth, *52 Ways of Looking at a Poem: A Poem for Every Week of the Year* (2002; London: Vintage, 2004; ISBN 0–099–42915–2).

Parrott, E. O., ed., *How to be Well-Versed in Poetry* (Harmondsworth: Penguin, 1991; ISBN 0–14–011275–8).

Peck, John, & Coyle, Martin, *Practical Criticism: How to Write a Critical Appreciation* (London: Macmillan, 1995; ISBN 0–333–63225–7).

Perrine, Laurence, & Arp, Thomas R., *Sound and Sense: An Introduction to Poetry* (1956; 8th edn, New York: Harcourt College Publishing/London: Thompson, 1992; ISBN 0–15–565732–1 [US], 0–15–582610–7 [UK]).

Preminger, Alex, et al., eds, *The New Princeton Encyclopedia of Poetry and Poetics* (Princeton: Princeton University Press, 1993; ISBN 0–691–02123–6).

Press, John, *The Chequer'd Shade: Reflections on Obscurity in Poetry* (1958; London: Oxford University Press, 1963).

B : Metre and Form

Attridge, Derek, *Well-Weighed Syllables: Elizabethan Verse in Classical Metres* (Cambridge: Cambridge University Press, 1974; ISBN 0–521–20530–1).

——*The Rhythms of English Poetry* (London: Longman, 1982; ISBN 0–582–55105–6).

Bibby, Cyril, *The Art of the Limerick* (Hamden, CT: Archon Books, 1978; ISBN 0–208–01761–5).

Fussell, Paul, *Poetic Meter and Poetic Form* (New York: McGraw-Hill, 1979; ISBN 0–07–553606–4).

Hollander, John, *Vision and Resonance: Two Senses of Poetic Form* (New York: Oxford University Press, 1975; ISBN 0–19–501898–2).

——*Rhyme's Reason: A Guide to English Verse* (1981; new, enlarged edn, New Haven and London: Yale University Press, 1989; ISBN 0–300–04307–4).

Malcolm, Noel, *The Origins of English Nonsense* (London: HarperCollins, 1997; ISBN 0–00–255827–0).

Nabokov, Vladimir, *Notes on Prosody and Abram Ganibal* (Princeton: Princeton University Press, 1964 [Bollingen Series]; ISBN 0–691–01760–3).

Read, Herbert, *Form in Modern Poetry* (1932; London: Vision Press, 1989; ISBN 0–85478–336–9).

Ridler, Anne, 'On Certain English Verse Rhythms', in *A Measure of English Poetry* (n.p.: Perpetua Press, 1991; ISBN 1–870882–05–9).

Roethke, Theodore, 'Some Remarks on Rhythm', in Ralph J. Mills, Jr., ed., *On the Poet and his Craft: Selected Prose of Theodore Roethke* (Seattle and London: University of Washington Press, 1966; ISBN 0–295–74003–5).

Silkin, Jon, *The Life of Metrical and Free Verse in Twentieth-Century Poetry* (Houndmills: Macmillan/New York: St Martin's Press, 1997; ISBN 0–333–59321–9 [UK], 0–312–17239–7 [US cloth]).

Spiller, Michael R. G., *The Development of the Sonnet: An Introduction* (London: Routledge, 1992; ISBN 0–415–08741–4).

Taylor, Dennis, *Hardy's Metres and Victorian Prosody* (Oxford: Clarendon Press, 1988; ISBN 0–19–812967–X).

Thompson, John, *The Founding of English Metre* (1966; repr. New York: Columbia University Press, 1989; ISBN 0–231–06755–0).

Winters, Yvor, *Forms of Discovery: Critical and Historical Essays on the Forms of the Short Poem in English* (Columbus: Ohio University Press, 1967; ISBN 0–804–00119–7).

C : Layout, Lineation, Punctuation

Cook, Elizabeth, *Seeing Through Words: The Scope of Late Renaissance Poetry* (New Haven and London: Yale University Press, 1986; ISBN 0–300–03675–2).

Grafton, Anthony, *The Footnote: A Curious History* (1995; rev, edn, Cambridge, MA: Harvard University Press; ISBN 0–674–90215–7).

Graham-White, Anthony, *Punctuation and Its Dramatic Value in Shakespearean*

Drama (Newark, NJ, and London: University of Delaware Press/Associated University Presses, 1995; ISBN 0–87413–542–7).

Griffiths, Eric, *The Printed Voice of Victorian Poetry* (Oxford: Clarendon Press, 1989; ISBN–0–19–812989–0).

Henry, Anne, Bray, Joe, & Fraser, Miriam, eds, *Ma(r)king the Text: The presentation of meaning on the literary page* (Aldershot: Ashgate, 2000; ISBN 0–7546–0168–4).

Hollander, John, Introduction to *Types of Shape* (new edn, New Haven and London: Yale University Press, 1991; ISBN 0–300–04925–0).

Honan, Park, *Browning's Characters: A Study in Poetic Technique* (New Haven: Yale University Press, 1961).

Jackson, H. J., *Marginalia: Readers Writing in Books* (New Haven and London: Yale University Press, 2001; ISBN 0–300–09720–4).

Jackson, Kevin, *Invisible Forms: A Guide to Literary Curiosities* (London: Picador, 1999/New York: Thomas Dunne Books, 2000; ISBN 0–330–37115–0 [UK], 0–312–26606–5 [US]).

Lennard, John, *But I Digress: The Exploitation of Parentheses in English Printed Verse* (Oxford: Clarendon Press, 1991; ISBN 0–19–811247–5).

——'Punctuation—and: "Pragmatics" ', in A. H. Jucker, ed., *Historical Pragmatics* (Amsterdam and Philadelphia: John Benjamins, 1995; ISBN 90–272–5047–2 [Eur.], 1–55619–328–9 [USA]).

——'Period', 'Punctuation', 'Apestail', 'Apostrophe', 'Guillemets', 'Mise-en-Page', 'Nota', 'Parenthesis', and 'Scriptio Continua', in Cuddon, *A Dictionary of Literary Terms and Literary Theory*.

——'Mark, Space, Axis, Function: towards a (new) theory of punctuation on historical principles', in Henry, Bray, & Fraser, *Ma(r)king the Text*.

Levertov, Denise, 'On the Function of the Line', in *Chicago Review,* 30/3 (1979), 30–6.

McCloud, Scott, *Understanding Comics: The Invisible Art* (New York: Harper Perennial, 1994; ISBN 0–06–097625–N).

McGann, Jerome, *The Textual Condition* (Princeton: Princeton University Press, 1991; ISBN 0–691–01518–X).

——*Black Riders: The Visible Language of Modernism* (Princeton: Princeton University Press, 1993; ISBN 0–691–01544–9).

Parkes, Malcolm B., *Pause and Effect: An Introduction to the History of Punctuation in the West* (Aldershot: Scolar Press, 1992; ISBN 0–85976–742–7).

Ricks, Christopher, 'Geoffrey Hill 1: "The Tongue's Atrocities" ' and 'Geoffrey Hill 2: At-one-ment', in *The Force of Poetry*.

Sutherland, Kathryn, 'Note on the Text', in Jane Austen, *Mansfield Park* (Harmondsworth: Penguin 1996 [Penguin Classic]).

——'Speaking commas/reading commas: punctuating *Mansfield Park*', in Henry, Bray, & Fraser, *Ma(r)king the Text*.

Vendler, Helen, *The Breaking of Style: Hopkins, Heaney, Graham* (Cambridge, MA, and London: Harvard University Press, 1995; ISBN 0–674–08121–8).

Zwicker, Steven N., *Lines of Authority: Politics and English Literary Culture, 1649–1689* (1993; Ithaca, NY, and London: Cornell University Press, 1996; ISBN 0–8014–8336–0).

D : Rhyme

Bradford, Richard, 'Rhyme', in *Silence and Sound: Theories of Poetics from the Eighteenth Century* (Rutherford/Madison/Teaneck, NJ, and London: Fairleigh Dickinson University Press/Associated University Presses, 1992; ISBN 0–8386–3435–4).

Daniel, Samuel, 'A Defence of Ryme' (1603), in A. C. Sprague, ed., *Samuel Daniel: Poems and A Defence of Ryme* (Chicago and London: University of Chicago Press, 1965; ISBN 0–226–13609–4).

Levi, Primo, 'Rhyming on the Counterattack', in *The Mirror Maker: Stories and Essays* (trans. Raymond Rosenthal, 1989; London: Minerva, 1990), 110–14.

Milton, John, 'The Verse', a note prefixed to the 2nd edn of *Paradise Lost* (1674), in e.g. Fowler, ed., *Paradise Lost* (London: Longman, 1976; ISBN 0–582–48455–3).

Ricks, Christopher, 'John Milton: Sound and Sense in *Paradise Lost*', in *The Force of Poetry*.

——'Frustration at a Recalcitrant World', in *T. S. Eliot and Prejudice* (London: Faber and Faber, 1988; ISBN 0–571–15254–6).

Stillman, Frances, *The Poet's Manual and Rhyming Dictionary* (London: Thames and Hudson, 1966; ISBN 0–500–27030–9).

E : Diction and Syntax

Auerbach, Erich, '*Sermo Humilis*', in *Literary Language and its Public in Late Latin Antiquity and in the Middle Ages* (1958; trans. Ralph Manheim, Princeton and Chichester: Princeton University Press, 1965, 1993 [Bollingen Series, 74]; ISBN 0–691–02468–5).

Baugh, Albert C., & Cable, Thomas, *A History of the English Language* (4th edn, London: Routledge and Kegan Paul, 1993; ISBN 0–415–09379–1).

Brathwaite, Edward Kamau, *History of the Voice: The Development of Nation Language in Anglophone Caribbean Poetry* (London and Port of Spain: New Beacon, 1984; ISBN 0–901241–55–5).

Coetzee, J. M., 'The Rhetoric of the Passive in English', in David Attwell, ed., *J. M. Coetzee: Doubling the Point: Essays and Interviews* (Cambridge, MA, and London: Harvard University Press, 1992; ISBN 0–674–21518–4).

Crystal, David, *The Cambridge Encyclopedia of Language* (Cambridge: Cambridge University Press, 1987; ISBN 0–521–42443–7).

——*The Cambridge Encyclopedia of the English Language* (Cambridge: Cambridge University Press, 1995; ISBN 0–521–40179–8).

Empson, William, *Seven Types of Ambiguity* (1930; London: Hogarth Press, 1984; ISBN 0–7012–0556–3).

——*The Structure of Complex Words* (1951; London: Hogarth Press, 1985; ISBN 0–7012–1006–0).

Landau, Sidney I., *Dictionaries: The Art and Craft of Lexicography* (1984; 2nd edn, Cambridge: Cambridge University Press, 2001; ISBN 0–521–78512–X).

Lewis, C. S., *Studies in Words* (1960; 2nd edn, Cambridge: Cambridge University Press, 1990 [Canto]; ISBN 0–521–39831–2).

Nash, Walter, *Jargon: Its Uses and Abuses* (Oxford: Blackwell, 1993; ISBN 0–631–18063–X).

Nowottny, Winifred, *The Language Poets Use* (1962; with corrections, London: Athlone Press, 1965; ISBN 0–485–12009–7).

Robinson, Ian, *The Foundations of English Prose: The Art of Prose Writing from the Middle Ages to the Enlightenment* (Cambridge: Cambridge University Press, 1996; ISBN 0–521–48088–4).

Sacks, Shelson, ed., *On Metaphor* (Chicago and London: University of Chicago Press, 1979; ISBN 0–226–73334–3).

Tillotson, Geoffrey, *Augustan Poetic Diction* (1961; London: Athlone Press, 1964).

Williams, Raymond, *Keywords: A Vocabulary of Culture and Society* (1976; rev. edn, London: Fontana, 1988; ISBN 0–00–686150–4).

F : History and Biography

Cunningham, Val, *British Writers of the Thirties* (Oxford: Oxford University Press, 1989; ISBN 0–19–282655–7).

Davenport, Guy, 'Ozymandias', in *The Geography of the Imagination.*

Eliot, T. S., 'Tradition and the Individual Talent', in *The Sacred Wood.*

Empson, William, *Using Biography* (London: Chatto and Windus/Hogarth Press, 1984; ISBN 0–7011–2889–5).

Everett, Barbara, *Poets in Their Time* (Oxford: Oxford University Press, 1991; ISBN 0–19–811281–5).

France, Peter, & St Clair, William, *Mapping Lives: The Uses of Biography* (London and New York: British Academy/Oxford University Press, 2002; ISBN 0–19–726269–4).

Hewison, Robert, *Under Siege: Literary Life in London 1939–45* (1977; London: Methuen, 1988; ISBN 0–413–40910–4).

Lowes, John Livingston, *The Road to Xanadu: A Study in the Ways of the Imagination* (1927; London: Picador, 1978; ISBN 0–330–25270–4).

McGann, Jerome J., *The Beauty of Inflections: Literary Investigations in Historical Method and Theory* (Oxford: Clarendon Press, 1985; ISBN 0–19–811730–2).

Morris, John N., *Versions of the Self: Studies in English Autobiography from John Bunyan to John Stuart Mill* (New York and London: Basic Books, 1966).

Phillips, Rodney, et al., *The Hand of the Poet: Poems and Papers in Manuscript* (New York: Rizzoli International, 1997; ISBN 0–8478–1958–2).

Plimpton, George, ed., *Poets at Work: The Paris Review Interviews* (New York: Penguin, 1989; ISBN 0–14–011791–1).

Ricks, Christopher, *Allusion to the Poets* (Oxford: Oxford University Press, 2002; ISBN 0–19–925032–4).

Scarry, Elaine, ed., *Fins de Siècle: English Poetry in 1590, 1690, 1790, 1890, 1990* (Baltimore and London: Johns Hopkins University Press, 1995; ISBN 0–8018–4929–2).

St Clair, William, *The Reading Nation in the Romantic Period* (Cambridge: Cambridge University Press, 2004; ISBN 0–521–81006–X).

Trelawny, Edward John, *Records of Shelley, Byron, and the Author* (1858; with an introduction by Anne Barton, New York: New York Review of Books, 2000; ISBN 0–940322–36–6).

Vendler, Helen, *Coming of Age as a Poet: Milton, Keats, Eliot, Plath* (Cambridge, MA, and London: Harvard University Press, 2003; ISBN 0–674–01383–2).

Walcott, Derek, *The Antilles: Fragments of Epic Memory* (New York: Farrar, Straus and Giroux, 1992/London: Faber and Faber, 1993; ISBN 0–374–10530–8 [US], 0–571–17080–3 [UK]).

Walcott, Derek, *Derek Walcott reads a selection of his work* [from] Collected Poems 1948–84 *and* Omeros (Argo/Polygram, 1994; catalogue no. 522–222–4).

Wilmer, Clive, ed., *Poets Talking:* Poet of the Month *Interviews from BBC Radio 3* (Manchester: Carcanet, 1994; ISBN 1–85754–075–1).

Young, James E., *Writing and Rewriting the Holocaust: Narrative and the Consequences of Interpretation* (Bloomington and Indianapolis: Indiana University Press, 1990; ISBN 0–253–36716–6).

G : Gender

Beauvoir, Simone de, *The Second Sex* (1949; trans. and ed. H. M. Parshley, London: Picador, 1988; ISBN 0–330–30338–4).

Cameron, Deborah, ed., *The Feminist Critique of Language: A Reader* (London: Routledge, 1990; ISBN 0–415–04260–7).

Cixous, Hélène, *Coming to Writing and Other Essays*, ed. Deborah Jensen (Cambridge, MA, and London: Harvard University Press, 1991; ISBN 0–674–14437–6).

Epstein, Julia, & Straub, Kristina, eds, *Body Guards: The Cultural Politics of Gender Ambiguity* (New York and London: Routledge, 1991; ISBN 0–415–90389–0).

Flynn, Elizabeth A., & Schweickart, Patrocinio P., eds, *Gender and Reading: Essays on Readers, Texts, and Contexts* (Baltimore and London: Johns Hopkins University Press, 1986; ISBN 0–8018–2907–0).

Kramarae, Cheris, & Treichler, Paula A., eds, *Amazons, Bluestockings and Crones: A Feminist Dictionary* (London: Pandora, 1992; ISBN 0–04–440863–3).

Montefiore, Jan, *Feminism and Poetry: Language, Experience, Identity in Women's Writing* (1987; 2nd edn, London: Pandora, 1994; ISBN 0–04–440893–5).

Yorke, Liz, *Impertinent Voices: Subversive Strategies in Contemporary Women's Poetry* (London: Routledge, 1991; ISBN 0–415–05204–1).

H : Writing Poetry

Brownjohn, Sandy, *To Rhyme or Not to Rhyme: Teaching Children To Write Poetry* (1982, as *What rhymes with 'secret'?*; new edn, London: Hodder and Stoughton, 1994; ISBN 0–340–61148–0).

Bugeja, Michael J., *The Art and Craft of Poetry* (Cincinatti: Writer's Digest Books, 1994; ISBN 0–89879–633–4).

Hart, David, ed., *Border Country: Poems in Process* (Birmingham: Wood Wind Publications, 1991; ISBN 1–871320–01–1).

Lees, Gene, *The Modern Rhyming Dictionary: A Practical Guide to Lyric Writing for Songwriters and Poets* (1981; rev. edn, New York: Cherry Lane Music Co., 2000; ISBN 0–89524–317–2).

Sansom, Peter, *Writing Poems* (Newcastle upon Tyne: Bloodaxe Books, 1994 [Bloodaxe Poetry Handbooks, 2]; ISBN 1–85224–204–3).

Singleton, John, & Luckhurst, Mary, eds, *The Creative Writing Handbook: Techniques for New Writers* (1996; 2nd edn, London: Macmillan, 2000; ISBN 0–333–79226–2).

Turner, Barry, ed., *The Writer's Handbook* (London: Macmillan/PEN, annually from 1987).

I : Critical Collections

Davenport, Guy, *The Geography of the Imagination: Forty Essays by Guy Davenport* (London: Picador, 1984; ISBN 0–330–28415–0).

Eliot, T. S., *The Sacred Wood: Essays on Poetry and Criticism* (London: Methuen, 1920).

Lodge, David, ed., *20th Century Literary Criticism: A Reader* (London and New York: Longman, 1972; ISBN 0–582–48422–7).

——*Modern Criticism and Theory: A Reader* (London and New York: Longman, 1988; ISBN 0–582–49460–5).

Ricks, Christopher, *The Force of Poetry* (Oxford: Clarendon Press, 1984; ISBN 0–19–811722–1).

——*Essays in Appreciation* (Oxford: Clarendon Press, 1996; ISBN 0–19–818344–5).

Vendler, Helen, *The Given and the Made: Recent American Poets* (London: Faber and Faber, 1995; ISBN 0–571–17078–1).

——*Soul Says: On Recent Poetry* (Cambridge, Mass., and London: Belknap Press of Harvard University Press, 1995; ISBN 0–674–82147–5).

Walder, Dennis, ed., *Literature in the Modern World* (1990; 2nd edn, Oxford and New York: Oxford University Press, 2004; ISBN 0–19–925301–3).

J : Anthologies

As all 'authors' are by definition editors, 'ed.' and 'eds' have been omitted.

Adcock, Fleur, *The Faber Book of 20th Century Women's Poetry* (London: Faber and Faber, 1987; ISBN 0–571–13693–1).

Alexander, Nigel, *Elizabethan Narrative Verse* (London: Arnold, 1967 [Stratford-upon-Avon Library, 3]).

Allen, Donald M., *The New American Poetry 1945–1960* (New York: Grove Press/London: Evergreen Books, 1960).

Alvarez, A., *The New Poetry* (1962; rev. edn, Harmondsworth: Penguin, 1966).

Amis, Kingsley, *The New Oxford Book of Light Verse* (Oxford and New York: Oxford University Press, 1978; ISBN 0–19–211862–5).

Anon., *Englands Helicon* (1600, 1614; ed. Hugh MacDonald, London: Routledge and Kegan Paul, 1949 [The Muses' Library]).

Ashraf, Mary, *Political Verse and Song from Britain and Ireland* (London: Lawrence and Wishart/Berlin: Seven Seas Books, 1975; SBN 83515–303–5).

Astley, Neil, *Poetry with an Edge* (1988; new edn, Newcastle upon Tyne: Bloodaxe, 1993; ISBN 1–85224–061–X).

——*Poems of the Year 2003* (Newcastle upon Tyne: Bloodaxe, 2003; ISBN 1–85224–654–5).

Auden, W. H., & Garret, John, *The Poet's Tongue* (2 vols, London: Bell and Sons, 1935, 1937).

Bassir, Olumbe, *An Anthology of West African Verse* (Ibadan: Ibadan University Press, 1957).

Benson, Judi, & Falk, Agneta, *The Long Pale Corridor: Contemporary Poems of Bereavement* (Newcastle upon Tyne: Bloodaxe, 1996; ISBN 1–85224–317–1).

Brett, Simon, *The Faber Book of Useful Verse* (London and Boston: Faber and Faber 1981; ISBN 0–571–11782–1).

Bullett, Gerald, *Silver Poets of the Sixteenth Century* (London: Dent, 1947 [Everyman]; ISBN 0–460–11985–0).

Select Bibliography and Further Reading

Burnett, Paula, *The Penguin Book of Caribbean Verse in English* (Harmondsworth: Penguin, 1986; ISBN 0–14–058511–7).

Causley, Charles, *Rising Early: Story Poems and Ballads of the Twentieth Century* (Leicester: Brockhampton Press, 1964; ISBN 0–340–03782–2).

Clark, Sandra, *Amorous Rites: Elizabethan Erotic Verse* (London: Dent, 1994 [Everyman]; ISBN 0–460–87530–2).

Clarke, A. M., *Best Poems of Trinidad* (1943; 2nd edn, Dover, MA: Majority Press, 1999; ISBN 0–912469–36–6).

Clayton, Thomas, *Cavalier Poets* (Oxford: Oxford University Press, 1978; ISBN 0–19–281204–1).

Cohen, J. M., *The Penguin Book of Comic and Curious Verse* (Harmondsworth: Penguin, 1952).

——*More Comic and Curious Verse* (Harmondsworth: Penguin, 1956).

——*Yet More Comic and Curious Verse* (Harmondsworth: Penguin, 1959).

Coote, Stephen, *The Penguin Book of Homosexual Verse* (1983; with revisions Harmondsworth: Penguin, 1986; ISBN 0–14–058551–6).

Cunningham, Val, *The Penguin Book of Spanish Civil War Verse* (Harmondsworth: Penguin, 1980; ISBN 0–14–042262–5).

Davies, R. T., *Medieval English Lyrics: A Critical Anthology* (1963; London: Faber and Faber 1966; ISBN 0–571–06571–6).

Donno, Elizabeth Story, *Elizabethan Minor Epic* (London: Routledge, 1963).

Dunn, Douglas, *A Rumoured City: New Poets from Hull* (Newcastle upon Tyne: Bloodaxe, 1982; ISBN 0–906427–41–X).

——*The Faber Book of Twentieth-Century Scottish Poetry* (1992; London: Faber and Faber 1993; ISBN 0–571–15432–8).

Evans, Maurice, *Elizabethan Sonnets* (London: Dent, 1977 [Everyman]; ISBN 0–460–11554–5).

Ferguson, Margaret, et al., *The Norton Anthology of Poetry* (5th edn, New York and London: Norton, 2005; ISBN 0–393–97920–2).

Field, Jonathan & Field, Moira, *The Methuen Book of Theatre Verse* (London: Methuen Drama, 1991; ISBN 0–413–66120–2).

Ford, Mark, *The New York Poets: An Anthology* (Manchester: Carcanet, 2004; ISBN 1–85754–734–9).

Fowler, Alastair, *The New Oxford Book of Seventeenth-Century Verse* (Oxford and New York: Oxford University Press, 1991; ISBN 0–19–248087–8).

——*The Country House Poem: A Cabinet of Seventeenth-Century Estate Poems and Related Items* (Edinburgh: Edinburgh University Press, 1994; ISBN 0–7486–0440–5).

France, Linda, *Sixty Women Poets* (Newcastle upon Tyne: Bloodaxe, 1993; ISBN 1–85224–252–3).

French, Philip, & Wlaschin, Ken, *The Faber Book of Movie Verse* (London and Boston: Faber and Faber 1993; ISBN 0–571–16660–1).

Fuller, John, *The Oxford Book of Sonnets* (2000; Oxford: Oxford University Press, 2002; ISBN 0–19–280389–1).

Gardner, Brian, *Up the Line to Death: The War Poets 1914–1918* (London: Eyre Methuen, 1964; ISBN 0–416–22380–X).

——*The Terrible Rain: The War Poets 1939–1945* (London: Methuen, 1966).

Gardner, Helen, *The Metaphysical Poets* (1957; rev. edn, Harmondsworth and New York: Viking/Penguin, 1966; ISBN 0–14–042038–X).

——*The New Oxford Book of English Verse* (Oxford and New York: Clarendon Press, 1972; ISBN 0–19–812136–9).

——*The Faber Book of Religious Verse* (London and Boston: Faber and Faber 1972; ISBN 0–571–11452–0).

Greer, Germaine, et al., *Kissing the Rod: An Anthology of 17th Century Women's Verse* (London: Virago, 1988; ISBN 0–86068–851–8).

Grigson, Geoffrey, *The Faber Book of Popular Verse* (London and Boston: Faber and Faber 1971; ISBN 0–571–10606–4).

——*The Faber Book of Nonsense Verse with a Sprinkling of Nonsense Prose* (London and Boston: Faber and Faber 1974; ISBN 0–571–11356–7).

——*The Oxford Book of Satirical Verse* (Oxford and New York: Oxford University Press, 1980; ISBN 0–19–214110–4).

——*The Faber Book of Reflective Verse* (London and Boston: Faber and Faber 1984; ISBN 0–571–13300–2).

Gross, John, *The New Oxford Book of Comic Verse* (Oxford and New York: Oxford University Press, 1994; ISBN 0–19–283207–7).

Gustafson, Ralph, *The Penguin Book of Canadian Verse* (1958; rev. edn, Harmondsworth: Penguin, 1967).

Habekost, Christian, *Dub Poetry: 19 poets from England and Jamaica* (Neustadt: Michael Schwinn, 1986; ISBN 3–925077–07–3).

Harold, John, *How Can You Write a Poem When You're Dying of AIDS ?* (London: Cassell, 1993; ISBN 0–304–32904–5).

Hayward, John, *The Penguin Book of English Verse* (Harmondsworth: Penguin, 1956; ISBN 0–14–042032–0).

Heaney, Seamus, & Hughes, Ted, *The Rattle Bag* (London and Boston: Faber and Faber, 1982; ISBN 0–571–11976–X).

Heuvel, Cor van den, *The Haiku Anthology* (New York: Touchstone, 1986; ISBN 0–671–74881–5).

Hodgart, Matthew, *The Faber Book of Ballads* (London and Boston: Faber and Faber 1965; ISBN 0–571–09688–3).

Hoffman, Michael, & Lasdun, James, *After Ovid: New Metamorphoses* (London and Boston: Faber and Faber 1994; ISBN 0–571–17691–7).

Hoover, Paul, *PostModern American Poetry* (New York and London: Norton, 1994; ISBN 0–393–31090–6).

Hulse, Michael, Kennedy, David, & Morley, David, *The New Poetry* (Newcastle upon Tyne: Bloodaxe, 1993; ISBN 1–85224–244–2).

Hunt, John Dixon, *The New Oxford Book of Garden Verse* (Oxford and New York: Oxford University Press, 1993; ISBN 0–19–214196–1).

James, Stephen, *The Tabla Book of New Verse 2004* (Bristol: Tabla, 2004; ISBN 0–9532981–4–0).

Jarman, Mark, & Mason, David, *Rebel Angels: 25 Poets of the New Formalism* (Brownsville, OR: Story Line Press, 1996; ISBN 1–885266–30–8).

Jerrold, Walter, & Leonard, R. M., *A Century of Parody and Imitation* (London and New York: Oxford University Press, 1913).

Jones, Emrys, *The New Oxford Book of Sixteenth Century Verse* (Oxford and New York: Oxford University Press, 1991; ISBN 0–19–282971–8).

Jones, Peter, *Imagist Poetry* (Harmondsworth: Penguin, 1972; ISBN 0–14–042147–5).

Kerrigan, John, *Motives of Woe: Shakespeare and 'Female Complaint': A Critical Anthology* (Oxford: Clarendon Press, 1991; ISBN 0–19–811770–1).

Kossman, Nina, *Gods and Mortals: Modern Poems on Classical Myths* (New York: Oxford University Press, 2001; ISBN 0–19–513341–2).

Larkin, Philip, *The Oxford Book of Twentieth Century English Verse* (1973; Oxford and New York: Oxford University Press, 1997; ISBN 0–19–812137–7).

Lee, John Robert, *Roseau Valley and other poems for Brother George Odlum: An Anthology* (Castries, St Lucia: Jubilee Trust Fund, 2003; ISBN 976–8180–74–9).

Levin, Phillis, *The Penguin Book of the Sonnet: 500 Years of a Classic Tradition in English* (Harmondsworth and New York: Penguin, 2001; ISBN 0–713–99529–7).

Lindsay, David W., *English Poetry 1700–1780: Contemporaries of Swift and Johnson* (London: Dent, and Totowa, NJ: Rowman and Littlefield, 1974; ISBN 0–460–11700–9 [UK], 0–87471–546–6 [US]).

Lonsdale, Roger, *The New Oxford Book of Eighteenth-Century Verse* (1984; with corrections, Oxford: Oxford University Press, 1987; ISBN 0–19–282054–0).

——*Eighteenth-Century Women Poets* (Oxford: Oxford University Press, 1989; ISBN 0–19–282775–8).

Macbeth, George, *The Penguin Book of Sick Verse* (Harmondsworth: Penguin, 1963).

Maja-Pearce, Adewale, *The Heinemann Book of African Poetry in English* (Oxford and Portsmouth, NH: Heinemann, 1990 [African Writers Series]; ISBN 0–435–91323–9).

Maidment, Brian, *The Poorhouse Fugitives: Self-taught poets and poetry in Victorian Britain* (Manchester: Carcanet, 1987; ISBN 0–85635–706–5).

Markham, E. A., *Hinterland: Caribbean Poetry from the West Indies and Britain* (Newcastle upon Tyne: Bloodaxe, 1989; ISBN 1–85224–087–3).

McGann, Jerome J., *The New Oxford Book of Romantic Period Verse* (Oxford and New York: Oxford University Press, 1993; ISBN 0–19–214158–9).

Montague, John, *The Faber Book of Irish Verse* (London and Boston: Faber and Faber 1974; ISBN 0–571–11218–8).

Mordecai, Pamela, & Morris, Mervyn, *Jamaica Woman: An Anthology of Poems* (London, Kingston, and Port of Spain: Heinemann, 1980 [Caribbean Writers Series]; ISBN 0–435–98600–7).

Norbrook, David, & Woudhuysen, H. R., *The Penguin Book of Renaissance Verse, 1509–1659* (Harmondsworth: Allen Lane/Penguin Press, 1992; ISBN 0–7139–9016–3).

Opie, Iona, & Opie, Peter, *The Oxford Book of Narrative Verse* (Oxford and New York: Oxford University Press, 1983; ISBN 0–19–214131–7).

Palgrave, Francis Turner, *The Golden Treasury of English Songs and Lyrics* (1861, 1896; enlarged edn, London and Melbourne: Dent, 1955 [Everyman]; ISBN 0–460–11096–9).

Parini, Jay, *The Columbia Anthology of American Poetry* (New York: Columbia University Press, 1995; ISBN 0–231–08122–7).

Parker, Alan Michael, & Willhardt, Mark, *The Routledge Anthology of Cross-Gendered Verse* (London and New York: Routledge, 1996; ISBN 0–415–11291–5).

Poole, Adrian, & Maule, Jeremy, *The Oxford Book of Classical Verse in*

Translation (Oxford and New York: Oxford University Press, 1995; ISBN 0–19–214209–7).

Reeves, James, *Georgian Poetry* (Harmondsworth: Penguin, 1960).

Reilly, Catherine, *Scars Upon My Heart: Women's Poetry and Verse of the First World War* (London: Virago, 1981; ISBN 0–86068–226–9).

Ricks, Christopher, *The New Oxford Book of Victorian Verse* (1987; Oxford and New York: Oxford University Press, 1990; ISBN 0–19–284084–3).

Riordan, Maurice, & Turney, Jon, *A Quark for Mister Mark: 101 Poems about Science* (London: Faber and Faber 2000; ISBN 0–571–20542–9).

Roberts, Michael, *The Faber Book of Modern Verse* (1936; rev. edn by Donald Hall, London and Boston: Faber and Faber 1965; ISBN 0–571–06348–9).

Sargent, Helen Child, & Kittredge, G. L., *English and Scottish Popular Ballads Edited from the Collection of Francis James Child* (Boston and New York: Houghton Mifflin, 1904).

Schiff, Hilda, *Holocaust Poetry* (London: Fount, 1995; ISBN 0–00–627875–2).

Sergeant, Howard, *Commonwealth Poems of Today* (London: English Association/John Murray, 1967).

——*The Swinging Rainbow: Poems for the Young* (London: Evans, 1969; ISBN 0–237–35106–4).

Silcock, Arnold, *Verse and Worse: A Private Collection* (London and Boston: Faber and Faber 1952; ISBN 0–571–05132–4).

Sissay, Lemn, *The Fire People: A Collection of Contemporary Black British Poets* (Edinburgh: Payback Press, 1998; ISBN 0–86241–739–2).

Skelton, Robin, *Poetry of the Thirties* (Harmondsworth: Penguin, 1964).

——*Poetry of the Forties* (Harmondsworth: Penguin, 1968).

Smith, Ken, & Benson, Judi, *Klaonica: Poems for Bosnia* (Newcastle upon Tyne: Bloodaxe, 1993; ISBN 1–85224–283–3).

Sola Pinto, Vivian de, & Rodway, Allan, *The Common Muse: Popular British Ballad Poetry from the 15th to the 20th Century* (1957; Harmondsworth: Penguin, 1965).

Squire, J. C., *Apes and Parrots: An Anthology of Parodies* (London: Herbert Jenkins Ltd [1929]).

Stevenson, Jane, & Davidson, Peter, *Early Modern Women Poets: An Anthology* (Oxford and New York: Oxford University Press, 2001; ISBN 0–19–924257–7).

Strand, Mark, & Boland, Eavan, *The Making of a Poem: A Norton Anthology of Poetic Forms* (New York and London: Norton, 2000; ISBN 0–393–04916–7).

Tomlinson, Charles, *Eros English'd: Classical Erotic Poetry in Translation from Golding to Hardy* (Bristol: Bristol Classical Press, 1992; ISBN 0–85399–159–7).

Wavell, Field Marshal Earl (A. P.), *Other Men's Flowers* (1944; London: Pimlico, 1992; ISBN 0–7126–5342–2).

Wright, David, *Longer Contemporary Poems* (Harmondsworth: Penguin, 1966).

——*The Mid Century English Poetry 1940–1960* (Harmondsworth: Penguin, 1965).

Wyndham Lewis, D. B., & Lee, Charles, *The Stuffed Owl: An Anthology of Bad Verse* (1930, 1948; London: Dent, 1963 [Aldine Paperbacks]).

Index of Poems and Poets Quoted and Cited

Collections cited as sources will be found in the same section as their citation, or in §I : Critical Collections (p. 397).

Initial definite and indefinite articles are omitted in titles, but not in first lines doing duty as titles.

I BY POEM

Index of Poems and Poets Quoted and Cited

Index of Poems and Poets Quoted and Cited

Index of Poems and Poets Quoted and Cited

Index of Poems and Poets Quoted and Cited

II BY POET

Index of Poems and Poets Quoted and Cited

Index of Poems and Poets Quoted and Cited

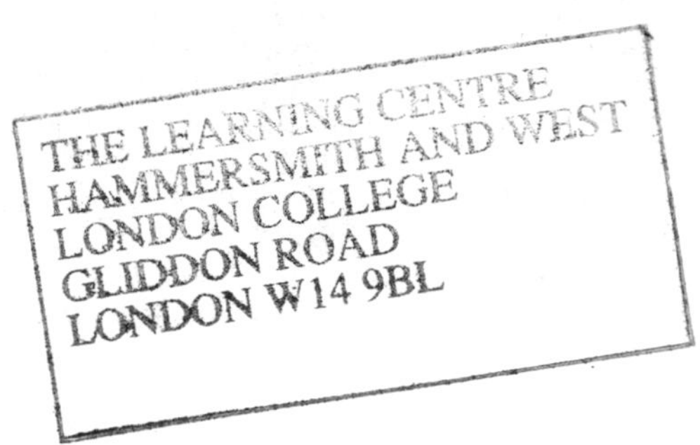